Using OS/2™

Using OS/2™

Kris Jamsa

Osborne **McGraw-Hill**
Berkeley, California

Osborne **McGraw-Hill**
2600 Tenth Street
Berkeley, California 94710
U.S.A.

For information on translations and book distributors outside of the U.S.A., write to Osborne **McGraw-Hill** at the above address.

A complete list of trademarks appears on page 749.

Using OS/2™

1234567890 DODO 898

ISBN 0-07-881306-9

Contents

DETACH (The OS/2 Background Dispatcher)

Preface

In 1981, IBM announced the IBM PC, a small yet powerful "personal" computer that has become the company's most influential machine. At that time, Microsoft and IBM each released a version of DOS (MS-DOS and PC-DOS, respectively), a disk-operating system that allowed the user to run programs, manipulate files, and perform basic utilities.

At first, many users were skeptical of both the IBM PC and DOS. They lacked the arcade-game flair offered by other personal computers, and the PC was expensive. Users and small businesses were hard pressed to justify acquisition of the computers. At that time spreadsheets provided the best reason to buy a PC, but over the years, word processing also became a major use of the PC. Although they were not yet fully accepted in the home, the IBM PC and DOS broke considerable ground in businesses and schools.

Users now wanted "integration," and DOS began to change by breaking away from the CP/M mindset and moving instead toward a UNIX orientation that provided for I/O redirection and hierarchical subdirectories. In retrospect, this was the first stage in developing DOS into a "multitasking" operating system that could execute several programs simultaneously.

As more and more applications became available for the PC, users became more sophisticated and demanded more sophisticated applications. A simple single-user database-management system written just a year before now had to execute with several concurrent users over a local area network. With the advent of the IBM PC AT, the microcomputer industry had its first fully functional, fast PC capable of managing such applications. In response to the demand for complete integration, increased CPU utilization, and multitasking, Microsoft announced Microsoft Windows.

Response to Microsoft Windows was mixed. Some users found it to be convenient and discovered that it allowed them to share data among several applications executing simultaneously. However, many complained that Windows was just too slow. Most users missed completely the significant impact that this package would have on the microcomputer industry. Windows was Microsoft's test product. At the time of the release of Windows, Microsoft had spent two years developing a multitasking operating system that would serve as the successor to DOS. Microsoft listened closely to the praise and criticism that Windows drew while continuing to plan the design goals and implementation for its new operating system.

In April 1987, IBM announced its new Personal Series line of computers (PS/2) that would upgrade an aging IBM PC. This line of systems included 8088, 80286, and 80386 computers that incorporated the latest hardware technologies. That same month, IBM and Microsoft announced their joint effort to develop and release an industry-standard operating system that would pave the way well into the 1990s. That operating system is OS/2.

OS/2 is an 80286-based operating system, which means that it requires at least an IBM PC AT or AT clone. Indeed, OS/2 fully supports the 80386. However, OS/2 does not run on the IBM PC (8088). The PC simply does not have the power to drive OS/2, nor the ability to support protected-mode programs. As you will see throughout this text, OS/2 is a powerful operating system. For the first time, PC users will have the same capabilities as those on minicomputer systems.

OS/2 is a multitasking operating system, which means that it not only allows users to run many programs at the same time, but also quickly changes from one program to another, even exchanging information among them. Thus, OS/2 provides the user and programmer with a myriad of new capabilities. This book presents each of them to you.

A Familiar Face

For those who are just starting with OS/2, do not be intimidated. Within minutes you will be at the OS/2 system prompt, which

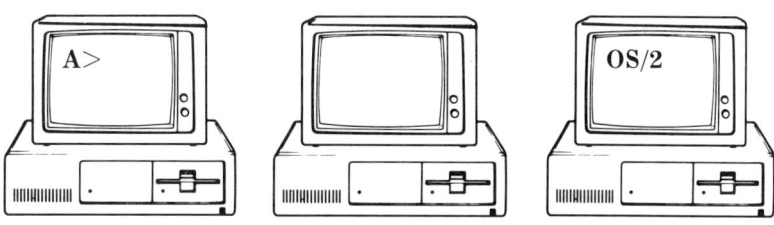

Figure P-1. *OS/2 providing capabilities of multiple computers*

looks amazingly similar to the DOS prompt. Although this may be comforting during your initial sessions, do not let it mislead you as to OS/2's tremendous capabilities. Unlike DOS (which gives you a single user prompt), OS/2 provides multiple system prompts, just as if you have several computers on your desk (see Figure P-1). However, for many of you, the DOS-like prompt will be a familiar face.

The Presentation Manager

When many users speak of OS/2, they also speak of a program called the Presentation Manager. At one time, the major OS/2 design goal was to produce an operating system that was user-friendly, yet allowed the user to fully exploit the operating system and its multitasking capabilities. The OS/2 Presentation Manager is a Windows-like shell that provides the user with a common interface to OS/2 and all OS/2 applications. Under the Presentation Manager, users no longer have to memorize nebulous commands for OS/2 or for new programs. Instead, OS/2 presents itself and its applications in a consistent graphical interface. Thus, the user will learn to use the operating system all the more quickly.

Early versions of OS/2 will not have the Presentation Manager. IBM and Microsoft are currently working on the joint development of the Presentation Manager code. It is currently scheduled for release in the last quarter of 1988. Chapter 14 of this book examines the OS/2 Presentation Manager in detail.

What's Inside

Here is a brief overview of each of the chapters in this book.

Chapter 1 provides an overview of OS/2. It discusses the need for OS/2 along with its design goals and implementations. By the end of this chapter, you should fully understand OS/2 from the big picture and the concept of multitasking.

Chapter 2 gets you started right away with OS/2 commands. You will traverse the OS/2 Session Manager and create real- and protected-mode sessions. By the end of this chapter you will be able to rapidly move around in OS/2.

Chapter 3 takes a look at the basic OS/2 commands. For those who are familiar with DOS, much of this chapter will be review. Watch each command carefully, however: OS/2 has several enhancements over DOS that are quite subtle.

Chapter 4 takes a look at the OS/2 system configuration parameters. Many users will be content to use the default OS/2 system configuration for quite some time. However, by reading this chapter, you will get a much better feel for multitasking and for OS/2 real- and protected-mode operations.

Chapter 5 examines OS/2 device control. You will learn the functional aspects of the OS/2 spooler, MODE command, and device drivers. By the end of this chapter everyone should have a fully functional system printer.

Chapter 6 examines OS/2 I/O redirection. OS/2 provides complete support for the DOS I/O redirection operators along with several more. As you will see, OS/2 command-line processing is powerful and functional, and remains quite straightforward.

Chapter 7 looks at OS/2 batch processing. Those who are familiar with DOS batch processing will find the concepts quite similar. However, OS/2 introduces several new key commands. As you will learn, OS/2 protected-mode batch files use the CMD extension as opposed to the BAT extension.

Chapter 8 examines OS/2 subdirectories in great detail. OS/2 subdirectories enable you to manage your file structure carefully and to obtain the best possible organization and system performance.

Chapter 9 looks at all of the remaining OS/2 commands. Because of the diversity of their functionality, they are simply grouped under the heading, "Advanced Commands." By the end of this chapter you will have seen all but two of the OS/2 commands.

Chapter 10 looks at the two remaining OS/2 commands, BACKUP and RESTORE. By implementing the procedures shown in this chapter, you can greatly reduce the possibility of data loss.

Chapter 11 looks at OS/2 from the perspective of the programmer. In this chapter you will learn how to create OS/2 protected-mode programs and how to migrate those programs to real mode.

Chapter 12 continues the OS/2 programming tutorial. This chapter looks at advanced programming techniques such as timer services, interprocess communication, and shared memory. Chapter 12 is the OS/2 programmer's toolbox. It will help you with any OS/2 programming application.

Chapter 13 takes a look at the OS/2 disk structure and explains how OS/2 disks have remained compatible with DOS. If you are to understand the operating system fully, you need to understand how it records information on disk.

Chapter 14 examines the OS/2 Presentation Manager. Although the Presentation Manager does not yet exist, it is based closely on Windows version 2.0. Using this as a baseline, you can gain an appreciation of the functional capabilities of the Presentation Manager.

Appendix A provides a standard ASCII chart.

Appendix B provides a complete OS/2 command reference. For the first time anywhere, OS/2 command syntax charts are provided for the reader.

Appendix C looks at several of the installation considerations involved in placing OS/2 onto your fixed disk.

Disk Package

All of the programming examples in this book are available on disk. The *Using OS/2* disk also includes an on-line help facility to give you information on each OS/2 command and system configuration parameter. With this disk you can put most of your OS/2 documentation back on the shelf. The disk package is shipped in a solid container that is ideal for carrying your disks to school or to the office.

This disk can be obtained for $17.45, plus $2.50 for shipping and handling. (Foreign orders, send $5.00 for shipping.) Make checks payable to Kris Jamsa Software, Inc.

Kris Jamsa Software, Inc.
P.O. Box 26031
Las Vegas, Nevada 89126

Please send me the diskette package that accompanies *Using OS/2*. My payment for $17.45 (plus $2.50 for shipping and handling or $5.00 for foreign orders) is enclosed.

Name ———————————————————————————

Address ————————————————————————————

City ———————————— State ————— ZIP —————————

Kris Jamsa Software, Inc.   P.O. Box 26031   Las Vegas, Nevada 89126

DOS User's Group

The DOS User's Group is an international user group composed of DOS, Windows, and OS/2 users. The members of the DOS User's Group are novice, intermediate, and advanced users, and range from MIS directors to housewives, students, authors, business executives, and even operating system developers. Our user base is growing into one of the most successful user groups ever.

The DOS User's Group provides new and exciting information for users at all levels. Since the April 1987 announcement of OS/2, the DOS User's Group newsletters have focused on OS/2, its development, and its ramifications. DOS User's Group members were among the first to see OS/2 commands. The DOS User's Group newsletter is currently the best source of OS/2 programming tips, command summaries, and tutorials. With several well-known contributing editors, the DOS User's Group can answer your PC, DOS, OS/2, Windows, and application questions. If you are serious about OS/2, join the DOS User's Group today. Annual membership is $25 ($35, Canada and Europe).

DOS User's Group   P.O. Box 26601   Las Vegas, NV 89126

Yes, I wish to join the DOS User's Group. My annual membership fee of $25 ($35 outside of U.S.A.) is enclosed.

Name _____

Address _____

City _____ State _____ ZIP _____

DOS USER'S GROUP
P.O. Box 26601
Las Vegas, Nevada 89126
(702) 363-3419

U.S. Members $25.00 annual fee
Canada, Mexico, and Europe $35.00 annual fee

Quarterly newsletter which includes:

DOS Command Tutorials
— Basic overview
— Tips, tricks, and traps
— Source code for implementation

DOS Customization Hints
— Thorough examination of CONFIG.SYS entries
— Tips, tricks, and traps

Question and Answer Forum
— Large user base of experience

Third Party Software Reviews and Discounts
— Indepth reviews of major software packages
— Discounts to user group members

Turbo Pascal Secrets
— Low level DOS programming techniques from Turbo Pascal

Programming Hints
— Linker and Librarian commands
— Tips, tricks, and traps

MS Windows
— User perspective
— Programmer prospective

OS/2
— General overview
— Programmer information
— Advanced concepts

Batch Processing
— DOS batch commands
— Tips, tricks, and traps

The DOS User's Group is an international user group consisting of members who are:

Novice Users, Programmers, Buyers, Manufacturers, Developers, Authors, MIS Directors

each of whom want to maximize their knowledge of DOS, MS Windows, and OS/2.

$25.00 Annual Membership Fee (U.S.)
$35.00 Annual Membership Fee (Canada - Europe)

☐ Money Order
☐ Personal Check

Name_____

Address_____

City_____ State_____ Zip_____

Osborne **McGraw-Hill** assumes no responsibility for this offer. This is solely an offer of Kris
Jamsa Software Inc. and not of Osborne **McGraw-Hill**.

DOS USERS GROUP
P.O. BOX 26601
Las Vegas, Nevada 89126

QUARTERLY NEWSLETTER
Latest MS and PC DOS News
New Product Reviews
Discounts on Third Party Products
DOS Utilities

DOS TUTORIALS
Configuring DOS
MS Windows
Advanced DOS Programming
Developing DOS Applications
8088-80386

THIRD PARTY DEMO DISKETTES
DOS Demo Disk
C Demo Disk
Pascal Demo Disk
FORTRAN Demo Disk

$25.00 Annual Membership Fee (U.S.)
$35.00 Annual Membership Fee (Canada - Europe)

_____ Money Order

_____ Personal Check

Name_____

Address _____

City _____State _____Zip_____

1 Introducing OS/2

Since its introduction, OS/2, the new operating system for the IBM PC AT and AT compatibles, has fueled much speculation. This chapter provides a basic overview of the factors that led to the development of OS/2, the functional aspects of OS/2, and the impact OS/2 will have on the microcomputer industry. Upon completion of this chapter, you will be able to begin fully utilizing OS/2.

What Is OS/2?

OS/2 is a new operating system that was developed by Microsoft (MS) and IBM. In general, OS/2, like any operating system, provides the interface between the user and the computer. Specifically, an operating system manages system resources such as disks, printers, and other peripheral devices (mouse, modem, plotter, and so on). In addition, the operating system provides the means for you to execute other programs, such as a word processor or database-management package, on your computer (see Figure 1–1).

OS/2 (like its predecessor, DOS) provides each of these functions and many more capabilities (such as multitasking, virtual memory management, and support for protected-mode applications). If any of these terms are new to you, don't worry. Each is discussed in great detail throughout this book.

In addition, OS/2, like DOS, has many faces, each of which is dependent on the end user (see Figure 1–2). At first, OS/2 will appear to be a command-line processor, which allows you to exe-

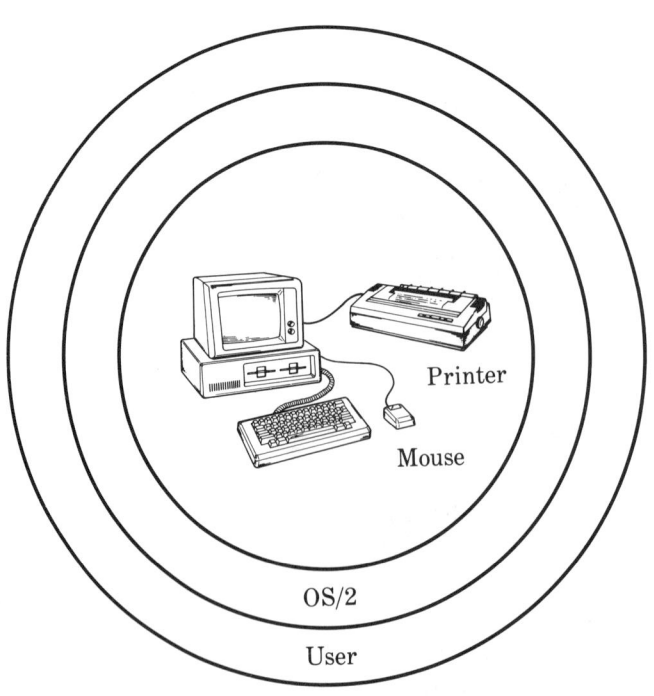

Figure 1-1.   *The function of an operating system*

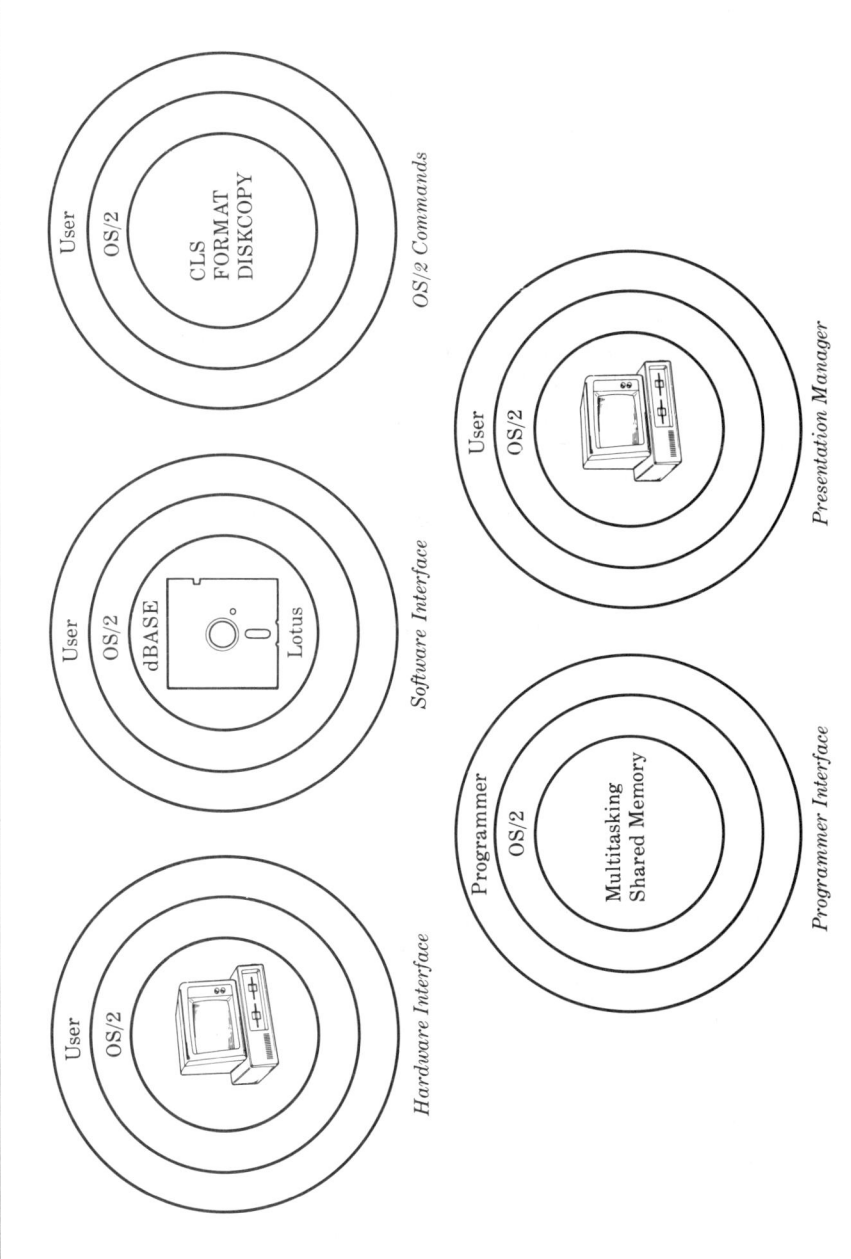

Figure 1-2. *The faces of OS/2*

cute commands by entering them from the keyboard. The OS/2 prompt, OS/2's most familiar face, closely resembles that of the DOS prompt.

```
[C:\]
```

Later in this text, you will learn about the OS/2 Presentation Manager, which is much like Microsoft Windows. In the future, many of you will issue each of your commands and execute your programs in the Presentation Manager environment.

To programmers, OS/2 provides the programming capabilities and development tools previously available only from minicomputer operating systems such as UNIX of VAX/VMS. As you will see in later chapters, OS/2's programming facilities make your applications virtually limitless.

Why OS/2?

Since its advent in 1981, DOS has been the standard operating system for personal computers. Originally, DOS provided simplistic file-manipulation capabilities and a mechanism for executing other applications (such as word processors or spreadsheets). Since that time, the personal computer market has exploded. Each day, thousands of new users begin working with DOS. In fact, more than 10 million people currently use DOS. As the number of DOS users has increased over the past few years, so too has their sophistication and the complexity of their applications. To meet these demands, DOS has increased its functional capabilities several times in the form of new versions. Table 1-1 and Table 1-2 describe the changes to DOS since 1981.

Version	Date	Functionality
1.0	1981	Original disk operating system
1.25	1982	Support for double-sided disks
2.0	1983	Support for subdirectories
2.01	1983	Support for international symbols
2.11	1983	Bug fixes
2.25	1983	Extended character set support
3.0	1984	Support for 1.2MB floppy disk
		Support for larger hard disk
3.1	1984	Support for PC networks
3.2	1986	Support for microfloppies
3.3	1987	Support for PS/2 series of computers

Table 1-1. *Versions of DOS*

Today, the needs of users are even more complex. What were once single-user programs now require simultaneous access by multiple users from several different computers linked together with a local area network. Office automation and integrated workstations are now realities. Users need a mechanism to easily exchange information (data) from one application to another.

Version	Date	Functionality
1.0	1981	Original disk operating system
2.0	1983	Support for subdirectories
2.10	1983	Bug fixes
3.0	1984	Support for 1.2MB floppy disk
		Support for larger hard disk
3.1	1984	Support for PC networks
3.2	1986	Support for microfloppies
3.3	1987	Support for PS/2 series of computers

Table 1-2. *IBM Versions of DOS*

"User-friendly" software has given way to "user-consistent" software that is based on dialog boxes, pull-down menus, and support for a mouse interface.

With the advent of the 80286 and 80386 processors, the capabilities of computer hardware now exceed current software utilization. The time is right for a new, powerful operating system, and OS/2 is the operating system that will carry personal computers far into the 1990s. To summarize, OS/2 was developed in response to these factors:

- The 640K of program space provided by DOS is insufficient for sophisticated applications.

- What were once single-user programs must be accessible to multiuser systems on local area networks.

- User applications require the sharing of information to ensure complete integration.

- The advent of the 80286 and 80386 provided a processor powerful enough to drive a multitasking operating system.

How OS/2 Increases Your Computing Capabilities

OS/2 allows you to execute multiple programs at the same time. DOS allows you to execute only one program at a time. For example, if you were developing a report that required you to simultaneously view information contained in a database, a spreadsheet, and a word processor, you would essentially need three computers (see Figure 1–3).

Under OS/2, however, you can execute all three of these programs simultaneously on the same computer. OS/2 allows you to switch quickly from one application to the next and to view the output of each on the screen. This process of executing several programs simultaneously is *multitasking*. A major benefit of

Figure 1-3. *Three computers needed to produce sales report*

multiple programs simultaneously running on the same computer is that each can easily exchange information, which greatly
reduces your workload.

Information Exchange

If several programs coexist in the same computer, they can easily
exchange information. For example, assume that you are producing an end-of-month summary report that lists sales percentages,
current inventory, and general-ledger information (accounts
receivable and accounts payable). To produce the report, you must
consolidate information readily available from a database, spreadsheet, and general-ledger package.

Using applications written to utilize OS/2 shared memory, you
can simultaneously execute all three programs along with your
word processor and allow each program to place its required
information into a shared region (called a *clipboard*) that each
program can access.

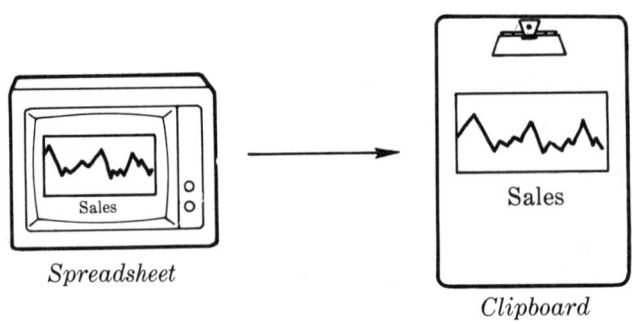

Figure 1-4.   *Placing graphics from spreadsheet into clipboard*

In this case, you would first place the graphics from your spreadsheet into the clipboard, as shown in Figure 1-4. Next, you could copy the contents of the clipboard into your word processing document, as shown in Figure 1-5. You would then repeat this process, first for the inventory database (see Figure 1-6) and then for the general-ledger information (see Figure 1-7). In so doing, OS/2 would actually integrate data from all three sources, greatly simplifying your task. Under OS/2, integrated products are a reality.

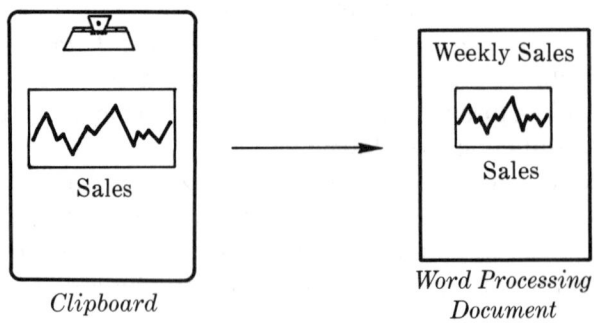

Figure 1-5.   *Copying contents of clipboard into document*

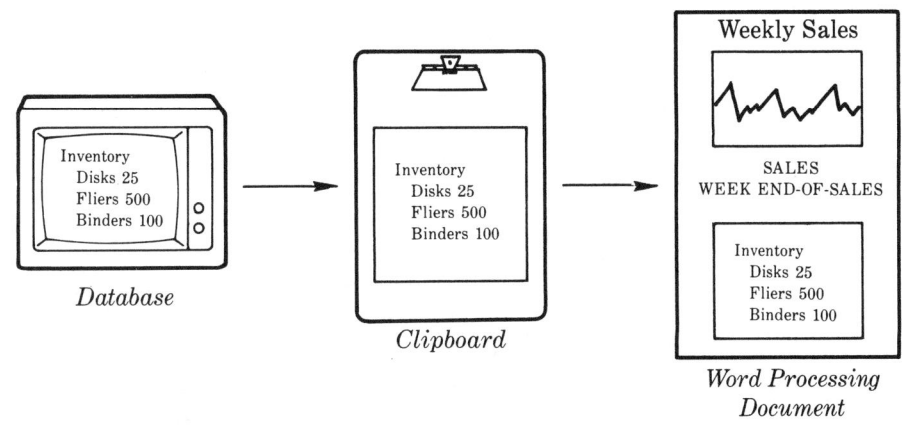

Figure 1-6. *Placing inventory database into clipboard and then into document*

It is important to note that applications using OS/2 features (such as shared memory) must be developed by third-party vendors. The availablity of such applications will greatly influence the number of users that make the transition to OS/2. There-

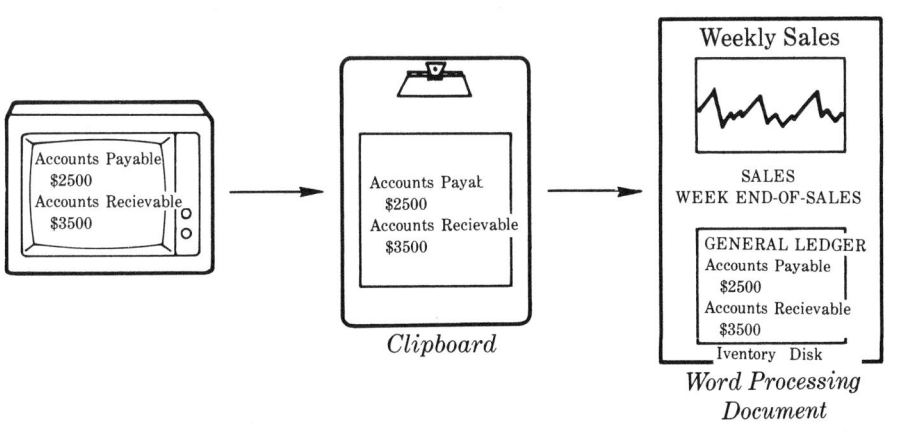

Figure 1-7. *Placing general-ledger information into clipboard and then into document*

fore, the key to OS/2's success is not necessarily its powerful capabilities, but rather the number of applications programs that make use of these capabilities.

Understanding Multitasking

Multitasking is the process of executing several programs simultaneously. If you are familiar with the DOS PRINT command, you have already experienced multitasking. Each time you issue the DOS PRINT command, DOS begins printing your files in the background, thus allowing you to continue to execute commands in the foreground (at the DOS prompt). In so doing, your computer appears to be performing two tasks simultaneously.

A multitasking operating system, therefore, is an operating system that gives the appearance of simultaneously performing more than one task. Always remember that personal computers can perform only one function at a time. OS/2 (just as the DOS PRINT command) must give the appearance that several events are occurring simultaneously. The computer is actually just switching from one program to the next, at high speed.

MULTITASKING

A multitasking system is one that gives the appearance of executing several programs simultaneously. If a computer only one has processor, the computer is physically restricted to performing only one task at a time. A multitasking system, therefore, gives the appearance of performing several functions concurrently by rapidly switching from one function to the next.

The key to multitasking lies in the ability to share resources between several programs in order to maximize CPU utilization. Although many users spend a great deal of time in front of the computer, they are actually using only a fraction of the computer's processing capabilities.

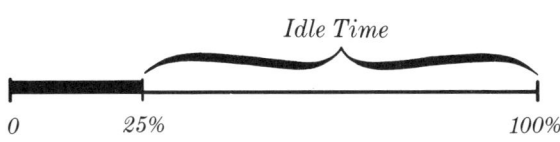

Figure 1-8. *Utilizing 25% of CPU processing capabilities*

Consider a word processing session at your computer. Each time you type a character at the keyboard, the word processing program must process the keystroke, either by adding the character to the document or by performing a predefined task. Although you may type at a rapid pace, the electronic components within the computer are working much faster. As a result, the CPU is actually sitting idle a large percentage of the time while waiting for your next keystroke. Each time you pause (either to turn a page or to relax), the percentage of CPU idle time increases to an even greater extent. Few users are capable of utilizing more than 25% of the CPU processing capabilities for a sustained period of time (see Figure 1-8).

Multitasking systems increase CPU utilization by allowing other programs to use the CPU during previously idle periods. For example, assume that you are editing a word processing document while the DOS PRINT command prints a file in the background. In this case you are obtaining a greater percentage of CPU utilization (see Figure 1-9).

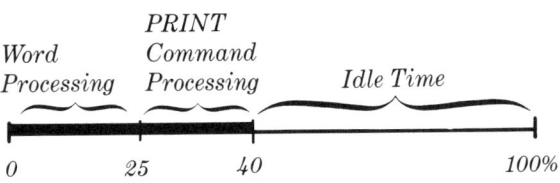

Figure 1-9. *Utilizing CPU capabilities with PRINT command*

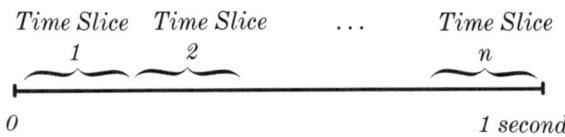

Figure 1-10.   *Concept of time slices in CPU utilization*

If you could simultaneously execute a third program, you could achieve an even higher percentage of CPU utilization and thus achieve more output from your hardware and computer sessions. Unfortunately, under DOS the PRINT command is essentially the only command that executes concurrently.

DOS appears to execute PRINT concurrently to your foreground processing by dividing each CPU processing second into smaller units called *time slices* (see Figure 1E10). Next, DOS distributes a time slice to your current application (the word processor in this scenario), allows it to process for a period of time, and then processes the PRINT command to print your file. DOS repeats this process by rapidly changing from the word processor to PRINT in succession, as shown in Figure 1E11. Since this switching occurs so fast, it is essentially transparent to the end user, thus making the CPU appear to be simultaneously performing two tasks.

OS/2 takes this distribution of the CPU even further by allowing you to execute several programs at the same time. Assume that you are simultaneously executing a word processor, spreadsheet, the DOS PRINT command, and a database-management package. In this case, OS/2 again divides the CPU processing time into time slices. The only difference is that it must now give a time slice to several programs in a round-robin fashion, as shown in Figure 1-12.

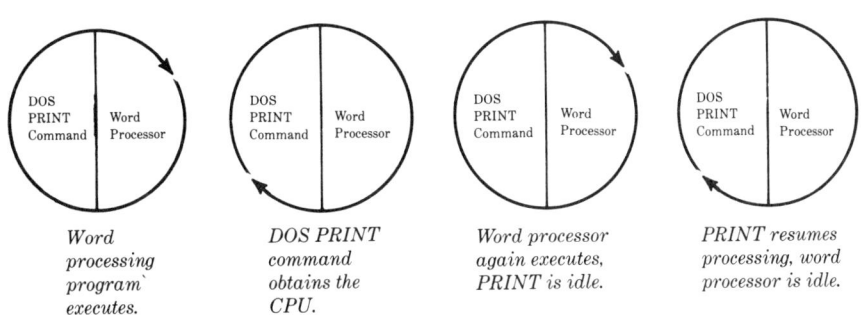

Figure 1-11. *Distribution of CPU time slices*

Because OS/2 switches between the programs so rapidly, the CPU time-sharing is normally undetectable to the end user. The net results are greater functionality and increased resource utilization.

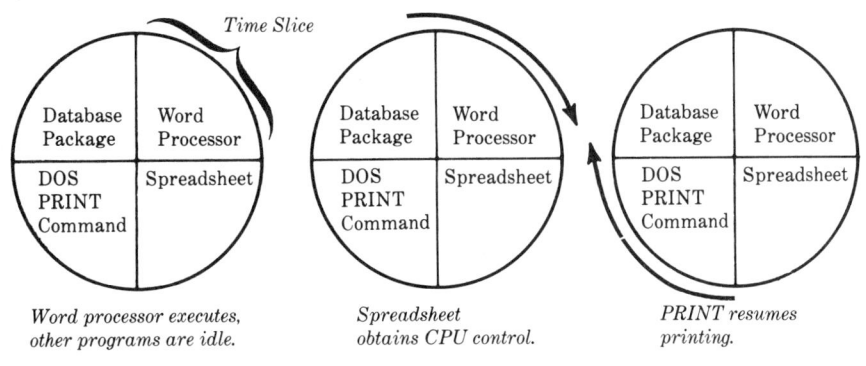

Figure 1-12. *Giving time slices in a round-robin fashion*

SYSTEM UTILIZATION

Multitasking improves the overall utilization of your computer resources and the productivity of your computer sessions by minimizing CPU idle time. By simultaneously executing several programs, you can fully exploit your system's capabilities.

This simple overview of the OS/2 multitasking capabilities has provided the foundation required for you to begin your simultaneous execution of several programs in Chapter 2. Later chapters discuss in detail the implementation of OS/2 multitasking.

Real Mode Versus Protected Mode

By now, many of you have probably heard the terms "real-mode applications" and "protected-mode applications." The difference between the real-mode applications and protected-mode applications is quite straightforward.

DOS programs execute while the CPU is in *real mode*. As such, they can directly access hardware devices and essentially dictate the state of the machine. Since only one program can execute at any given time under DOS, real-mode programs have no other program to affect. Under OS/2, however, several programs can execute simultaneously. However, allowing programs to perform input or output operations in an uncontrolled fashion can have devastating effects, and that is what *protected mode* is designed to prevent.

For example, assume that you are viewing the result of a graph produced by your spreadsheet program, as illustrated in Figure 1–13. You do not want a second program that is concurrently executing with your spreadsheet application to randomly output results to the screen. To do so would destroy the current screen contents. In a multitasking environment such as OS/2, programs must cooperate. To ensure this cooperation, OS/2 coordinates applications while it executes in protected mode.

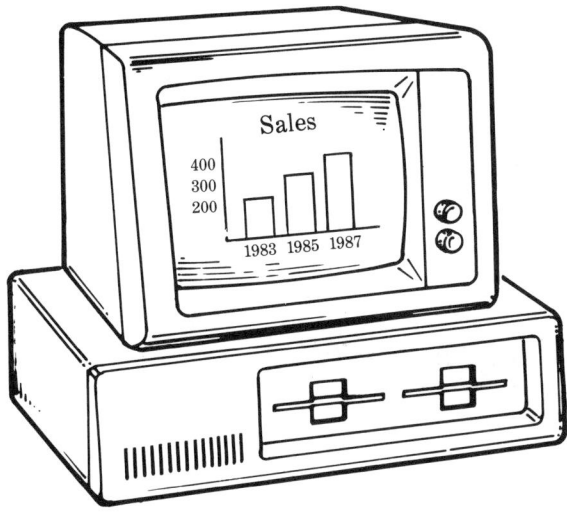

Figure 1-13. *Result of graph produced by spreadsheet program*

As the name implies, OS/2 protected mode exists to protect concurrent applications from harming one another. As such, protected-mode programs cannot generally access hardware devices directly, modify specific memory locations (such as the video-display memory), or perform other operations that will affect the harmony of the multitasking environment. Simply stated, OS/2 uses protected mode to support multitasking.

REAL MODE

DOS programs execute in real mode, which gives them complete control of the computer. Under real mode, programs can perform low-level I/O operations, directly access memory locations, and control hardware devices. Real-mode processing is unacceptable in a multitasking environment since it allows programs to affect each other.

PROTECTED MODE

OS/2 multitasking requires 80286/80386 protected mode. In this mode, OS/2 maintains strict control of each application. In essence, OS/2 protects each program from other programs. Unlike real mode, protected-mode programs must cooperate. They cannot directly access memory locations, perform low-level I/O operations, or directly access hardware devices. OS/2 protected mode ensures that concurrent applications cooperate.

Maintaining DOS Compatibility

Of the many design considerations confronting the OS/2 developers, the most critical was ensuring DOS compatibility. Since more than 10 million people currently use DOS, the number of software packages that execute under DOS are countless. In order for OS/2 to be successful, it had to provide a means of executing existing DOS programs. If OS/2 did not provide this capability, few users (if any) would migrate to OS/2. To do so simply would not be cost-effective.

Previous sections of this chapter stated that DOS applications execute in real mode, while OS/2 applications execute in protected mode. OS/2 provides complete support for each mode. This means that OS/2 is fully capable of concurrently executing several OS/2 protected-mode programs, or running your current DOS applications in real mode.

REAL MODE VERSUS PROTECTED MODE

DOS applications execute in *real mode.*
OS/2 concurrent applications execute in *protected mode.*
OS/2 provides complete support for real-mode and protected-mode applications. It allows you to perform multitasking of protected-mode applications while maintaining compatibility for your existing DOS (real-mode) applications.

Later chapters discuss how to quickly change from one mode to the other. The OS/2 developers have done a good job of providing full functional support for both real-mode and protected-mode programs, and making it easy for the end user to execute each.

The last compatibility issue concerns disks. OS/2 uses the identical disk format as that used by DOS. In this way, OS/2 can read disks created by DOS, and DOS can read disks created by OS/2. However, remember that many disks coming from OS/2 systems will likely be in 1.2MB format.

DISK COMPATIBILITY

OS/2 and DOS use identical disk formats. DOS can read a disk created under OS/2, and OS/2 fully supports DOS disks. However, remember that many OS/2 disks will be in 1.2MB format.

OS/2 Hardware Requirements

OS/2 is an operating system designed for the IBM PC AT (and compatibles). The PC AT uses a processor chip called the 80286. The 80286 is a descendant of the 8088 processor used in the IBM PC. In addition to increased processing speed, the 80286 provides hardware support for protected-mode applications that is not available under the IBM PC (8088). Thus, OS/2 executes only on the 80286 (IBM PC AT and AT compatibles).

80286-BASED OPERATING SYSTEM

OS/2 is an operating system based on the architecture of the IBM PC AT. OS/2 requires the additional processing speed, along with hardware support for protected-mode processing, that is not available on the IBM PC. OS/2 does not run on the IBM PC.

OS/2 does run on machines using the 80386 processor, the successor to the 80286 (the processor used in the IBM PC AT). The IBM PS/2 Model 80, for example, uses the 80386.

Note that, in addition to the 80286, OS/2 runs on the 80386 (the successor to the 80286); however, today OS/2 does not fully support the 80386. Figure 1–14 depicts OS/2's hardware requirements. OS/2 requires either an 80286 or 80386 processor in the CPU. OS/2 ships on 1.2MB floppy disks. Most PC ATs are configured with a minimum of one 1.2MB floppy drive. Quite probably the most noticeable hardware requirement is the 1.5MB of random-access memory (RAM) required for OS/2.

OS/2 provides tremendous functional enhancements over DOS. For years, DOS application developers and users have been complaining about the fact that DOS is restricted to 640K. OS/2 breaks this barrier and allows programs to be virtually any

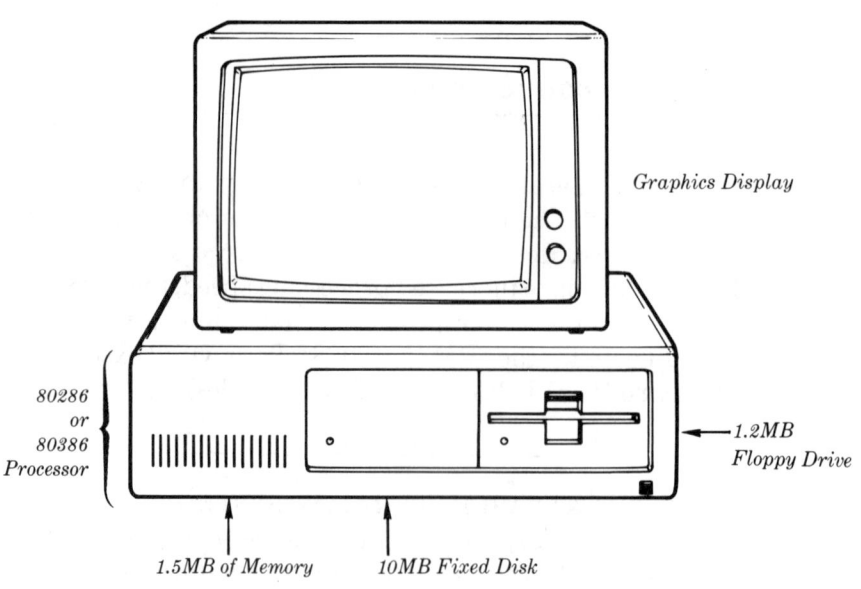

Figure 1-14. *Hardware requirements for OS/2*

length. To provide this functional enhancement, however, requires additional memory. For the first time, microcomputer users will have the same capabilities as those normally found on minicomputers. With this in mind, the OS/2 requirement for 1.5MB of memory is more than reasonable.

Virtual Memory and Devices

Under DOS, programs cannot exceed 640K in size. Before a program can execute, the program must reside in the computer's physical memory. Each time you start your computer, it loads DOS into memory (see Figure 1–15). Once in memory, DOS allows you to execute additional programs by bringing them into memory, as shown in Figure 1–16.

The IBM PC, PC AT, and PC compatibles use a technique known as *memory-mapped I/O* to display characters on your video

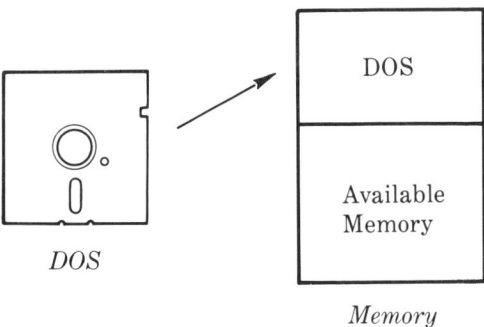

DOS

Memory

Figure 1–15. *DOS loaded into memory*

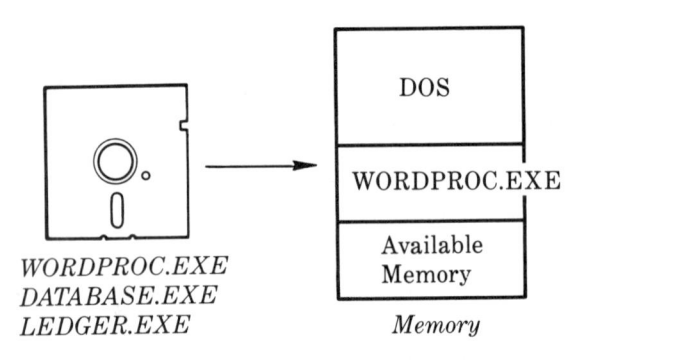

WORDPROC.EXE
DATABASE.EXE
LEDGER.EXE

Figure 1 - 16. *DOS loading more programs into memory*

screen. Under this technique, the values to be displayed on the screen are placed into specific memory locations. The computer's hardware then sends these values to specific locations on the screen display (see Figure 1–17). Depending upon your monitor

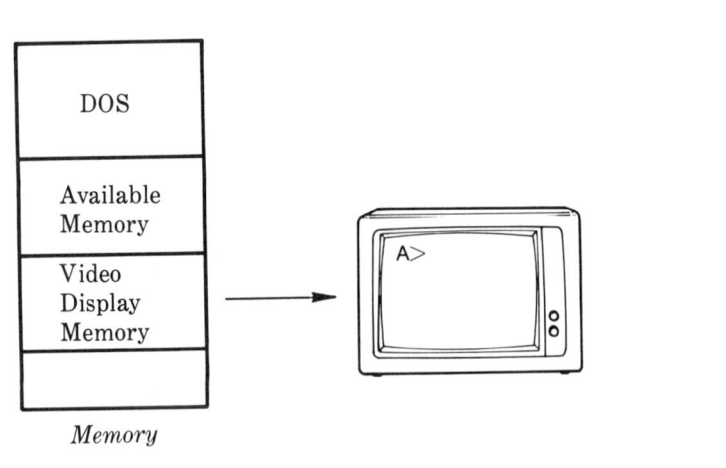

Figure 1 - 17. *Memory locations sent to screen display*

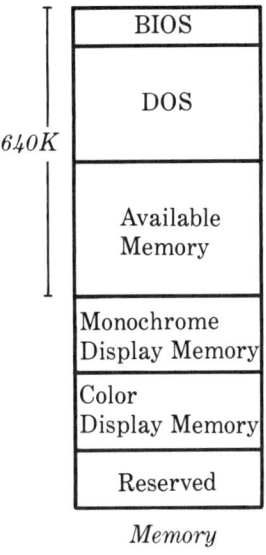

Memory

Figure 1-18. *Memory locations of monochrome and color display*

type (monochrome or color), memory-mapped I/O uses two distinct memory locations, as shown in Figure 1–18.

If you closely examine the DOS memory map, you will see that the 640K of memory is located below the start of the video memory region. This 640K region is the home for DOS applications. Unfortunately, as programs increase in functional capabilities, they also increase in size. The 640K of available memory for DOS applications is now a restriction.

OS/2 allows programs to exceed the 640K barrier by using protected-mode processing. In addition, OS/2 uses a technique known as *virtual memory management*. OS/2 virtual memory gives applications the appearance of having unlimited memory.

Under DOS, each time a program references a memory location, the memory reference is to a physical memory address in the computer's RAM (a function of real-mode processing). This technique is illustrated in Figure 1–19.

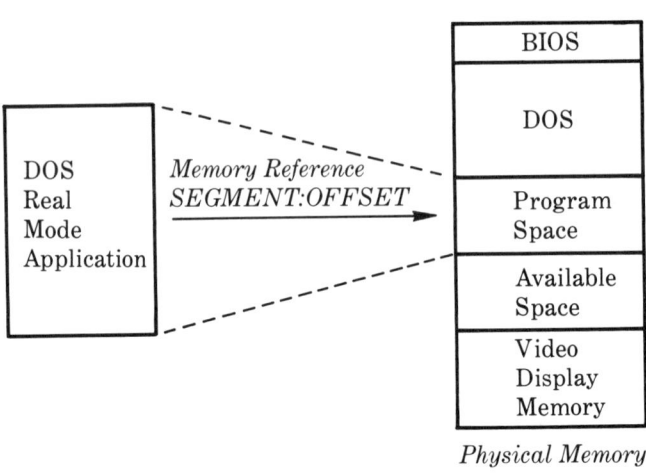

Figure 1-19.   *Memory reference to physical memory location in RAM*

Although this technique is straightforward, it prevents applications from exceeding the 640K and is unsuitable for multitasking. Each time a program executes, the program must reside in memory. If several programs are to execute concurrently, each must reside in memory (see Figure 1-20).

Unfortunately, since DOS applications can directly reference physical memory locations, you could not prevent one program from referencing the memory locations currently in use by a second program. Hence, one concurrent application could easily modify the code or data of a second application, either intentionally or accidentally (see Figure 1-21).

The mere possibility of such an occurrence in a multitasking environment is unacceptable. The operating system in a multitasking environment must provide a means of protecting applications from one another.

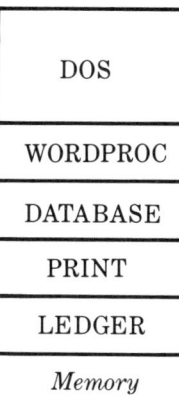

Memory

Figure 1-20. *Multiple programs residing in memory*

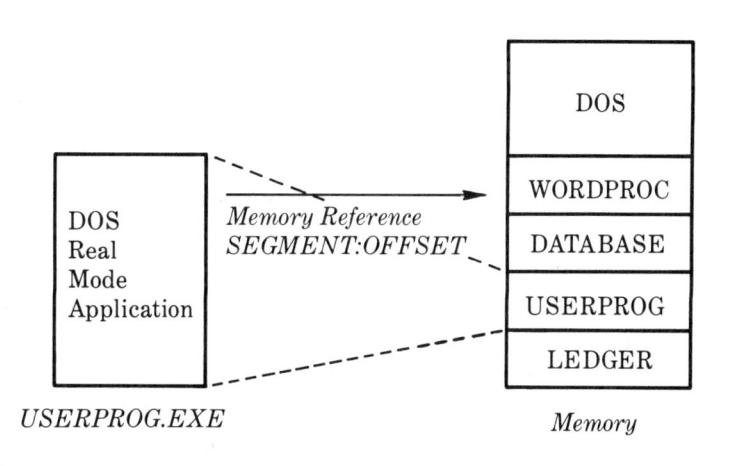

USERPROG.EXE *Memory*

Figure 1-21. *DOS inability to protect multiple programs in memory*

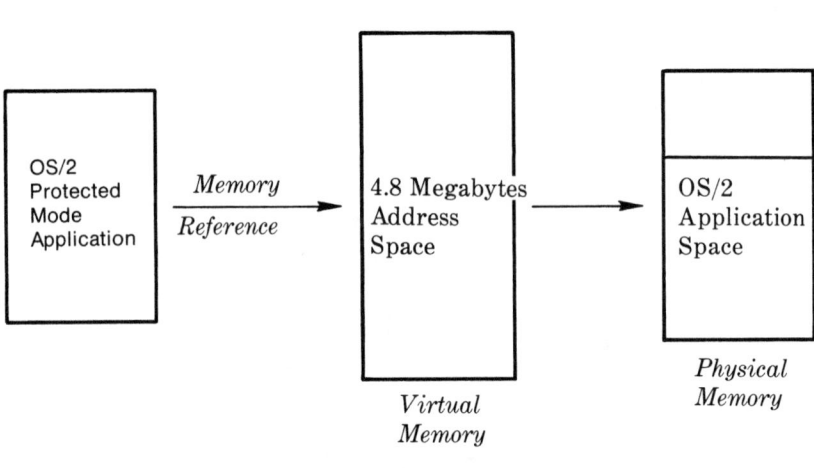

Figure 1-22.   *Virtual memory address space in OS/2*

OS/2 virtual memory management provides a level of indirection that allows it to control the specific memory locations addressable by each application. Rather than directly referencing physical memory locations (as happens under DOS), OS/2 applications instead access their own unique virtual memory address space that OS/2 maps to a physical memory location (see Figure 1-22). Remember that virtual memory is so named because the address space actually does not really exist. OS/2 once again simply gives the appearance of the memory being present.

OS/2 implements virtual memory by breaking a large program into several smaller pieces, as shown in Figure 1-23. When the user executes the program, OS/2 simply loads into memory the pages required for execution. The remainder of the program continues to reside on disk, as shown in Figure 1-24.

This technique is possible since, in most cases, only a small portion of a program performs the majority of the program's processing. When the program references a location in the pro-

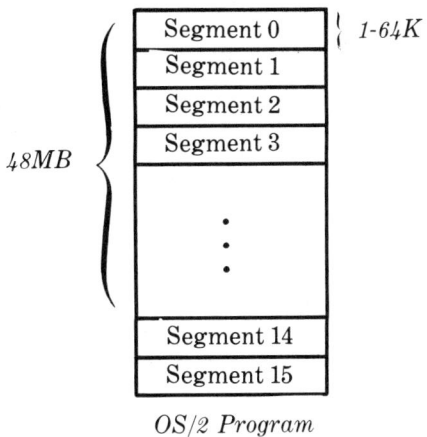

Figure 1-23. *OS/2 breaking a large program into smaller pieces*

gram that does not currently reside in memory, OS/2 brings the
segment containing the specific memory location into memory
from disk on demand. If there is no room in memory for the new

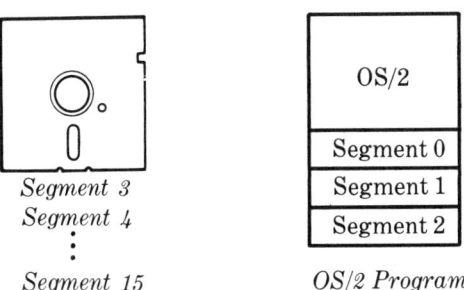

Figure 1-24. *OS/2 segments loaded into memory for execution*

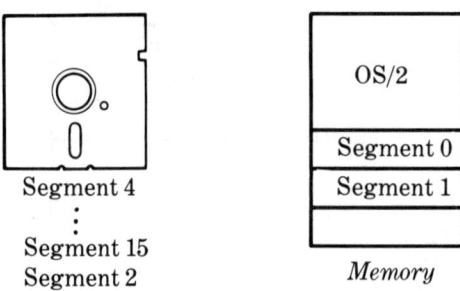

Figure 1-25.   *OS/2 moving a segment from memory*

segment, OS/2 first moves a segment from memory to disk to make memory space available, as shown in Figure 1-25. OS/2 then brings the desired segment into memory, as shown in Figure 1-26.

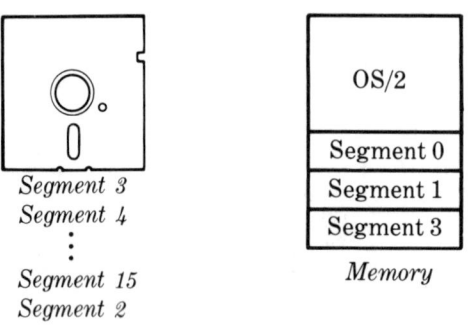

Figure 1-26.   *OS/2 bringing desired segment into memory*

This process of bringing segments into and out of memory in this fashion is called *segment swapping*.

Since OS/2 is a multitasking operating system, several programs can be executing simultaneously. Again, an OS/2 program must still reside in memory in order to execute. As shown in Figure 1-27, OS/2 brings into memory only those segments of each program that are required for immediate execution. In this case, if the user executes Program D, OS/2 must remove one of the other programs from memory temporarily to disk in order to make memory space available for Program D (see Figure 1-28).

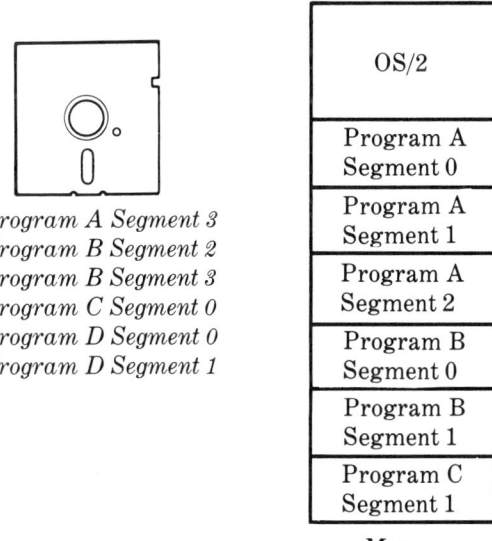

Program A Segment 3
Program B Segment 2
Program B Segment 3
Program C Segment 0
Program D Segment 0
Program D Segment 1

OS/2
Program A Segment 0
Program A Segment 1
Program A Segment 2
Program B Segment 0
Program B Segment 1
Program C Segment 1

Memory

Figure 1-27. *OS/2 virtual memory management*

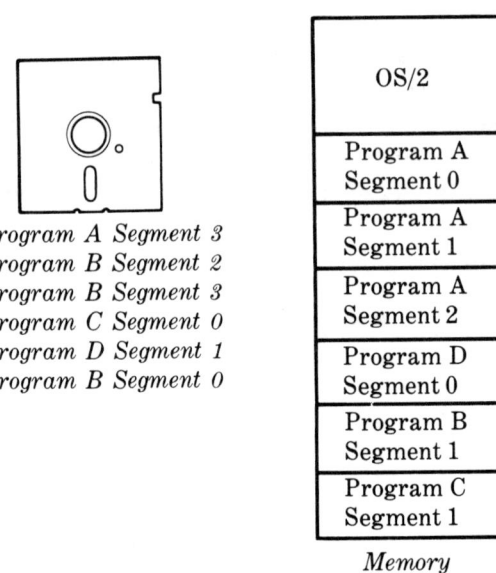

Program A Segment 3
Program B Segment 2
Program B Segment 3
Program C Segment 0
Program D Segment 1
Program B Segment 0

OS/2

Program A
Segment 0

Program A
Segment 1

Program A
Segment 2

Program D
Segment 0

Program B
Segment 1

Program C
Segment 1

Memory

Figure 1-28. *Example of virtual memory management*

By swapping segments in this manner, OS/2 can execute essentially an unlimited number of applications. However, swapping produces system overhead that limits the actual number of programs OS/2 can execute simultaneously. Although OS/2 can theoretically run an unlimited number of programs, to do so would simply be too slow.

A multitasking operating system succeeds by giving the appearance that unlimited resources (such as memory) exist for multiple applications. You have just seen how OS/2 uses virtual memory management to give applications the appearance of unlimited memory. In a similar fashion, OS/2 uses the concept of *virtual devices*. By using virtual devices, OS/2 gives each application the appearance of owning its own keyboard, screen, and printer. For example, if you are executing four programs simultaneously, each application uses its own virtual device for I/O operations. As you switch from one application to the next, OS/2 simply selects the application's virtual devices as active (see Figure 1–29). In so doing, when several programs are executing concurrently, the output of one program cannot affect another application's display or print output, since OS/2 maps individual applications to individual virtual devices.

Since OS/2 manages virtual devices, the user is not aware of the process of mapping input and output to and from each application to its virtual devices and activating an application's virtual devices.

VIRTUAL MEMORY

OS/2 virtual memory allows applications to exceed 640K in size and provides them with an address space of 48 megabytes. OS/2 uses segment swapping to implement virtual memory.

VIRTUAL DEVICES

OS/2 gives each application the appearance that it owns its own keyboard, screen display, printer, mouse, and so forth. Since each application uses its own unique devices in this manner, OS/2 protected-mode applications cannot interfere with one another. When you select a specific application for display, OS/2 maps the application's virtual devices to the actual physical devices in a fashion that is not obvious to the end user.

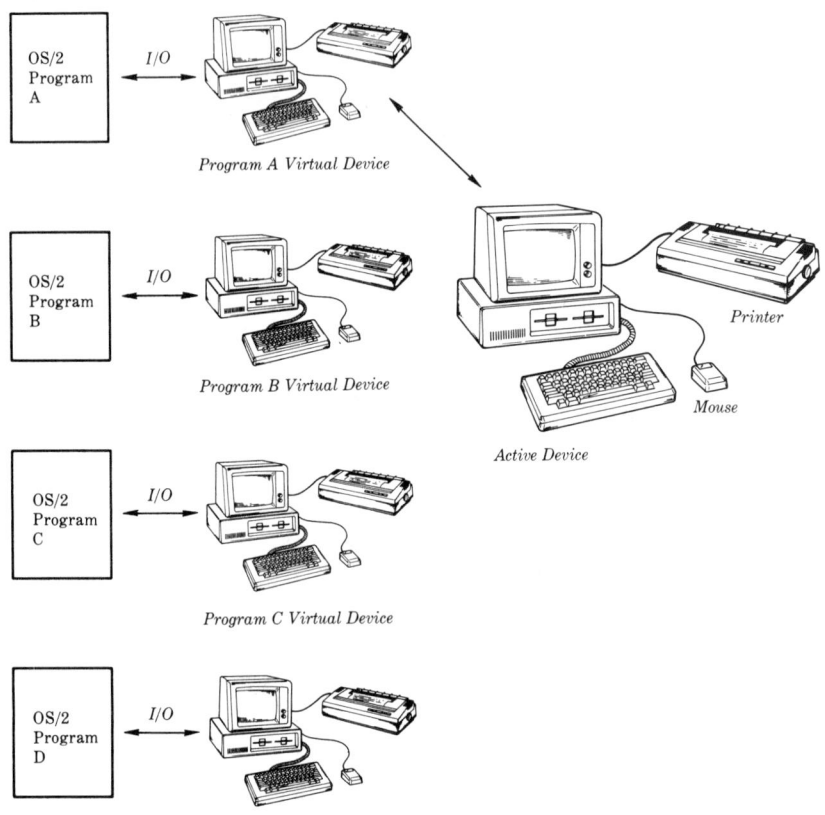

Program A Virtual Device

Program B Virtual Device

Program C Virtual Device

Program D Virtual Device

Printer

Mouse

Active Device

Figure 1-29. *OS/2 selection of virtual devices*

Future of DOS

DOS has been, and will continue to be, the mainstay for micro-computer operating systems. OS/2 is an 80286-based operating system that does not run on the IBM PC (8088). Because of the tremendous user base and software availability for the IBM PC, PC XT, and portable computers, these computers will continue to sell and be readily used for many years to come. In fact, you should even see new versions of DOS released that increase its functional capabilities.

Over the past few years, DOS has become fully accepted in the home, school, and business. Many of the requirements that led to OS/2's development (such as support for local area networks and integration of several software packages to support information exchange), have been driven strictly by business. Most home computer users do not have these requirements. As such, business will be the first sector to fully migrate to OS/2. Most home computer users will continue to use DOS for some time to come, thus ensuring that DOS remains fully utilized. Over the next few years, however, many users will begin to migrate to OS/2 as the prices of the 80286 and 80386 make them readily available to the general public.

History of OS/2

The concept of a multitasking operating system for personal computers is not new. In fact, many "old-time" personal computer users remember that CP/M provided limited concurrent capabil-ities. Although the need for a sophisticated multitasking operat-ing system has only recently become apparent, OS/2 has been on the planning table for a long time. In fact, the first release of OS/2 took more than four years to develop. Compare this to the devel-

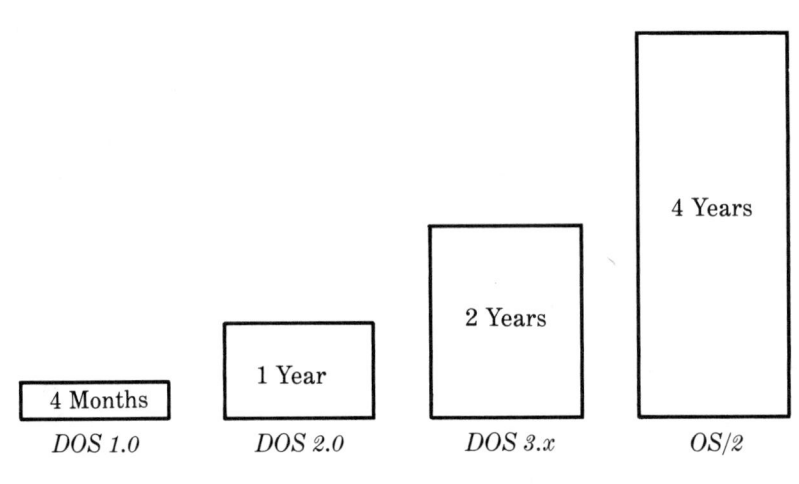

Figure 1-30   *Comparison of DOS development time with OS/2 development time*

opment time required for different versions of DOS, as shown in Figure 1-30.

In April 1987, Microsoft and IBM announced their joint venture to release a fully functional multitasking operating system capable of taking personal computers well into the 1990s. Because of the large DOS user base, OS/2 had to provide all of its functional enhancements while remaining fully DOS compatible. Hence, OS/2 had to be 100% functional before its release to the general public. In this light, the four-year development period for OS/2 is understandable.

The DOS developers have used many of the features that OS/2 provides in recent releases of DOS. For example, DOS code pages for international support and named parameters for batch processing (which are available under OS/2) are available under DOS 3.3.

It is important not to overlook the impact of MS Windows on OS/2. Although most people associate MS Windows strictly with the OS/2 Presentation Manager, Windows actually gave the OS/2 developers a dry run for such concepts as multitasking, virtual devices, and swapping. In addition, MS Windows taught everyone that if a multitasking operating system is slow (Windows is slow on an IBM PC), no one will use it. This is another reason OS/2 will not migrate to the IBM PC.

Although OS/2 is new to the public, it already has a long past. OS/2 is destined to have a significant place in microcomputer history.

User Interface

For DOS users, OS/2 provides a familiar interface, the command-line prompt:

```
[C:\]
```

For users new to both OS/2 and DOS, the command-line prompt is OS/2's means of prompting you for input. Simply stated, OS/2 is asking you to enter a command. If you were to simply press the ENTER key, OS/2 would process the input and redisplay its prompt for you to issue your next command, as follows:

```
[C:\]
[C:\]
```

If you were to type in CLS and press the ENTER key,

```
[c:\]
[c:\]
[c:\] CLS
```

OS/2 would clear the screen. As you can see, OS/2 erases the contents of the screen and places the cursor in the upper-left corner of the screen:

```
[c:\]
```

Once OS/2 completes a command, it redisplays its command-line prompt and requests your next command.

For most of you, the OS/2 command-line interface will be your interface to the operating system. Later chapters examine the OS/2 Presentation Manager, which provides an alternate user interface.

Chapter Highlights

OS/2 is a new operating system from Microsoft and IBM that is designed to run on the IBM PC AT and AT compatibles.

OS/2 provides increased functional capabilities over DOS by fully supporting multitasking.

Multitasking allows users to fully utilize the CPU's processing capabilities by reducing CPU idle time.

OS/2 implements multitasking by dividing each CPU processing second into smaller sections called time slices. OS/2 then distributes time slices to each program in the system.

OS/2 provides a user interface similar to the DOS command-line prompt. From this prompt, OS/2 commands are entered in the same manner as DOS commands.

More than 10 million users currently use DOS. OS/2 real mode provides compatibility for existing DOS applications.

OS/2 executes applications in either real mode or protected mode. Real mode exists to ensure compatibility for existing DOS commands. Protected mode exists to protect OS/2 concurrent applications from interfering with one another.

Unlike DOS, which restricts applications to 640K of memory, OS/2 uses virtual memory management, which gives applications a 48 megabyte virtual address space.

OS/2 virtual memory management breaks a large program into smaller sections called segments. OS/2 brings into memory only those segments that are required for the program to execute and leaves the remaining segments on disk. When the program later references a segment address that does not currently reside in the computer's physical memory, OS/2 brings the specific segment from disk into memory. This process is known as segment swapping.

OS/2 requires an 80286 or 80386 processor, 1.5MB of memory, a 1.2 MB floppy disk, and a graphics display. OS/2 does not execute on the IBM PC (8088).

Because of its tremendous user base, DOS will remain fully supported for many years to come.

OS/2 is not a recent idea. The initial version required more than four years to develop.

OS/2's multitasking capabilities make it well-suited to carry personal computers far into the 1990s.

2 *Getting Started with OS/2*

Chapter 1 provided a brief overview of OS/2, its design rationale, implementation, and functional capability. This chapter provides more technical information to get the novice PC user up to speed with the concepts and terminology to be used throughout the remainder of the book. By the end of this chapter you should be comfortable with your personal computer and with OS/2. For experienced DOS users, much of this chapter should be review. Pay close attention to each of the highlighted sections until discussion of the OS/2 Session Manager begins. At that point, you begin your use of OS/2.

Understanding Hardware

Simply stated, *hardware* is the boards, cables, and peripheral devices (printers, mouse, modem, and so on) that make up your

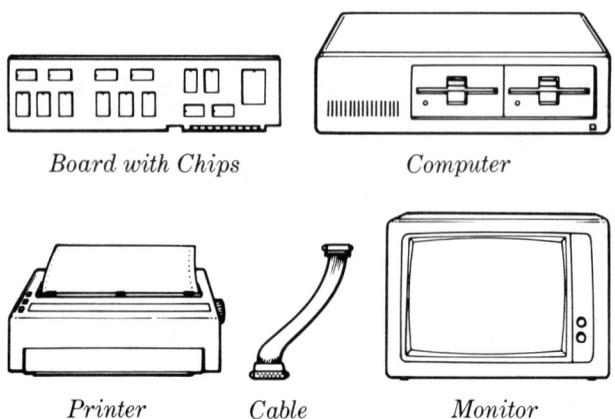

Figure 2-1. *Hardware components*

computer, as illustrated in Figure 2-1. By far the largest piece of your computer hardware is the chassis, which is home to the computer's central processing unit (CPU), the computer's memory, and also your floppy and fixed disk drives (see Figure 2-2).

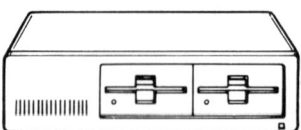

Figure 2-2. *Computer chassis*

Processor chip	Computer	Usage	Unique features
8088	IBM PC	16-bit processor 8-bit bus	First PC with an MB address space
80286	IBM PC AT	16-bit processor 16-bit bus	Protected mode
80386	IBM PS/2 Model 80 Deskpro 386	32-bit processor 32-bit bus	Protected mode Memory management by using hardware

Table 2-1. *Comparison of 8088, 80286, and 80386 Chips*

The CPU is the computer's main processor. In the IBM PC, the CPU is known as the 8088. The IBM PC AT uses a faster, more functional processor called the 80286. In addition, a processor chip known as the 80386 (which is found in such computers as the IBM PS/2 Model 80 and Compaq's DeskPro 386) is much faster and provides significant functional enhancements over both the 8088 and 80286. These three chips (the 8088, 80286, and 80386) are the primary processor chips found in IBM and compatible personal computers today, as depicted in Table 2-1. OS/2 runs on 80286 and 80386.

In addition to housing the computer's CPU, the chassis stores the computer's memory. Memory within a computer is defined in terms of bytes. A *byte* consists of eight binary digits. Each of the devices within the computer communicates with other devices based upon the presence or absence of electronic signals. A signal within the computer is in one of two states: present (on) or absent (off). These states can be defined by binary digits that are by definition either 1 or 0.

BINARY

The binary numbering system represents values as a series of 1's and 0's known as bits. If a bit is set, it has the value 1; otherwise, the bit is clear, or 0.

A bit within the computer is used to represent the presence or absence of an electronic signal. If the bit is set, the signal is on. If the bit is clear, the signal is off.

Eight binary digits (10010100) form a byte.

The computer stores information as a series of binary digits (1's and 0's). For example, assume that you want to add the values 2 + 5. Table 2-2 illustrates the binary values that the computer uses to store the values 0-10. In order to add the values 2 + 5, the computer uses binary digits, as follows:

```
  2      0010
 +5     +0101
 ───    ─────
  7      0111
```

A byte is simply a collection of eight binary digits. As shown in Table 2-3, a byte is capable of storing values ranging from 0 to 255.

Discussions about the computer's memory often refer to bytes in increments of "K" (for example, 256K). For simplification,

Decimal	Binary
0	0000
1	0001
2	0010
3	0011
4	0100
5	0101
6	0110
7	0111
8	1000
9	1001
10	1010

Table 2-2. *Conversion of Decimal Numbers to Binary*

Decimal	Binary
0	0000 0000
1	0000 0001
2	0000 0010
.	.
.	.
.	.
253	1111 1101
254	1111 1110
255	1111 1111

Table 2-3. *Maximum Possibilities of Decimal-to-Binary Conversion*

many computer users view a "K" as the value 1000. Therefore, 256K of storage provides space for 256,000 bytes. However, this is a simplification. A "K" actually equals 1024, so 256K is actually equal to

$$256 \times 1024 = 262,144$$

IF your computer has storage space for 256K, it is capable of storing 262,144 bytes of information, as shown in Figure 2-3.

Chapter 1 noted that OS/2 requires 1.5MB of memory. A *megabyte* is equal to 1 million bytes. OS/2, therefore, requires your computer to provide memory space for 1.5 million bytes of information.

Probably the easiest way to visualize a byte is as a character of the alphabet. As it turns out, each time you store a character in memory, the character occupies a byte of storage space. Therefore, 256K is actually space for 262,144 characters.

BYTE

A byte is eight binary digits (00101100). Within the computer, each character stored requires a byte of memory.

OS/2 requires 1.5MB of memory (a megabyte is 1 million bytes). OS/2, therefore, requires memory space for 1.5 million characters.

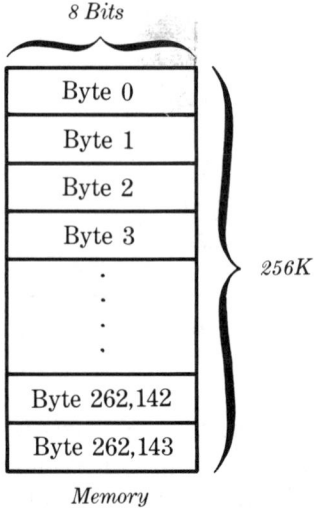

Figure 2-3.   *Storage space for 256K of memory*

Your computer's memory is a short-term (or *volatile*) memory. Each time you power your computer off, the computer loses the entire contents of its memory. Once this information is lost, you can never retrieve it. If you need to store information from one user session to the next, you must place the information to be saved on disk (as described in detail later in this chapter).

The computer uses memory to store programs and their data. A computer *program* is simply a list of instructions that tells the computer what to do. Before a program can execute, the program must reside in the computer's memory. This chapter later examines several OS/2 commands. At start-up time, OS/2 places several commands into memory. To execute these commands, you simply type the command's name at the OS/2 prompt. Most of your programs, however, will reside on disk. Before OS/2 can execute them, it must load them from disk into memory, as shown in Figure 2-4.

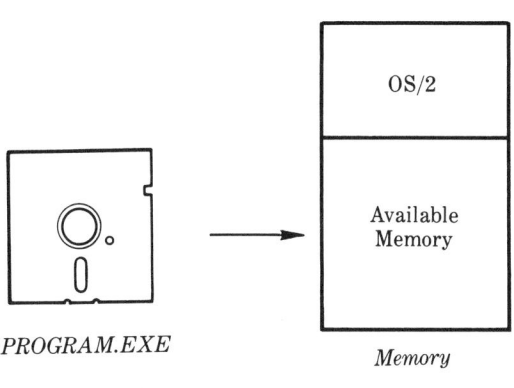

PROGRAM.EXE

Figure 2-4. *OS/2 loading programs from disk into memory*

In case you are curious, the maximum amount of memory that you can place into an 80286 is 16MB, or space enough for 16 million characters.

In addition to the CPU and memory, all of the remaining chips used by the PC reside in the chassis. If you purchase additional hardware (such as a modem or mouse), you must install in the chassis the device interface boards that allow the hardware device to communicate with the computer.

However, most users seldom need to open the computer chassis. If you do not need to add additional hardware to your system, leave the chassis closed.

Screen Display

Your *screen display* is the device that OS/2 uses to display a program's output (or result). The two most common types of PC display are monochrome (green, amber, or black and white) and color. A color display is produced with a color graphics adapter (CGA), extended graphics adapter (EGA), or video graphics

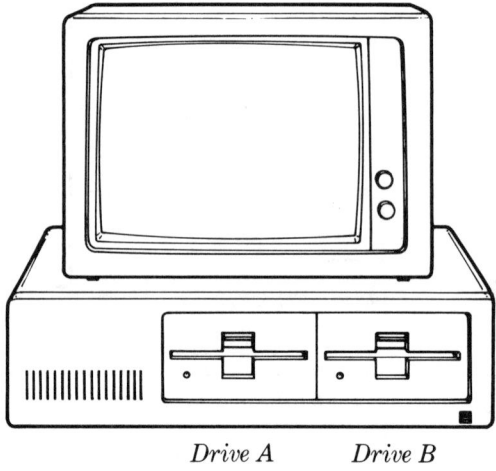

Drive A   Drive B

Figure 2-5.   *Drive configuration of standard IBM PC*

adapter (VGA). OS/2 provides complete support for each type of monitor. If you anticipate using the OS/2 Presentation Manager discussed in Chapter 14, you will need a color graphics adapter. If you are fully satisfied with the OS/2 command-line interface, a monochrome adapter is indeed acceptable. However, most of the programs you will see released for OS/2 will make extensive use of color, which in turn makes output more attractive than it would be with a monochrome display.

Disk Drives

Disk drive configurations may differ for each system. Most computers today have two floppy disk drives. Older PC systems use side-by-side floppy disk drives, as shown in Figure 2-5. Most IBM PC AT systems, however, use a more compact disk drive called a *half-height drive*, as shown in Figure 2-6.

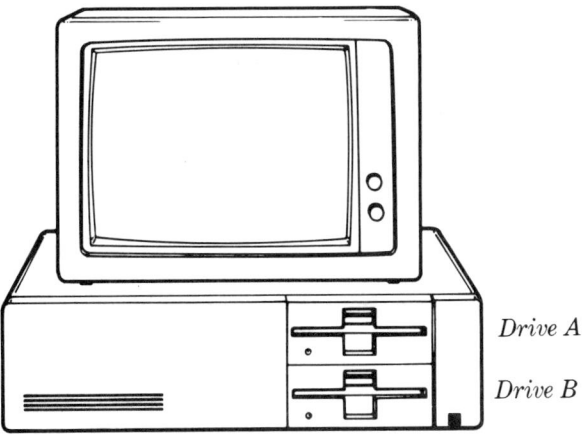

Drive A

Drive B

Figure 2-6. *Drive configuration with half-height drives*

Although most systems have two floppy drives, OS/2 requires your system to have only one floppy drive, as shown in Figure 2-7. Note, however, that OS/2 requires at least one 1.2MB floppy disk drive.

Figure 2-7. *Drive configuration with only one floppy drive*

If you closely examine the disk drive types shown in Figure 2-8, you see that each drive contains a latch that must be opened when you insert the disk into the drive, and closed once the disk is in place. Also, each drive has a small light that tells you when OS/2 is using the disk. When this light is on, the disk is in use. Never open the latch or turn off the computer while this light is illuminated. In so doing, you risk losing all of the data that the disk contains.

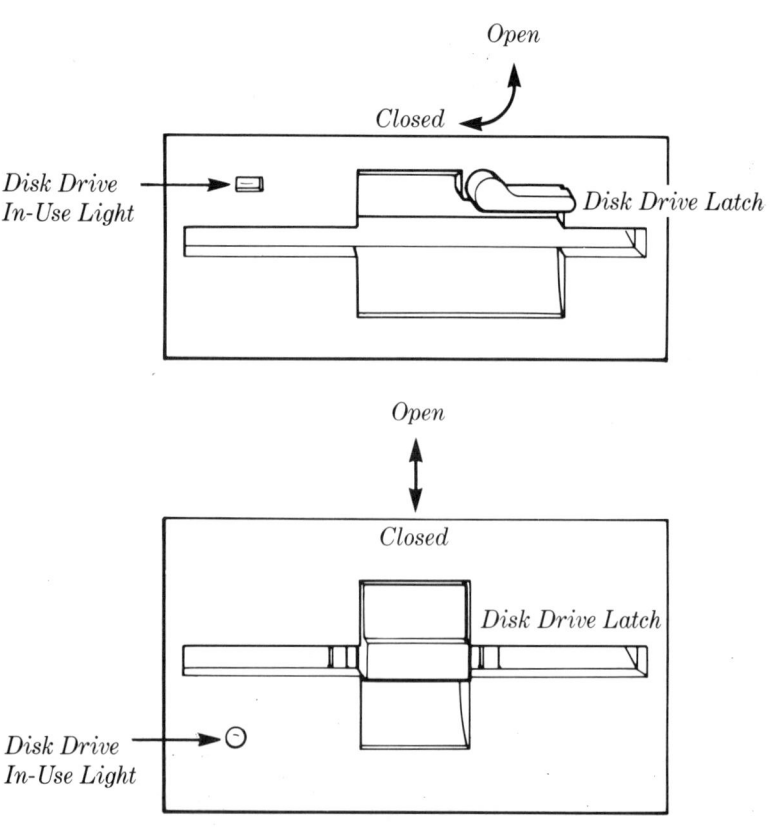

Figure 2-8. *Types of disk drives*

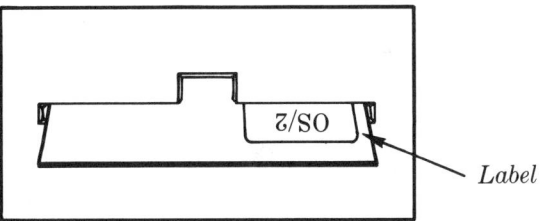

Figure 2-9. *Proper way to insert disk that has a label*

To insert a disk into a drive, always insert the disk so that its label is facing up and is fully visible, as shown in Figure 2-9. If the disk does not have a label, insert the disk so that the small notch in the disk is at the outer-left corner, as shown in Figure 2-10.

Always keep in mind that disks must be treated with great care. After you purchase your computer, you will probably find that a great deal of your computer cost outlay is for floppy disks. Since OS/2 makes extensive use of 1.2MB floppy disks, you will find that these disks are not inexpensive. With proper treatment,

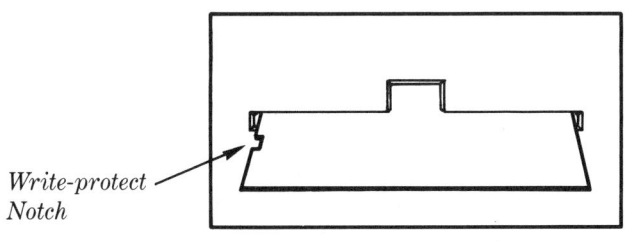

Figure 2-10. *Proper way to insert disk that has no label*

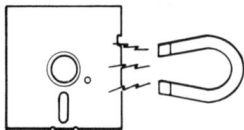

Never place the disk near magnetic devices.

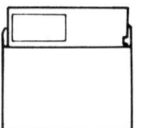

Always place disks back into a disk envelope when you are not using them.

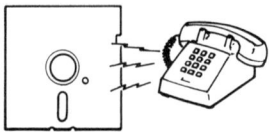

Keep the disk away from your telephone.

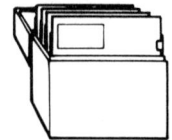

Store your floppies in a safe location.

Never touch your floppy disk media.

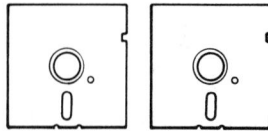

Always make a backup copy of your floppy disk.

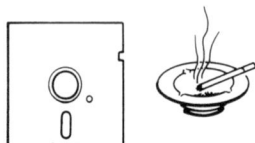

Never smoke near floppy disks.

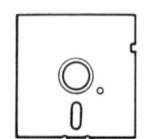

Keep room temperature in the range 50° F to 110° F.

Never bend floppy disks.

Figure 2-11. *Rules for handling floppy disks*

however, your floppy disks can last a long time. With proper care, you greatly reduce the possibility of losing the information contained on the disk. Always follow the rules for handling floppy disks that are shown in Figure 2-11.

Most personal computers today have an internal *fixed disk.* In most cases, the fixed disk is hidden from the user by the computer's chassis. The only visible portion of the fixed disk is the disk activation light, as shown in Figure 2-12.

Although fixed and floppy disk drives both exist to store information, fixed disks are different from floppies in several ways. First, fixed disks are not removable. Unlike floppy disks that you must insert into the disk drive whenever you need to access the information they contain, fixed disks are a permanent fixture within the computer. You cannot physically access a fixed disk's storage media (see Figure 2-13).

Second, fixed disks have greater storage capacity than floppy disks. In fact, common fixed disk sizes include 10MB, 20MB, and 30MB of storage. Third, since fixed disks are internal to the computer, their mechanical makeup is superior to that of floppy disks, thus making fixed disks much faster. OS/2 users should

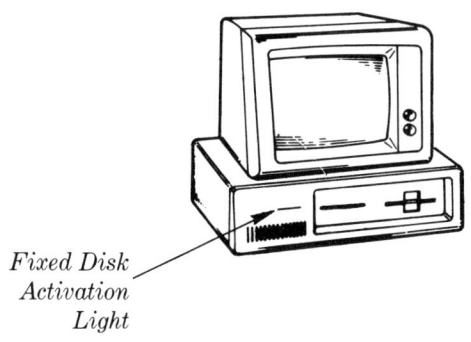

Fixed Disk
Activation
Light

Figure 2-12.   *Activation light on fixed disk*

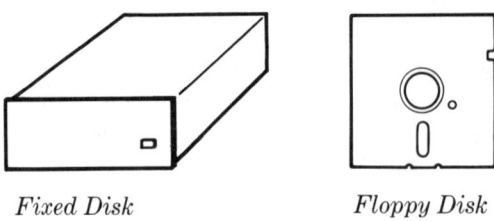

Fixed Disk   *Floppy Disk*

Figure 2-13.   *Fixed disk versus floppy disk*

have a minimum of a 10MB fixed disk. Table 2-4 summarizes the major differences between fixed disks and floppy disks.

Users are often curious about the makeup of a floppy disk. From the outside, a floppy disk appears as shown in Figure 2-14. The *disk jacket* is a cardboard cover that protects the disk storage media from scratches, dust, and fingerprints. The *write-protect notch* allows you to prevent the contents of your floppy disks from being changed. When the disk notch is visible (see Figure 2-15) OS/2 can modify the data contained on the disk. When you cover

Disk type	Speed	Common sizes	Removable	Cost	Susceptability to damage
Floppy disk	Significantly slower than fixed disk	360K 720K 1.2 MB	Yes	Relatively inexpensive	High
Fixed disk	Slower than RAM disk	10 MB, 20 MB, 30 MB	No	Several hundred dollars	Physically protected from user

Table 2-4.   *Comparison of Floppy Disk to Fixed Disk*

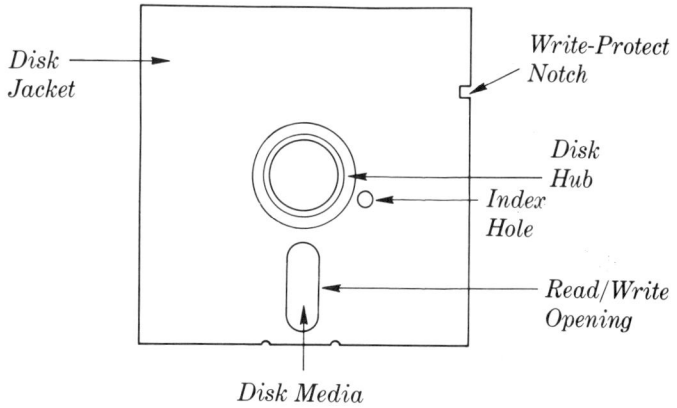

Figure 2-14.   *Parts of a floppy disk*

Figure 2-15.   *Write-protect notch on disk*

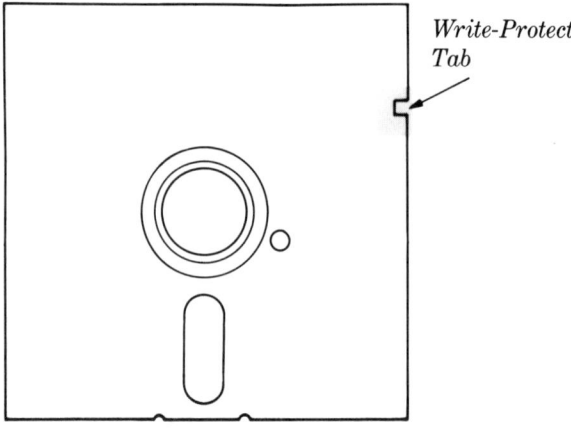

Write-Protect Tab

Figure 2-16.   *Tab covering write-protect notch*

this notch with a *write-protect tab* (provided with your new disks), OS/2 cannot modify the disk contents (see Figure 2-16). In so doing, the disk is said to be *write-protected*. When you write-protect a disk. OS/2 can only read or copy the contents of the disk to another source.

The *disk hub* is the portion of the disk that the disk drive uses to spin the disk once you place it in the drive. A disk works in a manner similar to the way a tape is played on a tape recorder. Once in the disk drive, the disk spins rapidly past the disk drive's *read/write head*, which reads data from or writes data to the floppy disk.

The disk's *read/write opening* provides the read/write head with access to the disk storage media. As the disk spins rapidly inside the disk drive, the read/write head records data to or from the disk. The *index hole* provides a timing mechanism as the disk spins rapidly within the drive. Be careful never to touch the disk storage media through any of these openings. In so doing, you could destroy the information stored on the disk.

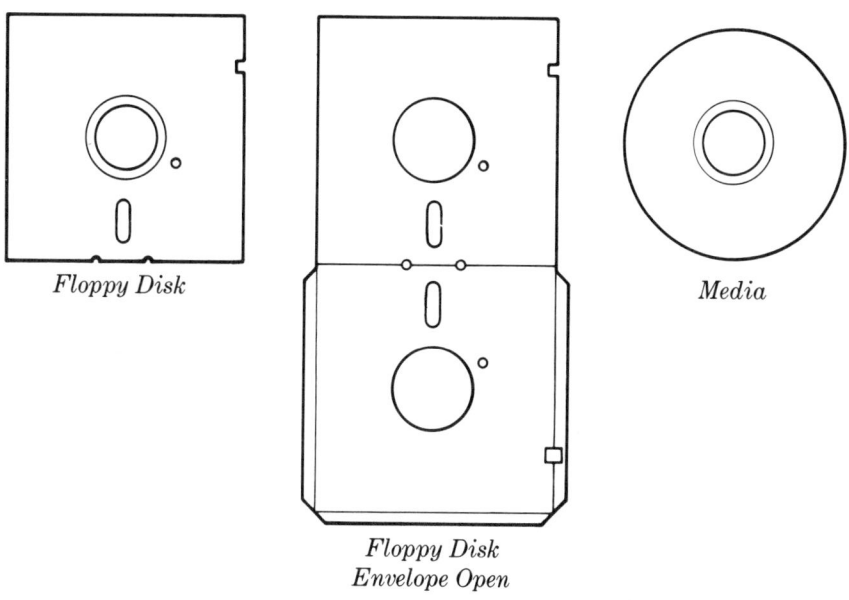

Floppy Disk

Media

*Floppy Disk
Envelope Open*

Figure 2-17. *Inner construction of floppy disks*

If you take apart a floppy disk, you will expose the storage media, as shown in Figure 2-17.

With the advent of the IBM PS/2 line of computers, more and more users are migrating to 3 1/2-inch disks called *microfloppies* (see Figure 2-18). Microfloppy disks are a unique size that requires a special disk drive. As more and more computers migrate to microfloppy disks, you will notice that more software also begins shipping on microfloppy disks. Because of their plastic containers, microfloppy disks are much more durable than standard 5 1/4-inch disks, as well as much less susceptible to dust, smoke, and other destructive particles.

If you look at the top of your microfloppy disks, you notice a small metal portion called a *shutter*, as shown in Figure 2-19.

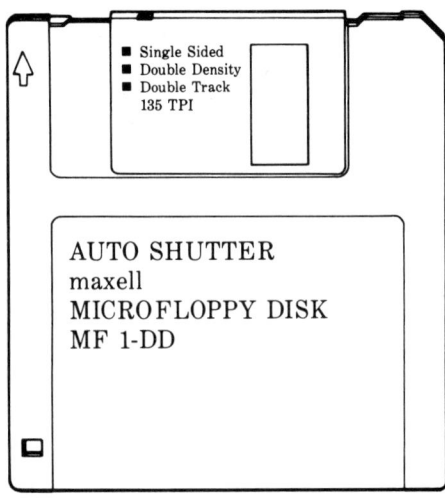

Figure 2-18. *Microfloppy disk*

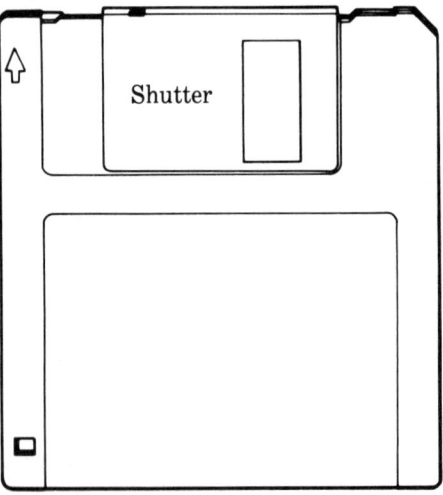

Figure 2-19. *Location of shutter*

Slide the shutter to the left and you expose the storage media of the microfloppy disk (see Figure 2-20). Each time that the computer directs the disk drive to read data from or write data to the disk, the drive slides this shutter to the left and exposes the disk media to the drive's read/write head.

If you turn over the microfloppy disk (see Figure 2-21), you will see the disk's write-protect notch. If you can see light through this opening, the disk is write-protected. If this opening is closed, OS/2 can access the disk in either read or write mode to change the disk's contents.

The second major element on the back of the microfloppy is the disk drive *spindle*. The disk drive uses this spindle to rotate the microfloppy disk within the drive in the same manner that floppy disk drives use the disk hub. Unlike floppy disk drives that use the index hole for timing, microfloppy disks use the sector notch.

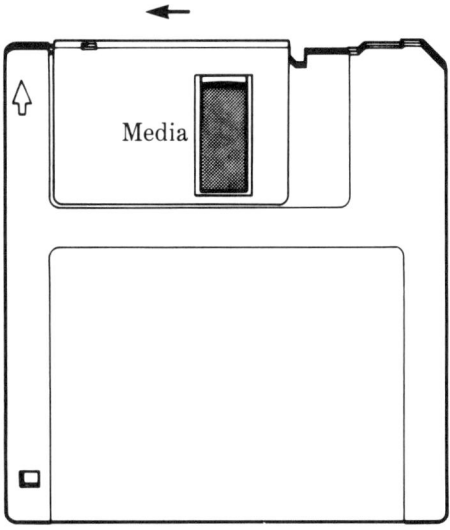

Figure 2-20. *Disk media*

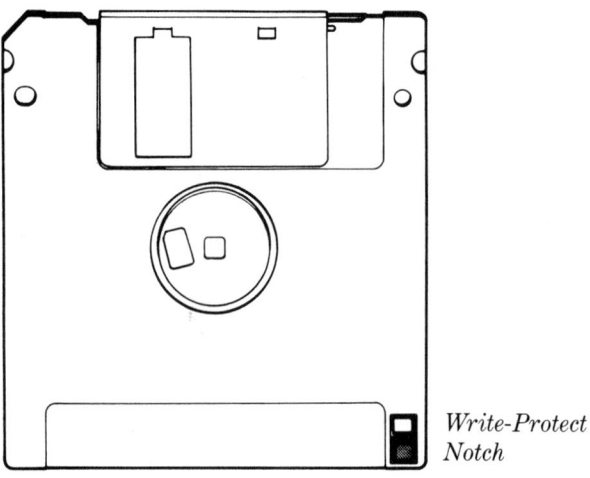

*Write-Protect
Notch*

Figure 2-21.   *Write-protect notch on microfloppy disk*

Before a microfloppy disk will spin, it must be properly seated in
the drive.

Microfloppy disks are on the verge of making an important
contribution to the microcomputer field. Their use should continue to grow in the future.

The Keyboard

Figure 2-22 illustrates a common keyboard for the IBM PC AT.
Before you begin using OS/2, you must understand the functions
of several basic keys. First, the keys on your keyboard that are
labeled F1 through F10 are called *function keys* (see Figure 2-23).
Later chapters will show how OS/2 allows you to use several of
these keys to simplify your command input.

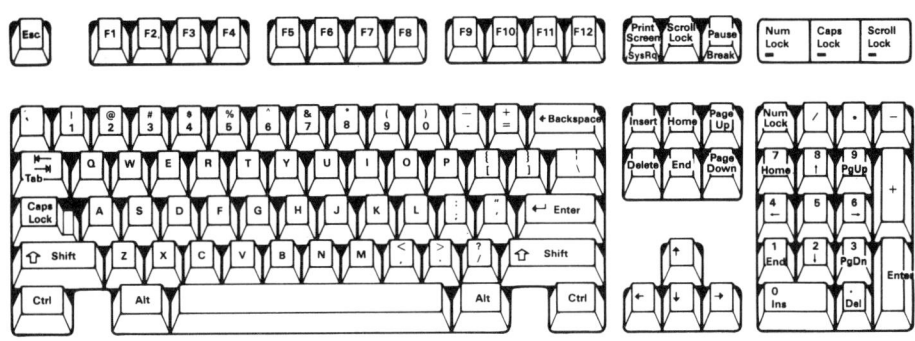

Figure 2-22. *IBM AT keyboard template*

Next, the BACKSPACE key allows you to erase the character that immediately precedes the cursor on your screen display (see Figure 2-24). Assume that your screen display contains the following:

A> DISKCOPY_

Pressing the BACKSPACE key one time results in the following:

A> DISKCOP_

Likewise, pressing the BACKSPACE key again results in

A> DISKCO_

OS/2 (as does DOS) uses the ENTER key to terminate each of the commands that you enter from the keyboard (see Figure

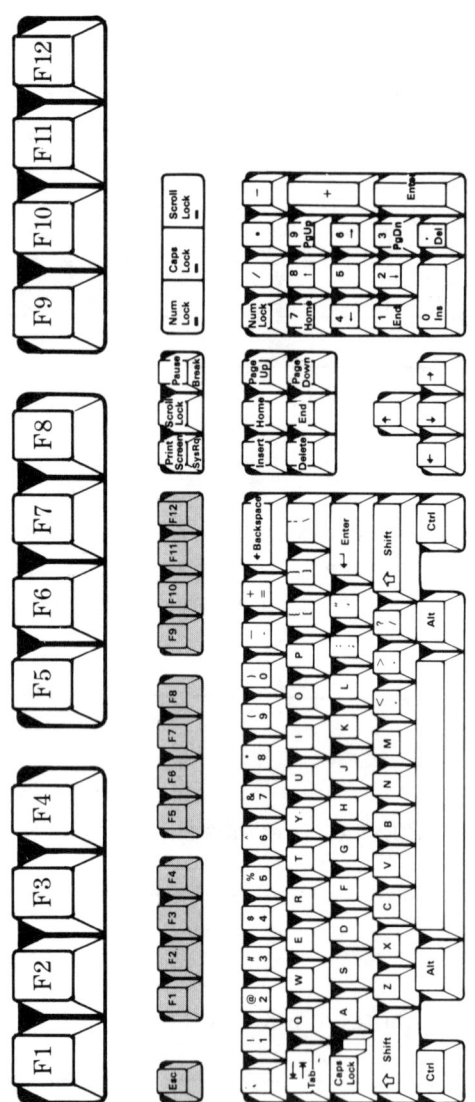

Figure 2-23. *Location of function keys*

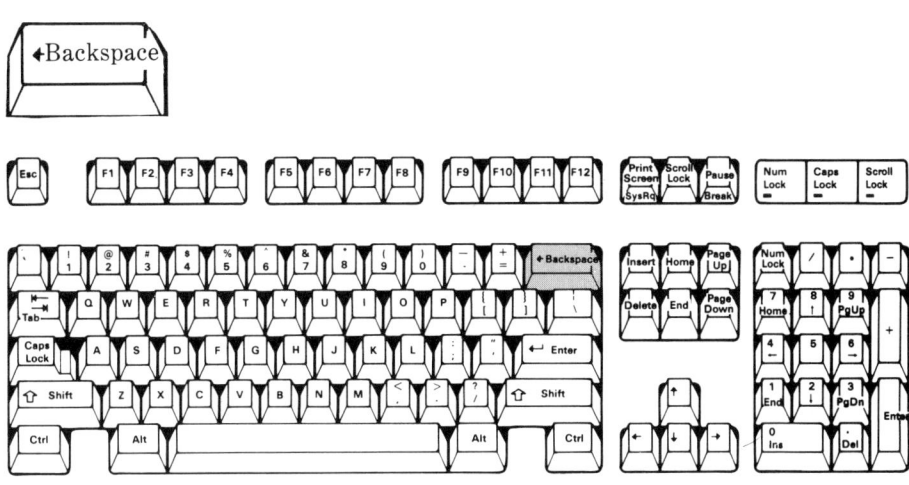

Figure 2-24. *Location of BACKSPACE key*

2-25). To execute the OS/2 "clear screen" command, for example, you would type CLS at the OS/2 prompt and press the ENTER key:

```
[A:\] CLS
```

OS/2 responds to the command by clearing the contents of the screen display and placing the cursor in the upper-left corner of the screen.

The next three keys play an important role in activating the OS/2 Session Manager, which allows you to quickly switch

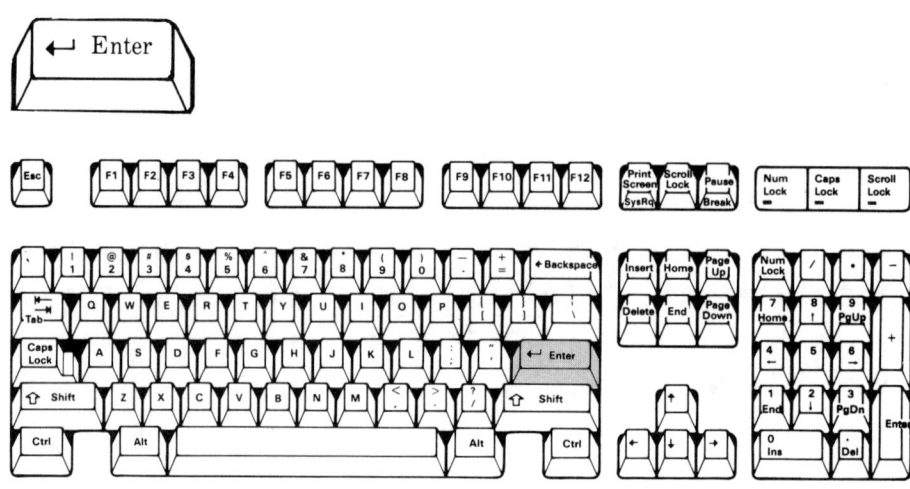

Figure 2-25.   *Location of ENTER key*

between OS/2 concurrent applications. First, locate the CTRL key (see Figure 2-26). Although this key is used for several additional functions, pressing the CTRL key and the ESC key (in that order and leaving both depressed) directs OS/2 to activate the Session Manager. See Figure 2-27 for the location of the ESC key.

In a similar manner, pressing the ALT key (see Figure 2-28) in conjunction with the ESC key directs the OS/2 Session Manager to select the next application (in its list of concurrent applications) as active for display. The remainder of the keyboard keys work in the same manner as standard typewriter keys.

Understanding Software

Just as your cables, boards, and peripheral devices comprise your computer's hardware, the programs that the computer executes constitute its software. Simply stated, *software* is computer pro-

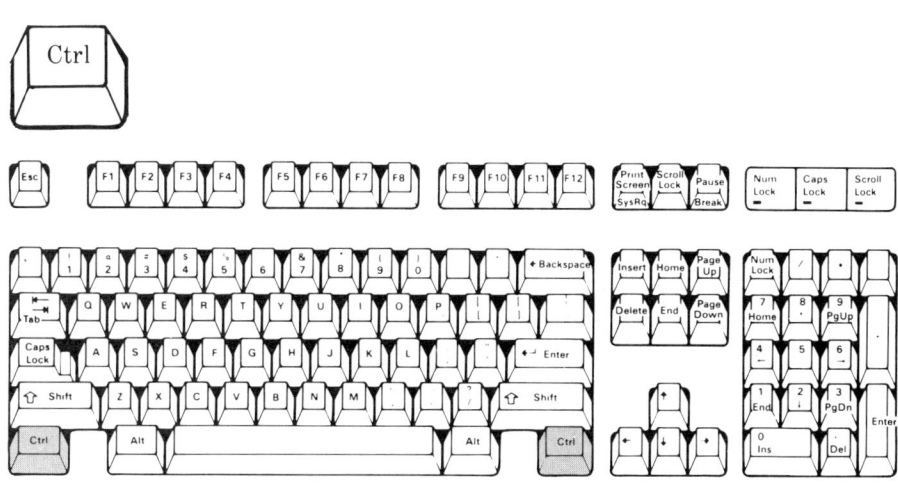

Figure 2-26. *Location of* CTRL *key*

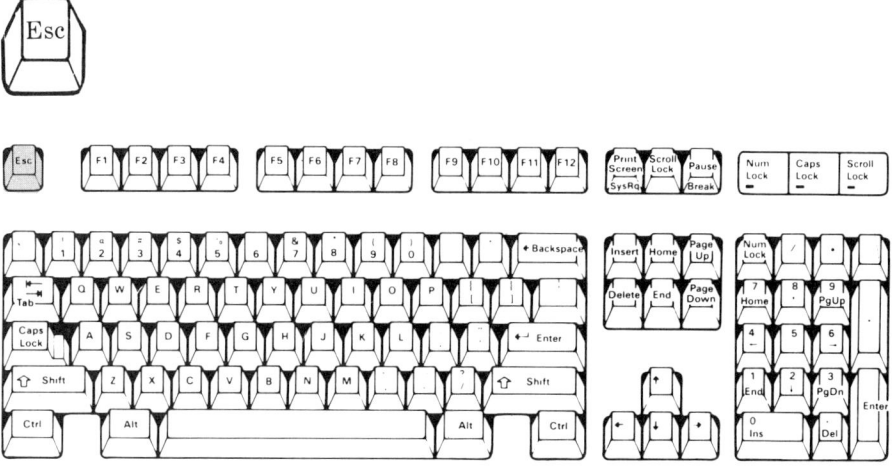

Figure 2-27. *Location of* ESC *key*

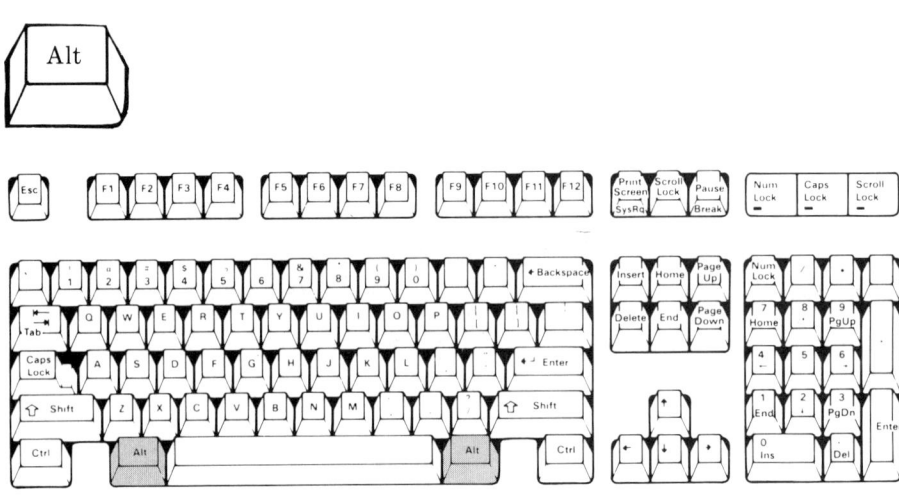

Figure 2-28. *Location of ALT key*

grams. A *computer program* is simply a list of instructions that the computer is to perform. The computer's hardware components rely on software to tell them what to do.

Software falls into one of two categories: *application software* and *system software.* Application software is programs written to perform a specific task (such as a word processing program, a spreadsheet, or a mailing-list program). Application software comprises the majority of the software on the market today. Each day, thousands of programmers develop simple programs to perform payroll, inventory, general-ledger and similar functions. As user sophistication has increased, the complexity of their applications (and subsequently the programming required to implement these applications) has increased tremendously. OS/2 provides the programmer with a myriad of capabilities aimed at aiding software developers with their programming tasks.

System software includes operating systems such as OS/2 and DOS, which allow users to execute application software programs. In addition to operating systems, device driver software (which allow the operating system to communicate with hardware devices) and local area network software fall into this category. System software generally provides the hardware interface for application software (see Figure 2-29).

Remember that, regardless of whether the software is categorized as system or application software, it is still only a list of instructions that the computer is to perform.

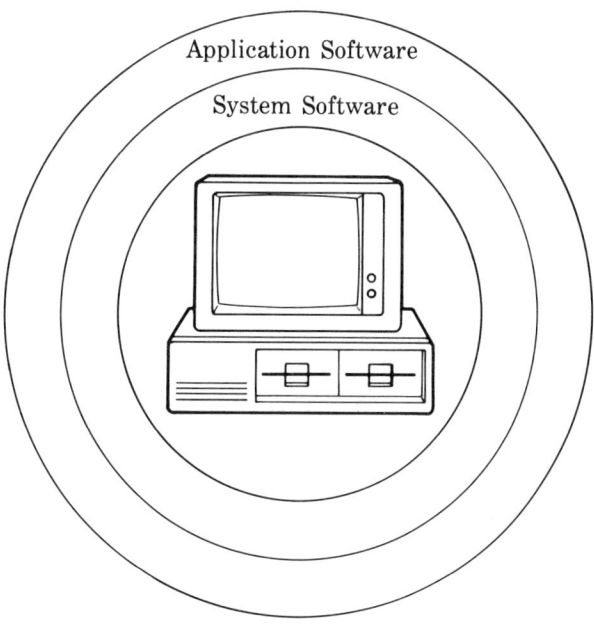

Figure 2-29. *Relationship between application and system software*

SOFTWARE

Software is computer programs. Computer scientists divide software into two categories: system software and application software.

System software includes operating systems such as OS/2, device drivers, and local area network software. System software is normally concerned with computer or device control.

Application software includes programs written to provide a specific task, such as a word processor or spreadsheet. Application software comprises the majority of software today.

Input-Processing-Output (IPO)

No matter what function your computer performs, it always follows three steps: input, processing, and output. *Input* is the process of getting data into the computer from an external source. Common avenues of input include the keyboard, a mouse, modem, or floppy disk, as shown in Figure 2-30. Before most programs can perform useful work, they must get data with which to work. Word processing programs get their input from the keyboard operator. Database programs use disks, while data-communications programs get their input from modems.

The result of a program's execution is its *output*. For example, a word processor produces letters and reports. Common sources of output include a monitor, printer, floppy disk, and a modem, as shown in Figure 2-31.

When a program performs an input or output operation, the action is often described as an *I/O operation*. I/O is simply an abbreviation for input/output.

Processing is the actual work the computer performs to convert the input to a meaningful output.

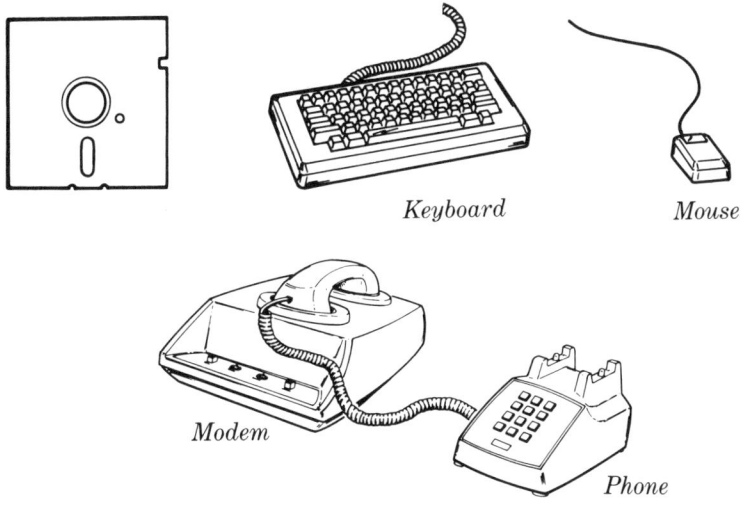

Figure 2-30. *Common input sources*

Getting Started

Most of you already have DOS running on an existing system. If you do, you can simply follow the installation procedures provided in your OS/2 documentation in order to install OS/2, or refer to Appendix D of this text (which walks you through an OS/2 installation). Before you do, however, read this section and start OS/2 from a floppy disk to gain familiarity with its functional capabilities.

If you have just purchased your computer, be sure that you have all of its cables properly installed. If you have DOS available on your fixed disk (your dealer may have installed DOS for you)

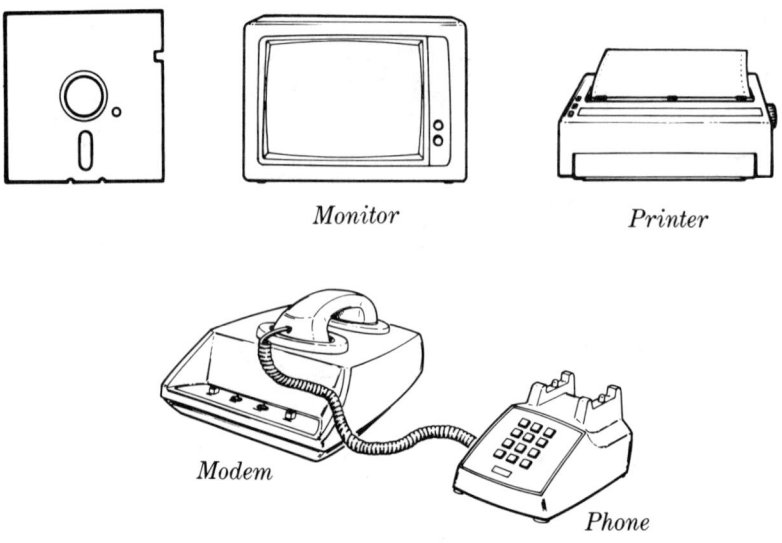

Monitor   *Printer*

Modem

Phone

Figure 2-31. *Common output sources*

turn on your system. If DOS is present, your system should display the DOS prompt, as shown here:

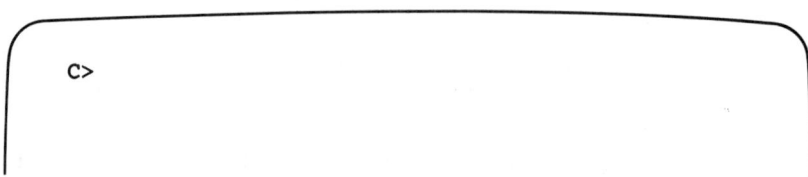

```
C>
```

If DOS is not present, your system should invoke a hardware-resident version of BASIC and display the following:

```
The IBM Personal Computer Basic
Version C1.10 Copyright IBM Corp 1981
62940 Bytes free
Ok
1LIST  2RUN    3LOAD"  4SAVE"  5CONT    6"LPT1  7TRON    8TROFF  9KEY   10SCREEN
```

If your system fails to display either of these prompts, recheck your cabling and repeat this process until you can successfully start your computer. Once you know that your hardware works and is correctly configured, getting started with OS/2 will be much easier. If you have problems, you will have fewer areas to troubleshoot.

Next, you will start OS/2 from floppy disk. Throughout this book the terms "start OS/2" and "boot OS/2" will be used interchangeably. Both refer to the process of loading OS/2 into memory from disk so that the computer can begin processing (see Figure 2-32). Now place your OS/2 system disk into drive A of your computer (see Figure 2-33).

If the computer is already turned on, press the CTRL, ALT, and DEL keys in that order and leave each key depressed (see Figure 2-34). This keyboard combination provides one method of restarting (rebooting) OS/2. Your second means of booting OS/2 is turning the power of your computer off and then back on.

RESTARTING OS/2

OS/2 can be restarted in one of two ways. First, pressing the CTRL-ALT-DEL keys in that order and leaving each key depressed boots OS/2. Second, powering your computer off and then back on reboots OS/2.

As the computer begins the OS/2 start-up process, you will see the disk activation light for drive A illuminate. The computer is attempting to read OS/2 from the disk in drive A into memory. If

1. Turn computer on.

2. Computer locates OS/2 on disk.

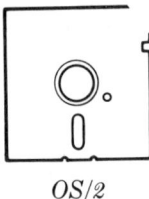

OS/2

3. Computer loads OS/2 from disk into memory.

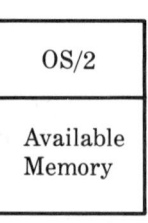

Memory

OS/2 startup is complete.
OS/2 displays its prompt.

Figure 2-32. *Process of loading OS/2 into memory*

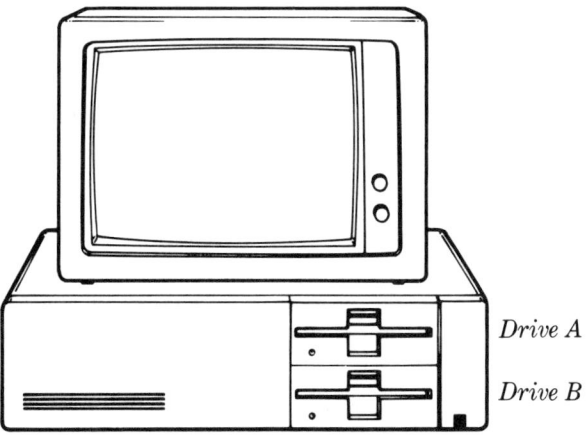

Figure 2-33. *Drive configuration*

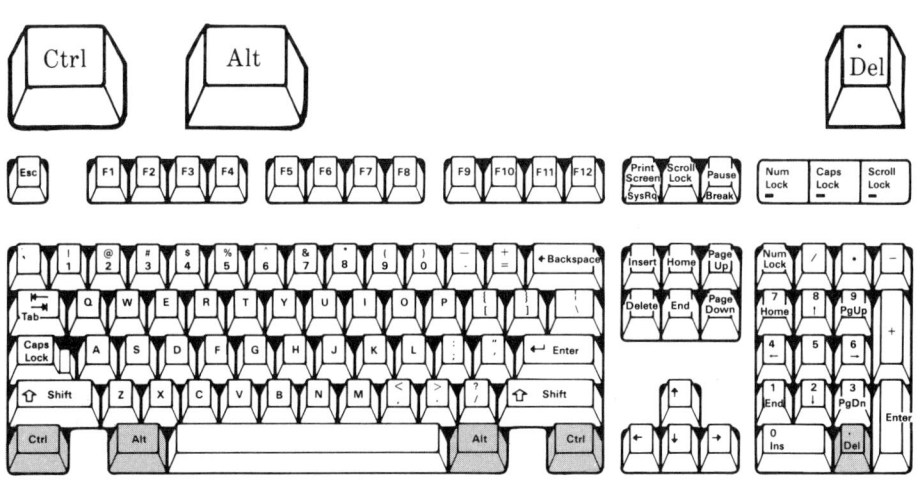

Figure 2-34. *Location of CTRL, ALT, and DEL keys*

your computer is not on, turn it on now. If your computer is already active, use the CTRL-ALT-DEL key combination to restart OS/2.

If you do not place the correct OS/2 system disk in drive A, OS/2 will respond with

```
The file "OS2BIO.COM" cannot be found.
Insert a system disk and restart the
system.
```

If this or a similar message occurs, the computer is simply telling you that you have placed the wrong disk in drive A. Simply insert the correct disk into drive A and once again press the CTRL-ALT-DEL key combination to restart OS/2.

Once the correct disk is in drive A, the system can complete the OS/2 start-up process and eventually display either the OS/2 prompt that you saw in Chapter 1

```
[A:\]
```

or a new OS/2 menu

```
Start a Program
COMMAND.COM                              R
```

This menu is the OS/2 Session Manager. Each OS/2 program runs in the context of an OS/2 *session.* OS/2 sessions, therefore, own their own virtual devices, as explained in Chapter 1. The OS/2 Session Manager oversees each of the OS/2 sessions, enables you to rapidly switch from one session to the next, and enables you to view the output of each session (program) on the screen.

OS/2 SESSION MANAGER

OS/2 is a multitasking operating system that allows you to execute several programs concurrently. The OS/2 Session Manager oversees each program and allows you to switch rapidly from one program to the next in order to view output from each.

If your system is currently displaying the OS/2 prompt

```
[A:\]
```

as opposed to the Session Manager menu, press the CTRL-ESC key combination to activate the OS/2 Session Manager.

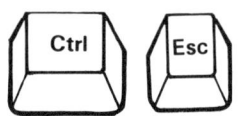

CTRL-ESC KEY COMBINATION

The CTRL-ESC key combination directs OS/2 to activate the Session Manager.

Your screen should now contain the Session Manager menu.

```
   Start a Program
   COMMAND.COM                                    R
```

Depending upon your specific version of OS/2, the Session Manager may present itself in a more formal manner, as shown here:

```
   Update                                    |  F1=Help

                         Program Selector
   Use  or → to move between Start a Program and Switch to a Running Program.
   Use ↑ or ↓ to select, then press Enter. Press F10 then Enter to Update lists.


   ┌─────────────────────────┐     ┌──────────────────────────────┐
   │  Start a Program        │     │ Switch to a Running Program  │
   │  ─────────────────      │     │ ───────────────────────────  │
   │                         │     │                              │
   │ ·* OS/2 Command Prompt *│     │ ·MS-DOS Command Prompt       │
   │                         │     │ ·* OS/2 Command Prompt *     │
   │                         │     │                              │
   │                         │     │                              │
   │                         │     │                              │
   │                         │     │                              │
   │                         │     │                              │
   └─────────────────────────┘     └──────────────────────────────┘
```

This implementation of the Session Manager is called the Program Selector. Although it appears differently on your screen, its functional goals are actually the same as those of the Session Manager — allowing you to move quickly from one OS/2 session to the next. If your screen contains the Program Selector, simply press the F1 key to obtain help.

Chapter 1 explained that OS/2 allows you to execute multiple OS/2 protected-mode programs or a single DOS real-mode application. In order to start an OS/2 protected-mode application, you must select the "Start a Program" option from the OS/2 Session Manager menu. To move from one Session Manager menu option to the next, simply use the arrow keys on your keyboard (see Figure 2-35).

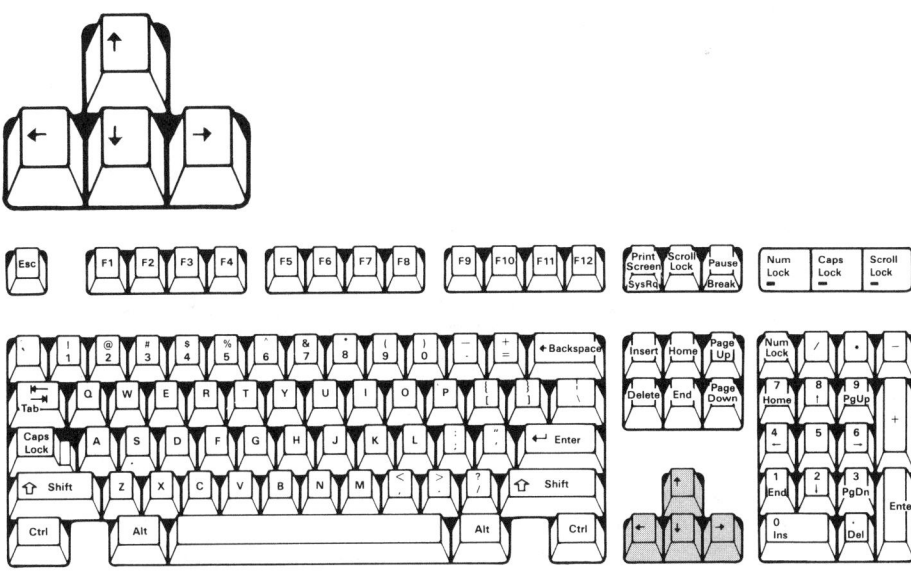

Figure 2-35.   *Location of arrow keys*

To execute your existing DOS programs, you must start an OS/2 real-mode session. The name of the OS/2 real-mode command-line processor is COMMAND.COM. The "R" to the right of COMMAND.COM reminds you that this is a real-mode session. To execute your DOS programs, simply select this option. OS/2 will create a real-mode session for your DOS applications and display a command-line prompt.

To select a Session Manager menu option, highlight the option by using the UP ARROW and DOWN ARROW keys. Once the option is highlighted, simply press the ENTER key.

SELECTING A SESSION MANAGER OPTION

From the OS/2 Session Manager menu, use your keyboard UP ARROW and DOWN ARROW keys to highlight the desired OS/2 session. Next, press the ENTER key to indicate your selection.

Now, select the "Start a Program" option to create an OS/2 protected-mode session. OS/2 creates the session and displays its command-line prompt, as follows:

```
[A:\]
```

Press the ENTER key several times:

```
[A:\]
[A:\]
[A:\]
```

OS/2 acknowledges your keyboard entry and immediately prompts you to enter a command. In this case, again type CLS and press the ENTER key to clear the screen display contents:

```
[A:\]
[A:\]
[A:\] CLS
```

You are currently executing commands in OS/2 protected mode. Once again, activate the Session Manager by pressing the CTRL-ESC keyboard combination. Your screen should now contain

```
Start a Program
COMMAND.COM                          R
CMD.EXE
```

As before, the "Start a Program" option allows you to start another OS/2 protected-mode session. COMMAND.COM still refers to the OS/2 real-mode session. The name of the session that you just created is CMD.EXE. Select this session and you will see the following:

```
[A:\]
```

This is the OS/2 protected-mode session in which you were just working. Later chapters will discuss CMD.EXE in detail. For now, simply view CMD.EXE as the OS/2 command-line processor that allows you to execute OS/2 commands and applications. Since you were not executing another program in your protected-mode session, the OS/2 Session Manager displayed CMD.EXE as the name of the active program.

From the OS/2 prompt type the word DATE and press the ENTER key:

```
[A:\] DATE
```

DATE is the OS/2 command to set your system date. OS/2 uses this date to track the date on which you modify or create files. If you simply want to view the current system date, press the ENTER key. OS/2 will leave the current system date unchanged.

```
[A:\] DATE

Current date is Mon  9-21-1987
Enter new date (mm-dd-yy):
[A:\]
```

Before examining the OS/2 DATE command in detail, first consider your third OS/2 command, TIME. At the OS/2 prompt, type TIME and press ENTER:

```
[A:\] TIME

Current time is 15:46:00.65
Enter new time:
```

OS/2 displays the current system time. Again, to simply display the system time and leave it unchanged, press the ENTER key.

```
[A:\] TIME

Current time is 15:46:00.65
Enter new time:
[A:\]
```

Once again, invoke the OS/2 DATE command. Upon invocation, DATE prompts you to enter the system date, as shown here:

```
[A:\] DATE

Current date is Mon   9-21-1987
Enter new date (mm-dd-yy):
```

DATE expects you to enter a date in the following format:

month/day/year

Table 2-5 shows valid dates accepted in OS/2. Note that OS/2 allows you to abbreviate a year (such as abbreviating 1988 to simply 88). If you enter an invalid date, DATE will notify you and again prompt you for another date:

```
[A:\] DATE

Current date is Mon   9-21-1987
Enter new date (mm-dd-yy): 31/12/88
Invalid date
Enter new date (mm-dd-yy):
```

Format	Date
9/30/88	September 30, 1988
9/30/1988	September 30, 1988
10/1/1988	October 1, 1988
12/8/1988	December 8, 1988

Table 2-5. *Accepted Date Formats*

The following is the complete format of the OS/2 DATE command:

DATE [mm-dd-yyyy]

Many OS/2 commands allow you to specify additional information when you invoke your commands. In the case of the OS/2 DATE command, you can include the date that you want OS/2 to use. (The brackets [ ] surrounding mm-dd-yyyy in the DATE command format indicate that the date is optional.) If you provide the date

```
[A:\] DATE 9/30/88
[A:\]
```

OS/2 will use it. If you do not supply the date,

```
[A:\] DATE
```

OS/2 will prompt you for the date, as follows:

```
[A:\] DATE
Current date is Mon  9-21-1987
Enter new date (mm-dd-yy):
```

For the remainder of this book, the brackets [ ] are used to indicate
optional command-line values. Now notice that the OS/2 DATE
command allows you to use a slash (/), a dash (-), or even a period (.)
to separate the date fields.

9.30.1988
9-30-1988
9-30.88
9/30/88

Invoke the OS/2 TIME command.

```
[A:\] TIME
```

TIME expects you to enter a time in the form

hh:mm[:ss[.hh]]

Once again, the brackets [ ] indicate optional fields. TIME only
requires you to enter the desired hours and minutes.

```
[A:\] TIME
Current time is 15:46:00.65
Enter new time: 12:45
```

However, if you want to include seconds, which are optional,

```
[A:\] TIME
Current time is 15:46:00.65
Enter new time: 12:45:15
```

the brackets surrounding [.hh] indicate that hundredths of seconds is also optional. A complete time specification would be the following:

```
[A:\] TIME·
Current time is 15:46:00.65
Enter new time: 12:45:15.66
```

Table 2-6 shows valid TIME formats.

Experienced IBM PC AT users who have used the AT SETUP disk to set the computer's system date and time, note that under OS/2 this is no longer required. The OS/2 DATE and TIME commands set the PC AT's nonvolatile system clock.

Format	Time
0:0:0.0	Midnight
12:00	12 noon
13:30	1:30 PM
16:00	4:00 PM
04:00	4:00 AM

Table 2-6. *Accepted Time Formats*

SYSTEM DATE AND TIME

OS/2 uses the DATE and TIME commands to set the system date and time. These commands set the nonvolatile clock on the IBM PC AT, which eliminates the need for the AT SETUP disk.

OS/2 Files

Floppy disks and fixed disks provide a means of storing your information from one user session so it can be used in other sessions. When OS/2 stores information on disk, it places the information into a storage facility called a *file*.

The files on your disk are much like the documents you place in a filing cabinet. Under OS/2 you can create disk files, modify their contents, rename them, and dispose of them when they are no longer needed.

Every OS/2 file has a name. An OS/2 file name is comprised of two parts: a file name and an extension. The OS/2 file name contains from one to eight characters. In addition to the standard characters of the alphabet, OS/2 allows you to use the following characters in OS/2 file names:

~!@N$%^&()−_{}'

The extension is optional and can contain from one to three characters. OS/2 uses a period to separate a file name from its extension, as follows:

filename[.ext]

The following names are valid for OS/2 files:

CMD.EXE	CONFIG.SYS
OCTOBER.PAY	BOOK.RPT
BUDGET	MY_NOTES
SALES.!!!	OS$2.NTS

These names are invalid for OS/2 files:

TOO_MANY_CHARACTERS	
.EXE	(No file name)
BOOK.EXE	(Period is an illegal character)
BLANK.EXE	(Blank character is invalid)
NEW.DATA	(Extension is too long)

OS/2 reserves several names for its devices. Since the following names are reserved, you cannot use them for files:

COM3	CON	COM1	KBD$
COM2	CLOCK$	NUL	
LPT1	LPT2	LPT3	
PRN	SCREEN$	POINTERS$	

OS/2 file names are discussed in detail later in this chapter.

DIR (Listing Your Files)

OS/2 provides many files on disk that you can list by issuing the OS/2 DIR command. From the OS/2 prompt, type DIR and press the ENTER key:

```
[A:\] DIR
```

OS/2 responds by displaying the files on drive A, as shown here:

```
[A:\] DIR

 Volume in drive A is OS2DISK
 Directory of  A:\

OS2BIO    COM      5120    5-27-87   12:00a
OS2DOS    COM    233016    5-27-87   12:00a
4201      DCP     17065    5-27-87   12:00a
5202      DCP       276    5-27-87   12:00a
ANSI      SYS      1651    5-27-87   12:00a
ANSICALL  DLL      3637    5-27-87   12:00a
AUTOEXEC  BAT       144    5-27-87   12:00a
AUTOEXEC  FLP       157    5-27-87   12:00a
BKSCALLS  DLL      5718    5-27-87   12:00a
BMSCALLS  DLL      2064    5-27-87   12:00a
BVSCALLS  DLL     26496    5-27-87   12:00a
CLOCK01   SYS      2237    5-27-87   12:00a
CMD       EXE     56144    5-27-87   12:00a
COM01     SYS     10806    5-27-87   12:00a
COMMAND   COM     25839    5-27-87   12:00a
CONFIG    FLP      1259    5-27-87   12:00a
CONFIG    HRD      1194    5-27-87   12:00a
CONFIG    SYS        54    8-30-87    7:17p
COUNTRY   SYS     14632    5-27-87   12:00a
DISK01    SYS     19142    5-27-87   12:00a
DOSCALL1  DLL      9810    5-27-87   12:00a
EGA       SYS      1963    5-27-87   12:00a
EXTDSKDD  SYS      1877    5-27-87   12:00a
FDISK     EXE     37488    5-27-87   12:00a
FORMAT    COM     63040    5-27-87   12:00a
FORMATS   TBL       560    5-27-87   12:00a
HARDERR   EXE     14272    5-27-87   12:00a
INITENV   FLP       166    5-27-87   12:00a
INSTBOOT  CMD       608    5-27-87   12:00a
INSTFLP   CMD       775    5-27-87   12:00a
```

```
KBD01     SYS     11731     5-27-87     12:00a
KBDCALLS  DLL      5166     5-27-87     12:00a
KEYBOARD  DCP     85917     5-27-87     12:00a
MONCALLS  DLL      7351     5-27-87     12:00a
MOUCALLS  DLL      4669     5-27-87     12:00a
MOUSEA02  SYS     13878     5-27-87     12:00a
MOUSEA03  SYS     14390     5-27-87     12:00a
MOUSEA04  SYS     13878     5-27-87     12:00a
MSG       DLL      6170     5-27-87     12:00a
NLS       DLL      5220     5-27-87     12:00a
OEMHLP    SYS      1330     5-27-87     12:00a
OSO001    MSG     73993     5-27-87     12:00a
OSO001H   MSG    121921     5-27-87     12:00a
POINTDD   SYS      4294     5-27-87     12:00a
PRINT01   SYS      5884     5-27-87     12:00a
QUECALLS  DLL     11524     5-27-87     12:00a
SCREEN01  SYS      1333     5-27-87     12:00a
SESMGR    DLL     23710     5-27-87     12:00a
SHELL     EXE     11744     5-27-87     12:00a
SPOOLCP   DLL      8932     5-27-87     12:00a
SWAPPER   EXE      4150     5-27-87     12:00a
VDISK     SYS      4662     5-27-87     12:00a
VIOCALLS  DLL     10359     5-27-87     12:00a
VIOTBL    DCP     52150     5-27-87     12:00a
INITENV   CMD       256     7-05-87      6:59p

        54 File(s)     126976 bytes free

[A:\]
```

The OS/2 DIR command displays several useful pieces of information. Examine the first few lines below:

```
[A:\] DIR

Volume in drive A is OS2DISK ———————— Disk Name
Directory of  A:\
```

Disk drive that the disk directory listing is from

These lines tell you the disk drive that the directory listing is from and the specific name of the disk. Later chapters will discuss how to assign names to each of your disks, along with the rationale for doing so.

Next, DIR provides you with specific information about each file, such as its size (in bytes) and its creation date and time.

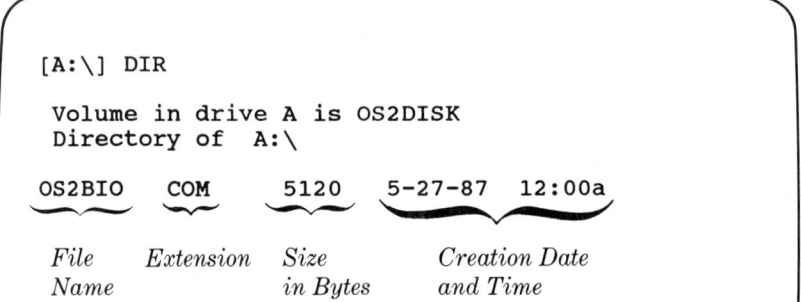

Last, DIR tells you how many bytes of available space remain on the disk. Remember that a byte is equivalent to a character.

```
 54 File(s)     126976 bytes free
```

The complete format of the OS/2 DIR command is

DIR [*file_specification*] [*/P*][*/W*]

where the following is true:

file_specification is the name of the file to list. If you do not provide a file specification, DIR lists all of the files contained on the disk. File specifications are examined in detail later in this chapter.

/P directs OS/2 to pause with each full screen of display to prompt the user, as follows:

```
Strike a key when ready . . .
```

Simply press a key and DIR will continue its listing.

/W directs DIR to display only the file name of each file on the disk and suppresses the size, date stamp, and time stamp for each file.

```
[A:\] DIR /W

 Volume in drive A is OS2DISK
 Directory of  A:\

OS2BIO    COM    OS2DOS    COM    4201      DCP    5202      DCP    ANSI      SYS
ANSICALL  DLL    AUTOEXEC  BAT    AUTOEXEC  FLP    BKSCALLS  DLL    BMSCALLS  DLL
BVSCALLS  DLL    CLOCK01   SYS    CMD       EXE    COM01     SYS    COMMAND   COM
CONFIG    FLP    CONFIG    HRD    CONFIG    SYS    COUNTRY   SYS    DISK01    SYS
DOSCALL1  DLL    EGA       SYS    EXTDSKDD  SYS    FDISK     EXE    FORMAT    COM
FORMATS   TBL    HARDERR   EXE    INITENV   BAK    INITENV   FLP    INSTBOOT  CMD
INSTFLP   CMD    KBD01     SYS    KBDCALLS  DLL    KEYBOARD  DCP    MONCALLS  DLL
MOUCALLS  DLL    MOUSEA02  SYS    MOUSEA03  SYS    MOUSEA04  SYS    MSG       DLL
NLS       DLL    OEMHLP    SYS    OSO001    MSG    OSO001H   MSG    POINTDD   SYS
        48 File(s)     146976 bytes free
```

Consider the following examples:

```
[A:\] DIR CMD.EXE
```

In this case, CMD.EXE is your file specification. OS/2 will display the following:

```
[A:\] DIR CMD.EXE

 Volume in drive A is OS2DISK
 Directory of  A:\

 CMD       EXE    56144   5-27-87  12:00a
         1 File(s)      126976 bytes  free
```

However, if you specify a nonexistent file,

```
 [A:\] DIR XXXX.YYY
```

OS/2 informs you that the file does not exist, as shown here:

```
 [A:\] DIR XXXX.YYY

 DOS0002: The system cannot find the file specified.
```

OS/2 Wildcard Characters

One of the most powerful features of OS/2 (and DOS) is the ability for you to substitute the characters * and ? for other characters in a file name during file search operations. The question mark character (?) in a file name tells OS/2 that any character can occupy that location in the file name. For example, if you enter the command

```
[A:\] DIR CHAPTER?.TXT
```

OS/2 will match files that begin with the word CHAPTER, regardless of the eighth letter. In this case, your output might be

```
[A:\] DIR CHAPTER?.TXT

 Volume in drive A is OS2BOOK
 Directory of  A:\

CHAPTER1 TXT        608    5-27-87   12:00a
CHAPTER2 TXT        775    5-27-87   12:00a
CHAPTER3 TXT        256    7-05-87    6:59p
          3 File(s)     126976 bytes free
```

In a similar manner, if you enter the command

```
[A:\] DIR ????????.EXE
```

OS/2 will list all files with the extension EXE, regardless of their file names. In this case, the eight question marks inform OS/2 that you do not care what characters occupy those locations in the file name.

The other OS/2 wildcard character, the asterisk (*), is more powerful than the question mark. The asterisk tells OS/2 not only that you do not care what character occupies a specific character location, but also that you do not care what characters occupy the positions that follow the asterisk. For example, the command

```
[A:\] DIR *.EXE
```

directs OS/2 to list every file with the extension EXE. Likewise, the command

```
[A:\] DIR *.*
```

directs OS/2 to match every file regardless of file names or extensions. The command

```
[A:\] DIR CHAP*.TXT

 Volume in drive A is OS2BOOK
 Directory of  A:\

CHAPTER1 TXT        608    5-27-87   12:00a
CHAPTER2 TXT        775    5-27-87   12:00a
CHAPTER3 TXT        256    7-05-87    6:59p
         3 File(s)      126976 bytes free
```

tells OS/2 to list any files whose first four characters are CHAP and that have a TXT extension.

OS/2 wildcard characters are a powerful feature that you will use on a continual basis.

OS/2 File Naming Conventions

Each OS/2 file stores one of two things: programs or data. Normally, you use the three-character file extension to distinguish between file types. Since OS/2 data files can contain a number of different things, use an OS/2 file extension to indicate specifically what the file contains. Commonly used examples are the following:

EXE   OS/2 executable program

CMD   OS/2 batch file

SYS   OS/2 installable device driver

TXT   Word processing file

DAT   Application program data file

BAT   DOS batch file

COM   DOS real-mode executable file

By examining OS/2 file extensions, you can categorize files as follows:

CMD.EXE   OS/2 executable file

ANSI.SYS   OS/2 device driver

STARTUP.CMD   OS/2 batch file

COMMAND.COM   DOS real-mode executable file

AUTOEXEC.BAT   DOS real-mode batch file

Write-Protecting Your Disk

Remember the write-protect notch on your floppy disk, as shown in Figure 2-15. If you cover the notch with a write-protect tab, OS/2 cannot modify the contents of the disks. In so doing, the files on the disk cannot be accidentally deleted. If OS/2 attempts to modify a file on a write-protected disk, the attempt will fail.

Always write-protect disks whose contents you do not want to change.

Selecting Disk Drives

Each of the commands discussed thus far has dealt only with files contained on drive A. OS/2 supports the concept of a default drive. Unless overridden, OS/2 will always search that drive for files or commands. Depending upon your computer's disk drive configuration, you may have several drives, as shown in Figure 2-36.

Assume that you have a second floppy disk drive (drive B). If you place a disk in that drive, you can examine its contents with the OS/2 DIR command, as follows:

```
[A:\] DIR B:
```

In this case, B: specifies the disk drive from which DIR is to list the files. If you omit drive B:, OS/2 lists the files contained on drive A (the default drive).

To select an alternate disk drive as the current default, type the drive letter (A, B, C, and so on) at the OS/2 prompt immediately followed by a colon, as shown here:

```
[A:\] B:
```

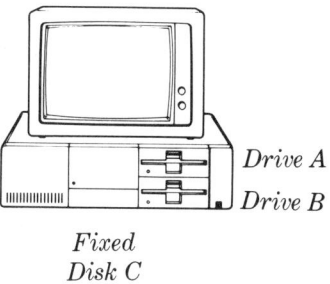

Fixed
Disk C

Figure 2-36. *Configuration with fixed disk and two floppy drives*

In this case, OS/2 selects drive B as the current default drive and acknowledges the change in the default drive by modifying the system prompt, as shown here:

```
[A:\] B:
[B:\]
```

If you again issue the OS/2 DIR command, OS/2 will list the files contained on drive B, which is the new default drive.

To once again make drive A the default drive, simply enter the letter A followed by a colon at the OS/2 prompt, as shown here:

```
[B:\] A:
[A:\]
```

Making a Working Copy of Your Disks

If treated properly, your floppy disks will last a long time. However, disks will fail periodically even under the best conditions because of the everyday wear and tear of being read from and written to. An immediate precaution against losing your OS/2 disks is to make a working copy of them, place the originals in a safe location, and use your new working copies.

To make a working copy of each of your OS/2 disks, get a blank 1.2MB floppy disk for each original OS/2 disk. Since most systems have only one 1.2MB floppy drive, use drive A for the disk copy. In this case, you will copy the contents of your original OS/2 disks to the working disks, as shown in Figure 2-37.

Before you begin, use write-protect tabs to protect each of your original OS/2 disks. This will prevent a processing error during

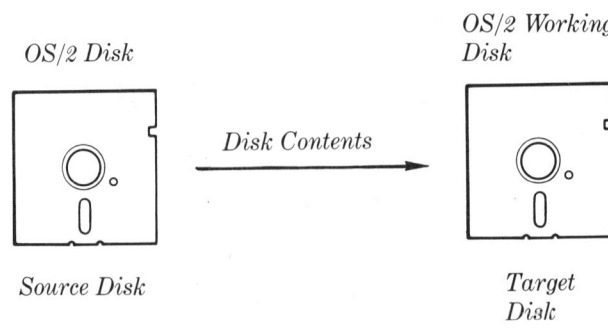

Figure 2-37. *Copying contents of original OS/2 disks to backup disks*

the execution of the DISKCOPY command from harming your original disks. Do not continue until you have write-protected each of your original OS/2 disks.

Place your OS/2 supplemental disk in drive A and issue the DISKCOPY command, as follows:

```
[A:\] DISKCOPY
```

Upon invocation, note that the disk activation light on drive A illuminates. OS/2 is reading the DISKCOPY command from disk into memory so that it can execute (see Figure 2-38).

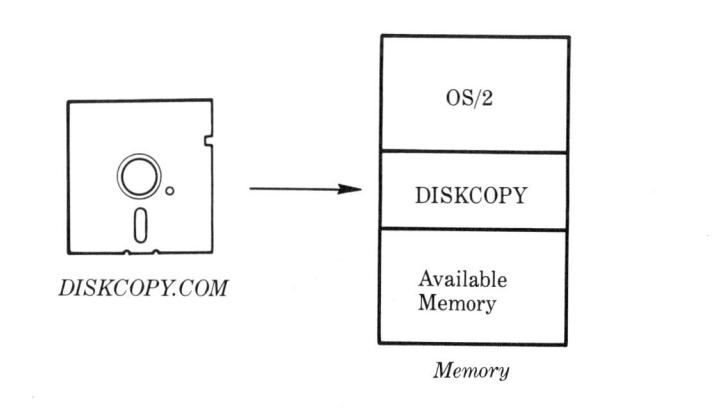

Figure 2-38. *OS/2 reading DISKCOPY from disk into memory*

The OS/2 Session Manager may respond with the following message:

```
Session Title: CMD.EXE

   DOS0034: The system has detected a wrong diskette
   in the drive.  Insert OS/2 into drive A and press
   enter.
─────────────────────────────────────────────────────
              Return the error to the program
              End the program
              Retry the operation
```

If this occurs, simply place your OS/2 system disk in drive A and select the "Retry the operation" option to continue execution of the DISKCOPY command.

In this case, your source disk is your original disk. The target disk is your working copy. Since you will be using drive A for both disks, respond to the DISKCOPY prompts as shown here:

```
[A:\] DISKCOPY
Enter drive letter for source. A:
Enter drive letter for target. A:
```

DISKCOPY will continue by prompting you to first place your source disk (the original OS/2 disk) and then your target disk (your working copy disk) into drive A at the correct times, as shown here:

```
[A:\] DISKCOPY
Enter drive letter for source. A:
Enter drive letter for target. A:
Insert source diskette in drive A:

Press Enter to continue.

Copying 80 tracks, 15 sectors per track, 2 side(s).
Insert target diskette in drive A:

Press Enter to continue.

Insert source diskette in drive A:

Press Enter to continue.

Insert target diskette in drive A:

Press Enter to continue.

Insert source diskette in drive A:

Press Enter to continue.

Insert target diskette in drive A:

Press Enter to continue.

Insert source diskette in drive A:

Press Enter to continue.

Insert target diskette in drive A:

Press Enter to continue.

Copy process ended.
Copy another diskette (Y/N)?
```

When DISKCOPY completes, it displays the following prompt:

```
Copy process ended.
Copy another diskette (Y/N)?
```

Press Y and continue this process for the remainder of your OS/2 disks.

Note that DISKCOPY cannot copy disks that are copy-protected. To do so, you need to purchase a third-party software package that breaks copy protection in order to back up your copy-protected disks. It is against the law to distribute copy-protected software.

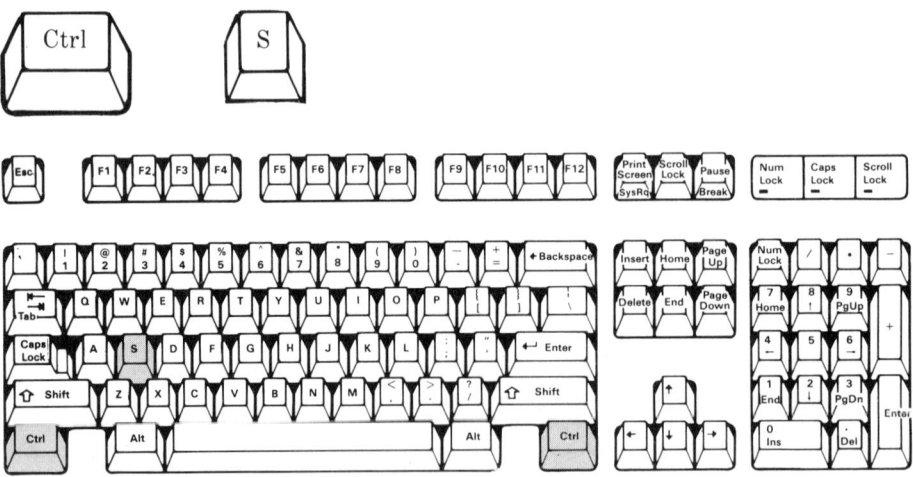

Figure 2-39. *Location of CTRL and S keys*

Controlling Screen Display
and Terminating OS/2 Commands

As OS/2 executes commands, it allows you to use several keyboard combinations to control a command's execution. You have already seen the use of the CTRL-ALT-DEL key combination to reboot OS/2, and CTRL-ESC to activate the OS/2 Session Manager. In a similar manner, OS/2 uses the CTRL-S key combination to temporarily suspend a command's screen display (see Figure 2-39).

If you execute the OS/2 DIR command, OS/2 will continue to list files and scroll previous file names off the top of the screen. By pressing the CTRL-S key combination, you can direct OS/2 to temporarily suspend the screen display so that you can view the directory listing on the screen. Consider the following directory listing:

```
[A:\] DIR

 Volume in drive A is OS2DISK
 Directory of  A:\

OS2BIO    COM     5120    5-27-87   12:00a
OS2DOS    COM   233016    5-27-87   12:00a
4201      DCP    17065    5-27-87   12:00a
5202      DCP      276    5-27-87   12:00a
ANSI      SYS     1651    5-27-87   12:00a
ANSICALL  DLL     3637    5-27-87   12:00a
AUTOEXEC  BAT      144    5-27-87   12:00a
AUTOEXEC  FLP      157    5-27-87   12:00a
BKSCALLS  DLL     5718    5-27-87   12:00a
BMSCALLS  DLL     2064    5-27-87   12:00a
BVSCALLS  DLL    26496    5-27-87   12:00a
CLOCK01   SYS     2237    5-27-87   12:00a
CMD       EXE    56144    5-27-87   12:00a

CTRL-S pressed here to suspend output
```

In this case the user has suspended the screen display to allow you to view the screen contents. To resume scrolling, simply press any key. The directory listing will continue, as shown here:

```
                                                          [A:\] DIR

       Volume in drive A is OS2DISK
       Directory of  A:\

       OS2BIO    COM      5120    5-27-87   12:00a
       OS2DOS    COM    233016    5-27-87   12:00a
       4201      DCP     17065    5-27-87   12:00a
       5202      DCP       276    5-27-87   12:00a
       ANSI      SYS      1651    5-27-87   12:00a
       ANSICALL  DLL      3637    5-27-87   12:00a
       AUTOEXEC  BAT       144    5-27-87   12:00a
       AUTOEXEC  FLP       157    5-27-87   12:00a
       BKSCALLS  DLL      5718    5-27-87   12:00a
       BMSCALLS  DLL      2064    5-27-87   12:00a
       BVSCALLS  DLL     26496    5-27-87   12:00a
       CLOCK01   SYS      2237    5-27-87   12:00a
       CMD       EXE     56144    5-27-87   12:00a
       COM01     SYS     10806    5-27-87   12:00a
       COMMAND   COM     25839    5-27-87   12:00a
       CONFIG    FLP      1259    5-27-87   12:00a
       CONFIG    HRD      1194    5-27-87   12:00a
       CONFIG    SYS        54    8-30-87    7:17p
       COUNTRY   SYS     14632    5-27-87   12:00a
       DISK01    SYS     19142    5-27-87   12:00a
       DOSCALL1  DLL      9810    5-27-87   12:00a
       EGA       SYS      1963    5-27-87   12:00a
       EXTDSKDD  SYS      1877    5-27-87   12:00a
       FDISK     EXE     37488    5-27-87   12:00a
       FORMAT    COM     63040    5-27-87   12:00a
       FORMATS   TBL       560    5-27-87   12:00a
       HARDERR   EXE     14272    5-27-87   12:00a
       INITENV   BAK       139    5-27-87   12:00a
       INITENV   FLP       166    5-27-87   12:00a
       INSTBOOT  CMD       608    5-27-87   12:00a
       INSTFLP   CMD       775    5-27-87   12:00a
       KBD01     SYS     11731    5-27-87   12:00a
       KBDCALLS  DLL      5166    5-27-87   12:00a
       KEYBOARD  DCP     85917    5-27-87   12:00a
       MONCALLS  DLL      7351    5-27-87   12:00a
       MOUCALLS  DLL      4669    5-27-87   12:00a
```

```
MOUSEA02 SYS     13878    5-27-87   12:00a
MOUSEA03 SYS     14390    5-27-87   12:00a
MOUSEA04 SYS     13878    5-27-87   12:00a
MSG      DLL      6170    5-27-87   12:00a
NLS      DLL      5220    5-27-87   12:00a
OEMHLP   SYS      1330    5-27-87   12:00a
OSO001   MSG     73993    5-27-87   12:00a
OSO001H  MSG    121921    5-27-87   12:00a
POINTDD  SYS      4294    5-27-87   12:00a
PRINT01  SYS      5884    5-27-87   12:00a
QUECALLS DLL     11524    5-27-87   12:00a
SCREEN01 SYS      1333    5-27-87   12:00a
SESMGR   DLL     23710    5-27-87   12:00a
SHELL    EXE     11744    5-27-87   12:00a
SPOOLCP  DLL      8932    5-27-87   12:00a
SWAPPER  EXE      4150    5-27-87   12:00a
VDISK    SYS      4662    5-27-87   12:00a
VIOCALLS DLL     10359    5-27-87   12:00a
VIOTBL   DCP     52150    5-27-87   12:00a
INITENV  CMD       256    7-05-87    6:59p
        54 File(s)    126976 bytes free
```

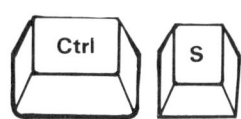

CTRL-S KEY COMBINATION

The CTRL-S key combination temporarily suspends the screen display. Once output is suspended by using CTRL-S, pressing any key will resume output.

In a similar manner, OS/2 allows you to terminate most commands by pressing the CTRL-C or CTRL-BREAK key combinations (see Figure 2-40). For example, assume that you want to terminate the OS/2 DIR command. As the file names scroll by on the screen, simply hold down the CTRL key and press the BREAK key. OS/2 will display a ^C on the screen, as shown here, and terminate the command:

```
[A:\] DIR

 Volume in drive A is OS2DISK
 Directory of  A:\

OS2BIO    COM     5120     5-27-87    12:00a
OS2DOS    COM   233016     5-27-87    12:00a
4201      DCP    17065     5-27-87    12:00a
5202      DCP      276     5-27-87    12:00a
ANSI      SYS     1651     5-27-87    12:00a
ANSICALL  DLL     3637     5-27-87    12:00a
AUTOEXEC  BAT      144     5-27-87    12:00a
AUTOEXEC  FLP      157     5-27-87    12:00a
BKSCALLS  DLL     5718     5-27-87    12:00a
BMSCALLS  DLL     2064     5-27-87    12:00a
BVSCALLS  DLL    26496     5-27-87    12:00a
CLOCK01   SYS     2237     5-27-87    12:00a
CMD       EXE    56144     5-27-87    12:00a
^C

[A:\]
```

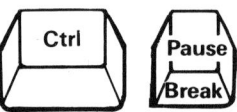

CTRL-BREAK KEY COMBINATION

The CTRL-BREAK key combination terminates the execution of the current application. OS/2 will respond to the CTRL-BREAK key combination by displaying a ^C, terminate the application, and redisplay the system prompt.

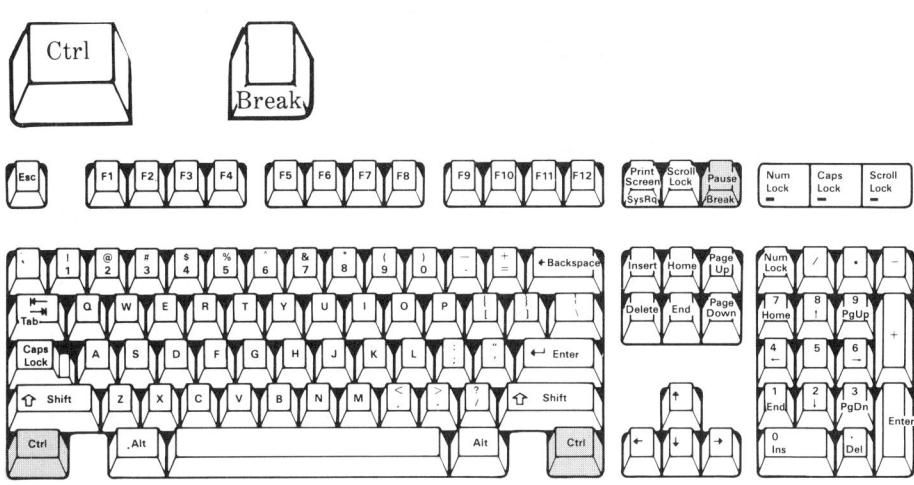

Figure 2-40. *Location of CTRL and BREAK keys*

Continuing Your OS/2 Installation

By now you should be fully conversant with OS/2 file manipulation, the OS/2 Session Manager, the manipulation of disk drives, and entering OS/2 commands. You should have successfully created a working copy of your OS/2 disks and placed the originals in a safe location. You are now ready to continue your OS/2 system installation. Refer to your OS/2 documentation or Appendix C of this text to complete installation.

Chapter Highlights

Hardware is the cables, boards, and peripheral devices that make up your computer.

Software is computer programs. A computer program is simply a list of instructions the computer is to perform. Software consists of system software, including operating systems such as OS/2 and DOS, and application software, which are programs written to provide a specific function, such as word processing.

Hardware devices within the computer communicate based upon the presence or absence of electronic signals. Since a signal. can be in only one of two states (either on or off), the computer uses the binary numbering system to represent these states. All data stored within the computer, therefore, is stored as a series of 1's and 0's (binary digits).

Eight binary digits combine to make a byte. Most of the computer's hardware devices (such as memory) manipulate bytes of information.

A "K" equals 1024 bytes; so 256K of memory is $256 * 1024$ bytes of memory.

OS/2 requires your system to have 1.5MB of memory. A megabyte is 1 million bytes.

I/O stands for input/output. Regardless of the application, computers perform three functions: they obtain input, process the input, and produce a meaningful output. These steps are often referred to as input-processing-output.

OS/2 predefines several keyboard combinations:

CTRL-ALT-DEL	Reboot OS/2
CTRL-ESC	Activate the OS/2 Session Manager
ALT-ESC	Switch to the next active session
CTRL-S	Temporarily suspend screen display
CTRL-BREAK	Terminate the current command

The OS/2 DATE and TIME commands allow you to examine or set the system's date and time. These commands set the non-volatile clock in the IBM PC AT and eliminate the need to use the AT SETUP disk.

OS/2 is a multitasking operating system that can execute multiple programs simultaneously. The OS/2 Session Manager allows you to move rapidly from one concurrent application to the next and to view the result of each on the screen.

OS/2 uses a storage facility called a file to store your information from one user session so it can be used in other sessions.

OS/2 files follow DOS naming conventions. Each OS/2 file name has an eight-character file name optionally followed by a three-character extension.

The OS/2 DIR command allows you to list the files contained on a disk and to display their sizes, creation date, and creation time stamps.

OS/2 supports the concept of a default disk drive. Unless over-ridden, OS/2 always examines the default drive for files and commands. To select a new drive as the system default, type in the drive letter, immediately followed by a colon, at the OS/2 prompt.

Before you continue your OS/2 processing, make working copies of each of your OS/2 disks. The OS/2 DISKCOPY command allows you to copy the contents of one disk to another.

3 Basic OS/2 Commands

Chapter 2 discussed the following five OS/2 commands:

CLS   OS/2 clear-screen command
DATE   OS/2 system date command
TIME   OS/2 system time command
DIR   OS/2 file-listing command
DISKCOPY   OS/2 disk-to-disk copy command

Chapter 2 also discussed the OS/2 Session Manager, which allows you to execute multiple OS/2 protected-mode programs or to select a real-mode session to execute your current DOS applications. By now you should know how to traverse the Session Manager menu, understand the functional aspects of the OS/2 prompt, be able to recognize valid OS/2 file names, understand the implication of the OS/2 wildcard characters (* and ?) and know how OS/2 uses the default disk drive. If you are unsure about any of these topics, quickly review Chapter 2.

This chapter presents a collection of OS/2 commands that you will need to get the most out of OS/2 in the shortest amount of time. For experienced DOS users, much of this chapter will be review. However, pay close attention to the example commands presented here. OS/2 expands the command-line capabilities of many commands, which at first appear to be subtle. The additional capabilities are quite useful. Users who are new to both OS/2 and DOS should take the time to enter each of the commands presented in this chapter. In so doing, you will greatly increase your learning, and hence your ability to work with OS/2.

Current Machine State

This chapter assumes that you have completed OS/2 installation and are currently using your fixed disk. If you are still running OS/2 off a floppy disk, be sure you are using a working copy of the disk. If you are still using your original OS/2 media, review Chapter 2 to see how to create working copies. All of the commands presented in this chapter will run from a floppy disk, but you will need to have your supplemental disk readily available because many of the OS/2 commands presented here reside on this disk. However, note that the system prompt that appears in most of the examples is for drive C. This is only because OS/2 resides on a fixed disk for these examples.

Internal Versus External Commands

If your system is not on, boot OS/2. Once OS/2 is running, use the CTRL-ESC key combination to enter the Session Manager menu:

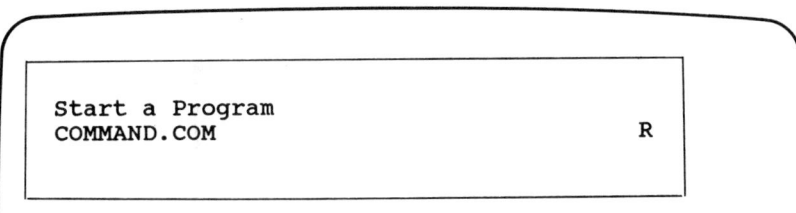

Create an OS/2 protected mode session by selecting Start a Program from the menu:

```
[c:\]
```

Each time OS/2 boots, it places several commands (called *internal commands*) into memory that you can execute simply by typing their names. These commands are internal commands; they always reside in memory within OS/2, as illustrated in Figure 3-1.

As discussed in Chapter 2, a program must reside in memory before it can execute. Since internal commands already reside in memory, OS/2 does not have to load them from disk into memory each time you execute them.

For example, issue the OS/2 CLS command:

```
[c:\] CLS
```

OS/2 executes this command by clearing your screen display and placing the system prompt in the upper-left corner of your screen.

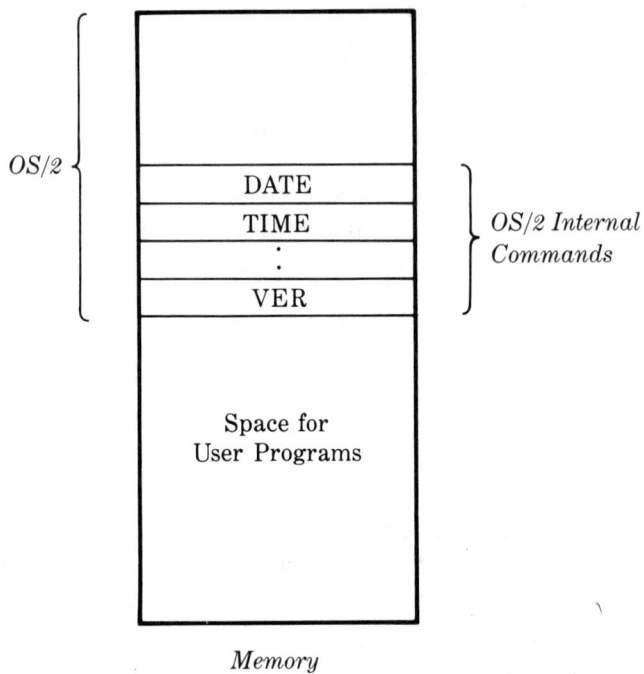

Figure 3-1.   *Internal commands within OS/2*

Issue the following directory command:

```
[C:\] DIR CLS.*
Volume in drive C is OS2
Directory of C:\

DOS0002: The system cannot find the file specified.

[C:\]
```

Notice that no such file resides on disk because CLS is an internal
command.

Next, issue the following command:

```
[C:\] DIR DISKCOPY.COM
Volume in drive C is OS2
Directory of C:\

DISKCOPY COM     33408    5-27-87   12:00a

     1 File(s)     10352640 bytes free

[C:\]
```

DISKCOPY.COM is an OS/2 *external command*. Unlike internal commands (which always reside in memory), OS/2 external commands reside on disk, as illustrated in Figure 3-2. Before

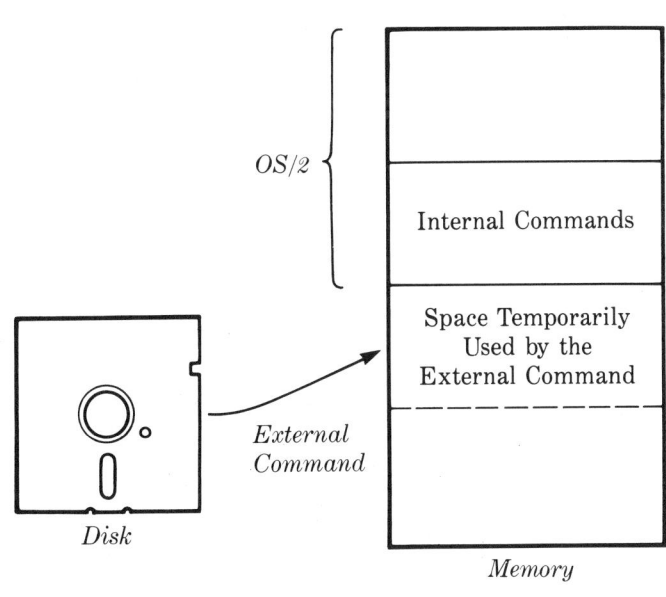

Figure 3-2. *External commands for OS/2*

OS/2 can execute the command, it must load the external command from disk into memory.

INTERNAL VERSUS EXTERNAL OS/2 COMMANDS

All OS/2 commands are either internal or external. OS/2 internal commands reside in memory within OS/2. OS/2 external commands reside on disk. Before OS/2 can execute an external command, it must first load the command into memory.

Issue the following directory commands:

```
[C:\] DIR *.COM

 Volume in drive C is OS2
 Directory of  C:\OS2

 APPEND    COM     5986    5-27-87   12:00a
 ASSIGN    COM     1689    5-27-87   12:00a
 BACKUP    COM    45232    5-27-87   12:00a
 CHKDSK    COM    46128    5-27-87   12:00a
 COMP      COM    29712    5-27-87   12:00a
 DISKCOMP  COM    31840    5-27-87   12:00a
 DISKCOPY  COM    33408    5-27-87   12:00a
 EDLIN     COM     8231    5-27-87   12:00a
 FIND      COM    23962    5-27-87   12:00a
 FORMAT    COM    63040    5-27-87   12:00a
 GRAFTABL  COM     7032    5-27-87   12:00a
 LABEL     COM    23392    5-27-87   12:00a
 MODE      COM    47726    5-27-87   12:00a
 MORE      COM    43898    5-27-87   12:00a
 PRINT     COM    36460    5-27-87   12:00a
 RESTORE   COM    49376    5-27-87   12:00a
 SYS       COM    27602    5-27-87   12:00a
 TREE      COM    26064    5-27-87   12:00a
       18 File(s)   10348544 bytes free

[C:\]
```

```
[C:\] DIR *.EXE

 Volume in drive C is OS2
 Directory of  C:\OS2

ANSI      EXE    10108    5-27-87   12:00a
ATTRIB    EXE    26220    5-27-87   12:00a
FDISK     EXE    37488    5-27-87   12:00a
GWBASIC   EXE    78864    5-27-87   12:00a
HELPMSG   EXE    23952    5-27-87   12:00a
JOIN      EXE    18528    5-27-87   12:00a
KEYB      EXE    12278    5-27-87   12:00a
PATCH     EXE    33644    5-27-87   12:00a
REPLACE   EXE    29072    5-27-87   12:00a
SORT      EXE    27056    5-27-87   12:00a
SPOOL     EXE    58006    5-27-87   12:00a
SUBST     EXE    18512    5-27-87   12:00a
XCOPY     EXE    22928    5-27-87   12:00a
        13 File(s)   10350592 bytes free

[C:\]
```

In both cases, OS/2 listed the names of external commands that reside in the current directory. Files with either the EXE or COM extension are executable files. Later chapters discuss why the distinction is made in these file names.

Real-Mode Session

Chapter 2 discussed how to select a protected-mode session by using the OS/2 Session Manager menu. Use the CTRL-ESC key combination to activate the Session Manager.

```
Start a Program
COMMAND.COM                              R
CMD.EXE
```

Next, select the COMMAND.COM option to start a real-mode session. In this case, OS/2 responds with its real-mode prompt:

```
C>
```

You can execute your existing DOS programs while in this mode. For example, a 1-2-3 user would enter the following:

```
C> 123
```

To return to the OS/2 Session Manager, press the CTRL-ESC key combination. If instead you press the ALT-ESC key combination, OS/2 displays your protected-mode session:

```
[C:\]
```

Pressing ALT-ESC again results in the display of your real-mode session. Just as the ALT-ESC key combination directs OS/2 to activate the Session Manager, pressing the ALT-ESC key combination one more time directs the Session Manager to select the next

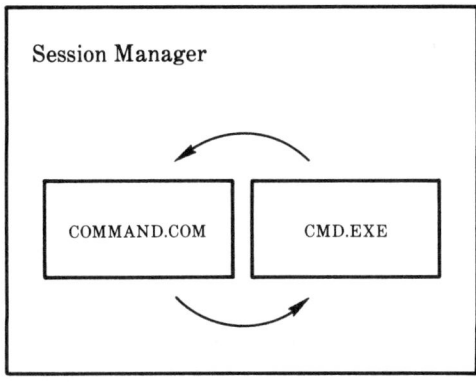

Figure 3-3.   *Toggling between sessions in Session Manager*

session in its list of active sessions. In this case, you have only two sessions active for the ALT-ESC combination to toggle between, as shown in Figure 3-3. If you have several sessions that are active, OS/2 will cycle from one to the next in a round-robin fashion, as shown in Figure 3-4.

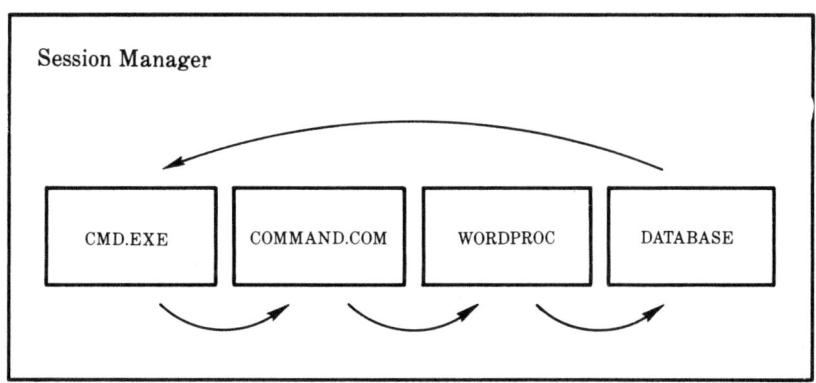

Figure 3-4.   *Round-robin shuffling between sessions in Session Manager*

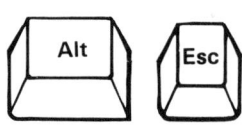

ALT-ESC KEY COMBINATION
Pressing the ALT-ESC keyboard combination directs
OS/2 to cycle through its list of active sessions in a
round-robin fashion.

More on the Session Manager

To prevent accidental deletion of files, place either a write-
protected or blank disk in drive A. Enter OS/2 protected mode
and, at the prompt, invoke the DISKCOPY command, as shown
here:

```
[C:\] DISKCOPY
```

DISKCOPY responds with its familiar prompt

```
[C:\] DISKCOPY
Enter drive letter for source.
```

Rather than selecting a source and target disk drive specification, instead activate the OS/2 Session Manager by pressing
CTRL-ESC.

```
Start a Program
COMMAND.COM                          R
DISKCOPY.COM
```

As you can see, when a protected-mode session is executing a program, the OS/2 Session Manager displays the name of the program that is currently executing. Thus, if you have several programs running simultaneously, you can select the desired session from this menu.

```
Start a Program
COMMAND.COM                          R
DISKCOPY.COM
WORDPROC.COM
DATABASE.COM
LEDGER.EXE
```

Select the DISKCOPY.COM session; the following appears on your screen:

```
[C:\] DISKCOPY
Enter drive letter for source.
```

Use the CTRL-BREAK key combination to terminate the command, as discussed in Chapter 2.

SESSION NAMES

When an OS/2 protected mode session is executing a program, the OS/2 Session Manager displays that program name on its Session Manager menu to simplify your session selection.

OS/2 Basic Commands

OS/2 commands are either internal (memory-resident) or external (reside on disk), as previously discussed. Each of the commands presented in this section executes in both real and protected mode. Experienced DOS users should not rush through the examples because OS/2 adds some enhancements to familiar commands (such as DIR and TYPE) that you will find quite useful.

DIR

Chapter 2 discussed the OS/2 DIR command, which allows you to list the files contained on your disk. For example, the command

```
[C:\] DIR *.TXT
```

lists all of the files with the extension TXT on the current disk. Likewise, the command

```
[C:\] DIR B:*.TXT
```

lists all of the files with the extension TXT that reside on drive B. You could also list all the files on drive A that contain this extension. Although you were able to view the names of all the files on drives A, B, and C with the extension TXT, you used three commands to do so. This is not required under OS/2 protected mode.

Consider the following command:

```
[C:\] DIR *.TXT B:*.TXT A:*.TXT
```

In this case, OS/2 first issues the DIR command with the file specification *.TXT. Upon completion of that directory listing, DIR lists all the files that match the file specification B:*.TXT. Last, DIR does the same with the file specification A:*.TXT. The flowchart in Figure 3-5 illustrates the processing involved in the execution of these commands.

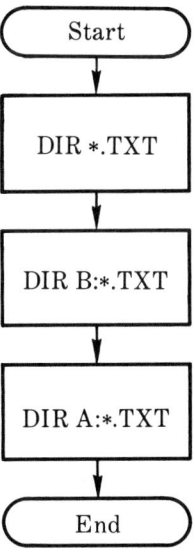

Figure 3-5. *Process of showing directories of multiple files*

On the screen, the output appears as follows:

```
[C:\] DIR *.TXT B:*.TXT A:*.TXT

Volume in drive C is OS2
Directory of C:\WS

CHAP3     TXT      46080    9-26-87     7:21p
ADD       TXT        512    9-14-87     9:19p
LTR       TXT       1152    9-14-87    10:16p

                3 File(s)       10323968 bytes free

Volume in drive B is MISC
Directory of B:\

NOTES     TXT       2233    9-17-87    10:12a
LTR       TXT       1152    9-14-87    10:16p

        2 File(s)      14336 bytes free

Volume in drive A is NOTES
Directory of A:\

NOTES     TXT       2233    9-17-87    10:12a

        1 File(s)      314336 bytes free

[C:\]
```

If DIR does not find files that match the specified files, it displays an error message so stating and terminates the command:

```
[C:\] DIR *.TXT *.SAV *.BAK

Volume in drive C is OS2
Directory of C:\WS

CHAP3     TXT      46080    9-26-87     7:21p
ADD       TXT        512    9-14-87     9:19p
LTR       TXT       1152    9-14-87    10:16p

DOS0002 The system cannot find the file specified.

[C:\]
```

The ability to provide multiple file specifications in this manner is new to OS/2.

ENHANCEMENT TO DIR

Under OS/2 protected mode, the OS/2 DIR command allows you to place multiple file specifications on the command line. DIR uses each file specification, one after another, to perform multiple directory listings.

TYPE (Displaying a File's Contents)

The OS/2 TYPE command enables you to display the contents of a text file on your screen. The format of the TYPE command is

TYPE *file_specification* [. . .]

where the following is true:

file_specification is the name of the file to display. It can contain a disk drive identification and an OS/2 path name (discussed in Chapter 8). TYPE supports the OS/2 wildcard characters * and ?.

TYPE allows you to display only the contents of text (or ASCII) files on your screen. If you attempt to TYPE the contents of a file with an EXE, COM, or OBJ extension, TYPE displays unrecognizable characters on your screen, and probably sounds the computer's built-in speaker.

Such files are not text files. They contain nonprintable (nonalphanumeric) characters. You can verify this by attempting to TYPE the contents of the file CMD.EXE:

```
[C:\] TYPE CMD.EXE
```

The nonalphanumeric characters in CMD.EXE result in strange characters on your display, along with the computer producing an intermittent beep. Text files are files that contain standard characters (such as book chapters or a letter).

Assume you have created the file CARS.DAT, which contains the following:

```
Mercedes
BMW
Supra
Rolls
300 ZX
Jaguar
```

If you issue the command

```
[C:\] TYPE CARS.DAT
```

TYPE displays the contents of the file on your screen:

```
[C:\] TYPE CARS.DAT
Mercedes
BMW
Supra
Rolls
300 ZX
Jaguar

[C:\]
```

If you enter a file name that does not exist,

```
[C:\] TYPE NOFILE.TXT
```

TYPE displays an error message, as shown here:

```
DOS0002 The system cannot find the file specified.
```

Assume your file FOOTBALL.DAT, on drive B, contains the following:

```
Bears
Jets
Seahawks
Broncos
49ers
Patriots
```

If you place a disk drive identification in the file specification

```
[C:\] TYPE B:FOOTBALL.DAT
```

TYPE displays the file's contents, as shown here:

```
[C:\] TYPE B:FOOTBALL.DAT

Bears
Jets
Seahawks
Broncos
49ers
Patriots

[C:\]
```

If you instead omit the disk drive identification,

```
[C:\] TYPE FOOTBALL.DAT
```

TYPE searches for the file FOOTBALL.DAT on the default drive, as discussed in Chapter 2.

TYPE supports the OS/2 wildcard characters. For example, if you have the files

MAR.BIL	Bills for the month of March
APR.BIL	Bills for the month of April
MAY.BIL	Bills for the month of MAY

on your current disk, the command

```
[C:\] TYPE *.BIL
```

results in the following display:

```
[C:\] TYPE *.BIL

March bills:
Electric          $125.00
Gas               $ 35.00
Food              $300.00
Beer              $300.00
Visa              $250.00
Rent              $455.00

April bills:
Electric          $100.00
Gas               $ 40.00
Food              $150.00
Beer              $450.00
Rent              $455.00

May bills:
Electric          $110.00
Gas               $ 34.00
Food              $ 50.00
Beer              $550.00
Rent              $455.00

[C:\]
```

If other files with the extension BIL also reside on the current disk, TYPE also displays their contents.

Closely examine the TYPE command format:

TYPE *file__specification* [...]

The [...] option means that you can repeat the file specification an unlimited number of times. As such, the following is a valid TYPE command:

```
[C:\] TYPE MAR.BIL APR.BIL MAY.BIL
```

Assuming these files exist on disk, this command displays the following:

```
March bills:
Electric          $125.00
Gas               $ 35.00
Food              $300.00
Beer              $300.00
Visa              $250.00
Rent              $455.00

April bills:
Electric          $100.00
Gas               $ 40.00
Food              $150.00
Beer              $450.00
Rent              $455.00

May bills:
Electric          $110.00
Gas               $ 34.00
Food              $ 50.00
Beer              $550.00
Rent              $455.00

[C:\]
```

OS/2 provides several files you can examine with TYPE. Use the DIR command to locate the files CONFIG.SYS, STARTUP.CMD, and AUTOEXEC.BAT. Use the TYPE command to display their contents.

ENHANCEMENTS TO THE OS/2 TYPE COMMAND

OS/2 protected mode provides several enhancements to the TYPE command. First, in protected mode, TYPE supports the OS/2 wildcard characters. Second, OS/2 protected mode allows you to place multiple file specifications on the command line. TYPE uses each file specification, one following another, and displays the contents of each specified file.

Figure 3-6.   *Copying a file from one disk to another disk*

COPY (Duplicating a File)

The OS/2 COPY command allows you to duplicate a file on disk by either placing it on a different disk (see Figure 3-6) or placing it on the same disk with a different name (see Figure 3-7). The OS/2

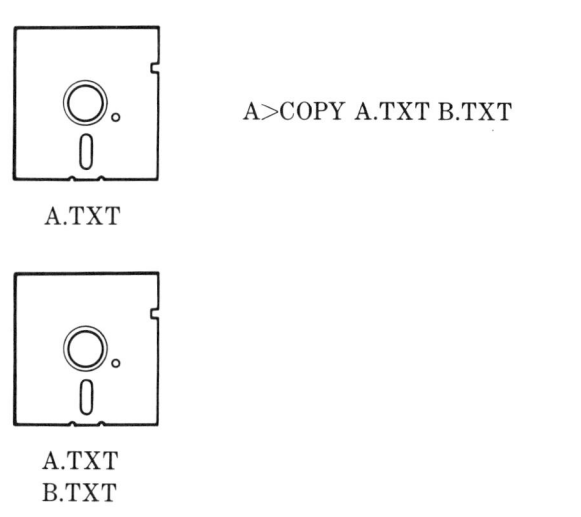

Figure 3-7.   *Copying a file on the same disk*

COPY command has tremendous capabilities. However, to avoid confusion, only the basics are discussed at this time.

The basic format of the COPY command is

COPY *source_file target_file*

where the following is true:

source_file is the complete OS/2 file specification of the file to duplicate. It can contain a disk drive identification, or an OS/2 path name (described in Chapter 8). COPY fully supports wildcard characters for the source file.

target_file is the complete OS/2 file specification of the new copy of the file. It can contain a disk drive identification, or an OS/2 path name (described in Chapter 8). COPY fully supports wildcard characters for the target file.

Consider the following example:

```
[C:\] COPY CONFIG.SYS CONFIG.SAV
```

In this case, COPY duplicates the contents of the file CONFIG.SYS and places the copy of the file into a new file called CONFIG.SAV. (Note, however, that if the write-protect tab is on the disk, COPY will not work.) If you perform a directory listing, OS/2 shows both files:

```
[C:\] DIR CONFIG.*

 Volume in drive C is OS2
 Directory of  C:\

CONFIG   SYS        24   9-24-87    4:14p
CONFIG   SAV        24   9-26-87    7:19p

        2 File(s)   10278912 bytes free

[C:\]
```

You can also copy the contents of CONFIG.SYS to drive B, as follows:

```
[C:\] COPY CONFIG.SYS B:CONFIG.SYS

   1 file(s) copied.
```

Note the following use of wildcard characters:

```
[C:\] COPY CONFIG.SYS B:*.*

        1 file(s) copied.
```

When you are using the OS/2 COPY command and the file name does not change when you copy it to a new target location, you can even omit the wildcard characters, as shown here:

```
[C:\] COPY CONFIG.SYS B:

        1 file(s) copied.
```

Each of the three previous examples have copied the file CONFIG.SYS to drive B and given the duplicate file the same name on that drive. Be careful because the OS/2 COPY command overwrites any files at the target location that have the same name as the specified target file.

Lastly, consider this COPY command:

```
[C:\] COPY *.BAK *.SAV
TEST.BAK
CHAP.BAK
PROGRAM.BAK

        3 file(s) copied.

[C:\]
```

In this case, COPY duplicates all files with the extension BAK and gives the copies the same file name with the extension SAV.

This command copies all of the files on drive A to the current default drive:

```
[C:\] COPY A:*.* B:*.*
```

As the following illustrates, COPY does not allow a file to be copied to itself:

```
[C:\] COPY CONFIG.SYS CONFIG.SYS
DOS1078: The file cannot be copied onto itself.

      0 file(s) copied.
```

RENAME (Changing a File's Name)

The OS/2 RENAME command enables you to change the name of an existing file. The format of the RENAME command is

RENAME *source_file target_file*

where the following is true:

source_file is the name of the file that you are renaming. This is a complete OS/2 file specification that may contain a disk drive identification and path name (discussed in Chapter 8). RENAME supports wildcard characters.

target_file is the new name of the file that you are renaming. This is a complete OS/2 file specification that may contain a disk drive identification and path name (discussed in Chapter 8). RENAME supports wildcard characters.

Note that OS/2 supports two forms of the RENAME command, each of which serves the same function. The command

```
[C:\] RENAME CONFIG.BAK CONFIG.SAV
```

is functionally identical to

```
[C:\] REN CONFIG.BAK CONFIG.SAV
```

In the previous examples, you listed the contents of the file CARS.DAT, as follows:

```
[C:\] TYPE CARS.DAT

Mercedes
BMW
Supra
Rolls
300 ZX
Jaguar

[C:\]
```

By using the OS/2 RENAME command, you can change the name of this file from CARS.DAT to DREAMS.DAT, as shown here:

```
[C:\] REN CARS.DAT DREAMS.DAT
```

Performing an OS/2 directory listing verifies that the name change has indeed taken place:

```
[C:\] DIR DREAMS.*

 Volume in drive C is OS2
 Directory of  C:\WS

DREAMS    DAT       45   9-26-87   6:37p
        1 File(s)  10303488 bytes free
```

To change the name of the file back to CARS.DAT, you can use the shorter version of the command (REN) as shown here:

```
[C:\] REN DREAMS.DAT CARS.DAT
```

RENAME does not create a new copy of a file, but instead simply changes the name of an existing file. RENAME fully supports the OS/2 wildcard characters * and ?. For example, the command

```
[C:\] REN *.DAT *.SAV
```

changes the name of all of the files with the extension DAT to SAV, as shown by this directory listing:

```
[C:\] DIR *.SAV

 Volume in drive C is OS2
 Directory of  C:\WS

LOAN     SAV     45952    9-26-87    7:19p
ACCTS    SAV       324    9-26-87    8:31p
         2 File(s)   10297344 bytes free

[C:\]
```

If you attempt to RENAME a nonexistent file, OS/2 responds with the following error message:

```
[C:\] REN NOFILE.TXT SOMEFILE.TXT

DOS0002: The system cannot find the file specified.

[C:\]
```

OS/2 does not allow you to RENAME a file to a name already in use by another file, as shown here:

```
[C:\] RENAME CARS.OLD CARS.DAT
```

If you attempt to do so, OS/2 responds with

```
[C:\] RENAME CARS.OLD CARS.DAT

DOS0005: The system cannot access the file specified.

[C:\]
```

Note that RENAME does not allow you to RENAME a file from one disk to another, as attempted here:

```
[C:\] RENAME CARS.DAT A:CARS.DAT
```

Keep in mind that OS/2 is simply changing the name of an existing file. RENAME in no way moves the file or makes a copy of it. If you attempt to do so, OS/2 responds with

```
[C:\] RENAME CARS.DAT A:CARS.DAT

DOS1043: The system cannot accept the parameter
specified.

[C:\]
```

OS/2 does not allow you to RENAME a file from one subdirectory to another. RENAME only allows you to change the name of standard files. RENAME will not change the name of an OS/2 directory.

DEL (Removing a File from Disk)

Just as OS/2 allows you to create and modify files, it also allows you to remove from disk when they are no longer required. The OS/2 DEL command allows you to erase a file or multiple files from disk. The format of the command is

DEL *file_specification* [...]

where the following is true:

file—specification is the name of the file to display. This can contain a disk drive identification, and an OS/2 path name (discussed in Chapter 8). DEL supports the OS/2 wildcard characters * and ?.

Assume that your disk contains the files shown in Figure 3-8. An OS/2 directory listing verifies the file's existence:

```
[C:\] DIR A:

 Volume in drive A has no label
 Directory of  A:\

MAR      BIL      92   9-26-87    8:31p
APR      BIL      77   9-26-87    8:31p
MAY      BIL      77   9-26-87    8:31p
CARS     DAT      45   9-26-87    6:37p
FOOTBALL DAT      49   9-26-87    8:31p
        5 File(s)     357376 bytes free
```

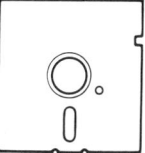

MAR.BIL
APR.BIL
MAY.BIL
CARS.DAT
FOOTBALL.DAT

Figure 3-8. *Sample files on disk*

If you enter the DEL command

```
[C:\] DEL A:MAR.BIL
```

OS/2 deletes the specified file (see Figure 3-9):

```
[C:\] DIR A:

 Volume in drive A has no label
 Directory of  A:\

 APR      BIL       77    9-26-87    8:31p
 MAY      BIL       77    9-26-87    8:31p
 CARS     DAT       45    9-26-87    6:37p
 FOOTBALL DAT       49    9-26-87    8:31p
          4 File(s)      358400 bytes free
```

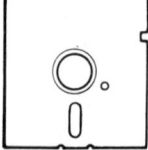

APR.BIL
MAY.BIL
CARS.DAT
FOOTBALL.DAT

Figure 3-9. *Deletion of sample file from disk*

Likewise, if you issue the command

```
[C:\] DEL A:APR.BIL
```

OS/2 deletes the file and leaves the following:

```
[C:\] DIR A:

 Volume in drive A has no label
 Directory of  A:\

MAY        BIL       77    9-26-87    8:31p
CARS       DAT       45    9-26-87    6:37p
FOOTBALL DAT         49    9-26-87    8:31p
         3 File(s)      359424 bytes free
```

The OS/2 DEL command fully supports the OS/2 wildcard characters * and ?. In this case, the command

```
[C:\] DEL A:*.DAT
```

deletes all of the files with the extension DAT and leaves the following:

```
[C:\] DIR A:

 Volume in drive A has no label
 Directory of  A:\

MAY        BIL       77    9-26-87    8:31p
         1 File(s)      361472 bytes free
```

Once you have deleted a file, OS/2 does not provide a means to retrieve it. If you are a programmer, the Osborne/McGraw-Hill text *DOS: Power User's Guide*, by Kris Jamsa (1988), shows you how to "unerase" a file that you have just deleted. However, OS/2 does not provide this facility.

Consider the following command:

```
[C:\] DEL *.*
```

DEL will erase all the files from the current directory of your disk. Because this can have devastating results if you entered the command in error, OS/2 first prompts you to ensure that you actually want to perform the command:

```
Are you sure (Y/N)?
```

To continue the command and delete the files as specified, press Y and press the ENTER key. If you do not want to execute the command, press N and press ENTER.

Early versions of DOS provided a similar form of this command called ERASE. The format of ERASE is identical to that of DEL:

ERASE *file_specification* [...]

where the following is true:

file_specification is the name of the file to display. This can contain a disk drive identification, and an OS/2 path name (discussed in Chapter 8). ERASE supports the OS/2 wildcard characters * and ?.

In order to maintain compatibility with existing DOS versions, OS/2 fully supports ERASE. For example, the commands

```
[C:\] DEL CONFIG.BAK
```

and

```
[C:\] ERASE CONFIG.BAK
```

are functionally identical. However, get in the habit of using the DEL command because it is the standard. ERASE only exists for compatibility with older versions of DOS.

Notice that the DEL command supports multiple files on the command line. If your directory contains

```
[C:\] DIR A:

Volume in drive A has no label.
Directory of A:\

A          TXT        45    9-26-87    6:37p
MAY        BIL        77    9-26-87    8:31p
B          TXT        49    9-26-87    8:31p

     3 File(s)     359424 bytes free
```

the command

```
[C:\] DEL A:A.TXT A:B.TXT
```

deletes both of the files A.TXT and B.TXT and leaves

```
[C:\] DIR A:

Volume in drive A has no label.
Directory of A:\

MAY       BIL       77    9-26-87   8:31p

      1 File(s)    361472 bytes free
```

In a similar manner, the command

```
[C:\] DEL *.BAK B:CONFIG.OLD A:DATA.SAV
```

first attempts to delete all files with the extension BAK. Next, it attempts to delete the file CONFIG.OLD from drive B. Last, it removes the file DATA.SAV from disk A. If DEL cannot match one of the file specifications, it displays the following message and terminates the command:

```
DOS0002: The system cannot find the file specified.

[C:\]
```

Chapter 2 examined write-protected disks. If you write-protect your disk (see Figure 3-10), OS/2 cannot modify its contents. As such, the command

```
[C:\] DEL A:*.BIL
```

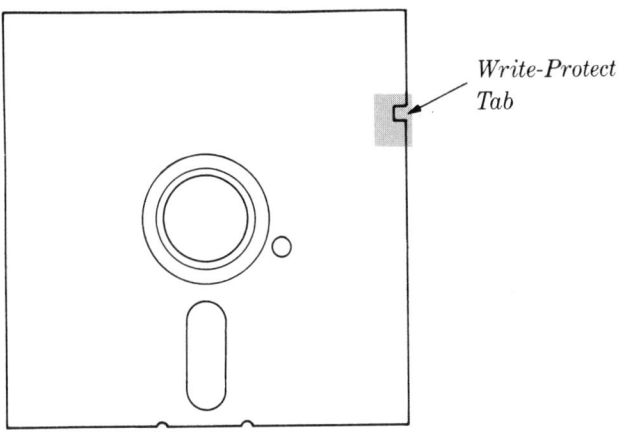

Figure 3 - 10. *Write-protected disk*

on a write-protected disk results in

```
Session Title: COMMAND.COM

        DOS0019: The system cannot write to
        a write-protected diskette.

        Return the error to the program
        End the program
        Retry the operation
```

This text later discusses how to set a file's attributes to read-only, which disallows OS/2 from modifying the file. If you attempt to delete such a file, OS/2 responds with

```
DOS0005: The system cannot access the file specified.
```

DEL is a powerful and necessary OS/2 command. Unfortunately, a user error involving DEL can have catastrophic effects, especially when you are using the OS/2 wildcard characters.

Later chapters explain that, unless the DEL command specifically references an OS/2 directory path, the OS/2 DEL command will only affect files in the current directory. In addition, DEL only deletes standard files and not subdirectories (see Chapter 8).

PROMPT (Changing the OS/2 System Prompt)

The OS/2 PROMPT command enables you to specify the prompt that OS/2 displays on your screen each time it is ready for you to enter a command. By default, OS/2 displays the following prompts, depending upon whether you are in a real- or protected-mode session. Assuming that you are currently in a protected-mode session, OS/2 by default uses the following:

```
[C:\]
```

Note the effect of changing the current default drive on the system prompt, as follows:

```
[C:\]
[C:\] B:
[B:\]
```

If you are in an OS/2 real-mode session, OS/2 displays the following prompt:

```
c>
```

To direct OS/2 to change its current system prompt, use the PROMPT command as shown here:

PROMPT [*prompt_string*]

where the following is true:

prompt_string is a character string that contains your desired system prompt. The prompt string can contain standard keyboard characters, along with several predefined metacharacters. PROMPT uses the following predefined metacharacters, which must be preceded by a $ in the form $*c*, where *c* is one of the following metacharacters:

a   Prompt displays the & character

b   Prompt displays the ¦ character

c   Prompt displays the (character

d   Prompt displays the current system date

e   Prompt writes the ASCII escape character

f   Prompt displays the) character

g   Prompt displays the > character

h   Prompt writes the backspace character

l   Prompt displays the < character

n   Prompt displays the current default drive

p   Prompt displays the current drive and directory

q   Prompt displays the = character

t   Prompt displays the current system time

v   Prompt displays the OS/2 version number

$ Prompt displays the $ character

—   Prompt writes a carriage return and linefeed

At the OS/2 prompt, enter the following command:

```
[C:\] PROMPT YES
```

OS/2 responds by changing the system prompt, as shown here:

```
YES
```

Press the ENTER key several times.

```
YES
YES
YES
```

Next, enter the following command:

```
YES PROMPT $t
```

OS/2 responds to the command by changing the prompt to the current system time.

Likewise, the command

```
21:45:23.44 PROMPT $d$g
```

results in

```
Sat   9-26-1987>
```

The command

```
Sat   9-26-1987> PROMPT $d$t$_$_$g
```

directs OS/2 to display

```
Sat   9-26-1987 21:45:23.44

>
```

Note the use of the $_ metacharacter to move the cursor down two lines. If you want to know the current system time

```
21:50:38.32
```

but do not like the amount of space it consumes on your screen, use the backspace character, as shown here:

```
21:50:38.32 PROMPT $t$h$h$h$h$h
```

In this case, OS/2 will respond with

```
21:51:
```

Note that the OS/2 PROMPT command only sets the system prompt for your current session. For example, if you set your system prompt to

```
WORDPROC>
```

and then created a second protected-mode session, the new session would use the default prompt, as shown here:

```
[C:\]
```

If you simply enter the PROMPT command without a prompt string, OS/2 sets your prompt back to its default.

```
YES PROMPT
[c:\]
```

Take a few minutes to experiment with PROMPT. It can be helpful in keeping track of your current file directory.

VER (Displaying the OS/2 Version Number)

The OS/2 VER command enables you to display the current OS/2 version number. The OS/2 version number is composed of two parts: a major version number and a minor version number. You should distinguish between the use of each version number. In most cases, these numbers provide you with significant insight to the degree of enhancements in a new release of a software package.

Most software developers use a specific standard when they release an upgrade to a new software package. If the upgrade is significant and results in major enhancements to the software package, the developers increment the major version number. In the case of version 1.0, the new release would become version 2.0. However, if the changes are relatively minor (perhaps to fix a bug), the developers only increment the minor version number. In the case of version 1.0, it would become version 1.1.

To determine your current version of OS/2, enter the VER command at the OS/2 prompt, as shown here:

```
[c:\] VER
```

Next, switch to a real-mode session and again execute the VER command. OS/2 displays the same version number in both modes. Whether you are working in real or in protected mode, you are still executing OS/2.

LABEL (Assigning a Name to a Disk)

The OS/2 LABEL command enables you to assign a name to a fixed or floppy disk. The name assigned to the disk is known as a volume label. The format of the LABEL command is

[*drive:*][*path*]LABEL [*target_drive:*][*volume_label*]

where the following is true:

drive: specifies the name of the disk drive containing the file LABEL.COM. LABEL is an external command, which means that it resides on disk. If you do not specify a drive, OS/2 uses the current default.

path is the subdirectory path to the file LABEL.COM. If you do not specify a path (see Chapter 8), OS/2 uses the current default.

target_drive: is the disk drive identification to which you are assigning the name. If you do not specify a target drive, LABEL uses the current default.

volume_label is the name that you are assigning to the disk. This can contain from 1 to 11 characters. If you do not specify a volume name, LABEL prompts you for one.

Consider the following directory listing:

```
[C:\] DIR

 Volume in drive C is OS2
 Directory of  C:\

OS2BIO    COM      5120    5-27-87   12:00a
OS2DOS    COM    233016    5-27-87   12:00a
OSO001    MSG     73993    5-27-87   12:00a
```

Notice that OS/2 lists the disk volume name. If the disk volume does not have a name

```
[C:\] DIR A:

 Volume in drive A has no label
 Directory of  A:\

MAY       BIL       77    9-26-87    8:31p
          1 File(s)     361472 bytes free
```

you can assign one to it by using the OS/2 LABEL command, as follows:

```
[C:\] LABEL
```

LABEL prompts you for the disk name, as shown here:

```
 Volume in drive C is OS2DISK
 Type a volume label of up to 11 characters
 or press Enter for no volume label update.
```

For example, to assign the disk in drive A the name "OS2DISK," issue the following command:

```
[C:\] LABEL A:OS2DISK
```

A directory listing of the disk shows

```
[C:\] DIR A:

Volume in drive A is OS2DISK
Directory of  A:\

MAY       BIL       77   9-26-87   8:31p
          1 File(s)     361472 bytes free
```

Many OS/2 users are confused by the need to use disk volume names. Consider this example. A computer user group always keeps track of its general ledger on floppy disks that contain the following files:

```
ACCOUNTS   PAY          156      11-04-87     11:22a
ACCOUNTS   REC          162      11-04-87     11:23a
PAYROLL    DAT          113      11-04-87     11:23a
SALARIES   DAT           89      11-04-87     11:23a
INCOME     TAX          151      11-04-87     11:24a
LEDGER     EXE        22042       8-14-84      8:00a
```

Each fiscal year, the company creates a new disk for the accounting data. Over the past three years the company has created the data disks shown in Figure 3-11. Obviously, the user now has several disks, each of which contains the same set of files. If the user mistakenly places the wrong floppy disk into the disk drive, he or she may inadvertently lose data files. By assigning

Figure 3-11.   *Software company's general-ledger system on disk*

volume labels to each disk, the general-ledger software can determine whether the user has placed the correct disk in the drive. Remember, a volume label can contain from 1 to 11 characters, so the company can use the volume labels LEDGER85, LEDGER86, and LEDGER87 for the disks.

A directory listing of the 1986 disk reveals the following:

```
    Volume in drive B is LEDGER87
    Directory of B:\

ACCOUNTS   PAY            156       11-04-87       11:23a
ACCOUNTS   REC            162       11-04-87       11:23a
PAYROLL    DAT            113       11-04-87       11:23a
SALARIES   DAT             89       11-04-87       11:23a
INCOME     TAX            151       11-04-87       11:24a
LEDGER     EXE          22042        8-14-84        8:00a
          6 File(s)          334848 bytes free
```

Since each disk is named, the general-ledger software can verify that the correct disk is in use.

If a disk already has a volume name, you can rename it with the LABEL command, as shown previously. If you decide that the name is already satisfactory, simply press the ENTER key or the CTRL-BREAK key combination. Otherwise, type in the desired new name.

Later this chapter discusses how you can specify a volume label for a disk during the formatting procedure.

VOL (Displaying a Disk's Name)

Closely related to the OS/2 LABEL command is the OS/2 VOL command, which displays the current name of a disk contained in the specified drive. The format of the command is

VOL [*target__drive:*][. . .]

where the following is true:

target__drive: is the disk drive name of which VOL is to return the volume label. If you do not specify a target disk, VOL uses the current default.

Consider the following command:

```
[C:\] VOL
```

VOL displays the name of the disk in the current drive, as shown here:

```
[C:\] VOL

  Volume in drive C is OS2DISK
```

If you instead enter the command

```
[C:\] VOL B:
```

VOL displays the name of the floppy disk in drive B. If the disk does not have a volume label, VOL displays

```
Volume in drive B has no label
```

If you examine the format of the VOL command, you find that you can specify several disk drives for which VOL is to return the volume label. Consider the following command:

```
[C:\] VOL A: B: C:
```

ENHANCEMENT TO THE OS/2 VOL COMMAND

In protected mode, OS/2 allows you to place several disk drive specifications on the VOL command line. VOL displays in succession the volume label (name) for each disk.

SET (Defining an Environment String)

Each time you create an OS/2 session, OS/2 creates an environment space for you to define specific pieces of information for that session. At the OS/2 prompt, type

```
[C:\] SET
```

OS/2 displays the session's default environment settings, as follows:

```
[C:\] SET

3XBOX=COMMAND.COM
COMSPEC=C:\CMD.EXE
PATH=C:\;C:\OS2;C:\TOOLS
INCLUDE=c:\include
LIB=c:\lib
INIT=c:\init

[C:\]
```

The OS/2 environment is simply a location where you can store information for use by OS/2 or your programs.

From the OS/2 prompt, issue the following commands and note their effects on the environment:

```
     [C:\] PROMPT YES
YES SET

3XBOX=COMMAND.COM
COMSPEC=C:\CMD.EXE
PATH=C:\;C:\OS2;C:\TOOLS
INCLUDE=c:\include
LIB=c:\lib
INIT=c:\init
PROMPT=YES

YES
```

The format of the OS/2 SET command is

SET [*string1*=[*string2*]]

where the following is true:

string1 is the name of an environment value to which you want to assign a value.

string2 is the name of the value assigned to *string1*.

Consider the following examples:

```
[C:\] SET
```

As you have seen, invoking SET without any parameters directs it to display its current settings. If you enter

```
[C:\] SET PROMPT=PROTECTED
PROTECTED
```

you change the system prompt by modifying the value assigned to the environment entry PROMPT. To restore the PROMPT, issue the OS/2 PROMPT command, as follows:

```
PROTECTED   PROMPT
[C:\]
```

Next, define your only environment entry called FILENAME by assigning it the value CONFIG.SYS. Later chapters discuss how to use the value of your variable FILENAME within OS/2 batch procedures.

```
[c:\] SET FILENAME=CONFIG.SYS
```

DISKCOMP (Comparing Two Floppy Disks)

The OS/2 DISKCOMP command enables you to compare the contents of two floppy disks and to display the side and track number of any differences. For example, if you have just created a backup copy of a disk by using the OS/2 DISKCOPY command, you can use the DISKCOMP command to ensure that the contents of the disks are identical. The format of the DISKCOMP command is

[*drive:*][path]DISKCOMP [d:[d:]]

where

drive: specifies the name of the disk drive containing the file DISKCOMP.COM. DISKCOMP is an external command, which means that it resides on disk. If you do not specify a drive, OS/2 uses the current default.

path is the subdirectory path to file DISKCOMP.COM. If you do not specify a path (see Chapter 8), OS/2 uses the current default.

d: is the disk drive containing one of the two disks that DISKCOMP is to compare. If you do not specify two disk drives, DISKCOMP prompts you to enter the disks in a drive as required.

DISKCOMP allows you to use the same or current disk drives for the disk comparison. If you use the same disk drive, DISKCOMP prompts you to place the floppy disks in the drive at the correct times, as shown here:

```
Enter drive letter for source. a:
Enter drive letter for target. a:

Insert source diskette in drive A:

Press Enter to continue.
Comparing 40 tracks 9 sectors per
track 2 side(s).

Insert target diskette in drive A:

Press Enter to continue.
```

If the two disks that DISKCOMP compared are identical, DISKCOMP displays the following message:

```
Compare OK.
Compare process has ended.
```

However, if a difference exists, DISKCOMP displays this message:

```
Comparison error on side n track n.
```

DISKCOMP only works with floppy disk drives. If you attempt to use DISKCOMP with a fixed or virtual drive, DISKCOMP displays the following message:

```
DOS1231: The system cannot accept the drive specified
or you specified a fixed disk.
```

The most common use of DISKCOMP is to verify the correct performance of a DISKCOPY command. If DISKCOPY was successful, DISKCOMP should not find any differences.

COMP (Comparing the Contents of Two Files)

The OS/2 COMP command compares two files and displays the byte (or character) location of the first 10 differences between the two files. The format of the COMP command is

[*drive:*][*path*]COMP[*file_specification*][*file_specification*]

where the following is true:

drive: specifies the name of the disk drive containing the file COMP.COM. COMP is an external command, which means that it resides on disk. If you do not specify a drive, OS/2 uses the current default.

path is the subdirectory path to the file COMP.COM. If you do not specify a path (see Chapter 8), OS/2 uses the current default.

file_specification is the complete OS/2 file specification for one of the files that COMP is to compare. If you omit either file, COMP prompts you for them, as shown here:

```
[C:\] COMP
Enter the first filename.
CONFIG.SYS

Enter the second filename.
CONFIG.BAK
```

Assume that the files DAYS.DAT, WORKDAYS.DAT, WEEKDAYS.DAT, and WEEKEND.DAT contain the following:

SUNDAY MONDAY TUESDAY WEDNESDAY THURSDAY FRIDAY SATURDAY	MONDAY TUESDAY WEDNESDAY THURSDAY FRIDAY	MONDAY TUESDAY WEDNESDAY THURSDAY FRIDAY	SATURDAY SUNDAY
DAYS.DAT	WORKDAYS.DAT	WEEKDAYS.DAT	WEEKEND.DAT

Enter the command

```
[C:\] COMP DAYS.DAT WORKDAYS.DAT
```

COMP displays the information shown in Figure 3-12. If you want to compare additional files, simply press Y and the ENTER key. Otherwise, press N and then press ENTER. One of the difficulties of using the COMP command is that it displays the location of each difference as a hexadecimal offset from the beginning of the file. Appendix A provides you with the hexadecimal values ranging from 0 to 127.

Consider the following command

```
[C:\] COMP
Enter the first filename.
CONFIG.SYS
Enter the second filename.
CONFIG.BAK
```

In this example, COMP prompts you for the primary and secondary file names to compare. Unless otherwise specified, COMP assumes that the specified files reside on the current drive.

```
Compare file C:DAYS.DAT and file C:WORKDAYS.DAT

A COMPARE error occurred at OFFSET 0
Mismatching byte of file 1 = 53

Mismatching byte of file 2 = 4D

A COMPARE error occurred at OFFSET 1
Mismatching byte of file 1 = 55

Mismatching byte of file 2 = 4F

A COMPARE error occurred at OFFSET 8
Mismatching byte of file 1 = 4D

Mismatching byte of file 2 = 54

A COMPARE error occurred at OFFSET 9
Mismatching byte of file 1 = 4F

Mismatching byte of file 2 = 55

A COMPARE error occurred at OFFSET A
Mismatching byte of file 1 = 4E

Mismatching byte of file 2 = 45

A COMPARE error occurred at OFFSET C
Mismatching byte of file 1 = 44

Mismatching byte of file 2 = 53

A COMPARE error occurred at OFFSET D
Mismatching byte of file 1 = 59

Mismatching byte of file 2 = 41

A COMPARE error occurred at OFFSET E
Mismatching byte of file 1 = 0D

Mismatching byte of file 2 = 59

A COMPARE error occurred at OFFSET F
Mismatching byte of file 1 = 0A

Mismatching byte of file 2 = 0D
```

Figure 3-12. *Screen display of COMPARE process*

There were 10 or more mismatches in comparing
the files. The system is ending the COMPARE command.

Do you want to compare more files (Y/N)?

Figure 3-12. *Screen display of COMPARE process (continued)*

COMP fully supports OS/2 wildcard character processing.
Assume that your directory listing contains the following:

```
   Volume in drive A has no label
   Directory of A:\

AUG        DAT         156        11-04-87        11:22a
JUL        DAT         156        11-04-87        11:22a
JUN        DAT          89        11-04-87        11:23a
JUL        OLD         156        11-04-87        11:22a
SEPT       DAT         156        11-04-87        11:22a
        5 File(s)              357376 bytes free
```

Enter the command

```
 [C:\] COMP A:*.DAT A:*.OLD
```

COMP compares the files with matching file names, unless one of
the files does not exist. If one of the files to be compared does not
exist, OS/2 indicates that it cannot find the specified file and
terminates the command.

If you simply specify a drive for the secondary file

```
[C:\] COMP CONFIG.SYS B:
```

COMP searches that drive for a file with the same name as the primary file. If COMP cannot find a matching file, it displays the following:

```
[C:\] COMP CONFIG.SYS A:

Compare file C:CONFIG.SYS and file A:CONFIG.SYS

DOS1490: The system cannot find A:CONFIG.SYS

Do you want to compare more files (Y/N)?
```

Just as you can use the DISKCOMP command to verify the success of a DISKCOPY command, you can use COMP to verify a file copy, as shown here:

```
[C:\] COPY CONFIG.SYS A:
[C:\] COMP CONFIG.SYS A:
```

If COMP finds differences between the two files, repeat your COPY command. If COMP again finds differences, attempt to COPY to a different target disk.

By default, COMP does not compare files of different lengths. If you attempt to do so, COMP displays the following:

```
The files are different sizes.
Do you want to continue (Y/N)?
```

Simply type Y and press ENTER to perform the comparison, or type N and press ENTER to terminate the command.

CHKDSK (Displaying a Disk's Current Status)

The OS/2 CHKDSK command provides several useful pieces of information about a specific disk. The format of the CHKDSK command is

*[drive:][path]*CHKDSK
[target_drive:][file_specification][/F][/V]

where the following is true:

drive: specifies the name of the disk drive containing the file CHKDSK.COM. CHKDSK is an external command, which means that it resides on disk. If you do not specify a drive, OS/2 uses the current default.

path is the subdirectory path to file CHKDSK.COM. If you do not specify a path (see Chapter 8), OS/2 uses the current default.

target_drive: is the disk drive identification containing the disk that CHKDSK is to examine. If you do not specify a target drive, CHKDSK uses the current default drive.

file_specification is the complete name of a file to examine for disk fragmentation. It can contain a disk drive identification and OS/2 path name (discussed in Chapter 8). CHKDSK supports the OS/2 wildcard characters.

/F directs CHKDSK to fix errors found in the file allocation table (FAT) or in directories. When /F is present, CHKDSK writes the corrections to disk. Periodically, OS/2 may lose one or more of the internal pointers that it uses to track files on disk. The /F qualifier directs CHKDSK to attempt to correct as many damaged pointers as possible.

/V directs CHKDSK to display the names and paths of all files on the target disk.

CHKDSK provides you with a summary listing of the following:

Disk volume label (if present)
Total disk space (in bytes)
Space consumed by hidden files (in bytes)
Space consumed by user files (in bytes)
Available disk space (in bytes)

If you are executing in real mode, OS/2 also displays

Total memory present (in bytes)
Total memory available (in bytes)

CHKDSK assumes that the disk you want to examine is already present in the target drive. Unlike other OS/2 commands, CHKDSK does not prompt you to place the target disk in the specified drive. If you do not specify a target disk drive, CHKDSK uses the current default drive.

If you invoke CHKDSK in protected mode, your output is

```
  362496 bytes total disk space.
  360448 bytes in 11 user files.
    2048 bytes available on disk.
```

If you invoke CHKDSK in real mode, CHKDSK displays

```
    362496 bytes total disk space.
    360448 bytes in 11 user files.
      2048 bytes available on disk.

[DOS mode storage report]
    524288 bytes total storage
    401728 bytes free
```

Note the additional lines of information on system memory utilization. If CHKDSK finds damaged pointers, it displays the following:

```
nnnn lost clusters found in nnnn chains
Convert lost chains to files (Y/N)?
```

Remember, for CHKDSK to actually write the corrections to disk, you must include the /F qualifier. If you then respond to the prompt with Y, CHKDSK begins creating files with the name FILE*nnnn*.CHK, where *nnnn* begins with 0000. These files contain the information that CHKDSK has recovered from the damaged pointers.

A convenient method of listing all of the files on a disk is to use the /V qualifier with CHKDSK, as shown here:

```
[C:\] CHKDSK A: /V

Directory A:\
A:\ANSI.EXE
A:\ATTRIB.EXE
A:\FDISK.EXE
A:\GWBASIC.EXE
A:\HELPMSG.EXE
A:\JOIN.EXE
A:\KEYB.EXE
A:\PATCH.EXE
A:\REPLACE.EXE
A:\SORT.EXE
A:\SPOOL.EXE

   362496 bytes total disk space.
   360448 bytes in 11 user files.
     2048 bytes available on disk.
```

FORMAT (Preparing a Disk for Use by OS/2)

Each time you buy a box of floppy disks, the original manufacturer of the disks has no way of knowing on what type of computer the disks will eventually be used, or with what specific operating system. Therefore, you must format each disk to meet your system's specific requirements.

The OS/2 FORMAT command prepares a disk for use by OS/2. The format of the command is

*[drive:][path]*FORMAT*[target—drive:][/N:sectors][/S][/T:tracks]*
[/V:label][/4]

where the following is true:

drive: specifies the name of the disk drive containing the file FORMAT.COM. FORMAT is an external command, which means that it resides on disk. If you do not specify a drive, OS/2 uses the current default.

path is the subdirectory path to file FORMAT.COM. If you do not specify a path (see Chapter 8), OS/2 uses the current default.

target—drive: specifies the disk drive identification containing the disk to format. If you do not specify a target drive, FORMAT uses the current default.

/N:sectors allows you to override the number of sectors per track on the disk. For 720K disks, use the value 9. If you omit this qualifier, FORMAT will choose the best value for the disk that you are formatting.

/S directs FORMAT to place in the target drive the operating system files that are required to boot OS/2. If you do not specify */S*, FORMAT creates a usable disk that cannot boot the operating system. The operating system files consume a significant amount of file space and are probably not required on most disks.

/T:tracks allows you to specify the number of tracks per side on the disk. For 720K disks, use the value 80.

/V:label directs FORMAT to assign a volume label as specified for the new disk.

/4 directs FORMAT to format a 360K floppy disk in a drive normally used for 1.2MB disks.

Place a blank disk in drive A and issue the following command:

```
[C:\] FORMAT A:
```

FORMAT responds with the following:

```
[C:\] FORMAT A:

Insert a new diskette in drive A:
and press Enter when ready.
```

If you have not yet placed the blank disk in drive A, do so now. Be careful that the disk is indeed blank. FORMAT destroys the current contents of a disk if it is not blank. Once you are ready, press the ENTER key to continue, and the disk formatting will begin. If you want to cancel the command, simply use the CTRL-BREAK key combination.

Upon completion, FORMAT displays the following:

```
Format another diskette (Y/N)?
```

To format another disk, press Y and ENTER. Otherwise, press N and press ENTER.

Besides readying a disk for use by OS/2, FORMAT makes a list of damaged locations on the disk. This list prevents OS/2 from trying to write data to these locations. If FORMAT finds bad sectors (locations) on the disk, it displays the following:

```
 362496 bytes total disk space
   2048 bytes in bad sectors
 360448 bytes available on disk
```

If the number of bad sectors is excessive (more than 15,000 on a 1.2MB disk), be leery of using the disk. Some users attempt a second FORMAT. If this also fails, they discard the disk. Floppy disks have improved so much in quality over the past few years that very rarely do disks have bad sectors.

Most fixed disks are shipped to you already formatted. If yours was not, the FORMAT command behaves in the identical manner for fixed disks.

EXIT (Terminating an OS/2 Session)

Throughout this chapter, you have seen how to create multiple OS/2 protected-mode sessions. The OS/2 EXIT command enables you to get rid of these sessions when you no longer require them. The format of the command is

EXIT

Assume that you have the following sessions active:

```
Start a Program
COMMAND.COM                          R
CMD.EXE
CMD.EXE
```

If you select one of the CMD.EXE sessions

```
[C:\]
```

and enter the EXIT command

```
[C:\] EXIT
```

OS/2 returns control to the Session Manager. One less protected-mode session exists, as shown here:

```
Start a Program
COMMAND.COM                          R
CMD.EXE
```

Chapter Highlights

OS/2 commands are classified as either internal or external commands.

Internal commands are commands that reside in memory, internal to OS/2.

External commands reside on disk. OS/2 must load external commands into memory from disk before it can execute them.

To select a real-mode session, select the COMMAND.COM entry from the OS/2 Session Manager menu. Once in real mode, you can execute your existing DOS programs.

Just as the CTRL-ESC key combination directs OS/2 to activate the Session Manager, pressing the ALT-ESC key combination directs OS/2 to switch to its next session.

When a protected-mode session is executing a program, the OS/2 Session Manager displays the name of the program on its menu, thus simplifying your task of session selection.

Several OS/2 commands allow you to place multiple files in the command line when you execute them in protected mode. The OS/2 commands will then use each file name, one after another, as the input to the command.

The OS/2 TYPE command enables you to display the contents of a file on your screen display. Unlike the DOS TYPE command, OS/2 TYPE supports multiple file specifications and the OS/2 wildcard characters.

The OS/2 COPY command enables you to duplicate a file.

The OS/2 RENAME command enables you to change the name of an existing file.

The OS/2 DEL command enables you to erase a file from disk when you no longer need it.

The OS/2 PROMPT command enables you to customize the command-line prompt that OS/2 displays on your screen.

The OS/2 LABEL command enables you to name a disk volume.

The OS/2 VOL command enables you to display the name of a disk.

OS/2 reserves a section of memory for each session (called the environment) in which you can place information that OS/2 or your applications can access. The OS/2 SET command allows you to display the current contents of the environment, or to create entries.

To ensure that the OS/2 DISKCOPY command successfully completed its processing, the OS/2 DISKCOMP command compares the contents of two floppy disks.

Just as the OS/2 DISKCOMP command compares the contents of two disks, the OS/2 COMP command compares two OS/2 files displaying the location of the first 10 differences.

The OS/2 CHKDSK command reports on the state of a disk. Optionally, CHKDSK can repair lost file pointers on the disk and create files through which you can possibly recover lost data.

The OS/2 FORMAT command prepares a disk for use by OS/2.

The OS/2 EXIT command allows you to terminate an OS/2 session, returns control to the Session Manager, and returns resources to OS/2.

4 OS/2 System Configuration

Previous chapters in this text have assumed that you always want OS/2 to support real- and protected-mode processing. Recall that real-mode processing exists solely to allow you to execute existing DOS applications. If you do not expect to run real-mode programs, you may restrict their use by using the OS/2 system configuration parameters. Most users are interested in ways to improve system performance and hence allow systems to run faster.

This chapter discusses in detail the OS/2 system configuration parameters and how each affects your overall system performance. If you are already familiar with the DOS CONFIG.SYS file and its entries, a few of the concepts discussed in this chapter will be review. However, OS/2 provides a tremendous collection of configuration parameters that relate to multitasking and protected-mode processing. By examining these system parameters in detail, you should develop a better understanding of OS/2 and its complexities.

System Configuration

Each time OS/2 boots, the OS/2 start-up procedures search the root directory on the boot drive for the CONFIG.SYS file. If OS/2 finds this file, it opens it, reads it, and uses its contents to configure the operating system in memory. If OS/2 does not find this file, it uses its default values to configure the operating system. Figure 4–1 illustrates the processing involved.

CONFIG.SYS is an ASCII text file that you can create by using a text editor or by copying it from the console device, as shown here:

```
[C:\] COPY KBD$ CONFIG.SYS
```

This file contains entries that OS/2 uses to define specific operating system attributes. The following is a list of the CONFIG.SYS entries that OS/2 supports:

BREAK
BUFFERS
CODEPAGE
COUNTRY
DEVICE
DEVINFO
FCBS
IOPL
LIBPATH
MAXWAIT
MEMMAN
PRIORITY
PROTSHELL
PROTECTONLY
RMSIZE
RUN
SHELL
SWAPPATH
THREADS
TIMESLICE

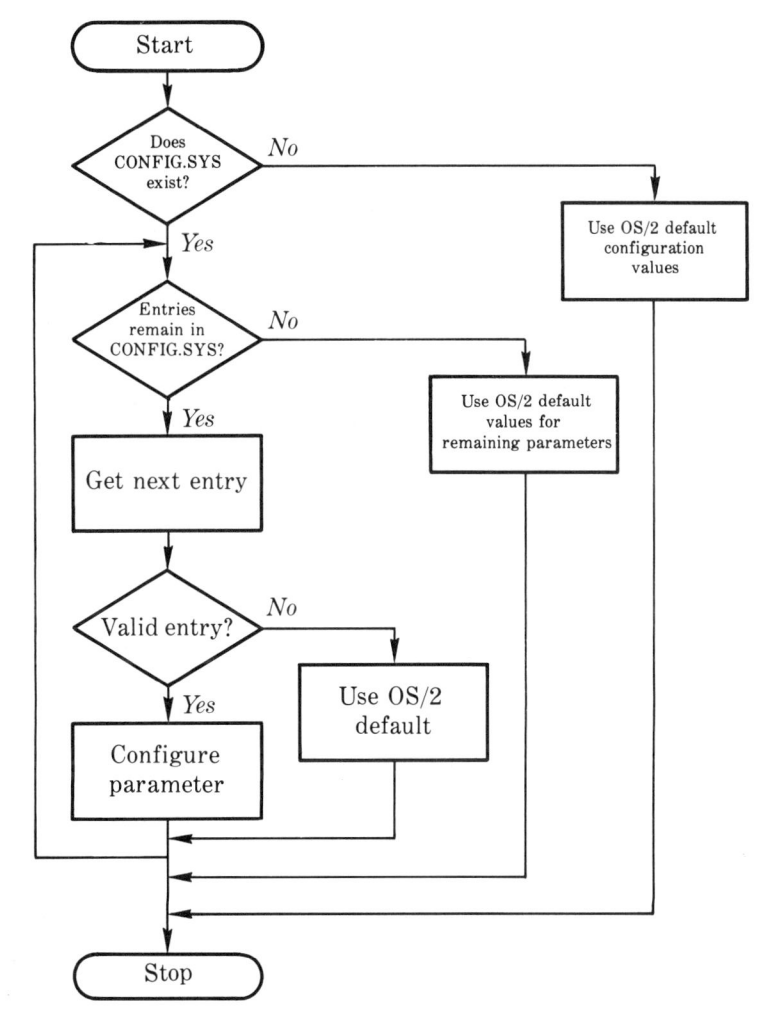

Figure 4-1. *System configuration process*

Be careful when you place entries into the CONFIG.SYS file. Each entry directly affects a specific portion of the operating system. Incorrect entries can significantly degrade your system performance. As a rule, make a copy of your existing CONFIG.SYS file before you modify its contents, as follows:

```
[C:\] COPY CONFIG.SYS CONFIG.SAV
```

In this way, you will always have a backup copy of the CONFIG.SYS file available. This copy contains valid system configuration entries should you need to restore the original file.

When you modify an entry in CONFIG.SYS you must reboot the operating system to make the change take effect. This is because OS/2 already has used the previous CONFIG.SYS file to configure itself in memory. The only time system configuration takes place is during system startup. To modify OS/2 system configuration parameters, follow these steps:

- Save the contents of the current CONFIG.SYS file.
- Edit or create the CONFIG.SYS file in the root directory.
- Place the desired entries in the file.
- Reboot the operating system.

The remainder of this chapter discusses each of the OS/2 system configuration entries.

BREAK (Default: BREAK=OFF)

Recall that you can terminate most applications by pressing the CTRL-BREAK or the CTRL-C key combinations. This is often your only means of terminating runaway programs other than by rebooting. By default, each time OS/2 writes to the screen or printer, or reads from the keyboard, it checks to see if the user has pressed the CTRL-BREAK key combination. If the user has done so, OS/2 normally terminates the execution of the program.

By using the BREAK=ON entry in the CONFIG.SYS file, you can increase the number of functions that OS/2 will check for a user-entered CTRL-BREAK upon completion of a command file in real mode. When BREAK=ON, OS/2 not only checks for CTRL-BREAK after screen and keyboard I/O operations, but the system also checks upon completion of each OS/2 system service (such as a disk read or write operation). The BREAK=ON setting increases real-mode system overhead since OS/2 must check for CTRL-BREAK after each disk operation. This, in turn, makes your applications run slower. Most users will leave BREAK=OFF. However, programmers may want to set BREAK=ON during program development and debugging. To turn CTRL-BREAK checking on, place the following entry in the CONFIG.SYS file and reboot:

```
BREAK=ON
```

BREAK

The OS/2 BREAK entry in the CONFIG.SYS file enables you to increase the number of functions that OS/2 (upon completion of a command) will examine the keyboard buffer for a user-entered CTRL-BREAK. If OS/2 encounters a CTRL-BREAK, it terminates execution of the program. This entry has no effect on protected-mode sessions.

BUFFERS (Default: BUFFERS=3)

Each time OS/2 reads or writes data to or from disk, it uses storage locations in memory to hold the transferred data. These storage locations are called *disk buffers*. Each time your applica-

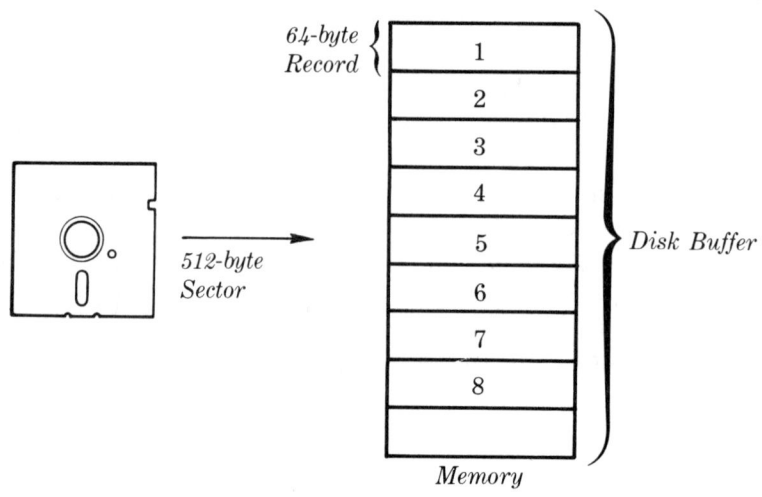

Figure 4-2.   *Storage of 8 records in 64-byte sector*

tion program reads or writes a record of data that is not equivalent to the disk sector size (a sector is normally 512 bytes), OS/2 buffers the record. A *sector* defines the smallest unit OS/2 disk operations will transfer.

If your application uses 64-byte records, a single sector can store 8 of them, as shown in Figure 4-2. For example, if your program reads Record 1 from disk, OS/2 reads the entire sector that contains Record 1 into a buffer, as shown in Figure 4-3. This means that records 2 through 8 are also available in memory.

Record 1	Record 2	Record 3	Record 4	Record 5	Record 6	Record 7	Record 8

0   64   128   192   256   320   384   448   512

Figure 4-3.   *Records within an application*

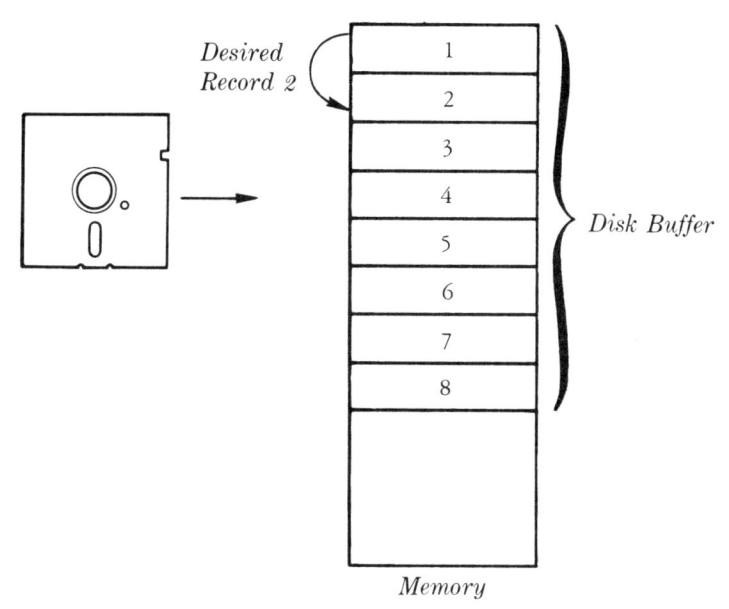

Figure 4-4. *Searching memory buffers for a record*

When your program later requests Record 2, OS/2 first searches its memory buffers for the record (see Figure 4-4). If it finds the record, OS/2 must not read a new sector from disk (a slow process). Therefore, by using disk buffers, OS/2 satisfies your I/O request much faster.

If you increase the number of file buffers that OS/2 supports, applications performing random-access file I/O (such as database and word processing applications) will note considerable performance improvement.

Note that file I/O buffering affects disk output. If your application writes records to disk that are smaller than a sector, OS/2 buffers each record. Once the buffer is full, OS/2 writes (or flushes) the buffer to disk. The following guidelines may prove helpful in determining the proper number of buffers to allocate for your applications:

- Database applications should use 20 to 35 disk buffers.

- Fixed disk systems should use 10 disk buffers (minimum).

- Disks with a large number of subdirectories should use 30 disk buffers.

- Word processing applications should use 20 to 30 disk buffers.

BUFFERS

Each time OS/2 reads or writes a record to disk that is not a multiple of the disk sector size, OS/2 places the record into a disk buffer. When OS/2 performs read operations, it first checks its buffers to see if the desired data already resides in memory, thus eliminating the need for a disk I/O. The OS/2 BUFFERS entry in the CONFIG.SYS file enables you to define the number of disk buffers that OS/2 supports.

CODEPAGE (Default: CODEPAGE=437)

The table that OS/2 uses to define a character set is called a *code page*. Each piece of information that the computer stores is a numeric value. When the computer displays the value on the screen, OS/2 uses code pages to map the numeric value to a specific character set.

For example, Figure 4–5 illustrates the code page used for the United States. The character "A" is represented in ASCII by the hexadecimal value 41. If you move (from left to right) to the column labeled "4," and then down to the row labeled "1," you find the character "A."

Figure 4–6 illustrates several of the code pages that OS/2 supports. Most users will never use a code page other than the system default. However, if you are using a foreign character set, you may need to specify the alternate code page in the CONFIG.SYS

Code page 437 (United States)

Hex Digits 1st → 2nd ↓	0-	1-	2-	3-	4-	5-	6-	7-	8-	9-	A-	B-	C-	D-	E-	F-
-0		►		0	@	P	`	p	Ç	É	á	░	└	╨	α	≡
-1	☺	◄	!	1	A	Q	a	q	ü	æ	í	▒	┴	╤	β	±
-2	☻	↕	"	2	B	R	b	r	é	Æ	ó	▓	┬	╥	Γ	≥
-3	♥	‼	#	3	C	S	c	s	â	ô	ú	│	├	╙	π	≤
-4	♦	¶	$	4	D	T	d	t	ä	ö	ñ	┤	─	╘	Σ	⌠
-5	♣	§	%	5	E	U	e	u	à	ò	Ñ	╡	┼	╒	σ	⌡
-6	♠	▬	&	6	F	V	f	v	å	û	ª	╢	╞	╓	µ	÷
-7	•	↨	'	7	G	W	g	w	ç	ù	º	╖	╟	╫	τ	≈
-8	◘	↑	(	8	H	X	h	x	ê	ÿ	¿	╕	╚	╪	Φ	°
-9	○	↓	)	9	I	Y	i	y	ë	Ö	⌐	╣	╔	┘	Θ	∙
-A	◙	→	*	:	J	Z	j	z	è	Ü	¬	║	╩	┌	Ω	·
-B	♂	←	+	;	K	[	k	{	ï	¢	½	╗	╦	█	δ	√
-C	♀	∟	,	<	L	\	l	|	î	£	¼	╝	╠	▄	∞	ⁿ
-D	♪	↔	-	=	M	]	m	}	ì	¥	¡	╜	═	▌	∅	²
-E	♫	▲	.	>	N	^	n	~	Ä	₧	«	╛	╬	▐	ε	■
-F	☼	▼	/	?	O	_	o	△	Å	ƒ	»	┐	╧	▄	∩	

Reprinted by permission, from *Disk Operating Systems Version 3.30 Reference* (International Business Machines Corporation, 1987), C-3.

Figure 4-5. *Code page for United States*

file by using one of the following code page entries:

437	United States
850	Multilingual
860	Portuguese
863	French/Canadian
865	Nordic

The following entry defines the Nordic code page at system startup:

```
CODEPAGE=865
```

Code page 865 (Norway)

Hex Digits 1st→ 2nd↓	0-	1-	2-	3-	4-	5-	6-	7-	8-	9-	A-	B-	C-	D-	E-	F-
-0		►		0	@	P	`	p	Ç	É	á	▓	└	╨	α	≡
-1	☺	◄	!	1	A	Q	a	q	ü	æ	í	▒	┴	╤	β	±
-2	☻	↕	"	2	B	R	b	r	é	Æ	ó	▓	┬	╥	Γ	≥
-3	♥	‼	#	3	C	S	c	s	â	ô	ú	│	├	╙	π	≤
-4	♦	¶	$	4	D	T	d	t	ä	ö	ñ	┤	─	╘	Σ	⌠
-5	♣	§	%	5	E	U	e	u	à	ò	Ñ	╡	┼	╒	σ	⌡
-6	♠	▬	&	6	F	V	f	v	å	û	ª	╢	╞	╓	μ	÷
-7	•	↨	'	7	G	W	g	w	ç	ù	º	╖	╟	╫	τ	≈
-8	◘	↑	(	8	H	X	h	x	ê	ÿ	¿	╕	╚	╪	Φ	°
-9	○	↓	)	9	I	Y	i	y	ë	Ö	⌐	╣	╔	┘	Θ	•
-A	◙	→	*	:	J	Z	j	z	è	Ü	¬	║	╩	┌	Ω	·
-B	♂	←	+	;	K	[	k	{	ï	ø	½	╗	╦	█	δ	√
-C	♀	∟	,	<	L	\	l			î	£	¼	╝	╠	▄	∞	ⁿ
-D	♪	↔	-	=	M	]	m	}	ì	Ø	¡	╜	═	█	φ	²
-E	♫	▲	.	>	N	^	n	~	Ä	₧	«	╛	╬	█	ε	■
-F	☼	▼	/	?	O	_	o	△	Å	ƒ	¤	┐	╧	▬	∩	

Code page 863 (Canada-French)

Hex Digits 1st→ 2nd↓	0-	1-	2-	3-	4-	5-	6-	7-	8-	9-	A-	B-	C-	D-	E-	F-
-0		►		0	@	P	`	p	Ç	É	¦	▓	└	╨	α	≡
-1	☺	◄	!	1	A	Q	a	q	ü	È	´	▒	┴	╤	β	±
-2	☻	↕	"	2	B	R	b	r	é	Ê	ó	▓	┬	╥	Γ	≥
-3	♥	‼	#	3	C	S	c	s	â	ô	ú	│	├	╙	π	≤
-4	♦	¶	$	4	D	T	d	t	Â	Ë	¨	┤	─	╘	Σ	⌠
-5	♣	§	%	5	E	U	e	u	à	Ï	¸	╡	┼	╒	σ	⌡
-6	♠	▬	&	6	F	V	f	v	¶	û	³	╢	╞	╓	μ	÷
-7	•	↨	'	7	G	W	g	w	ç	ù	·	╖	╟	╫	τ	≈
-8	◘	↑	(	8	H	X	h	x	ê	¤	Î	╕	╚	╪	Φ	°
-9	○	↓	)	9	I	Y	i	y	ë	Ô	⌐	╣	╔	┘	Θ	•
-A	◙	→	*	:	J	Z	j	z	è	Ü	¬	║	╩	┌	Ω	·
-B	♂	←	+	;	K	[	k	{	ï	¢	½	╗	╦	█	δ	√
-C	♀	∟	,	<	L	\	l			î	£	¼	╝	╠	▄	∞	ⁿ
-D	♪	↔	-	=	M	]	m	}	=	Ù	¾	╜	═	█	φ	²
-E	♫	▲	.	>	N	^	n	~	À	Û	«	╛	╬	█	ε	■
-F	☼	▼	/	?	O	_	o	△	§	ƒ	»	┐	╧	▬	∩	

Reprinted, by permission, from *Disk Operating Systems Version 3.30 Reference* (International Business Machines Corporation, 1987), C-5 and C-4

Figure 4-6. *Code pages supported by OS/2*

Code page 850 (Multilingual)

Hex Digits 1st→ 2nd↓	0-	1-	2-	3-	4-	5-	6-	7-	8-	9-	A-	B-	C-	D-	E-	F-
-0		►		0	@	P	`	p	Ç	É	á	░	└	ð	Ó	
-1	☺	◄	!	1	A	Q	a	q	ü	æ	í	▒	┴	Ð	β	±
-2	●	↕	"	2	B	R	b	r	é	Æ	ó	▓	┬	Ê	Ô	=
-3	♥	‼	#	3	C	S	c	s	â	ô	ú	│	├	Ë	Ò	¾
-4	♦	¶	$	4	D	T	d	t	ä	ö	ñ	┤	─	È	õ	¶
-5	♣	§	%	5	E	U	e	u	à	ò	Ñ	Á	┼	ı	Õ	§
-6	♠	▬	&	6	F	V	f	v	å	û	ª	Â	ã	í	µ	÷
-7	•	↨	'	7	G	W	g	w	ç	ù	º	À	Ã	Î	þ	¸
-8	◘	↑	(	8	H	X	h	x	ê	ÿ	¿	©	└	Ï	Þ	°
-9	○	↓	)	9	I	Y	i	y	ë	Ö	®	╣	┌	┘	Ú	¨
-A	◙	→	*	:	J	Z	j	z	è	Ü	¬	║	┴	┌	Û	·
-B	♂	←	+	;	K	[	k	{	ï	ø	½	┐	┬	█	Ù	¹
-C	♀	∟	,	<	L	\	l	|	î	£	¼	┘	├	▄	ý	³
-D	♪	↔	-	=	M	]	m	}	ì	Ø	¡	¢	=	¦	Ý	²
-E	♫	▲	.	>	N	^	n	~	Ä	×	«	¥	╪	Ì	¯	■
-F	☼	▼	/	?	O	_	o	△	Å	ƒ	»	¬	¤	▀	´	

Code page 860 (Portugal)

Hex Digits 1st→ 2nd↓	0-	1-	2-	3-	4-	5-	6-	7-	8-	9-	A-	B-	C-	D-	E-	F-
-0		►		0	@	P	`	p	Ç	É	á	░	└	╨	α	≡
-1	☺	◄	!	1	A	Q	a	q	ü	À	í	▒	┴	╤	β	±
-2	●	↕	"	2	B	R	b	r	é	È	ó	▓	┬	╥	Γ	≥
-3	♥	‼	#	3	C	S	c	s	â	ô	ú	│	├	╙	π	≤
-4	♦	¶	$	4	D	T	d	t	ã	õ	ñ	┤	─	╘	Σ	⌠
-5	♣	§	%	5	E	U	e	u	à	ò	Ñ	╡	┼	╒	σ	⌡
-6	♠	▬	&	6	F	V	f	v	Á	Ú	ª	╢	╞	╓	µ	÷
-7	•	↨	'	7	G	W	g	w	ç	ù	º	╖	╟	╫	τ	≈
-8	◘	↑	(	8	H	X	h	x	ê	Ì	¿	╕	╚	╪	Φ	°
-9	○	↓	)	9	I	Y	i	y	Ê	Õ	Ò	╣	┌	┘	Θ	∙
-A	◙	→	*	:	J	Z	j	z	è	Ü	¬	║	┴	┌	Ω	·
-B	♂	←	+	;	K	[	k	{	Ì	¢	½	╗	╦	█	δ	√
-C	♀	∟	,	<	L	\	l	|	Ô	£	¼	╝	╠	▄	∞	ⁿ
-D	♪	↔	-	=	M	]	m	}	ì	Ù	¡	╜	=	▌	φ	²
-E	♫	▲	.	>	N	^	n	~	Ã	Pt	«	╛	╬	▐	ε	■
-F	☼	▼	/	?	O	_	o	△	Â	Ó	»	┐	┴	▬	∩	

Reprinted, by permission, from *Disk Operating Systems Version 3.30 Reference* (International Business Machines Corporation, 1987), C-7 and C-6.

Figure 4-6. *Code pages supported by OS/2 (continued)*

OS/2 also allows you to define a secondary code page:

```
CODEPAGE=865,863
```

In this case, Nordic is the primary code page, while French/Canadian is secondary.

For each device that is to use the code page, you must include a DEVINFO entry in the CONFIG.SYS file (discussed later in this chapter). Once you define a code page for use by OS/2, the OS/2 CHCP command allows you to select the code page for use in the current session.

CODEPAGE

Each time OS/2 writes a character, it maps the character to a character set by way of a code page. The OS/2 CODEPAGE entry in the CONFIG.SYS file enables you to define alternate character sets for devices to support international concerns.

COUNTRY (Default: COUNTRY=001)

The OS/2 COUNTRY configuration parameter enables you to define the OS/2 international country characteristics. By default, OS/2 configures itself for the United States symbol set:

```
Country Code 1 United States

Date format mm dd yy
Currency symbol  $
Thousands separator  ,
Decimal separator  .
Time separator  :
Decimal significant digits  2
Currency format 0
12 hour format  (1-12)
Data list separator  ,
```

Country	Country Code	Code Pages	KEYB XX
United States	001	437,850	KEYB US
Canada (French)	002	863,850	KEYB CF
Latin America	003	437,850	KEYB LA
Netherlands	031	437,850	KEYB NL
Belgium	032	437,850	KEYB BE
France	033	437,850	KEYB FR
Spain	034	437,850	KEYB SP
Italy	039	437,850	KEYB IT
Switzerland	041	437,850	KEYB SG, KEYB SF
United Kingdom	044	437,850	KEYB UK
Denmark	045	865,850	KEYB DK
Sweden	046	437,850	KEYB SV
Norway	047	865,850	KEYB NO
Germany	049	437,850	KEYB GR
Portugal	351	860,850	KEYB PO
Finland	358	437,850	KEYB SU

Table 4-1. *Countries Supported by OS/2*

In order to support its ever-increasing foreign market, OS/2 provides support for the countries listed in Table 4-1.

For those who are not familar with the use of KEYB XX files in DOS, here is how they work. OS/2 allows you to install alternate keyboard templates for international support. For example, Figure 4-8 illustrates the Italian keyboard template. Each keyboard file name starts with the four characters "KEYB" and is followed by two country-specific characters.

For example, if you need to provide support for the Finland symbol set, the entry in the CONFIG.SYS file is as follows:

```
COUNTRY=358
```

Italian KEYBIT.COM

From *Disk Operating System Technical Reference*, 1986. Reprinted by permission of International Business Machines Corporation.

Figure 4-7.   *Italian keyboard layout*

COUNTRY

The OS/2 COUNTRY entry in the CONFIG.SYS file enables you to define international support by defining a code page and keyboard template for a specific country.

Device

Every hardware device on your system (whether disk, keyboard, or mouse) has a device driver associated with it. By default, OS/2 provides support for the standard devices (such as the disk, keyboard, system clock, and so forth). Each time OS/2 boots, it loads into memory software (called *device drivers*) required to communicate with these devices. When your programs later need to access these devices, the device driver provides the necessary interface (see Figure 4-8).

However, many users add additional devices (such as a mouse or plotter) to their systems. These "nonstandard" devices often require additional software support. Normally, the device manufacturer provides you with the device-driver software on floppy disk when you purchase the device.

Once you add the new hardware to your system, you must inform OS/2 of its existence by installing the device driver. To do so, you must place an entry in the CONFIG.SYS file. Use the entry

device=*file_specification*

where the following is true:

file_specification is the complete OS/2 path name for the file containing the device driver.

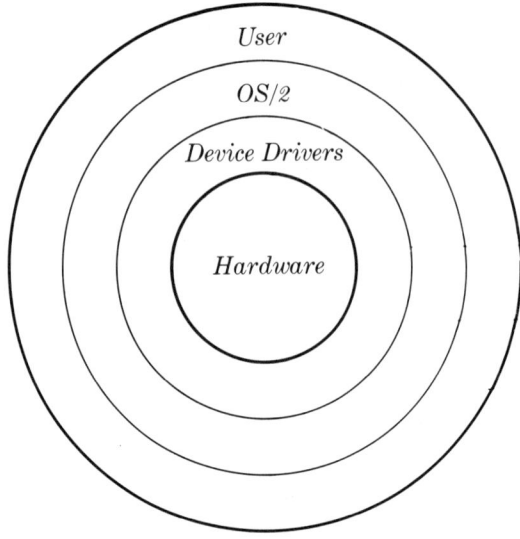

Figure 4-8. *Interface provided by device driver*

For example, to install a driver for a brand X mouse, you need to place something like the following entry in the CONFIG.SYS file:

```
DEVICE=XMOUSE.SYS
```

Most developers use the SYS extension to signify a device driver. The documentation that accompanies your hardware device normally includes the required entry for the CONFIG.SYS file.

Although your OS/2 disk may contain several device drivers, the most commonly used are

ANSI.SYS	Loads ANSI support for OS/2 real mode
COM.SYS	Loads asynchronous driver for the serial ports COM1 to COM8
EGA.SYS	Provides mouse support for EGA modes
MOUSEAnn.SYS	Loads support for specific mouse devices
RAMDISK.SYS	Installs a virtual disk drive in your computer's memory
VDISK.SYS	Installs a virtual disk drive in your computer's memory

The first device driver, ANSI.SYS, enables you to enhance your real-mode keyboard and video output processing. The ANSI driver is simply software that captures keyboard and screen data. In so doing, the driver can replace or enhance one sequence of characters with another.

The ANSI driver provides escape sequences to set character colors and attributes, clear lines of text on the screen, and position the cursor. Table 4-2 summarizes many of these commands.

ANSI Function	ANSI Code
Set cursor position	Esc[Row;COLH
Clear screen	Esc[HEsc[J
Cursor up n rows	Esc[nA
Cursor down n rows	Esc[nB
Cursor right n columns	Esc[nC
Cursor left n columns	Esc[nD
Save cursor position	Esc[s
Restore cursor position	Esc[u
Erase to end of line	Esc[K
Erase to bottom of screen	Esc[2J
Device status report	Esc[6n
Report cursor position	Esc[n;nR

Table 4-2. *Character Codes Supported by ANSI*

To install ANSI support for your real-mode processing, install the ANSI device driver into memory at system startup by placing the following entry in the CONFIG.SYS file:

```
DEVICE=ANSI.SYS
```

Remember that you must reboot the operating system for the change to take effect. The ANSI.SYS driver only provides support for real mode. In OS/2 protected mode, the OS/2 ANSI command enables or disables ANSI support for individual sessions.

ANSI.SYS

The OS/2 ANSI.SYS device driver enables you to install ANSI support for your real-mode applications. For protected mode, the ANSI command allows you to enable ANSI support for individual sessions.

The OS/2 COMn.SYS device driver enables you to install the device driver required for asynchronous communication through your computer's serial ports. As discussed in Chapter 5, data communications can occur serially one bit at a time over a single wire, or in a parallel fashion when multiple wires are used. Most systems include at least one serial and one parallel port. Your serial ports are called COM ports. The OS/2 COMn.SYS device driver allows you to utilize these ports. To install a serial port device driver, use the CONFIG.SYS entry

device=COMn.SYS

where the following is true:

COMn: specifies one of the following device drivers:

COM01.SYS specifies an IBM PC AT COM device.

COM02.SYS specifies an IBM PS/2 COM device.

For example, to install a driver for an IBM PC AT serial port, enter the following:

```
DEVICE=COM01.SYS
```

COM*n*.SYS

The OS/2 COM*n*.SYS device driver provides support for asynchronous serial devices. Serial device names are in the form COM*n*.

Depending upon the type of mouse that you are using, your system may or may not support certain graphics modes of the EGA monitor. The OS/2 EGA.SYS device driver allows you to install a device driver that aids many mouse devices in support of the EGA. If your mouse documentation specifies the EGA.SYS driver, include the following entry in CONFIG.SYS and reboot:

```
DEVICE=EGA.SYS
```

EGA.SYS

The OS/2 EGA.SYS device driver provides additional mouse support for EGA graphics modes.

The OS/2 MOUSEA*nn*.SYS driver exists to provide support for various mouse devices. Your system disk may distinguish several mouse drivers as follows:

MOUSEA00.SYS	Support for Mouse System's PC Mouse
MOUSEA01.SYS	Support for Visi-On's serial mouse
MOUSEA02.SYS	Support for Microsoft's serial mouse
MOUSEA03.SYS	Support for Microsoft's parallel mouse
MOUSEA05.SYS	Support for Microsoft's InPort mouse
MOUSEB00.SYS	Support for Mouse System's PC Mouse (PS/2)
MOUSEB01.SYS	Support for Visi-On's serial mouse (PS/2)
MOUSE0B2.SYS	Support for Microsoft's serial mouse (PS/2)
MOUSEB05.SYS	Support for PS/2 Inboard mouse

To install a mouse device driver, use the format

device=MOUSEA*nn*.SYS [,SERIAL=*COMn*]
[,MODE=*OS2_mode*][,QSIZE=*n*]

where the following is true:

COMn specifies a serial port (COM1 through COM8).
OS2_mode specifies real mode (r), protected mode (p), or both (b).
*n_* specifies the mouse queue size.

For example, to install the Microsoft parallel mouse, use the following:

DEVICE=MOUSEA03.SYS

MOUSEA*nn*.SYS

The OS/2 MOUSEAnn.SYS device driver provides support for various mouse devices. The two numeric values represented by *nn* signify specific mouse device drivers.

The OS/2 RAMDISK.SYS and VDISK.SYS device drivers enable you to define a virtual or RAM disk in your computer's random-access memory (RAM). If you have never used a RAM drive, here is how it works. The RAMDISK and VDISK device drivers allow you to emulate the existence of an OS/2 disk in your computer's memory. This disk can store files or directories, and is treated by OS/2 in the same manner as any other disk. The one exception is that when you turn off the power for your computer, the contents of the RAM disk are lost. The computer's main memory is volatile, which means it loses its contents when power is lost. Since the RAM disk resides here, its contents are also destroyed.

The main advantage of a RAM disk is speed. Floppy and fixed disks are mechanical; by their very nature they are slower than the computer's electronic counterparts. RAM disks are electronic, which means they are not constrained by the slow speed of mechanical arms.

Many people use RAM drives constantly and periodically save their files to fixed or floppy drives to avoid loss of data. The format to install the VDISK device driver is

DEVICE=VDISK.SYS [*disk_space* [[*sector_size*] [*file_limit*]]] [*/E*]

or, if your disk contains RAMDISK.SYS

DEVICE=RAMDISK.SYS [*disk_space* [[*sector_size*] [*file_limit*]]] [*/E*]

where the following is true:

disk_space specifies the number of kilobytes of memory OS/2 is to allocate for the RAM drive. The default size is 64K.

sector_size defines the size of each RAM disk sector in bytes. The default sector size is 128 bytes.

file_limit is the maximum number of files that the RAM disk will support. The default is 64 files.

/E directs OS/2 to place the RAM disk in extended memory for the IBM PC AT.

Each of the following entries is valid for VDISK.SYS. In this case, VDISK is installed with its default values:

```
DEVICE=VDISK.SYS
```

This entry installs a RAM disk with space for 360K of files, 512-byte sectors, and a maximum of 128 files:

```
DEVICE=VDISK.SYS 360 512 128
```

When OS/2 boots, it displays the following to notify you that it has installed the RAM drive:

```
VDISK Version 1.0 virtual disk D:
    Directory entries adjusted
    Buffer size        128 KB
    Sector size        512
    Directory entries   16
```

Once OS/2 installs the RAM disk, you access it just as you would any standard drive from either real or protected mode, as follows:

drive_id:

For example, if your RAM disk installation results in drive D, you would use D:.

DEVICE

The OS/2 DEVICE entry in the CONFIG.SYS file enables you to specify device drivers for unique hardware devices that OS/2 installs at system startup.

DEVINFO (Default: none)

The OS/2 DEVINFO configuration entry informs OS/2 that code-page switching is in use for the specified device. The format for the entry is

DEVINFO=*device_name, subtype, file_specification,*
      [*ROM*=[(code_page1[,code_page2)]]

where the following is true:

device_name is the name of the device that is using code-page switching (KBD$, LPT#, PRN, SCREEN$).

subtype specifies the physical device type (EGA, CGA, and so forth).

file_specification is the complete OS/2 path name of the file containing the desired code-page tables for output devices, or the keyboard translation tables.

ROM optionally specifies the primary and secondary code pages for output devices that reside in the device's read-only memory (ROM), or in a cartridge.

The following example defines a code page for the screen device:

```
DEVINFO=SCREEN$,CGA,COLOR.TBL
```

DEVINFO

The OS/2 DEVINFO entry in the CONFIG.SYS file enables you to associate OS/2 code pages to a specific device.

FCBS (Default: FCBS=4,0)

The FCBS entry in the CONFIG.SYS file exists to support your real-mode processing. Early versions of DOS used file-control blocks (FCBS) to track each open file. A file-control block contains the state and structure of a specific file. If you are not running older application programs (pre-DOS version 2.0), you should never have to specify this parameter in CONFIG.SYS. However, if you experience a problem with older programs as you migrate to newer versions of DOS, you may need to modify this entry by using the format

FCBS=*max_files, protected_files*

where the following is true:

max_files specifies the maximum number of files that OS/2 can open concurrently by using file-control blocks. This value must be in the range 1 to 255.

protected_files specifies the minimum number of files that OS/2 must leave open when it needs to open other files. This value must be in the range 1 to 255.

DOS 2.0 replaced file-control blocks with file handles. Most users, therefore, will never require this parameter. The following example allows DOS to open 16 files concurrently by using FCBS and ensuring that at least four are protected:

```
FCBS=16,4
```

FCBS

The OS/2 FCBS entry in the CONFIG.SYS file enables you to specify the number of file-control blocks that OS/2 sets aside for real-mode applications.

IOPL (Default: IOPL=NO)

Since OS/2 is a multitasking operating system, it must strictly control which programs can perform I/O operations at specific times. For example, if you are executing a word processing program on the screen, a second program that is also executing should not be allowed to overwrite the current screen contents randomly. To enforce this, OS/2 strictly controls I/O operations and grants only the most privileged applications the ability to perform low-level I/O by defining rings of I/O protection levels.

The IOPL (input/output protection level) defines the minimum ring level of protection an application must possess before it can perform low-level I/O operations. If an application outside of this ring attempts a low-level I/O (IN or OUT instruction), OS/2 generates a general-protection fault and the operation fails. OS/2 does not prevent programs from performing I/O. It requires that the applications cooperate in a multiprogramming environment.

Program I/O operations normally go through predefined OS/2 services defined in the Application Program Interface (API).

If you set IOPL to YES

```
IOPL=YES
```

OS/2 allows applications to perform low-level I/O operations. However, most users want the programs running in a concurrent environment to cooperate and therefore leave IOPL set to NO.

IOPL

By default, OS/2 protected-mode applications cannot perform low-level I/O operations that require privilege. In so doing, OS/2 maintains coordination in a multitasking environment. The OS/2 IOPL entry in the CONFIG.SYS file enables you to direct OS/2 to allow applications to perform such operations. Most users should leave this entry set at IOPL=NO.

LIBPATH (Default: boot_device: \)

OS/2 allows programmers to link modules in one of two ways. The first (and most familiar) is to link OBJ and LIB files with the LINK command. In this case, OS/2 combines files from disk to produce an executable file, as shown in Figure 4-9.

The second (and most powerful) method of combining modules is by using dynamic-link libraries (DLLs). Unlike static modules that the DOS linker resolves prior to execution of your code, dynamic-link libraries are not combined with the program code until program execution. This means that the OS/2 program

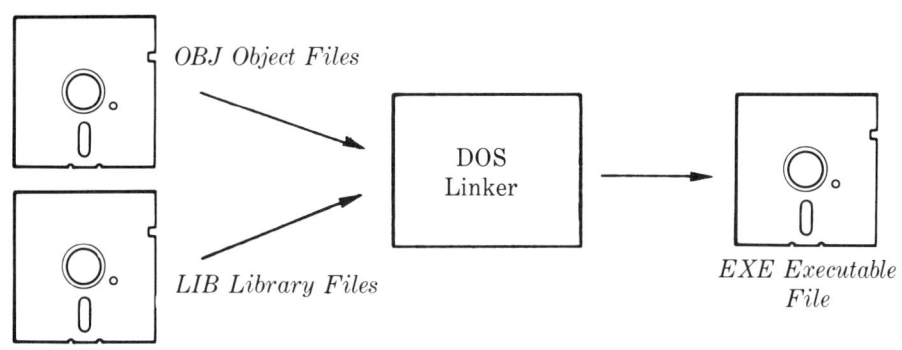

Figure 4-9. *Static linking to produce executable file*

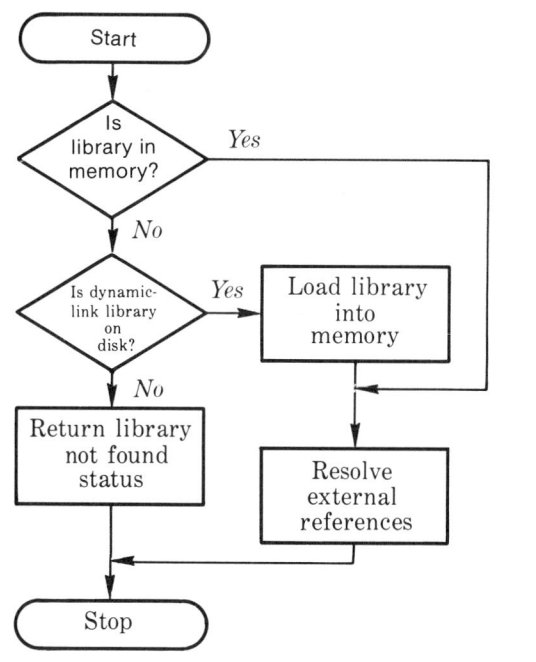

Figure 4-10. *Process of dynamic linking*

loader not only loads the program into memory to execute, but also resolves any external references to dynamic-link modules. These libraries can reside in memory or on disk prior to the execution of the program that references them. If the libraries are on disk, the OS/2 loader must load the library file into memory from disk (see Figure 4-10).

Dynamic-link libraries provide your application programs with several advantages. First, since the code contained in the dynamic-link library is not linked to an executable file, the sizes of the files for your programs are much smaller. Second, the code in dynamic-link libraries is shareable. If you have several programs simultaneously executing in memory, only one copy of the dynamic-link library must be present in memory, which each application can share (see Figure 4-11).

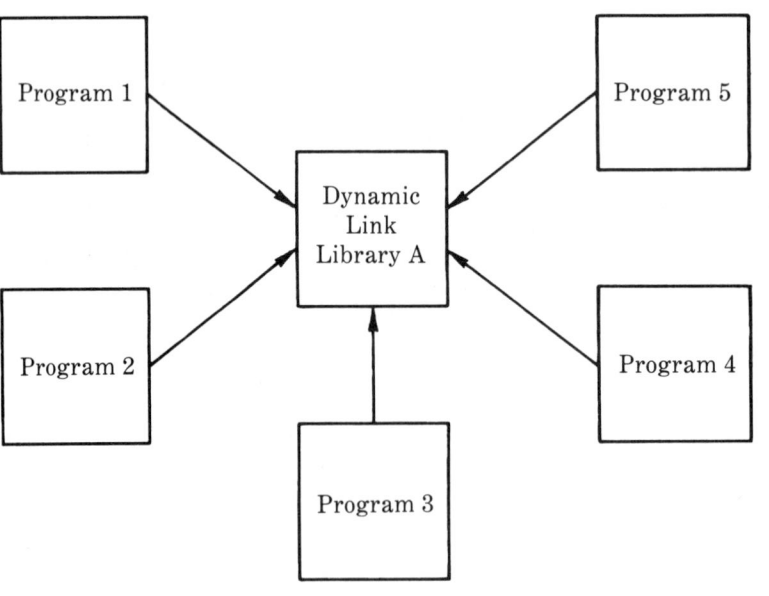

Figure 4-11. *Shared dynamic-link libraries*

Dynamic-link libraries indirectly make program updates easier. Since programmers can create their own DLLs, they can have several programs refer to a DLL. If the code in the DLL needs to be modified later, the programmer modifies the DLL, compiles, and reloads it into memory. None of the applications that utilize the library are affected and no relinking is required.

The OS/2 LIBPATH system configuration entry specifies where (on disk) OS/2 looks for DLLs by default. The OS/2 loader searches this location each time it must load a DLL from disk into memory. If you place all of your DLL files into the DOS subdirectory file \DLL, your CONFIG.SYS entry will be as follows:

```
LIBPATH=C:\DLL
```

By default, OS/2 searches the root directory on the boot device.

LIBPATH

The OS/2 LIBPATH entry defines the default locations on disk that OS/2 searches for its dynamic-link libraries.

MAXWAIT (Default: MAXWAIT=3)

Because OS/2 is a multitasking environment, it must have facilities to determine what applications should execute at what times. Under OS/2, these facilities are contained in the *scheduler*. The OS/2 scheduler is responsible for examining the list of programs available for execution and selecting the specific application to receive control of the CPU.

OS/2 determines which process to execute by assigning a priority to each program in the system. For example, assume you have three programs that execute simultaneously. The first, CALCULATE_PAYROLL, generates your company payroll. The second, STOCKS, monitors the stock market by way of a modem and notifies you of significant trends. The third, PAY_CHECKS, prints the company payroll checks. Since OS/2 is a multitasking system, each of these applications appears to be running simultaneously.

Because it has a direct influence on whether the company makes money, the stock market monitor (STOCKS) is the most critical program. Whenever data is available for this program, it should get control of the CPU. Therefore, this program has a priority of 3.

If no data exists on the modem for the monitor program, OS/2 should give the CPU to the program CALCULATE_PAYROLL to ensure that payroll is complete. This program is given the priority 2.

Last, if neither the stock monitor nor the payroll program has processing to perform (each may be waiting on a disk I/O to complete), OS/2 should execute the PAY_CHECKS program, which has a priority of 1. Figure 4-12 illustrates how OS/2 selects the program to execute.

Sometimes several programs with high priorities may exist simultaneously (see Figure 4-13). In these cases, OS/2 first checks the first program at priority 3 to see if it can execute. If it can, OS/2 executes it. After a period of time (a time slice), OS/2 gives the processor to the next available program at a higher-than or equal-to priority. OS/2 continues distributing the CPU until no programs exist with a priority equal to or greater than the priority of the previous program. OS/2 then moves to the next lower priority and begins distribution of the CPU among the programs at that level in a round-robin fashion.

However, processes with low priorities may never execute. To prevent a process from being locked out of the CPU, OS/2 provides the system of *dynamic priorities*. This means that although a process may have an initial priority level of 1, OS/2 may periodi-

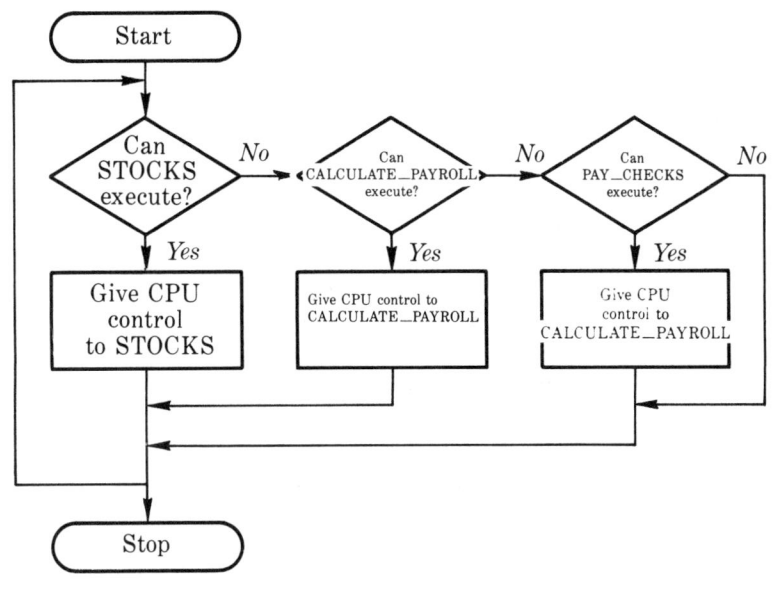

Figure 4-12. *Process of selecting program to execute*

cally increment this priority if it appears to OS/2 that the process is never getting the CPU. Once the process gets the CPU for a time slice, OS/2 reinstalls its initial priority, and this process begins its climb up the ladder of priorities.

The OS/2 MAXWAIT system configuration parameter defines the maximum amount of time a process must wait before it gets the CPU. By default, OS/2 uses the following parameter:

```
MAXWAIT=3
```

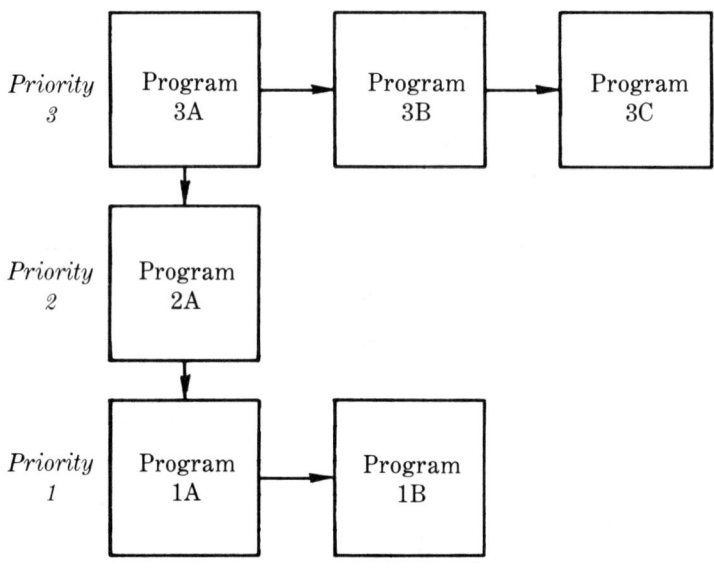

Figure 4-13. *Several programs with high priority levels*

This means that every three seconds OS/2 increments the priority for the processes waiting for the CPU. Most users will find this default value satisfactory.

MAXWAIT

The OS/2 MAXWAIT entry in the CONFIG.SYS file defines the maximum amount of time that an OS/2 application must wait until it receives a CPU time slice.

MEMMAN (Floppy Default: MEMMAN=NOSWAP,MOVE Fixed Default: MEMMAN=SWAP,MOVE)

With the flexibility of a multitasking environment comes a significant number of memory-management considerations. *Memory management* refers to the steps OS/2 takes to determine how much memory a program can use, whether or not OS/2 can move segments temporarily to disk to make room for other segments (swapping), and whether or not OS/2 can perform memory compaction (by moving segments of code to prevent memory fragmentation and thrashing).

By temporarily swapping a segment from memory to disk, OS/2 can allow more programs to execute than actually fit into memory (see Figure 4-14). Each time the OS/2 scheduler selects a process for execution, OS/2 attempts to resume execution where it left off. If it can, OS/2 continues. If it cannot, OS/2

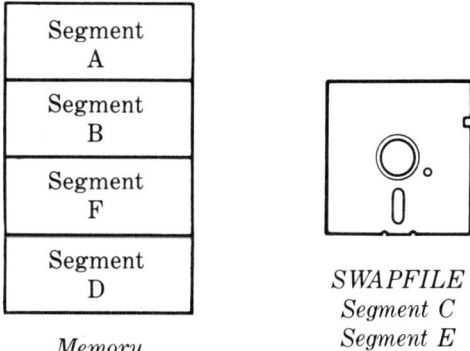

Memory

SWAPFILE
Segment C
Segment E

Figure 4-14. *OS/2 allowing more than one segment into memory*

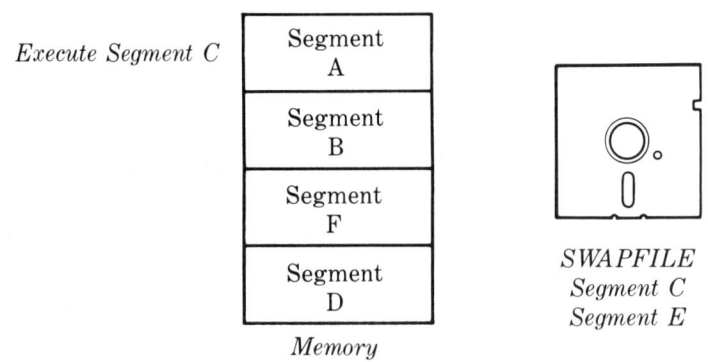

Figure 4-15. *OS/2 bringing segment from disk into memory*

brings the required segment from disk into memory, as illustrated in Figure 4-15. If insufficient space exists in memory for the segment, OS/2 swaps another segment temporarily to disk, as shown in Figure 4-16.

As you might expect, the greater the number of currently executing programs, the more swapping OS/2 must perform. Since swapping requires a large number of disk I/O operations, it produces significant system overhead. Therefore, OS/2 allows you to disable swapping. In so doing, you also limit the number of programs that OS/2 can execute concurrently.

A major memory-management concern in all multitasking environments is the prevention of memory fragmentation. Consider the following scenario. OS/2 has three programs to execute (A, B, and C), as shown in Figure 4-17. OS/2 loads each into memory, as shown in Figure 4-18. Later, program A completes and OS/2 removes it from memory (see Figure 4-19).

Next, OS/2 needs to load program D. Unfortunately, OS/2 does not have enough contiguous memory to load the program. By shifting the other two applications downward in memory, OS/2 gains sufficient space, as shown in Figure 4-20.

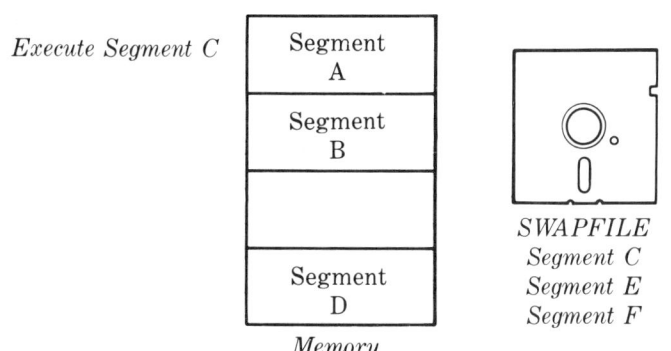

Step 1: Make room in memory for Segment C by swapping Segment F.

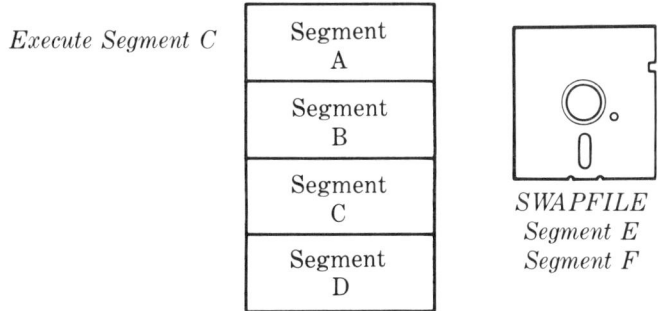

Step 2: Move Segment C from SWAPFILE on disk into memory.

Figure 4-16. *OS/2 swapping segment temporarily to disk*

The OS/2 virtual memory model performs memory compaction in this way, a relatively easy task for the operating system to perform. OS/2 performs the entire memory compaction transparently to the executing programs.

The OS/2 MEMMAN entry allows you to disable movement of memory sections in the fashion previously shown by specifying NOMOVE. Under normal circumstances, users in an office environment who run several programs concurrently should

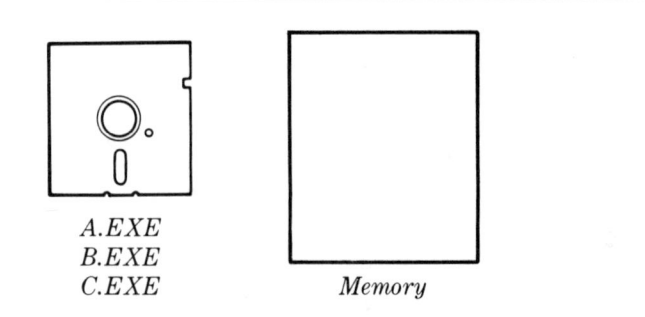

A.EXE
B.EXE
C.EXE
Memory

Figure 4-17. *Three programs to execute*

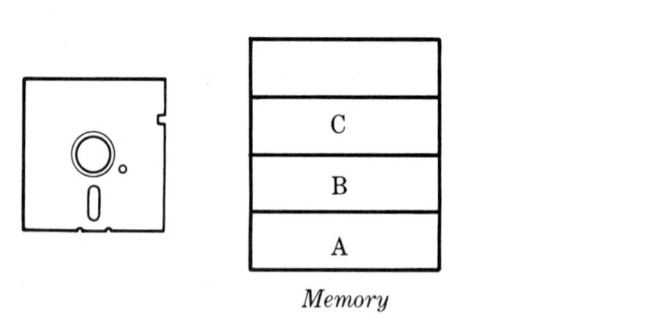

C

B

A

Memory

Figure 4-18. *OS/2 loading three programs into memory*

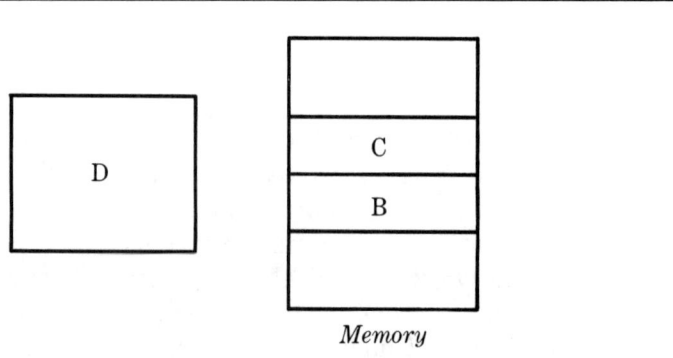

D

C

B

Memory

Figure 4-19. *Program A removed from memory after completion*

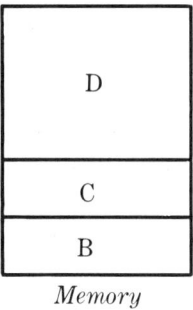

Memory

Figure 4-20.   *Programs B and C shifted downward to make room for D*

never set NOSWAP and NOMOVE. In so doing, they greatly restrict their own capabilities. Indeed, restricting each option reduces system overhead (swapping and moving are expensive in terms of CPU and disk I/O time), but flexibility outweighs performance considerations in most multiprogramming environments. The syntax for the MEMMAN entry is

MEMMAN=NOSWAP,NOMOVE

or

MEMMAN=SWAP,MOVE

or

MEMMAN=NOSWAP,MOVE

MEMMAN

The OS/2 MEMMAN entry in the CONFIG.SYS file allows you to enable or disable swapping and OS/2 memory management. Most fixed disk users will want OS/2 memory management fully supported.

PRIORITY (Default: PRIORITY=DYNAMIC)

As stated in the section on the MAXWAIT system configuration parameter, OS/2 is a priority-driven operating system. By default, OS/2 grants CPU control to the process with the highest priority and periodically increments the priority of processes. This priority scheme is called dynamic priority. OS/2 can change program priority on the fly (dynamically) as it considers necessary to ensure fairness of CPU distribution.

Most people use the default PRIORITY setting of DYNAMIC to ensure fairness. However, the need sometimes arises to ensure that OS/2 will execute the highest priority programs without tuning application priorities. If your application requires that you prevent dynamic priority boost (a real-time monitor program, for example), specify the following entry in the CONFIG.SYS file and reboot:

```
PRIORITY=ABSOLUTE
```

In so doing, OS/2 ensures that the priority for every program in the system remains constant.

PRIORITY

By default, OS/2 increments the priority of each application depending on the application's operational characteristics. Boosting priorities in this fashion is called dynamic scheduling. The OS/2 PRIORITY entry in the CONFIG.SYS file allows you to enable a dynamic priority boost or restrict dynamic priorities, thus yielding absolute scheduling. Most users enable dynamic priorities to maximize fairness of CPU distribution.

PROTECTONLY (Default: PROTECTONLY=NO)

OS/2 executes programs in two modes: real and protected. In real mode (DOS mode), applications can directly access memory, hardware, ports, and the video display. Although this mode of program execution has been the mainstay of DOS since its advent, it is unacceptable in a multitasking environment like OS/2. When multiple programs execute simultaneously, each program must cooperate in terms of hardware access and control.

OS/2 meets the requirement of upward compatibility. That is, OS/2 has the ability to execute DOS 3.x programs by switching from real mode to protected mode as program needs require.

If you do not expect to run DOS 3.x applications (such as Lotus 1-2-3, WordStar, or dBASE), you can specify the following in the CONFIG.SYS file:

```
PROTECTONLY=YES
```

In this mode, OS/2 will only support OS/2 applications. However, this mode is unacceptable for most users. Therefore, the following default value is used:

```
PROTECTONLY=NO
```

PROTECTONLY

The OS/2 PROTECTONLY entry in the CONFIG.SYS file enables you to restrict OS/2 to executing only protected-mode applications. In so doing, you free memory that OS/2 would allocate for real-mode applications.

PROTSHELL

The OS/2 PROTSHELL entry in the CONFIG.SYS file enables you to define the SHELL that oversees your protected-mode sessions, your protected-mode command interpreter, and an optional OS/2 batch file that OS/2 executes each time that you create a protected-mode session.

Consider the following CONFIG.SYS entry:

```
PROTSHELL=SHELL.EXE CMD.EXE /K INITENV.CMD
```

The OS/2 program SHELL.EXE is the Session Manager, discussed previously in this book. The CMD.EXE file defines your protected-mode command interpreter and INITENV.CMD is a batch file that OS/2 executes each time you create a protected-mode session.

PROTSHELL

The OS/2 PROTSHELL entry in the CONFIG.SYS file enables you to define your protected-mode shell, command processor, and a batch file that OS/2 executes each time you create a protected-mode session.

RMSIZE (Default: System-Dependent)

OS/2 executes programs in real mode or protected mode. As stated previously, real mode exists so that OS/2 can execute DOS 3.x applications. To support real-mode processing, OS/2 sets aside memory for real-mode processing, as shown in Figure 4-21.

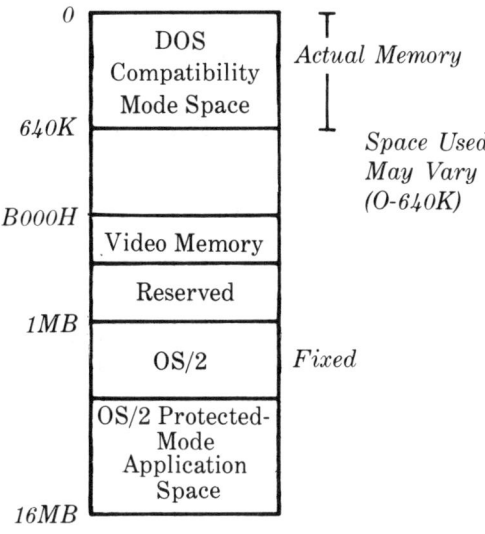

Figure 4-21. *OS/2 memory usage*

Unlike OS/2 virtual memory applications, real-mode programs cannot exceed 640K in size. The OS/2 RMSIZE configuration parameter allows you to specify the number of kilobytes of memory you want OS/2 to reserve for your real-mode applications. The format for the entry is

RMSIZE=*KBYTES*

where the following is true:

KBYTES specifies the number of kilobytes OS/2 is to reserve for real-mode applications. This value must be in the range of 0 to 640.

The actual memory available to real-mode applications is the value of *KBYTES* minus the space required for DOS. Therefore,

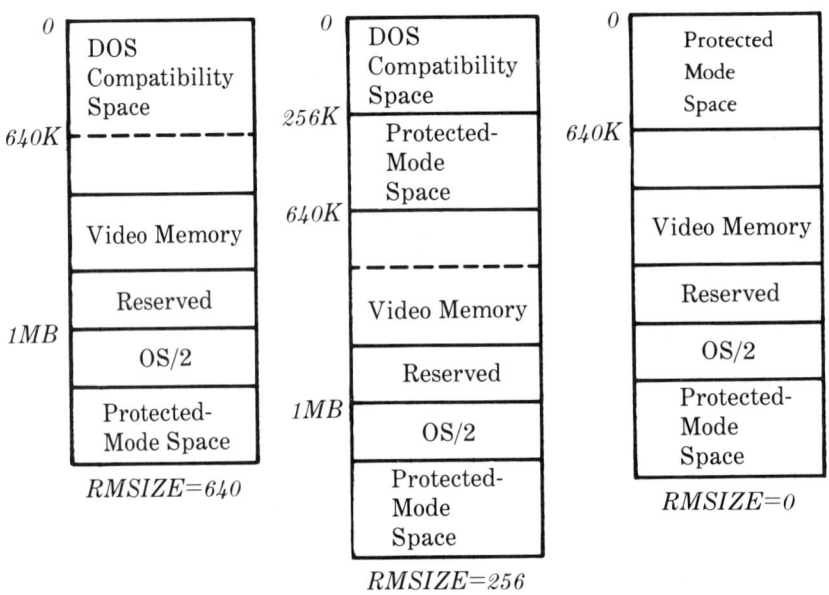

Figure 4-22. *Use of RMSIZE startup parameter*

most users set this value from 512 to 640, as shown in Figure 4-22.

If you do not anticipate running real-mode applications, you can set this value to 0, thus providing OS/2 with more memory for protected-mode programs.

RMSIZE

By default, OS/2 sets aside memory to support its real-mode processing. The OS/2 RMSIZE entry in the CONFIG.SYS file enables you to specify the amount of memory OS/2 sets aside for real-mode processing.

RUN (Default: None)

The OS/2 RUN system configuration parameter enables you to execute an application in background mode during system start-up. The format of the entry is

RUN *file__specification* [*command__line__arguments*]

where the following is true:

file__specification is the complete OS/2 path name of the command to execute.

command__line__arguments specify each command-line argument the program uses to execute.

The following entry installs a third-party network software product each time the system starts.

```
RUN =NETWORK
```

Starting an application in this mode differs from running the application from STARTUP.CMD. By starting in this mode, the program runs in the background as system startup completes. Programs in STARTUP.CMD run in the foreground unless you invoke them by using the DETACH command.

RUN

The OS/2 RUN entry in the CONFIG.SYS file enables you to execute a program at system startup. The specified program is executed in the background mode, which allows OS/2 to continue its start-up processing.

SHELL (Default: SHELL=COMMAND.COM)

The SHELL entry in the CONFIG.SYS file enables you to invoke an alternate command processor other than COMMAND.COM as your real-mode command-line processor. The format for this entry is

SHELL=*file_specification* [*/C string*] [*/E:nnnnn*] [*/P*]

where the following is true:

file_specification is the complete OS/2 path name of the file OS/2 is to use as the command interpreter.

/C string specifies a string that the command processor is to execute. If you omit this qualifier, COMMAND displays the familiar OS/2 prompt.

/E:nnnnn specifies the number of bytes that DOS (OS/2 real mode) reserves for the command processor's environment space.

/P installs the command processor permanently in memory.

Most users probably will not modify this entry. Those who do so will want to specify a new location for COMMAND.COM, as shown here:

```
SHELL=\DOS\COMMAND.COM
```

SHELL

The OS/2 SHELL entry in the CONFIG.SYS file enables you to specify an alternate real-mode command processor. Most users use SHELL simply to define an alternate location for COMMAND.COM.

SWAPPATH (Default: boot—device: \)

When OS/2 executes multiple programs concurrently, it must periodically swap segments from memory to disk to make space for others. When OS/2 swaps a segment, it places the segment temporarily in a swap file on disk. The OS/2 SWAPPATH system configuration entry allows you to specify the location of the swap file. The format of the entry is

SWAPPATH=*drive:[path name]*

where the following is true:

drive: specifies the disk drive identification OS/2 uses for the swap device.
path name is the OS/2 path name for the file OS/2 is to use as the swap file.

For example, the following entry directs OS/2 to use the file SWAPFILE.DAT in the root directory on drive C:

```
SWAPPATH=C:\
```

To minimize the system overhead associated with swapping, always be sure your target disk is a fixed disk. Some users wonder why you do not place the swap file in a RAM drive, which is much faster than even fixed disks. To do so actually affects your system adversely. The RAM disk allocates memory for a virtual disk drive. If you install a RAM drive to support your swap file, you would be reducing the available memory and thus increasing the amount of swapping that must occur. Although OS/2 might be faster at reading and writing to the swap file, it would also be performing much more swapping because of the reduction in available memory consumed by the RAM disk.

SWAPPATH

In order to execute multiple programs simultaneously, OS/2 must periodically make space available in memory for additional programs by temporarily moving segments from memory to disk. The OS/2 SWAPPATH entry in the CONFIG.SYS file defines the location where OS/2 temporarily places the segment on disk.

THREADS (Default: THREADS=48)

This chapter has made the assumption that OS/2 schedules processes for execution. OS/2 actually schedules an entity, called a *thread*. OS/2 applications are composed of one or more threads, which OS/2 treats as individual items to be scheduled. Therefore, OS/2 can concurrently execute multiple portions of the same program. Each part of the program is a thread (path of execution) to which the scheduler grants the CPU.

Users who are conversant with DOS can view the THREADS entry in the CONFIG.SYS file as being similar to the DOS FILES entry. The FILES entry specifies the maximum number of file handles DOS and OS/2 will support. Likewise, THREADS specifies the maximum number of threads (paths of execution) that can exist in the system. For most users, the default value of 48 is sufficient. However, if you are running many applications concurrently (each with multiple threads), you may have to increase this parameter. The format for the entry is

THREADS=*max_threads*

where the following is true:

max_threads defines the maximum number of threads OS/2 will support in the system. This value must be in the range 48 to 255.

The following entry sets the maximum number of threads to 128:

```
THREADS=128
```

THREADS

An OS/2 thread is a path of execution. The OS/2 scheduler dispatches CPU time slices to threads as opposed to processes. Each OS/2 process can consist of multiple threads. The OS/2 THREADS entry in the CONFIG.SYS file enables you to specify the maximum number of threads the system supports.

TIMESLICE (Default: None)

OS/2 shares the processor with each executing program by dividing processor time into time slices. The OS/2 system configuration parameter TIMESLICE allows you to specify the minimum and maximum amount of time on the CPU that OS/2 can grant to a process. The format for the entry is

TIMESLICE=*minimum[,maximum]*

where the following is true:

minimum specifies the minimum number of milliseconds that OS/2 can use for the CPU time slice. This value must be greater than 31.

maximum specifies the maximum number of milliseconds that OS/2 can grant as a time slice. This value must exceed the value specified for *minimum*.

If you only specify one value

```
TIMESLICE=45
```

OS/2 uses the value for both the maximum and minimum time slice.

TIMESLICE

To support the concurrent execution of multiple programs, OS/2 distributes CPU processing time slices to each application. The OS/2 TIMESLICE entry in the CONFIG.SYS file enables you to define the minimum and maximum CPU time slices.

Chapter Highlights

The OS/2 system configuration file CONFIG.SYS allows you to customize OS/2 for your personal needs. OS/2 supports the following CONFIG.SYS entries:

BREAK	Increases the number of functions that, upon completion of a command, OS/2 will examine the keyboard buffer for a user-entered CTRL-BREAK. Default: BREAK=OFF
BUFFERS	Defines the number of disk buffers that OS/2 places in memory to enhance disk I/O operations. Default: BUFFERS=3
CODEPAGE	Allows you to specify the code pages that OS/2 supports for international considerations. Default: CODEPAGE=437
COUNTRY	Defines the country symbol set that OS/2 supports for international considerations. Default: COUNTRY=001

DEVICE	Allows you to install OS/2 device drivers at system startup.
DEVINFO	Specifies the devices for which the OS/2 code pages will be used.
FCBS	Allows you to specify the number of file-control blocks that OS/2 supports for real mode programs. Default: FCBS=4,0
IOPL	Allows you to enable or disable applications to perform operations normally requiring privilege. Most users do not want this qualifier enabled in a multitasking environment. Default: IOPL=NO
LIBPATH	Specifies the location on disk that OS/2 examines for its dynamic-link libraries. Default: boot__dev: \
MAXWAIT	Specifies the maximum time interval that applications must wait before obtaining a CPU time slice. Default: MAXWAIT=3
MEMMAN	Enables or disables OS/2 memory management. Default: MEMMAN=SWAP,MOVE (fixed disk); MEMMAN= NOSWAP,MOVE (floppy disk)
PRIORITY	Specifies whether OS/2 will enable dynamic priority adjustments of process priorities. Default: PRIORITY= DYNAMIC
PROTSHELL	Defines the protected-mode command-line interpreter.
PROTECT-ONLY	Enables or disables OS/2 real-mode processing. Default: PROTECTONLY=NO
RMSIZE	Specifies the number of kilobytes that OS/2 allocates for real-mode processing. Default: RMSIZE= system-dependent
RUN	Allows you to execute a background task during system startup.
SHELL	Invokes an alternate command processor as real mode command-line processor. Default: SHELL= COMMAND.COM

SWAPPATH   Defines the location that OS/2 uses for swapping files from memory to disk. Default: boot_device: \

THREADS   Defines the maximum number of threads of execution that OS/2 supports. Default: THREADS=48

TIMESLICE   Defines the minimum and maximum OS/2 time slice values. Default: TIMESLICE= Determined by OS/2

If you modify a CONFIG.SYS entry, you must reboot the system in order for the change to take effect.

5 *Device Control Under OS/2*

Chapter 1 defined hardware as the cables, boards, and peripherals that comprise your computer. OS/2 assigns names to many of the peripheral devices attached to your computer, as illustrated in Figure 5–1. The following list summarizes what OS/2 reserves for your device names:

COM1:   The first asynchronous communications port on your computer (serial communication)

COM2:   The second asynchronous communications port on your computer (serial communication)

COM3:   The third asynchronous communications port on your computer (serial communication).

CLOCK$ The system real-time clock

CON: For input, CON refers to your keyboard. For output, CON refers to your screen

KBD$ Your keyboard device

LPT1:	The first parallel printer port on your computer
LPT2:	The second parallel printer port on your computer
LPT3:	The third parallel printer port on your computer
NUL:	The OS/2 null (or nonexistent) device. Often used as a "bit bucket"
PRN:	The first parallel printer port on your system
SCREEN$	Your screen device

Several of the devices appearing on this list are classified as serial or parallel devices. When your computer communicates with most peripheral devices, it does so with serial or parallel

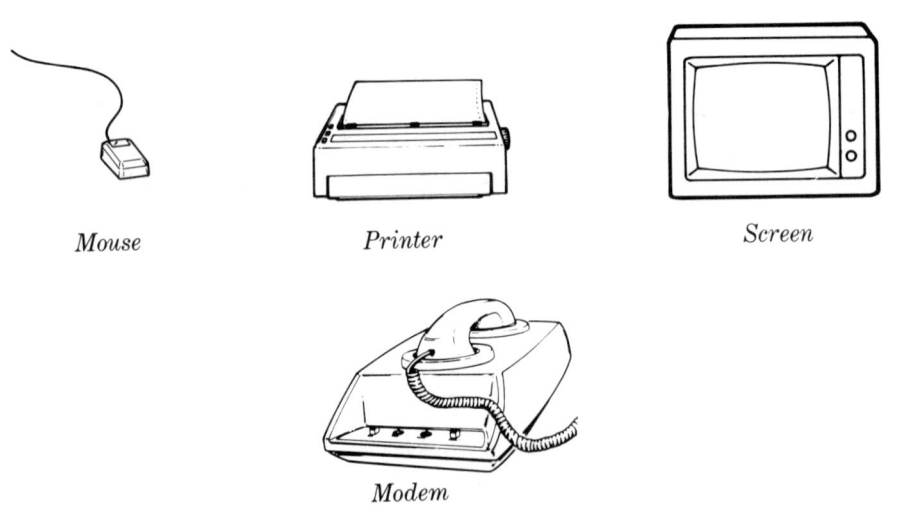

Mouse   *Printer*   *Screen*

Modem

Figure 5-1.   *Peripheral devices*

Character	Binary representation
O	01001111
S	01010011
/	00101111
2	00110010

Table 5 - 1. *Series of Bits for "OS/2" String*

data communication. Using either method, the computer sends data to peripheral devices character by character. Each character that the computer sends to a peripheral device is represented by eight binary digits, or bits. Recall that eight binary digits constitute a byte. For the computer to send the string "OS/2" to your printer, it transmits a series of bits shown in Table 5-1.

Serial devices use one wire to transmit data. Characters are sent character by character, bit by bit, as illustrated in Figure 5-2. Serial data communication also requires additional embed-

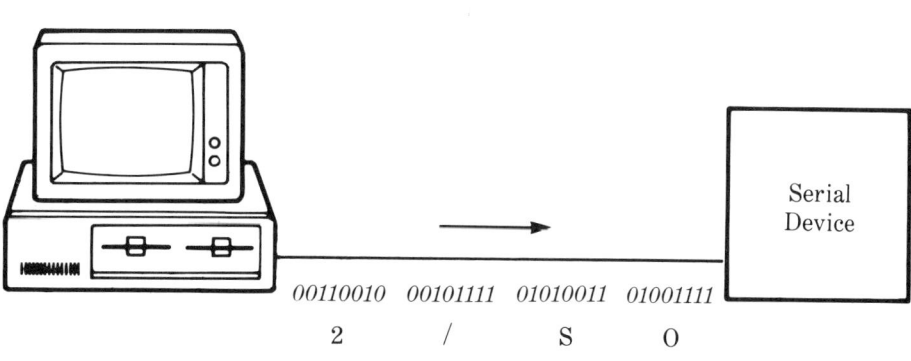

Figure 5 - 2. *Serial transmission of data*

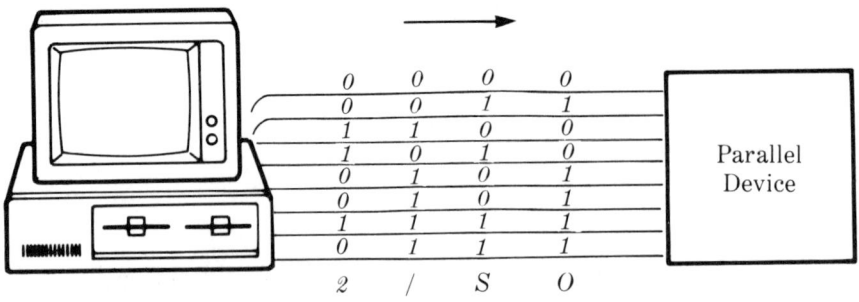

Figure 5-3. *Parallel transmission of data*

ded bits that ensure the coordination of the two communicating devices. For now, however, you only need to understand that serial communication occurs one bit at a time, over a single wire.

Parallel devices use eight wires to transmit data, which means that eight bits of a word can be sent at one time (see Figure 5-3). Unlike serial data (which requires embedded bits for coordination), parallel devices use additional wires. Because parallel communication occurs eight bits at a time, it is much faster than serial data communication. Most printers now use parallel data communication, whereas most modems use serial communication.

PARALLEL VERSUS SERIAL DATA COMMUNICATION

Devices on your computer are categorized as serial or parallel devices.

Serial devices use one wire for data transmission over which a byte of data is transmitted a single bit at a time. Most modems are serial devices.

Parallel devices use multiple wires for data transmission. As such, parallel devices can transfer a byte of data eight bits at a time. Most printers are parallel devices.

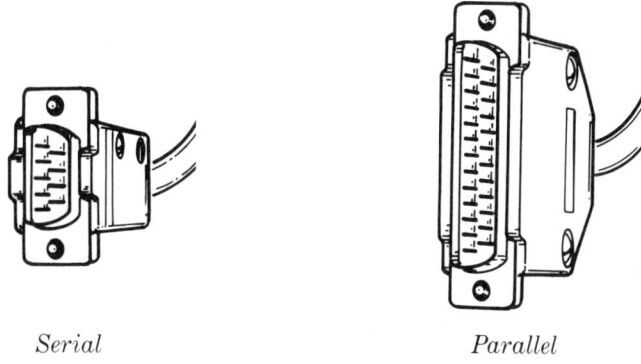

Serial   *Parallel*

Figure 5 - 4.   *Parallel and serial connectors*

To determine whether your printer is a serial or parallel device, first refer to the documentation that accompanied the printer. If you are still unsure, examine the cable used to connect the printer to your computer. Figure 5-4 illustrates commonly used serial and parallel connectors.

Using OS/2 Device Names

Throughout your daily use of OS/2, you will need to frequently reference OS/2 device names. For example, issue the following command:

```
[C:\] COPY CON NEWFILE.TXT
```

Your screen should now contain the following:

```
[c:\] COPY CON NEWFILE.TXT
```

The OS/2 device name CON serves two purposes. During keyboard input operations, CON references your keyboard, as shown
in Figure 5-5.

  Examine the previous command. In this case, OS/2 places into
the file NEWFILE.TXT any information that you type. In this
case, type in the following:

For input, CON points to the keyboard.
For output, CON points to the screen display.

Your screen should now contain the following:

```
[c:\] COPY CON NEWFILE.TXT
For input, con points to the keyboard.
For output, con points to the screen display.
```

Press the F6 function key to indicate the end of the file. OS/2
displays the following:

```
[c:\] COPY CON NEWFILE.TXT
For input, con points to the keyboard.
For output, con points to the screen display.
^Z
```

[C:\] COPY CON NEWFILE.TXT

Input Source   *Output Source*

Figure 5-5. *CON referencing the keyboard*

Next, simply press the ENTER key. OS/2 acknowledges the end of the file, as shown here:

```
    [C:\] COPY CON NEWFILE.TXT
For input, con points to the keyboard.
For output, con points to the screen display.
^Z
        1 File(s) copied.

[C:\]
```

OS/2 uses the ^Z (CTRL-Z) to mark the end of a text file. The F6 key allows you to insert the ^Z at the end of the file when you create a file using CON in this manner.

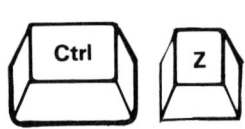

^Z

OS/2 uses the CTRL-Z key combination to signify the end of a text file. When you create files by copying them from the keyboard, press either the F6 key or the CTRL-Z key combination to signify the end of your file.

To verify that OS/2 indeed created the file NEWFILE.TXT, issue the following command:

```
[C:\] TYPE NEWFILE.TXT

For input, con points to the keyboard.
For output, con points to the screen display.

[C:\]
```

OS/2 displays the contents of the file that you just entered.

When used for output, CON refers to your screen display. For example, consider the following command:

```
[C:\] COPY NEWFILE.TXT CON
```

In this case, OS/2 copies the existing file, NEWFILE.TXT, to your screen display, as illustrated in Figure 5-6.

This chapter later discusses how to use similar commands to write to your system printer (LPT1: or PRN:).

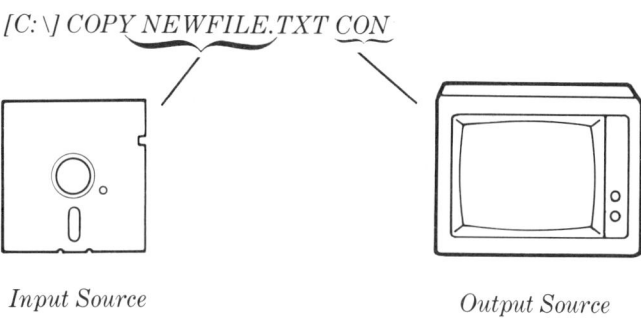

[C:\] COPY NEWFILE.TXT CON

Input Source   *Output Source*

Figure 5-6. *OS/2 copying NEWFILE.TXT to the screen display*

In a similar manner, OS/2 defines the devices KBD$ and SCREEN$ to reference your keyboard and screen, as shown in Figure 5–7. To create a new version of the file NEWFILE.TXT,

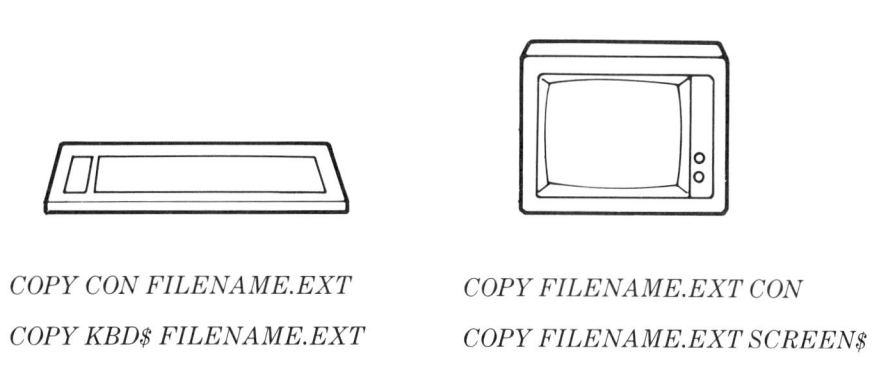

COPY CON FILENAME.EXT   *COPY FILENAME.EXT CON*

COPY KBD$ FILENAME.EXT   *COPY FILENAME.EXT SCREEN$*

Figure 5-7. *Use of KBD$ and SCREEN$ to reference keyboard and screen*

simply enter the following:

```
[C:\] COPY KBD$ NEWFILE.TXT
For input, con points to the keyboard.
For output, con points to the screen display.
^Z
         1 File(s) copied.

[C:\]
```

OS/2 copies into the file the keystrokes that you entered from the keyboard.

```
[C:\] DIR NEWFILE.TXT

 Volume in drive C is OS2DISK
 Directory of  C:\

NEWFILE   TXT         79  11-24-87    5:26p
        1 File(s)     9949184 bytes free

[C:\]
```

You can also use the SCREEN$ device name to display the contents of a file.

```
[C:\] COPY NEWFILE.TXT SCREEN$

For input, con points to the keyboard.
For output, con points to the screen display.

         1 File(s) copied.

[C:\]
```

KBD$ AND SCREEN$

OS/2 predefines your keyboard with the device KBD$. By using this device name, you can create files by typing them at the keyboard.

OS/2 also defines your screen display as SCREEN$. You can display files on your screen by copying the file to the device SCREEN$. However to simplify your transition from real to protected mode, use CON instead of KBD$ or SCREEN$.

MODE (Customizing Your Peripheral Devices)

The OS/2 MODE command enables you to set the characteristics of your computer's asynchronous communication adapters, the color/graphics adapter, and the system printer. For your video display, MODE allows you to alternate between 40-column and 80-column screen displays, or to enable or disable color that appears on the screen. Note that the video MODE commands work only on the color-graphics or extended-graphics-adapter (EGA) systems.

The OS/2 MODE command also allows you to modify your system printer characteristics (such as the character size). In addition, MODE enables you to define data communication parameters for each of your serial ports (such as their baud rates and the numbers of data bits to be used).

Video Display

MODE allows you to control the attributes of your video display. The format of the MODE command for this function is

[*drive:*][*path*]MODE N [, C]

where the following is true:

drive: is the disk identification of the disk containing the file MODE.COM. If you do not specify a disk drive, OS/2 uses the current default drive.

path is the OS/2 path name of the directory containing the file MODE.COM. If you do not specify an OS/2 directory path (discussed in Chapter 8), OS/2 uses the current default drive.

N is the desired video display mode and must be one of the following values:

40	Set the display to 40 columns per line
80	Set the display to 80 columns per line
BW40	Set the display to 40 columns per line with color disabled
BW80	Set the display to 80 columns per line with color disabled
CO40	Set the display to 40 columns per line with color enabled
CO80	Set the display to 80 columns per line with color enabled
C	Specifies the number of lines on the screen 25, 43, or 50.

Consider the following example:

```
[C:\] MODE 40
```

In this case, OS/2 changes your display attributes to 40 columns per line (as opposed to 80) and expands the size of your characters, as shown here:

```
[C:\]
```

To return to 80 columns per line, enter the following command:

```
[C:\] MODE 80
```

OS/2 responds by clearing your screen display and restoring its prompt, as shown here:

```
[C:\]
```

Printer Device

Just as OS/2 allows the MODE command to set the attributes of your screen display, it also allows you to define attributes for your system printer. For this function, the format of your MODE command is

[drive:][path]MODE *LPT#*[:] [*cpl*][,[*lpi*][,*P*]]

where the following is true:

LPT#: is the printer port (LPT1, LPT2, or LPT3) whose attributes MODE is to set.

cpl is the number of characters per line (either 80 or 132). OS/2 uses the 80-characters-per-line setting as its default.

lpi is the number of lines per inch on the output page. This value can be either 6 or 8. OS/2 uses the value of 6 as its default setting.

P specifies that MODE should perform continuous retries if a time-out error occurs.

Consider the following examples:

```
[C:\] MODE LPT1: 132,8
```

In this case, OS/2 sets the printer to 132 characters per line and 8 lines per inch.

```
[C:\] MODE LPT1: 80,6
```

To restore the printer to its default settings, OS/2 uses the values of 80 characters per line and 6 characters per inch.

Asynchronous Ports

Each serial port on your system is classified an *asynchronous port*. To define the port's characteristics, the format of MODE is

[drive:][path]MODE *COM#*[:] *baud* [*,parity*[*,databits*[*,stopbits*][*,P*]]]

where the following is true:

COM# is the asynchronous port of which MODE sets the attributes (such as COM1 or COM2). The value of # can range from 1 to 8.

baud defines the port's baud rate. The value must be 110, 150, 300, 600, 1200, 2400, 4800, 9600, or 19200. MODE only requires that you use the first two digits of the baud rate.

parity specifies the port's parity, as follows:

E Even parity (OS/2 default)
N No parity
O Odd parity

databits defines the number of data bits in a transmission as either 7 or 8. OS/2 uses 7 data bits by default.

stopbits defines the number of stop bits in a transmission as either 1 or 2. For 110 baud, OS/2 uses 2 stop bits. For all other baud rates, OS/2 uses 1.

P specifies that MODE is using a COM port for a serial printer and should perform continuous retries if a time-out error occurs.

Consider the following examples:

```
[c:\] MODE COM1: 96
```

In this case, OS/2 sets COM1 to 9600 baud. Note that since no other values require modification, MODE allows you to leave them out of the command line.

```
[c:\] MODE COM1: 48,N,7
```

In this case, MODE sets COM1 to 4800 baud, no parity, 7 data bits.

Using Your System Printer

This chapter previously discussed how OS/2 allows you to copy files from the keyboard by referencing the device name CON. In a similar manner, you could display the contents of a file by copying it to the CON device. Therefore, to send a file to the system printer, you should be able to issue the following command:

```
[C:\] COPY NEWFILE.TXT LPT1:
```

This command directs OS/2 to copy the contents of the file NEWFILE.TXT to your printer device, as shown in Figure 5-8. However, if you attempt to do so, your command probably will fail and the following will be displayed:

```
Session Title: CMD.EXE

     DOS0028: The printer is out of paper.

     Return the error to the program.
     End the program.
     Retry the operation.
     Ignore the error and continue.
```

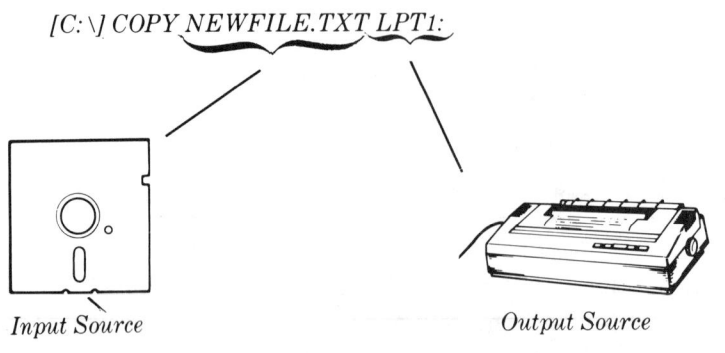

[C:\] COPY NEWFILE.TXT LPT1:

Input Source   *Output Source*

Figure 5-8. *OS/2 copying NEWFILE.TXT to the printer device*

OS/2 is a multitasking operating system (meaning that you can execute several programs simultaneously). As such, OS/2 must provide certain precautions to prevent several programs from writing to the printer device all at the same time. If each program were allowed to do so, your printed listings would be a collection of garbled letters.

To coordinate the access and use of your system printer, OS/2 provides a tool called a *print spooler*. Once installed by using the OS/2 SPOOL command, the print spooler oversees all information sent to the printer, as shown in Figure 5-9. In so doing, the spooler can ensure that data is printed in a coordinated manner.

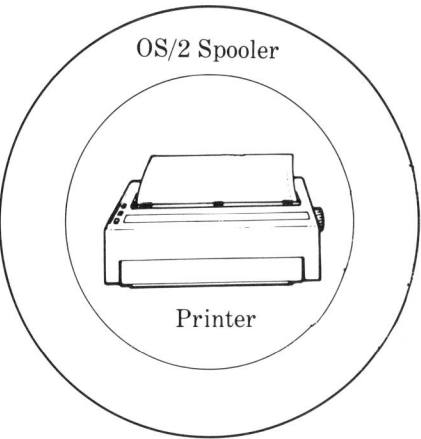

Figure 5-9. *Print spooler overseeing all information sent to printer*

OS/2 PRINT SPOOLER

Since OS/2 can execute multiple programs simultaneously, it is possible (and most likely) that several programs will attempt to access the system printer. To maintain coordination of printer output in this environment, OS/2 uses a print spooler.

The OS/2 SPOOL command installs a print spooler that, in turn, controls printer operations.

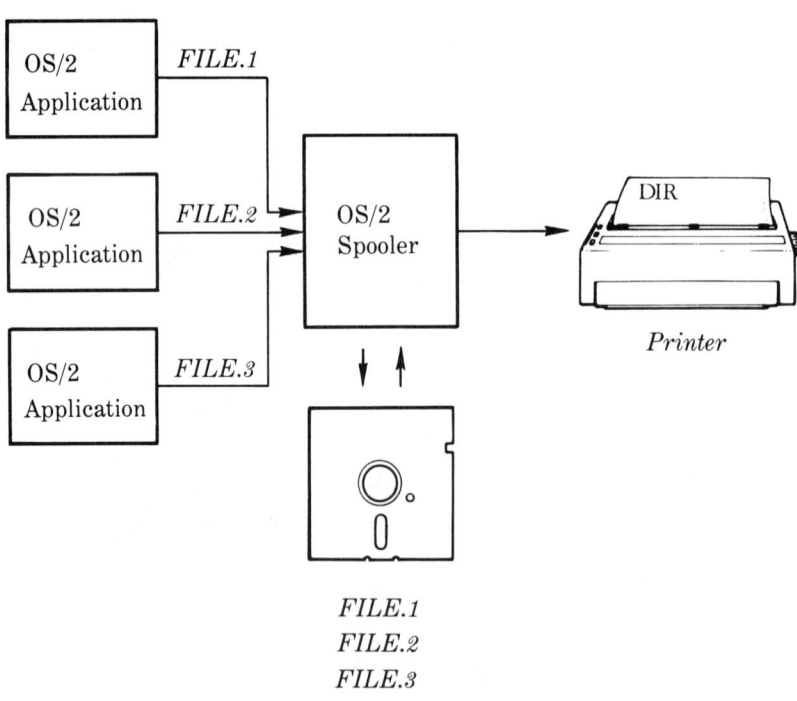

Figure 5-10.   *Print spooler temporarily writing data to disk*

The print spooler works by writing temporarily to disk all of the data an application is sending to the system printer (see Figure 5-10). Once the application has completed its printing, SPOOL closes the file it has created and places it in line to be printed (see Figure 5-11). In so doing, SPOOL maintains strict control of printer data.

The format of the SPOOL command is

[*drive:*][*path*]SPOOL [*d:*][*spool—path*] [*/D:device1*] [*/O:device2*]

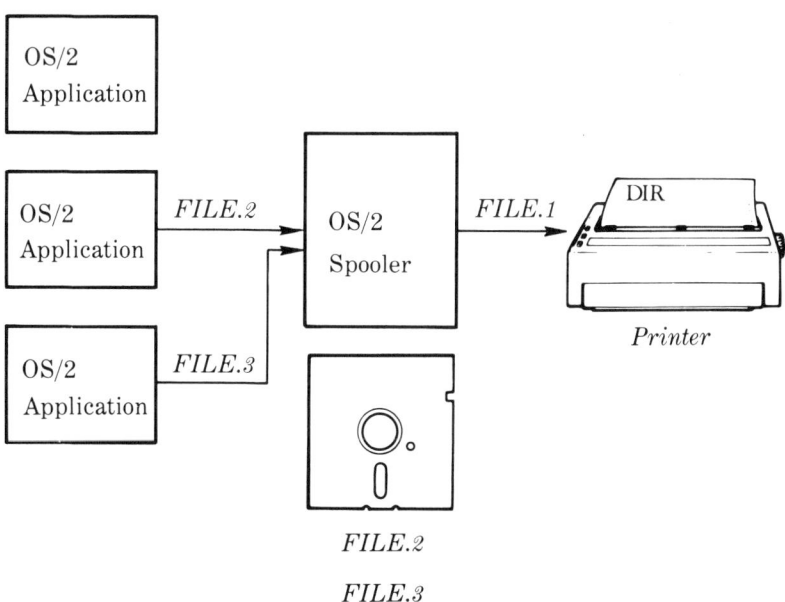

Figure 5-11. *File being placed in line to be printed*

where the following is true:

drive: is the disk drive identification of the disk containing the file SPOOL. EXE. If you do not specify a disk drive, OS/2 uses the current default.

path is the OS/2 path name of the directory containing the file SPOOL.EXE. If you do not specify a directory path (discussed in Chapter 8), OS/2 uses the current default.

d: specifies the disk drive where SPOOL is to temporarily place the files that it is creating until it can print them.

spool_path defines the OS/2 path name that SPOOL uses to store its temporary files (discussed in Chapter 8). By default, SPOOL uses a path name of \SPOOL.

/D:device1 specifies the port to which the printer is connected (LPTn or COMn).

/O:device2 specifies the name of the printer device. By default, SPOOL uses the device you specify for /O. Most users can ignore this qualifier and use the OS/2 default value.

Consider the following example:

```
[C:\] SPOOL C:\   /d:LPT1
```

In this case, SPOOL writes its files to the root directory on drive C (C: \). The printer device being spooled is LPT1. For now, most of you can simply use C: \ or A: \ as your spool directory. Chapter 8 discusses this parameter in detail.

Once installed, SPOOL consumes one of your OS/2 sessions since it never returns you to an OS/2 prompt. Many users use the CONFIG.SYS RUN entry to load the spooler.

```
SPOOL is running printing data on device LPT1.
```

Simply select the Session Manager menu by pressing CTRL-ESC. Note the addition of the session SPOOL.EXE. To create another protected-mode program, select the "Start a Program" option. Now you are ready to copy data to your printer.

Type the following command:

```
[C:\] COPY CON LPT1:
The input source is CON (the keyboard)
The output source is LPT1: (the system printer)
```

In this case, OS/2 is receiving its input from the keyboard device. Once you press the F6 key to signify the end of the file, OS/2 will begin printing the information that you type.

```
[C:\] COPY CON LPT1:
The input source is CON (the keyboard)
The output source is LPT1: (the system printer)
^Z

            1 File(s) copied.

[C:\]
```

Although the data appears to go directly to the printer, the OS/2 print spooler first temporarily writes the information to disk to ensure that the printer is available before it begins printing (see Figure 5-12). Because OS/2 spools its output in this manner, every application in the system appears to have its own printer. Rather than sending a busy signal when multiple programs attempt to simultaneously access a printer in use by one of them, OS/2 instead spools the output and allows the programs to proceed with their processing.

[C:\] COPY CON LPT1:

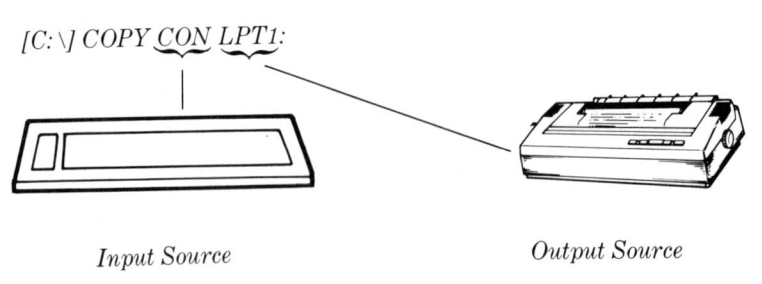

Input Source   *Output Source*

Figure 5-12. *Apparent individual printer for individual file*

Issue the following command:

```
[C:\] COPY NEWFILE.TXT LPT1:
```

OS/2 prints your file as desired.

Echoing Terminal Output
to the Printer (CTRL-PRINT SCREEN)

Once you have installed the OS/2 spooler, you can press the CTRL-PRINT SCREEN key combination to direct OS/2 to print every character that it writes to this session's screen display (see Figure 5–13).

Press the CTRL-PRINT SCREEN key combination and issue the following command:

```
[C:\] DIR
```

As OS/2 writes the directory listing on your screen it also writes the same information to your printer. To turn off character echoing, simply press the CTRL-PRINT SCREEN key combination. Once you have done this, again enter the following command:

```
[C:\] DIR
```

In this case, OS/2 simply writes the output to the screen display.

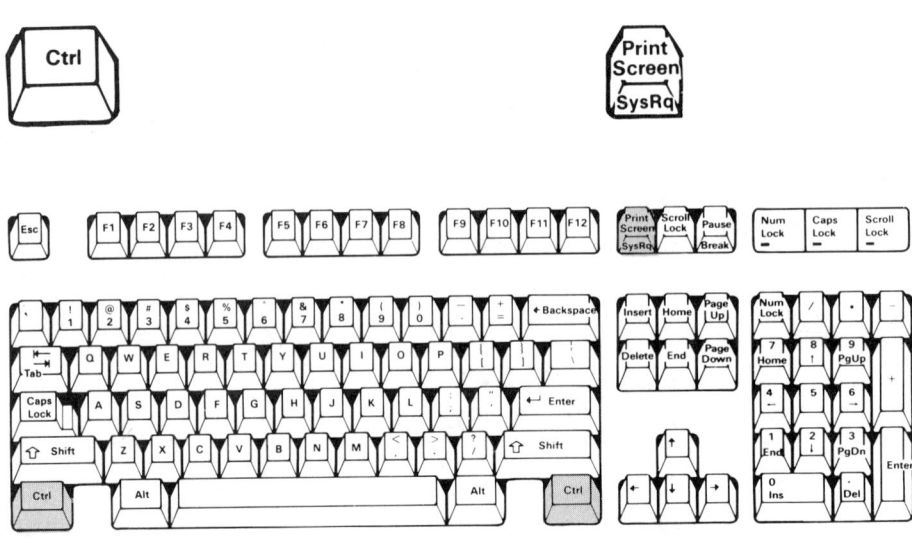

Figure 5 - 13. *Location of* CTRL *and* PRINT SCREEN *keys*

Many programmers find the CTRL-PRINT SCREEN echo a convenient method of getting a hard-copy listing of their compile error or link error messages. Before they invoke the compiler, they simply press CTRL-PRINT SCREEN. Any error messages that the compiler writes are then echoed to the printer.

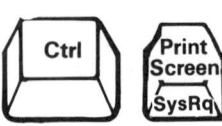

ECHOING OUTPUT TO THE SYSTEM PRINTER

Once you install the OS/2 spooler, you can press the CTRL-PRINT SCREEN key combination to direct OS/2 to print every character it writes to the screen display. CTRL-PRINT SCREEN is a toggle. The first time you press this combination, it will turn on echoing. The second invocation turns it off.

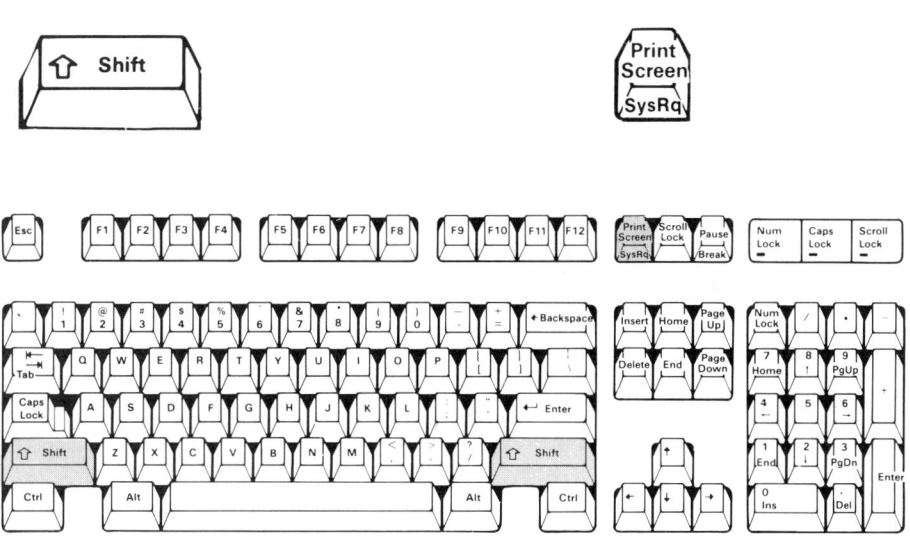

Figure 5-14. *Location of SHIFT and PRINT SCREEN keys*

Printing Your Screen Contents
(SHIFT-PRINT SCREEN)

Just as the CTRL-PRINT SCREEN key combination allows you to echo the characters written to your screen display, pressing the SHIFT-PRINT SCREEN key combination directs OS/2 to print the current contents of your screen display. For example, issue the following command:

```
[C:\] DIR
```

As your directory listing scrolls by on your screen, press the SHIFT-PRINT SCREEN key combination (see Figure 5-14). OS/2 stops the display and prints its current contents. If the computer beeps instead, you have probably not yet installed the OS/2 print spooler as previously discussed.

PRINTING YOUR SCREEN CONTENTS

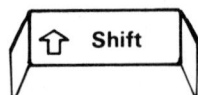 

Once you have installed the OS/2 spooler, you can press the SHIFT-PRINT SCREEN key combination that directs OS/2 to copy the current screen contents to your printer.

PRINT

This chapter previously discussed how to copy files to your system printer. This section examines the OS/2 PRINT command, which allows you to send your files to the printer in a controlled manner. Consider the following command:

```
[C:\] COPY NEWFILE.TXT PRN:
```

Once you have installed your spooler, this command copies the contents of the file to your printer. However, the command has some drawbacks. Once the command completes, you must manually form-feed your printer by first taking it off-line, issuing a form-feed, and then placing it back on-line.

The OS/2 PRINT command provides you with a solution to this drawback. The print spooler is a background process, which means it works behind the scenes to perform a function (such as printing a file) while you execute other commands. As previously discussed, background commands share CPU time slices with the other programs that are executing in the system, thus giving your computer the appearance that it is doing several things at once.

Using the COPY CON command, create the following files:

```
The OS/2 PRINT command is a background
command which gives you more control over
your printed output.
```

```
The OS/2 PRINT command uses a storage
facility called a queue.  A queue is simply
a waiting line.  In this case, files are
waiting to be printed.
```

Your screen should now contain the following:

```
[C:\] COPY CON: PRINTER.TXT
The OS/2 PRINT command is a background
command that gives you more control over
your printed output.
^Z
        1 File(s) copied.

[C:\] COPY CON: QUEUE.TXT
The OS/2 PRINT command uses a storage
facility called a queue. A queue is simply
a waiting line. In this case, files are
waiting to be printed.
^Z
        1 File(s) copied.

[C:\]
```

Once you have created the files, issue the following command:

```
[C:\] PRINT PRINTER.TXT QUEUE.TXT
```

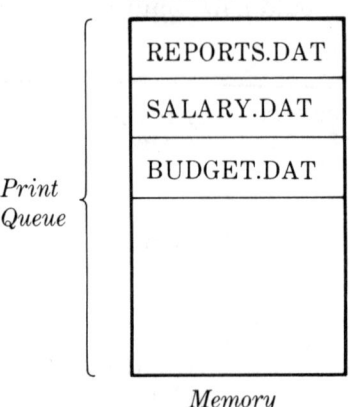

[C:/] PRINT REPORTS.DAT,SALARY.DAT,BUDGET.DAT

Results in

REPORTS.DAT
SALARY.DAT
BUDGET.DAT

Print Queue

Memory

Figure 5 - 15. *Storage of files in the queue*

The files should begin printing and OS/2 will redisplay its system prompt.

The OS/2 PRINT command uses a storage facility called a *queue* to keep track of your print files. Simply stated, a queue is a waiting line. OS/2 sets aside an area called the spooler queue that contains the files that you wish to print. Each time you issue an OS/2 PRINT command to print files, PRINT places the names of the files to print in this area, as shown in Figure 5-15.

■ The queue can be empty (see Figure 5-16).

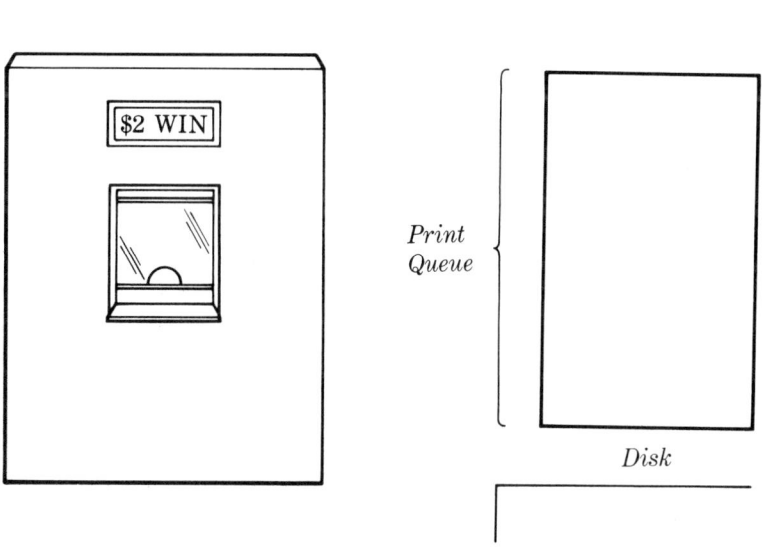

Figure 5- 16. *Empty queue*

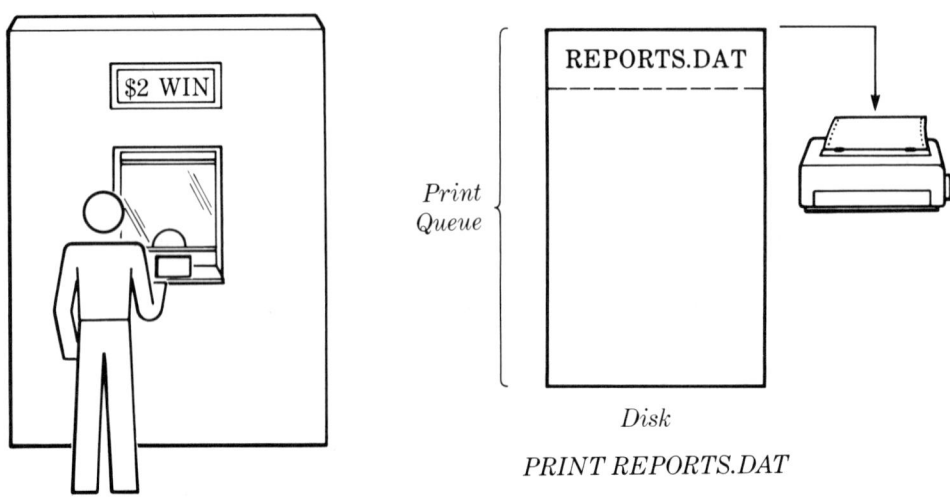

Figure 5-17. *Immediate action from queue*

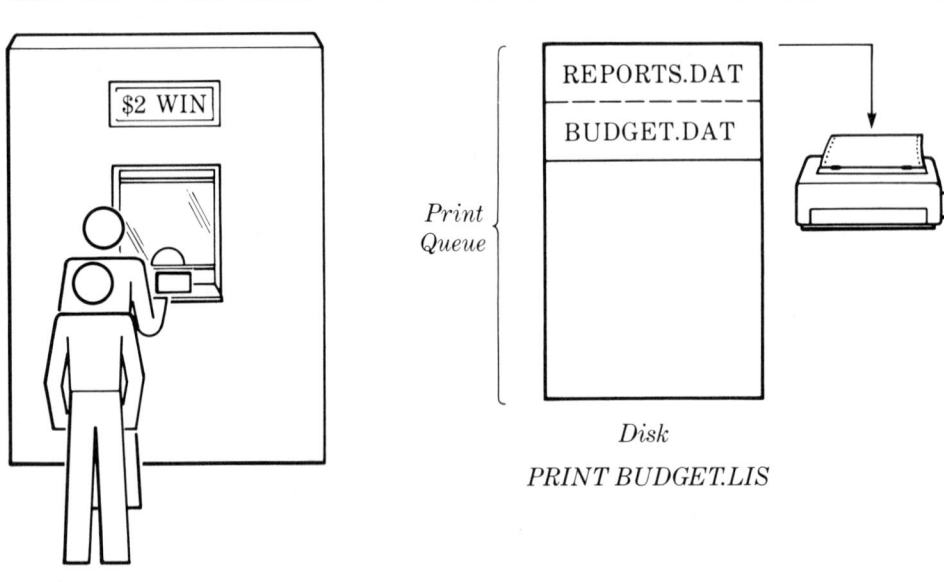

Figure 5-18. *Waiting in the queue*

- An entry can enter the queue and receive immediate service (see Figure 5-17).

- If service is not immediately available, the entry must wait (see Figure 5-18).

- Additional entries can also be queued (see Figure 5-19).

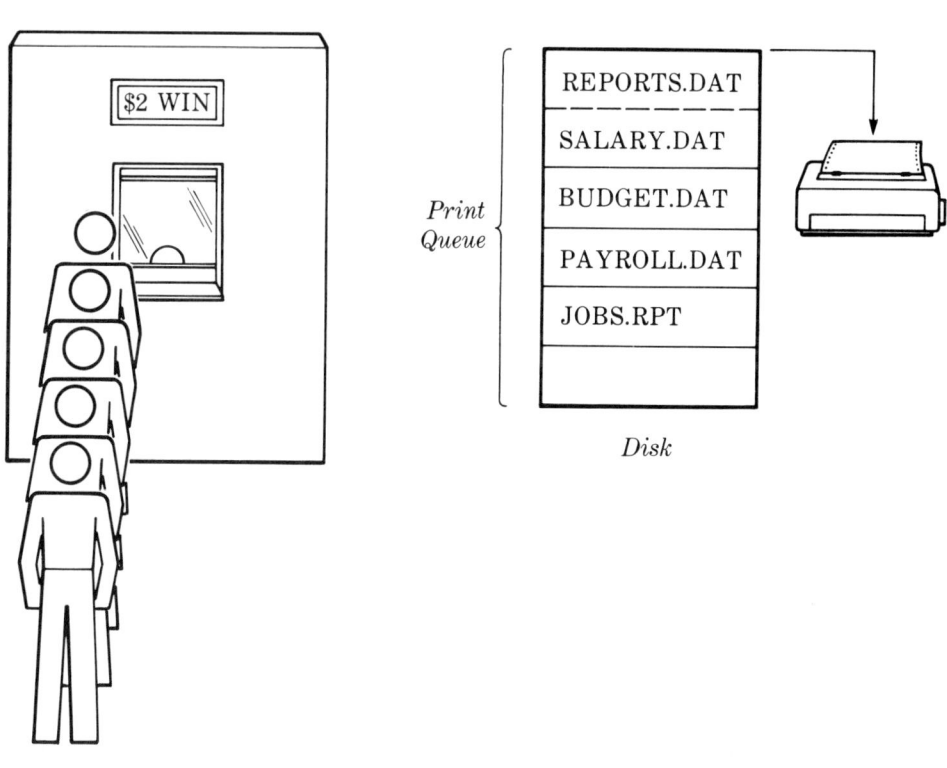

Figure 5-19. *Additional entries queued*

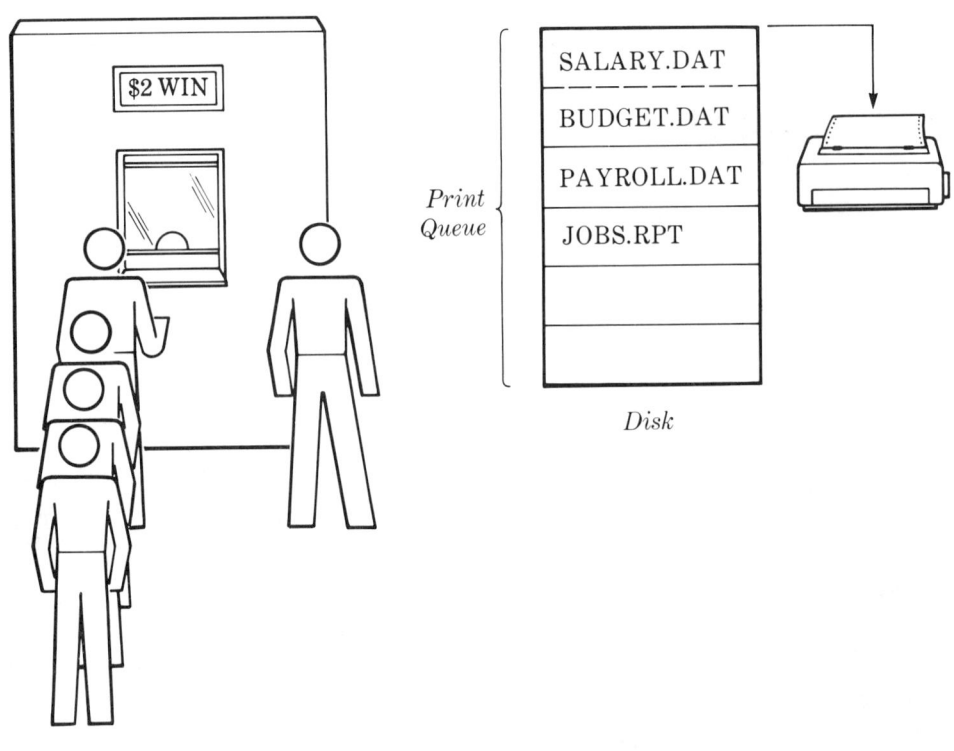

Figure 5-20. *Entry leaving queue*

■ Once service is available, an entry leaves the queue (see Figure 5-20).

The queue has a limited amount of space for entries. Once this disk space is full, entries are denied, as shown in Figure 5-21. It is also possible for an entry to leave the queue prior to obtaining service (see Figure 5-22).

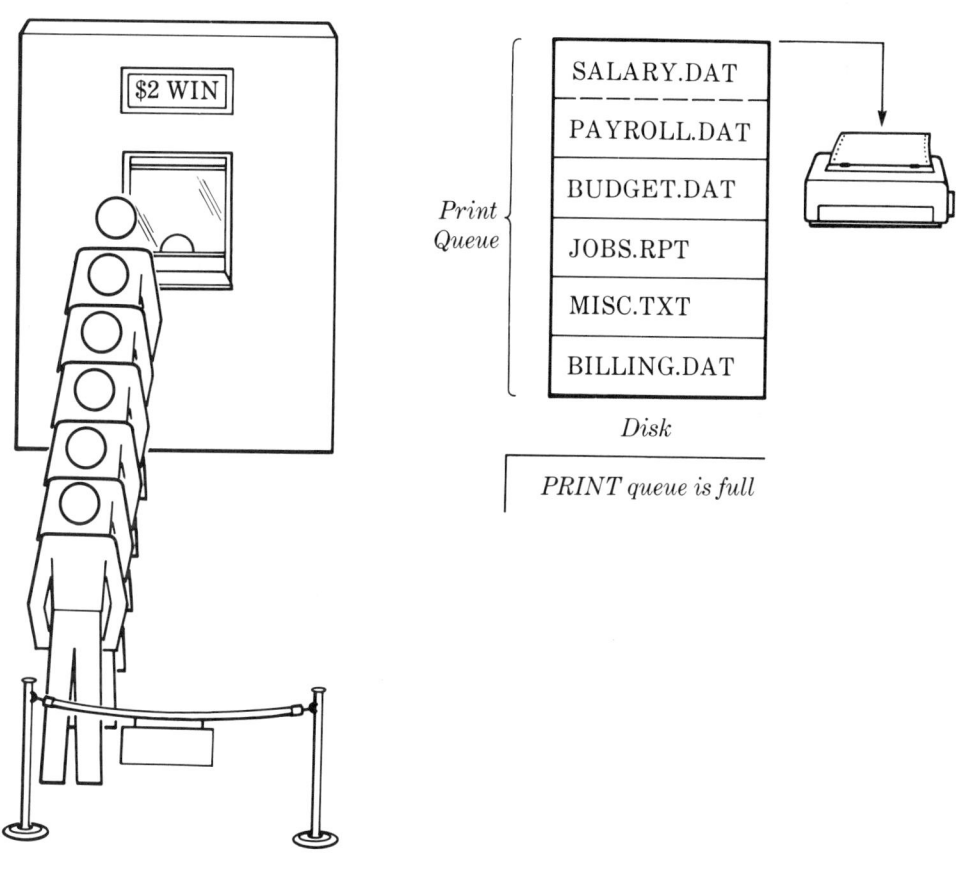

Figure 5-21. *Entries denied access to queue*

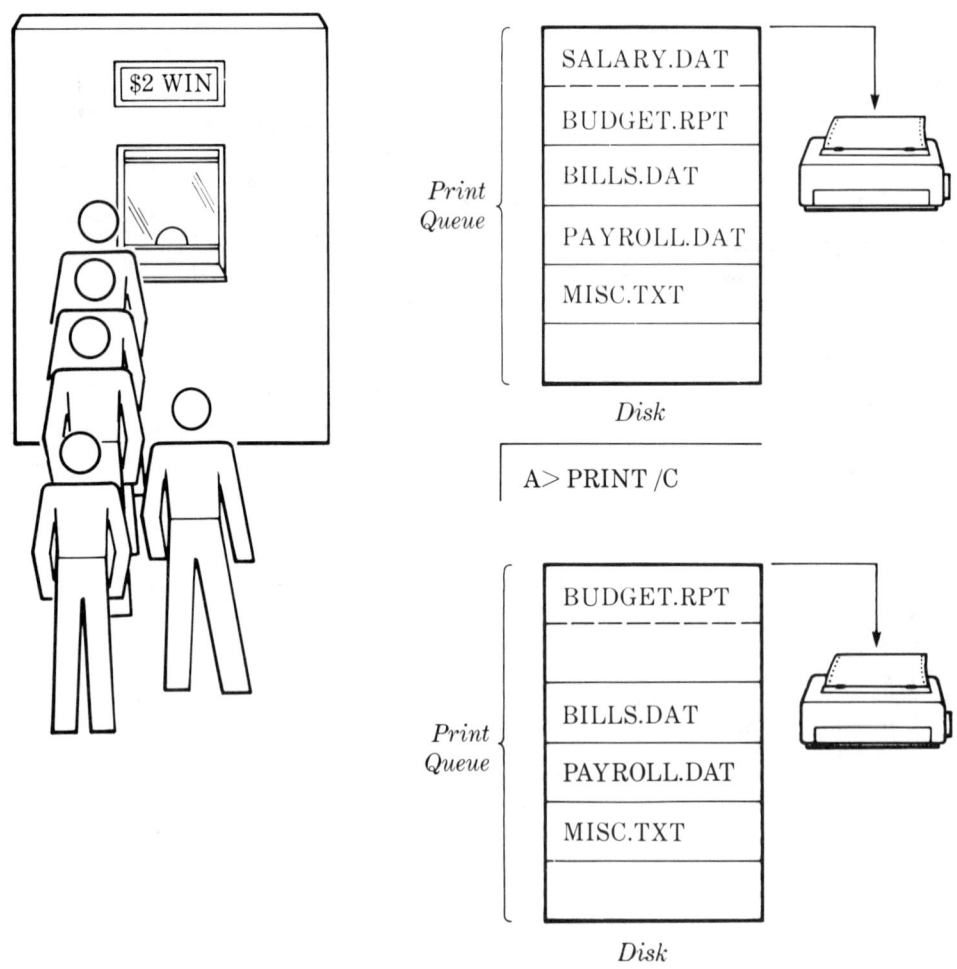

Figure 5-22.   *Entry leaving queue before being serviced*

The complete format of the OS/2 PRINT command is

[*drive:*][*path*]PRINT[*/D:device*][*/C*][*/T*][*/B*]file__specification [...]

where the following is true:

drive: is the disk drive identification of the disk containing the file PRINT.EXE. If you do not specify a disk drive, OS/2 uses the current default.

path is the OS/2 path name of the directory containing the file PRINT.EXE. If you do not specify a directory path (discussed in Chapter 8), OS/2 uses the current default.

/D:device specifies the port to which the printer is connected (LPTn or COMn).

/C directs PRINT to stop printing the current file.

/T directs PRINT to stop printing the current file, and to remove all remaining entries from the print queue. When you use this qualifier, OS/2 terminates the printing of the current file and displays the following message on the printout:

/B directs PRINT to treat the first ^Z as an end of file.

```
All SPOOL files cancelled by operator.
```

Consider the following examples:

```
[C:\] PRINT CONFIG.SYS AUTOEXEC.BAT STARTUP.CMD
```

This command places the files CONFIG.SYS, AUTOEXEC.BAT, and STARTUP.CMD into the print queue for printing. OS/2 prints the files in the order that they appear in the PRINT command.

```
[C:\] PRINT A:CONFIG.SYS B:CONFIG.SYS
```

PRINT prints the file A:CONFIG.SYS and B:CONFIG.SYS. The PRINT command supports full OS/2 file specifications.

```
[C:\] PRINT *.TXT
```

In this case, OS/2 prints all of the files with the extension TXT. PRINT fully supports OS/2 wildcard characters.

```
[C:\] PRINT /C
```

To remove a file from the print queue, simply use the /C qualifier as shown. In a similar manner, the command

```
[C:\] PRINT /T
```

directs PRINT to remove all of the files currently in the print queue.

You will use the OS/2 PRINT command during the majority of your computer sessions. Take time now to experiment with its functional capabilities.

Chapter Highlights

Most of the peripheral devices on your system (mouse, printer, and so forth) are classified as either serial or parallel.

Serial devices transmit a byte of data one bit at a time over a single wire.

Parallel devices transmit a byte of data eight bits at a time over multiple wires.

Most printers today use parallel data transmission, while most modems use serial transmission.

The OS/2 MODE command allows you to specify attributes for your screen display, system printer, and asynchronous (serial) devices.

OS/2 reserves several names that it associates with its peripheral devices. You cannot use these names as file names because OS/2 reserves them for devices. The following names are reserved: COM1:, COM2:, COM3:, CLOCK$, CON:, KBD$, LPT1:, LPT2:, LPT3:, NUL:, PRN:, and SCREEN$.

In order to maintain control over its printer output in a multitasking environment, OS/2 uses a resource called a spooler to oversee all printer output. To use the OS/2 spooler, you must invoke the OS/2 SPOOL command.

Once you have installed the OS/2 spooler, you can press the CTRL-PRINT SCREEN key combination to direct OS/2 to echo the output sent to the screen display also to the system printer. In addition, by pressing the SHIFT-PRINT SCREEN key combination, you direct OS/2 to print its current screen contents.

6 OS/2 I/O Redirection

Thus far, all of your OS/2 commands have obtained input from the keyboard and written output to the screen display, as illustrated in Figure 6-1. However, OS/2 provides a large collection of command-line operators that enable you to redirect I/O (input/output) from one source to another.

Consider the following OS/2 command:

```
[C:\] DIR
```

In this case, OS/2 displays the output of the DIR command to your screen display, as illustrated in Figure 6-2.

Most OS/2 commands send output to a predefined destination called *stdout* (for standard output). By default, stdout points to your screen display.

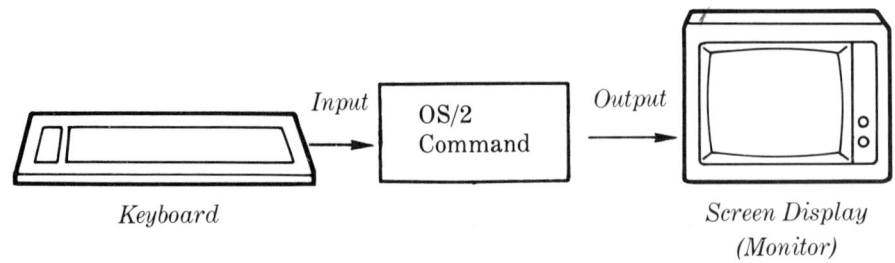

Figure 6-1. *Input from keyboard and output to screen display*

This chapter examines in detail each of the OS/2 I/O redirection operators. These operators enable you to route a command's input or output (or both) to a new source. Just as OS/2 defines stdout to point to your screen display, OS/2 defines *stdin* (standard input source) to point to your keyboard (see Figure 6-3).

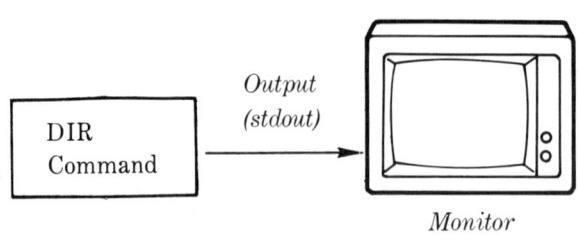

Figure 6-2. *Output of DIR command to screen display*

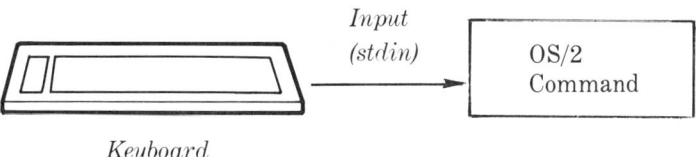

Figure 6-3. *OS/2 stdin pointing to keyboard*

From the OS/2 prompt, issue the following command:

```
[C:\] DIR > FILES.DAT
```

OS/2 does not display the output of the command to your screen. Instead, the OS/2 output redirection operator > directs OS/2 to place the output of the command into the file FILES.DAT, as shown in Figure 6-4. Using this same operator, OS/2 allows you to write the output of your directory listing to your system printer, as follows:

```
[C:\] DIR > PRN:
```

Figure 6-5 illustrates this process.

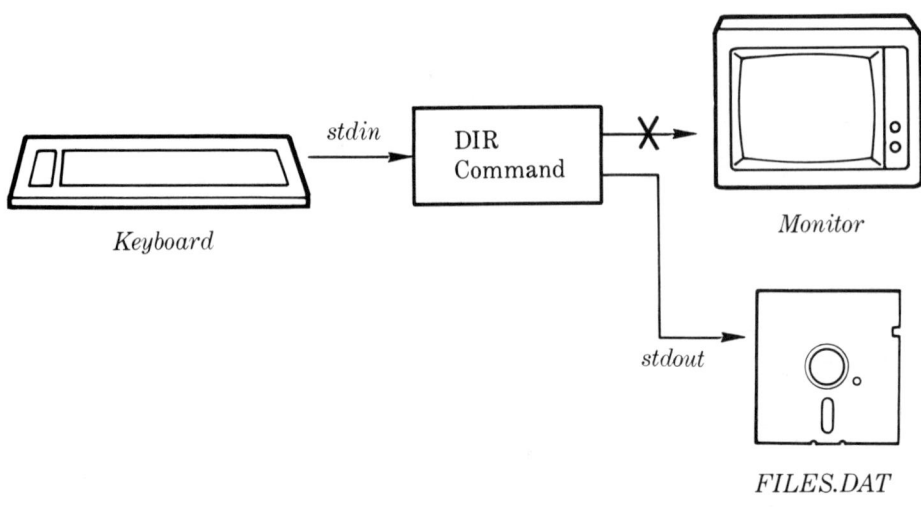

Figure 6-4. *OS/2 output redirection to FILES.DAT*

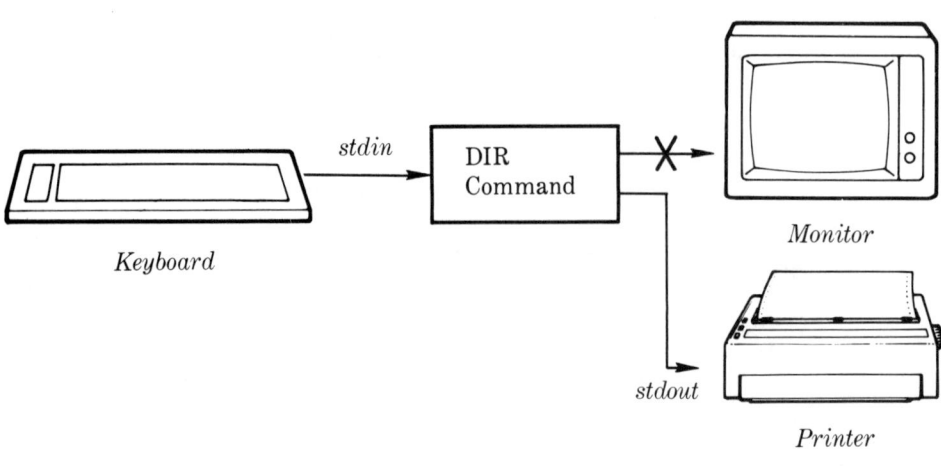

Figure 6-5. *OS/2 process of redirecting output to printer*

If your system printer is turned on, the output of your directory listing should begin printing. OS/2 allows you to redirect the output of most of its commands in this manner. For example, to obtain a quick listing of all the files on your disk, use the CHKDSK command, as shown here:

```
[C:\] CHKDSK /V > PRN:
```

OUTPUT REDIRECTION >

The OS/2 output redirection operator > allows you to redirect the output of a command from your screen display to a file or device.

The OS/2 append redirection operator >> enables you to append the output of a command to the file that you specify. Assume that you have the following files:

MARCH.BIL   Contains your expenses for March

APRIL.BIL   Contains your expenses for April

MAY.BIL   Contains your expenses for May

If you type the contents of the file MARCH.BIL and display the output to your screen, OS/2 responds as follows:

```
[C:\] TYPE MARCH.BIL

Electric         $125.00
Gas              $ 35.00
Food             $300.00
Beer             $300.00
Visa             $250.00
Rent             $455.00

[C:\]
```

However, if you use the append redirection operator >> as follows,

```
[C:\] TYPE MARCH.DAT >> TOTAL.DAT
```

OS/2 appends the contents of the file MARCH.BIL to the file TOTAL.BIL. If the target file (in this case TOTAL.BIL) does not exist, OS/2 creates it (see Figure 6-6).

Next, you can simply issue the commands

```
[C:\] TYPE APRIL.BIL >> TOTAL.BIL
```

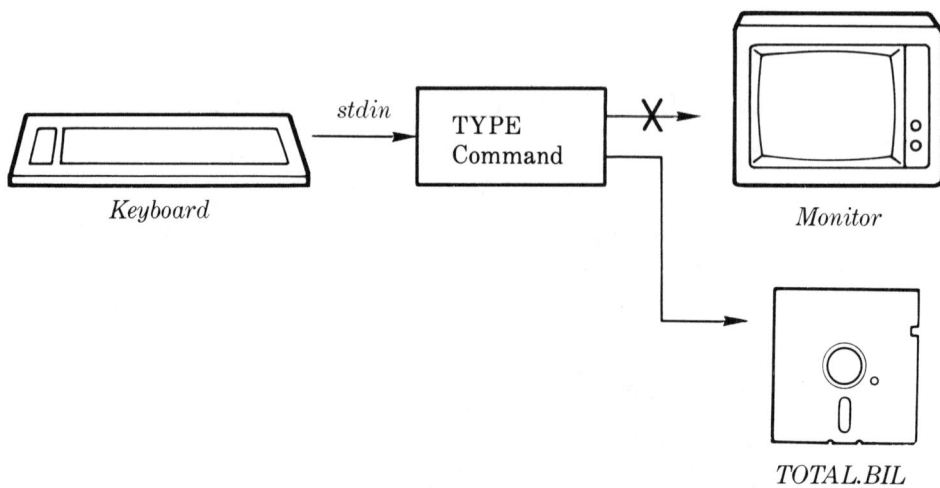

Figure 6-6. *OS/2 using append redirection operator*

and

```
[C:\] TYPE MAY.BIL >> TOTAL.BIL
```

to append the contents of APRIL.BIL and MAY.BIL to the file TOTAL.BIL, as shown here:

```
[C:\] TYPE TOTAL.BIL

Expenses for March

Electric          $125.00
Gas               $ 35.00
Food              $300.00
Beer              $300.00
Visa              $250.00
Rent              $455.00

Expenses for April

Electric          $100.00
Gas               $ 40.00
Food              $150.00
Beer              $450.00
Rent              $455.00

Expenses for May

Electric          $110.00
Gas               $ 34.00
Food              $ 50.00
Beer              $550.00
Rent              $455.00

[C:\]
```

OS/2 appended the contents of each specified file to TOTAL.BIL.

In a similar manner, you can obtain a directory listing of several disks by issuing the following commands:

```
[C:\] DIR A: >> FILES.LIS
[C:\] DIR B: >> FILES.LIS
[C:\] DIR C: >> FILES.LIS
```

By using multiple command-line parameters as illustrated in Chapter 3, you can obtain the same result by issuing the following command:

```
[C:\] DIR A: B: C: > FILES.LIS
```

APPEND REDIRECTION>>

The OS/2 append redirection operator >> allows you to redirect the output of a command from a screen display and append the results to the specified file.

Just as the output and append redirection operators enable you to redirect the output of a command (stdout) to a new source, OS/2 provides the input redirection operator < to redirect stdin from the keyboard to a new source, as shown in Figure 6-7.

Consider the OS/2 MORE command. MORE obtains its input from stdin and displays it to stdout a screenful at a time; the user presses the ENTER key to resume the screen display, as shown here:

```
-- More --
```

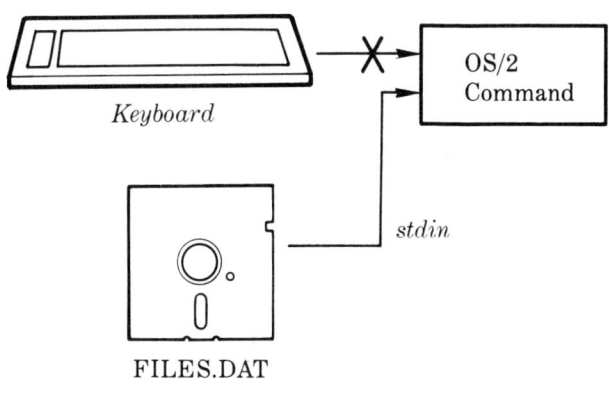

Figure 6-7. *Redirecting stdin from keyboard to new source*

Many users issue the MORE command as follows to display the contents of large files, a screenful at a time:

```
[C:\] TYPE FILES.DAT ¦ MORE
```

In this case, MORE obtains its input from the file FILES.DAT (as opposed to your keyboard), as shown in Figure 6-7.

```
[C:\] TYPE FILES .DAT ¦ MORE

Volume in drive C is OS2DISK
  Directory of  C:\OS2

   .              <DIR>       9-03-87    9:49p
   ..             <DIR>       9-03-87    9:49p
   ANSI    EXE    10108       5-27-87   12:00a
   APPEND  COM     5986       5-27-87   12:00a
   ASSIGN  COM     1689       5-27-87   12:00a
```

```
ATTRIB    EXE     26220    5-27-87    12:00a
BACKUP    COM     45232    5-27-87    12:00a
CHKDSK    COM     46128    5-27-87    12:00a
COMP      COM     29712    5-27-87    12:00a
DISKCOMP  COM     31840    5-27-87    12:00a
DISKCOPY  COM     33408    5-27-87    12:00a
EDLIN     COM      8231    5-27-87    12:00a
FDISK     EXE     37488    5-27-87    12:00a
FIND      COM     23962    5-27-87    12:00a
FORMAT    COM     63040    5-27-87    12:00a
FORMATS   TBL       366    5-27-87    12:00a
GRAFTABL  COM      7032    5-27-87    12:00a
GWBASIC   EXE     78864    5-27-87    12:00a
HELPMSG   EXE     23952    5-27-87    12:00a
JOIN      EXE     18528    5-27-87    12:00a
-- More --
```

When you press the ENTER key, MORE displays the next full page (if a page exists) or to the end of the file, as shown here:

```
KEYB      EXE     12278    5-27-87    12:00a
LABEL     COM     23392    5-27-87    12:00a
MODE      COM     47726    5-27-87    12:00a
MORE      COM     43898    5-27-87    12:00a
PATCH     EXE     33644    5-27-87    12:00a
PRINT     COM     36460    5-27-87    12:00a
REPLACE   EXE     29072    5-27-87    12:00a
RESTORE   COM     49376    5-27-87    12:00a
SORT      EXE     27056    5-27-87    12:00a
SPOOL     EXE     58006    5-27-87    12:00a
SUBST     EXE     18512    5-27-87    12:00a
SYS       COM     27602    5-27-87    12:00a
TREE      COM     26064    5-27-87    12:00a
XCOPY     EXE     22928    5-27-87    12:00a
         35 File(s)    6537216 bytes free
```

INPUT REDIRECTION<

The OS/2 input redirection operator < allows you to redirect a command input from the keyboard to a file.

The OS/2 FIND command also supports I/O redirection. FIND locates and displays each occurrence of a string within a file. The format of the command is

[*drive:*][*path*]FIND [*/C*][*/N*][*/V*] "string" [file—spec[...]]

where the following is true:

drive: specifies the disk drive identification containing the file FIND.EXE. If you do not specify a drive, OS/2 uses the current default.

path is the OS/2 directory path to the file FIND.EXE. If you do not specify a path name, OS/2 uses the current default. Chapter 8 discusses OS/2 path names in detail.

/C directs FIND to display a count of the number of occurrences of the string in the file.

/N directs FIND to display the line number of each line containing the specified string.

/V directs FIND to display all lines that do not contain the specified string.

string is the string to search for.

file—spec is the name of the file to search.

Assume that the file STATES.LIS contains the following:

```
ALASKA, JUNEAU
ALABAMA, MONTGOMERY
ARIZONA, PHOENIX
ARKANSAS, LITTLE ROCK
CALIFORNIA, SACRAMENTO
NEVADA, LAS VEGAS
WASHINGTON, OLYMPIA
```

Enter the following command:

```
[C:\] FIND "ARIZ" STATES.LIS
```

In this case, FIND displays the following:

```
---------- STATES.LIS
ARIZONA, PHOENIX
```

Likewise, if you issue the command

```
[C:\] FIND/N "ALA" STATES.LIS
```

FIND displays the following:

```
---------- STATES.LIS
[1]ALASKA, JUNEAU
[2]ALABAMA, MONTGOMERY
```

To obtain a count of the number of occurrences of the letter "A," enter the command

```
[C:\] FIND /C "A" STATES.LIS
```

and FIND displays the following:

```
---------- STATES.LIS: 7
```

This chapter later discusses how FIND fully supports another OS/2 redirection operator, the OS/2 pipe.

The OS/2 SORT command also supports I/O redirection. The OS/2 SORT command sorts the data that it receives from stdin and writes the sorted information to stdout. The format of the OS/2 SORT command is

[*drive:*][path]SORT [/+*n*][/*R*]

where the following is true:

drive: specifies the disk drive identification containing the file SORT.EXE. If you do not specify a drive, OS/2 uses the current default.

path is the OS/2 directory path to the file SORT.EXE. If you do not specify a path name, OS/2 uses the current default. Chapter 8 discusses OS/2 path names in detail.

/+*n* directs SORT to perform the sort based upon the data beginning in column *n*.

/*R* directs SORT to perform the sort in reverse (descending) order.

Assume that the file NAMES.LIS contains the following:

```
BARNES
VOHS
BRYANT
RICH
EUBANK
GUEBARD
ANDERSON
HUTCHINSON
SCHMAUDER
BOY
```

The OS/2 command

```
[C:\] SORT < NAMES.LIS
```

results in the following:

```
ANDERSON
BARNES
BOY
BRYANT
EUBANK
GUEBARD
HUTCHINSON
RICH
SCHMAUDER
VOHS
```

Likewise, if you have the file MAIL.LIS that contains

```
1234567890123456789

WA SEATTLE    93244
AZ PHOENIX    85023
NV LAS VEGAS  89126
NY NEW YORK   22021
OR PORTLAND   91122
CA OAKLAND    83233
MA BOSTON     01123
```

you can sort it by city, as shown here:

```
[C:\] SORT /+4 < MAIL.LIS

MA BOSTON       01123
NV LAS VEGAS    89126
NY NEW YORK     22021
CA OAKLAND      83233
AZ PHOENIX      85023
OR PORTLAND     91122
WA SEATTLE      93244
```

You could use the SORT command to display the information sorted by ZIP code, as shown here:

```
[C:\] SORT /+15 < MAIL.LIS

MA BOSTON       01123
NY NEW YORK     22021
CA OAKLAND      83233
AZ PHOENIX      85023
NV LAS VEGAS    89126
OR PORTLAND     91122
WA SEATTLE      93244
```

Note that OS/2 allows you to place multiple redirection operators on the same line. In the following command line, SORT obtains its information from the file MAIL.LIS and then writes its output to the file ZIP.SRT:

```
[C:\] SORT /+15 < MAIL.LIS > ZIP.SRT
```

OS/2 Pipe

The OS/2 I/O pipe redirection operator (¦) redirects the output of one program to become the input of a second program. For example, if you enter the command

```
[C:\] DIR ¦ MORE
```

the output of the DIR command is not written to the screen, but rather to the stdin of the MORE command, as shown in Figure 6-8.

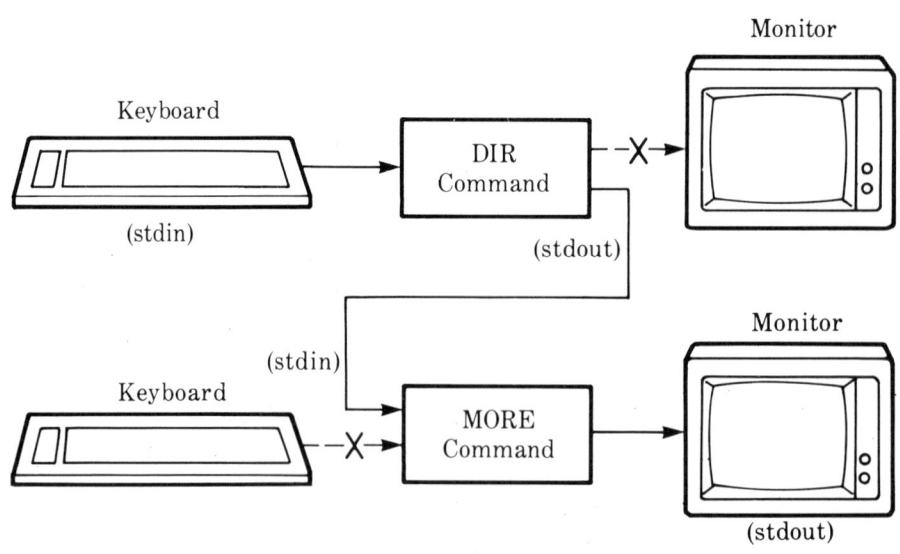

Figure 6-8. *Output of DIR written to stdin of MORE*

OS/2 allows you to use the MORE, FIND, and SORT commands with the OS/2 pipe. For example, the following command displays a sorted directory listing on your screen:

```
[C:\] DIR ¦ SORT
```

Likewise, you can write the sorted directory listing to a file, as follows:

```
[C:\] DIR ¦ SORT > DIR.SRT
```

You can use multiple pipe operators on the command line, as shown here:

```
[C:\] DIR ¦ SORT ¦ MORE
```

In this case, OS/2 displays a sorted listing of your files on the screen, a page at a time. The OS/2 pipe and redirection operators are quite powerful. Spend a few minutes to experiment with them.

OS/2 PIPE ¦

The OS/2 pipe operator ¦ allows you to direct the output of the program to become the input of a second program.

Additional Command-Line Operators

In addition to the I/O redirection operators (which are also found under DOS), OS/2 provides several command-line operators that may increase your command-line processing capabilities.

Consider the OS/2 command separator &, which allows you to place multiple commands on a single line, as shown here:

```
[C:\] COPY A.TXT B.TXT & COMP A.TXT B.TXT
```

In this case, OS/2 first executes the OS/2 COPY command, immediately followed by the COMP command. By separating your commands in this manner, you can place several OS/2 commands on the same line:

```
[C:\] DISKCOPY A: B: & DISKCOMP A: B: & LABEL B: & CLS
```

From the OS/2 prompt issue the following command:

```
[C:\] CHKDSK A: & CHKDSK B: & CHKDSK C:
```

As soon as the command begins executing, start typing characters on your keyboard as fast as you can. Eventually, if you are faster at typing than OS/2 is at executing the command, you will fill up the buffer into which OS/2 places each character you type.

This buffer is called the *keyboard buffer* or *type-ahead buffer*. When this occurs, the computer begins beeping with each key that you press and ignores the keys that you type.

Users often issue one command and, while that command executes, they type the next command OS/2 is to execute. In some cases, they type so many commands in advance that they fill up the OS/2 type-ahead buffer. By allowing users to place multiple commands on the initial command line and separating each command with an ampersand, OS/2 reduces the possibility of filling the keyboard buffer.

COMMAND SEPARATOR &

The OS/2 command-line separator & allows you to place multiple commands on a single command line. OS/2 executes each command, one line after another, from left to right.

The AND command-line operator && enables you to execute multiple commands that are dependent upon the result of the first command. For example, consider the following command:

```
[C:\] DIR FILES.DAT && TYPE FILES.DAT
```

If OS/2 successfully executes the DIR FILES.DAT command, it then executes the TYPE FILES.DAT command, as shown in Figure 6-9. The OS/2 AND operator only executes the second command when the first command has completed without errors. If the first command fails, OS/2 ignores the second command.

Using the AND operator as follows, you can develop an enhanced version of the RENAME command to be able to rename a file to a different device.

```
[C:\] COPY CONFIG.SAV A: && DEL CONFIG.SAV
```

In this case, if OS/2 successfully copies the file to the new location, it then deletes the file from its present disk.

To enhance your capabilities to an even greater extent, OS/2 allows you to group commands within parentheses. This enables you to perform complex command lines as shown in the following examples.

OS/2 always executes commands from left to right. In the following example, OS/2 first executes the commands contained

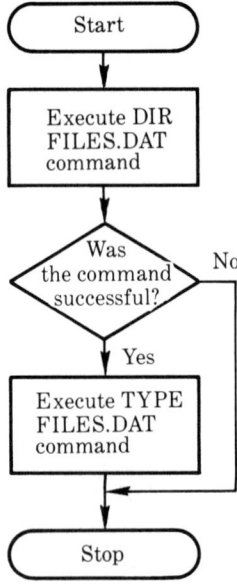

Figure 6-9. *Process of OS/2 successfully executing first command and executing a second command*

within the parentheses:

```
[C:\] (DIR FILES.DAT && TYPE FILES.DAT) && DEL FILES.DAT
```

Because this command uses the OS/2 AND operator, OS/2 executes the first command

```
    DIR FILES.DAT
```

and examines its success. If the command is successful, OS/2 then executes the next command, as follows:

```
    TYPE FILES.DAT
```

However, if the first command fails, OS/2 completes the processing of the commands remaining on the command line and starts with a "false" value at the first command-line operator.

```
    FALSE && DEL FILES.DAT
```

If both commands are successful, OS/2 continues its processing with a "true" value at the first command-line operator.

```
TRUE && DEL FILES.DAT
```

Figure 6-10 summarizes the processing involved.

GROUPING OPERATORS ( )

To enable you to perform complex logical expressions within your command line, OS/2 allows you to group commands with parentheses.

AND OPERATOR &&

The OS/2 AND command-line operator && allows you to conditionally execute a second command based on the result of the first command. If OS/2 successfully executes the first command, it then executes the second command. If the first command fails, OS/2 ignores the second command.

Similar to the OS/2 AND command-line operator (&&) is the OR operator (¦ ¦). Consider the following command:

```
[C:\] DIR A:CONFIG.SYS ¦¦ COPY B:CONFIG.SYS A:
```

In this case, OS/2 first executes the following command:

```
DIR A:CONFIG.SYS
```

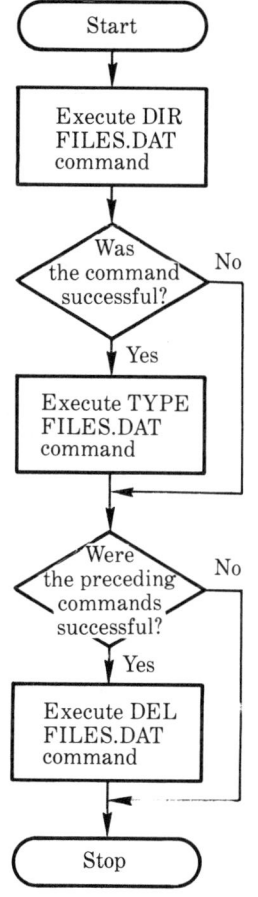

Figure 6-10. *Process of OS/2 executing commands in parentheses*

If this command is successful, the processing of the command line is complete. However, if the command fails, OS/2 performs the command to the right of the OR operator. In this case, if the file CONFIG.SYS does not exist in drive A (that is, the DIR command fails), then OS/2 copies the file CONFIG.SYS from drive B to

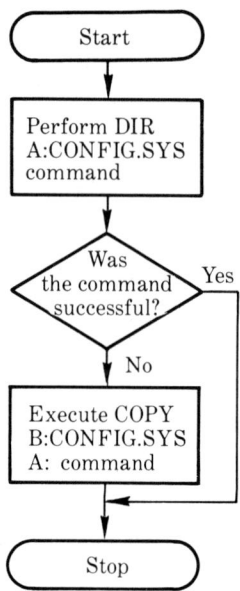

Figure 6-11. *Process of OS/2 executing commands with OR operator*

drive A. Figure 6-11 summarizes the processing involved.

Note that by grouping commands within parentheses, it is possible to combine the OS/2 OR and AND operators, as shown here:

```
[C:\] (DIR A:CONFIG.SYS && TYPE A:CONFIG.SYS) || COPY B:CONFIG.SYS A:
```

OR OPERATOR ¦¦

The OS/2 OR command-line operator ¦¦ allows you to conditionally execute a second command based on the result of the first command. If OS/2 successfully executes the first command, it ignores the second command. If the first command fails, OS/2 executes the second command.

    The OS/2 AND and OR operators may appear confusing at first. Experiment with them in order to get a better feel for their capabilities.

    OS/2 obviously has increased the number of special characters that you can place on the command line (>, >>, <, ¦ , &, &&, ¦¦). However, you may want to use one of these characters as a parameter within the command line. For example, the ampersand character "&" is a valid character in OS/2 file names. As a result, you could create an OS/2 file with the name "&":

```
C> DIR &

 Volume in drive C is OS2DISK
 Directory of  C:\WS

&               7   9-27-87  10:41a
        1 File(s)  10022912 bytes free
```

If you attempt to type the file in OS/2 protected mode, the command fails.

```
[C:\] TYPE &

DOS0002: The system cannot find the file specified.

[C:\]
```

OS/2 is using the ampersand as an operator instead of a file name. In such cases, the OS/2 command-line operator ^, called the *escape character*, directs OS/2 not to use a special symbol (such as &) as an operator. In this case, you can type the contents of "&" by using the escape character, as shown here:

```
[C:\] TYPE ^&
AAAAAAA

[C:\]
```

OS/2 ESCAPE CHARACTER ^

The OS/2 escape character ^ directs OS/2 not to use the symbol that immediately follows the escape character as an I/O redirection command-line operator.

The combinations of the commands that you can create with the OS/2 command-line operators are virtually limitless. Take some time to have some fun with these operators. In so doing, you will greatly increase your understanding of their functional capabilities.

Chapter Highlights

Most OS/2 commands write output to a predefined source called stdout (for standard output). By default, stdout points to your screen display.

In a similar manner to stdout, OS/2 defines a standard input source for commands called stdin. By default stdin points to the keyboard.

The OS/2 I/O redirection operators allow you to modify the source of input or output (or both) for a command.

The output redirection operator > allows you to direct the output of a command to a file or device.

The append redirection operator >> allows you to append the output of a command to a file.

The OS/2 input redirection operator < allows you to modify a command's source of input from the keyboard to a file.

The OS/2 pipe operator ¦ makes the output of one program become the input of a second command.

OS/2 uses the ampersand (&) as a command separator so you can place several OS/2 commands on one line.

The OS/2 logical AND operator (&&) allows you to conditionally execute one command based upon the result of the first command. If the first command is successful, OS/2 executes the second command. If the first command fails, OS/2 does not execute the second command.

The OS/2 logical OR operator (¦ ¦) allows you to conditionally execute one command based upon the result of the first command. If the first command fails, OS/2 executes the second command. However, if the first command is successful, OS/2 ignores the second command.

To increase the number of logical expressions that you can place on the command line, OS/2 allows you to group expressions by using parentheses.

The OS/2 escape character (^) allows you to direct OS/2 not to treat the character that it precedes as a redirection or command-line operator.

7 OS/2 Batch Processing

Throughout this text, you have typed in at the keyboard all of the commands that you have executed under OS/2. Processing of this type (where OS/2 obtains the commands to execute from your keyboard entry) is called *interactive processing*. OS/2 generally receives each command from your keyboard entry, processes the command, and redisplays its prompt to indicate that it is ready for another command (see Figure 7-1).

During your processing, you must wait for OS/2 to complete the execution of the current command before you can issue subsequent commands within that session. Most of the processing done on personal computers today occurs in this fashion. OS/2 allows you to group several commands into a single file, so you can execute the entire series of commands with one keyboard entry. The files that contain these lists of commands are called *batch files*. An OS/2 batch file is a text file that you can create

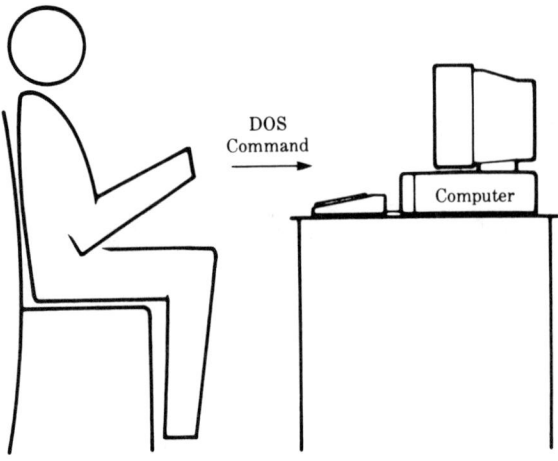

Figure 7-1. *Interactive processing*

with a text editor, word processor, or by copying the file contents from your keyboard, as shown here:

```
[C:\] COPY CON: FILENAME.CMD
```

In this case, the batch file that you are creating has the CMD extension. For users who are conversant with DOS, this differs from the BAT extension used for DOS batch files. OS/2 executes CMD batch files in protected mode and BAT batch files in real mode.

BATCH FILE EXTENSIONS

OS/2 protected-mode batch files use the file extension CMD (for example, STARTUP.CMD). OS/2 real-mode batch files use the file extension BAT (for example, AUTOEXEC.BAT). If you attempt to execute a CMD batch file in real mode, or a BAT batch file in protected mode, OS/2 will not locate the file.

OS/2 batch files provide several advantages. First, OS/2 batch files allow you to abbreviate long commands, which reduces your typing and saves you time. Second, by specifying several commands for OS/2 to execute in succession, your constant presence at the computer is no longer required, thus freeing you to do other things. Third, OS/2 batch files are programmable, so you can build a degree of "intelligence" into your processing.

OS/2 batch files allow you to abbreviate a long command or series of commands that you use on a regular basis. For example, consider the SPOOL command examined in Chapter 5.

```
[C:\] SPOOL C:\ /D:LPT1
```

Rather than typing in this command each time you start your system (or worse, trying to remember the format of the command from one computer session to the next), place it in a batch file instead, as shown here:

```
[C:\] COPY CON: SP.CMD
SPOOL C:\ /D:LPT1

        1 File(s) copied.
```

Then, each time you need to install the spooler, type the following command:

```
[C:\] SP
```

Next, consider the following Microsoft C compiler command line that compiles the contents of the file HELLO.C:

```
[C:\] cl -d -c -AS -Gsw -Oas -Zpe -Fpa -FoHello.obj Hello.c
```

Rather than typing this command line each time you need to compile the program, you can create the following OS/2 batch file to perform the same task:

```
[C:\] COPY CON: C.BAT
cl -d -c -AS -Gsw -Oas -Zpe -Fpa -FoHello.obj Hello.c
        1 File(s) copied.

[C:\]
```

Instead of typing the entire command, you can now simply type in the name of a batch file (C), which is a significant savings in keystrokes.

In addition to saving you time by reducing keystrokes, OS/2 batch files often make your time at the computer more productive. For example, consider a database application that generates a list of books for a specific topic, sorts the list by title, and then prints the list. The processing requires the following commands:

GENLIST   Creates a list of books on the given topic
SORTLIST   Sorts the list of books by title
PRTLIST   Prints the list of books

Most of the time, a user simply enters the first command at the OS/2 prompt, as shown here:

```
[C:\] GENLIST "OS/2"
```

When GENLIST completes, the user enters the command

```
[C:\] SORTLIST
```

Lastly, the user can print the book list by issuing the command

```
[C:\] PRTLIST
```

None of these commands requires user intervention once it begins. However, the user must remain close to the computer to execute the next command, preventing him or her from performing other tasks away from the computer.

OS/2 batch files provide you with a solution to this problem. First, the user creates a batch file that contains the desired commands, as shown here:

```
[C:\] COPY CON: BOOKLIST.CMD
GENLIST "OS/2"
SORTLIST
PRTLIST
^Z

        1 File(s) copied.
```

Assume that BOOKLIST.CMD is the name of the batch file. To execute the commands, the user enters

```
[C:\] BOOKLIST
```

OS/2 executes the series of commands in the batch file BOOKLIST.CMD without further user intervention. After issuing the batch file name, the user is free to perform other tasks away from the computer.

A batch file contains one or more OS/2 commands that you want to execute in succession. Most of the time you will want OS/2 to execute these commands sequentially. However, OS/2 batch files are programmable. For example, the OS/2 IF command allows you to perform one or more commands based on a specific condition (*conditional processing*), and the OS/2 FOR command allows you to repeat a specific command for a given set of files (*iterative processing*).

The following list summarizes the advantages that OS/2 batch files provide over interactive processing:

■ Batch files minimize keystrokes—and save you time—by allowing you to abbreviate a command or a series of commands.

■ Batch files allow you to group logically related commands into one file, so you can execute the series of commands without being constantly present at the computer.

■ Batch files are programmable.

The majority of your OS/2 batch processing will be sequential processing. In other words, the batch file contains a list of commands that OS/2 executes in succession (one after another) until no commands remain in the file.

For example, consider the following batch file, TEST.CMD:

```
CLS
DATE
TIME
```

When you have created this file, use the OS/2 TYPE command to display its contents, as follows:

```
[c:\] TYPE TEST.CMD

CLS
DATE
TIME

[c:\]
```

OS/2 executes this file sequentially, starting first with the CLS command, then DATE, and followed by TIME. Upon invocation, the batch file first clears the screen contents:

```
[c:\]
```

Next, it issues the OS/2 DATE command:

```
[c:\] DATE

Current date is Sat 10-03-1987
Enter new date (mm-dd-yy):
```

Lastly, the batch file invokes the OS/2 TIME command:

```
[c:\] DATE
Current date is Sat 10-03-1987
Enter new date (mm-dd-yy):
[c:\] TIME
Current time is 13:52:05.43
Enter new time:
```

OS/2 executed each command in the batch file in succession.

Since you are already familiar with the required OS/2 commands, create a batch file that clears the screen display, sets the default drive to drive A, and displays the current disk volume label.

```
CLS
A:
VOL
```

On invocation, the batch file displays the following:

```
[C:\] CLS                    OS/2 would clear the screen here.

[C:\] A:

[A:\] VOL
Volume in drive A is TESTTEST

[A:\]
```

In a similar manner, create an OS/2 batch file that clears the screen display, displays the current environment entries, and sets the system prompt to OS/2>.

```
[C:\] COY CON: TEST2.CMD
CLS
SET
PROMPT OS/2$g

        1 File(s) copied.
```

On invocation, the procedure displays the following:

```
[C:\] TEST2

[C:\] CLS                         OS/2 would clear the screen here.

[C:\WS] SET
3XBOX=command.com
COMSPEC=C:\CMD.EXE
PATH=C:\;C:\OS2;C:\TOOLS
INCLUDE=c:\include
LIB=c:\lib
INIT=c:\init

[C:\] PROMPT.OS/2$g

OS/2>
```

You should now understand the creation and execution of OS/2 batch files. Rather than getting the command from the user entry at the keyboard (as in interactive processing), OS/2 reads a command from the batch file, executes it, and reads the next command in the file (batch processing). OS/2 repeats this process until no commands remain in the batch file.

To create and execute a protected-mode OS/2 batch file, complete the following steps:

1. Create a file with the extension CMD.

2. Enter the commands you want to execute with the batch file.

3. At the OS/2 prompt, direct OS/2 to execute the commands contained in the file by entering the name of the batch file.

Thus far, all of your batch commands have had fairly simple names (TEST.CMD, BOOKLIST.CMD, and so forth). As with all OS/2 files, you must give your batch files names that are as meaningful as possible. However, keep in mind that you cannot use any of the OS/2 reserved names for batch file names, nor can you use OS/2 command names.

Each time you enter a command at the OS/2 prompt, OS/2 first checks its list of internal commands in search of a match for the command. If the command is not found, OS/2 then looks for a file that matches the command name and that has the EXE or COM extension. Last, OS/2 searches for batch files. Figure 7-2 illustrates the processing involved.

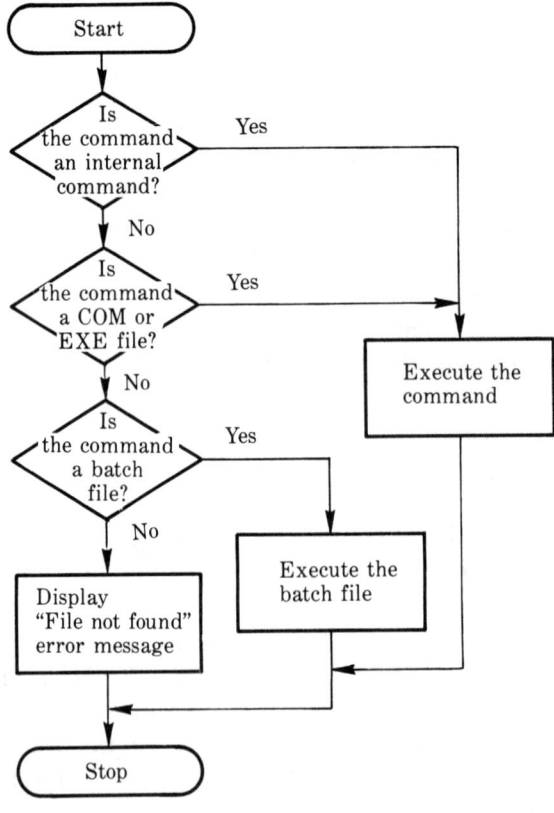

Figure 7-2. *Process of OS/2 searching for batch files*

For example, create the following batch file called PROMPT.CMD, which sets the system prompt to PROMPT>:

```
[C:\] COPY CON: PROMPT.CMD
PROMPT PROMPT$g
^Z

        1 File(s) copied.

[C:\]
```

When you attempt to execute this batch file, OS/2 does not find it. Instead, OS/2 first finds its internal PROMPT command. You have no way to execute PROMPT.CMD.

BATCH FILE NAMES

OS/2 protected-mode batch files have the extension CMD and real-mode batch files have the extension BAT. Name your batch files as meaningfully as possible. Do not use the same names that OS/2 assigns to its internal or external commands. If you do, OS/2 will never execute your batch files since it will always find the command first.

Error Processing

Occasionally, a user will place an invalid or incorrect command in a batch file. The following batch file contains a typographical error:

```
    GATE
    TIME
```

Here, the user entered the DATE command as GATE. When the user invokes this procecure, OS/2 displays

```
[C:\WS] GATE
DOS1041: The system cannot find the filename specified.

[C:\WS] TIME
The current time is: 14:10:07.28
Enter the new time:
```

If your batch file contains an error, OS/2 skips that command and processes the next command in the file. OS/2 handles the error as if the user had entered the invalid command from the keyboard, as shown here:

```
[C:\] GATE
DOS1041: The system cannot find the filename specified.
```

INVALID BATCH COMMANDS

If your batch file contains an invalid command, OS/2 displays an error message stating this and continues its processing with the next command.

File Termination

Once OS/2 begins executing the commands in your batch file, it continues until it encounters the end of the batch file. If you need to terminate the batch-file processing for any reason, press the CTRL-BREAK key combination. In protected mode, OS/2 immediately terminates the batch-file processing and returns you to the OS/2 prompt. In real mode, however, OS/2 prompts you as follows:

```
Terminate batch job (Y/N)?
```

To terminate the procedure, simply type the letter Y. If you want the batch file to execute to completion, type the letter N.

BATCH FILE TERMINATION

To terminate an OS/2 batch file, use the CTRL-BREAK key combination. In protected mode, OS/2 immediately terminates the batch job. In real mode, OS/2 first prompts you to ensure that you really want to terminate the command.

For example, consider the following batch file:

```
DATE
TIME
```

Upon invocation, the batch file displays the following:

```
[C:\] DATE
The current date is: Sat 10-03-1987
Enter the new date: (mm-dd-yy)
```

If you press the CTRL-BREAK key combination at the DATE prompt, OS/2 protected mode terminates the batch file and returns you to the system prompt.

```
[c:\]
```

However, if you are in real mode, OS/2 prompts you as follows:

```
C> DATE
The current date is: Sat 10-03-1987
Enter the new date: (mm-dd-yy) ^C

Terminate batch job (Y/N)?
```

In this case, if you type Y, OS/2 terminates the batch file. However, if you type N, OS/2 continues processing, as shown here:

```
C> DATE
The current date is: Sat 10-03-1987
Enter the new date: (mm-dd-yy) ^C

Terminate batch job (Y/N)? N

C> TIME
The current time is: 14:19:03.37
Enter the new time:
```

OS/2 Batch Commands

By now you should be conversant with the basics of OS/2 batch file processing. This section examines several OS/2 commands that will enhance your batch-processing capabilities.

REM

The OS/2 REM command displays messages during the execution of OS/2 batch files. These messages inform the user as to the state of the batch processing. For example, to enhance the book list database application, you might include the following REM statements:

```
REM Preparing list of books on the TOPIC OS/2
GENLIST "OS/2"
REM Sorting the list of books by title
SORTLIST
REM Sending the list of books to the printer
PRTLIST
```

On invocation, the procedure displays the following:

```
[C:\WS] REM Preparing list of books on the TOPIC OS/2

[C:\WS] GENLIST "OS/2"

[C:\WS] REM Sorting the list of books by title

[C:\WS] SORTLIST

[C:\WS] REM Sending the list of books to the printer

[C:\WS] PRTLIST
```

Even a user who is relatively unfamiliar with the processing performed by the database application is enlightened by the messages from REM. The format of the REM command is

REM [*message*]

where the following is true:

message is an optional string of up to 123 characters. This text is to provide the user with a meaningful message. Take time to make your messages as meaningful as possible.

The following batch file illustrates another use of REM:

```
REM allows us to display a message to the end user
REM can be used for remarks within a batch file
REM doesn't require a remark as shown next
REM
```

On invocation, the batch file displays the following:

```
[C:\]REM allows us to display a message to the end user

[C:\]REM can be used for remarks within a batch file

[C:\]REM doesn't require a remark as shown next

[C:\]REM
```

Many users also use REM to increase the readability of their batch files. For example, consider the following batch file:

```
CLS
DATE
TIME
VER
DEL *.BAK
DEL *.SAV
GENLIST "OS/2"
SORTLIST
PRTLIST
PRINT *.LOG
DEL *.LOG
```

Using REM, you can greatly increase its readability, as shown here:

```
REM
REM Clear the screen display and prompt the user
REM for the system date and time
REM
CLS
DATE
TIME

REM
REM Display the current version of OS/2
REM
VER

REM
REM Get rid of old LIST files
REM
DEL *.BAK
DEL *.SAV

REM
REM Create a new list based on OS/2, sort the list, and print it.
REM
GENLIST "OS/2"
SORTLIST
PRTLIST
PRINT *.LOG

REM
REM Delete today's log file of activities.
REM
DEL *.LOG
```

In this case, even the novice can easily understand the processing that the file performs.

PAUSE

In a manner similar to REM, the OS/2 PAUSE command displays a message to the user. Unlike REM, PAUSE suspends processing and requires the user to strike any key to continue, as shown in the following:

```
Press any key when ready.
```

The format of the OS/2 PAUSE command is

PAUSE [*message*]

where the following is true:

message is an optional message containing up to 123 characters.

If you simply place PAUSE in a batch file without any parameters,

```
PAUSE
```

the batch file displays the following:

```
Press any key when ready.
```

At this point, the user can press any key to continue execution of the batch file, or press the CTRL-BREAK key combination to terminate the batch file. Such processing is convenient when you need to suspend processing temporarily in order to perform a task (such as placing a new disk into a disk drive):

```
PAUSE Place a formatted diskette in drive A.
```

On invocation, the batch file displays the following:

```
[C:] PAUSE Place a formatted diskette in drive A.
Place a formatted diskette in drive A.
Press any key when ready.
```

Consider the following use of PAUSE:

```
PAUSE Ready to create book list.
GENLIST "OS/2"
SORTLIST
PAUSE Need a floppy diskette in drive A.
PRTLIST
```

This batch file displays

```
[C:\] PAUSE Ready to create book list.
Ready to create book list.
Press any key when ready.
[C:\] GENLIST "OS/2"
[C:\] PAUSE Need a floppy diskette in drive A.
Need a floopy diskette in drive A.
Press any key to continue.
[C:\] PRTLIST
```

However, be careful not to overuse PAUSE. In this example,

```
PAUSE Ready to create book list.
GENLIST "OS/2"
PAUSE Ready to sort book list.
SORTLIST
PAUSE Need a floppy diskette in drive A.
PRTLIST
```

the batch file pauses after each command to display a message
to the user and prompts the user to press any key to continue.

```
[C:\] PAUSE Ready to create book list.
Ready to create book list.
Press any key when ready.
[C:\] GENLIST "OS/2"
PAUSE Ready to sort book list.
Ready to sort book list.
Press any key when ready.
[C:\] SORTLIST
PAUSE Need a floppy diskette in drive A.
Need a floppy diskette in drive A.
[C:\] PRTLIST
```

In this way one of the major advantages of batch file processing
is lost, because the commands can no longer execute without
user intervention.

ECHO

So far, all of the batch files have displayed on the screen the
names of the commands that they are executing:

```
[C:\] GENLIST "OS/2"

[C:\] SORTLIST

[C:\] PRTLIST
```

However, you may sometimes want to suppress the command
names or messages normally displayed by REM. The OS/2
ECHO command allows you to suppress batch-file command
names and messages from display to the end user. The format
of the OS/2 ECHO command is

ECHO [*ON* ¦ *OFF* ¦ *message*]

where the following is true:

ON directs OS/2 to display the names of the commands as they execute within OS/2 batch files.

OFF directs OS/2 to suppress the display of command names as the commands execute within OS/2 batch files. Messages normally displayed by REM are also suppressed.

message directs OS/2 to display an optional string of up to 123 characters.

The bar (¦) that appears between the words *ON*, *OFF*, and *message* means that you must select one of the three options. This bar is the OR operator. You can use the *ON*, *OFF*, or *message* options, but not a combination of the three.

If you simply invoke ECHO from the OS/2 prompt, ECHO displays its current state (on or off):

```
[C:\] ECHO
ECHO is on.

[C:\]
```

Consider this database batch file example:

```
GENLIST "OS/2"
SORTLIST
PRTLIST
```

On invocation, the file displays the following:

```
[C:\] GENLIST "OS/2"

[C:\] SORTLIST

[C:\] PRTLIST
```

If you place the command ECHO OFF at the start of the file

```
ECHO OFF
GENLIST "OS/2"
SORTLIST
PRTLIST
```

OS/2 indeed suppresses the display of the command names as they execute.

```
[c:\] ECHO OFF
[c:\]
```

The following batch procedure verifies that ECHO OFF also suppresses messages normally displayed by REM:

```
REM SHOULD DISPLAY
REM ALSO DISPLAYED
ECHO OFF
REM NOT DISPLAYED
REM NOT SEEN
```

On invocation, the procedure displays the following:

```
[C:\WS]REM SHOULD DISPLAY

[C:\WS]REM ALSO DISPLAYED

[C:\WS]ECHO OFF
```

Many people use ECHO to display a series of messages to the end user, as shown here:

```
ECHO OFF
ECHO "-------------------------------------------------"
ECHO "|                Book List Generation            |"
ECHO "|                                                 |"
ECHO "|   This program executes three commands:         |"
ECHO "|      GENLIST "TOPIC"                             |"
ECHO "|      SORTLIST                                    |"
ECHO "|      PRTLIST                                     |"
ECHO "|                                                 |"
ECHO "-------------------------------------------------"
```

On invocation of this batch procedure, OS/2 displays the following:

```
[C:\WS]ECHO OFF
"-------------------------------------------------"
"|                Book List Generation            |"
"|                                                 |"
"|   This program executes three commands:         |"
"|      GENLIST "TOPIC"                             |"
"|      SORTLIST                                    |"
"|      PRTLIST                                     |"
"|                                                 |"
"-------------------------------------------------"
```

The ECHO OFF command at the top of the previous batch file is essential. Without it, OS/2 would display (echo) the name of each command as it executed within the file (including ECHO). As such, the batch file

```
ECHO "-------------------------------------------------"
ECHO "-------------------------------------------------"
ECHO "|                Book List Generation            |"
ECHO "|                                                 |"
ECHO "|   This program executes three commands:         |"
ECHO "|      GENLIST "TOPIC"                             |"
ECHO "|      SORTLIST                                    |"
ECHO "|      PRTLIST                                     |"
ECHO "|                                                 |"
```

would display

```
[C:\WS]ECHO "--------------------------------------------------"
"--------------------------------------------------"

[C:\WS]ECHO "|                    Book List Generation        |"
"|              Book List Generation           |"

[C:\WS]ECHO "|                                                |"
"|                                          |"

[C:\WS]ECHO "|  This program executes three commands:         |"
"|  This program executes three commands:   |"

[C:\WS]ECHO "|        GENLIST "TOPIC"                          |"
"|      GENLIST "TOPIC"                      |"

[C:\WS]ECHO "|        SORTLIST                                |"
"|      SORTLIST                             |"

[C:\WS]ECHO "|        PRTLIST                                 |"
"|      PRTLIST                              |"

[C:\WS]ECHO "|                                                |"
"|                                          |"

[C:\WS]ECHO "--------------------------------------------------"
"--------------------------------------------------"
```

Chapter 6 discussed OS/2 I/O redirection. You can use the ECHO command as a source of input for a program that obtains its input from the standard input device. For example, consider the following command:

```
[C:\] ECHO "OS2DISK" ¦ LABEL A:
```

In this case, OS/2 redirects the message OS2DISK to the OS/2 LABEL command, which uses the message as the desired label for the disk in drive A.

Conditional Batch Processing

All of the batch procedures examined thus far have been sequential — executing commands in order, beginning with the first command and ending with the last. Sequential batch files exhibit no decision-making capabilities. The OS/2 IF command enables your batch files to perform simple decision-making. The format of the IF command is

IF [*NOT*] *condition OS2__COMMAND*

where the following is true:

NOT directs OS/2 to perform a Boolean NOT of the result of the condition. For example, if the condition is TRUE, a NOT condition results in a FALSE. Likewise, if the condition is FALSE, a NOT condition results in a TRUE.

condition must be one of the following:

    ERRORLEVEL number
    EXIST file__specification
    STRING1==STRING2

OS2__COMMAND is the command that you want OS/2 to execute when the condition is TRUE.

The first condition, ERRORLEVEL number, works as follows. Most programs return a status value to OS/2 when they terminate. The ERRORLEVEL condition tests the value of this status. For example, the following batch procedure first executes the program GENLIST. If GENLIST exists with a status value greater than or equal to 1, the batch file then executes the command SORTLIST. If the exit status of GENLIST is less than 1, the batch file terminates without executing SORTLIST.

```
GENLIST "OS/2"
IF NOT ERRORLEVEL 1 SORTLIST
```

The OS/2 IF command enables your batch files to perform simple decision-making. Figure 7-3 summarizes the processing of the previous batch file.

In a similar manner, the following batch file (DISPLAY.CMD) searches the current disk for the file TEST.TXT. If the file is found, the DIR command returns the status value 0. If the file is not found, DIR returns a status value of 1.

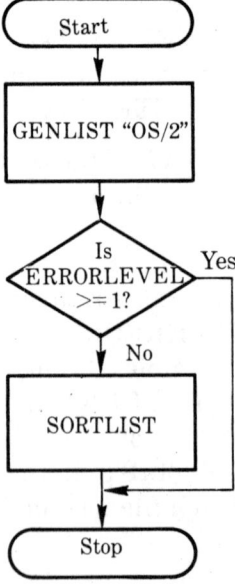

Figure 7-3. *Processing of sample batch file*

```
ECHO OFF
DIR TEST.TXT
IF ERRORLEVEL 1 ECHO NO SUCH FILE -- TEST.TXT
IF NOT ERRORLEVEL 1 TYPE TEST.TXT
```

With this in mind, the batch file can use the ERRORLEVEL condition either to display the contents of the file or to display the following message:

```
NO SUCH FILE -- TEST.TXT
```

The second IF condition, EXIST file—specification, evaluates as TRUE when the file name specified in file—specification exists as stated. For example, the following conditions are valid uses of the IF EXIST expression:

```
IF EXIST C:STARTUP.CMD TYPE C:STARTUP.CMD
IF EXIST A:\SUBDIR\A.NTS   COPY A:\SUBDIR\A.NTS B:
IF EXIST B.TXT COMP B.TXT A.TXT
```

Using this condition, you can change the previous batch file from

```
ECHO OFF
DIR TEST.TXT
IF ERRORLEVEL 1 ECHO NO SUCH FILE -- TEST.TXT
IF NOT ERRORLEVEL 1 TYPE TEST.TXT
```

to

```
ECHO OFF
IF EXIST TEST.TXT TYPE TEST.TXT
IF NOT EXIST TEST.TXT ECHO NO SUCH FILE -- TEST.TXT
```

If the file TEST.TXT exists, OS/2 displays its contents. Otherwise, OS/2 displays the following message:

```
NO SUCH FILE -- TEST.TXT
```

Note the use of the Boolean NOT in the following expression:

```
IF NOT EXIST TEST.TXT ECHO NO SUCH FILE -- TEST.TXT
```

The file specification in the IF EXIST condition is a complete OS/2 path name containing an optional disk drive identifier. The following batch procedure checks to see if the file CONFIG.SYS exists on drive A. If not, the procedure copies the file from drive B.

```
IF NOT EXIST A:CONFIG.SYS COPY B:CONFIG.SYS A:
```

Figure 7-4 illustrates the processing performed.

The OS/2 IF STRING1==STRING2 condition evaluates as TRUE when the characters contained in STRING1 are identical to those contained in STRING2. Consider the following example:

```
IF OS/2==OS/2 ECHO SAME STRINGS
```

Since both strings are identical, the batch procedure displays the following message:

SAME STRINGS

In order for OS/2 to evaluate the strings as equal, the characters in each string must match identically. OS/2 does not consider the following strings to be identical:

```
OS/2==os/2
```

Later in this chapter, during the discussion of batch-file parameters, the use of this condition will become clearer.

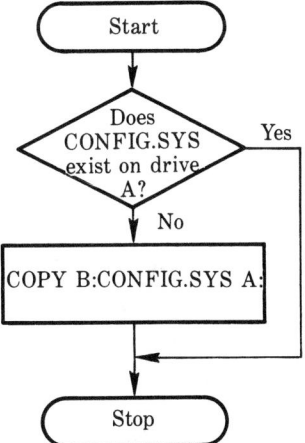

Figure 7-4. *Process of checking IF EXIST condition*

OS/2 IF COMMAND

The OS/2 IF command enables you to develop decision-making capabilities within your batch files. The IF command supports the following three conditions:

    ERRORLEVEL value
    EXIST file—specification
    STRING1==STRING2

If the specified condition is true, IF executes the OS/2 command that follows.

Branching with GOTO

The OS/2 GOTO command provides your batch files with an even greater degree of programmability. The format of the GOTO command is

GOTO *label—name*

where the following is true:

label—name is a unique sequence of characters that defines a location within the batch file to which OS/2 is to branch. OS/2 distinguishes labels from batch commands by preceding the label with a colon (:OS2LABEL). (Keep in mind that OS/2 uses only the first eight characters of a label, although labels may be virtually any length. For example, OS/2 considers the label names OS2—LABEL1 and OS2—LABEL2 to be identical.) When OS/2 reads a line from the batch file that begins with a colon, OS/2 knows that it has a label, and does not attempt to execute the label as a command.

The following OS/2 batch file verifies that OS/2 only distinguishes between the first eight characters of a label name:

```
GOTO OS2_LABEL2
:OS2_LABEL1
ECHO OS2_LABEL1
:OS2_LABEL2
ECHO OS2_LABEL2
```

Although the GOTO command specifies the label name OS2_LABEL2, OS/2 first matches the label with OS2_LABEL1 (remember only the first eight characters are used, thus yielding OS2_LABE). On invocation, the procedure displays the following:

```
[c:\] GOTO OS2_LABEL2

[c:\] ECHO OS2_LABEL1
OS2_LABEL1

[c:\] ECHO OS2_LABEL2
OS2_LABEL2
```

The following OS/2 batch file uses the GOTO command to produce an infinite loop that will run indefinitely and display the message "Infinite Loop":

```
ECHO OFF
:LOOP
ECHO INFINITE LOOP
GOTO LOOP
```

On invocation, the procedure displays the following:

```
[C:\] ECHO OFF
INFINITE LOOP
INFINITE LOOP
INFINITE LOOP
INFINITE LOOP
INFINITE LOOP
INFINITE LOOP
INFINITE LOOP
INFINITE LOOP
INFINITE LOOP
```

The only way to terminate this procedure is to press the CTRL-BREAK key combination.

The following batch procedure checks for the file STARTUP.CMD on drive C.

```
ECHO OFF
IF EXIST C:STARTUP.CMD GOTO DISPLAY
ECHO FILE DOES NOT EXIST
GOTO DONE
:DISPLAY
TYPE STARTUP.CMD
:DONE
```

If the file does not exist, the batch file displays the following message:

```
FILE DOES NOT EXIST
```

If the file does exist, the procedure displays the contents of the file.

The OS/2 GOTO command used in conjunction with the IF command provides considerable programmability of your batch files.

If a GOTO command references a nonexistent label, OS/2 terminates the batch processing. Consider the following batch file:

```
GOTO NO_LABEL
:N
:NO
:NO_
:NO_L
:NO_LA
:NO_LAB
```

On invocation, the procedure displays the following:

```
[C:\] GOTO NO_LABEL
DOS1039: The system cannot find the batch label specified.
```

NONEXISTENT BATCH LABELS

If your batch file uses GOTO to branch to a label that does not exist in the batch file, OS/2 displays an error message and terminates the batch-file processing.

The OS/2 IF and GOTO commands are examined in more detail later in this chapter when OS/2 batch-file parameters are introduced.

Iterative Processing

An iterative process repeats itself during a specific interval of time. In programming, iterative processing allows a program to repeat a series of instructions for a given duration. You have already seen one form of iterative processing when you used the OS/2 GOTO command:

```
ECHO OFF
:LOOP
ECHO INFINITE LOOP
GOTO LOOP
```

In this case, OS/2 repeated a series of instructions for a given period of time (until the user pressed CTRL-BREAK).

OS/2 also provides a second iterative construct, the FOR command. FOR directs OS/2 to repeat a specific instruction for a given set of files. The format of the OS/2 FOR command is

FOR *%%variable* IN (*set*) DO *OS2_COMMAND*

where the following is true:

%%variable is the name of a memory location in which OS/2 stores the name of a file it is to use during the current iteration of the loop.

set is a collection of OS/2 file names separated by commas. OS/2 wildcard characters are valid file names for use within the set. For example, the following are valid OS/2 file names:

STARTUP.CMD, CONFIG.SYS

*.CMD, *.BAT

.

OS2_COMMAND is the name of the OS/2 command that FOR is to execute with each iteration of the loop. The OS/2 FOR command cannot be used as the *OS2_COMMAND*. In other words, the FOR command cannot appear twice on the command line.

OS/2 executes the FOR command as follows. On the first iteration (first loop), OS/2 places the first file name in the set into the variable *%%variable*. OS/2 then issues the command associated with *OS2—COMMAND*.

For example, consider the following FOR loop:

FOR %%V in (STARTUP.CMD, CONFIG.SYS) DO TYPE %%V

On the first pass through the loop, OS/2 assigns the variable %%V the value STARTUP.CMD and executes the command TYPE %%V. Since the variable %%V actually contains the name STARTUP.CMD, the command is identical to TYPE STARTUP.CMD. When the command completes, OS/2 performs the second pass through the loop assigning %%V the name CONFIG.SYS. In this case, the command TYPE %%V is equivalent to the command TYPE CONFIG.SYS. OS/2 then attempts to loop for a third time. However, no more files remain in the set of file names, so the FOR loop terminates. Figure 7-5 illustrates the processing involved.

The following batch file clears the screen display and then types the contents of all of your protected-mode batch files (*.CMD). In this case, OS/2 expands *.CMD to match each of the files with the CMD extension.

```
CLS
FOR %%V IN (*.CMD) DO TYPE %%V
```

Likewise, the following procedure displays all of your protected- and real-mode batch files:

```
CLS
FOR %%V IN (*.CMD, *.BAT) DO TYPE %%V
```

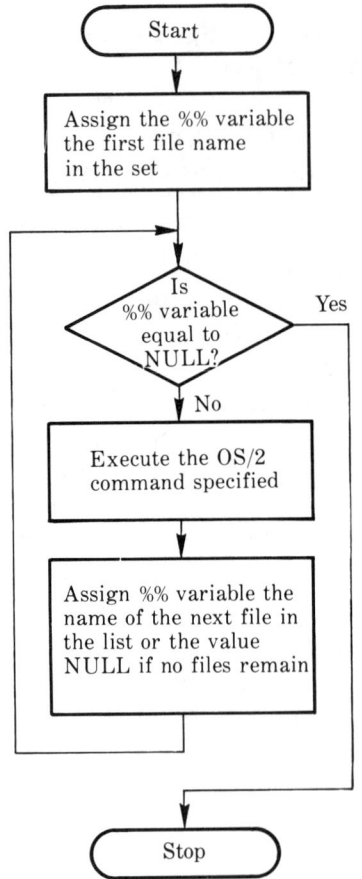

Figure 7-5. *Iterative processing*

Although the FOR command is most frequently used for batch processing, OS/2 also allows you to issue the FOR command from the OS/2 prompt. In this case, use a single percent sign (%) in front of your variable name, as shown here:

```
FOR %V IN (*.CMD, *.BAT) DO TYPE %V
```

Just as with the OS/2 batch file, this command displays the contents of each of your OS/2 batch files.

The use of OS/2 batch parameters will enhance the OS/2 FOR command, as shown later in this chapter.

OS/2 Batch-File Parameters

OS/2 batch files provide you with tremendous flexibility and time savings. You have seen how to abbreviate OS/2 commands by using batch files and how to add a degree of "intelligence" to your batch files by using the OS/2 IF, GOTO, and FOR commands. This section discusses how to increase the number of applications that your batch files support by using OS/2 batch-file parameters. In essence, you will make your batch files more generic, and in turn increase their flexibility. Your batch files will meet the requirements for many applications instead of just one specific command.

Consider the following batch file:

```
IF NOT EXIST B.TXT COPY A.TXT B.TXT
```

Although the batch file serves its function (copying the contents of the file A.TXT to the file B.TXT), it has no other use. In other words, the only time that you would execute this command is when the file that you want to copy happens to be named A.TXT, and the destination file just happens to be named B.TXT. A more useful batch file would allow you to execute this command for any two files.

A *batch parameter* is a value that you place in the command line each time you invoke the batch procedure from the OS/2 prompt. For example, consider the following command:

```
[C:\] MYCOPY SOURCE.TXT TARGET.TXT
```

In this case, MYCOPY is assumed to be an existing batch file. SOURCE.TXT and TARGET.TXT are the batch-file parameters (or values) that you want the command to use.

```
[C:\] MYCOPY SOURCE.TXT TARGET.TXT
        Batch file    Batch-file parameters
```

You access batch file parameters within your files by using the variables %0 to %9. In the following command,

```
[C:\] MYCOPY SOURCE.TXT TARGET.TXT
```

the parameters contain the following:

%0 contains MYCOPY
%1 contains SOURCE.TXT
%2 contains TARGET.TXT
%3 contains NULL
.
.
.
%9 contains NULL

Note that OS/2 assigns the NULL value to batch parameters not having a corresponding command-line parameter. The previous batch file

```
IF NOT EXIST B.TXT COPY A.TXT B.TXT
```

becomes

```
IF NOT EXIST %2 COPY %1 %2
```

You have used the OS/2 batch parameters to increase the number of applications that the batch file supports. If you invoke the procedure with

```
[C:\] MYCOPY A.TXT B.TXT
```

OS/2 substitutes A.TXT into %1 and B.TXT in %2 to yield the following:

```
IF NOT EXIST B.TXT COPY A.TXT B.TXT
```

In a similar manner, the following batch file allows you to abbreviate the OS/2 DIR command as D:

```
[C:\] COPY CON: D.CMD
DIR %1
^Z
        1 File(s) copied.
```

If you invoke the batch file with

```
[C:\] D STARTUP.CMD
```

the procedure performs a directory listing of the file STARTUP.CMD. Likewise, if you invoke the file as

```
[C:\] D *.TXT
```

the procedure lists the directory entries for each file with the TXT extension. Finally, if you invoke the procedure without any command-line arguments

```
[C:\] D
```

the file simply issues the OS/2 DIR command and displays a directory listing of all files.

The OS/2 protected-mode DIR command, however, allows you to perform directory listings of multiple files, as follows:

```
[C:\] DIR A.TXT B.TXT C:*.*
```

In this case, you can use the remaining parameters to obtain a similar command, as follows:

```
DIR %1 %2 %3 %4 %5 %6 %7 %8 %9
```

If you invoke the procedure with

```
[C:\] D STARTUP.CMD CONFIG.SYS
```

OS/2 performs a directory listing of the file STARTUP.CMD and then a directory listing of CONFIG.SYS. Likewise, if you invoke the procedure with

```
[C:\] D *.CMD *.BAT *.SYS
```

OS/2 first lists all of the files with the CMD extension, then those with BAT, and, last, those with the SYS extension.

The OS/2 batch parameter %0 always contains the name of the batch file that is executing. In this case, the following batch file displays its own contents:

```
TYPE %0.CMD
```

On invocation, %0 contains the name of the batch file. By simply adding the CMD extension, you create a complete OS/2 file specification.

You can use OS/2 batch parameters with the IF command.

As such, you can test for nonexistent batch parameters. For example, the following batch file (T.CMD) checks for the existence of the file specified by %1.

```
ECHO OFF
IF NOT '%1'=='' TYPE %1
IF '%1'=='' ECHO NO FILE SPECIFIED
```

If the file exists, the procedure displays the contents of the file. If the file does not exist, the procedure displays the following message:

```
NO FILE SPECIFIED
```

Note the following test:

```
IF '%1'=='' ECHO NO FILE SPECIFIED
```

If OS/2 does not have a value for a batch parameter, it assigns the parameter the value NULL. When this occurs, the following test for the NULL string becomes TRUE.

```
'%1'==''
```

Sometimes you may need more than nine batch parameters (%0 though %9). The OS/2 SHIFT command provides you with a solution. The format of the SHIFT command is

SHIFT

SHIFT rotates the values of each batch parameter one location to the left. For example, the command line

```
[C:\] TEST ONE TWO THREE
```

results in the following batch parameters:

%0 contains TEST
%1 contains ONE
%2 contains TWO
%3 contains THREE
%4 contains NULL
.
.
.
%9 contains NULL

Invoking the SHIFT command one time results in the following:

%0 contains ONE
%1 contains TWO
%2 contains THREE
%3 contains NULL
.
.
.
%9 contains NULL

Likewise, the next invocation of SHIFT produces the following:

%0 contains TWO
%1 contains THREE
%2 contains NULL
.
.
.
%9 contains NULL

If your command line has more than nine parameters on the command line

```
[C:\] TEST A B C D E F G H I J K L
```

SHIFT rotates a new parameter in %9 with each invocation. When no new parameters exist, SHIFT replaces %9 with the NULL parameter. The following batch procedure uses the fact that SHIFT will eventually shift a NULL value into %9 (or place a NULL in %9) to start. The procedure displays each of its batch parameters one at a time and shifts each to the left with each iteration. Once the value in %1 is NULL, the procedure terminates.

```
ECHO OFF
:LOOP
IF '%1'=='' GOTO DONE
ECHO %1
SHIFT
GOTO LOOP
:DONE
```

For example, if you invoke the procedure with

```
[C:\] TEST A B C D E F G
```

the procedure displays the following:

```
[C:\] TEST A B C D E F G
[C:\] ECHO OFF
A
B
C
D
E
F
G
```

If you want to watch the actual shift of parameters occur, use ECHO as shown here:

```
ECHO OFF
:LOOP
IF '%1'=='' GOTO DONE
ECHO %1 %2 %3 %4 %5 %6 %7 %8 %9
SHIFT
GOTO LOOP
:DONE
```

In this case, invoking the procedure with

```
[C:\] TEST A B C D E
```

results in the following:

```
[C:\] TEST A B C D E
[C:\] ECHO OFF
A B C D E
B C D E
C D E
D E
E

[C:\]
```

Removing a Batch-File Disk

At times during your batch processing, you may have to remove
the floppy disk containing the procedure in order to continue
processing. When this occurs, OS/2 displays the following message when it completes the command:

```
Insert the diskette that contains the batch file
and press any key when ready.
```

Place the original disk that contains the batch file in the disk
drive and press the ENTER key. Once the disk containing the
batch file is in the drive, OS/2 continues processing the batch
file.

Changing Your Default Drive

OS/2 allows you to change the current default drive during the
execution of an OS/2 batch file. For example, consider the following batch file:

```
A:
VOL
```

On invocation, OS/2 displays

```
[C:\] A:

[A:\] VOL
Volume in drive A is DOSHELP

[A:\]
```

When OS/2 completes the processing of the batch file, the default remains drive A.

The OS/2 batch file commands SETLOCAL and END-LOCAL work in conjunction within a batch file. OS/2 allows you to change the default disk drive within your batch files. When the batch file completes, your default disk drive remains the same as the last disk drive identifier to which the disk was set. The OS/2 SETLOCAL and ENDLOCAL commands work in conjunction to save and restore the default disk drive, directory, and environment contents.

In a manner similar to the previous batch file, this batch procedure changes the system prompt to OS/2>:

```
PROMPT OS/2$g
```

On completion of the command, the prompt is changed, as shown here:

```
OS/2>
```

However, frequently you do not want changes such as this to remain in effect on completion of the batch procedure. In such cases, use SETLOCAL and ENDLOCAL, as shown here:

```
SETLOCAL
A:
VOL
ENDLOCAL
```

In this case, the first command executed is SETLOCAL, which saves the current disk drive, directory, and environment entries. Next, the batch file changes the default drive. The batch procedure then invokes the ENDLOCAL command, which restores the previously saved disk, directory, and environment entries and prevents them from being changed by the batch procedure.

PRESERVING SETTINGS

The OS/2 SETLOCAL and ENDLOCAL commands work in conjunction to save and later restore the current disk drive, directory, and environment settings. As such, no matter what processing a batch file performs, SETLOCAL and ENDLOCAL ensure that no adverse effects occur.

OS/2 Nested Batch Procedures

Sometimes one batch procedure must invoke a second batch procedure in order to complete its processing. If the second batch procedure is the last command in your file, you have no problems.

```
CLS
DATE
BATFILE
```

However, if the batch procedure is nested in the middle of your batch file,

```
CLS
BATFILE
DATE
```

you must invoke the procedure by using the OS/2 CALL command, as shown here:

```
CLS
CALL BATFILE
DATE
```

The format of the CALL command is

CALL *batch__file* [*argument*]

where the following is true:

batch__file is the complete OS/2 file specification of the batch file to invoke.

argument is an optional batch parameter OS/2 passes to the nested batch procedure. OS/2 can access the argument within the nested batch file by using variables %1 to %9.

Consider the batch file VOLUME.CMD, which sets the default drive to disk specified by %1 and then invokes the OS/2 VOL command:

```
SETLOCAL
%1
VOL
ENDLOCAL
```

The following batch file invokes VOLUME.CMD as a nested batch procedure by using CALL:

```
CLS
CALL VOLUME A:
LABEL
```

On invocation, the procedure clears the screen contents, invokes VOLUME.CMD with the parameter A:, and issues the OS/2 LABEL command for the current drive. This processing could be easily implemented with one batch file. However, there may be times when you have developed a useful batch file that you want to use within another batch file. Rather than having to include that file within your new batch file, you can simply invoke it by using CALL.

Changing the Command Processor

By default, each time you invoke an OS/2 batch file, the file CMD.EXE serves as the command-line processor that examines the contents of each line of the file and executes the required commands. The CMD.EXE file also serves as the OS/2 command-line processor. Each time you enter a command at the keyboard, the program contained in CMD.EXE actually reads and processes the command.

CMD.EXE

The CMD.EXE file contains the command-line processor. Each time you enter a command from the keyboard, CMD.EXE reads and executes the command.

In rare cases, a user may need to specify an alternate command-line processor for a specific batch file. The OS/2 EXTPROC command allows you to specify a command-line processor other than CMD.EXE for the current batch file. The format of the command is

EXTPROC *file___specification*

where the following is true:

file___specification is the complete OS/2 file specification for the file that will serve as the command-line processor in this batch file.

Consider the following example:

```
EXTPROC MYSHELL.EXE
X1
Y1
RESULT
```

Here, the batch file has substituted the file MYSHELL.EXE as the command-line processor for this batch file (replacing CMD.EXE). The EXTPROC command must be the first command in the batch file. (Most users will never require this command.)

OS/2 Named Batch File
Parameters

This chapter previously discussed the OS/2 batch-file parameters %0 to %9. Recall that using these parameters allows you to greatly increase the functionality of your commands. In a similar manner, OS/2 allows you to create a named parameter by using the SET command, as follows:

SET NAMED_PARAMETER=VALUE

For example, this command creates a named parameter, called FILE, and assigns it the value STARTUP.CMD:

```
[C:\] SET FILE=STARTUP.CMD
```

Once you have created a named parameter by using the SET command, you can access the named parameter within your batch files by grouping the named parameter within percent signs, as shown here:

```
CLS
TYPE %FILE%
```

In this case, the batch file displays the contents of the file STARTUP.CMD. If you have not yet assigned a value to the named parameter, the batch file displays the following:

```
DOS0002: The system cannot find the file specified.
```

STARTUP.CMD

Each time your system boots, OS/2 examines the root directory on the boot disk for the file STARTUP.CMD. If it does not find this file, OS/2 displays the familiar Session Manager menu.

If the file exists, OS/2 executes it in the same manner as all of the batch files examined thus far. In this way, you can define a list of commands that you want OS/2 to execute each time the system boots. Consider the following batch file:

```
[C:\] COPY CON: STARTUP.CMD
CLS
PROMPT PROT>
^Z

        1 File(s) copied.
```

In this case, when OS/2 boots, it clears the screen display and sets the system prompt. OS/2 will automatically retain a protected-mode session.

STARTUP.CMD

Each time OS/2 boots, it searches the root directory of the boot device for the file STARTUP.CMD. IF OS/2 finds this batch file, it executes its contents. Otherwise, OS/2 displays the Session Manager menu. OS/2 only invokes STARTUP.CMD at boot time and not with each new session.

However, note that OS/2 only executes STARTUP.CMD at boot time. It does not invoke the batch file each time you create a protected-mode session.

/Q Qualifier

Earlier this chapter explained how to suppress the display of command names within a batch file by setting ECHO OFF. Similarly, you can suppress command-name display by placing a /Q at the end of the command line, invoking the batch file as shown here:

[C:\] CMDFILE /Q

You can also precede command names with @, and OS/2 will suppress command name display. Consider this batch file:

@DATE
@TIME

OS/2 will suppress each command as the file executes.

STARTUP.CMD Versus AUTOEXEC.BAT

For experienced DOS users, STARTUP.CMD looks like the AUTOEXEC.BAT file, which allows you to define a list of commands DOS executes at system boot time. Under OS/2, AUTOEXEC.BAT does not go away. Recall that OS/2 real-mode batch files have the extension BAT. As such, AUTOEXEC. BAT is a real-mode batch file. The first time you select the real-mode session, OS/2 examines the root directory of the boot device for the AUTOEXEC.BAT file. If the file exists, OS/2 executes its contents. If not, OS/2 displays the real-mode prompt.

However, note that OS/2 only invokes STARTUP.CMD the first time you start the system.

DETACH (The OS/2 Background Dispatcher)

OS/2 takes the convenience of batch-file processing one step further and allows you to execute programs in the background mode of your current session while you issue commands from the foreground mode.

The OS/2 DETACH command allows you execute other programs as background tasks. The format of the DETACH command is

DETACH *OS2_COMMAND_LINE*

where the following is true:

OS2_COMMAND_LINE specifies the command you want OS/2 to execute in the background. The command must be one that does not require user intervention while it executes.

Consider the following examples. The following command writes a directory listing of the current disk to the file DIR.DAT in the background, leaving you free to execute other tasks in the foreground:

```
[C:\] DETACH DIR > DIR.LST
```

Likewise, the following command writes the output of the CHKDSK command to the file DISK.STS:

```
[C:\] DETACH CHKDSK > DISK.STS
```

On invocation, the command displays the following:

```
The Process identification number is 34.
```

The process identification number is the means by which OS/2 tracks processes within the system. Although this message is purely informational, it does assure you that OS/2 has started the background processing.

The OS/2 DETACH command is most convenient. Spend some time now becoming familiar with its capabilities.

Chapter Highlights

Most of the commands that OS/2 executes are interactive commands. The user enters the command at the keyboard, OS/2 processes the command, and then redisplays the system prompt for the next command.

In addition to interactive commands, OS/2 allows you to group logically related commands, or to abbreviate a long command, by using a batch file. A batch file is a text file that contains the names of the commands you want OS/2 to execute.

OS/2 protected-mode batch files have the CMD extension (such as STARTUP.CMD). OS/2 real-mode batch files have the BAT extension (such as AUTOEXEC.BAT).

Batch processing has the following advantages over interactive processing:

■ Batch files minimize keystrokes by allowing you to abbreviate a command or a series of commands, saving you time.

■ Batch files enable you to group logically related commands into one file. This allows you to execute a series of commands without having to be constantly present at the computer.

■ Batch files are programmable.

The OS/2 REM command allows your batch files to display messages to the end user as your batch file executes.

Like REM, the OS/2 PAUSE command displays a message to the end user. In addition, PAUSE temporarily suspends processing and requests the user to press a key to continue.

If your batch file contains an invalid command, OS/2 simply displays an error message and continues its processing by going on to the next command in the batch file.

To terminate a batch file, press the CTRL-BREAK key combination. In protected mode, OS/2 immediately terminates the batch file. In real mode, OS/2 first prompts you to ensure that you really want to terminate processing.

The OS/2 ECHO command allows you to suppress the display of command names as they execute within a batch file. In addition, ECHO allows you to display messages to the end user.

The OS/2 IF command allows your batch files to perform simple decision-making based on the following conditions:

ERRORLEVEL number
EXIST file_specification
STRING1==STRING2

The OS/2 GOTO command allows your batch procedure to branch from one location in the batch file to another. OS/2 uses labels as the target for the GOTO command.

The OS/2 FOR command allows you to repeat a specific command for a given set of files. The FOR command is an OS/2 iterative batch processing construct.

Just as many OS/2 commands support command-line arguments, OS/2 allows you to pass values into your batch procedures. OS/2 stores these values in variables named %1 to %9. If your batch file requires more than nine parameters, you can use the OS/2 SHIFT command to expand the parameter-processing capabilities.

Each time you change a default drive, directory, or environment entry within an OS/2 batch file, that change remains in effect when the procedure has completed execution. To prevent such changes from being permanent, OS/2 provides the SETLOCAL and ENDLOCAL commands. These two commands work in conjunction to save and restore the current disk, directory, and environment contents.

Many batch files must invoke a second batch procedure to complete their processing. The OS/2 CALL command allows you to invoke another batch procedure from within your current batch file.

Each time you enter a command from the keyboard or execute a command from within an OS/2 protected-mode batch file, the program CMD.EXE serves as the command-line processor. In rare cases, you may need to specify a batch command-line processor other than CMD.EXE. The OS/2 EXTPROC command allows you to do this.

In addition to the parameters %0 to %9, OS/2 allows you to define named parameters by using the OS/2 SET command. Once the named parameter is defined, you can access its value later by grouping the parameter within quotes.

Each time OS/2 boots, it examines the boot disk for the STARTUP.CMD file. If OS/2 finds this file, it executes the contents of the file and leaves you with a protected-mode prompt. If OS/2 does not find this file, it displays the Session Manager menu.

In a manner similar to STARTUP.CMD, the first time that OS/2 selects the real-mode session, it executes the contents of the AUTOEXEC.BAT file. This file allows you to define the commands that you want OS/2 to execute before you receive the real-mode prompt for the first time.

In a manner similiar to ECHO OFF, OS/2 allows you to append /Q qualifier when you invoke OS/2 batch procedure. Likewise, if you precede each command name within a batch file with an @ symbol, OS/2 will suppress the command-name display.

Last, the OS/2 DETACH command allows you to execute a command in background mode. The command must be such that it requires no user intervention once it begins execution. Once you execute a background command by using DETACH, OS/2 displays its system prompt to allow you to continue executing commands in the foreground.

8 *Using OS/2 Subdirectories*

Most OS/2 users will find that everyday use of OS/2 quickly produces a large number of files on their fixed or floppy disks. Unfortunately, having a large number of files often leads to confusion and a cluttered directory listing. This makes locating a specific file difficult at best. If this is indeed your case, OS/2 subdirectories may provide a solution.

OS/2 subdirectories exist for one purpose—file management. Subdirectories provide you with many advantages such as increased file organization, faster file access, and increased flexibility because of such OS/2 commands as PATH, APPEND, DPATH, JOIN, and SUBST. As you examine each of these commands, it should become apparent that the advantages these commands provide is a direct result of increased file organization.

Consider the following scenario. A manager of a computer resale store must track the following types of information:

Hardware sales
Hardware inventory
Hardware on order
Software sales
Software inventory
Software on order
General-ledger information

One solution would be for the manager to combine all of this information into one location on the disk. To do so would require no additional setup to the computer or disk configuration. Although this may at first appear to be the easiest solution to implement, a closer look reveals that it has several disadvantages. First, by combining all of the files required to track these items into one location, the disk becomes cluttered with files. Retrieving a specific file becomes almost impossible. Second, if the manager does not use OS/2 subdirectories, the company's disk is restricted to the number of files shown in Table 8-1.

Each disk type sets aside a specific area in which it records the names of the files in the root directory of that disk. The

Disk space	Maximum number of files in the root directory
160K	64
180K	
320K	112
360K	
1.2MB	224
Fixed disk	Based on partition size

Table 8-1. *Maximum Number of Files in Root Directory*

Disk space	Sectors allocated for directory entries
160K	4
180K	
320K	7
360K	
1.2MB	14
Fixed disk	Based on partition size

Table 8-2. *Amount of Space Allotted for Directory Entries*

amount of space set aside for these entries depends upon the disk type (see Table 8-2).

Sectors are 512 bytes in length. Each directory entry (file name) requires 32 bytes (see Table 8-3.

With these basic numbers, you can calculate the maximum number of files per disk as shown here.

number of entries = (number of sectors * sector size)/32

The computer store manager's second choice is to create OS/2 subdirectories. View subdirectories in the same manner as you

Field	Offset
File name	0
Extension	8
Attribute byte	11
Reserved for DOS	12
Time	22
Date	24
Starting cluster number	26
File size	28

Table 8-3. *Entry in Directory Structure*

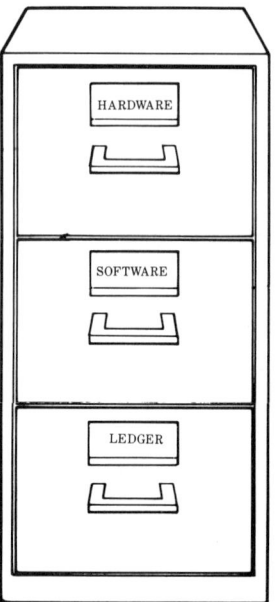

Figure 8-1. *Filing cabinet signifying root directory*

would the drawers in a filing cabinet. In this case, to increase the company's organization, divide the files as shown in Figure 8-1.

As you create these same drawers (subdirectories) under OS/2, visualize them as the tree structure shown here:

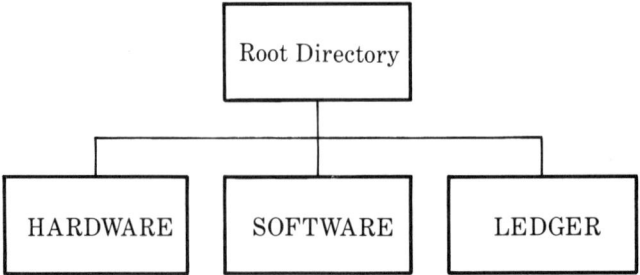

Every OS/2 disk has a root directory. Thus far, all of your commands have manipulated the files contained in the root directory. Place in drive A a formatted disk that contains no files. Issue the OS/2 DIR command, and the following is displayed:

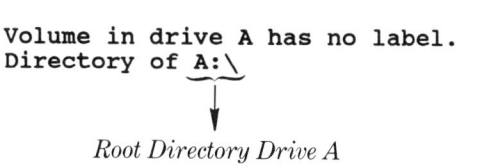

```
Volume in drive A has no label.
Directory of A:\
```

Root Directory Drive A

OS/2 represents the root directory as a backslash (\ ). In this case, the A: \ specifies that the directory listing is from the disk in drive A. The backslash tells you that you are examining the root directory. All directory names (OS/2 path names) grow from the root directory. Given this directory structure

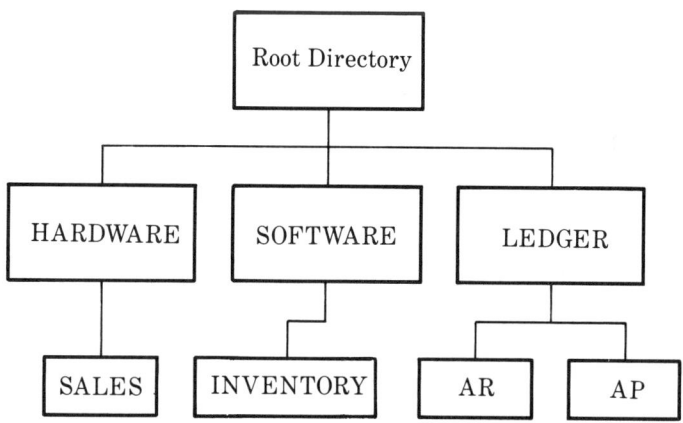

the following are valid OS/2 directory names:

\HARDWARE
\HARDWARE \SALES
\SOFTWARE
\SOFTWARE \INVENTORY

\LEDGER
\LEDGER \AR
\LEDGER \AP

The disk in drive A does not yet have any subdirectories. To create a subdirectory, you must issue the OS/2 MKDIR command. The format of the MKDIR comand is

MKDIR[*drive:*][*path*] [...]

or

MD [*drive:*][*path*] [...]

where

drive: is the disk drive on which you create the subdirectory. If you omit the disk drive identifier, MKDIR uses the current default.

path is the name of the subdirectory that OS/2 is to create.

... states that you can place multiple subdirectory names on the command line.

Again issue the OS/2 DIR command for the disk in drive A. The following is displayed:

```
Volume in drive A has no label.
Directory of A:\
```

View the disk as only containing the root directory, as shown here:

```
┌──────────────────┐
│                  │
│  Root Directory  │
│                  │
└──────────────────┘
```

To create the directory HARDWARE, issue the following command:

```
[A:\] MKDIR \HARDWARE
```

If you examine the path name \HARDWARE, you see the path starts with the root directory (\ ) and then specifies the name of the subdirectory to create HARDWARE. If you now issue the DIR command, OS/2 displays the following:

```
Volume in drive A has no label.
Directory of A:\

HARDWARE      <DIR>      10-05-87    2:20p

    1 File(s)     1213440 bytes free
```

As you can see, the disk now contains the subdirectory HARD-WARE. View the disk as now containing the following structure:

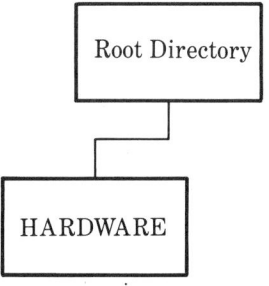

Next, issue the following command:

```
[A:\] MKDIR \SOFTWARE \LEDGER
```

As you can see, the OS/2 MKDIR command (in protected mode) allows you to place multiple subdirectory names on a single command line. Again, issue the OS/2 DIR command and the following is displayed:

```
Volume in drive A has no label.
Directory of A:\

HARDWARE     <DIR>       10-05-87     2:20p
SOFTWARE     <DIR>       10-05-87     2:24p
LEDGER       <DIR>       10-05-87     2:24p

     3 File(s)     1212416 bytes free
```

View the disk as containing the following structure:

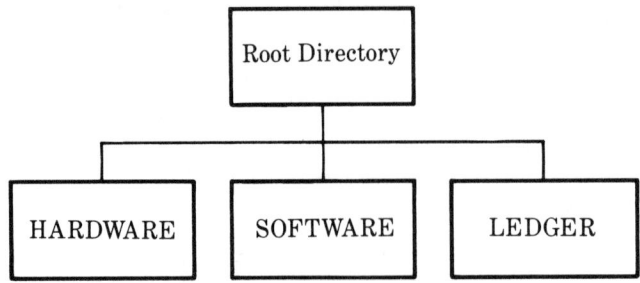

To improve the company's organization even further, subdivide each subdirectory into quarters, as shown here:

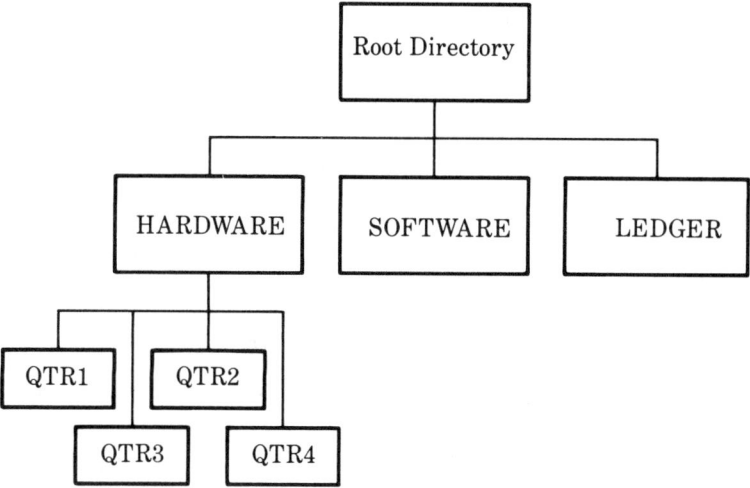

Visualize this further division in the same way that you would files within each drawer of the filing cabinet (see Figure 8-2).

To create the subdirectories within the HARDWARE directory enter the following commands:

```
[A:\] MKDIR \HARDWARE\QTR1 \HARDWARE\QTR2
[A:\] MKDIR \HARDWARE\QTR3 \HARDWARE\QTR4
```

The complete OS/2 path names for each quarter subdirectory are as follows:

\HARDWARE \QTR1
\HARDWARE \QTR2
\HARDWARE \QTR3
\HARDWARE \QTR4

Assuming that the user places the files into each directory as shown here,

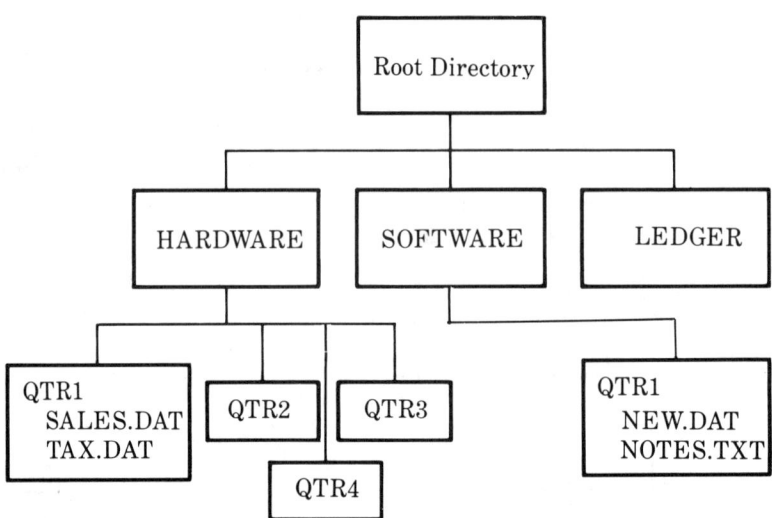

the complete file specifications become the following:

\HARDWARE \QTR1 \SALES.DAT
\HARDWARD \QTR1 \TAX.DAT
\SOFTWARE \QTR1 \NEW.DAT
\SOFTWARE \QTR1 \NOTES.TXT

In this way OS/2 allows you to issue any of the following commands:

```
[A:\] DIR \HARDWARE
[A:\] DIR \HARDWARE\QTR1
[A:\] TYPE \HARDWARE\QTR1\SALES.DAT
[A:\] TREE /F
[A:\] TYPE \SOFTWARE\QTR1\NOTES.TXT
[A:\] COPY \SOFTWARE\QTR1\NEW.DAT B:
```

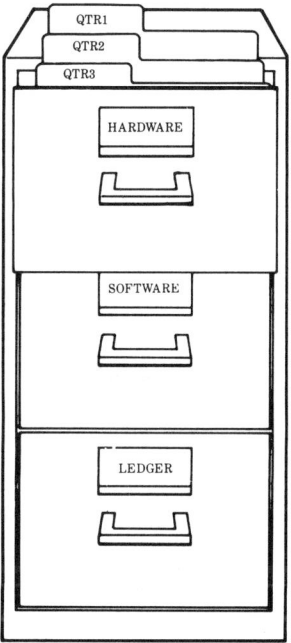

Figure 8-2. *Filing cabinet with subdirectories*

You have divided your disk into several subdirectories. You can repeat this process several times to create essentially whatever logical division of your files is required. The only OS/2 restriction is that a path name cannot exceed 63 characters in length, as shown here:

\HARDWARE \QTR1 \SALES \COMPUTER \DISKDRIV \REPAIR \ORDERS \NEWPART.A

Now that you have seen how to create OS/2 subdirectories, you must learn how to traverse your subdirectory structure easily.

The OS/2 CHDIR allows you to change your current working directory.

Issue a directory listing of the disk in drive A and the following is displayed:

```
Volume in drive A has no label.
Directory of A:\

HARDWARE     <DIR>        10-05-87    2:20p
SOFTWARE     <DIR>        10-05-87    2:24p
LEDGER       <DIR>        10-05-87    2:24p

     3 File(s)     1212416 bytes free
```

In this case, the directory listing is of the root directory, which is the current directory. Issue the following command:

```
[A:\] CHDIR \HARDWARE
```

Again issue the DIR command and the following is displayed:

```
Volume in drive A has no label.
Directory of A:\HARDWARE

 .              <DIR>        10-05-87    2:20p
 ..             <DIR>        10-05-87    2:20p
QTR1            <DIR>        10-05-87    2:20p
QTR2            <DIR>        10-05-87    2:20p
QTR3            <DIR>        10-05-87    2:20p
QTR4            <DIR>        10-05-87    2:20p

     6 File(s)     1212416 bytes free
```

In this case, the directory listing is of the subdirectory \HARD-WARE. The previous OS/2 CHDIR command enabled you to change the current directory.

The format of the CHDIR command is

CHDIR [*drive:*][*path*]

where the following is true:

drive: specifies the disk drive identifier of the disk on which you want to change the current directory.

path specifies the name of the desired directory.

Again, issue the DIR command and the following is displayed:

```
Volume in drive A has no label.
Directory of A:\HARDWARE

.               <DIR>        10-05-87     2:20p
..              <DIR>        10-05-87     2:20p
QTR1            <DIR>        10-05-87     2:20p
QTR2            <DIR>        10-05-87     2:20p
QTR3            <DIR>        10-05-87     2:20p
QTR4            <DIR>        10-05-87     2:20p

    6 File(s)      1212416 bytes free
```

The DIR command displays the current working directory. In addition, OS/2 predefines the subdirectories . and .. as follows:

.   OS/2 defines the period as the current directory.

..   OS/2 defines the double periods as the parent directory. In the case of the subdirectory \HARDWARE, the root is its parent directory. Likewise, given the directory \HARDWARE \QTR1, the subdirectory \HARDWARE is the parent of QTR1.

Issue the following OS/2 DIR command:

```
[A:\] DIR .

Volume in drive A has no label.
Directory of A:\HARDWARE

.                <DIR>        10-05-87      2:20p
..               <DIR>        10-05-87      2:20p
QTR1             <DIR>        10-05-87      2:20p
QTR2             <DIR>        10-05-87      2:20p
QTR3             <DIR>        10-05-87      2:20p
QTR4             <DIR>        10-05-87      2:20p

        6 File(s)     1212416 bytes free
```

In this case, OS/2 performs a directory listing of the current directory (.). Likewise, the command

```
[A:\] DIR ..

Volume in drive A has no label.
Directory of A:\

HARDWARE         <DIR>        10-05-87      2:20p
SOFTWARE         <DIR>        10-05-87      2:24p
LEDGER           <DIR>        10-05-87      2:24p

        3 File(s)     1212416 bytes free
```

lists the files contained in \HARDWARE parent directory, which in this case is the root.

To change the current directory back to the root, you have two choices. First, you know that the parent directory is the root in this case. Therefore, the command

```
[A:\] CD ..
```

sets the current default to the root directory (\). Likewise, you know that OS/2 defines the backslash (\) as the root directory. Therefore, the command

```
[A:\] CD \
```

also sets the current directory to the root.

OS/2 supports the notion of the current directory. Assuming that your current directory is the root, the following commands are equivalent:

```
[A:\] CD \HARDWARE
```

and

```
[A:\] CD HARDWARE
```

If a subdirectory is immediately below the current directory, you can access it simply by specifying its name without the complete path specification starting at the root directory. For example, if the subdirectory QTR1 resides immediately below the directory HARDWARE, you can use the CHDIR command as follows to select the directory as the current default:

```
[A:\] CD QTR1
```

The MKDIR command works in a similar way. Previously in this chapter you created directories by specifying complete path names, as shown here:

```
[A:\] MKDIR \SOFTWARE \LEDGER
```

If the directory that you are creating is to reside immediately below the current directory, you can simply reference it by name, as shown here:

```
[A:\] MKDIR HARDWARE SOFTWARE
```

Therefore, assume you have the following directory structure:

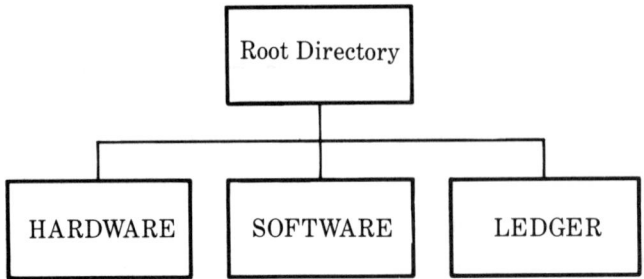

If your current directory is HARDWARE, the command

```
[A:\] MKDIR QTR1
```

changes the structure to the following:

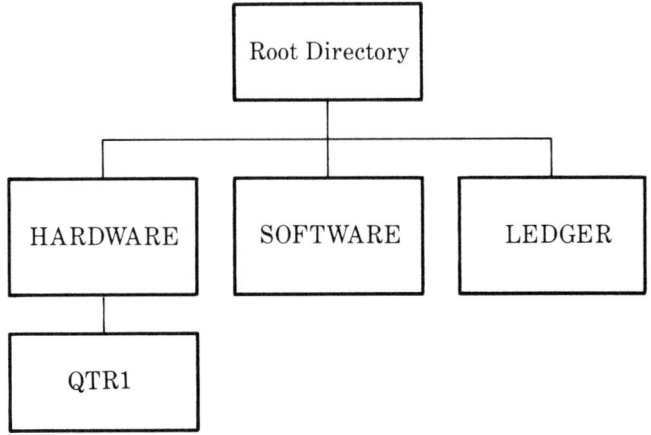

You could have also issued the command as follows:

```
[A:\] MKDIR \HARDWARE\QTR1
```

However, if you enter the command

```
[A:\] MKDIR \QTR1
```

OS/2 starts at the root directory (\ ) and creates the subdirectory QTR1, as shown next.

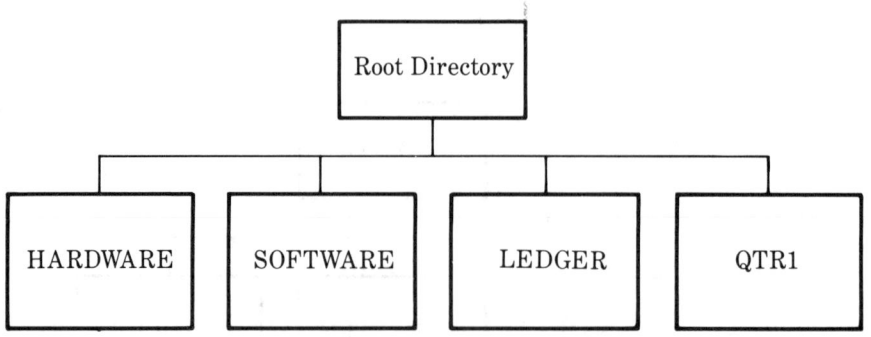

OS/2 PREDEFINED DIRECTORY NAMES

OS/2 predefines the following directory names:

\Root directory	The upper-level directory from which all other directories grow.
.Current directory	Similar to the current disk drive. OS/2 first searches the current directory for commands or data unless otherwise specified by the user.
..Parent directory	The directory immediately above a directory in the directory structure. Given the path name \HARDWARE \QTR1, the root directory is the parent directory for HARDWARE, while HARDWARE is the parent of QTR1.

Just as the MKDIR command enables you to create OS/2 subdirectories, the RMDIR command removes them. The format of the command is

RMDIR [*drive:*][*path*] [...]

or

RD [*drive:*][*path*] [...]

where the following is true:

drive: specifies the disk drive identifier of the disk containing the directory you want to remove.

path specifies the name of the OS/2 subdirectory to delete.

... states that you can place multiple subdirectory names on the command line.

Now once again, assume that you have the following directory structure:

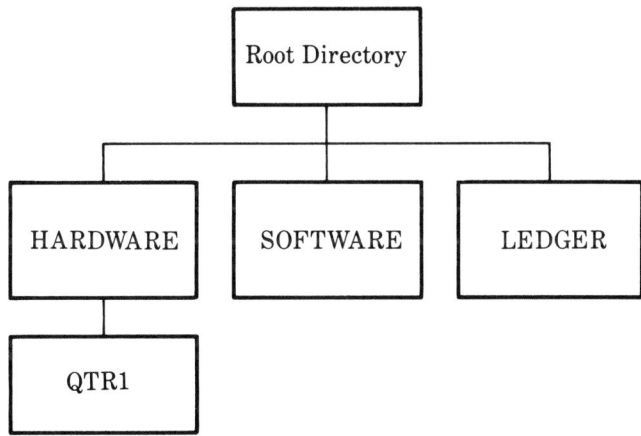

The command

```
[A:\] RMDIR \HARDWARE\QTR1
```

results in the structure shown next:

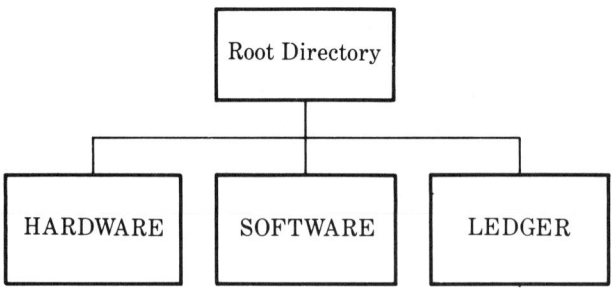

Likewise, the command

```
[A:\] RMDIR \SOFTWARE \LEDGER
```

produces the following:

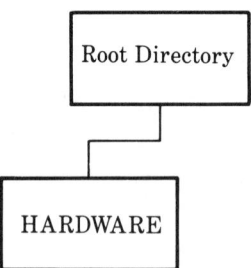

RMDIR does not allow you to remove a subdirectory containing files or subdirectories. If you attempt to do so, RMDIR displays the following:

```
DOS1042: The system cannot find the path, the
name specified is not a directory, or the directory
is not empty.
```

If you really want to remove the directory, you must first use the OS/2 DEL command to delete the files contained in the directory and then issue RMDIR to remove the directory. DEL will not delete an OS/2 subdirectory. Also, OS/2 does not allow you to delete a directory that is the current directory for any session.

REMOVING AN OS/2 DIRECTORY

The OS/2 RMDIR command enables you to delete a subdirectory when it is no longer needed. OS/2 does not allow you to delete a subdirectory that contains files. You must first use the OS/2 DEL command to delete the files and then issue the RMDIR command. The DEL command will not delete an OS/2 subdirectory.

Recall that unless overridden by an OS/2 path name, the DEL command only deletes files contained in the current directory. Assuming that your directory structure contains

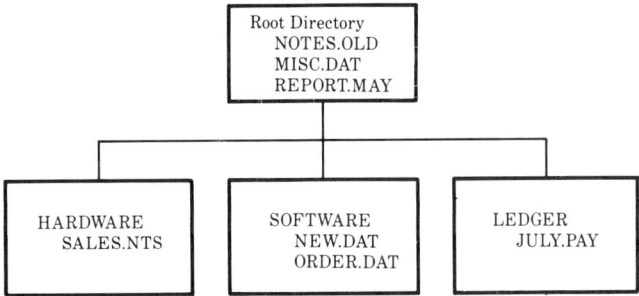

and that the root is your current directory, the command

```
[A:\] DEL *.*
```

only deletes files contained in the current directory and leaves files contained in other subdirectories intact, as shown here:

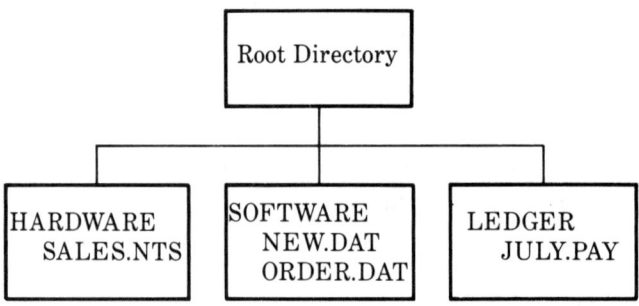

Executing Programs Contained in Subdirectories

This chapter has described how you could easily access files contained in OS/2 subdirectories simply by providing complete path names, as follows:

```
[A:\]  DIR  \HARDWARE
[A:\]  DIR  \HARDWARE\QTR1
[A:\]  TYPE  \HARDWARE\QTR1\SALES.DAT
[A:\]  TREE  /F
[A:\]  TYPE  \SOFTWARE\QTR1\NOTES.TXT
[A:\]  COPY  \SOFTWARE\QTR1\NEW.DAT  B:
```

If you have an executable file that is contained in a subdirectory, you execute it by typing its complete path name at the OS/2 prompt. For example, if you assume that your directory structure contains

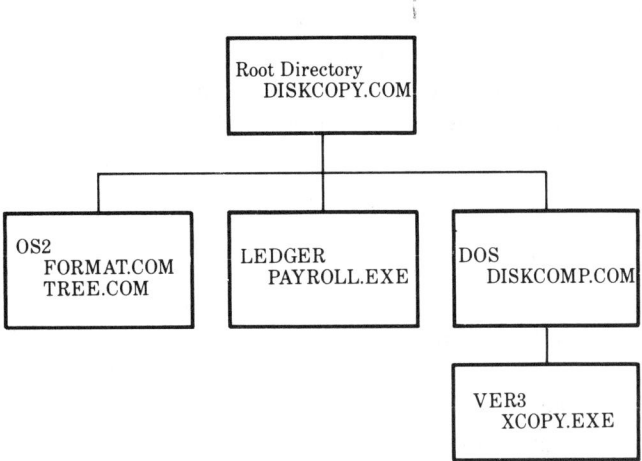

the following are valid OS/2 command paths:

\DISKCOPY
\OS2 \FORMAT
\OS2 \TREE
\LEDGER \PAYROLL
\DOS \DISKCOMP
\DOS \VER3 \XCOPY

EXECUTING COMMANDS
CONTAINED IN SUBDIRECTORIES

OS/2 allows you to execute commands contained in subdirectories in the same manner as all OS/2 commands. However, you must include the complete subdirectory path name of the command (for example, [A: \] \OS2 \DISKCOPY).

OS/2 TREE Command

The OS/2 TREE command enables you to display on your screen the directory structure of the specified disk. By default, this command lists all of the subdirectories on your disk. If you include the /F command-line qualifier, TREE displays each of the files contained in each subdirectory. The format of the TREE command is

[*drive:*][*path*]TREE [*disk_drive:*][/*F*]

where the following is true:

drive: is the disk drive identifier of the disk containing the TREE.COM file.

path is the OS/2 subdirectory that contains the TREE.COM file.

disk_drive is the disk drive identifier of the file of which TREE is to display the structure.

/*F* directs TREE to display the name of each file contained in the subdirectories of the specified disk drive.

Assume that your directory structure contains the following:

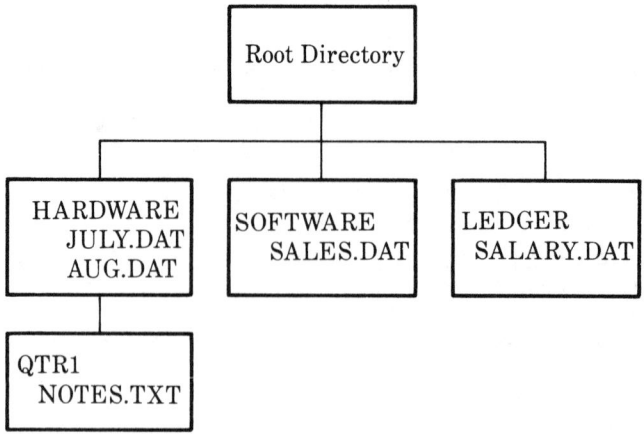

The command

```
[A:\] TREE
```

displays the following:

```
Directory path listing
Path: \HARDWARE
Subdirectories:  QTR1


Path: \HARDWARE\QTR1
Subdirectories:  None


Path: \SOFTWARE
Subdirectories:  None


Path: \LEDGER
Subdirectories:  None
```

Likewise, the command

```
[A:\] TREE /F
```

will display the names of every file in each directory on the disk.

Many people use TREE in conjunction with the OS/2 pipe to determine if a specific file resides on disk, as shown here:

```
[A:\] TREE /F ¦ FIND "AUG"
```

OS/2 PATH Command

The OS/2 PATH command enables you to define to OS/2 where it should look for external commands that it does not find in the current directory. Thus far, each time you have issued a command, the command has resided in the current directory. This chapter previously discussed how to execute commands that are contained in other directories by specifying complete path names. Before examining the format of the OS/2 PATH command, you should understand how OS/2 locates the files that it executes.

Each time you enter a command, OS/2 first searches for the command that you entered in its list of internal commands. If OS/2 finds the command it executes it. If not, OS/2 searches the current directory for an EXE, COM, or CMD file matching the specified file name. Again, if OS/2 finds the file, it executes it. If not, OS/2 checks to see if you have defined a command path.

A *command path* is a list of OS/2 subdirectories that OS/2 will search in succession until it either finds a file matching the name of the command entered, or until it exhausts all of the subdirectories in its list. Figure 8-3 summarizes the processing performed.

The format of the OS/2 PATH command is

PATH [*drive:*][*path*] [;[*drive:*][*path*]...]

or

path ;

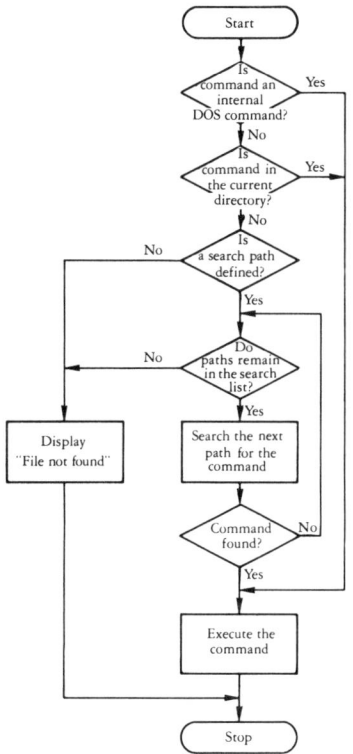

Figure 8-3. *Flowchart showing PATH searching root directories for files*

where the following is true:

drive: specifies a disk identifier that OS/2 is to include in the command search path.

path specifies an OS/2 subdirectory that OS/2 is to include in the command search path.

... states that you can repeat the series of drives and path names to the 63-character limit.

Before examining the PATH command, issue the SET command and the following is displayed:

```
3XBOX=command.com
COMSPEC=C:\CMD.EXE
PATH=C:\;C:\OS2;C:\TOOLS
INCLUDE=c:\include
LIB=c:\lib
INIT=c:\init
```

As you can see, PATH defines an environment entry. If your system already has a command path defined, you have been using PATH for some time without even realizing it. This explains why many of the commands that you have issued have not resided in the current directory, yet OS/2 was still able to locate them.

Consider the following command:

```
[A:\] PATH C:\
```

In this case, if OS/2 does not find the command as an internal command, or an executable file in the current directory, it will search the root directory of drive C for the command.

Consider the following command:

```
[A:\] PATH A:\;B:\;C:\
```

In this case, if OS/2 does not locate a command, it will search the root directories of the disk in drives A, B, and C in that order as shown in Figure 8-4.

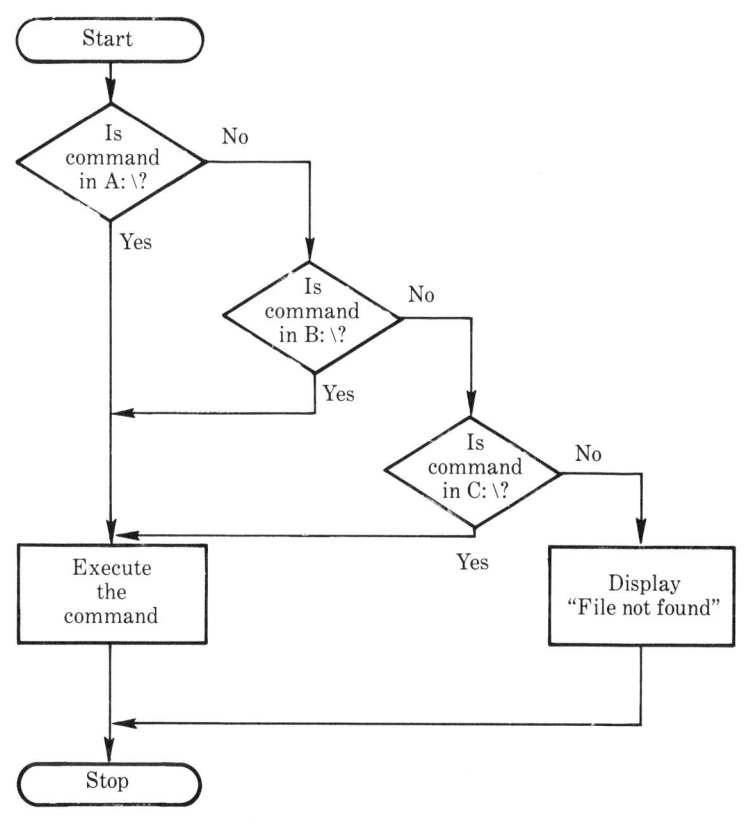

Figure 8-4. *OS/2 searching root directories of drives A, B, and C*

If you invoke the PATH command without any parameters, PATH displays its current command path, as shown here:

```
[A:\] PATH
PATH=C:\;C:\OS2;C:\TOOLS
```

If you invoke PATH with a semicolon

```
[A:\] PATH ;
```

PATH removes the previously defined command path.

```
[A:\] PATH
No Path
```

In this case, OS/2 only searches for the command as an internal command followed by the files in the current directory.

OS/2 PATH COMMAND

OS/2 allows you to define a command-file search path that the system examines each time it does not locate the command entered as an internal command or in the current directory.

OS/2 APPEND and DPATH Commands

Just as the OS/2 PATH command allows you to define a search path for executable commands, the OS/2 APPEND command allows you to define a search path for data files in real mode and the OS/2 DPATH command allows you to define a search path for data files in protected mode.

Data-file search paths work in the identical manner to command search paths. If OS/2 cannot open a file as specified, OS/2 searches the subdirectories specified in the data-file search path until the file is found, or until the path is exhausted. The format of the APPEND command is

APPEND [*drive:*][*path*][;[*drive:*][*path*]...]

where the following is true:

drive: specifies a disk identifier that OS/2 is to include in the real-mode data-file search path.

path specifies an OS/2 subdirectory that OS/2 is to include in the real-mode data-file search path.

... states that you can repeat the series of drives and path names to the 63-character limit.

Likewise the format of the OS/2 DPATH command is

DPATH [*drive:*][*path*][;[*drive:*][*path*]...]

where the following is true:

drive: specifies a disk identifier that OS/2 is to include in the protected-mode data-file search path.

path specifies an OS/2 subdirectory that OS/2 is to include in the protected-mode data-file search path.

... states that you can repeat the series of drives and path names to the 63-character limit.

Consider the following command:

```
[A:\] APPEND C:\;B:\;A:\
```

In this case, OS/2 defines a real-mode data path consisting of the root directories of drives C, B, and A, in that order. If OS/2 does not find the data file specified in the command line, or in a file open statement from an application, it searches the paths specified in the data-file search list. The protected-mode equivalent to APPEND in this case is as follows:

```
[A:\] DPATH C:\;B:\;A:\
```

If you invoke APPEND without any parameters, APPEND displays its current search list, as shown here:

```
[A:\] APPEND
APPEND=C:\;B:\;A:\
```

Likewise, DPATH displays the following:

```
[A:\] DPATH
DPATH=C:\;B:\;A:\
```

If you invoke either APPEND or DPATH with a semicolon, each will delete the current data-file search path. Most users immediately define command-file search paths by using the PATH command. The APPEND and DPATH commands usually are used by programmers who are developing applications for end users. If they are not sure from which directory users may invoke their programs, the programmers can ensure that the data files the programs use will be found because of a data-file search path.

OS/2 APPEND AND DPATH COMMANDS

Just as the OS/2 PATH command allows you to define command-file search paths, the OS/2 APPEND and DPATH commands allow you to define a data-file search path. Once defined, OS/2 searches this path each time it fails to locate a data file as specified. APPEND defines real-mode data-file search paths. Likewise, DPATH allows you to define a protected-mode data-file search path.

OS/2 SUBST Command (Real Mode)

The more you divide your disk into subdirectories, the larger your OS/2 path names become. Although you will indeed have good disk management, most users would dislike having to enter commands such as the following:

```
[A:\] COPY \HARDWARE\QTR1\SALES\COMPUTER\DISKDRIV\REPAIR\ORDERS\NEWPART.A B:
```

For your convenience, OS/2 provides the SUBST command, which allows you to abbreviate a long OS/2 path name with a disk drive identifier. Although SUBST was originally introduced to aid file control blocks (FCBs) in manipulating directories, its use can still be exploited today. The format of the SUBST command is

SUBST [*drive:*][*path*][*/D*]

where the following is true:

drive: specifies the disk drive identifier that OS/2 is to use as the abbreviation for the OS/2 subdirectory name.

path specifies the OS/2 path name to abbreviate with the disk drive name.

/D directs SUBST to delete a previous join.

Consider the following example:

```
[A:\] SUBST D: \HARDWARE\QTR1\SALES\COMPUTER\DISKDRIV\REPAIR\ORDERS
```

In this case, rather than having to repeatedly type the directory name \HARDWARE \QTR1 \SALES \COMPUTER \DISKDRIV \REPAIR \ORDERS, you can simply reference the disk drive D. For example, the following command issues a directory listing of the subdirectory:

```
[A:\] DIR D:
```

If the subdirectory that you are abbreviating has subdirectories below it, you reference them as shown here:

```
[A:\] DIR D:\SUBDIR
```

If you invoke SUBST without any parameters, SUBST displays its current substitutions, as shown here:

```
[A:\] SUBST
D: is substituted for A:\HARDWARE\QTR1\SALES\COMPUTER\DISKDRIV\REPAIR\ORDERS
```

To delete a previous substitution, use the /D qualifier, as shown here:

```
[A:\] SUBST D: /D
```

OS/2 SUBST COMMAND

The OS/2 SUBST command allows you to abbreviate long directory path names with a disk drive identifier. The SUBST command only executes in real mode and only affects the DOS session.

OS/2 JOIN Command (Real Mode)

The OS/2 real-mode JOIN command enables you to join a disk drive to a directory on the current disk, thus giving the appearance that the disk in the other drive is actually part of the current directory structure.

The format of the JOIN command is

JOIN [*drive:*][*path*][*/D*]

where the following is true:

drive: specifies the disk drive to be joined to the directory structure.

path specifies the name of an empty OS/2 directory on the device that drive is being joined to.

/D directs JOIN to delete a previous JOIN.

Create an empty directory, as shown here:

```
[A:\] MKDIR \JOINDIR
```

Next, invoke the JOIN command with the disk drive that you want to add to the directory structure.

```
[A:\] JOIN B: \JOINDIR
```

You can now access the disk contained in drive B simply by referencing JOINDIR. As such, you can access all of the files contained in drive B as if they were actually contained in the subdirectory JOINDIR. JOIN does not care if you change the disks contained in drive B. It will treat the new series of files as if they also resided under JOINDIR.

If you invoke JOIN without any parameters, JOIN displays its current joins, as follows:

```
[A:\] JOIN
B: is joined to A:\JOINDIR
```

To remove a JOIN, use the /D qualifier, as shown here:

```
[A:\] JOIN B: /D
```

OS/2 JOIN COMMAND

The OS/2 JOIN command allows you to join a disk contained in a different drive to the directory structure of the specified disk drive. The JOIN command works only in real mode.

General Guidelines

Use the following rules of thumb when you create your OS/2 directories:

- OS/2 directory names conform to the same format as OS/2 file names, with an eight-character file name followed by an optional three-character extension. The following are valid OS/2 directory names: FILENAME.EXT, HARDWARE.SAL, and SOFTWARE.INV.

- If you do not specify a complete OS/2 path name when you create a subdirectory, OS/2 assumes that you are creating the subdirectory in the current directory.

- To manipulate directories contained on other disks, simply precede the directory name with a disk drive identifier such as B:\FINANCE\CAR.

- Do not create directory names identical to names of files contained in the same directory.

- Do not create a directory called \DEV. OS/2 uses a hidden directory called \DEV to communicate with hardware devices.

- OS/2 path names cannot exceed 63 characters.

- Root directories on each disk are restricted to a specific number of files because of the disk layout. However, subdirectories can contain an unlimited number of files.

- Logically divide your disk into subdirectories.

■ Do not create directories with the OS/2 reserved names \QUEUES, \SEM, or \SHAREMEM.

Disk space	Maximum number of files in the root directory
160K	64
180K	
320K	112
360K	
1.2MB	224
Fixed disk	Based on partition size

Table 8-4. *Files Supported by Root Directory*

Chapter Highlights

OS/2 subdirectories exist for one purpose—file management.

If you do not use OS/2 subdirectories, your disks are restricted to a limited number of files, as shown in Table 8-4.

Every OS/2 directory has a root directory (\ ) from which all other subdirectories grow.

The OS/2 MKDIR command enables you to create OS/2 subdirectories. Unlike the DOS MKDIR command, under OS/2 protected mode you can specify on one command line multiple subdirectory names that you want MKDIR to create.

The OS/2 CHDIR command enables you to traverse the directory structure that you create by using the OS/2 MKDIR command. CHDIR selects a new directory as the current default.

Just as the OS/2 MKDIR command enables you to create subdirectories, the OS/2 RMDIR command enables you to delete them when they are no longer required. The RMDIR command does not allow you to remove subdirectories that contain files or child subdirectories. You must first use the OS/2 DEL command to delete the files, and then RMDIR to remove the directory. DEL cannot delete an OS/2 directory.

To access files contained in an OS/2 subdirectory, you simply specify a complete path name for the file, starting at the root directory, traversing the parent subdirectories, and finally specifying the file name.

To execute a command that resides in an OS/2 subdirectory, again simply specify a complete path name by entering it at the OS/2 prompt.

The OS/2 TREE command enables you to display your directory structure on your screen. By using the /F command-line qualifier, you can direct TREE to display the file names of each file residing in all of the directories on the disk.

The OS/2 PATH command enables you to specify a command-file search path that OS/2 examines each time it cannot locate the file that you have entered as either an internal command, or external command residing in the current directory.

In a manner similar to the PATH command, the OS/2 APPEND and DPATH commands enable you to define data-file search paths that OS/2 examines each time it cannot open a file as specified in the command line or in a program OPEN statement.

The OS/2 SUBST command enables you to abbreviate long OS/2 path names as a disk drive identification. Once a path name has been substituted, you refer to the path by using the disk drive identifier.

The OS/2 JOIN command enables you to join a disk contained in another drive to the current directory structure.

9 OS/2 Advanced Commands

The preceding chapters have examined the majority of the OS/2 commands. This chapter completes your OS/2 command coverage. It contains the remaining commands, an ad hoc collection of "advanced commands." You should issue each of the commands presented in the "Example" sections to increase your understanding of OS/2.

ANSI

Function   Enable ANSI support for a protected-mode session.

Mode   Protected

Format

ANSI [*ON* ¦ *OFF*]

where the following is true:

ON directs OS/2 to support ANSI terminal commands for the current protected-mode session.

OFF directs OS/2 to disable ANSI support in the current protected-mode session.

Notes If you invoke ANSI without a command-line parameter, ANSI displays the current state of ANSI support (ON or OFF).

The ANSI command is a protected-mode command. To provide ANSI support for real mode, you must install the ANSI.SYS driver in the CONFIG.SYS file.

Examples In the following case, OS/2 supports ANSI escape sequences in the current protected-mode session:

```
[C:\] ANSI ON
The ANSI extended screen and
keyboard control are on.

[C:\]
```

If you invoke ANSI without a command-line parameter, ANSI displays the current state of support (ON or OFF), as follows:

```
[C:\] ANSI
The ANSI extended screen and
keyboard control are on.

[C:\]
```

The ANSI escape sequence

```
Esc[HEsc[J
```

clears the current screen contents and places the cursor in the upper-left (home) cursor position. You can verify this by issuing the OS/2 PROMPT command once ANSI support is enabled. Use the following system prompt:

```
[C:\] PROMPT $e[H$e[J$n$g
```

OS/2 clears the screen and displays the current disk drive followed by a > character each time the prompt is displayed.

ASSIGN

Function Route disk drive references from one disk drive to another.

Mode Real

Format

ASSIGN [*source_drive=target_drive* [...]]

where the following is true:

source_drive is the disk drive identifier of the disk from which to route disk I/O references.

target_drive is the disk drive identifier of the disk to which disk I/O operations will be routed.

... states that the command can be repeated several times.

Notes Many older software packages always look to drive A for data or overlay files. If you want to install this software on your fixed disk, you must trick the software into looking for the files on the fixed disk. ASSIGN enables you to do this.

If you invoke ASSIGN without any command-line parameters, ASSIGN restores its original disk drive assignments.

Do not place a colon after each disk drive identifier in the ASSIGN command line.

Examples   In the following case, OS/2 real-mode disk I/O operations that reference drive A are routed to drive C:

```
C> ASSIGN A=C
```

If you invoke the following command, OS/2 actually lists the files contained on drive C.

```
C> DIR A:
```

If you invoke ASSIGN without any command-line parameters, OS/2 restores its original disk drive assignments:

```
C> ASSIGN
```

ATTRIB

Function   Display or modify the attribute byte of a file.

Mode   Real/Protected

Format

[*drive:*][*path*]ATTRIB [+A ¦ −A] [+R ¦ −R] *file_specification* [/S]

where the following is true:

drive: specifies the disk drive containing the file ATTRIB.EXE. If you do not specify a disk drive identifier, OS/2 uses the current default.

path is the OS/2 path name of the subdirectory that contains the file ATTRIB.EXE. If you do not specify an OS/2 path name, OS/2 uses the current default.

+A directs ATTRIB to set the archive bit of a file(s).

−A directs ATTRIB to clear the archive bit of a file(s).

+R directs ATTRIB to set the read-only bit of a file(s).

−R directs ATTRIB to clear the read-only bit of a file(s).

file_specification is the complete OS/2 file specification (including a disk drive and path name) of the file(s) to modify. ATTRIB supports OS/2 wildcard characters.

/S directs ATTRIB to process all of the files below the given file specification.

Notes Each OS/2 file has a directory entry that contains the fields shown in Table 9-1.

The OS/2 ATTRIB command modifies the attribute byte of a file.

Field	Offset
File name	0
Extension	8
Attribute byte	11
Reserved for DOS	12
Time	22
Date	24
Starting cluster number	26
File size	28

Table 9-1. *Entry in Directory Structure*

Several OS/2 commands (such as BACKUP, RESTORE, and XCOPY) use the attribute of a file to enable selective file processing. By using these commands in conjunction with ATTRIB, you can gain considerable file-processing control.

Examples If you do not specify the A or R qualifier,

```
[C:\] ATTRIB *.*
```

ATTRIB displays the current attributes of each file, as shown here:

```
A         C:\OS2\ANSI.EXE
A    R    C:\OS2\APPEND.COM
A    R    C:\OS2\ASSIGN.COM
A         C:\OS2\ATTRIB.EXE
A    R    C:\OS2\BACKUP.COM
A    R    C:\OS2\CHKDSK.COM
A    R    C:\OS2\COMP.COM
A    R    C:\OS2\DISKCOMP.COM
A    R    C:\OS2\DISKCOPY.COM
A    R    C:\OS2\EDLIN.COM
A         C:\OS2\FDISK.EXE
A    R    C:\OS2\FIND.COM
A    R    C:\OS2\FORMAT.COM
A         C:\OS2\FORMATS.TBL
A    R    C:\OS2\GRAFTABL.COM
A         C:\OS2\GWBASIC.EXE
A         C:\OS2\HELPMSG.EXE
A         C:\OS2\JOIN.EXE
A         C:\OS2\KEYB.EXE
A    R    C:\OS2\LABEL.COM
A    R    C:\OS2\MODE.COM
A    R    C:\OS2\MORE.COM
A         C:\OS2\PATCH.EXE
A    R    C:\OS2\PRINT.COM
A         C:\OS2\README
A         C:\OS2\REPLACE.EXE
A    R    C:\OS2\RESTORE.COM
A         C:\OS2\SORT.EXE
A         C:\OS2\SPOOL.EXE
A         C:\OS2\SUBST.EXE
A    R    C:\OS2\SYS.COM
A    R    C:\OS2\TREE.COM
A         C:\OS2\XCOPY.EXE
```

In this case,

```
[C:\] ATTRIB +R CONFIG.SYS
```

ATTRIB sets the CONFIG.SYS file to read-only. In so doing, OS/2 cannot modify the contents of the file. For example, if you attempt to delete a read-only file, OS/2 displays the following:

```
[C:\] DEL FILENAME.EXT
SYS0005: The system cannot access the file specified.
[C:\]
```

The OS/2 BACKUP /M qualifier directs BACKUP to only back up those files modified since the previous backup. By issuing the command

```
[C:\] ATTRIB +A \*.* /S
```

you can set the archive bit of every file on disk as requiring a backup. Likewise, the following command marks each file as being backed up:

```
[C:\] ATTRIB -A \*.* /S
```

BREAK

Function Enable or disable OS/2 extended CTRL-BREAK checking in real mode.

Mode Real

Format

BREAK [*ON* | *OFF*]

where the following is true:

ON enables extended real-mode CTRL-BREAK checking.

OFF disables extended real-mode CTRL-BREAK checking.

Notes By default, OS/2 real mode checks for a user-entered CTRL-BREAK after it completes keyboard, screen, and printer I/O operations. If you enable extended CTRL-BREAK checking, OS/2 also checks for a user-entered CTRL-BREAK when it completes each system service (such as disk read or write operations).

If you invoke BREAK without a command-line parameter, the command displays the current state of processing (either ON or OFF).

By enabling extended CTRL-BREAK processing, you increase the system overhead since OS/2 must check for a CTRL-BREAK when it completes each system service. Programmers may want to enable this checking during program development. However, most users will leave BREAK=OFF.

Example The following command enables OS/2 real mode extended CTRL-BREAK checking:

```
C> BREAK ON
```

If you invoke BREAK without a command-line parameter, it displays the current state of extended CTRL-BREAK checking (either ON or OFF) as follows:

```
C> BREAK
BREAK is on

C>
```

CHCP

Function   Display or change the current code page.

Mode   Real/Protected

Format

CHCP [*code—page*]

where the following is true:

code—page specifies the desired code page. The *code—page* variable must have been previously prepared by the system as either the primary or secondary code page in the CONFIG.SYS file.

Notes   Valid code page entries include the following:

437   United States
850   Multilingual
860   Portugal
863   French-Canadian
865   Nordic

If you invoke CHCP without a command-line parameter, CHCP displays the current code page.

Example   The following command directs CHCP to select the Nordic code page. Remember that this code page must have been previously prepared by the system with an entry in the CONFIG.SYS file.

```
[C:\] CHCP 865
```

If you enter CHCP without a command-line parameter, the command displays the current code page.

```
[C:\] CHCP
Active character set:      437
Prepared system character set(s):     437
```

CMD

Function Invoke a secondary protected-mode command-line processor.

Mode Protected

Format

CMD [*drive:*][*path*] [*/C string*] [*/K string*]

where the following is true:

drive: specifies the drive containing the secondary command processor. If you do not specify a disk drive, OS/2 uses the current default.

path specifies the OS/2 subdirectory that contains the secondary command processor. If you do not specify a path name, OS/2 uses the current default.

/C string directs OS/2 to load the secondary command processor into memory only long enough to execute the command specified by *string*. Once the command completes, OS/2 removes the secondary command processor.

/K string directs OS/2 to load the secondary command processsor permanently into memory. Once the command specified by *string* completes, OS/2 leaves the secondary command processor in memory.

Notes Each time you invoke a secondary command processor, the secondary command processor gets its own copy of the environment.

Refer to the OS/2 PROTSHELL entry in the CONFIG.SYS file (see Chapter 4) for more specifics on the protected-mode command processor.

To terminate a secondary command processor, use the OS/2 EXIT command.

Examples The following command directs OS/2 to load a command processor into memory and to display the prompt of the secondary command processor:

```
[C:\] CMD
```

Likewise, the following command directs OS/2 to load the secondary command processor into memory long enough to execute the DIR command:

```
[C:\] CMD /C DIR > DIR.LST
```

On completion of the command, the secondary command processor terminates.

The following entry in the CONFIG.SYS file directs OS/2 to use CMD.EXE as its protected-mode command processor:

```
PROTSHELL=SHELL.EXE CMD.EXE /K INITENV.CMD
```

Each time OS/2 creates a protected-mode session, it loads the secondary command processor permanently into memory and executes the batch file INITENV.CMD.

COMMAND

Function   Load a secondary real-mode command processor.

Mode   Real

Format

COMMAND [*drive:*][*path*] [*/C string*][*/E:num_bytes*][*/P*]

where the following is true:

drive: specifies the disk drive identifier of the disk containing the secondary command processor. If you do not specify a disk drive, OS/2 uses the current default.

path is the OS/2 subdirectory that contains the command processor. If you do not specify a path name, OS/2 uses the current default.

/C string directs OS/2 to execute the command specified by *string*. Most people use this parameter for nested batch-file invocations.

/E:num_bytes specifies the size OS/2 is to allocate for the secondary command processor environment space. The value of *num_bytes* must be between 160 and 32,767. The default is 160 bytes.

/P directs OS/2 to leave the secondary command processor permanently in memory.

Notes   Each time you load a secondary command processor, it obtains its own copy of the OS/2 environment space.

Most people use COMMAND to invoke nested batch procedures, as shown here:

```
CLS
DATE
COMMAND /C BATFILE
TIME
```

To terminate a secondary command processor, use the OS/2 EXIT command.

Example   In the following command, OS/2 loads the secondary command processor into memory only long enough to execute the CHKDSK command:

```
C> COMMAND /C CHKDSK
```

Once the command terminates, OS/2 removes the secondary command processor.

EXIT

Function   Terminate a secondary command processor.

Mode   Real/Protected

Format

EXIT

Notes   EXIT enables you to terminate either a real- or protected-mode secondary command processor.

If you invoke EXIT from a protected-mode command processor, OS/2 returns control to the OS/2 Session Manager.

Example EXIT terminates a protected- or real-mode secondary command processor, as shown here:

```
[C:\] EXIT
```

GRAFTABL

Function Enable real mode to display the extended character set when the display is in graphics mode.

Mode Real

Format

*[drive:][path]*GRAFTABL *[codepage ¦ ? ¦ /STA]*

where the following is true:

drive: specifies the disk drive containing the file GRAFTABL.COM. If you do not specify a disk drive identifier, OS/2 uses the current default.

path is the OS/2 path name of the subdirectory that contains the file GRAFTABL.COM. If you do not specify an OS/2 path name, OS/2 uses the current default.

codepage specifies the code page to be used for display:

437 United States
850 Multilingual
860 Portugal
863 French-Canadian
865 Nordic

? directs GRAFTABL to display its command-line options.

/STA directs GRAFTABL to display the code page that is currently in use.

Notes GRAFTABL loads memory-resident code when it is invoked. As such, GRAFTABL can only be invoked one time.

GRAFTABL only affects the real-mode session.

Examples If you specify the *?* in the GRAFTABL command line, GRAFTABL displays its command-line options, as shown here:

```
C> GRAFTABL ?

The English version of the graphic character
set table is already loaded.
The acceptable GRAFTABL parameters are:

  /STA - Request status only
  ?    - Display this summary of parameters

  437  - English graphic character set
  860  - Portuguese graphic character set
  863  - Canadian French graphic character set
  865  - Nordic graphic character set

C>
```

In the following case, GRAFTABL uses the code page for the United States when it displays extended characters:

```
C> GRAFTABL 437
```

The following command directs GRAFTABL to display the current code page:

```
C> GRAFTABL  /STA
The English version of the graphic character
set table is already loaded.

C>
```

HELPMSG

Function   Provide additional help on each OS/2 error message.

Mode   Real/Protected

Format

[*drive:*][*path*]HELPMSG *message—id*

where the following is true:

drive: specifies the disk drive containing the file HELPMSG.EXE.
If you do not specify a disk drive identifier, OS/2 uses the current
default.

path is the OS/2 path name of the subdirectory that contains the
file HELPMSG.EXE. If you do not specify an OS/2 path name,
OS/2 uses the current default.

message—id is the OS/2 message on which to display additional
help text. Each OS/2 error message comes in the form
SYS*nnnn*, where *nnnn* is a four-digit number.

Notes   Each time OS/2 displays a protected-mode error message, it uses the format SYS*nnnn*, where *nnnn* is a four-digit
number that uniquely identifies the error.
    Although most OS/2 error messages are fairly self-explana-
tory, HELPMSG provides you additional help text.

Example As shown by the following, the text displayed by HELPMSG is quite helpful:

```
[C:\] TYPE XXX
SYS0002: The system cannot find the file specified.

[C:\] HELPMSG SYS0002

SYS0002: The system cannot find the file specified.

EXPLANATION: The file named in the command
does not exist in the directory or the drive
specified.  You may have typed the filename
incorrectly, or you may have used an
unacceptable character.  Unacceptable
characters are: . " / \ [ ] : | < > + ; ,
and all control characters.
ACTION: Retry the command using a correct filename.

[C:\]
```

PATCH

Function Make changes to an executable file.

Mode Real/Protected

Format

[*drive:*][*path*]PATCH *file_specification* [/A]

where the following is true:

drive: specifies the disk drive containing the file PATCH.EXE. If you do not specify a disk drive identifier, OS/2 uses the current default.

path is the OS/2 path name of the subdirectory that contains the file PATCH.EXE. If you do not specify an OS/2 path name, OS/2 uses the current default.

file—specification is the complete OS/2 file specification of the file to which PATCH is to apply the changes. The *file—specification* variable can contain a disk drive identifier and OS/2 path name.

/A directs PATCH to execute in automatic mode and obtain its inputs from a file (as opposed to the user).

Notes Executable files are difficult to change in cases where a solution to a known bug is found. In the past, most people used the DOS DEBUG command to apply fixes (patches) to an executable file.

PATCH provides a standard for changing files.

Most people will never use this command. In many cases, software developers will publish fixes (called *patches*) for software programs. The OS/2 PATCH command enables you to apply these fixes.

All values specified to patch are in hexadecimal.

Examples In the following case, you are applying a patch to the file FILENAME.EXE:

```
[C:\] PATCH FILENAME.EXE
```

PATCH prompts you for the hexadecimal offset in the file for the first patch, as shown here:

```
Patching FILENAME.EXE
End of file is at AFE
Enter the hexadecimal offset of patch:
```

Enter 0 and press the ENTER key:

```
00000000    4D 5A 40 00 01 00 00 00 04 00 FF FF FF FF 00 00    MZ@...........
```

PATCH displays the current byte value at this location. Enter 11 to change the current value. PATCH moves the cursor to the right, thus allowing you to change the next value.

```
00000000    11 5A 40 00 01 00 00 00 04 00 FF FF FF FF 00 00    MZ@...........
```

Press ENTER and PATCH responds with the following:

```
Do you want to continue patching FILENAME.EXE? (Y/N)
```

To continue with the patch, type Y. Otherwise, type N. In this case type N.

```
Patching FILENAME.EXE
End of file is at AFE
Enter the hexadecimal offset of patch: 0

00000000    11 5A 40 00 01 00 00 00 04 00 FF FF FF FF 00 00    .Z@...........

Do you want to continue patching FILENAME.EXE? (Y/N)

Patches entered for FILENAME.EXE

00000000    11 5A 40 00 01 00 00 00 04 00 FF FF FF FF 00 00    .Z@...........

Do you want these patches applied to FILENAME.EXE? (Y/N) Y

Patches applied to FILENAME.EXE
```

PATCH displays the changes that you have made to the file and prompts you as to whether you want the patch actually written to disk. To write the patch, type Y. Otherwise, type N.

RECOVER

Function   Recover a damaged disk or file.

Mode   Real/Protected

Format

[*drive:*][*path*]RECOVER [*d:*][*p*]*filename.ext*

or

[*drive:*][*path*]RECOVER[*d:*]

where the following is true:

drive: specifies the disk drive containing the file RECOVER. COM. If you do not specify a disk drive identifier, OS/2 uses the current default.

path is the OS/2 path name of the subdirectory that contains the file RECOVER.COM. If you do not specify an OS/2 path name, OS/2 uses the current default.

d: is the disk drive identifier of the file or disk to recover. If you do not specify a disk drive, RECOVER uses the current default.

p is the OS/2 path name of the subdirectory containing the file to recover. If you do not specify an OS/2 path name, OS/2 uses the current default.

filename.ext is the name of the damaged file to recover.

Notes If an OS/2 disk or file becomes damaged and loses sectors, the OS/2 RECOVER command enables you to retrieve portions of the file up to the point of the corruption.

If the file is a text file, you can later edit the file to restore the missing contents. However, if the file is an executable file, you should not execute it. Remember, the file is missing sectors. Instead, maintain a good backup of your files so that you do not have to rely on RECOVER.

If you use RECOVER to recover a complete disk, the command creates files in the root directory with names in the form FILE*nnnn*.REC, where *nnnn* is a four-digit number beginning with 0001 (FILE0001.REC).

Examples The following command attempts to recover the contents of the disk in drive A.

```
C> RECOVER A:
```

RECOVER creates several files whose names are in the format FILE*nnnn*.REC.

The following command recovers the contents of the file FILENAME.EXT up to the point of the damaged sector.

```
C> RECOVER FILENAME.EXT
```

REPLACE

Function Allow selective file replacements and updates when new versions of software become available.

Mode Real/Protected

Format

[*drive:*][*path*] REPLACE *source_filespec* [*target_filespec*]
[*/A*][*/P*][*/R*][*/S*][*/W*]

where the following is true:

drive: specifies the disk drive containing the file REPLACE.EXE. If you do not specify a disk drive identifier, OS/2 uses the current default.

path is the OS/2 path name of the subdirectory that contains the file REPLACE.EXE. If you do not specify an OS/2 path name, OS/2 uses the current default.

source_filespec is the complete OS/2 file specification of the files that REPLACE is to use in the file replacement. REPLACE supports OS/2 wildcard characters.

target_filespec is the complete OS/2 file specification of the destination of the files being added or released.

/A directs REPLACE to add files to the target directory instead of replacing them. With this qualifier, REPLACE only places those files onto the target that are not currently present.

/P directs REPLACE to prompt you with either

```
Do you want to replace FILENAME.EXT (Y/N)?
```

or

```
Do you want to add FILENAME.EXT (Y/N)?
```

before adding or replacing files.

/R directs REPLACE to also replace files on the target location that are currently marked as read-only. Without this qualifier,

REPLACE stops replacement operations with the first file marked read-only.

/S directs REPLACE to search the subdirectories on the target location for other occurrences of the file to replace. This qualifier cannot be used with */A*.

/W directs REPLACE to prompt either

```
Press Enter to begin replacing files.
```

or

```
Press Enter to begin adding files.
```

before starting the file-replacement operations.

Notes REPLACE is a convenient utility for software developers. It enables them easily to select specific files for replacement.

Examples Assume that your target disk in drive A has the following directory structure:

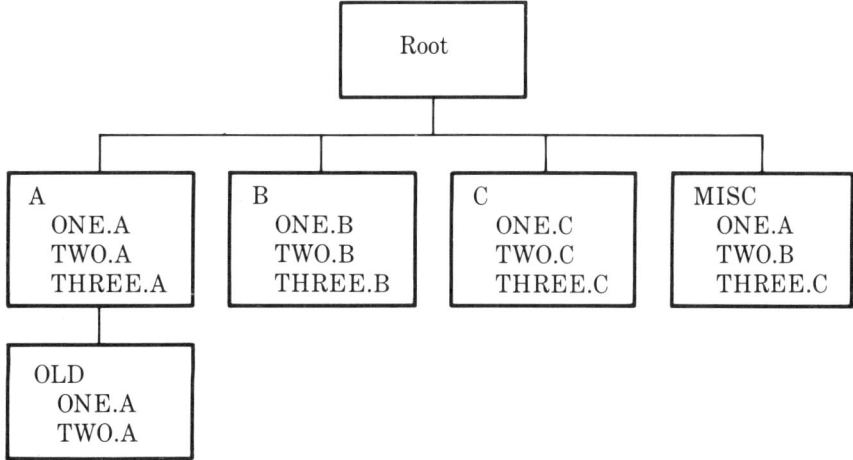

Also assume that the source disk contains the following files:

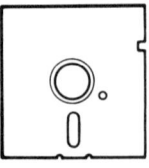

ONE.A
ONE.B
ONE.C
TWO.A
TWO.B
THREE.A

The REPLACE command

```
C> REPLACE *.A A:\
```

will not replace any files since the root directory on drive A does not contain any files. However, the command

```
C> REPLACE *.A A:\A
```

will replace the files, as shown here:

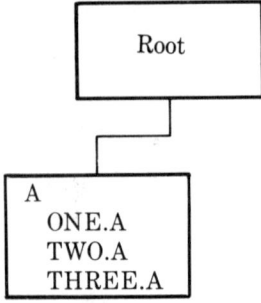

In a similar manner, the command

```
C> REPLACE *.* A:\ /S
```

will replace the following files on the target disk:

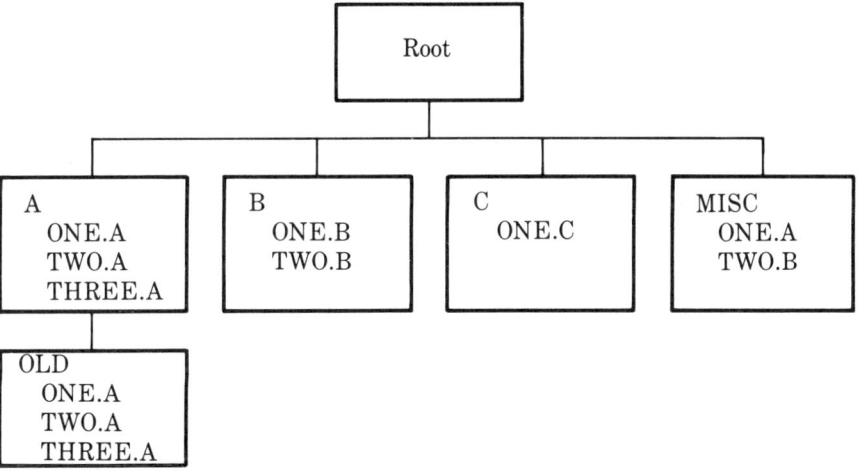

As you can see, REPLACE makes your file updates straight-forward.

SYS

Function   Transfer to the target disk the hidden operating system files that perform the initial system start-up processing.

Mode   Real/Protected

Format

[*drive:*][*path*]SYS *target_drive*: [/S]

where the following is true:

drive: specifies the disk drive containing the file SYS.COM. If you do not specify a disk drive identifier, OS/2 uses the current default.

path is the OS/2 path name of the subdirectory that contains the file SYS.COM. If you do not specify an OS/2 path name, OS/2 uses the current default.

target__drive specifies the target disk drive for the hidden operating system files.

/S directs SYS also to copy the files specified by the file FORMAT.TBL to the target drive.

Notes SYS does not copy either of the files CMD.EXE or COMMAND.COM to the target disk. You must do so by using the OS/2 COPY command.

SYS does not work with a disk that has used the JOIN or SUBST commands.

OS/2 only transfers files to an empty, formatted target disk.

Example If you enter the following command, SYS transfers the hidden operating system files to the disk in drive A.

```
[C:\] SYS A:
```

Verify this by issuing the CHKDSK command, as shown here:

```
[C:\] CHKDSK A:

    362496 bytes total disk space.
    238592 bytes in 2 hidden files.
    123904 bytes available on disk.

[C:\]
```

VERIFY

Function   Enable or disable disk verification.

Mode   Real/Protected

Format

VERIFY [*ON ¦ OFF*]

where the following is true:

ON enables OS/2 disk verification.

OFF disables OS/2 disk verification.

Notes   Periodically a disk drive may not correctly record the information on disk as intended by OS/2. Although rare, such occurrences can leave incorrect data on disk.

   If you enable disk I/O verification, OS/2 double checks the data it writes to disk by rereading each sector and comparing it with the original data, as shown in Figure 9-1. If a discrepancy exists, OS/2 can detect it. Figure 9-2 illustrates the processing that OS/2 normally performs for a command such as

```
[C:\] COPY SOURCE.DAT TARGET.DAT
```

However, once you enable disk verification, OS/2 performs the processing shown in Figure 9-3.

   If you invoke VERIFY without a command-line parameter, VERIFY displays its current state (ON or OFF).

   Because OS/2 must now reread each sector that it writes to disk, disk verification has significant system overhead.

Examples   The following command enables disk I/O verification:

```
[C:\] VERIFY ON
```

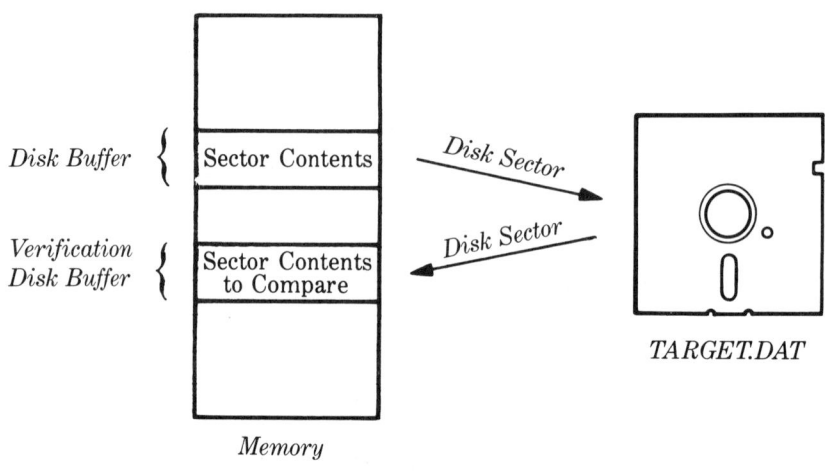

Figure 9-1.   *OS/2 verifying that target and source sectors are the same*

If you invoke VERIFY without command-line parameters, VERIFY displays its current state (ON or OFF), as shown here:

```
[C:\] VERIFY
VERIFY is on.
```

XCOPY

Function   Copy source files and subdirectories to a target destination.

Mode   Real/Protected

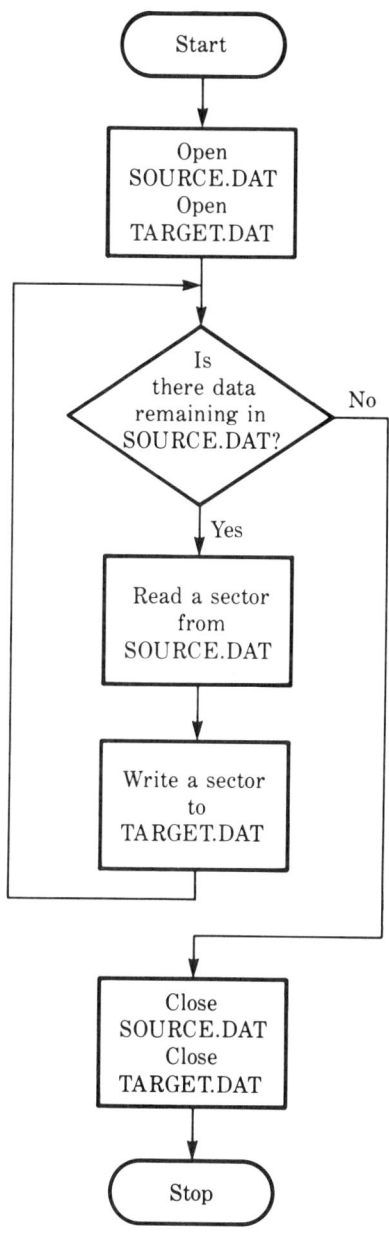

Figure 9-2. *Process of OS/2 reading and writing sectors*

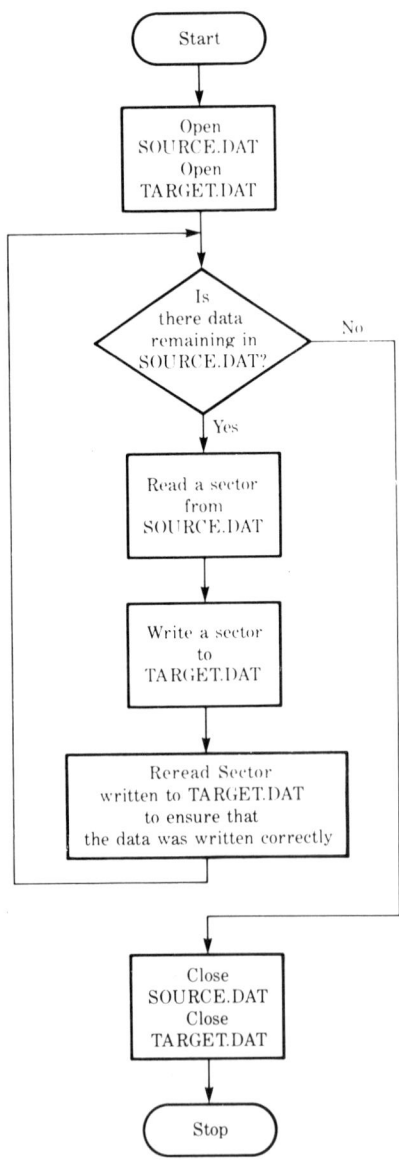

Figure 9-3. *OS/2 recognizing differences between source and target sectors*

Format

[*drive:*][*path*]XCOPY *source__filespec* [*target__filespec*]
[*/A*][*/D:mm-dd-yy*][*/E*][*/M*][*/P*][*/V*]

where the following is true:

drive: specifies the disk drive containing the file XCOPY.EXE. If you do not specify a disk drive identifier, OS/2 uses the current default.

path is the OS/2 path name of the subdirectory that contains the file XCOPY.EXE. If you do not specify an OS/2 path name, OS/2 uses the current default.

source__filespec is the complete OS/2 file specification for the source files that XCOPY is to copy.

target__filespec is the destination name for the files copied by XCOPY.

/A directs XCOPY to only copy files that have the archive bit set.

/D:mm-dd-yy directs XCOPY only to copy files created since the specified date.

/E directs XCOPY to place subdirectories on the target disk if the subdirectory is currently empty. This qualifier must be used with the /S switch.

/M has the same functionality as the /A qualifier. However, /M directs XCOPY to clear the archive bit of each file as it copies the file.

/P directs XCOPY to prompt

```
FILENAME.EXT (Y/N)?
```

before copying each file.

/S directs XCOPY to copy directories and subdirectories (unless they are empty).

/V directs XCOPY to verify the contents of the target file compared to the source file to ensure that the file copy was successful.

Notes XCOPY provides increased functionality over COPY and DISKCOPY. XCOPY copies files contained in OS/2 subdirectories on a selective basis. In fact, many people use XCOPY to repair disk fragmentation or as a system back-up mechanism.

Examples Assume that your source disk in drive A contains the following file structure:

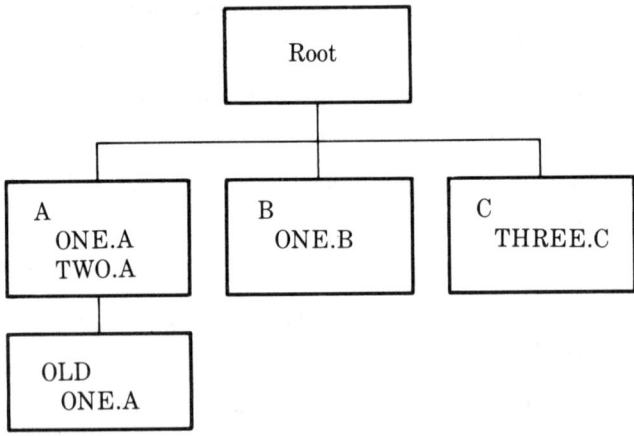

Place a blank disk in drive B. The following command creates an identical disk structure on the disk in drive B.

```
[C:\] XCOPY A:\*.* B:\ /S
```

Likewise, the command

```
[C:\] XCOPY A:\A\*.* B: /S
```

creates a disk with the following structure:

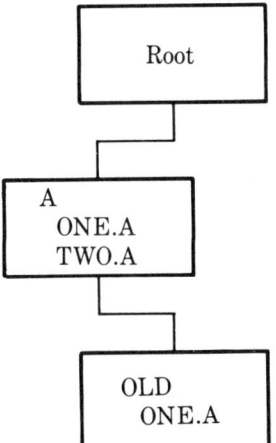

To use XCOPY to copy the entire contents of a fixed disk to floppy disks, first set each file on the fixed disk as requiring a backup, as shown here:

```
[C:\] ATTRIB +A \*.* /S
```

Next, issue the following command:

```
[C:\] XCOPY \*.* A: /S /M
```

XCOPY begins transferring files to the floppy disk and maintains the existing disk structure. Once the target disk becomes full, insert a new floppy disk in drive A and again invoke the following command:

```
[C:\] XCOPY \*.* A: /S /M
```

XCOPY continues right where it left off since it has been clearing the archive bit on each file it successfully copies to the target disk.

Chapter Highlights

The OS/2 ANSI command provides ANSI terminal support for the current OS/2 protected-mode session. To give real-mode ANSI support, you must install the ANSI.SYS device driver in the CONFIG.SYS file and reboot.

The OS/2 ASSIGN command enables you to route disk drive operations from one disk drive to another disk drive in real mode.

Each OS/2 file has an attribute byte in its directory entry. The OS/2 ATTRIB command enables you to change or display file attribute bytes.

The OS/2 BREAK command enables you to increase the number of times that OS/2 checks for a user-entered CTRL-BREAK in OS/2 real mode.

OS/2 uses code pages to map values to a character set. The OS/2 CHCP command enables you to change or display the current code page of a protected-mode session.

The CMD command enables you to invoke a secondary OS/2 protected-mode command processor. In a similar manner, COMMAND enables you to load a secondary command processor in OS/2 real mode. In both cases, the secondary processor can be permanent or temporary.

The OS/2 EXIT command enables you to terminate a secondary command processor. Invoking EXIT from an OS/2 protected-mode session returns control to the OS/2 Session Manager.

When the display is in graphics mode, real-mode applications have difficulty displaying characters in the extended character set. The OS/2 GRAFTABL command loads memory-resident code that aids character display.

Each OS/2 error message has the format SYS*nnnn*, where *nnnn* is a four-digit number that uniquely identifies the error. The OS/2 HELPMSG command displays additional text on each OS/2 error.

Changes to executable files are normally difficult, if not impossible. The OS/2 PATCH command enables you to make such changes in a consistent fashion.

Occasionally, a disk will become damaged and lose sectors. The OS/2 RECOVER command enables you to recover damaged files up to the point of corruption.

The OS/2 SYS command transfers the hidden operating system files required to start the OS/2 boot process on the target disk. OS/2 does not copy CMD.EXE or COMMAND.COM to the target disk.

The OS/2 VERIFY command enables disk-verification operations. On rare occasions, a disk drive may not correctly record information. If you enable disk verification, you increase the possibility of OS/2 detecting the error.

The OS/2 XCOPY command provides you with a powerful alternative to the COPY and DISKCOPY commands. The XCOPY command enables you selectively to copy files and subdirectories.

10 Performing Disk Backups

The most critical function you must perform on a regular basis is backing up your system disk. Anyone who has ever lost data knows the frustration and inconvenience that a single command or hardware malfunction can cause. You perform backups for only one reason—to minimize the impact of the loss of data. No foolproof scheme exists to ensure that you will never lose data. Your goal is to minimize the impact of such a loss, should one occur.

Data loss can result from a number of sources. Your data can be destroyed by a power failure, fire, theft, accidental spills of food or drink, accidental deletion, a hardware error, and even programming errors. However, by performing backups on a regular basis, the likelihood of (and the impact from) losing data is greatly reduced.

Many users fail to perform backups and claim that "backups simply take too long." Such users are setting themselves up for a catastrophic data loss. The key to a successful back-up policy is taking time to ensure that your backups are done regularly. By following the few steps presented in this chapter, maintaining complete system backups is straightforward and requires minimal time.

Before you get started, choose a safe (yet convenient) location for the storage of your back-up disks. Both your working and back-up disks can be destroyed at the same time by, for example, theft or fire. In fact, many users make one or more copies of their disks and place the originals in a safe-deposit box. At the minimum, you should store your disks in a disk storage box to protect them against dust and damage (see Figure 10-1). Such storage containers are available at all computer supply stores.

Once you store your back-up disks in a container, place the container in a safe location away from your computer. They are less likely to be affected by the same source that may destroy your working disks.

Also, create a log for your disks by using a notebook—a three-ring notebook is a good choice. Use one section for tracking your computer software (see Figure 10-2). Likewise, track your hardware purchases and maintenance (see Figure 10-3). Last, keep track of your back-up dates, as shown in Figure 10-4.

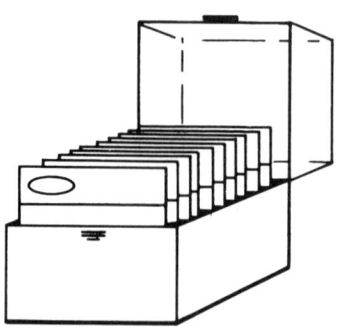

Figure 10-1.   *Media box for disk storage*

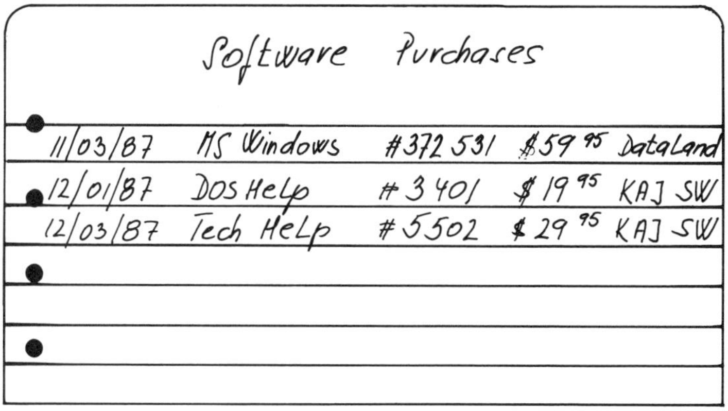

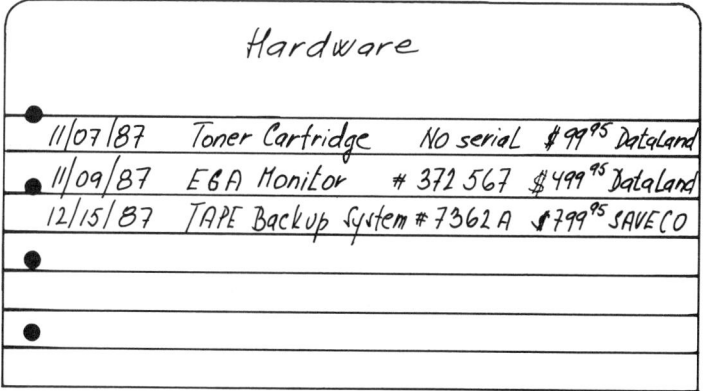

Figure 10-2. *Sample log for software purchases*

Figure 10-3. *Sample log for hardware*

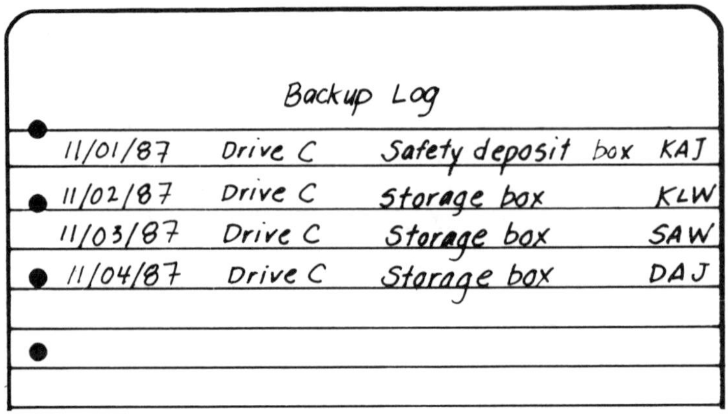

Figure 10-4.   *Back-up log*

If you later have a catastrophic loss because of fire or theft, all your records will be fully intact for insurance purposes. Admittedly, all this may sound a little paranoid. However, the people who are the most concerned about maintaining thorough backups are the least likely to be affected. If they lose an entire hard disk, their paranoia guarantees that they have complete backups on hand.

Floppy Disk Backup

The most common method of backing up your floppy disks is by using the OS/2 DISKCOPY command, examined in Chapter 2. Most software today is not copy-protected. Place your original disks (write-protected) in drive A and your working disks in drive B. Next, issue the following command:

```
[C:\] DISKCOPY A: B:
```

OS/2 copies the contents of your original disk to the target disk and produces a working copy.

If you cannot create a working copy of your disk, you may need to purchase a third-party software package that bypasses software copy protection. In so doing, you can make back-up copies of your working disks. However, remember that it is against the law to distribute licensed software.

Third-Party Back-Up Products

Many users ask whether they should use the OS/2 BACKUP command or instead purchase a third-party product that performs file backups. The answer is, use either. Many users like third-party products because they are menu-driven and therefore easy to use. In terms of functionality, each back-up product performs basically the same task: saving your files to a back-up disk. But whichever you choose, use it on a regular basis.

This chapter develops two back-up procedures that provide complete system backups. Because the actual back-up procedures are performed by batch procedures, the user does not have to memorize the required back-up commands. As such, the back-up procedure is not complex.

For those of you who are using critical development systems where a large percentage of your disk changes on a daily basis, you might consider a tape back-up system, as shown in Figure 10-5. Such systems provide speed advantages over slower floppy disks.

Many very good tape back-up systems are available today. The major difference between each system is the back-up software available for each. If you decide to buy such a system, be sure that

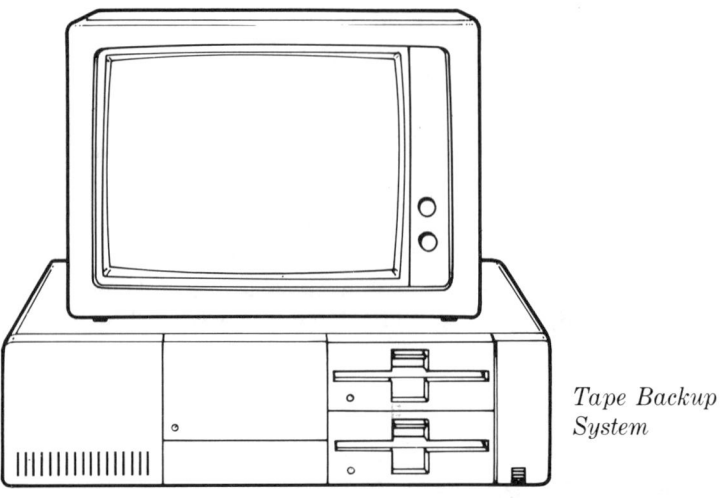

Tape Backup System

Figure 10-5. *Tape back-up system*

it can perform a complete disk backup, incremental backups of modified files, and that it provides complete support for OS/2 subdirectories and wildcard characters.

The key point to remember is that no back-up system (whether the OS/2 BACKUP command or an expensive third-party back-up product) can prevent data loss if you do not use it on a regular basis.

OS/2 BACKUP Command

The OS/2 BACKUP command enables you to back up files contained on floppy disks. In most cases, however, if you are using floppy disks, the OS/2 DISKCOPY or XCOPY commands will better serve your needs. This section concentrates strictly on the use of BACKUP with fixed disks.

The format of the OS/2 BACKUP command is

[*drive:*][*path*]BACKUP [*d:*][*p*][*file*] [*backup—disk:*]
[*/A*][*/D:mm-dd-yy*][*/F*][*/L:logfile*][*/M*][*/S*][*/T:hh:mm:ss*]

where the following is true:

drive: is the disk drive identifier of the disk containing the file BACKUP.COM. If you do not specify a disk drive identifier, OS/2 uses the current drive.

path is the OS/2 path name of the OS/2 subdirectory containing the file BACKUP.COM. If you do not specify a path, OS/2 uses the current default.

d: is the disk drive identifier of the disk containing the files that you want backed up.

p is the OS/2 path name of the OS/2 subdirectory containing the files that you want backed up.

file is the file name of the file(s) that you want backed up.

backup—disk: is the disk drive containing the back-up floppy disks.

/A directs BACKUP to add the files to be backed up to those already residing on the back-up disk. If you omit this qualifier, BACKUP overwrites the files on the back-up disk. The /A qualifier is not accepted if files exist that were backed up by using the DOS 3.2 BACKUP command.

/D:mm-dd-yy directs BACKUP to only back up files that were created or modified since the specified date.

/F directs BACKUP to format the disks contained in the target drive. BACKUP does not use this qualifier to FORMAT a fixed disk.

/L:logfile directs BACKUP to create a log file of each of the files that it is backing up by recording the date, time, and specific back-up disk on which each file resides.

/M directs BACKUP only to back up those files created or modified since the last backup.

/S directs BACKUP to back up all of the files contained in subdirectories below the directory to be backed up.

/T:hh:mm:ss directs BACKUP only to back up those files created or modified after the specified time.

Before you begin your hard disk backup, determine how many floppy disks you will need to store the data contained on your hard disk. To do so, first set the default drive to your fixed disk. Next, invoke the OS/2 CHKDSK command, as follows:

```
[C:\] CHKDSK

Volume OS2DISK created Sep 3, 1987   9:47pm

 21309440 bytes total disk space.
        0 bytes in 1 hidden files.
   182272 bytes in 82 directories.
 11681792 bytes in 1171 user files.
    20480 bytes in bad sectors.
  9406464 bytes available on disk.

[C:\]
```

Subtract the number of bytes available on the disk from the total disk space, as shown here:

bytes in use = total disk space − bytes available

Next, use the following equation to determine the number of floppy disks that your backup will require:

number of disks = bytes in use / storage capacity

Table 10-1 lists the storage capacity of commonly used floppy disks.

Disk type	Storage capacity
Single-sided Double-density	184,320 bytes
Double-sided Double-density	368,640 bytes
Double-sided Double-density 3.5	737,280 bytes
Quad-density	1,228,800 bytes
High-capacity 3.5	1,474,560 bytes

Table 10-1. *Number of Bytes Available on Different Types of Disks*

For example, assume that the CHKDSK command displayed the following:

```
[C:\] CHKDSK

Volume OS2DISK created Sep 3, 1987  9:47pm

 21309440 bytes total disk space.
        0 bytes in 1 hidden files.
   182272 bytes in 82 directories.
 11681792 bytes in 1171 user files.
    20480 bytes in bad sectors.
  9406464 bytes available on disk.

[C:\]
```

You can determine the number of floppy disks required for the backup as follows:

bytes in use = total disk space − bytes available

= 21309440 − 9406464

= 11902976

number of disks = bytes in use / storage capacity

= 11902976 / 1228800

= 9.69

= 10 disks

Unlike DOS, the OS/2 BACKUP command does not require formatted target disks. If you have previously formatted disks, your backup will proceed faster since BACKUP does not have to format each disk during the backup. However, if your disks are not formatted, simply place the /F qualifier in the back-up command line.

UNFORMATTED TARGET DISKS

Unlike the DOS BACKUP command (which requires the target disks to be previously formatted), the OS/2 BACKUP command allows you to use unformatted disks. In such cases, simply place the /F qualifier on the command line.

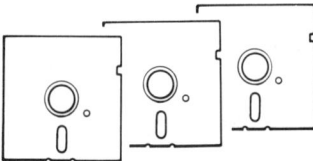

New Monthly Backups

Consider the following examples:

```
[C:\] BACKUP C:\PAYROLL.DAT A:
```

BACKUP will back up the file PAYROLL.DAT from the root directory to the disk contained in drive A. In this case, BACKUP will overwrite the contents of the disk in drive A and display the following warning message:

```
DOS1681: Warning!   The files in target
drive A:\root will be erased.

Press Enter to continue or Ctrl+Break to cancel.
```

If you do not want the files on the target disk to be destroyed, you can cancel the command by pressing the CTRL-C key combination.

BACKUP TERMINATION

To terminate the BACKUP command at any time, simply press the CTRL-BREAK key combination.

If instead you press the ENTER key to continue the backup, BACKUP will copy the file to drive A and display the following:

```
The system is backing up files to drive A:
Diskette number 01

\PAYROLL.DAT
```

Likewise, the command

```
[C:\] BACKUP C:\*.TXT A:
```

will back up all of the files in the root directory with the TXT extension to the disk in drive A. Again enter the following command:

```
[C:\] BACKUP C:\*.TXT A: /M
```

This time you have added the /M qualifier to the command line.

All OS/2 files use a 32-byte directory entry that contains the information shown in Table 10-2. Many OS/2 commands use the attribute byte to track changes to the file. Whenever the file is backed up, BACKUP sets the value of this byte to indicate that. When you later change the file, the value of the attribute byte is changed and thus indicates that it needs to be backed up. The /M qualifier in the BACKUP command line directs BACKUP to only back up those files created or modified since that last backup. BACKUP does this processing by examining the attribute byte of each file. Issuing the command

```
[C:\] BACKUP C:\*.TXT A:
```

immediately followed by

```
[C:\] BACKUP C:\*.TXT A: /M
```

results in no files being backed up by the second command. This should make sense because the first command set the attribute byte of each file as being backed up. The second command is looking for files requiring a backup and there should not be any.

Field	Offset
File name	0
Extension	8
Attribute byte	11
Reserved for DOS	12
Time	22
Date	24
Starting cluster number	26
File size	28

Table 10-2. *Entries in Directory Structure*

Thus far, all of the BACKUP commands examined have affected only files contained in the root directory. However, the OS/2 BACKUP command enables you to back up files contained in OS/2 subdirectories by using the /S qualifier. Assume that your directory structure on drive C is as shown in Figure 10-6.

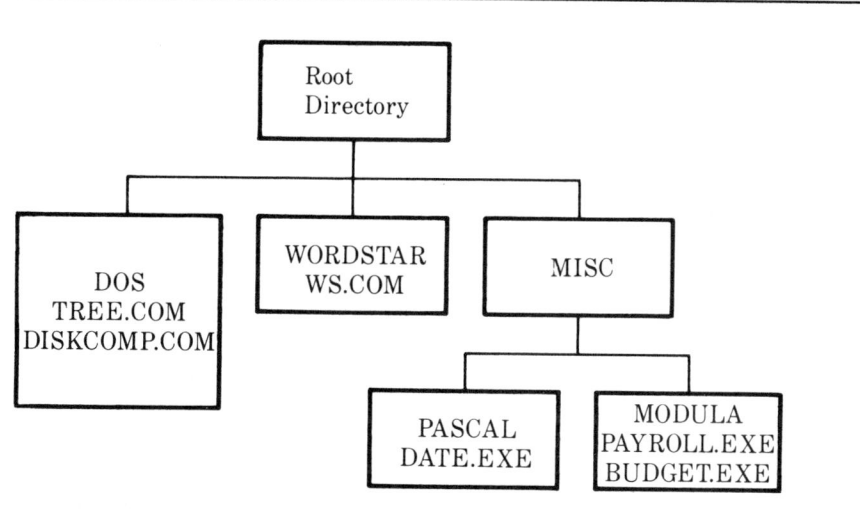

Figure 10-6. *Directory structure with DOS, WORDSTAR, and MISC directories*

The OS/2 BACKUP command

```
[C:\] BACKUP C:\ A: /S
```

will back up the entire directory structure to the back-up disks, thus providing a complete backup of your entire disk.

If the disks that you are using for the backup have not yet been formatted, simply add the /F qualifier to the previous command, as shown here:

```
[C:\] BACKUP C:\ A: /F/S
```

In this case, BACKUP backs up your disk as well as formats the target disks. Therefore, you may have to respond to several FORMAT prompts presented previously in this text. If so, simply press the ENTER key in response to the prompt for a volume label and type the letter N in response to the prompt for additional disks.

Once BACKUP fills the first floppy disk, it will prompt you to enter the second disk, as shown here:

```
Insert the backup diskette 02 in drive A:
DOS1681: Warning! The files in target
drive A:\root will be erased.

Press Enter to continue or Ctrl+Break to cancel.
```

Simply place a new disk in the drive and press the ENTER key to continue.

The BACKUP command enables you to specify date and time by using the /D and /T qualifiers. If you use these qualifiers, specify the date and time formats in the same manner as you would for the OS/2 DATE and TIME commands. For example, the following command backs up all the files on your disk that were created after 6 PM on December 25, 1987.

```
[C:\] BACKUP C:\ A: /D:12-25-87 /T:18:00:00
```

Previously in this chapter you saw that the following command overwrote the contents of the disk in drive A:

```
[C:\] BACKUP C:\ A:
```

In many cases, however, you will simply want BACKUP to add files to files that already reside on the back-up disk in drive A. In such cases, simply add the /A qualifier to the BACKUP command line, as shown here:

```
[C:\] BACKUP C:\ A: /A
```

Later in this chapter, during a discussion of back-up procedures that you should perform on a daily basis, the /A qualifier will be used to append today's files to those backed up yesterday.

The OS/2 BACKUP command provides the /L qualifier that allows you to create a log file of each of the files that BACKUP places on the back-up disk. If you simply place the /L qualifier on the BACKUP command line,

```
[C:\] BACKUP C:\ A: /L
```

BACKUP will write its log to the file BACKUP.LOG in the root directory of the disk being backed up. The format of the BACKUP log file is

```
10-4-1987  10:41:54
001   \OS2\ANSI.EXE
001   \OS2\APPEND.COM
001   \OS2\ASSIGN.COM
001   \OS2\ATTRIB.EXE
001   \OS2\BACKUP.COM
001   \OS2\CHKDSK.COM
001   \OS2\COMP.COM
001   \OS2\DISKCOMP.COM
```

When you later need to locate for restoration a file on the back-up disks, you can quickly examine the log file to locate the file.

Developing a Back-Up Policy

Backups *must* be performed on a regular basis. Depending on the importance of your data, your back-up procedures may vary slightly. However, if you follow these procedures, you will greatly reduce the possibility of data loss.

The first day of each month you will perform a complete system backup. Make sure that before you start, you have an adequate number of floppy disks available.

Each day, throughout the remainder of the month, you will back up only those files created or modified since the previous backup. Since backups are done on a daily basis, you will only be

---

BACKUP PROCEDURES

The first of each month, issue the following command:

BACKUP C:\ A: /L /S

This command will back up your entire disk. Each day of the month, enter the following command:

BACKUP C:\ A: /L /S /A /M

This command backs up each of the files created or modified since the previous backup.

---

backing up the files that you have created each day. Your daily backups should only take a few minutes to complete.

Always remember to place your back-up disks in a safe location. Since your backups will require multiple disks, make sure that you label each disk in a meaningful way. For monthly backups, use the label shown in Figure 10-7. Likewise, for daily backups use the label shown in Figure 10-8.

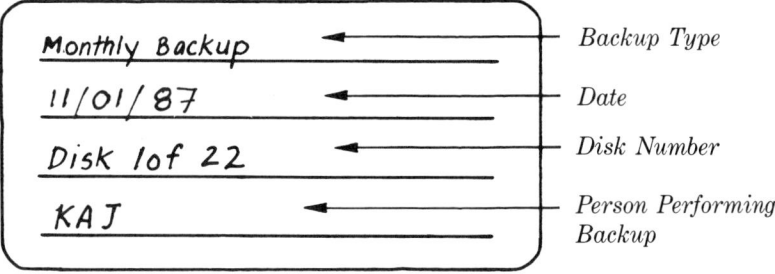

Figure 10-7. *Example of labels for monthly disk backups*

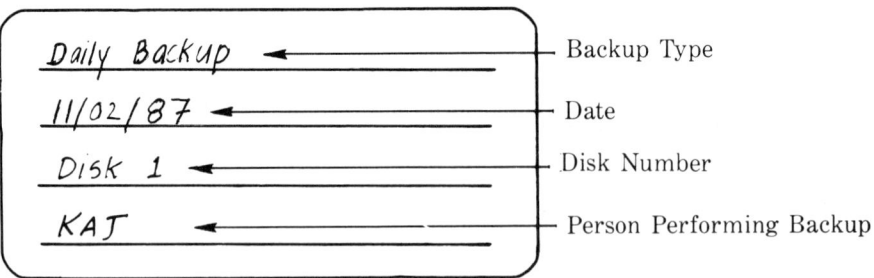

Figure 10-8. *Example of labels for daily disk backups*

Use the following batch procedure (MONTHLY.CMD) to create your monthly backups:

```
ECHO OFF
REM MONTHLY BACKUP PROCEDURES
BACKUP C:\ A: /S /L
IF ERRORLEVEL 4 GOTO FATAL_ERROR
IF ERRORLEVEL 3 GOTO USER_TERMINATED
IF ERRORLEVEL 2 GOTO SHARING_CONFLICT
IF ERRORLEVEL 1 GOTO NO_FILES
:SUCCESSFUL_BACKUP
ECHO BACKUP SUCCESSFUL
GOTO DONE
:FATAL_ERROR
ECHO FATAL ERROR IN PROCESSING
GOTO DONE
:USER_TERMINATED
ECHO USER TERMINATION
GOTO DONE
:SHARING_CONFLICT
ECHO SOME FILES NOT BACKED UP DUE TO SHARING LOCKS
GOTO DONE
:NO_FILES
ECHO NO FILES FOUND TO BACKUP
:DONE
```

BACKUP uses the following error-status values to support the development of batch procedures to perform your backups:

0   BACKUP completed successfully

1   BACKUP found no files to backup

2   BACKUP could not back up files because of sharing conflicts

3   BACKUP was terminated by a CTRL-C

4   BACKUP was terminated by an error

On a daily basis invoke the following batch procedure :

```
ECHO OFF
REM DAILY BACKUP PROCEDURES
BACKUP C:\ A: /S /L /A /M
IF ERRORLEVEL 4 GOTO FATAL_ERROR
IF ERRORLEVEL 3 GOTO USER_TERMINATED
IF ERRORLEVEL 2 GOTO SHARING_CONFLICT
IF ERRORLEVEL 1 GOTO NO_FILES
:SUCCESSFUL_BACKUP
ECHO BACKUP SUCCESSFUL
GOTO DONE
:FATAL_ERROR
ECHO FATAL ERROR IN PROCESSING
GOTO DONE
:USER_TERMINATED
ECHO USER TERMINATION
GOTO DONE
:SHARING_CONFLICT
ECHO SOME FILES NOT BACKED UP DUE TO SHARING LOCKS
GOTO DONE
:NO_FILES
ECHO NO FILES FOUND TO BACKUP
:DONE
```

At the end of each month you should have multiple disks, as shown next.

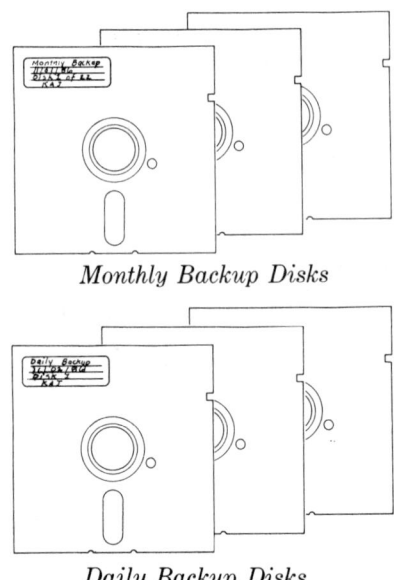

Monthly Backup Disks

Daily Backup Disks

Once you successfully complete the next month's backup

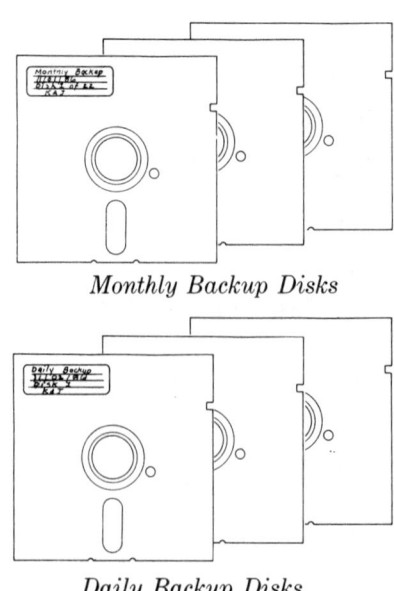

Monthly Backup Disks

Daily Backup Disks

you can re-use the previous month's disks.

Note that these batch files assume you are using previously formatted disks. This should greatly reduce the amount of time that BACKUP requires. If not, simply change the line

```
[C:\] BACKUP C:\ A: /S /L
```

to

```
[C:\] BACKUP C:\ A: /S /L /F
```

Eventually, you should have enough formatted disks to be able to remove the /F qualifier.

OS/2 RESTORE Command

You should never have to invoke the OS/2 RESTORE command to restore files from your back-up disks. But if you do, the OS/2 RESTORE command is quite straightforward. The format of the OS/2 RESTORE command is

*[drive:][path]*RESTORE *source_disk*: [*d:*][*p*][*file*]
    [/*A*:mm-dd-yy][/*B*:mm-dd-yy][/*E*:hh:mm:ss][/*L*:hh:mm:ss]
    [/*M*][/*N*][/*P*][/*S*]

where the following is true:

drive: is the disk drive identifier of the disk containing the file RESTORE.COM. If you do not specify a disk drive identifier, OS/2 uses the current drive.

path is the OS/2 path name of the OS/2 subdirectory containing the file RESTORE.COM. If you do not specify a path, OS/2 uses the current default.

source—disk: is the disk drive identifier of the disk containing the back-up disks.

d: is the disk drive to which you want to restore the files.

p is the OS/2 path name of the subdirectory to which you want to restore the files.

file is the name of the file to be restored.

/A directs RESTORE to restore only those files modified on or after the specified date.

/B directs RESTORE to restore only those files modified on or before the specified date.

/E directs RESTORE to restore only those files modified on or before the specified time.

/L directs RESTORE to restore only those files modified on or after the specified time.

/M directs RESTORE to restore only those files modified since the last backup.

/N directs RESTORE to restore only those files no longer contained on the disk.

/P directs RESTORE to prompt you before restoring files that have been changed or marked read-only since the backup.

/S directs RESTORE also to restore subdirectories below the target path name.

If you are preparing to restore files from your back-up disks, you should first write-protect your back-up disks, as shown in Figure 10-9. In so doing, you reduce the possibility of losing your only back-up copies of a file.

If you are looking for a specific file, again refer to the file BACKUP.LOG that the /L BACKUP qualifier creates. If it exists, simply print it and locate each reference to the file that you desire.

Figure 10-9.   *Write-protected disk for monthly backup*

Consider the following commands:

```
[C:\] RESTORE A: C:\ /S
```

In this case, RESTORE restores the entire fixed disk from the back-up disks contained in drive A. The /S qualifier works in an identical manner for BACKUP and RESTORE.

```
[C:\] RESTORE A: C:\*.SAL /S
```

In this case, RESTORE only restores files with the SAL extension from the disk contained in drive A.

In some cases, you may have files that you do not want the RESTORE command to overwrite. If so, use the /P qualifier, as shown here:

```
[C:\] RESTORE A: C:\ /P
```

In this case, RESTORE prompts you with the following message when it encounters such files:

```
Warning! File FILENAME was changed after backed up.
Replace the file (Y/N)?
```

If you are not sure which files you may have lost from your disk, use the /N option during the restoration, as shown here:

```
[C:\] RESTORE A: C:\ /S /N
```

In this case, RESTORE only restores the files that are no longer on disk.

Just as BACKUP provides exit-status values for batch processing, so too does RESTORE. The following are the exit-status values for RESTORE:

0   RESTORE completed successfully

1   RESTORE found no files to restore

2   RESTORE could not restore files because of sharing conflicts

3   RESTORE was terminated by a CTRL-C

4   RESTORE was terminated by an error

Multitasking Concerns

Backups are a critical function that you must perform on a regular basis. Under DOS, BACKUP was the only program that could run without the fear of another application modifying the disk structure during the middle of a backup. However, under OS/2 this is not the case. During your monthly backups, the only program that you should have running on your system is BACKUP. In so doing, you can be sure that you have a good foundation on which to start your daily backups.

Chapter Highlights

Data loss may occur from any of several sources (fire, theft, programming errors, spills, and so forth). Therefore, you should perform system backups on a regular basis.

Many third-party products exist that perform system backups. Normally, the advantage of such products is user interface. The fundamental processing is similar to the OS/2 BACKUP command.

Use either the OS/2 DISKCOPY or XCOPY commands to make copies of your disks. Use BACKUP for your fixed disks.

You will find the OS/2 BACKUP command useful throughout your work. By defining a few simple batch commands, you can easily perform backups on a regular basis in little time.

If you should lose data, the OS/2 RESTORE command enables you to recover it in a straightforward manner from the back-up disks.

Since OS/2 is a multitasking operating system, it is possible that other programs may be running during your monthly backups. To be sure that you have a solid foundation for your daily backups, make sure that BACKUP is the only program running during your system backups.

11 OS/2 Programming Introduction

Each of the preceding chapters has examined OS/2 strictly from the perspective of the end user. This chapter takes a closer look at OS/2's inner workings, this time from a programmer's viewpoint. You will learn how to develop protected-mode applications and how to migrate these programs to OS/2 real mode (and DOS). You will be introduced to the OS/2 system services and learn how to access these services from within your programs. This chapter examines the MAKE utility and how it can simplify your program maintenance. This chapter also discusses several OS/2 applications that you can execute in both real mode and protected mode.

Chapter 12 also examines OS/2 programming considerations. However, the concepts in Chapter 12 are much more advanced. You must be fully conversant with each of the concepts presented in this chapter before going on to Chapter 12.

A First Look

With a text editor (or by copying it from the keyboard device), enter the following C program called FIRST.C:

```
main ()
  {
   printf ("First OS/2 program\n");
  }
```

On invocation, this program displays the following message:

```
[C:\] FIRST
First OS/2 program

[C:\]
```

Using the Microsoft C compiler, compile this program by using the /Lp compiler directive (the protected-mode default) to create a protected-mode executable file, as shown here:

```
[C:\] CL /Lp FIRST.C
```

Microsoft C provides the CL command to compile and link your C source files (see Figure 11-1).

Using the CTRL-ALT keyboard combination, select a real-mode

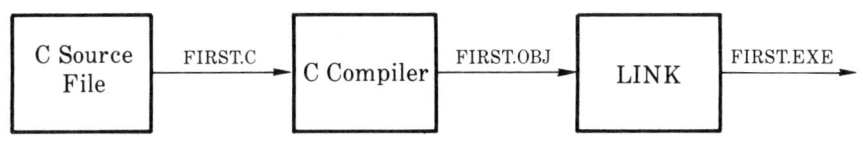

Figure 11–1.   *The CL command in C used for compiling and linking source files*

session. Again, invoke the program as shown here:

```
C> FIRST
Program too big to fit in memory

C>
```

As you can see, the program invocation fails in real mode, as it should. The /Lp compiler directive produced a protected-mode executable file that cannot execute in real mode.

Again select your protected-mode session. Compile the program by using the CL command, but this time replace the /Lp compiler directive with /Lc, as shown here:

```
[C:\] CL /Lc FIRST.C
```

The /Lc directive instructs the C compiler to produce a real-mode (compatibility) executable file. Once the compilation completes, again select a real-mode session and execute the program, as follows:

```
C> FIRST
First OS/2 program

C>
```

Although the program now executes in real mode, it no longer works in protected mode, as shown here:

```
[C:\] FIRST
SYS0193: The system has detected an unacceptable
executable format in the file C:\FIRST.EXE

[C:\]
```

Admittedly, you could keep two copies of the executable file on disk, one for protected mode and one for real mode. However, as the number of your applications increased, you would soon have an unmanageable collection of files. Ideally, you need a method of producing EXE files that execute in either real or protected mode. In this way, you only have a single copy of the program file. Each time it is invoked, the program itself determines in which mode of execution it should operate. The OS/2 BIND utility enables you to migrate protected-mode programs to real mode.

BIND

By default, OS/2 applications do not run in protected mode and real mode. However, by following these three simple steps, you are able to build programs that run in both modes. Such programs are called *OS/2 family applications*.

1. Create your program source code.

2. Compile the program by using the /Lp option to produce a protected-mode executable file.

3. Use BIND to create a compatibility mode executable file.

Using the previous C program, you implement these steps as follows:

1. Create your program source code.

```
main ()
{
  printf ("First OS/2 program\n");
}
```

2. Compile the program by using the /Lp option to produce a protected-mode executable file.

```
[C:\] CL /Lp FIRST.C
```

3. Use BIND to create a compatibility mode executable file.

```
[C:\] BIND FIRST \LIB\DOSCALLS.LIB
```

This program now executes in protected mode

```
[C:\] FIRST
First OS/2 program

[C:\]
```

as well as in real mode

```
C> FIRST
First OS/2 program

C>
```

You can run this program on DOS. Later, this chapter examines in detail the module-definition files and the OS/2 BIND utility. For now, simply understand that they are required steps for running your programs in both protected mode and real mode.

The next example program uses OS/2 system services to display the current mode of processing (real or protected). If you invoke the program in real mode, it displays the following:

```
C> SHOWMODE
Current mode is REAL

C>
```

Likewise, in protected mode the output is as follows:

```
[C:\] SHOWMODE
Current mode is PROTECTED

[C:\]
```

Using the previous four steps, the processing becomes the following:

1. Create your program source code.

```
#include <doscalls.h>

main()
 {
   char mode;

   DOSGETMACHINEMODE(&mode);        /* Get mode */

   printf("Current mode is %s\n",(mode == 1) ? "PROTECTED": "REAL");
 }
```

2. Compile the program by using the /Lp option to produce a protected-mode executable file.

```
[C:\] CL /Lp SHOWMODE.C
```

3. Use BIND to create a compatibility mode executable file.

```
[C:\] BIND SHOWMODE \LIB\DOSCALLS.LIB
```

Although both of these example programs perform simple processing, each illustrates the steps required to build a program that runs in either real or protected mode. Follow these steps throughout the applications presented in the remainder of this chapter.

OS/2 FAMILY APPLICATIONS

By default, OS/2 protected-mode programs do not execute in real mode and OS/2 real-mode programs do not execute in protected mode. By using the OS/2 BIND utility, you can create a compatibility mode executable file that executes in both modes. Not all protected-mode programs can be migrated to compatibility mode in this manner. However, many can, thus reducing your file duplication.

Module-Definition File (DEF File)

Many OS/2 applications also use a special file called a *module-definition file*. This file tells the linker specifics about the program.

In most cases, your module-definition files will be straightforward. However, you should note that module-definition files can become quite complex, as illustrated by the following entries. Each of the following entries is valid for OS/2 module-definition files.

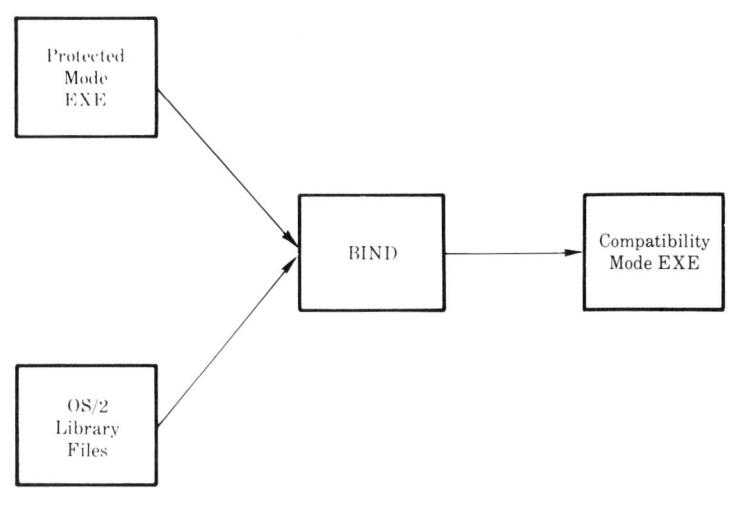

Figure 11-2.   *Module-definition file as part of input for BIND*

CODE

This statement specifies how OS/2 treats the application code segments:

CODE [*load_option*] [*share_option*] [*execute_option*] [*privilege*]

where the following is true:

load_option specifies when the code segments are loaded.

> PRELOAD   All segments are automatically loaded. (This is the default setting.)

> LOADONCALL   Segments are loaded only when called.

share_option specifies whether or not the code segments can be shared by other applications.

> SHARED   Segments are available to other applications (default for library).
>
> NONSHARED   Segments are not shareable. (This is the default for application programs.)

execute_option states whether a segment can only be executed, or executed and read.

> EXECUTEONLY   Segments cannot be read.

> EXECUTEREAD   Segments can be read. (This is the default.)

privilege states whether or not the application has I/O privilege.

> IOPL

PURE code does not contain data. For example,

CODE LOADONCALL

DATA

This statement specifies how OS/2 treats the application data segments:

DATA [*load_option*] [*instance_option*] [*share_option*]
    [*write_option*] [*privilege*]

where the following is true:

load_option specifies when the data segments are loaded.

> PRELOAD   All segments are automatically loaded. (This is the default.)

> LOADONCALL   Segments loaded only when referenced.

instance_option specifies the manipulation of DGROUP data space.

NONE	No automatic data segment is created.
SINGLE	All instances share same DGROUP data space.
MULTIPLE DGROUP	Data space is copied for each instance.

share_option specifies whether or not the data segments can be shared by other applications.

SHARED	Segments are available to other applications.
NONSHARED	Segments are not shareable. (This is the default.)

write_option states whether a segment can only be read, or read and written to.

READONLY	Segments can only be read.
READWRITE	Segments can be read or written to. (This is the default.)

privilege states whether or not the application has I/O privilege.

IOPL

For example,

DATA READONLY

DESCRIPTION

This statement enables you to insert a text string within the executable file:

DESCRIPTION 'text message'

For example,

DESCRIPTION 'OS/2 Publications 1988'

EXPORTS

This statement defines the names of routines contained in this module that will be exported to other modules:

EXPORTS *entry_name*[=*internal_name*] [*@ordinal_value*]
   [*RESIDENTNAME*][*NODATA*][*privilege*][...]

where the following is true:

entry_name defines the name other modules must use to reference the routine.

internal_name specifies the actual name of this routine within this module.

@ordinal_value is a numeric value that serves as an index to the routines named in the string table.

RESIDENTNAME is a keyword that specifies that the function's name must be resident at all times. It is used in conjunction with ordinal values.

NODATA is a keyword that specifies that the function is not bound to a global data segment.

privilege is a numeric value that specifies the number of bytes to reserve for parameters to the function.

For example,

EXPORTS
   NEWFILE=CREATE_FILE GETDIR NODATA

HEAPSIZE

This statement specifies the size of the heap for the application. *num_bytes* must range from 0 to 65,536.

HEAPSIZE *num_bytes*

For example,

HEAPSIZE 4096

IMPORTS

This statement defines the names of functions that the program imports from other modules:

IMPORTS [*internal_name*=[*module_name*.[*entry_name* ¦ *ordinal_value*]]]

where the following is true:

internal_name is the name that the program will use for the routine.

module_name specifies the name of the module from which the routine is imported.

entry_name is the name of the routine within the import module.

ordinal_value is a numeric index into the string table that specifies the name of the imported function.

For example,

```
IMPORTS
   UTIL=SP_UTIL
   GETVER=DOSUTIL.VERSION_NUMBER
```

LIBRARY

This statement identifies the executable file as a library as opposed to an application. If no library name is given, OS/2 uses the file name minus the extension.

LIBRARY [*library_name*]

For example,

LIBRARY OS2LIB

NAME

This directive identifies the executable file as an application program as opposed to a library file. If no application name is given, OS/2 uses the file name minus the extension.

NAME [*application_name*]

For example,

NAME FIRST

PROTMODE

This statement specifies that the application runs only in OS/2 protected mode. For example,

PROTMODE

SEGMENTS

This statement allows you to define the attributes of specific segments (overriding the DATA and CODE default segment types).

SEGMENTS [']*segment_name*['][CLASS[']*class_name*[']]
   [*minimum_bytes*] [*segment_flags*]

where the following is true:

segment—name defines the name of the segment of which you are setting the attributes.

class—name specifies the class of the specific segment (such as CODE).

minimum—bytes is the minimum number of bytes to allocate for this segment (0 to 65,536).

segment—flags defines the attributes of the segment:

EXECUTEONLY	EXECUTEREAD	IOPL
LOADONCALL	NONSHARED	PRELOAD
READONLY	READWRITE	SHARED

For example;

SEGMENTS 'CODE' READONLY

STACKSIZE

This statement specifies the size of the local stack for the application. *num—bytes* must range from 0 to 65,536.

STACKSIZE *num—bytes*

For example,

STACKSIZE 4096

STUB

This statement attaches the specified file to the beginning of the application. If the application is executed under DOS 3.x, the program runs first, possibly displaying a message that states the application is an OS/2 program.

STUB *file__name*

For example,

STUB NOTDOS.OBJ

Although module-definition files may seem threatening to some users, in most cases the use of these files will be quite straightforward, as shown here:

```
NAME FIRST
DATA MOVEABLE
CODE MOVEABLE PURE
HEAPSIZE 2048
STACKSIZE 2048
```

MODULE-DEFINITION FILE

To create an OS/2 executable file, you can optionally create a module-definition file that defines the attributes of the executable file. The module-definition file is simply a text file that you create with your text editor. Module-definition files should have the DEF extension.

BIND Processing in Detail

For each of the previous example programs, you used BIND in a straightforward manner, as shown here:

```
[C:\] BIND FILENAME \LIB\DOSCALLS.LIB
```

However, BIND also allows several command-line arguments. This section provides a complete overview of the processing capabilities of BIND.

The format of BIND is

BIND *input_file*[.ext] [*import_libraries*] [*link_libraries*]
  [−*o output_file*[.exe]] [−*n @filename*] [−*n name* [...]]
  [−*m map_filename*]

where the following is true:

input_file is the name of the OS/2 executable file to bind.

import_libraries specifies the names of the import libraries used to resolve external references in the *link_libraries* when the IMPORT by ORDINAL option is used in the LINK command.

link_libraries specifies the names of the libraries OS/2 binds to the application when it executes under OS/2.

−*o output_file* specifies an alternate name for the executable file BIND produces.

−*n @filename* specifies a file of names of calls to map to the BadDynLink service.

−*n name* specifies a name of a call to map to the BadDynLink service.

−*m map_filename* directs BIND to produce a link map of the DOS 3.x executable file.

If you plan never to migrate your applications from protected mode to real mode, you will never need to use BIND. For most programmers, however, BIND will play an important role in program development.

BIND

The OS/2 BIND utility creates your compatibility mode executable file that will execute in real mode or protected mode. BIND examines the executable file and library files to produce a new executable file with an EXE extension.

MAKE

As your programs increase in complexity, maintaining them can become more of a challenge. To simplify your program maintenance, some OS/2 programming languages include a utility called MAKE that helps you update your programs when you have to change code. MAKE is an intelligent application manager that recompiles, reassembles, or links only those programs affected by a code change. It does this by analyzing the date and time stamps associated with every file used by the application.

To begin, you must create a MAKE description file (by using a text editor) that consists of one or more descriptions in the following form:

target_file: dependent_file [*,dependent_file . . .*]
   command
   [command . . .]

where the following is true:

target_file: specifies the name of a file that may or may not need to be updated because of a code change.

dependent_file specifies the name of a file from which the target file is built. If the date stamp on the dependent file is newer than the target file, the commands that follow are executed. If the number of dependent files exceeds one line, place a backslash at the end of the line and continue listing the names on the following line.

command specifies a DOS command to be executed when the dependent file has changed.

Think of the MAKE description file as a series of IF-THEN statements. If the dependent file is newer than the target file (or if the target file does not exist), then the series of DOS commands that follow are executed. For example:

```
FIRST.EXE:     FIRST.C,FIRST.DEF

               CL /Lp FIRST.C

               BIND FIRST \LIB\DOSCALLS.LIB
```

In this case, if FIRST.EXE is older than either FIRST.C or FIRST.DEF, or if FIRST.EXE does not exist, MAKE will compile, link, and bind the file. Figure 11-3 illustrates this processing.

Invoke MAKE as

MAKE [*options*][macro_definitions] filename

where the *options* include the following:

/d directs MAKE to display the date of each file as it examines the file.

/i directs MAKE to ignore error-code values returned by commands as they execute.

/n directs MAKE to display each command it would normally execute, instead of actually executing the command.

/s directs MAKE to suppress the names of files as they are processed.

MAKE supports embedded macros that are later substituted during the MAKE execution. The format of a MAKE macro is

$(macro_name)

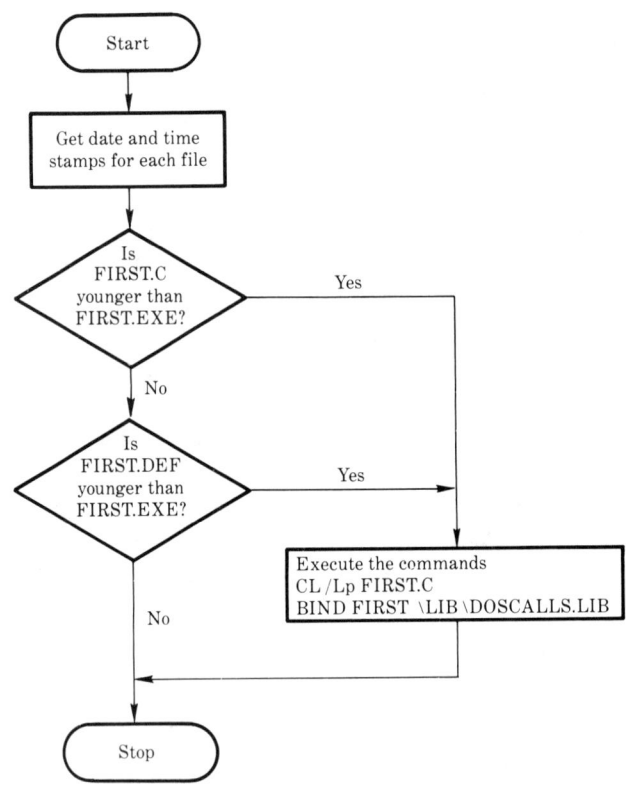

Figure 11-3. *Process of MAKE determining execution order of files*

For example, consider the following:

$(NAME).EXE: $(NAME).C,$(NAME).DEF

                  CL $(NAME).C

                  BIND $(NAME) \LIB\DOSCALLS.LIB

If you later invoke MAKE with

MAKE NAME=FIRST

MAKE will substitute the macro, as shown here:

FIRST.EXE: FIRST.C,FIRST.DEF

               CL /Lp FIRST.C

               BIND FIRST \LIB\DOSCALLS.LIB

In addition, MAKE predefines three macros, as follows:

$*   Use target file name without the extension

$A   Use the complete target file name

$**   Use the complete list of dependent files

MAKE also allows you to define inference rules to specify how MAKE should convert one file type to another. The format of an inference rule is:

```
.dependent_extension.target_extension
command
```

For example, to convert from C to EXE, you would use the following:

```
.C.EXE
   CL $*.C
```

MAKE is a powerful and convenient programming utility. Many of you will find it useful for all applications, not just OS/2. Most OS/2 sample programs have a MAKE description file accompanying them. The ability to decipher this file greatly simplifies your development tasks.

MAKE

MAKE is a program development and maintenance utility that examines the date and time stamps of each dependent file and compares them to that of the target file. If a dependent file is younger, or the target file does not exist, MAKE performs the commands that follow.

API Services

For the first time, OS/2 brings microcomputer programmers capabilities previously available only under minicomputer operating systems like UNIX or VAX/VMS. Because of its complexity, OS/2 took a considerable time to develop (more than four years). Including utility programs, OS/2 consists of more than 350,000 lines of code. To simplify their development efforts, the OS/2 developers broke the large programming task into a series of smaller, more manageable subtasks called *functions* or *services*.

Since these routines are required for OS/2 to execute, the OS/2 developers make them readily available to your application programs.

Under DOS, your programs accessed system services by way of INT 21H. In OS/2 protected mode, INT 21H no longer exists. Instead, your programs use the Application Program Interface (API) services. The following is a list of the API services available under OS/2:

DosAllocHuge	DosDevConfig
DosAllocSeg	DosDevIOCtl
DosAllocShrSeg	DosDupHandle
DosBeep	DosEnterCritSec
DosBufReset	DosErrClass
DosCaseMap	DosError
DosChdir	DosExecPgm
DosChgFilePtr	DosExit
DosCLIAccess	DosExitCritSec
DosClose	DosExitList
DosCloseQueue	DosFileLock
DosCloseSem	DosFindClose
DosCreateCSAlias	DosFindFirst
DosCreateQueue	DosFindNext
DosCreateSem	DosFlagProcess
DosCreateThread	DosFreeModule
DosCWait	DosFreeSeg
DosDelete	DosGetCollate

DosGetCP
DosGetCtryInfo
DosGetDateTime
DosGetDBCSEv
DosGetEnv
DosGetHugeShift
DosGetInfoSeg
DosGetMachineMode
DosGetMessage
DosGetModHandle
DosGetModName
DosGetProcAddr
DosGetPrty
DosGetResource
DosGetSeg
DosGetShrSeg
DosGetVersion
DosGiveSeg
DosHoldSignal
DosInsMessage
DosKillProcess
DosLoadModule
DosLockSeg
DosMakePipe
DosMemAvail
DosMkdir
DosMonClose
DosMonOpen
DosMonRead
DosMonReg
DosMonWrite
DosMove
DosMuxSemWait
DosNewSize
DosOpen
DosOpenQueue
DosOpenSem
DosPeekQueue
DosPFSActivate

DosPFSCloseUser
DosPFSInit
DosPFSQueryAct
DOSPFSVerifyFont
DosPhysicalDisk
DosPortAccess
DosPtrace
DosPurgeQueue
DosPutMessage
DosQCurDir
DosQCurDisk
DosQFHandState
DosQFileInfo
DosQFileMode
DosQFSInfo
DosQHandType
DosQueryQueue
DosQVerify
DosRead
DosReadAsynch
DosReadQueue
DosReAllocHuge
DosReAllocSeg
DosResumeThread
DosRmdir
DosScanEnv
DosSearchPath
DosSelectDisk
DosSelectSession
DosSemClear
DosSemRequest
DosSemSet
DosSemSetWait
DosSemWait
DosSetCP
DosSetDateTime
DosSetFHandState
DosSetFileInfo
DosSetFileMode

DosSetFSInfo	KbdStringIn
DosSetMaxFH	KbdSynch
DosSetPtry	KbdXlate
DosSetSession	MouClose
DosSetSigHandler	MouDeRegister
DosSetVec	MouDrawPtr
DosSetVerify	MouFlushQue
DosSleep	MouGetDevStatus
DosStartSession	MouGetEventMask
DosStopSession	MouGetHotKey
DosSubAlloc	MouGetNumButtons
DosSubFree	MouGetNumMickeys
DosSubSet	MouGetNumQueEl
DosSuspendThread	MouGetPtrPos
DosSystemService	MouGetPtrShape
DosTimerAsynch	MouGetScaleFact
DosTimerStart	MouInitReal
DosTimerStop	MouOpen
DosUnlockSeg	MouReadEventQue
DosWrite	MouRegister
DosWriteAsynch	MouRemovePtr
DosWriteQueue	MouSetDevStatus
KbdCharIn	MouSetEventMask
KbdClose	MouSetHotKey
KbdCustCP	MouSetPtrPos
KbdDeRegister	MouSetPtrShape
KbdFlushBuffer	MouSetScaleFact
KbdFreeFocus	MouShellInit
KbdGetFocus	MouSynch
KbdGetStatus	VioDeRegister
KbdGetXT	VioEndPopUp
KbdOpen	VioGetAnsi
KbdPeek	VioGetBuf
KbdRegister	VioGetCP
KbdSetFgnd	VioGetConfig
KbdSetStatus	VioGetCurPos
KbdSetXT	VioGetCurType
KbdShellInit	VioGetFont

VioGetMode
VioGetPhysBuf
VioGetState
VioModeUndo
VioModeWait
VioPopUp
VioPrtSc
VioPrtScToggle
VioReadCellStr
VioReadCharStr
VioRegister
VioSaveReDrawUndo
VioSavReDrawWait
VioScrLock
VioScrollDn
VioScrollLf
VioScrollRt

VioScrollUp
VioScrUnLock
VioSetAnsi
VioSetCP
VioSetCurPos
VioSetCurType
VioSetFont
VioSetMode
VioSetState
VioShowBuf
VioWrtCellStr
VioWrtCharStr
VioWrtCharStrAtt
VioWrtNAttr
VioWrtNCell
VioWrtNChar
VioWrtTTY

As you examine this list of services, note the similarity to many of the DOS INT 21H and BIOS services. This chapter later discusses how OS/2 defines a subset of these services as the *family API*. Your programs can use family API services from either real mode or protected mode by way of BIND. As long as your program only uses this subset of the API, BIND can create an OS/2 family executable file. As stated, an OS/2 family application determines the mode it is executing in and processes accordingly. The following is a list of family API services:

DOSBEEP
DOSCHDIR
DOSCHGFILEPTR
DOSCLOSE
DOSDELETE
DOSDEVCONFIG
DOSDEVIOCTL
DOSDUPHANDLE
DOSERROR
DOSFILELOCKS

DOSFINDCLOSE
DOSFINDFIRST
DOSFINDNEXT
DOSMKDIR
DOSMOVE
DOSNEWSIZE
DOSOPEN
DOSQCURDIR
DOSQCURDISK
DOSQFHANDSTATE

DOSQFSINFO	VIOGETCURTYPE
DOSQFILEINFO	VIOGETMODE
DOSQFILEMODE	VIOGETPHYSBUF
DOSQVERIFY	VIOREADCELLSTR
DOSREAD	VIOREADCHARSTR
DOSRMDIR	VIOSCRLOCK
DOSSELECTDISK	VIOSCRUNLOCK
DOSSETFHANDSTATE	VIOSCROLLDN
DOSSETFSINFO	VIOSCROLLLF
DOSSETFILEMODE	VIOSCROLLRT
DOSSETVEC	VIOSCROLLUP
DOSSETVERIFY	VIOSETCURPOS
DOSWRITE	VIOSETCURTYPE
KBDCHARIN	VIOSETMODE
KBDFLUSHBUFFER	VIOSHOWBUFF
KBDGETSTATUS	VIOWRTCELLSTR
KBDPEEK	VIOWRTCHARSTR
KBDREGISTER	VIOWRTCHARSTRATT
KBDSETSTATUS	VIOWRTNATTR
KBDSTRINGIN	VIOWRTNCELL
VIOGETBUF	VIOWRTNCHAR
VIOGETCURPOS	VIOWRTTTY

API SERVICES

The OS/2 system services are called Application Program Interface (API) services. These services provide the same functionality as those found under DOS INT 21H and BIOS INT 10H and 16H. OS/2 defines a subset of the API services as the family API. The family API routines have direct DOS INT 21H or BIOS counterparts. As long as your programs only use the family API services, BIND will be able to create a compatibility mode executable file.

OS/2 Family Application EXE Structure

The OS/2 API provides your interface to the OS/2 system services. For example, each time your program sets the current directory, it uses the OS/2 API service DOSCHDIR.

A *dynamic-link library* is a library of routines accessed by programs during execution. Under DOS, each time you link a file, you must specify the names of the OBJ and LIB files that LINK is to combine to build the EXE file. Linking applications in this manner is *static linking*, since all of the routines required must be present at link time (see Figure 11-4). With dynamic-link libraries, the actual resolution of externals is done by the OS/2 loader when it places a program into memory. In this way, both the program and the executable code reside in memory (see Figure 11-5).

The advantages of using dynamic-link libraries include the following: shared source code, since many programs can map to the same library (see Figure 11-6); smaller executable files on disk, since the library code is external to the program; and easier modification of code.

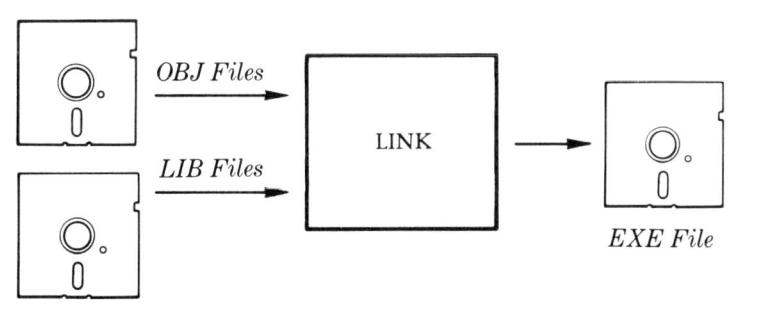

Figure 11-4. *Static linking*

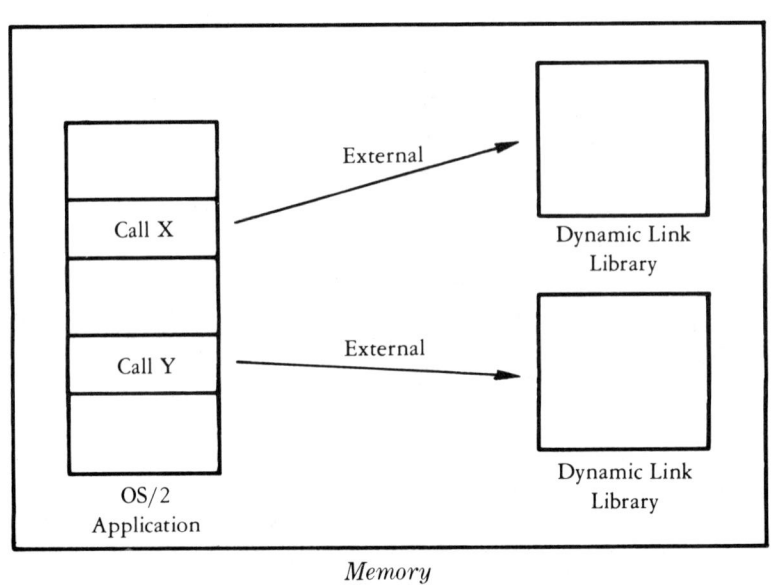

Figure 11-5. *Dynamic linking*

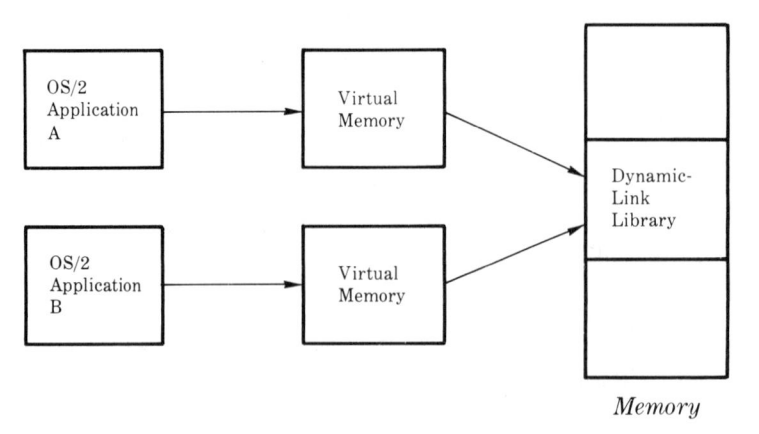

Figure 11-6. *Many programs linking to same library*

In the past, each time you changed a routine contained in a library, you had to relink every application that accessed the routine. With dynamic-link libraries, this is not required. You need only compile and reload the updated dynamic-link library. Programs will map to this new code transparently. Since each program does not actually contain any code from the library, a change in the library does not affect the program. The next time OS/2 loads a program that references the updated routine, the loader simply maps the program to the updated library routine transparently. In this way, every program that references the library routine is updated when the new dynamic-link library is loaded.

The OS/2 API is implemented as a dynamic-link library. Each time an OS/2 application requests a system service, the program does so by using the OS/2 API.

Consider the following C program that uses the API routine DOSQCURDIR to display the current directory. Using the previous four steps, the processing is as follows:

1. Create the source file with a text editor.

```
#include <doscalls.h>

main ()
  {
   int status, length;

   char dir[64];

   status = DOSQCURDIR (0, dir, &length);

   printf ("\\%s\n", dir);
  }
```

2. Compile and link the program by using the protected-mode directive /Lp in the compiler command line.

```
[C:\] CL /Lp SHOWDIR.C
```

3. Use BIND to build the compatibility mode executable file.

```
[C:\] BIND SHOWDIR \LIB\DOSCALLS.LIB
```

This program runs in protected mode

```
[C:\] SHOWDIR
\OS2DIR

[C:\]
```

as well as real mode

```
C> SHOWDIR
\OS2DIR

C>
```

Under OS/2, this processing makes sense. Each time the program loads, OS/2 maps the DOSQCURDIR call to the OS/2 API dynamic-link library (see Figure 11-7). However, under DOS the API dynamic-link library does not exist. How does the program succeed? The secret lies in the family application EXE structure.

OS/2 EXE files have two headers. The first header appears

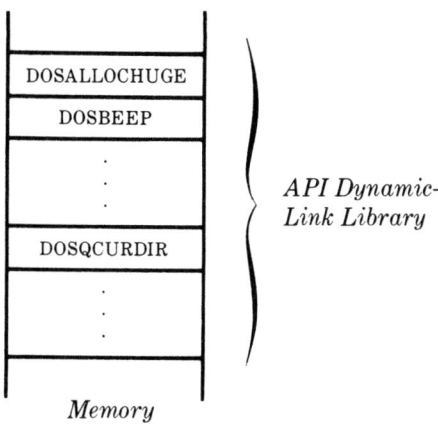

Figure 11-7. *Mapping the DOSQCURDIR call to dynamic-link library*

in DOS 3.x format and the second is an OS/2 extension. Each time your compatibility mode program executes under OS/2 protected mode, it ignores the DOS 3.x header and maps API calls to the dynamic-link library. However, when the application executes under DOS 3.x, it uses the DOS header. In this case, the program does not map to the OS/2 API dynamic-link library, since the API dynamic-link library only exists under OS/2.

Instead, each of the OS/2 API calls (such as DOSQCURDIR) are mapped to a set of routines called the DOS 3.x family API. The DOS 3.x family API examines the parameters specified in the call and, in turn, invokes the corresponding INT 21H service (see Figure 11-8). In so doing, the loader actually dictates in which mode the program executes—real or protected. The BIND facility simply allows the DOS 3.x family API routines to be included, thus making the program compatible to both modes of processing.

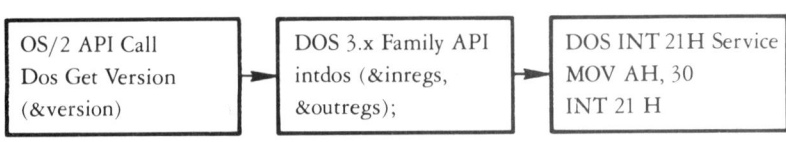

Figure 11-8. *DOS 3.x family API examining call and invoking INT 21H service*

As you might suspect, not all of the OS/2 API services are DOS 3.x compatible. This is simply because many of the OS/2 services exceed the capabilities of INT 21H or BIOS services.

EXE HEADER

OS/2 programs have two file headers—one for real mode and one for protected mode. Depending on the current mode, the corresponding header is used. The real-mode header contains code that maps OS/2 API calls to the corresponding INT 21H services. As such, the executable file itself determines in which mode to execute.

OS/2 Applications

The following programs use many of the OS/2 family API services. Each application is easily migrated from protected mode to real mode. Since the processing required for each will be the same, you might consider creating a MAKE file as shown here:

```
$(NAME).EXE $(NAME).C,$(NAME).DEF
            CL /Lp $(NAME).C
            BIND $(NAME) \LIB\DOSCALLS.LIB
```

Then, to produce your compatibility mode EXE, enter the command line

```
MAKE NAME=FIRST
```

MAKE will perform each step of your processing for you.

The first program you will examine is BEEP.C.

```
#include <doscalls.h>
#include <stdlib.h>

main ()
  {
   while (1)
     DOSBEEP (rand(), rand() % 255);
  }
```

The program loops forever (or until CTRL-C), generating sounds on your computer's speaker. Once you invoke this program, use the Session Manager to create another OS/2 session. The BEEP.EXE file continues to execute and generates sounds concurrently to your other sessions. This is a simple way to illustrate OS/2 multitasking.

To create a compatibility mode EXE file, use BIND as shown here:

```
[C:\] BIND BEEP \LIB\DOSCALLS.LIB
```

The program OS2EXIT.C shows you how to terminate a program and return a status value to OS/2.

```
#include <doscalls.h>

main ()
 {

   DOSEXIT (1, 3);

 }
```

In so doing, the OS/2 IF statement can perform conditional processing based upon ERRORLEVEL, as shown here:

```
OS2EXIT
IF ERRORLEVEL 1 command
```

The following program DELFILE.C

```
#include <doscalls.h>

main (argc, argv)
  int argc;
  char *argv[];
 {
  int status;

  if (argc > 1)
   {
     status = DOSDELETE (argv[1], 0);

     switch (status) {
      case 0: break;
      case 2: printf ("File not found\n");
              break;
      case 3: printf ("Path not found\n");
              break;
      case 5: printf ("Access Denied\n");
              break;
      default: printf ("File not deleted\n");
              break;
     }
   }
 }
```

deletes the file specified by the first command-line argument, as follows:

```
[C:\] DELFILE FILENAME.EXT
```

OS/2 fully supports command-line programming in the same fashion as DOS. The DELFILE.C program does not support wildcard characters.

The following sample programs provide OS/2 subdirectory manipulation. The first, MDIR.C, creates the subdirectory specified by the first command-line argument.

```c
#include <doscalls.h>

main (argc, argv)
  int argc;
  char *argv[];
  {
  int status;

  if (argc > 1)
    {
      status = DOSMKDIR (argv[1], 0);

      switch (status) {
       case 0: break;
       case 3: printf ("Path not found\n");
               break;
       default: printf ("Invalid directory\n");
                break;
      }
    }
  }
```

Invoke MDIR as follows:

```
[C:\] MDIR \DIRNAME
```

The second program, CDIR.C, sets the current directory to the specified directory.

```
#include <doscalls.h>

main (argc, argv)
  int argc;
  char *argv[];
 {
  int status;

  if (argc > 1)
    {
      status = DOSCHDIR (argv[1], 0);

      switch (status) {
       case 0: break;
       case 3: printf ("Path not found\n");
               break;
       default: printf ("Invalid directory\n");
                break;
      }
    }
 }
```

Again, the program is invoked as follows:

```
[C:\] CDIR \DIRNAME
```

The code that is shown on the following page implements the program REMDIR.C.

```
#include <doscalls.h>

main (argc, argv)
  int argc;
  char *argv[];
  {
  int status;

  if (argc > 1)
    {
      status = DOSRMDIR (argv[1], 0);

      switch (status) {
        case 0: break;
        case 3: printf ("Path not found\n");
                break;
        case 5: printf ("Access denied\n");
                break;
        default: printf ("Invalid directory\n");
                break;
      }
    }
  }
```

The REMDIR program enables you to remove the subdirectory specified by the first command-line argument, as shown here:

```
[C:\] REMDIR \DIRNAME
```

The program SHOWDIR.C displays the current directory.

```
#include <doscalls.h>

main ()
  {
  int status, length;

  char dir[64];

  status = DOSQCURDIR (0, dir, &length);

  printf ("\\%s\n", dir);
  }
```

The following code implements MOVE.C:

```
#include <doscalls.h>

main (argc, argv)
  int argc;
  char *argv[];
 {
  int status;

  if (argc > 2)
    {
      status = DOSMOVE (argv[1], argv[2], 0);

      switch (status) {
        case 0: break;
        case 2: printf ("File not found\n");
                break;
        case 3: printf ("Path not found\n");
                break;
        case 5: printf ("Access Denied\n");
                break;
        default: printf ("File not renamed\n");
                break;
        }
    }
  else
    printf ("Specify source and target file names\n");
 }
```

The program MOVE.C allows you to rename the file specified by the first command-line argument to the name specified by the second.

```
[C:\] MOVE SOURCE.EXT TARGET.EXT
```

The code that is snown on the next page implements FILE-MODE.C.

```
#include <doscalls.h>

char *attr[33];

main (argc, argv)
  int argc;
  char *argv[];
 {
  int status, attribute;

  attr[0] = "Normal";
  attr[1] = "Readonly";
  attr[2] = "Hidden";
  attr[4] = "System";
  attr[16] = "Subdirectory";
  attr[32] = "Archive";

  if (argc > 1)
   {
     status = DOSQFILEMODE (argv[1], &attribute, 0L);

     switch (status) {
      case 0: printf ("File attribute = %s\n", attr[attribute]);
              break;
      case 2: printf ("File not found\n");
              break;
      case 3: printf ("Path not found\n");
              break;
     }
   }
 }
```

The FILEMODE.C program displays an attribute of a file based
on the information shown in Table 11-1. Invoke FILEMODE as
shown here:

```
[C:\] FILEMODE FILENAME.EXT
```

Note that this program makes several simplifying assump-
tions. For example, a file can have multiple attributes such as
hidden and read-only (3).

In a similar manner, SHOWDISK.C displays the current disk drive.

```
#include <doscalls.h>

main ()
  {
  int status, drive ;
  long int logical_drive;

  status = DOSQCURDISK (&drive, &logical_drive);

  printf ("Current drive is %c\n", drive+64);
  }
```

The next two programs, READSTR.C and VIDEO.C, use API services defined in the file SUBCALLS.H. Take time now to print the contents of DOSCALLS.H and SUBCALLS.H (which are provided with the OS/2 software development kit). Both should be helpful to your programming.

The READSTR.C program reads and displays the character string entered by the user at the keyboard.

Value	Attribute
0	Normal
1	Read-only
2	Hidden
4	System
16	Subdirectory
32	Archive

Table 11-1. *File Attribute Information*

```
#include <subcalls.h>

main ()
 {
    char buffer[255];

    struct len {
        int inlength,
            outlength;
     } length;

    length.inlength = 255;

    KBDSTRINGIN (buffer, &length, 0, 0);

    printf ("\n%s\n", buffer);
    printf ("%d\n", length.outlength);
 }
```

To create a compatibility mode program, use BIND as shown here:

```
[C:\] BIND READSTR \LIB\DOSCALLS.LIB
```

Lastly, VIDEO.C displays the letter "A" 256 times in the middle of your screen, with each of the video-display attributes supported by the color graphics adapter.

```
#include <subcalls.h>

main ()
  {
   int row = 5, column = 10, i;

   char cell_string[2];

   cell_string[0] = 'A';

   for (i = 0; i < 255; i++)
     {
       cell_string[1] = i;
       VIOWRTCELLSTR (cell_string, 2, row, column, 0);
       if (column < 50)
         column++;
       else
         {
          column = 10;
          row++;
         }
     }
  }
```

Use BIND as shown here to create a compatibility mode EXE file:

```
[C:\] BIND VIDEO \LIB\DOSCALLS.LIB
```

Chapter Highlights

To create a protected-mode C program, use the CL command along with the /Lp directive of the Microsoft C compiler:

CL /Lp FILENAME.C

In a similar manner, to create a real-mode executable file, use the CL command along with the /Lc compiler directive:

CL /Lc FILENAME.C

Real-mode executable files do not execute in protected mode. Likewise, protected-mode executable files do not execute in real mode.

OS/2 allows you to create a family executable file that will execute in either real mode or protected mode. To do so, follow these three steps:

1. Create the source file with a text editor.

2. Compile and debug the program by using the protected-mode directive /Lp in the compiler command line.

3. Use BIND to build the compatibility mode executable file.

OS/2 module-definition files define the attributes of an executable file. In most cases, this file will be quite straightforward, as shown here:

```
NAME FIRST
DATA MOVEABLE
CODE MOVEABLE PURE
HEAPSIZE 2048
STACKSIZE 2048
```

OS/2 system services are called application program interface (API) routines. The OS/2 API services provide the equivalent functionality for OS/2 as INT 21H and BIOS INT 10H and 16H do for DOS.

OS/2 defines a subsystem of the API as the family API. These routines have direct counterparts under INT 21H and BIOS services. As long as your programs only use family API services, BIND can create a compatibility mode executable file from it.

12 *Advanced Programming Considerations*

Chapter 11 examined the basics of creating OS/2 protected-mode applications and how to migrate those applications to real mode by using the OS/2 BIND facility. You were introduced to the OS/2 Application Program Interface (API), which provides your programs with access to the OS/2 system services. This chapter will not be restricted to the DOS compatible subset of the API (family API services). Rather, this chapter discusses OS/2 timer services, semaphores, shared memory, pipes, exit lists, threads, and Vio-PopUp screens.

With OS/2 system services, your programs gain tremendous flexibility and allow you to perform the same functions that were previously available only through DOS interrupt-trapping and memory-resident (TSR) programs. Each OS/2 API service is easily accessible from your programs. In most cases, you can treat each API service as a black box, ignoring how the service works while concentrating instead on the function that the service performs.

Timer Services

In the past (under DOS), when you were tasked with displaying a message on the screen for a brief period of time, you simply created a FOR loop, as shown here:

```
for (i = 0; i < delay_value; ++i)
    ; /* do nothing but delay */
```

Under DOS, such processing was fully acceptable. Your program was the only active program in the system, so CPU time was not really wasted. However, in a multitasking operating system such as OS/2, tying up the CPU in a FOR loop like this wastes CPU cycles that OS/2 could otherwise fully utilize by assigning them to another program. OS/2 provides several API timer services that allow your programs to delay in an effective, yet CPU-efficient, manner.

Consider the following program that uses the API service DosSleep to delay for a 10-second period:

```
#include <doscalls.h>

main ()
 {
  printf ("About to delay\n");
  DOSSLEEP (10000L);
  printf ("Delay complete\n");
 }
```

On invocation, the program displays the following:

```
About to delay
```

After the 10-second period elapses, the program continues and displays the following message:

```
Delay complete
```

The following program expands on the previous application by allowing you to develop a chime clock, which sounds a chime at each half hour:

```c
#include <doscalls.h>
#include <stdio.h>

main ()
  {
   struct datetime {
       char hour, minute, second, hundredth, day, month;
       int year, zone;
       char dow;
     } time;

   int count;

   do
     {
      DOSGETDATETIME (&time);

      if (time.minute == 0)
        {
          if (time.hour > 12)
            time.hour -= 12;
          for (count = 1; count <= time.hour; count++)
            {
              putchar(7);
              DOSSLEEP (500L);
            }
        }
      else if (time.minute == 30)
        putchar(7);

      DOSGETDATETIME (&time);

      if (time.minute > 30)
        DOSSLEEP ((60 - time.minute) * 60000L);
      else
        DOSSLEEP ((30 - time.minute) * 60000L);

     }
   while (1);
  }
```

Invoke the program as a background task, as shown here:

```
[C:\] DETACH CHIME
```

As discussed later in this chapter, OS/2 provides several timer services that manipulate OS/2 semaphores.

Interprocess Communication

OS/2 is a multitasking operating system, which means that it executes several programs simultaneously. To fully exploit the capabilities of each process, OS/2 must provide a means for each process to communicate. *Interprocess communication* (IPC) is the process of exchanging information between two or more concurrent programs. OS/2 includes the following facilities to provide IPC support:

Shared memory
Semaphores
Pipes
Queues

Shared memory allows you to set aside a specific region of memory that two or more processes can access, as shown in Figure 12-1. The advantages of shared memory include less overhead and greater simplicity. The disadvantage is that there are no controls on the memory access. Any process that can access the shared-memory region can modify its contents at any time. Shared memory requires the communicating programs to develop their own internal protocols.

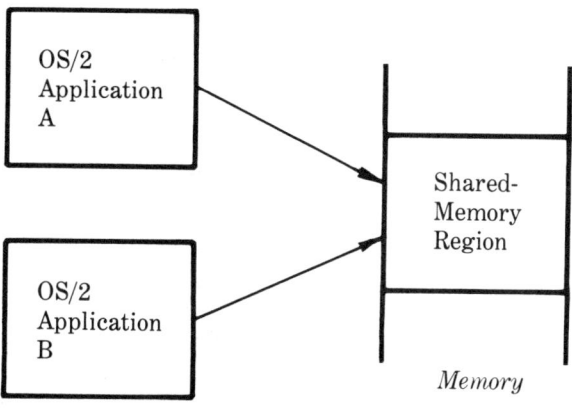

Figure 12 - 1. *Shared memory*

An OS/2 *semaphore* is a flag or counter that OS/2 applications use to synchronize or restrict access to resources. In the same manner as shared memory, a semaphore resides in a region that each OS/2 process can access, as shown in Figure 12-2.

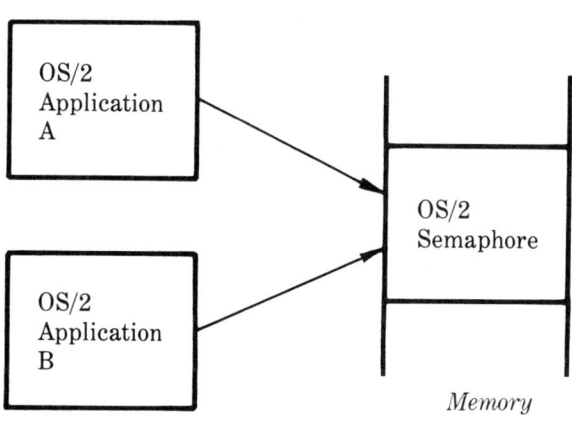

Figure 12 - 2. *Region of memory for semaphore*

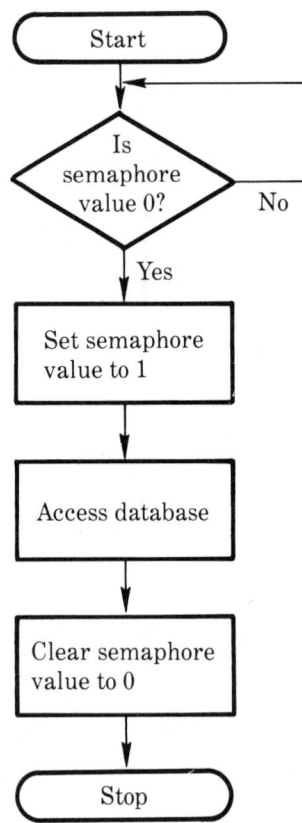

Figure 12-3. *Process of semaphore controlling access to a database*

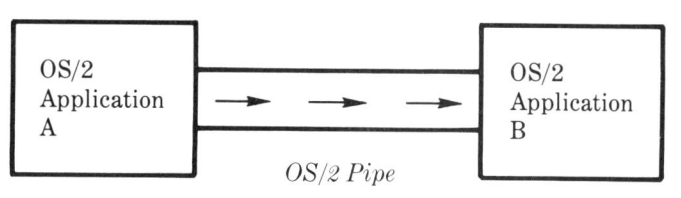

Figure 12-4. *OS/2 pipe*

Again, each communicating process must follow a predefined protocol. For example, assume that several programs need to concurrently access a database file. To be sure that two programs do not simultaneously update the same record, you use a semaphore to control the database access. In this case, before any process can update the database, the semaphore must have the value of 0 (see Figure 12-3). Once a process is ready to access the database and the semaphore is 0, the updating process sets the semaphore to the value 1 and restricts other processes from updating the database. Although Figure 12-3 indicates a polling mechanism, the actual OS/2 implementation of semaphores is much more efficient.

One process can possibly lock the other processes out of the database forever. Each program must be fully cooperative and applications must be carefully written to ensure fairness.

An OS/2 *pipe* is a one-way channel (message path) between two processes, as shown in Figure 12-4. One process puts messages into the pipe while the other process reads them. OS/2 includes several API service routines that provide pipe manipulation. Much of the data-flow control in the pipe is transparent to the end programmer. OS/2 pipes are easily implemented.

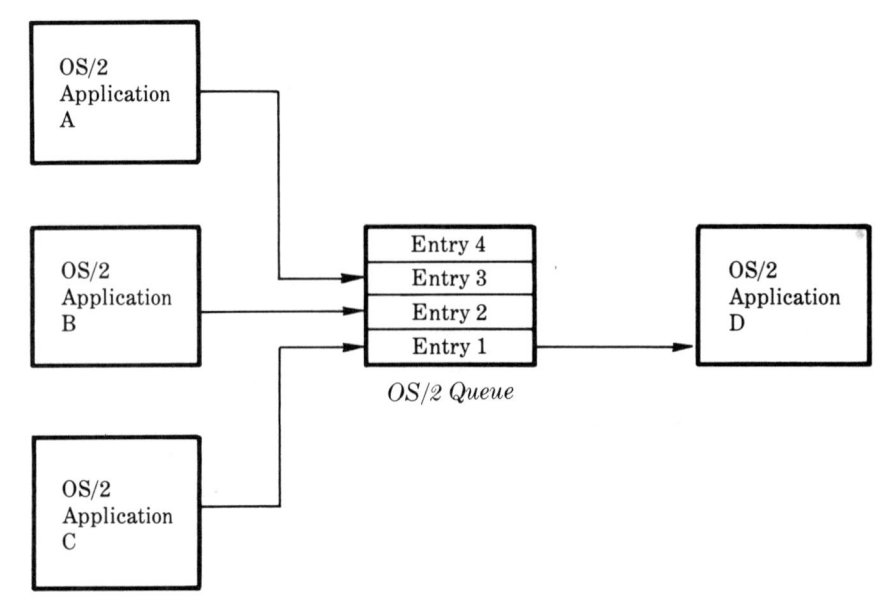

Figure 12-5. *OS/2 queue*

An OS/2 queue is similar in concept to a pipe in that a process reads each of the messages contained in the queue. OS/2 allows several processes to place data into a queue, as shown in Figure 12-5. Again, OS/2 provides a complete set of API services for queue manipulation.

OS/2 interprocess communication is a critical facility for the success of a multitasking operating system. The next few sections examine several of the OS/2 IPC capabilities in detail. By the time you have finished these sections, you should have a good understanding of how the OS/2 Presentation Manager will develop certain facilities, such as the Clipboard, which allows information to be cut and pasted from one OS/2 application to the next (see Figure 12-6).

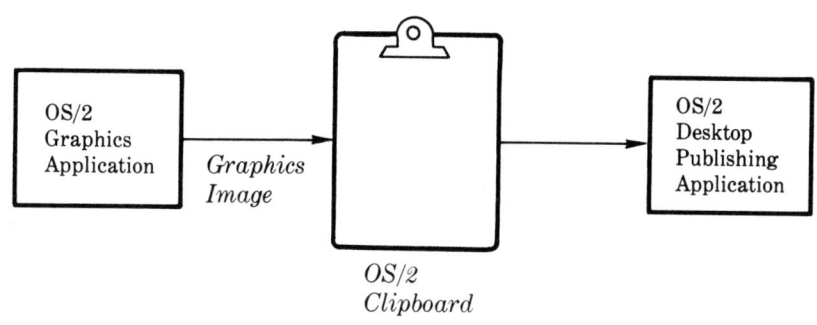

Figure 12-6. *OS/2 Clipboard*

Shared Memory

Most of the interprocess communication capabilities that will be examined use shared memory in one form or another. To create a shared-memory region, one process must use the OS/2 API service DosAllocShrSeg. For example, the following program creates a shared-memory region called \SHAREMEM \MEM:

```
#include <doscalls.h>
#include <dos.h>          /* contains FP_SEG and FP_OFF macros */

main ()
{
  char far *SharedSeg; /* pointer to shared segment */

  char letter;

  unsigned SharedSel;

  DOSALLOCSHRSEG ((unsigned) 10, "\\SHAREMEM\\MEM", &SharedSel);

  FP_SEG(SharedSeg) = SharedSel;  /* get segment address */
  FP_OFF(SharedSeg) = 0;

  while (1)
    for (letter = 'A'; letter <= 'Z'; ++letter)
      *SharedSeg = letter;

  DOSFREESEG (SharedSel);
}
```

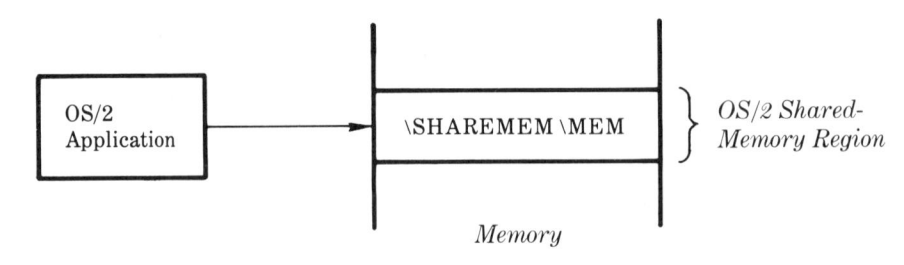

Figure 12-7.   *Example program creating \SHAREMEM \MEM*

Figure 12-7 illustrates how this program works.

All OS/2 shared-memory segments must have the prefix \SHAREMEM. Once the example program creates the shared-memory segment, it loops forever and places the uppercase letters of the alphabet into the memory region.

When a process has created a shared-memory region, other processes that wish to access the shared-memory region must use the OS/2 API service DosGetShrSeg, which provides access as shown in Figure 12-8.

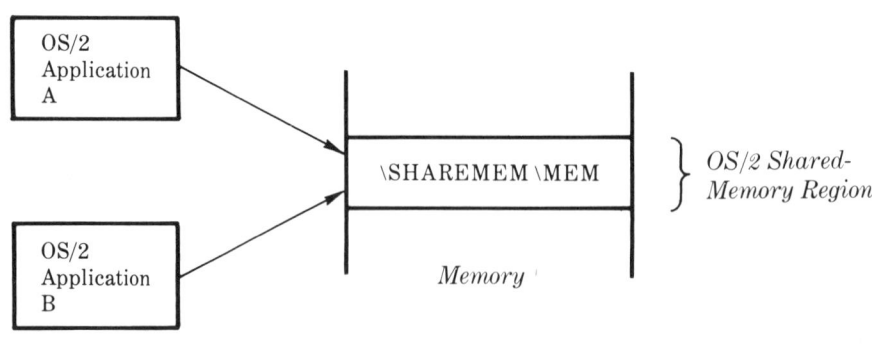

Figure 12-8.   *OS/2 allocating access to \SHAREMEM \MEM*

Once the program obtains access to the shared-memory region, it begins displaying the characters that the region contains, as in the following program:

```
#include <doscalls.h>
#include <dos.h>        /* contains FP_SEG and FP_OFF macros */

main ()
 {
  char far *SharedSeg; /* pointer to shared segment */

  unsigned SharedSel;

  DOSGETSHRSEG ("\\SHAREMEM\\MEM", &SharedSel);

  FP_SEG(SharedSeg) = SharedSel;
  FP_OFF(SharedSeg) = 0;

  while (1)
    printf ("%c\n", *SharedSeg);

  DOSFREESEG (SharedSel);
 }
```

On invocation, this program displays the following:

```
B
B
W
W
W
Q
C
D
D
D
I
U
U
U
U
W
W
```

```
Y
Y
Y
Y
J
J
J
J
K
K
B
```

Note that the program does not get every letter. This is because the two programs are not synchronized in any way. In this case, add the following third program, which places the characters 0 to 9 into the memory region in a similar manner:

```c
#include <doscalls.h>
#include <dos.h>          /* contains FP_SEG and FP_OFF macros */

main ()
{
  char far *SharedSeg; /* pointer to shared segment */

  char letter;

  unsigned SharedSel;

  DOSGETSHRSEG ("\\SHAREMEM\\MEM", &SharedSel);

  FP_SEG(SharedSeg) = SharedSel;  /* get segment address */
  FP_OFF(SharedSeg) = 0;

  while (1)
    for (letter = '0'; letter <= '9'; ++letter)
      *SharedSeg = letter;

  DOSFREESEG (SharedSel);
}
```

Now the previous program displays the characters that are shown on the following page.

As illustrated, processes that use shared memory must use some type of protocol to be fully functional.

The next two programs illustrate a more functional aspect of shared memory. The first program creates three shared-memory segments (VALUE1, VALUE2, and SUM), as shown in Figure 12-9. The program then places two values into the regions

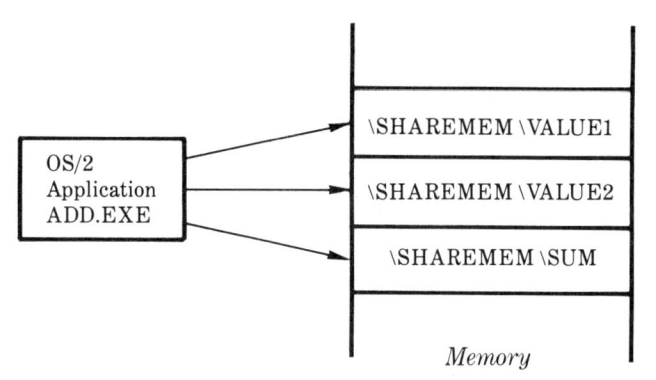

Figure 12-9. *Sample program creating three shared-memory segments*

VALUE1 and VALUE2.

```
#include <doscalls.h>
#include <dos.h>          /* contains FP_SEG and FP_OFF macros */

main ()
{
  char far *V1Seg;  /* pointer to shared segment */
  char far *V2Seg;  /* pointer to shared segment */
  char far *SumSeg; /* pointer to shared sum */

  unsigned V1Sel;
  unsigned V2Sel;
  unsigned SumSel;

  DOSALLOCSHRSEG ((unsigned) 10, "\\SHAREMEM\\VALUE1", &V1Sel);
  DOSALLOCSHRSEG ((unsigned) 10, "\\SHAREMEM\\VALUE2", &V2Sel);
  DOSALLOCSHRSEG ((unsigned) 10, "\\SHAREMEM\\SUM", &SumSel);

  FP_SEG(V1Seg) = V1Sel;     /* get segment address */
  FP_OFF(V1Seg) = 0;

  FP_SEG(V2Seg) = V2Sel;     /* get segment address */
  FP_OFF(V2Seg) = 0;

  FP_SEG(SumSeg) = SumSel;   /* get segment address */
  FP_OFF(SumSeg) = 0;

  *V1Seg = 7;
  *V2Seg = 10;

  DOSSLEEP (15000L);

  printf ("Sum = %d\n", *SumSeg);

  DOSFREESEG (V1Sel);
  DOSFREESEG (V2Sel);
  DOSFREESEG (SumSel);
}
```

Next, a second OS/2 program examines these two values and places their sum into the memory region SUM (see Figure 12-10).

```
#include <doscalls.h>
#include <dos.h>            /* contains FP_SEG and FP_OFF macros */

main ()
{
  char far *V1Seg;  /* pointer to shared segment */
  char far *V2Seg;  /* pointer to shared segment */
  char far *SumSeg; /* pointer to shared sum */

  unsigned V1Sel;
  unsigned V2Sel;
  unsigned SumSel;

  DOSGETSHRSEG ("\\SHAREMEM\\VALUE1", &V1Sel);
  DOSGETSHRSEG ("\\SHAREMEM\\VALUE2", &V2Sel);
  DOSGETSHRSEG ("\\SHAREMEM\\SUM", &SumSel);

  FP_SEG(V1Seg) = V1Sel;     /* get segment address */
  FP_OFF(V1Seg) = 0;

  FP_SEG(V2Seg) = V2Sel;     /* get segment address */
  FP_OFF(V2Seg) = 0;

  FP_SEG(SumSeg) = SumSel;   /* get segment address */
  FP_OFF(SumSeg) = 0;

  *SumSeg = *V1Seg + *V2Seg;

  DOSFREESEG (V1Sel);
  DOSFREESEG (V2Sel);
  DOSFREESEG (SumSel);
}
```

The first program places the values into the memory and then delays for 15 seconds, which gives you time to create a session containing the SUM.EXE program. However, you may not be able to get the second session started in time. In that case, the program would display an incorrect result.

To prevent this "window of error" from happening, use the OS/2 API service DosExeCPgm to create a child process. As before, the program places the values to be summed into the memory regions. Next, the program creates the child process that sums the values and places the result into SUM. When the first program again receives control, the values are summed correctly.

```c
#include <doscalls.h>
#include <dos.h>

main ()
{
  char far *V1Seg;  /* pointer to shared segment */
  char far *V2Seg;  /* pointer to shared segment */
  char far *SumSeg; /* pointer to shared sum */

  char *child = "SUM.EXE", exe_buffer[100];

  struct ResultCodes codes;

  unsigned V1Sel;
  unsigned V2Sel;
  unsigned SumSel;

  DOSALLOCSHRSEG ((unsigned) 10, "\\SHAREMEM\\VALUE1", &V1Sel);
  DOSALLOCSHRSEG ((unsigned) 10, "\\SHAREMEM\\VALUE2", &V2Sel);
  DOSALLOCSHRSEG ((unsigned) 10, "\\SHAREMEM\\SUM", &SumSel);

  FP_SEG(V1Seg) = V1Sel;    /* get segment address */
  FP_OFF(V1Seg) = 0;

  FP_SEG(V2Seg) = V2Sel;    /* get segment address */
  FP_OFF(V2Seg) = 0;

  FP_SEG(SumSeg) = SumSel;  /* get segment address */
  FP_OFF(SumSeg) = 0;

  *V1Seg = 7;
  *V2Seg = 10;

  DOSEXECPGM (exe_buffer, 100, 0, 0L, 0L,
              (struct ResultCodes far *) &codes, child);

  printf ("Sum = %d\n", *SumSeg);

  DOSFREESEG (V1Sel);
  DOSFREESEG (V2Sel);
  DOSFREESEG (SumSel);
}
```

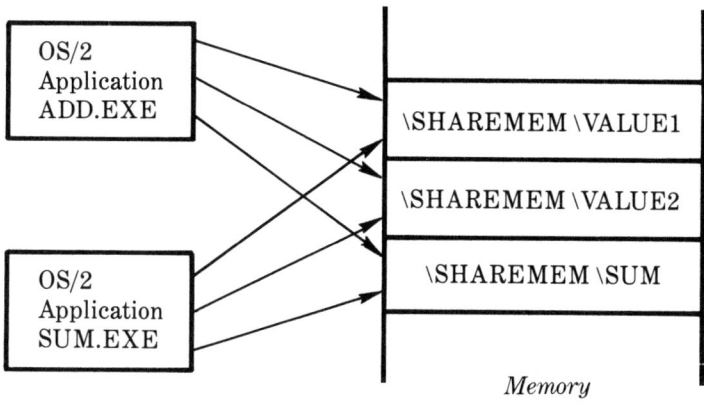

Figure 12-10. *Sample program placing sum of values into SUM*

OS/2 Semaphores

A semaphore is a flag that several programs can access in order to synchronize their activities. OS/2 provides several routines that manipulate OS/2 semaphores. To create an OS/2 semaphore, use the OS/2 API service DosCreateSem, which creates a semaphore with the specified name. All OS/2 semaphores must have the prefix \SEM.

In this case, the first example program creates a semaphore called \SEM \WAIT and sets it to the value 1, as shown in Figure 12-11.

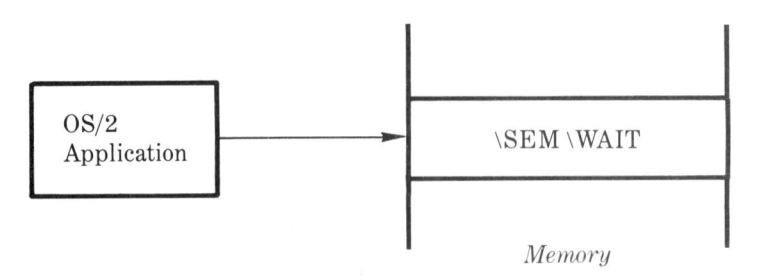

Figure 12-11. *Creating of \SEM \WAIT semaphore*

```
#include        <doscalls.h>     /* contains 286DOS function declarations */

main ()
 {
   unsigned long SemHandle;
   unsigned TimerHandle;

   DOSCREATESEM (1, &SemHandle, "\\SEM\\WAIT");

   DOSSEMSET (SemHandle);

   DOSTIMERASYNC (5000L, SemHandle, &TimerHandle);

   printf ("Waiting for asynchronous timer to clear semaphore\n");

   DOSSEMWAIT (SemHandle, (long) -1);  /* -1 no time out */

   printf ("Semaphore cleared\n");
 }
```

Next, the program creates an asynchronous timer that, on completion, clears the specified semaphore. Last, the program waits until the semaphore is cleared. On invocation the program displays the following:

```
Waiting for asynchronous timer to clear semaphore
```

After the timer service's specified time period expires, the semaphore is cleared, the program completes, and the following message is displayed:

```
Semaphore cleared
```

In a similar manner, the following program creates a semaphore and waits for it to be cleared by some external means:

```c
#include <doscalls.h>
#include <stdlib.h>

main ()
 {
   unsigned long SemHandle;

   DOSCREATESEM (1, &SemHandle, "\\SEM\\WAIT");

   DOSSEMSET (SemHandle);

   printf ("Waiting for concurrent application to clear semaphore\n");

   do
    DOSBEEP (rand(), rand() % 255);
   while (DOSSEMWAIT (SemHandle, 0));

   printf ("Semaphore cleared\n");
 }
```

In order for the previous program to complete, you must execute the following program to clear the semaphore, as shown in Figure 12-12.

```
#include        <doscalls.h>    /* contains 286DOS function declarations */

main ()
 {
   unsigned long SemHandle;

   DOSOPENSEM (&SemHandle, "\\SEM\\WAIT");

   DOSSLEEP (10000L);   /* delay long enough to watch other program */

   DOSSEMCLEAR (SemHandle);

   DOSCLOSESEM (SemHandle);
 }
```

On invocation, the first program begins generating random sounds from the computer's speaker. It will continue to do so until the semaphore is cleared.

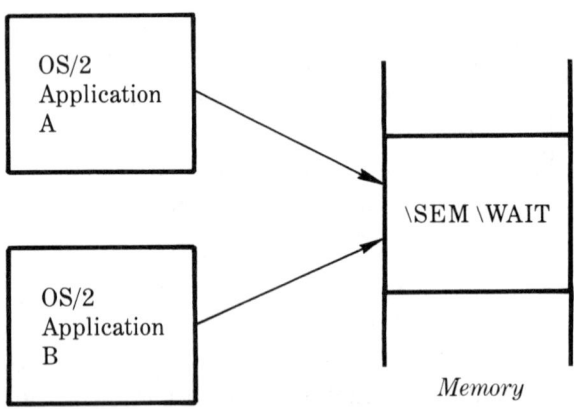

Figure 12-12. *Clearing the \SEM \WAIT semaphore*

OS/2 SEMAPHORE

An OS/2 semaphore is a flag that several OS/2 applications can access in order to synchronize their processing or resource accesses. OS/2 provides a large collection of API services that manipulate semaphores.

Pipes

An OS/2 pipe provides a means for two processes to open a direct channel of communication, as shown in Figure 12-13.

The following program uses OS/2 pipes and shared memory:

```c
#include <doscalls.h>
#include <dos.h>          /* contains FP_SEG and FP_OFF macros */

main ()
{
  unsigned HandleSel;

  struct handles { unsigned int readhandle, writehandle; } far *pipe;

  int letter, len;

  char *child = "PIPE2.EXE", exe_buffer[100];

  struct ResultCodes codes;

  int status;

  DOSALLOCSHRSEG ((unsigned) sizeof(struct handles),
          "\\SHAREMEM\\HANDLE", &HandleSel);

  FP_SEG(pipe) = HandleSel;
  FP_OFF(pipe) = 0;

  DOSMAKEPIPE (&pipe->readhandle, &pipe->writehandle, 1024);

  for (letter = 'A'; letter <= 'Z'; ++letter)
    DOSWRITE (pipe->writehandle, &letter, 1, &len);

  DOSEXECPGM (exe_buffer, 100, 0, 0L, 0L,
          (struct ResultCodes far *) &codes, child);

  DOSCLOSE (pipe->writehandle);
  DOSCLOSE (pipe->readhandle);
  DOSFREESEG (HandleSel);
}
```

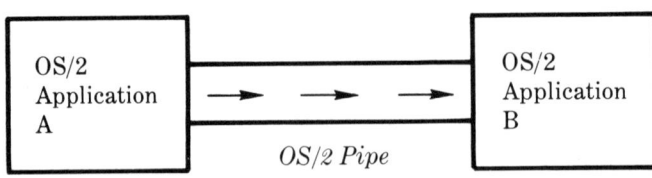

Figure 12-13. *OS/2 pipe providing channel of communication*

The program first allocates a region of shared memory into which it will place the pipe handle from which the second program will read. Next, the program invokes the OS/2 API service DosMake-Pipe to create the pipe and the service DosWrite to fill the pipe with the uppercase letters of the alphabet. The program then creates a child process that reads the data contained in the pipe and converts each uppercase letter to lowercase.

The following program is the child process that reads the pipe data. The program uses the DosRead to read the pipe data.

```
#include <doscalls.h>
#include <dos.h>          /* contains FP_SEG and FP_OFF macros */

main ()
{
  unsigned HandleSel;

  struct handles { unsigned int readhandle, writehandle; } far *pipe;

  int letter, len;

  DOSGETSHRSEG ("\\SHAREMEM\\HANDLE", &HandleSel);

  FP_SEG(pipe) = HandleSel;
  FP_OFF(pipe) = 0;

  while (! DOSREAD (pipe->readhandle, &letter, 1, &len))
    {
      if ((letter >= 'A') && (letter <= 'Z'))
        letter = letter + 32;

      printf ("%c %d\n", letter, len);
      if (letter == 'z')
        break;
    }
}
```

As just illustrated, your IPC requirements in OS/2 can be implemented in a myriad of ways.

OS/2 PIPES

OS/2 pipes allow two processes to open a direct communications channel. Once a pipe is created by way of the OS/2 DosMakePipe API service, processes access the pipe by way of the DosRead and DosWrite API services. Pipes may only be used by parent-child processes. The parent must create the pipe.

OS/2 Threads

An OS/2 thread is a path of execution. Therefore, each OS/2 program is made up of one or more threads. Each time the OS/2 scheduler assigns a CPU time slice, it does so in terms of threads (as opposed to processes). This fact opens up a new spectrum of programming. By using OS/2 threads, you can easily generate concurrent programming languages such as Ada, Modula II, and even a concurrent C.

Consider the following C program:

```
main ()
  {
   file_weekly_sales ();
   print_attendence ();
   display_accounts ();
  }
```

The program begins its execution and invokes each function in a serial fashion, one function immediately following the previous function. However, note that none of the functions is dependent on another. By using OS/2 threads, the program could easily execute all three functions in parallel (see Figure 12-14).

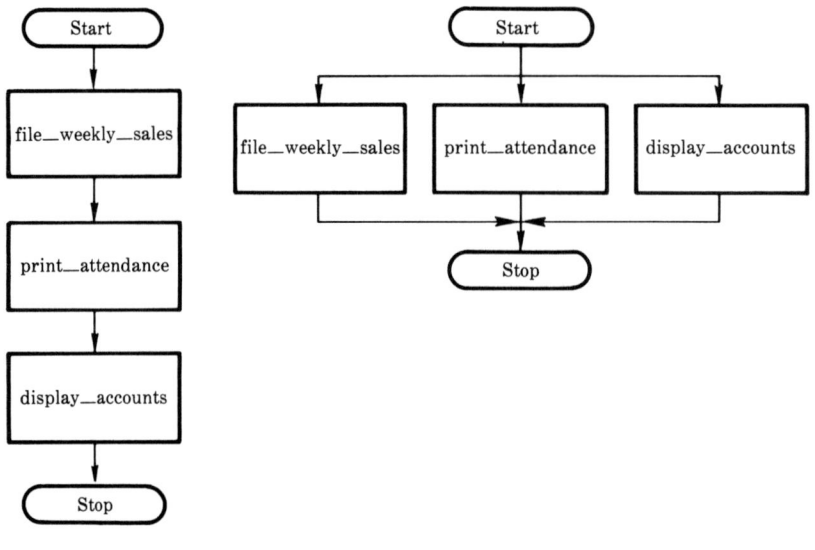

Figure 12-14. *Execution of three functions in parallel*

The following C program creates an OS/2 thread that executes the function **file—it** concurrently with the remainder of the program's processing. The net result is that while the program is displaying the message

```
Threads Work
```

on the screen, the concurrent thread is writing the message

```
THREADS WORK!
```

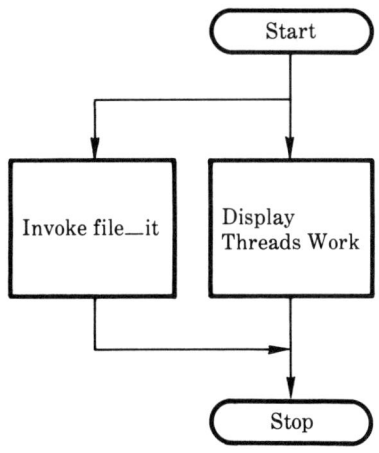

Figure 12-15. *OS/2 executing threads concurrently*

to the file THREADS.DAT. OS/2 executes the threads concurrently, as shown in Figure 12-15. The following program implements THREADS.C:

```c
#include <doscalls.h>
#include <stdio.h>

main ()
  {
  unsigned id, stack[512];

  void far file_it (void);

  DOSCREATETHREAD (file_it, &id, (char far *) &stack[511]);

  printf ("Threads Work\n");
  }

void far file_it ()
  {
  FILE *fopen(), *fp;

  fp = fopen ("THREADS.DAT", "w");

  fprintf (fp, "THREADS WORK!\n");

  fclose (fp);
  }
```

Compile the program as follows:

```
[C:\] CL -AL -G2 -Lp -Gs THREADS.C
```

Note that the program passes the last element of the stack to the API service. Remember that OS/2 stacks grow downward toward lower memory addresses.

OS/2 THREADS

OS/2 threads are paths of execution. Each OS/2 program is comprised of one or more paths of execution. The OS/2 scheduler distributes time slices to threads as opposed to processes. The OS/2 API service DosCreateThread enables your applications to create additional threads.

Exit List

Since OS/2 programs allocate many resources (semaphores, shared memory, and so forth), OS/2 allows you to define a list of functions that OS/2 executes each time the program terminates. This list of functions is called a *program termination list*. The following program (EXITLIST.C) uses the OS/2 service DosExit-List to place three functions into the list that OS/2 executes on program termination. As such, each time the program terminates, it displays the following:

```
First exit routine
Second exit routine
Third exit routine
```

The following program implements EXITLIST.C:

```
#include <doscalls.h>

#define EXLIST_ADD      1    /* add routine to exit list */
#define NEXT            3    /* pass to next routine in the list */

main()
 {
  void first(), second(), third();

  DOSEXITLIST(EXLIST_ADD, first);
  DOSEXITLIST(EXLIST_ADD, second);
  DOSEXITLIST(EXLIST_ADD, third);
 }

void first ()
 {
  printf ("First exit routine\n");
  DOSEXITLIST(NEXT, (char *) 0);
 }

void second ()
 {
  printf ("Second exit routine\n");
  DOSEXITLIST(NEXT, (char *) 0);
 }

void third ()
 {
  printf ("Third exit routine\n");
  DOSEXITLIST(NEXT, (char *) 0);
 }
```

Again compile the program as follows:

```
[C:\] CL -AL -G2 -Lp -Gs EXITLIST.C
```

OS/2 EXIT LIST

Since most OS/2 applications allocate resources such as semaphores and shared memory, OS/2 allows you to define a list of functions that it invokes when the program terminates. The OS/2 API routine DosExitList enables you to place functions into and remove functions from this termination list.

VioPopUp

Thus far, you have executed several programs by using the OS/2 DETACH command. As you have seen, once these programs begin executing, they cannot receive input from, or write output to, the user. However, OS/2 does allow background programs to use a VioPopUp screen to display a screenful of information.

Consider the following example program:

```c
#include <doscalls.h>
#include <stdio.h>
#include <subcalls.h>

main ()
{
  struct datetime {
      char hour, minute, second, hundredth, day, month;
      int year, zone;
      char dow;
    } time;

  int count;

  int flags = 1;

  do
    {
      DOSGETDATETIME (&time);

      if (time.minute == 0)
        {
            if (time.hour > 12)
              time.hour -= 12;

            VIOPOPUP (&flags, 0);

            for (count = 1; count <= time.hour; count++)
              {
                  putchar(7);
                  DOSSLEEP (500L);
              }
            printf ("%02d:%02d:%02d\n", time.hour, time.minute, time.second);
            DOSSLEEP (10000L);
            VIOENDPOPUP (0);
        }
      else if (time.minute == 30)
        {
            putchar(7);
            VIOPOPUP (&flags, 0);
            printf ("%02d:%02d:%02d\n", time.hour, time.minute, time.second);
            DOSSLEEP (10000L);
            VIOENDPOPUP (0);
        }

      DOSGETDATETIME (&time);

      if (time.minute > 30)
        DOSSLEEP ((60 - time.minute) * 60000L);
      else
        DOSSLEEP ((30 - time.minute) * 60000L);

    }
  while (1);
}
```

In this case, the example program modifies the previous chime clock to wake up every half hour and display the time on the screen, as follows:

```
12:00:00
```

Again invoke the program by using the DETACH command, as shown here:

```
[C:\] DETACH CLOCK
```

Each half hour the example program wakes up and displays the current time after clearing the screen display. Once the time has been on the screen for 15 seconds, the program restores the previous screen and goes back to sleep for another 30 minutes.

VioPopUp

By default, OS/2 background processes cannot perform I/O operations to the screen and keyboard. The OS/2 VioPopUp service allows background tasks to display a screenful of information. When the popup screen is done, OS/2 restores the original screen display.

Chapter Highlights

To allow your programs to delay in an effective (yet CPU-efficient) manner, OS/2 provides a series of timer services.

Interprocess communication (IPC) is the process of two or more processes exchanging information. To fully exploit its processing capabilities, OS/2 provides the following IPC implementations:

Shared memory
Semaphores
Pipes
Queues

OS/2 shared memory allows you to set aside a region of memory that processes can access in order to place information readily available to other processes. The advantages of shared memory include simplicity and low overhead. However, the disadvantage is that the communicating processes must use an internal protocol to access the information contained in the shared-memory region.

An OS/2 semaphore is a flag that OS/2 applications use to synchronize their processing or device accesses. In a manner similar to shared memory, a semaphore is a named resource that any application can access.

An OS/2 pipe is a communications channel that two processes can use for direct information exchange. Once a process creates an OS/2 pipe, it must have a means to provide the cooperating process with a handle that is used to read or write data into the pipe.

An OS/2 queue is similar to a pipe in that one process reads the data contained in queue. OS/2 allows many processes to place information into a queue.

An OS/2 thread is a path of execution. As such, each OS/2 program is comprised of one or more threads. OS/2 distributes CPU time slices to threads as opposed to processes. Using the OS/2 API service DosCreateThread, your applications programs can easily create threads of execution.

Since most OS/2 applications allocate resources such as semaphores or shared memory, OS/2 allows you to define a list of routines that OS/2 invokes each time the program terminates. The OS/2 API service DosExitList allows you to add and remove functions to and from this list.

By default, OS/2 background processes cannot perform console I/O operations. However, by using a VioPopUp service, screen background processes can interrupt the current screen contents to display a screenful of information. On completion, the original screen contents are redisplayed.

13 *OS/2 Disk Layout*

By now you should have a solid foundation in OS/2. You have seen all of the OS/2 commands and you should be comfortable with OS/2 directory manipulation. This chapter discusses OS/2 disk structures and examines a couple of ways you can increase your system performance by enhancing your disk operations.

This text has discussed 5 1/4-inch floppy disks, microfloppy disks, quad-density disks, and fixed disks. Most of the discussions have ignored the specific disk type in use. This is because OS/2 treats all disks in the same manner at the lowest levels of disk structure and access. This, in turn, greatly simplifies the OS/2 disk I/O services that are built into OS/2 and ensures that OS/2 disks remain fully compatible with DOS. Most users will never have to access disks at OS/2's lowest levels. However, a basic understanding of how OS/2 records information on disk is beneficial to all users.

Most of the examples presented in this chapter are based on floppy disks because of their widely varied uses. Keep in mind, however, that each of the concepts presented in this chapter also applies to fixed disks.

A disk is best viewed as a record album. Each time you place a floppy disk into a disk drive, the disk begins spinning past a recording mechanism called the read/write head (see Figure 13-1).

The read/write head simply records data to and from the disk storage media. Both floppy disks and fixed disks work in this manner. Each time the disk drive must read a specific location, it waits until that location spins past the read/write head.

Many people have heard the term *head crash*. The disk read/write head is very close to the disk surface, and head crash occurs when the read/write head makes physical contact with the disk storage media, scarring it and preventing further use of the

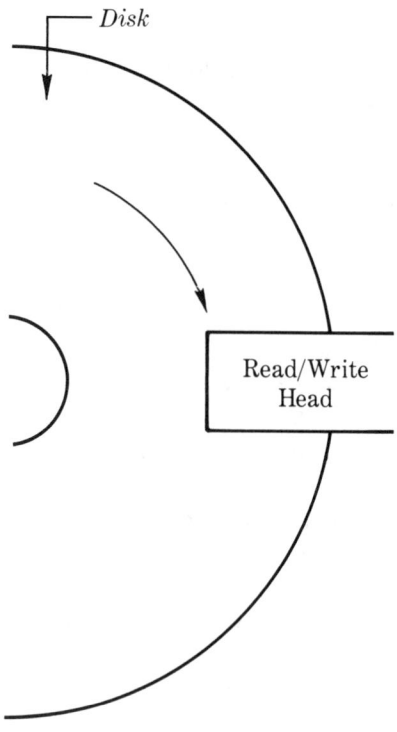

Figure 13-1. *Disk spinning past read/write head*

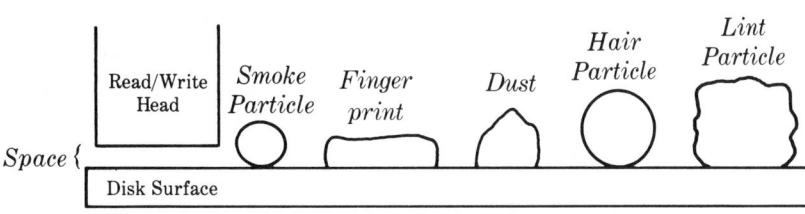

Figure 13-2. *Causes of head crash*

disk. In most cases, head crashes are a direct result of minute particles on the disk surface. Dust, smoke, or a hair fragment can result in a head crash (see Figure 13-2). You should keep your computer environment as clean as possible.

Each disk is composed of tracks that begin at the outer edge and work to the center, as shown in Figure 13-3. The actual

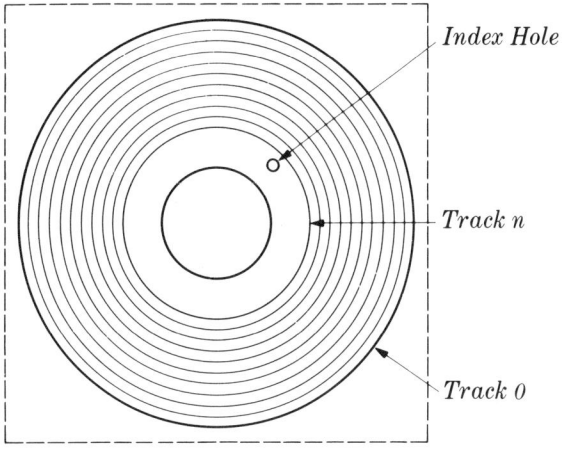

Figure 13-3. *Tracks that make up a disk*

number of tracks on the disk depends on the type of disk. Standard floppy disks (360K) use 40 tracks per side; quad-density disks use 80. As you will see later in this chapter, fixed disks are also made up of tracks that may number several hundred.

OS/2 further divides your disk's tracks into equal-sized units called sectors (see Figure 13-4). In a manner similar to tracks, the number of sectors per track also depends upon the disk type, as shown in Table 13-1.

Each sector must be of equal length in bytes. OS/2 disks use 512-byte sectors. Disk storage capacity is a function of the sector size, number of sectors per track, and the number of tracks per disk, as shown here:

storage = (bytes per sector) * (sectors per track) *
        (tracks per side) * (sides per disk)

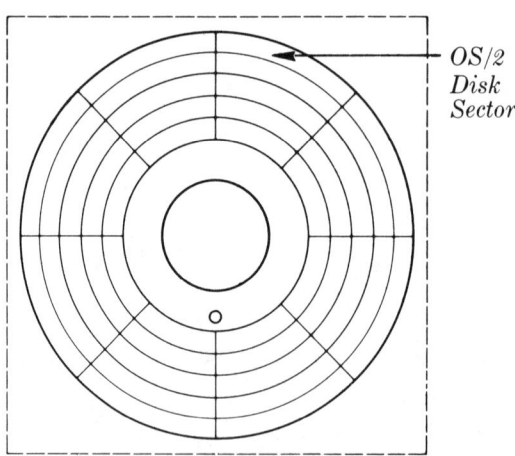

OS/2
Disk
Sector

Figure 13-4.   *Sectors that make up tracks*

Disk type	Tracks per side	Total sectors
Single-sided, 8 sectors per track	40	320
Single-sided, 9 sectors per track	40	360
Double-sided, 8 sectors per track	40	640
Double-sided, 9 sectors per track	40	720
Quad-density, 9 sectors per track	80	1440
Quad-density, 15 sectors per track	80	2400

Table 13-1. *Configurations of Disk Types and Sectors*

Consider a 1.2MB disk that can store up to 1,228,800 bytes of information. These disks use

512 bytes per sector
15 sectors per track
80 tracks per side
2 sides per disk

Compute the storage capacity as follows:

$$\text{storage} = (\text{bytes per sector}) * (\text{sectors per track}) *$$
$$(\text{tracks per side}) * (\text{sides per disk})$$
$$= 512 * 15 * 80 * 2$$
$$= 1{,}228{,}800 \text{ bytes}$$

Disk Utilization

Not all of the 1.2MB of a quad-density disk is available space for storage of your data. When you format a disk, OS/2 reserves disk sectors for the following:

Boot record
File-allocation tables
Root directory entries

The first sector on all OS/2 disks contains a *boot record* that either begins the OS/2 start-up process or displays the following message:

```
The file "OS2BIO.COM" cannot be found.
Insert a system diskette and restart
the system.
```

Specifically, this sector contains the information shown in Figure 13-5.

BOOT RECORD

Every OS/2 disk contains a boot record as its first sector. If the disk is bootable, the boot record starts the boot process. Otherwise, the boot record displays the nonsystem-disk error message.

OS/2 uses the *file-allocation table* (FAT) to track the utilization of disk space. Specifically, the FAT contains entries for sectors currently used to store files, sectors available for file allocation, and sectors that are unavailable because of media corruption. The FAT, therefore, serves as your disk road map. Because of its importance, OS/2 places two copies of the FAT on your disk to prevent disk corruption from rendering a disk unusable. If one FAT becomes corrupted, another is available.

Although most users speak in terms of disk sectors, the FAT tracks disk *clusters*, which are sets of contiguous sectors. Table 13-2 illustrates the number of sectors per cluster used by each disk type.

8086 JMP instruction
IBM or Microsoft name and version number
Bytes per disk sector
Sectors per cluster
Number of reserved sectors
Max root directory entries
Total sectors
Media description
Number of sectors per file allocation table
Sectors per track
Number of disk heads
Number of hidden sectors
Bootstrap program

Figure 13-5.   *Example boot record*

Disk type	Sectors per cluster
Single-sided, 8 sectors per track	1
Single-sided, 9 sectors per track	2
Double-sided, 8 sectors per track	1
Double-sided, 9 sectors per track	2
Quad-density, 8 sectors per track	2
Quad-density, 9 sectors per track	1
Fixed disk, 17 sectors per track (less than 15MB)	4
Fixed-disk, 17 sectors per track (greater than 15MB)	8

Table 13-2.   *Number of Sectors Per Cluster*

Each time OS/2 allocates space for a file, it does so in terms of clusters, not sectors. You can verify this by invoking the OS/2 CHKDSK command, as shown here:

```
[A:\] CHKDSK

Volume CHAP13 created Oct 20, 1987   5:38am

   362496 bytes total disk space.
        0 bytes in 1 hidden files.
    20480 bytes in 2 user files.
   342016 bytes available on disk.

[A:\]
```

Note the amount of available disk space. Next, create a simple file as shown here:

```
[A:\] COPY CON: A
1
2
3
4
5
^Z
          1 File(s) copied.

[A:\]
```

Again invoke CHKDSK.

```
[A:\] CHKDSK

Volume CHAP13 created Oct 20, 1987   5:38am

   362496 bytes total disk space.
        0 bytes in 1 hidden files.
    21504 bytes in 3 user files.
   340992 bytes available on disk.

[A:\]
```

The simple file resulted in OS/2 allocating 1024 bytes (1024 in this case is equal to 2 sectors or 1 cluster). Each time your file grows beyond its 1024-byte boundary, OS/2 allocates another cluster to the file.

CLUSTER

A cluster is the OS/2 unit of file allocation. Each time OS/2 allocates space for a file, it does so in terms of a cluster. A cluster is two or more contiguous disk sectors (depending on the disk type).

From the previous example, you may have recognized a possible problem from this type of disk space allocation: If most of your files are small (using less than 512 bytes), each file has a wasted sector of disk space, as shown in Figure 13-6.

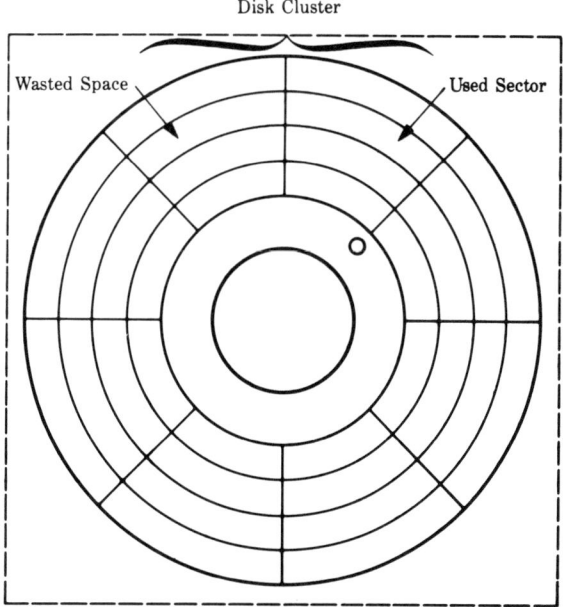

Figure 13-6. *One sector of wasted space*

However, in most cases, the standard file usage makes clusters a viable file-allocation unit. If instead of clusters, OS/2 used sectors as its file-allocation unit, this might indeed prevent wasted space within files. However, the size of the FAT would double (since the number of entries would double), which would consume a considerable amount of disk space. More important, if disk sectors were employed as the unit of file allocation, the amount of disk fragmentation (discussed later) would increase.

View the FAT as a table that contains an entry for each cluster on disk. Assuming that you are using a double-sided, double-density disk (360K) that uses 2 sectors per cluster, the FAT appears as shown in Table 13-3.

OS/2 uses the first two FAT entries to specify media information. The remaining entries contain one of the following values:

0	Cluster available
FFF	End of file (last cluster)
FF7	Corrupted (unusable) file
nnn	Where *nnn* is the next cluster in the file chain

Cluster number	Status
0	
.	.
.	.
.	.
5 (Starting Cluster)	6
6	13
7	0
8	0
9	FF7
10	FF7
11	0
12	0
13	FFF
14	0
.	.
.	.
.	.
355	0

Table 13-3. *Sample File-Allocation Table for 360K Disk*

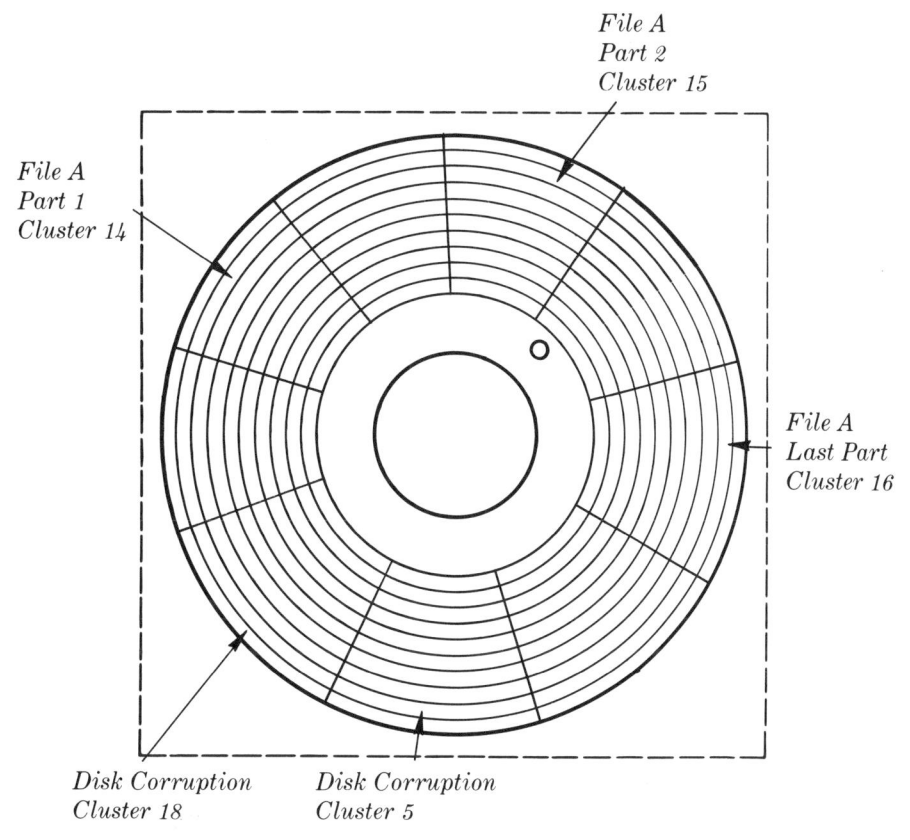

File A
Part 2
Cluster 15

File A
Part 1
Cluster 14

File A
Last Part
Cluster 16

Disk Corruption
Cluster 18

Disk Corruption
Cluster 5

Figure 13-7. *Example disk structure*

Therefore, a file is made up of a chain of cluster entries.

For example, given the disk structure shown in Figure 13-7, the FAT entries might be those shown in Table 13-4.

OS/2 finds the starting cluster of a file by way of the file's directory entry. Once it locates the starting entry, it traverses the list of cluster entries until the end-of-file (FFF) entry is found. Each time OS/2 needs additional space for a file, it traverses the FAT for available clusters.

Note that OS/2 places the value FF7 in the FAT for any corrupted sectors that appear on the disk during formatting. This prevents OS/2 from later attempting to use the corrupted sectors.

Cluster number	Status
0	Reserved
1	Reserved
2	n
3	n
4	n
5	FF7
6	n
.	.
.	.
.	.
14	15
15	16
16	FFF
.	.
.	.
.	.
355	n

Table 13-4. *File-Allocation Table for Example Disk*

The FORMAT command is the only mechanism that records corrupted sectors on disk. Whenever you suspect corrupted sectors, formatting is a good step.

FILE-ALLOCATION TABLE

Every OS/2 disk has a file-allocation table (FAT) that tracks disk space usage. The FAT records sectors that are corrupted and should not be used for storing files, sectors that are available for file allocation, and which sectors relate to each file. Each cluster on the disk has a FAT entry. The FAT, therefore, is your disk road map.

Disk type	Directory sectors	Directory entries
Single-sided	4	64
Double-sided	7	112
Quad-density	14	224
Fixed disk	32	512

Table 13-5.   *Entries for Directories*

Chapter 8 stated that if you do not use OS/2 subdirectories, your disks are restricted to a fixed number of files, as shown in Table 13-5. Each OS/2 file requires a 32-byte directory entry, as shown in Table 13-6.

If you are using a 1.2MB disk, you can determine the maximum number of files that the root directory can store, as shown here:

max_files=(sectors * sector_size) / entry_size
           =14 * 512 / 32
           =224

Field	Offset
File name	0
Extension	8
Attribute byte	11
Reserved for DOS	12
Time	22
Date	24
Starting cluster number	26
File size	28

Table 13-6.   *Entry in Directory Structure*

ROOT DIRECTORY FILES

OS/2 reserves a limited amount of space on each disk for files in the root directory. Each OS/2 file requires a 32-byte entry. Because of this, each disk is restricted to a limited number of files in the root directory. To place more files than this limit on the disk, you must use OS/2 subdirectories.

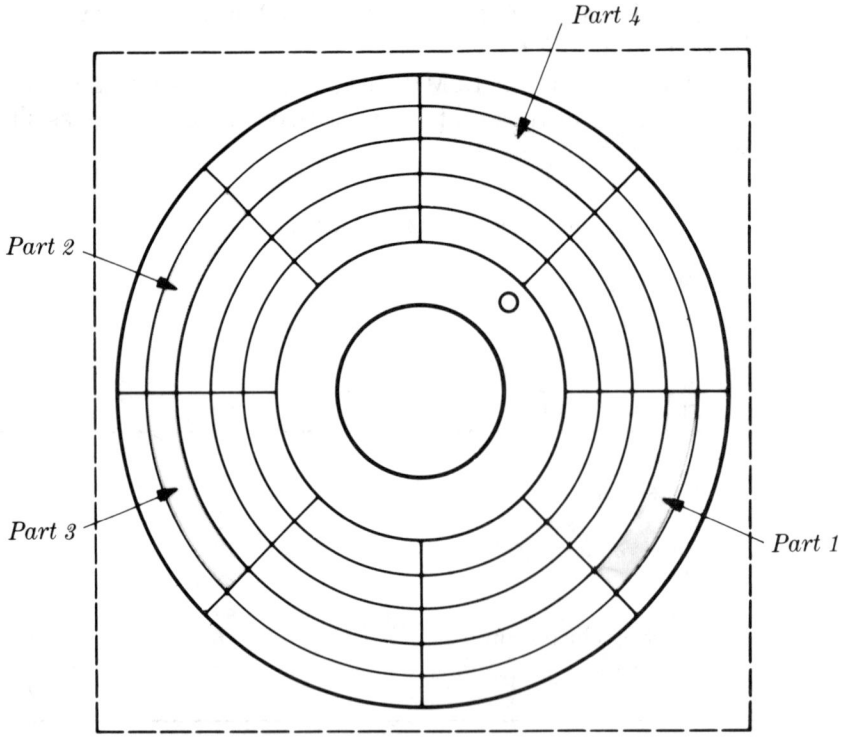

Figure 13-8.   *Example of disk fragmentation*

Disk Fragmentation

Disk fragmentation occurs when the files on your disk are contained in sectors that are physically dispersed around the disk, as shown in Figure 13-8. In this example, all four parts of the file (clusters) are physically dispersed. Contrast this file with a contiguous file, shown in Figure 13-9.

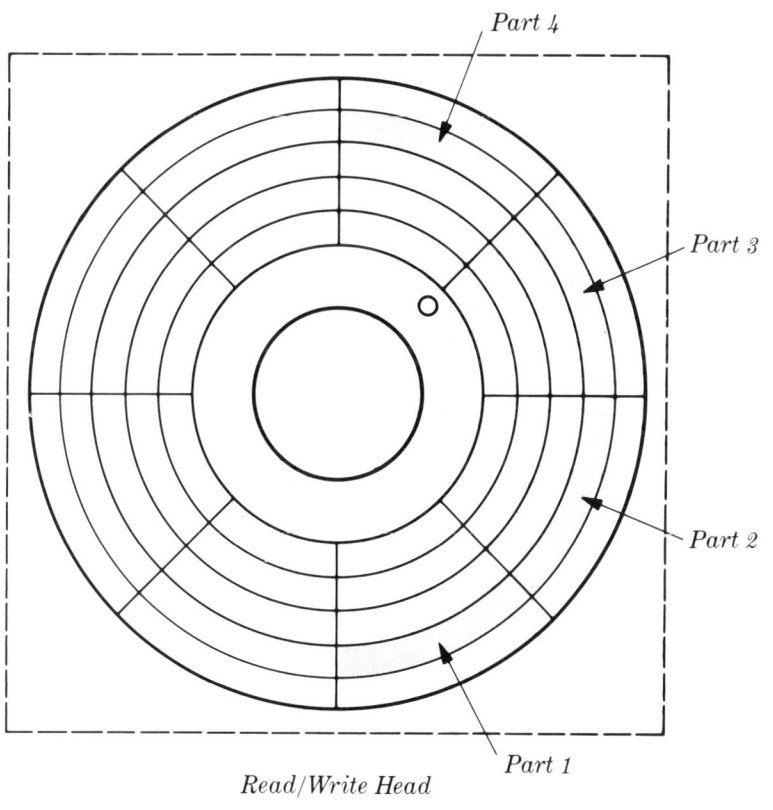

Figure 13-9. *Sample file*

Fragmented files can increase the amount of time required for the disk to access sectors, since additional disk rotations may be required to read the contents of the file. This in turn makes your application run slower. If many files are fragmented, overall system performance may decrease sharply.

Consider a scenario where two OS/2 concurrent programs must read the contents of a file from two different disk drives. One file is contiguous (see Figure 13-10), while the other is badly fragmented, as shown in Figure 13-11. The programs begin by reading the first cluster, as shown in Figure 13-12.

Next, each program must read the second cluster. The first program must now rotate the disk a half revolution before the second cluster can be read. However, the contiguous disk has the data immediately available, as shown in Figure 13-13. This process repeats again for the third cluster (see Figure 13-14) and then the fourth (see Figure 13-15).

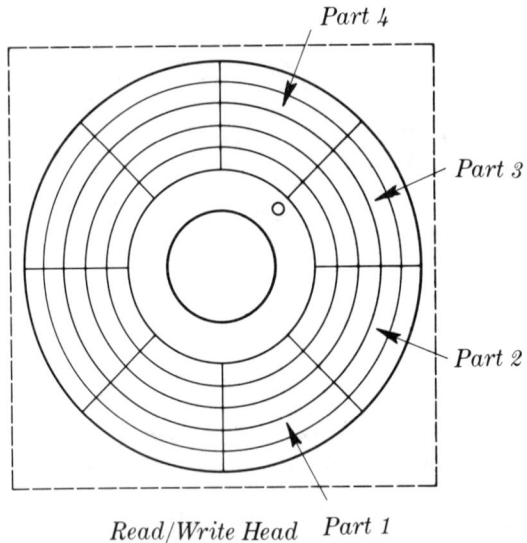

Figure 13-10. *Contiguous file*

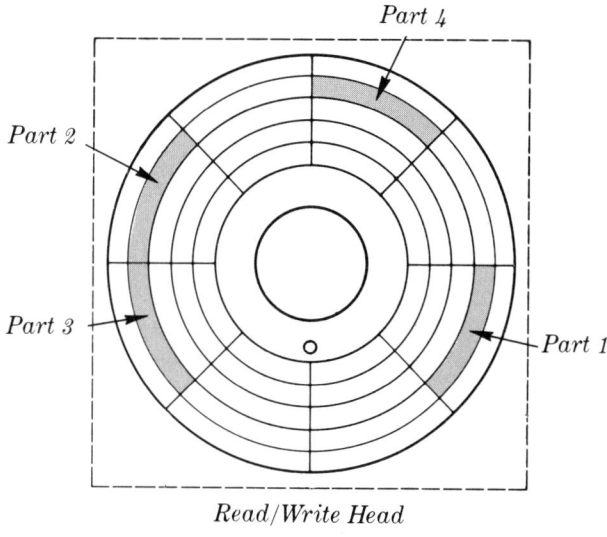

Read/Write Head

Figure 13-11. *Noncontiguous file*

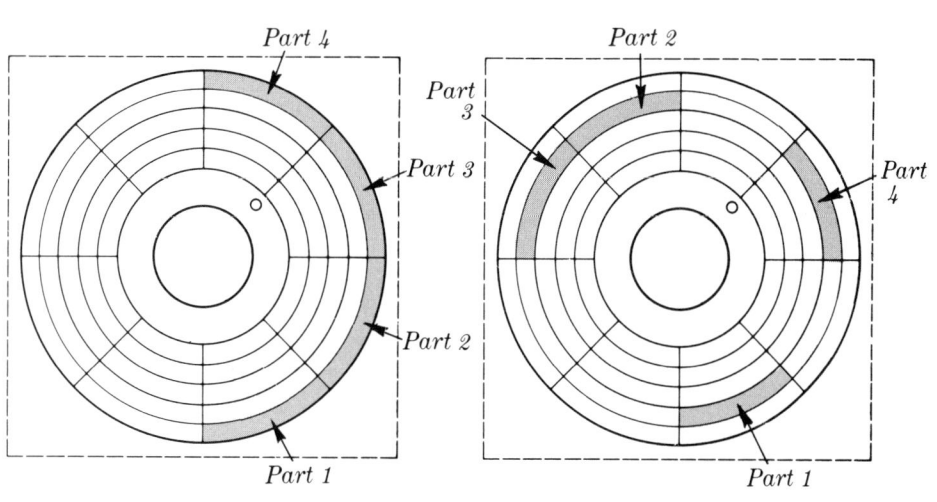

Figure 13-12. *Programs reading first cluster*

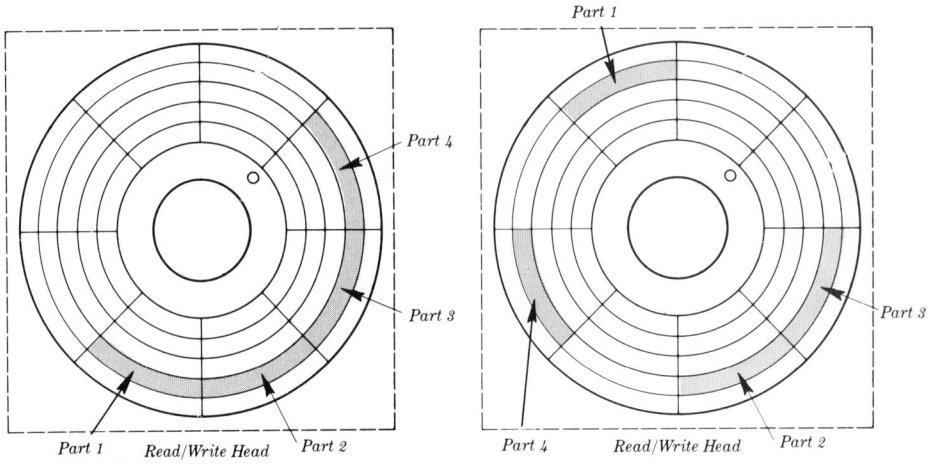

Figure 13-13.   *Data immediately available on contiguous disk*

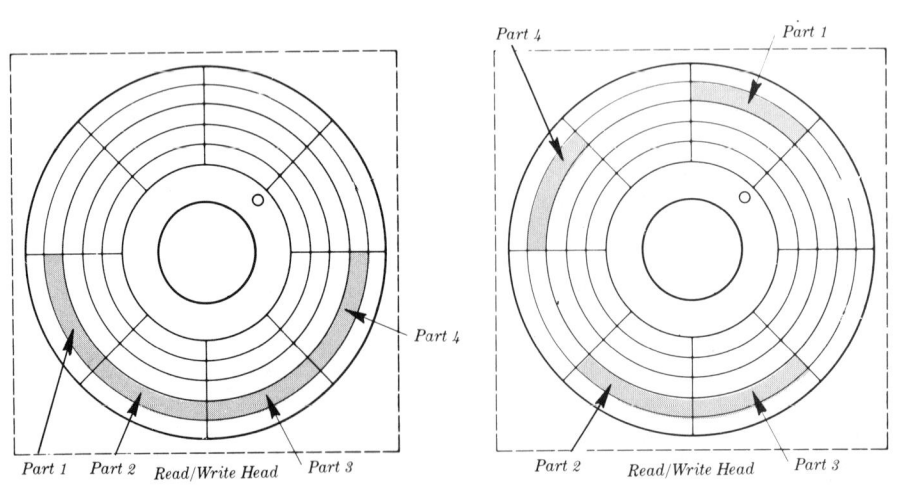

Figure 13-14.   *Process repeating for third cluster*

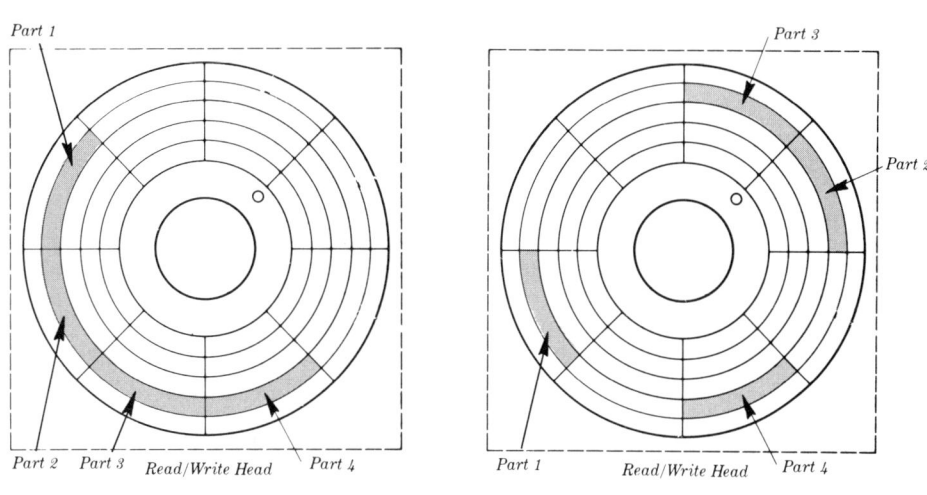

Figure 13-15. *Process repeating for fourth cluster*

In this example, the files were quite small. However, it should be readily apparent how disk fragmentation can affect your overall system performance. To determine whether or not your disk or a specific file is fragmented, use the OS/2 CHKDSK command, as shown here:

```
[A:\] CHKDSK *.*
```

If any of your files are not contiguous, CHKDSK reports the condition, as shown here:

```
A:\FILENAME.EXT
contains n non-contiguous blocks.
```

To repair a noncontiguous fixed disk, you must perform a complete disk backup and restoration. Immediately following the backup, you must either erase all the files from the disk or format the drive prior to restoration. Many users make two copies of their disks before performing the disk format and file restoration. This prevents a single floppy-disk corruption from rendering the restoration incomplete.

To repair your floppy disks, use the OS/2 XCOPY command. The OS/2 DISKCOPY command will not correct disk fragmentation.

DISK FRAGMENTATION

Disk fragmentation occurs when parts of your files (clusters) become physically spread out across a disk. Fragmentation causes the disk drive to rotate the disk several additional times in order to read the file contents. This, in turn, decreases system performance. The OS/2 CHKDSK command informs you as to the state of fragmentation on a disk. Once a disk becomes fragmented, you must use the OS/2 BACKUP, RESTORE, or XCOPY commands.

Hard Disks

Each of the preceding concepts applies to fixed disks as well as floppies. This section examines several of the factors that make fixed disks unique.

Unlike floppy disks (which are exposed to the environment), fixed disks are sealed in a protective casing, as shown in Figure 13-16, making them less susceptible to damage from dust, smoke, and fingerprints. In addition, since you do not have access to the fixed-disk storage medium, the disk is less flexible and spins at a much faster rate than a floppy disk. This provides fixed disks

Read/Write
Head

Platter

Figure 13-16. *Fixed disk in sealed casing*

with greater storage capacity and faster access time.

Floppy disks normally record data on both sides, as shown in Figure 13-17. Fixed disks, on the other hand, are composed of multiple sections called *platters.* Most computer fixed disks use two platters, thus providing four sides on which to record information, as shown in Figure 13-18.

Just as floppy disks use tracks to organize the information that they contain, fixed disks combine multiple tracks to form *cylinders* (see Figure 13-19). In most cases, data is recorded on a fixed disk based upon cylinders as opposed to individual tracks.

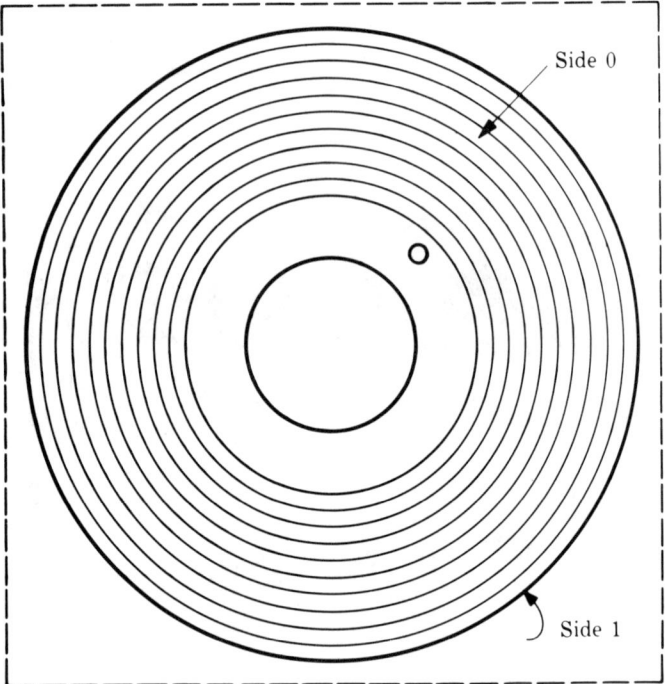

Figure 13-17. *Storage by floppy on two sides of disk*

In the past, many users divided up the space of their fixed disk into areas called *partitions*. In this way, users could place multiple operating systems on different partitions, as shown in Figure 13-20. Today, however, partitions are used most commonly with large disks. OS/2 (as well as DOS) only supports partitions up to 32MB in length. If your fixed disk is quite large, you must divide it into several distinct partitions.

The OS/2 FDISK command enables you to define your disk partitions. OS/2 uses the first sector on the fixed disk as the master boot record. This sector contains information on each of the partitions on the disk. This is how the computer determines

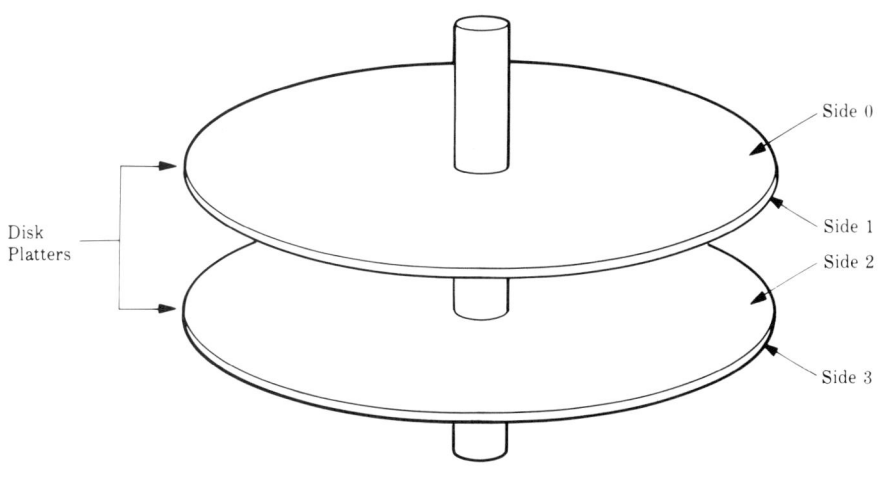

Figure 13-18. *Two platters of fixed disk*

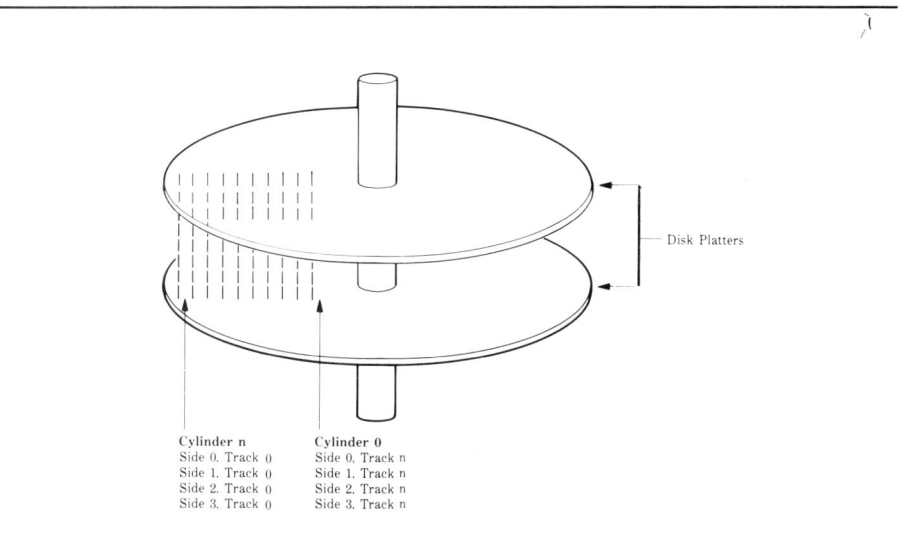

Figure 13-19. *Cylinders on fixed disk*

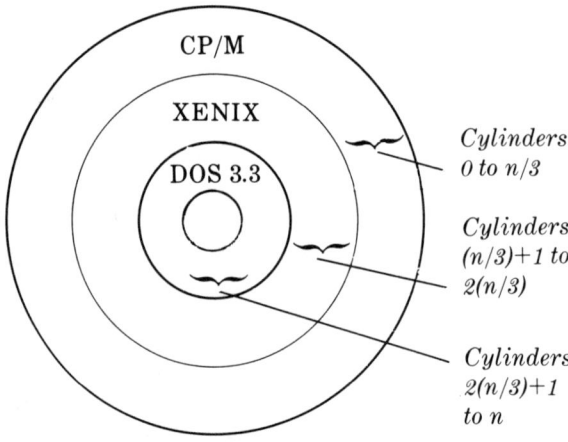

Figure 13-20.   *Multiple partitioning*

from which operating system it should boot and how large each partition is. The OS/2 FDISK command provides the user interface to this data storage area. The FDISK command is examined in detail in the Osborne/McGraw-Hill text, *DOS: The Complete Reference* (1987).

Using Directories to Improve System Performance

Most users are interested in ways to make their systems run faster. Many install expensive hardware upgrades, which might include faster disks, system clocks, or coprocessors. In many cases, these users can achieve significant performance increases simply by using OS/2 directories to their fullest extent.

Assume that your disk has the directory structure shown in Figure 13-21. Executable files are located in several different directories. You can simplify your program execution by defining command-file and data-file search paths through the PATH and APPEND commands. Depending on the order in which you place

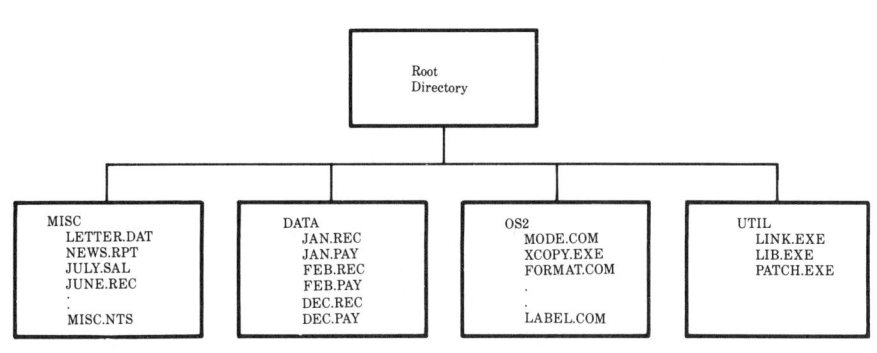

Figure 13-21. *Sample directory structure*

the directory names within these commands, your system performance can increase or decrease accordingly.

For example, if you issue the command

```
[C:\]  PATH C:\MISC;C:\DATA;C:\OS2;C:\UTIL
```

OS/2 will first search the directories DATA and MISC each time it fails to find the command specified in the current directory. The directories UTIL and OS2 are far more likely to contain the executable files, but OS/2 in this case must search every directory entry in the subdirectories DATA and MISC before it searches UTIL and OS2. This can result in considerable system overhead. If the files in DATA are most likely to be used as data files, the subdirectory DATA should be the first directory specified in the OS/2 APPEND or DPATH commands.

In this same way, if the user again logically divides the files contained in DATA and MISC into further subdirectories, file-search overhead may be reduced to an even greater degree.

If you are not fully utilizing OS/2 subdirectories, you should be. The time you spend today organizing your disk into logical collections of files will pay substantial dividends in the future.

Chapter Highlights

At its lowest levels of disk access, OS/2 treats fixed, floppy, and microfloppy disks in the same way. OS/2's disk I/O operations are standard and remain fully compatible with DOS.

The disk drive records data onto and off of the disk media by way of the read/write head. Each time that you place a floppy disk into a drive, the disk begins spinning past the read/write head. This allows the disk drive to access the entire storage area of the disk.

OS/2 physically divides disks into a collection of concentric rings called tracks. Next, OS/2 divides each track into equally sized sections called sectors. Disk storage capacity is determined from the following equation:

storage = (bytes per sector) * (sectors per track) *
        (tracks per side) * (sides per disk)

Not all of the storage space on a disk is available for data. OS/2 allocates space on each disk to store the following:

Boot record
File-allocation table
Root directory entries

As you can see, every OS/2 disk has a boot record. If the disk is bootable, the boot record starts the boot process. Otherwise, the boot record is responsible for displaying the nonsystem disk-error message.

The file allocation table (FAT) is your disk road map. The FAT records available disk space, which disk space is associated with specific files, and corrupted disk sectors. Because of its importance, OS/2 maintains two copies of the FAT on disk.

Each OS/2 file requires a 32-byte directory entry. OS/2 sets aside a specific number of disk sectors to store root directory entries. Hence, each disk is restricted to a specific number of files in the root directory.

Each time OS/2 allocates space to a file, it does so in terms of a cluster. A cluster is a collection of two or more contiguous sectors. The entries in the FAT, therefore, actually track clusters rather than sectors. By allocating space in clusters, OS/2 reduces disk fragmentation.

Disk fragmentation occurs when your files contain several clusters that are physically dispersed across the disk. Because the disk drive must rotate the disk several times to read a fragmented file, disk I/O operations become slower, and system performance suffers. The OS/2 CHKDSK command informs you as to the state of fragmentation on your disk. If your disk becomes fragmented, you must use either the OS/2 BACKUP or XCOPY command to make a new copy of the disk.

Many users improve their system performance by minimizing the number of directory entries OS/2 must examine when it searches for command files and data files. Users accomplish this by using subdirectories. A carefully planned directory structure will have a significant impact on system performance.

14 OS/2 Presentation Manager

More than 10 million people currently use DOS, and the number of users who will in the next few years use OS/2 is far greater. OS/2 is the operating system destined to carry personal computers well into the 1990s.

For users to be able to exploit OS/2 to its fullest capabilities, it must be easy to use. IBM and Microsoft are working in a joint effort to produce the OS/2 Presentation Manager. The OS/2 Presentation Manager will provide a standard user interface not only for OS/2, but also for OS/2 applications. It is slated for release late in 1988. This chapter will base most of its discussion about the Presentation Manager on a three-manual description package called the Presentation Manager specification, which is available in the OS/2 software development kit. The examples presented will use MS Windows version 2.0, from which a large percentage of the Presentation Manager will be derived. However, keep in mind that until the Presentation Manager is actually released, much of this discussion is speculation.

OS/2 PRESENTATION MANAGER

The OS/2 Presentation Manager is a Microsoft Windows-like graphical display of the system. It allows the user to quickly invoke and display several applications at one time. The Presentation Manager provides a consistent view not only of OS/2, but also of OS/2 applications.

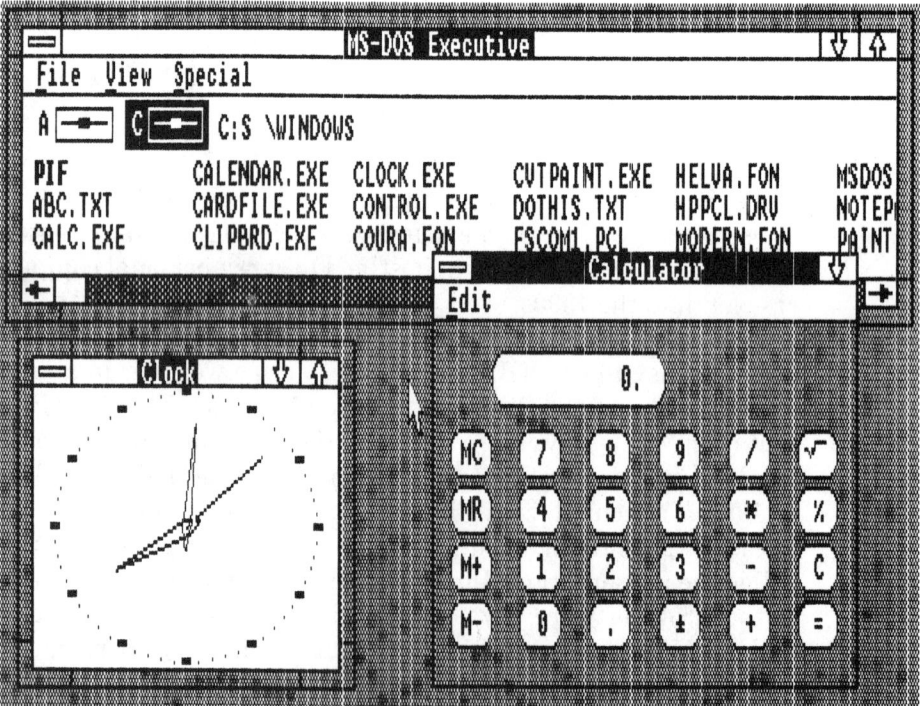

Figure 14-1. *Displaying concurrent programs on screen*

What Is the Presentation Manager?

OS/2 is a multitasking operating system, which means that it can execute multiple programs simultaneously. The OS/2 Presentation Manager is an MS Windows-like graphical display of the applications currently executing within the system. Using the Presentation Manager, you can display the output of several concurrent programs on the screen at one time, as shown in Figure 14-1.

Specifically, the Presentation Manager is a shell that is layered on OS/2. It provides a consistent user interface for all OS/2 applications (see Figure 14-2).

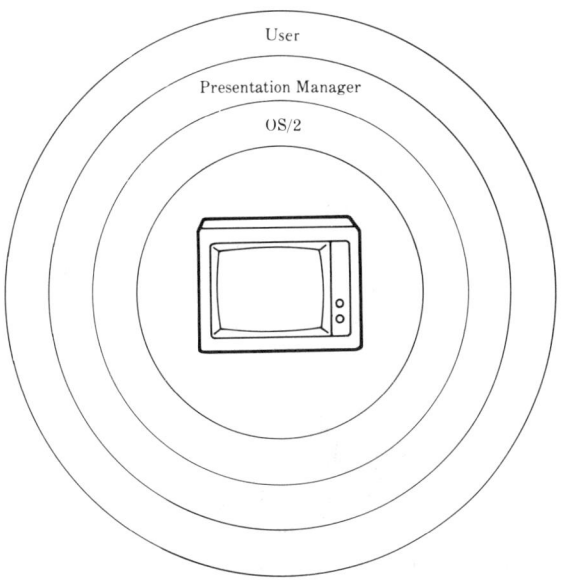

Figure 14-2.   *Presentation Manager shell*

From within the OS/2 Presentation Manager, you can execute an application, make another application active, modify the size and attributes of the application's display screen, and provide the user with easy access to device controls (such as screen color or printer characteristics).

Essentially, the Presentation Manager eliminates the need to remember nebulous commands and replaces the commands with an easy-to-use, consistent set of pull-down menus, as shown in Figure 14-3.

Since you can already create and display multiple applications at one time by using OS/2, why do you need the Presentation Manager? Simply stated, the Presentation Manager gives you a

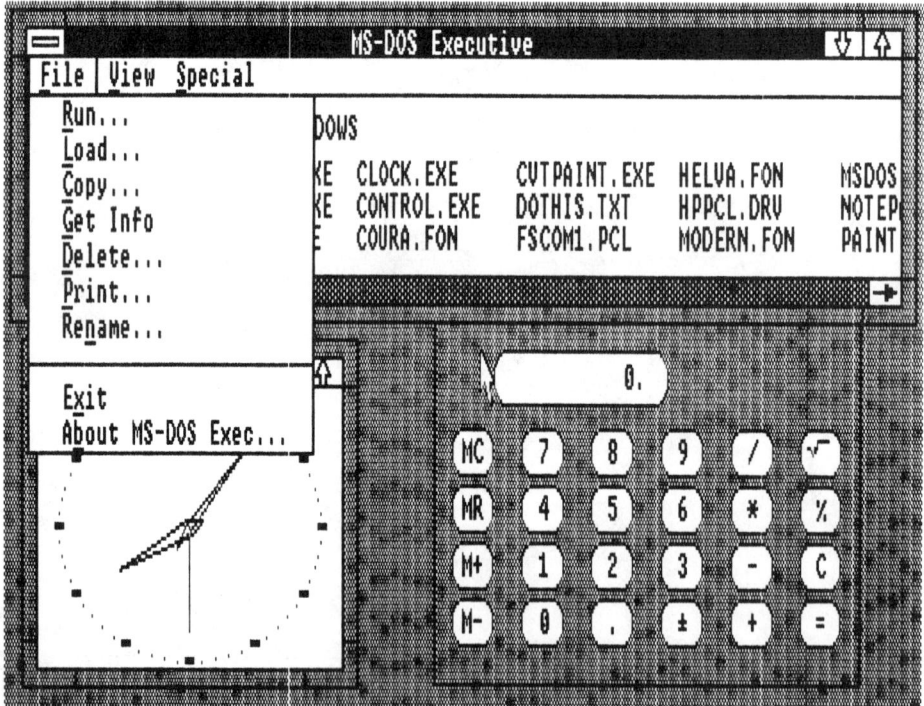

Figure 14-3. *Pull-down menu*

Figure 14-4. *Screen groups of OS/2*

view of the entire system, not merely of one application screen group. Under OS/2, each time you want to monitor the output of a different program, you must select that program's screen group as the active display and overwrite the current contents of your screen (see Figure 14-4). However, the Presentation Manager enables you to simultaneously display the results of several programs on your screen, as shown in Figure 14-5. The Presentation Manager enables you to change the size and position of each window, as shown in Figure 14-6.

Many users may recall the tiled appearance of applications under previous versions of MS Windows (see Figure 14-7). By using this screen-display facility, each time the user activated a window, Windows would simply squeeze it into the display area, as shown in Figure 14-8.

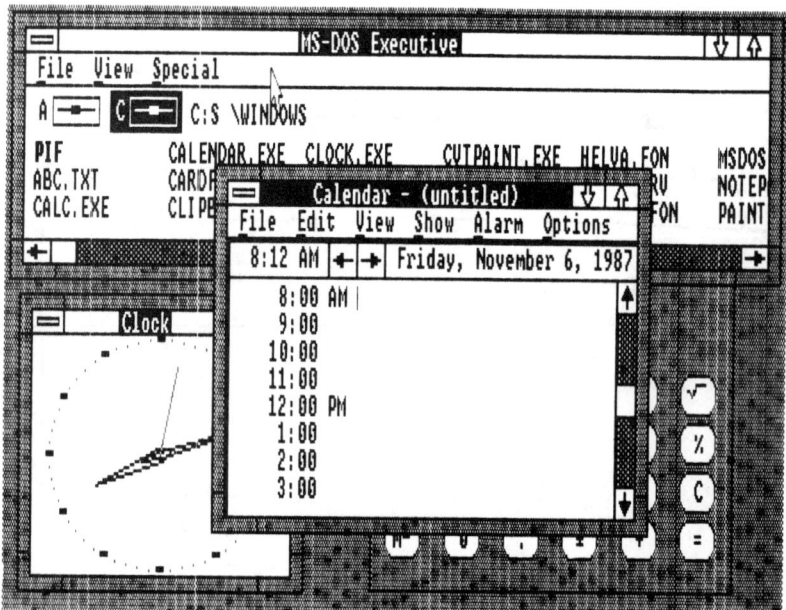

Figure 14-5. *Simultaneously displaying results of programs*

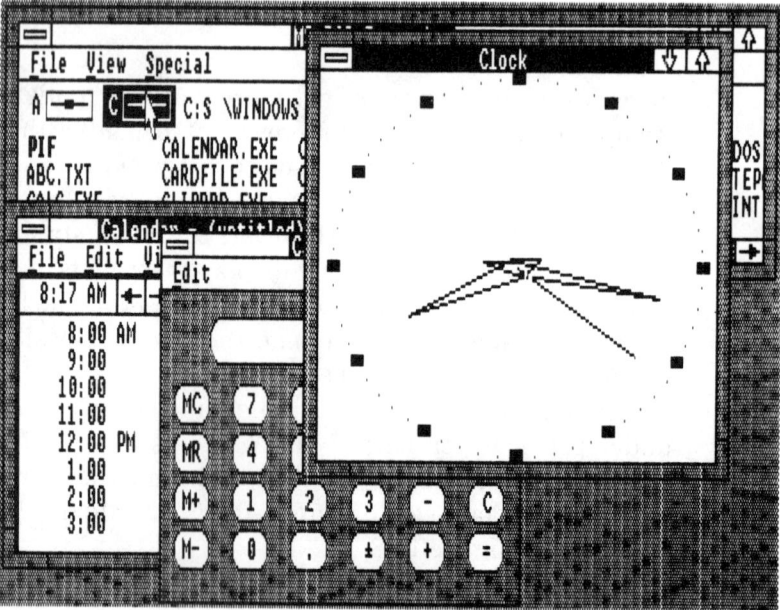

Figure 14-6. *Changing the size and position of windows*

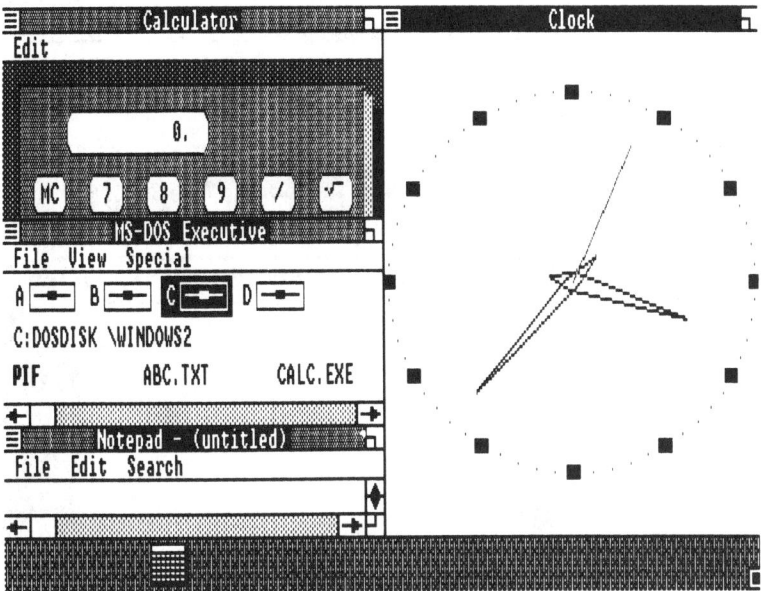

Figure 14-7. *Tiled appearance of windows*

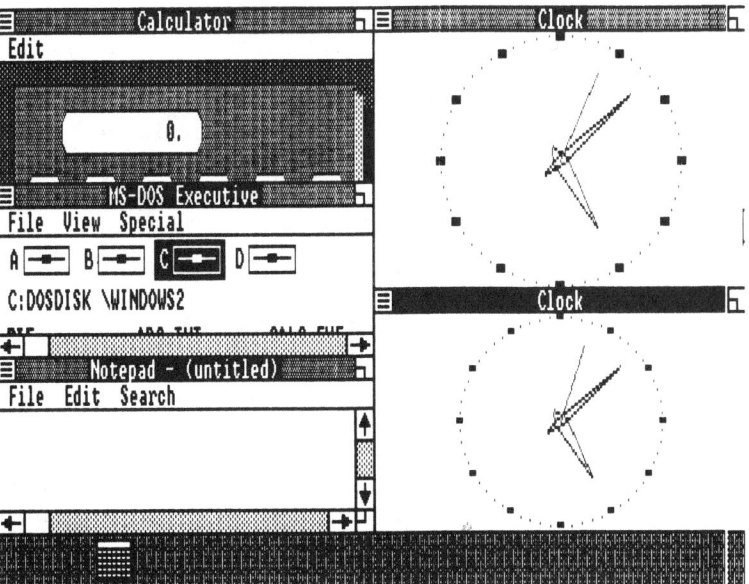

Figure 14-8. *Windows squeezing in display*

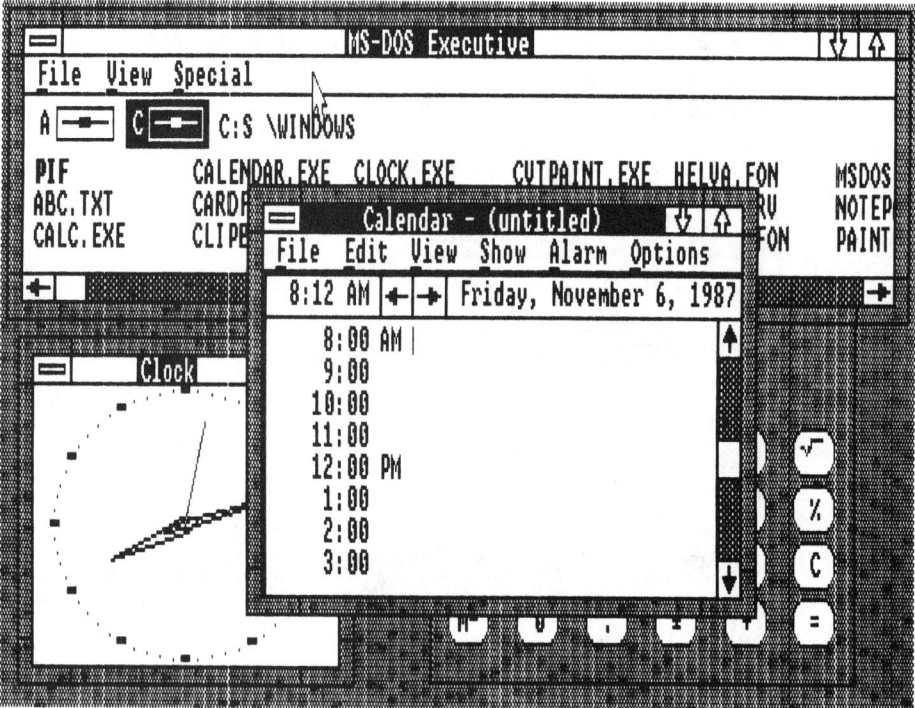

Figure 14-9.   *Overlaying one window on another window*

The OS/2 Presentation Manager uses overlay windows. You
can simply lay one window on top of another, as shown in Figure
14-9. In this way, the Presentation Manager provides full control
of how OS/2 presents itself to the end user.

PRESENTATION MANAGER SCREEN DISPLAY

The OS/2 Presentation Manager provides a complete display on the screen of
all of the applications that are currently active in the system. Users can
easily switch from one application to another and leave previous applications
on the screen if required.

Unlike previous versions of Windows that appeared tiled on the screen,
the Presentation Manager uses overlay windows, allowing one window to be
placed on top of another.

Window Structure

For those who are familiar with previous versions of MS Windows, Windows 2.0 is similar in its functional capabilities, although the appearance of each window differs slightly on the screen display.

Under the OS/2 Presentation Manager, each window frame will contain six features, as illustrated in Figure 14-10.

- Border area
- Client area
- Scroll bars (vertical and horizontal)
- Menu bars
- System icon
- Size (maximize and minimize) icons

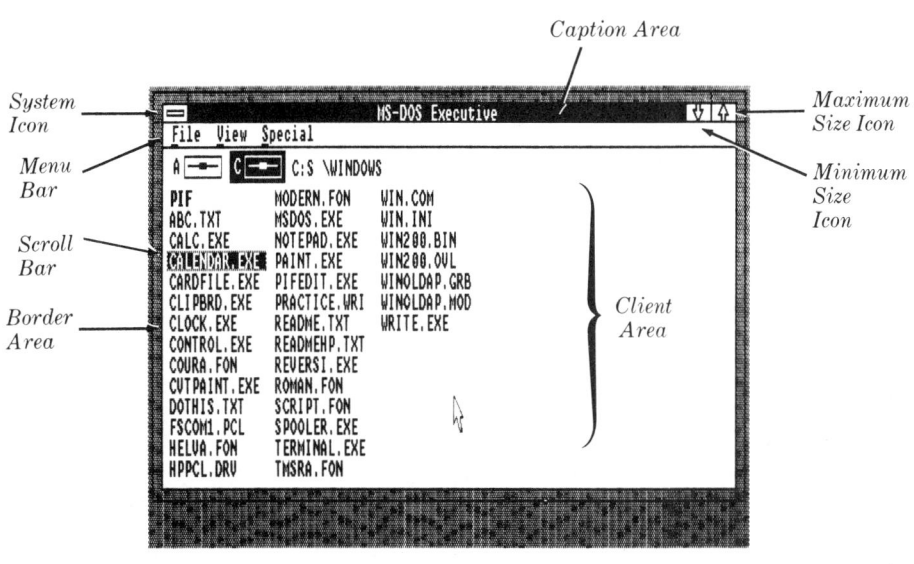

Figure 14-10. *Features of window frame*

The function of each menu section is as follows:

■ The border section separates each window display from another window display.

■ The caption is an area that contains a descriptive name to describe the function of the window.

■ The client area is the actual space for program display.

■ Each window can have one or two scroll bars (vertical and horizontal). These scroll bars allow you to scroll the window text up or down and left or right.

■ The menu bar is a region at the top of each window that contains pull-down menus.

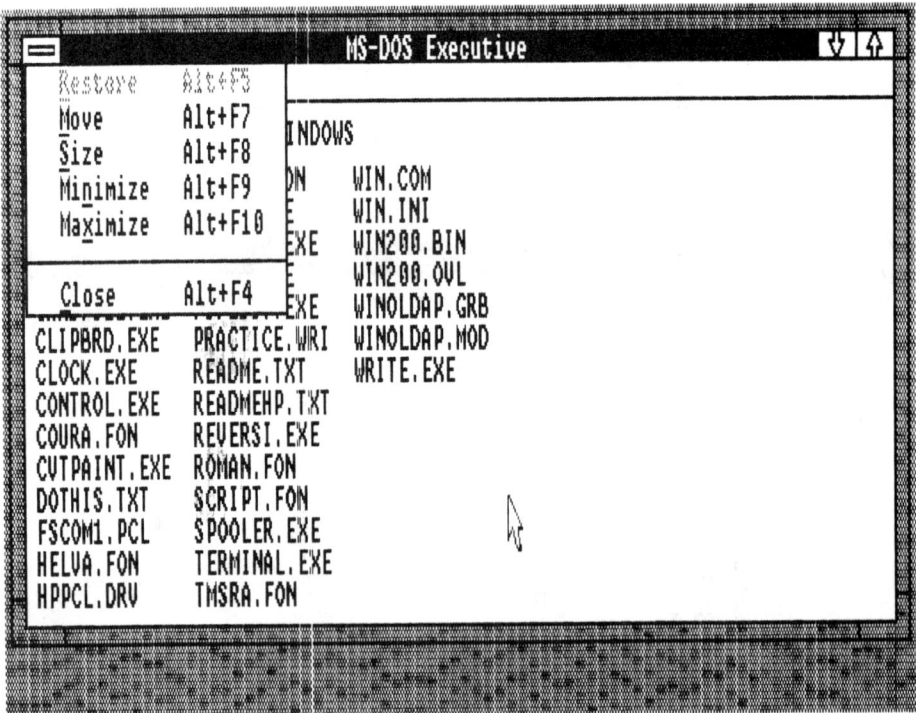

Figure 14-11. *System icon*

■ The system icon is an icon that allows the user to activate the system menu, as in Figure 14-11.

■ The maximum icon enables the user to expand the window to the full screen size, as shown in Figure 14-12.

■ The minimum icon enables the user to switch the window display to an icon, as shown in Figure 14-13.

Just as MS Windows provides dialog boxes, so will the OS/2 Presentation Manager (see Figure 14-14). In the same manner as MS Windows, these dialog boxes can have scroll bars, buttons, and list boxes, as in Figure 14-15.

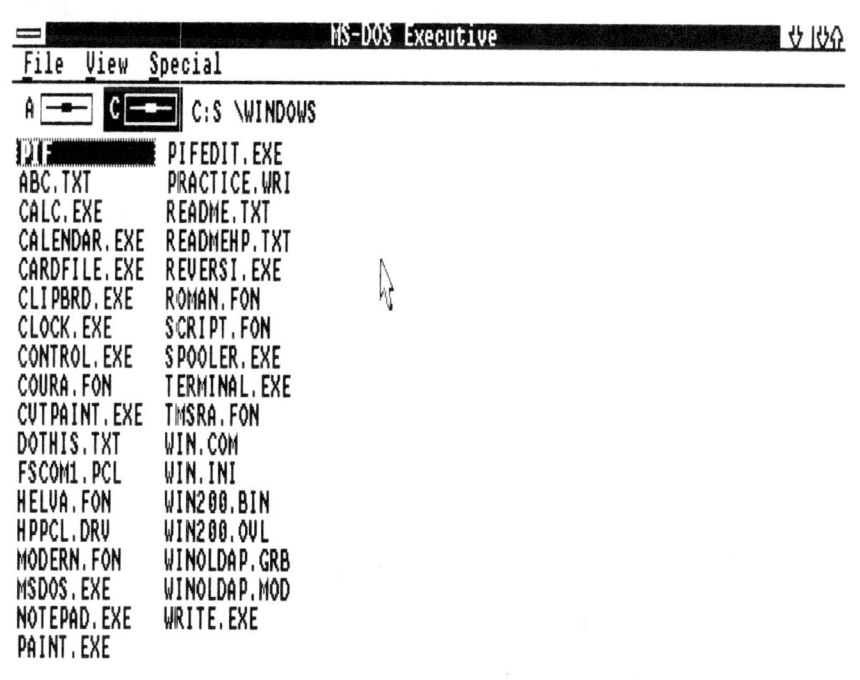

Figure 14-12. *Expanding a window to full size*

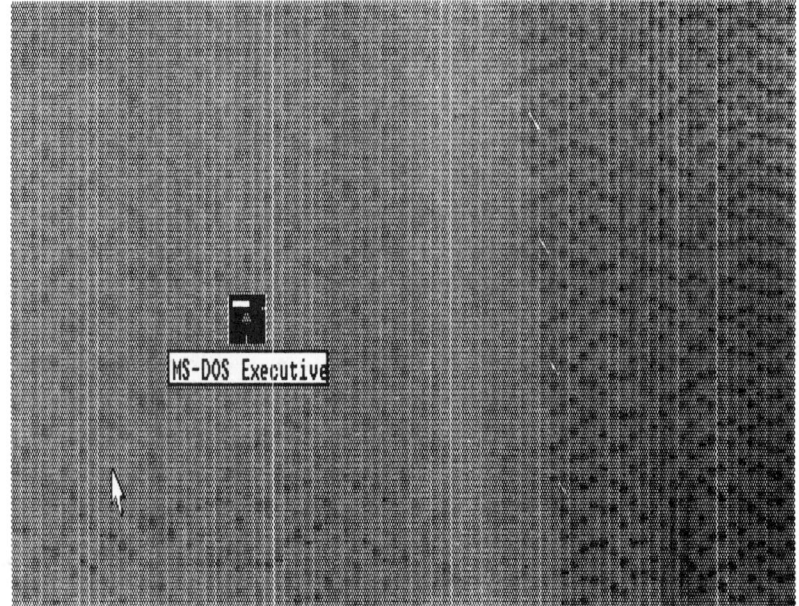

Figure 14-13. *Switching window display to icon*

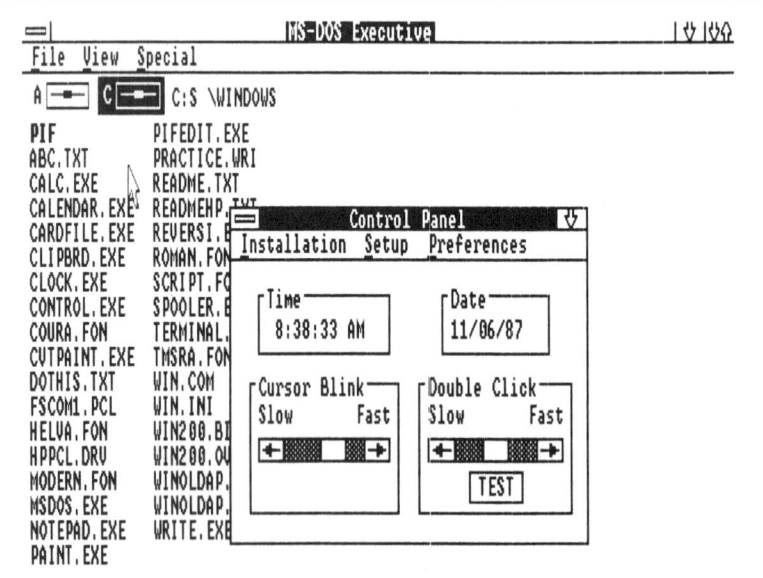

Figure 14-14. *Dialog box*

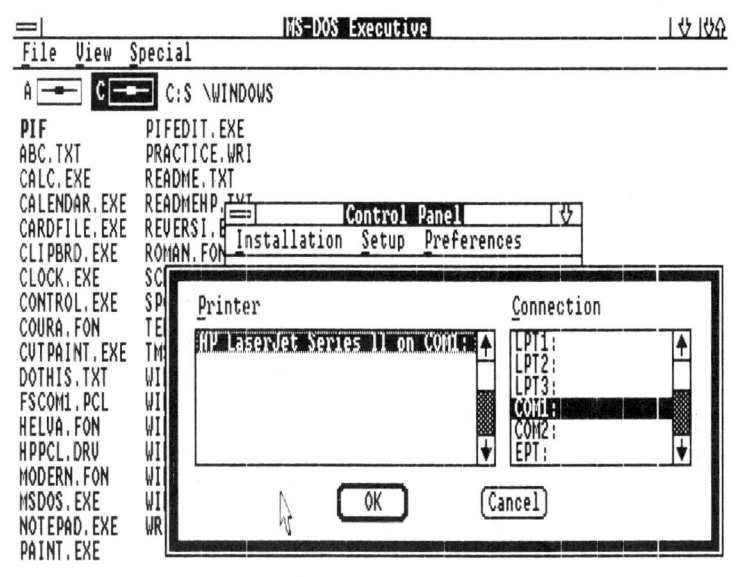

Figure 14-15. *Scroll bars, buttons, and list boxes in dialog box*

WINDOW STRUCTURE

The appearance of the Presentation Manager windows may be slightly different from that of Microsoft Windows, but its main components are the same, as follows:

- Border section
- Client area
- Menu bar
- Maximum size icon
- Caption area
- Scroll bar
- System icon
- Minimum size icon

Presentation Manager Programming

The OS/2 Presentation Manager provides a tremendous collection of interprocess communication routines, virtual-device support, and a large graphical interface. Each routine is accessed by your programs as a simple function call. The Presentation Manager Specification document contains several volumes of text about programming the Presentation Manager. However, it is similar in functionality to programming MS Windows applications. As such, serious OS/2 developers should begin developing MS Windows applications immediately by way of the MS Windows software development kit.

PRESENTATION MANAGER FUTURE

Most software developers will agree that the key to a successful package is its user interface. The OS/2 Presentation Manager gives OS/2 and OS/2 applications a consistent user-friendly interface. The learning curve for users at all levels for all OS/2 applications will be low. The OS/2 Presentation Manager will be a powerful influence into the 1990s.

Putting the Pieces Together

OS/2 is destined to be one of the most influential software packages ever released. The OS/2 Presentation Manager will have a considerable say in the overall success of OS/2. If OS/2 is slow, people will not use it. Likewise, if OS/2 is difficult, users will not fully exploit its capabilities. The OS/2 Presentation Manager must be both functional and fast.

As the future will show, the OS/2 Presentation Manager will provide tremendous capabilities not only to the end user, but also to the programmer. Although it will remain a mystery until it releases, the best way to fully prepare for the Presentation Manager is to use and develop programs for MS Windows.

Chapter Highlights

More than 10 million people currently use DOS. The number of users who will some day run OS/2 is much larger.

To be successful, OS/2 must have a consistent, easy-to-use, fast user interface. The OS/2 Presentation Manager will provide this critical user interface.

To date, the OS/2 Presentation Manager does not exist. IBM and Microsoft are currently in a joint development effort to complete the Presentation Manager. Its current release is scheduled for late in 1988.

Unlike OS/2 sessions that only display the result of one program on the screen, the OS/2 Presentation Manager allows several programs to be displayed on the same screen in differently sized windows.

Unlike previous versions of Windows that used tiled windows, Windows 2.0 and the OS/2 Presentation Manager use overlay windows that allow one window to be placed on top of another.

For those who are familar with MS Windows, the functionality of Presentation Manager windows will be identical. Each window will consist of the following:

- Border area

- Caption area

- Client area

- Scroll bars (vertical and horizontal)

- Menu bars

- System icon

- Size (maximize and minimize) icons

Just as OS/2 provides a myriad of programming tools, so, too, does the OS/2 Presentation Manager. Specifically, the Presentation Manager provides a powerful collection of device-independent graphics routines. Users who are serious about programming the OS/2 Presentation Manager should begin programming MS Windows applications today.

OS/2 will be a strong force in the PC marketplace for some time. The Presentation Manager can only make that force more powerful.

A ASCII Codes

Table A-1 lists the ASCII codes for characters.

DEC	OCTAL	HEX	ASCII	DEC	OCTAL	HEX	ASCII
0	000	00	NUL	16	020	10	DLE
1	001	01	SOH	17	021	11	DC1
2	002	02	STX	18	022	12	DC2
3	003	03	ETX	19	023	13	DC3
4	004	04	EOT	20	024	14	DC4
5	005	05	ENQ	21	025	15	NAK
6	006	06	ACK	22	026	16	SYN
7	007	07	BEL	23	027	17	ETB
8	010	08	BS	24	030	18	CAN
9	011	09	HT	25	031	19	EM
10	012	0A	LF	26	032	1A	SUB
11	013	0B	VT	27	033	1B	ESC
12	014	0C	FF	28	034	1C	FS
13	015	0D	CR	29	035	1D	GS
14	016	0E	SO	30	036	1E	RS
15	017	0F	SI	31	037	1F	US

Table A-1. *ASCII Character Codes*

DEC	OCTAL	HEX	ASCII	DEC	OCTAL	HEX	ASCII
32	040	20	SPACE	67	103	43	C
33	041	21	!	68	104	44	D
34	042	22	"	69	105	45	E
35	043	23	#	70	106	46	F
36	044	24	$	71	107	47	G
37	045	25	%	72	110	48	H
38	046	26	&	73	111	49	I
39	047	27	'	74	112	4A	J
40	050	28	(	75	113	4B	K
41	051	29	)	76	114	4C	L
42	052	2A	*	77	115	4D	M
43	053	2B	+	78	116	4E	N
44	054	2C	,	79	117	4F	O
45	055	2D	−	80	120	50	P
46	056	2E	.	81	121	51	Q
47	057	2F	/	82	122	52	R
48	060	30	0	83	123	53	S
49	061	31	1	84	124	54	T
50	062	32	2	85	125	55	U
51	063	33	3	86	126	56	V
52	064	34	4	87	127	57	W
53	065	35	5	88	130	58	X
54	066	36	6	89	131	59	Y
55	067	37	7	90	132	5A	Z
56	070	38	8	91	133	5B	[
57	071	39	9	92	134	5C	\
58	072	3A	:	93	135	5D	]
59	073	3B	;	94	136	5E	^
60	074	3C	<	95	137	5F	_
61	075	3D	=	96	140	60	`
62	076	3E	>	97	141	61	a
63	077	3F	?	98	142	62	b
64	100	40	@	99	143	63	c
65	101	41	A	100	144	64	d
66	102	42	B	101	145	65	e

Table A-1. *ASCII Character Codes (continued)*

DEC	OCTAL	HEX	ASCII	DEC	OCTAL	HEX	ASCII
102	146	66	f	115	163	73	s
103	147	67	g	116	164	74	t
104	150	68	h	117	165	75	u
105	151	69	i	118	166	76	v
106	152	6A	j	119	167	77	w
107	153	6B	k	120	170	78	x
108	154	6C	l	121	171	79	y
109	155	6D	m	122	172	7A	z
110	156	6E	n	123	173	7B	{
111	157	6F	o	124	174	7C		
112	160	70	p	125	175	7D	}
113	161	71	q	126	176	7E	~
114	162	72	r	127	177	7F	DEL

Table A-1. *ASCII Character Codes (continued)*

B OS/2 Command Summary

This appendix provides a summary of the commands used in OS/2.

ANSI

Function   Enable ANSI support for a protected-mode session.

Mode   Protected

Format

ANSI [ON¦ OFF]

where the following is true:

ON directs OS/2 to support ANSI terminal commands for the current protected-mode sesson.

OFF directs OS/2 to disable ANSI support in the current protected-mode session.

Syntax Chart

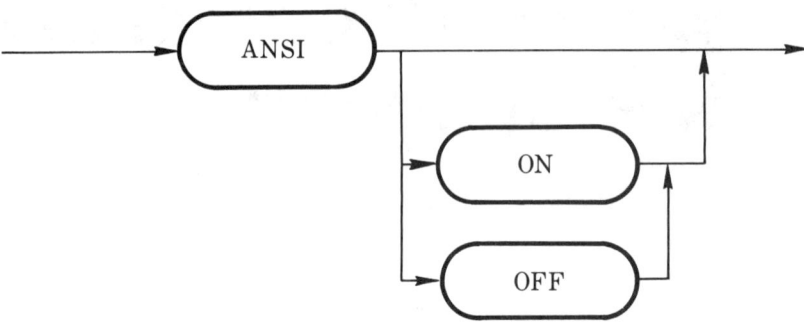

Notes ANSI escape sequences are combinations of characters that direct the terminal to perform special functions (such as clearing the screen display or erasing the current line).

If you invoke ANSI without a command-line parameter, ANSI displays the current state of ANSI support (ON or OFF).

The ANSI command is a protected-mode command. To provide ANSI support for real mode you must install the ANSI.SYS driver in the CONFIG.SYS.

```
DEVICE=ANSI.SYS
```

Table B-1 defines the supported ANSI escape sequences.

Examples In the following case, OS/2 supports ANSI escape sequences in the current protected-mode session:

```
[C:\] ANSI ON
The ANSI extended screen and
keyboard control are on.

[C:\]
```

ANSI function	ANSI code
Set cursor position	Esc[Row;COLH
Clear screen	Esc[HEsc[J
Cursor up *n* rows	Esc[nA
Cursor down *n* rows	Esc[nB
Cursor right *n* columns	Esc[nC
Cursor left *n* columns	Esc[nD
Save cursor position	Esc[s
Restore cursor position	Esc[u
Erase to end of line	Esc[K
Erase to bottom of screen	Esc[2J
Device status report	Esc[6n
Report cursor position	Esc[n;nR

Table B-1. *Character Codes Supported by ANSI*

Invoking ANSI without a command-line parameter directs ANSI to display its current state of support (ON or OFF), as shown here:

```
[C:\] ANSI
The ANSI extended screen and
keyboard control are on.

[C:\]
```

The following command turns ANSI support OFF in the current protected-mode session:

```
[C:\] ANSI OFF
The ANSI extended screen and
keyboard control are off.

[C:\]
```

The ANSI escape sequence

esc[Hesc[J

clears the current screen contents and places the cursor in the upper-left (home) cursor position. You can verify this by issuing the OS/2 PROMPT command once ANSI support is enabled. Use the following system prompt:

```
[C:\] PROMPT $e[H$e[J$n$g
```

OS/2 clears the screen and displays the current disk drive followed by a > character each time the prompt is displayed.

APPEND

Function   Define the data-file search path that OS/2 uses each time it fails to locate a file in the current directory, or as specified.

Mode   Real

Format

[*drive:*][*path*]APPEND [*d:*][*p* [;[*d:*][*p*]...]

where the following is true:

drive: specifies the disk drive containing the file APPEND.COM. If you do not specify a disk drive identifier, OS/2 uses the current default.

path is the OS/2 path name of the subdirectory that contains the file APPEND.COM. If you do not specify an OS/2 path name, OS/2 uses the current default.

d: specifies a disk drive that OS/2 is to include in the data search path.

p specifies an OS/2 subdirectory to include in the data search path.
... states that the disk drive and subdirectories may be specified several times.

Syntax Chart

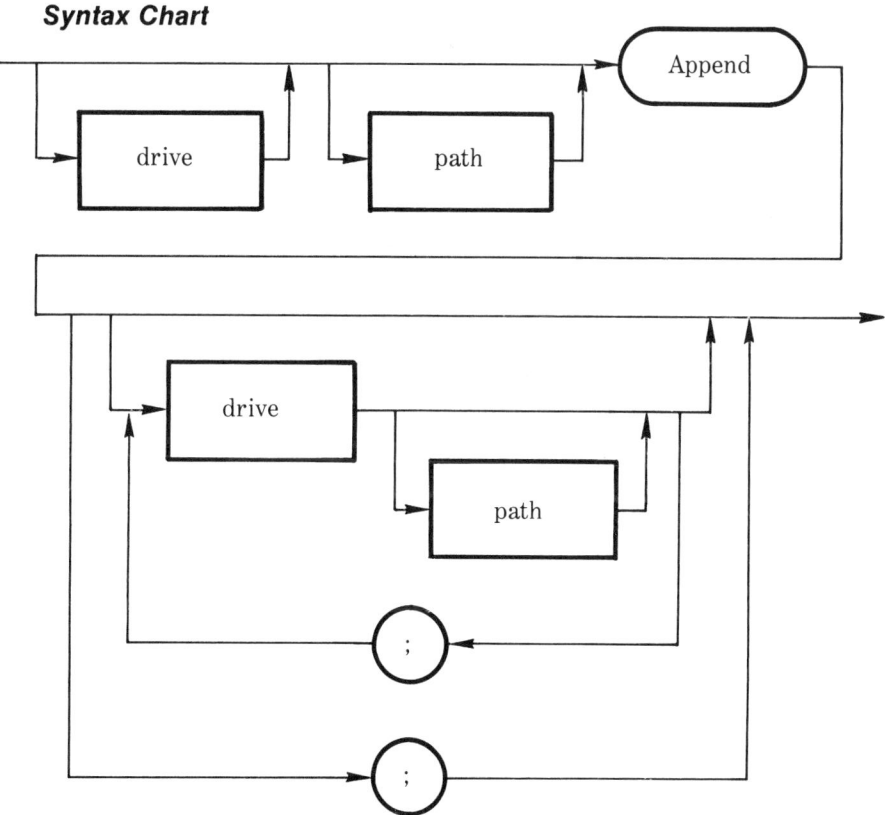

Notes Each time OS/2 real mode cannot find a specified data file or a data file in the current directory, it searches to see if the user has defined a data file search path (see Figure B-1). The OS/2 APPEND command enables you to define disk drives and sub-directories to be included in the real-mode data-file search path. In a similar manner, the OS/2 DPATH command enables you to define a protected-mode data-file search path.

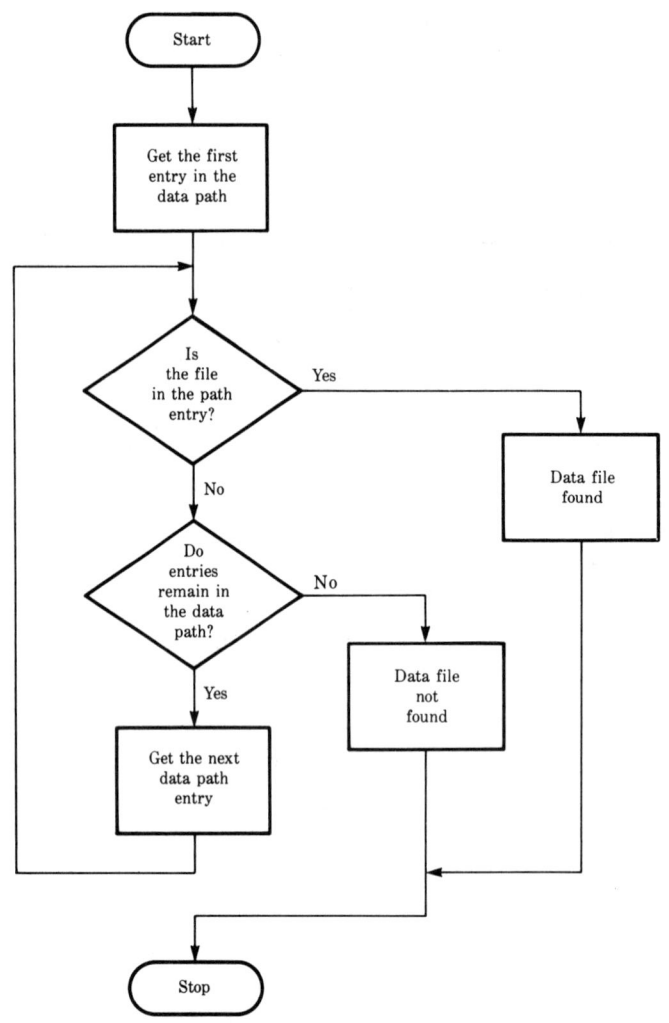

Figure B-1.   *Flowchart to determine if file is in data path*

Examples   If OS/2 cannot find the data file in the current directory, OS/2 searches the root directories in drives C, B, and A, in
that order, as shown in Figure B-2.

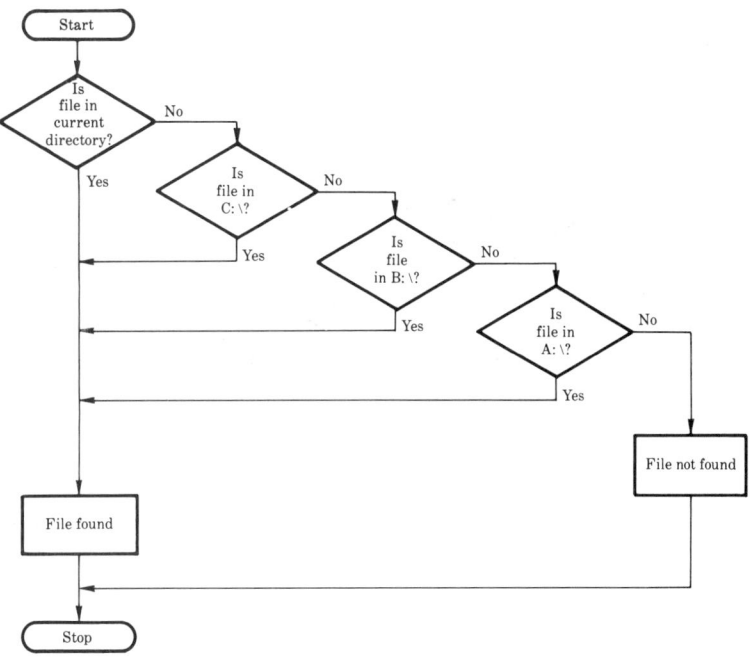

Figure B-2. *OS/2 searching root directories on drives C, B, and A*

```
C> APPEND C:\;B:\;A:\
```

In similar manner, the following APPEND command directs OS/2 to search \OS2, \UTIL, and then \MISC, in that order:

```
C> APPEND \OS2;\UTIL;\MISC
```

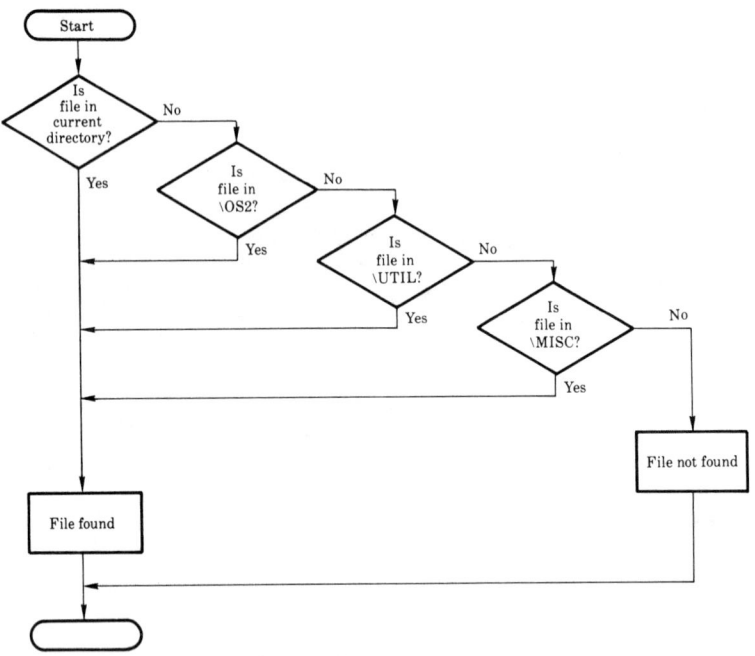

Figure B-3. *OS/2 searching root directories for \OS/2, \UTIL, and \MISC*

Figure B-3 illustrates the processing performed.

ASSIGN

Function Route disk drive references from one disk drive to another.

Mode Real

Format

ASSIGN [*source_drive=target_drive* [. . .]]

where the following is true:

source_drive is the disk drive identifier of the disk from which to route disk I/O references.

target_drive is the disk drive identifier of the disk to which disk I/O operations will be routed.

. . . states that the command can be repeated several times.

Syntax Chart

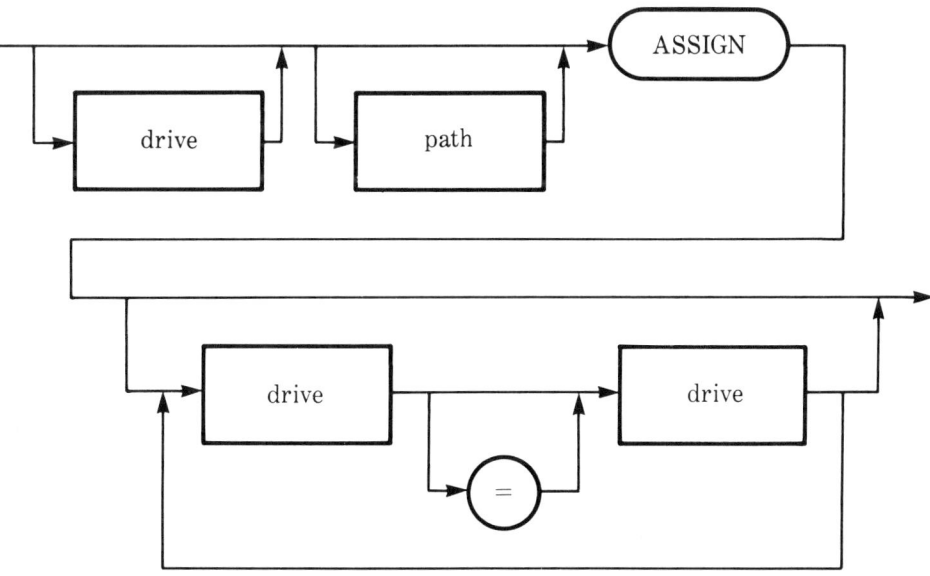

Notes   Many older software packages always look to drive A for data or overlay files. If you want to install this software on your fixed disk, you must trick the software into looking on the fixed disk for the files. The ASSIGN command enables you to do this.

If you invoke ASSIGN without any command-line parameters, ASSIGN will restore its original disk drive assignments.

Do not place a colon after each disk drive identifier in the ASSIGN command line.

Most users should consider using the OS/2 SUBST command instead of ASSIGN.

Do not use a disk on which ASSIGN has been invoked with the following commands:

BACKUP
DISKCOPY
FORMAT
JOIN
LABEL
PRINT
RESTORE
SUBST

Examples In the following case, OS/2 real-mode disk I/O operations that reference drive A are routed to the disk in drive C:

```
C> ASSIGN A=C
```

If you invoke a command such as

```
C> DIR A:
```

OS/2 actually lists the files contained on drive C.

If you invoke ASSIGN without any command-line parameters, OS/2 restores its original disk drive assignments, as shown here:

```
Volume in drive C has no label
Directory of  C:\MISC

HARDWARE      <DIR>        10-05-87    2:20p
SOFTWARE      <DIR>        10-05-87    2:24p
LEDGER        <DIR>        10-05-87    2:24p
        3 File(s)    1209344 bytes free
```

Note that you can perform multiple disk drive assignments on one command line.

ATTRIB

Function Display or modify the attribute byte of a file.

Mode Real/Protected

Format

[*drive:*][*path*]ATTRIB [+*A*¦ −*A*] [+*R*¦ −*R*] *file_specification* [/*S*]

where the following is true:

drive: specifies the disk drive containing the file ATTRIB.EXE. If you do not specify a disk drive identifier, OS/2 uses the current default.

path is the OS/2 path name of the subdirectory that contains the file ATTRIB.EXE. If you do not specify an OS/2 path name, OS/2 uses the current default.

+*A* directs ATTRIB to set the archive bit of a file.

−*A* directs ATTRIB to clear the archive bit of a file.

+*R* directs ATTRIB to set the read-only bit of a file.

−*R* directs ATTRIB to clear the read-only bit of a file.

file_specification is the complete OS/2 file specification including a disk drive and path name of the file(s) to modify. ATTRIB supports OS/2 wild-card characters.

/*S* directs ATTRIB to process all of the files below the given file specification.

Syntax Chart

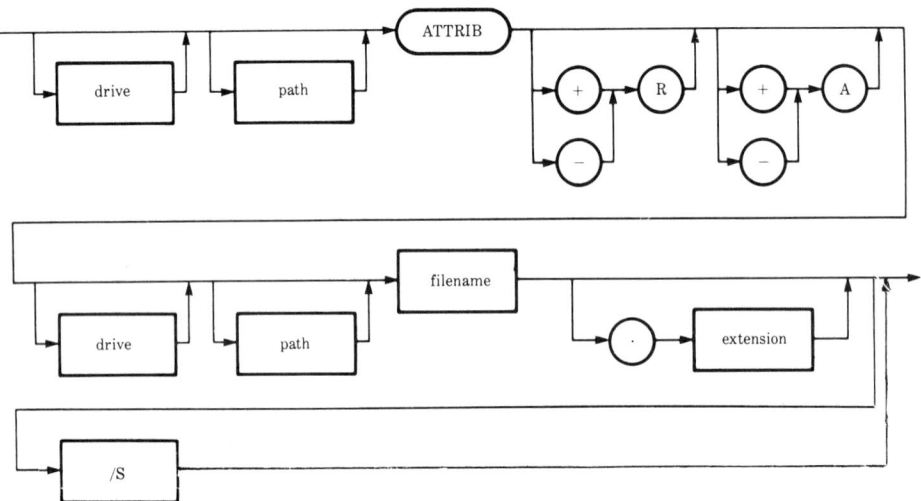

Notes   Each OS/2 file has a directory entry that contains the fields shown in Table B-2.

The OS/2 ATTRIB command modifies the attribute byte of a file.

Several OS/2 commands (such as BACKUP, RESTORE, and XCOPY) use a file's attribute to enable selective file processing. By using these commands in conjunction with ATTRIB, you can

Field	Offset
File name	0
Extension	8
Attribute byte	11
Reserved for DOS	12
Time	22
Date	24
Starting cluster number	26
File size	28

Table B-2.   *Fields for Directory Entries*

gain considerable file-processing control.

Examples If you do not specify the A or R qualifier,

```
[C:\] ATTRIB *.*
```

ATTRIB displays the current attributes of each file, as shown here:

```
A           C:\OS2\ANSI.EXE
A           C:\OS2\ATTRIB.EXE
A           C:\OS2\FDISK.EXE
A           C:\OS2\GWBASIC.EXE
A           C:\OS2\HELPMSG.EXE
A           C:\OS2\JOIN.EXE
A           C:\OS2\KEYB.EXE
A           C:\OS2\PATCH.EXE
A           C:\OS2\REPLACE.EXE
A           C:\OS2\SORT.EXE
A           C:\OS2\SPOOL.EXE
A           C:\OS2\SUBST.EXE
A           C:\OS2\XCOPY.EXE
```

In the following case, ATTRIB sets the file CONFIG.SYS to read-only:

```
[C:\] ATTRIB +r CONFIG.SYS
```

In so doing, OS/2 cannot modify the contents of the file. For example, if you attempt to delete a read-only file, OS/2 displays the following:

```
DOS0005: The system cannot access the file specified.
[C:\]
```

The OS/2 BACKUP /M qualifier directs BACKUP to only back up those files modified since the previous backup. By issuing the command

```
[C:\] ATTRIB +A \*.* /S
```

you can set the archive bit of every file on disk as requiring a backup. Likewise, the following command marks each file as being backed up:

```
[C:\] ATTRIB -A \*.* /S
```

Many people use ATTRIB in conjunction with XCOPY to copy the entire contents of their fixed disk to floppy disks and to maintain the original disk structure. To do so, first mark all of the files on disk as requiring a backup, as shown here:

```
[C:\] ATTRIB +A \*.* /S
```

Next, simply invoke XCOPY, as shown here:

```
[C:\] XCOPY C:\*.* A: /S /M
```

When the floppy disk fills, XCOPY displays a message and terminates. Simply insert a new floppy disk in the drive and again repeat this process. The XCOPY command picks up with the first file marked as archived and resumes the process at the correct location. Simply repeat this process until XCOPY finds no files to copy.

BACKUP

Function Back up one or more files to a new disk.

Mode Real/Protected

Format

[*drive:*][*path*]BACKUP *source:*[*file_spec*] *target:* [/*A*][/*D:mm-dd-yy*] [*L:logfile*][/*M*][/*S*][*T:hh:mm:ss*][/*F*]

where the following is true:

drive: specifies the disk drive containing the file BACKUP.COM. If you do not specify a disk drive identifier, OS/2 uses the current default.

path is the OS/2 path name of the subdirectory that contains the file BACKUP.COM. If you do not specify an OS/2 path name, OS/2 uses the current default.

source: specifies the source disk that contains the file(s) to be backed up.

file_spec is the OS/2 path name(s) for the file(s) to back up.

target: specifies the target disk.

/*A* directs BACKUP to append source files to files on the target disk. This switch is not valid for back-up disks created with DOS version 3.2.

/*D:mm-dd-yy* directs BACKUP to back up files modified since the specified date.

/*L:logfile* places an entry for all of the files in the specified log file (BACKUP.LOG is the default).

/*M* directs BACKUP to back up files modified since the last backup.

/*S* directs BACKUP to back up all subdirectory files.

/*T:hh:mm:ss* backs up files modified since specified time.

/*F* tells BACKUP that the target disk is unformatted.

Syntax Chart

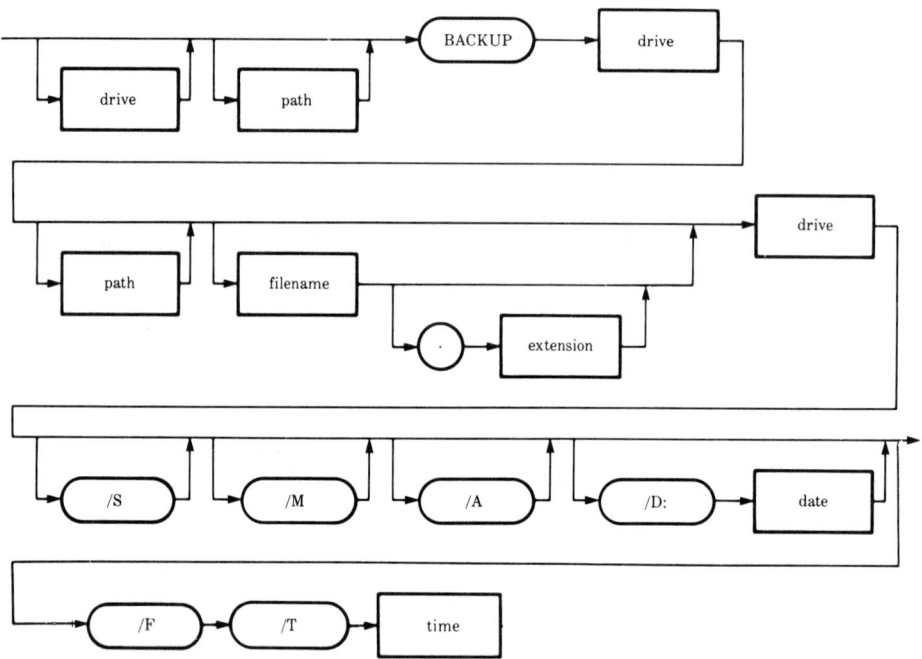

Notes BACKUP works closely with each of the system's directory entries to select specific files for backup. Note how OS/2

Field	Offset
File name	0
Extension	8
Attribute byte	11
Reserved for DOS	12
Time	22
Date	24
Starting cluster number	26
File size	28

Table B-3. *BACKUP Command-Line Qualifiers*

directory fields closely relate to the BACKUP command-line qualifiers, as shown in Table B-3.

A 10MB disk requires approximately 26 360K floppy disks or 9 1.2MB disks for a complete backup. To determine the exact number of disks required to perform a backup, first use the OS/2 CHKDSK command, as shown here:

```
[C:\] CHKDSK

Volume OS2DISK created Oct 30, 1987   9:46pm

 21309440 bytes total disk space.
        0 bytes in 1 hidden files.
   206848 bytes in 90 directories.
 13946880 bytes in 1694 user files.
    20480 bytes in bad sectors.
  7084032 bytes available on disk.

[C:\]
```

The number of disks required is computed by

Disks required = (Total space − Available space)/Floppy disk size

In this case, the equation becomes

Disks required = (21309440 − 7084032)/1213952
$$= 11.718$$
$$= 12 \text{ (1.2MB) floppy disks}$$

Examples   The following command backs up all of the files in drive C (including those in OS/2 subdirectories) to the floppy disk in drive A:

```
[C:\] BACKUP C:\*.* A: /S
```

The following command uses the BACKUP/A qualifier to add the file C:TEST.DAT to the files contained on the back-up disk in drive B:

```
[C:\] BACKUP C:TEST.DAT B: /A
```

The following command directs BACKUP to only back up the files created since 31 December 1987.

```
[C:\] BACKUP C:\*.* A: /S /D:12:31:87
```

BREAK

Function   Enable or disable OS/2 extended CTRL-BREAK checking in real mode.

Mode   Real

Format

BREAK [*ON¦ OFF*]

where the following is true:

ON enables extended real-mode CTRL-BREAK checking.
OFF disables extended real-mode CTRL-BREAK checking.

Syntax Chart

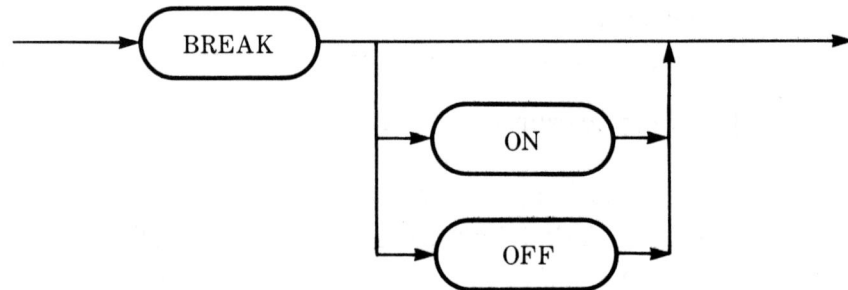

Notes By default, OS/2 real mode checks for a user-entered CTRL-BREAK after completion of keyboard, screen, and printer I/O operations. If you enable extended CTRL-BREAK checking, OS/2 also checks for a user-entered CTRL-BREAK upon completion of each system service (such as disk read or write operations).

If you invoke BREAK without a command-line parameter, BREAK displays the current state of processing (either ON or OFF).

By enabling extended CTRL-BREAK processing, you increase the system overhead since OS/2 must check for a CTRL-BREAK upon completion of each system service. As such, programmers may want to enable this checking during program development. However, most users will leave BREAK=OFF.

Examples This command enables OS/2 real-mode extended CTRL-BREAK checking:

```
C> BREAK ON
```

If you invoke BREAK without a command-line parameter, BREAK displays its current state of extended CTRL-BREAK checking (either ON or OFF).

```
C> BREAK
BREAK is on

C>
```

CALL

Function Invoke a nested batch procedure from within an OS/2 batch file.

Mode Real/Protected

Format

CALL [*drive:*][*path*]BatchFile [*argument* [...]]

where the following is true:

drive: specifies the disk drive containing the batch file to be executed. If you omit the drive specifier, CALL uses the current disk drive.

path specifies the OS/2 subdirectory name of the directory containing the batch file to execute. If you do not specify a path name, CALL uses the current directory.

argument is the command-line parameter for the nested batch procedure.

... specifies that there can be several command-line parameters.

Syntax Chart

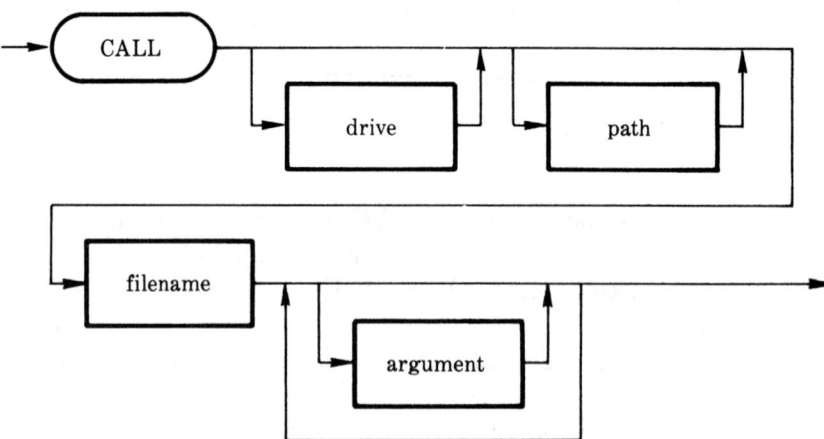

Notes OS/2 and DOS have difficulty invoking one batch file from within a second batch file when the invocation of the procedure appears in the middle of the batch file, as shown here:

```
CLS
BATFILE
DATE
```

If you must invoke a batch procedure in this manner, the OS/2 CALL command enables you to do so.

This command is similar in functionality to the DOS COMMAND /C within a batch file.

Examples   In the following case, BATFILE is either a BAT or CMD file, depending on the mode (real or protected). Since the nested batch file invocation appears in the middle of the first batch file, you must use the OS/2 CALL command, as shown here:

```
CLS
CALL BATFILE
DATE
```

CHCP

Function   Display or change the current code page.

Mode   Real/Protected

Format

CHCP [*code_page*]

where the following is true:

code_page specifies the desired code page. The *code_page* variable must have been previously prepared by the system as either the primary or secondary code page in the CONFIG.SYS file.

Syntax Chart

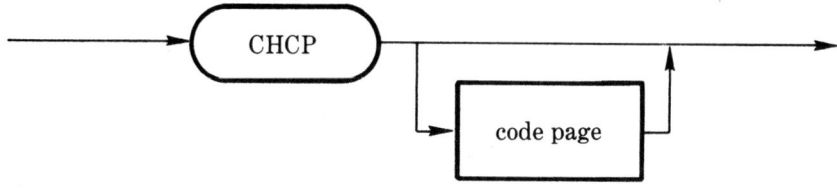

Notes Each time OS/2 displays a character on the screen, it must first map the ASCII value of a character to a specific letter of a character set. OS/2 uses code pages to map letters to specific characters. For example, consider the U.S. code page shown in Figure B-4.

If OS/2 is to display the letter "A" on the screen (A is represented by the ASCII hex value 41), it first starts at column 4 and moves down to row 1. This value contains the letter "A."

OS/2 allows you to establish a different character set for your OS/2 session. This, in turn, increases the international support provided by OS/2. In order to select an alternate code page, you

Code page 437 (United States)

Hex Digits 1st → 2nd ↓	0-	1-	2-	3-	4-	5-	6-	7-	8-	9-	A-	B-	C-	D-	E-	F-
-0		►		0	@	P	`	p	Ç	É	á	▓	└	╨	α	≡
-1	☺	◄	!	1	A	Q	a	q	ü	æ	í	▒	┴	╤	β	±
-2	●	↕	"	2	B	R	b	r	é	Æ	ó	▓	┬	╥	Γ	≥
-3	♥	‼	#	3	C	S	c	s	â	ô	ú	│	├	╙	π	≤
-4	♦	¶	$	4	D	T	d	t	ä	ö	ñ	┤	─	╘	Σ	⌠
-5	♣	§	%	5	E	U	e	u	à	ò	Ñ	╡	┼	╒	σ	⌡
-6	♠	▬	&	6	F	V	f	v	å	û	ª	╢	╞	╓	μ	÷
-7	•	↕	'	7	G	W	g	w	ç	ù	º	╖	╟	╫	τ	≈
-8	◘	↑	(	8	H	X	h	x	ê	ÿ	¿	╕	╚	╪	Φ	°
-9	○	↓	)	9	I	Y	i	y	ë	Ö	⌐	╣	╔	┘	Θ	•
-A	◙	→	*	:	J	Z	j	z	è	Ü	¬	║	╩	┌	Ω	•
-B	♂	←	+	;	K	[	k	{	ï	¢	½	╗	╦	█	δ	√
-C	♀	∟	,	<	L	\	l	|	î	£	¼	╝	╠	▄	∞	ⁿ
-D	♪	↔	-	=	M	]	m	}	ì	¥	¡	╜	═	▐	φ	²
-E	♫	▲	.	>	N	^	n	~	Ä	Pt	«	╛	╬	▌	ε	■
-F	☼	▼	/	?	O	_	o	△	Å	ƒ	»	┐	╧	▀	∩	

Reprinted, by permission, from *Disk Operating System Version 3.30 Reference* (International Business Machines Corporation, 1987), C-3.

Figure B-4. *Code page for United States*

must place a CODEPAGE= entry in the CONFIG.SYS file, as shown here:

```
CODEPAGE=437,865
```

Valid code page entries include the following:

437 United States
850 Multilingual
860 Portugal
863 French-Canadian
865 Nordic

If you invoke CHCP without a command-line parameter, CHCP displays the current code page.

Examples The following command directs CHCP to select the Nordic code page. Remember that this code page must have been previously prepared by the system with an entry in the CONFIG.SYS file.

```
[C:\] CHCP 865
```

The invocation of CHCP without a command-line parameter results in the display of the current code page, as shown here:

```
[C:\] CHCP
Active character set: 437
Prepared system character set(s):    437
```

CHDIR

Function   Change or display the default directory.

Mode   Real/Protected

Format

CHDIR [*drive:*][*path*]

or

CD [*drive:*][*path*]

where the following is true:

drive: specifies the disk drive for which you are setting the default subdirectory. If you omit the disk drive, CHDIR uses the current default.

path specifies the OS/2 path name that you want as the current directory. If you omit the path, CHDIR displays the current directory.

Syntax Chart

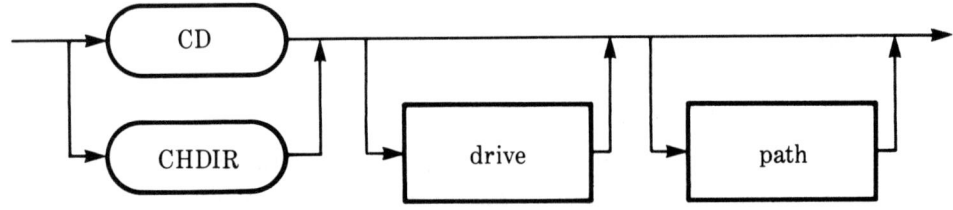

Notes   The CHDIR command changes or displays the current directory name for the specified disk drive. If you do not specify a drive, CHDIR uses the current default drive. If you do not specify a path name, CHDIR displays the current default directory name.

Each time you specify an OS/2 path name to CHDIR, CHDIR performs the following processing: If the path name is preceded with a backslash (such as \SUBDIR), OS/2 begins its search for the directory at the root. However, if the path name does not begin with a backslash (such as SUBDIR), the subdirectory must reside below the current default directory.

OS/2 predefines the following two directory names:

.. Parent directory of the current directory
. Current default directory

Verify this by performing a directory listing of an OS/2 subdirectory, as shown here:

```
Volume in drive C is OS2DISK
Directory of C:\SUBDIR

.               <DIR>       11-01-87   11:34a
..              <DIR>       11-01-87   11:34a

     2 File(s)     7182336 bytes free
```

If you simply issue the following directory command,

```
[C:\] DIR .

Volume in drive C is OS2DISK
Directory of C:\SUBDIR

.               <DIR>       11-01-87   11:34a
..              <DIR>       11-01-87   11:34a

     2 File(s)      7182336 bytes free

[C:\]
```

OS/2 displays a directory listing of the current directory. However, if you instead use

```
[C:\] DIR ..
```

OS/2 displays the files in the parent directory.

Examples   If you simply invoke CHDIR without a path name,
CHDIR displays the current directory, as shown here:

```
[C:\] CD
C:\SUBDIR

[C:\]
```

This command is valid with a disk drive specifier, as shown
here:

```
[C:\] CHDIR B:
B:\UTIL

[C:\]
```

In a similar manner, the following OS/2 CHDIR command selects
the subdirectory \OS2\CMDFILES in drive B as the current
default directory:

```
[C:\] CHDIR B:\OS2\CMDFILES
```

The user could actually issue this command as two separate commands, first selecting the subdirectory \OS2

```
[C:\]  CD B:\OS2
```

and then selecting CMDFILES

```
[C:\]  CD B:CMDFILES
```

Note the use of the leading backslash in the following command:

```
[C:\]  CD B:\OS2
```

By using the backslash, OS/2 looks for the subdirectory OS2 in the root directory of drive B. However, in the second command

```
[C:\]  CD B:CMDFILES
```

you do not want CHDIR to look for the directory in the root, but rather as a subdirectory below the current directory (which is \OS2). If you had instead issued the command

```
[C:\]  CHDIR B:\CMDFILES
```

CHDIR would not have found the directory (since it would have looked in the root directory as opposed to the current directory).

CHKDSK

Function   Check the current status of a disk.

Mode   Real/Protected

Format

CHKDSK [*drive:*][*path*][*filename*] [/F] [/V]

where the following is true:

drive: is the disk drive that CHKDSK is to examine.
path specifies an OS/2 subdirectory containing files that CHKDSK is to examine for disk fragmentation.
filename is the file name and extension of file(s) that CHKDSK is to examine for disk fragmentation.
/F directs CHKDSK to fix errors found in a directory or FAT.
/V directs CHKDSK to display the names of all files on the disk.

Syntax Chart

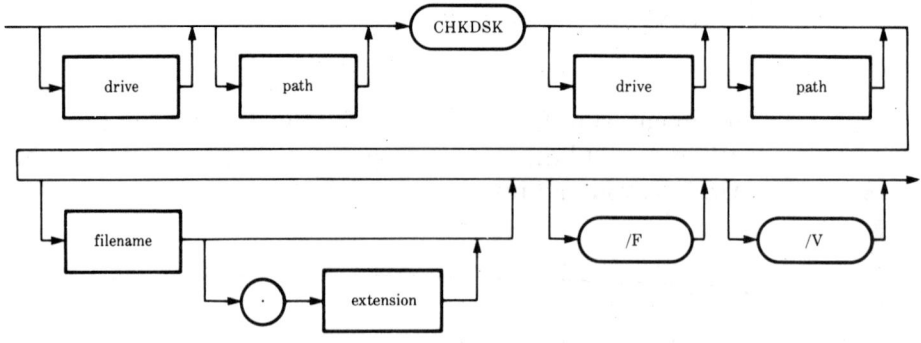

Notes CHKDSK reports on the following:

- The amount of free, used, and corrupted disk space
- The number of hidden files
- The amount of free and used memory (only in real mode)

Periodically, files become corrupted (losing sectors) in normal day-to-day operations because disk usage causes wear and tear on the storage media. The OS/2 CHKDSK enables you to view and optionally repair such discrepancies.

Also, it is possible for OS/2 files to become fragmented. A fragmented file is a file whose contents are dispersed around the entire contents of the disk. The problem with fragmented files is that they increase system overhead on file I/O operations because the disk drive must rotate the disk several additional times in order to read the disk. The OS/2 CHKDSK command displays information on fragmented files. Once your disk becomes severely fragmented, you should consider a system backup-and-restore operation as described in Chapter 13.

CHKDSK does not work with disks that have been used with the JOIN or SUBST commands.

If you have several OS/2 sessions active, do not try to repair your disk. When OS/2 has files open (as would the OS/2 spooler, for example), it cannot correctly update the file-allocation table (FAT).

By default, CHKDSK only reports disk errors, but will not attempt to fix them. In order to write the actual corrections to disk, use the /F qualifier.

Examples The following command displays the state of the current disk:

```
[C:\] CHKDSK
```

In real mode the output might be as follows:

```
Volume OS2DISK created Oct 30, 1987   9:46pm

 21309440 bytes total disk space.
        0 bytes in 1 hidden files.
   208896 bytes in 91 directories.
 13871104 bytes in 1714 user files.
    20480 bytes in bad sectors.
  7206912 bytes available on disk.

[DOS mode storage report]
   524288 bytes total storage
   401184 bytes free

C>
```

In protected mode, OS/2 suppresses the display of memory utilization, as shown here:

```
  Volume OS2DISK created Oct 30, 1987   9:46pm

 21309440 bytes total disk space.
        0 bytes in 1 hidden files.
   208896 bytes in 91 directories.
 13873152 bytes in 1715 user files.
    20480 bytes in bad sectors.
  7204864 bytes available on disk.

[C:\]
```

If you use a file specification (or OS/2 wildcard characters), CHKDSK reports on disk fragmentation, as shown here:

```
 [C:\] CHKDSK *.*
```

In the following case, if fragmented files exist, CHKDSK displays

```
C:\FILENAME.EXT
contains n non-contiguous blocks.
```

If CHKDSK discovers errors while examining your disk contents, it displays the following:

```
Volume OS2DISK created Oct 30, 1987  9:46pm

Errors found.  F parameter not specified.
Corrections will not be written to disk.

1 lost clusters found in 1 chains.
Convert lost chains to files (Y/N)?
DOS1359: 2048 bytes disk space would be freed.
```

To direct CHKDSK to repair the errors, use the /F qualifier, as shown here:

```
[C:\] CHKDSK /F
```

Many people use CHKDSK to quickly locate a file. If you invoke CHKDSK with the /V qualifier, CHKDSK displays the name of every file on the disk.

```
[C:\] CHKDSK /V
```

CLS

Function   Clear the screen display.

Mode   Real/Protected

Format

CLS

Syntax Chart

```
─────────────────────────────( CLS )─────────────────────────────▶
```

Notes   The CLS command does not affect video attributes. The CLS command places the cursor and OS/2 prompt in the home (upper-left) position.

Example   In the following case, OS/2 erases the current screen contents and places the cursor and the current OS/2 prompt in the home position.

```
[C:\] CLS
```

CMD

Function   Invoke a secondary protected-mode command-line processor.

Mode   Protected

Format

CMD [*drive:*][*path*] [*/C string*] [*/K string*]

where the following is true:

drive: specifies the drive containing the secondary command processor. If you do not specify a disk drive, OS/2 uses the current default.

path specifies the OS/2 subdirectory that contains the secondary command processor. If you do not specify a path name, OS/2 uses the current default.

/C string directs OS/2 to load the secondary command processor into memory only long enough to execute the command specified by *string*. Once the command completes, OS/2 removes the secondary command processor.

/K string directs OS/2 to load the secondary command processor permanently into memory. Once the command specified by *string* completes, OS/2 leaves the secondary command processor in memory.

Syntax Chart

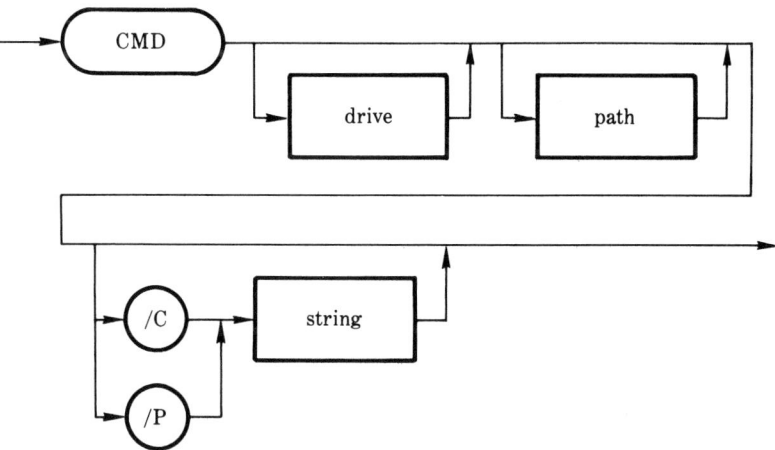

Notes Each time you invoke a secondary command processor, the secondary command processor gets its own copy of the environment.

Refer to the OS/2 PROTSHELL entry in the CONFIG.SYS file (see Chapter 4) for more specifics on the protected-mode command processor.

To terminate a secondary command processor, use the OS/2 EXIT command.

Examples The following command directs OS/2 to load a command processor into memory and to display the secondary command processor's prompt:

```
[C:\] CMD
```

The following command directs OS/2 to load the secondary command processor into memory long enough to execute the DIR command:

```
[C:\] CMD /C DIR > DIR.LST
```

Upon completion of the command, the secondary command processor terminates.

The following entry in the CONFIG.SYS file directs OS/2 to use CMD.EXE as its protected-mode shell:

```
PROTSHELL=SHELL.EXE CMD.EXE /K INITENV.CMD
```

Each time OS/2 creates a protected-mode session, it loads the secondary command processor permanently into memory and executes the batch file INITENV.CMD.

COMMAND

Function　Load a secondary real-mode command processor.

Mode　Real

Format

COMMAND [*drive:*][*path*] [*/C string*][*/E:num_bytes*][*/P*]

where the following is true:

drive: specifies the disk drive identifier of the disk containing the secondary command processor. If you do not specify a disk drive, OS/2 uses the current default.

path is the OS/2 subdirectory that contains the command processor. If you do not specify a path name, OS/2 uses the current default.

/C string directs OS/2 to execute the command specified by *string*. Most people use this parameter for nested batch file invocations.

/E:num_bytes specifies the size OS/2 is to allocate for the secondary command processor environment space. *num_bytes* must be between 160 and 32,767. The default is 160 bytes.

/P directs OS/2 to leave the secondary command processor permanently in memory.

Syntax Chart

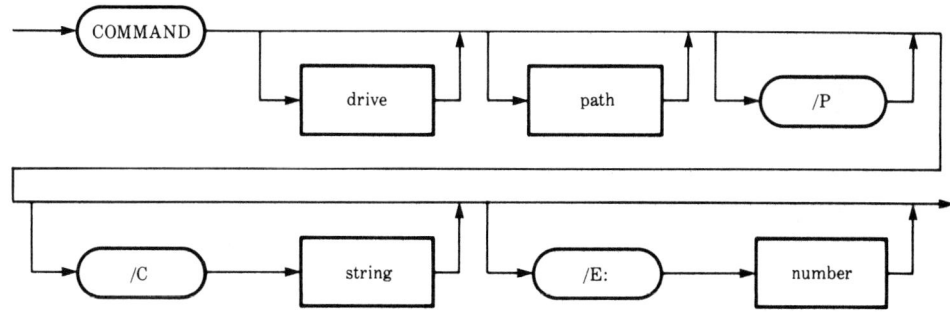

Notes Each time you load a secondary command processor, the secondary command processor obtains its own copy of the OS/2 environment space.

Most people use COMMAND to invoke nested batch procedures, as shown here:

```
CLS
COMMAND /C BATFILE
DATE
```

To terminate a secondary command processor, use the OS/2 EXIT command.

Examples In the following case, OS/2 loads the secondary command processor into memory only long enough to execute the CHKDSK command:

```
[C:\] COMMAND /C CHKDSK
```

Once the command terminates, OS/2 removes the secondary command processor.

COMP

Function Display the first 10 differences between two files.

Mode Real/Protected

Format

[*drive:*][*path*]COMP *file__spec file__spec2*

where the following is true:

drive: specifies the disk drive identifier of the disk containing the file COMP.COM. If you do not specify a disk identifier, OS/2 uses the current default.

path specifies the OS/2 subdirectory name of the subdirectory that contains the file COMP.COM. If you do not specify a subdirectory name, OS/2 uses the current default.

file__spec and *file__spec2* are the complete OS/2 path names of the files to compare. The COMP command supports OS/2 wildcard characters.

Syntax Chart

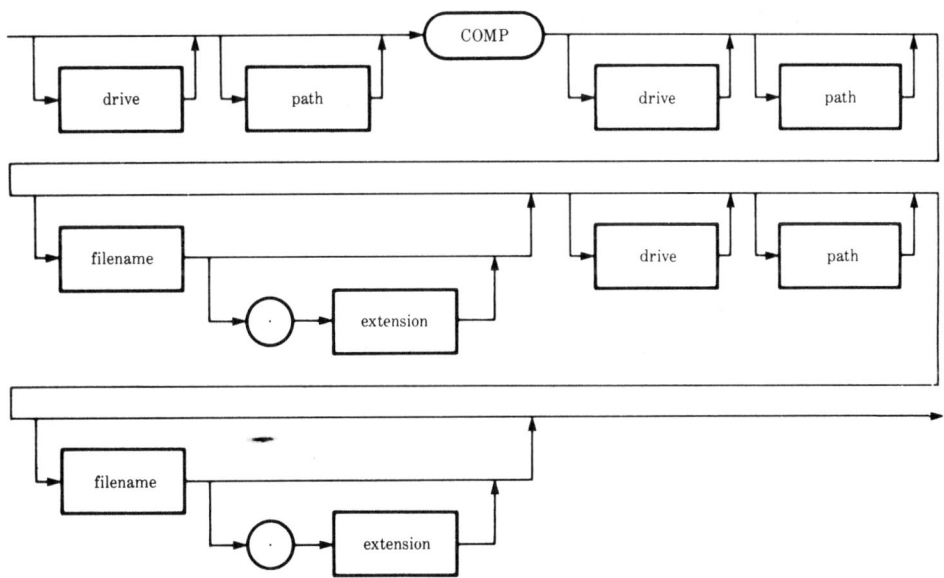

Notes The COMP command displays the differences as hexadecimal offsets into the file.

If the files are identical, COMP displays the following message:

```
The files compare OK.
```

Upon completion of the file comparison, COMP displays the following:

```
Do you want to compare more files (Y/N)?
```

To compare additional files type Y. Otherwise, type N.

Examples In the following case, COMP compares the contents of the file A.DAT to B.DAT:

```
[C:\] COMP A.DAT B.DAT
```

Assuming that each file contains

```
[C:\] TYPE A.DAT
A
AA

[C:\] TYPE B.DAT
B
BB

[C:\]
```

the command displays the following:

```
Compare file C:A.DAT and file C:B.DAT

A COMPARE error occurred at OFFSET 0
Mismatching byte of file 1 = 41

Mismatching byte of file 2 = 42

A COMPARE error occurred at OFFSET 3
Mismatching byte of file 1 = 41

Mismatching byte of file 2 = 42

A COMPARE error occurred at OFFSET 4
Mismatching byte of file 1 = 41

Mismatching byte of file 2 = 42

Do you want to compare more files (Y/N)?
```

If you omit the file name from the secondary file, OS/2 matches the file name on the specified drive with the primary file, as shown here:

```
[C:\] COMP A.DAT B:
```

If you do not specify the files in the COMP command line, COMP prompts you for them, as shown here:

```
[C:\] COMP
Enter the first filename.
A.DAT

Enter the second filename.
B.DAT
```

COPY

Function   Copy one or more files to a new destination.

Mode   Real/Protected

Format

COPY *source_file target_file* [/V][/A][/B]

or

COPY *source1*+source2 [...] *target_file* [/V][/A][/B]

where the following is true:

source_file specifies the complete OS/2 file specification of the file to be copied.

target_file is the name of the destination file. If a file matching the name of *target_file* exists, COPY overwrites it.

/V requests COPY to use disk verification to ensure a successful copy has occurred. This qualifier adds processing overhead. However, it prevents a hardware error from rendering the contents of the source and target files inconsistent.

/A informs COPY that the preceding file was an ASCII file.

/B informs COPY that the preceding file was a binary file.

Syntax Chart

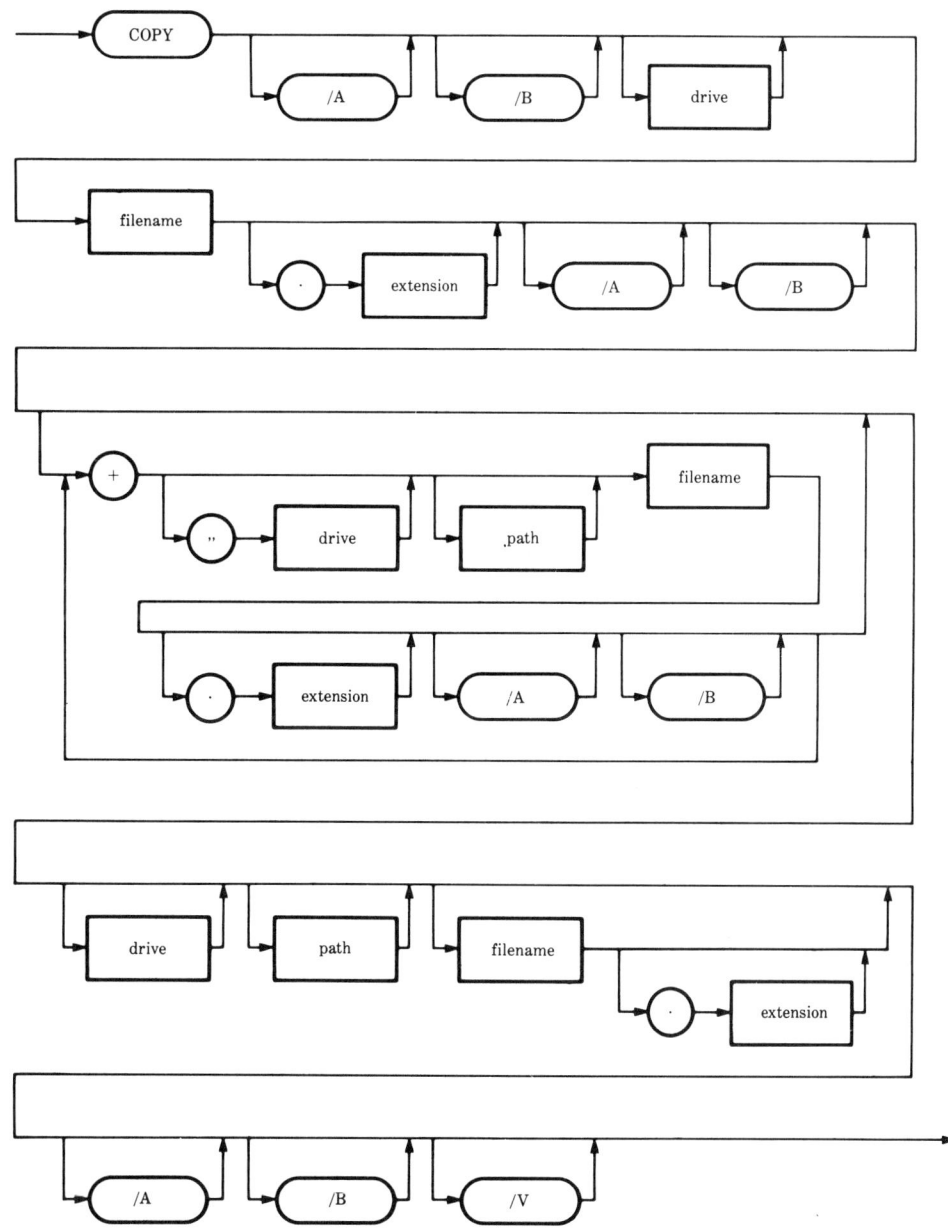

Notes COPY fully supports OS/2 wildcard characters.

Warning: COPY overwrites target files with the same name.

To combine multiple files into one file, use the plus sign (+) between the desired source files.

COPY will not allow you to copy a file to itself. If you attempt to do so, COPY displays the following:

```
DOS1078: The file cannot be copied onto itself.
        0 file(s) copied.

[C:\]
```

Examples The following command copies the contents of the file CONFIG.SYS to a file in drive B with the same name:

```
[C:\] COPY A:CONFIG.SYS B:CONFIG.SYS
```

The following command copies all of the files in drive A to drive B. If you want to copy files contained in subdirectories below the current directory, use the XCOPY command.

```
[C:\] COPY A:*.* B:*.*
```

The following command uses the plus sign to append the files B and C to the file A and create a file called D:

```
[C:\] COPY A+B+C D
```

The following command allows you to append text from the keyboard to an existing file, thus creating a new file:

```
[C:\] COPY FILENAME+KBD$ NEWFILE.EXT
```

DATE

Function   Set the OS/2 system date.

Mode   Real/Protected

Format

DATE [*mm-dd-yy*]

or

DATE [*dd-mm-yy*]

or

DATE [*yy-mm-dd*]

where the following is true:

mm is the desired month (1-12).
dd is the desired day (1-31).
yy is the desired year (80-99). OS/2 also allows you to include the century in the form 19yy or 20yy.

Syntax Chart

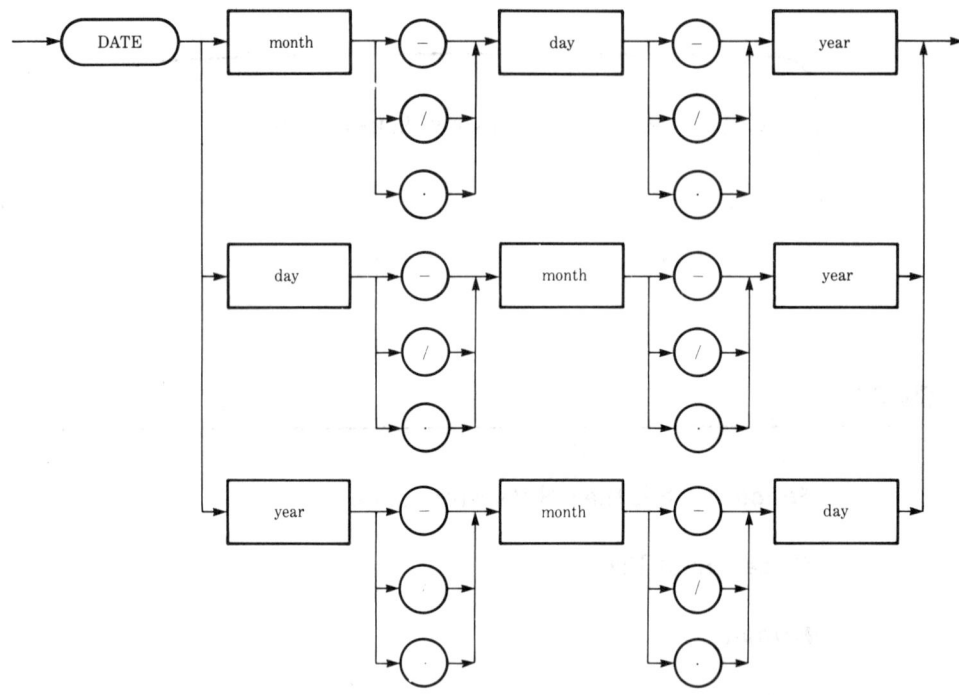

Notes The date format mm-dd-yy is dependent upon the COUNTRY= specifier in the CONFIG.SYS file. If you do not specify a date, DATE displays the current date.

DATE does modify the PC AT system clock. In the past, you had to use the SETUP disk provided with the guide to operations in order to change the AT system clock. The OS/2 TIME and DATE commands actually set this clock.

The actual date is an optional command-line parameter. If you omit the date, DATE prompts you for it.

Examples In the following case, since the date was not present on the OS/2 command line, DATE prompted the user for it:

```
[C:\] DATE

The current date is: Sun 11-01-1987
Enter the new date: (mm-dd-yy)
```

If you simply want to display the system date without modifying it, press the ENTER key at the date prompt, and DATE leaves the system date unchanged.

If you enter the following

```
[C:\] DATE 12/08/87
```

DATE sets the system date to 8 December 1987. This command is identical to

```
[C:\] DATE 12/08/1987
```

As you can see, DATE fully supports a four-digit year.

The following command illustrates a date setting from the DATE prompt:

```
[C:\] DATE

The current date is: Sun 11-01-1987
Enter the new date: (mm-dd-yy) 12-08-87
```

DEL

Function   Delete a file from disk.

Mode   Real/Protected

Format

DEL [*drive:*][*path*]*filename*[.*ext*] [. . .]

where the following is true:

drive: specifies the disk drive containing the file to delete. If you omit the drive qualifier, DEL uses the current default drive.

path specifies the name of the OS/2 subdirectory that contains the file to be deleted. If you omit the path entry, DEL uses the current directory.

filename[.*ext*] is the name of the file to delete. DEL fully supports OS/2 wildcard characters.

. . . OS/2 protected mode allows you to place on the same command line several files to be deleted.

Syntax Chart

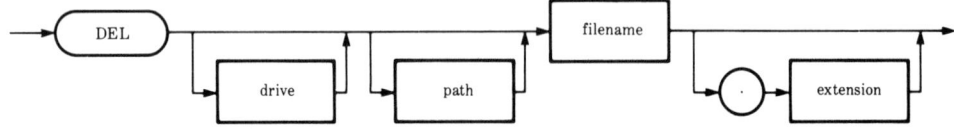

Notes   DEL will not remove subdirectories. Instead, use RMDIR.

Warning: Once you have deleted a file, OS/2 cannot retrieve it.

Unless overridden with a drive or path specifier, DEL only deletes files in the current directory.

OS/2 protected mode allows you to delete several specific files at one time by placing each file name on the command line.

If you attempt to delete all of the files in a directory, OS/2 first prompts you with the following message to ensure that you actually want the command performed:

```
Are you sure (Y/N)?
```

If you want to delete the files type Y and press ENTER. Otherwise, simply type N and press ENTER.

Examples In the following case, DEL erases the contents of the file CONFIG.OLD from drive B:

```
[C:\] DEL B:CONFIG.OLD
```

In a similar manner, the following command deletes a file from within an OS/2 subdirectory:

```
[C:\] DEL \OS2\COMMANDS\STARTUP.BAK
```

If you attempt to delete all of the files in the current directory,

```
[C:\] DEL *.*
```

DEL responds with the following:

```
Are you sure (Y/N)?
```

If you want to delete the files type Y and press ENTER. Otherwise, simply type N and press ENTER.

In OS/2 protected mode, DEL allows you to place several files on the command line, as shown here:

```
[C:\] DEL A.TXT B.TXT C.TXT
```

If one of the files does not exist, DEL terminates the command.

DETACH

Function   Execute an OS/2 command in the background mode. OS/2 creates a process and displays its process identification number (pid), which executes the specified command. OS/2 returns control to the process by invoking DETACH and allows it to continue its processing while the command invoked with DETACH completes in the background mode.

Mode   Protected

Format

DETACH *OS2_command* [*argument* [...]]

where the following is true:

OS2_command is the OS/2 command DETACH is to execute as a detached process.
argument is a command-line argument for the command.
... states that several arguments can appear in the command line.

Syntax Chart

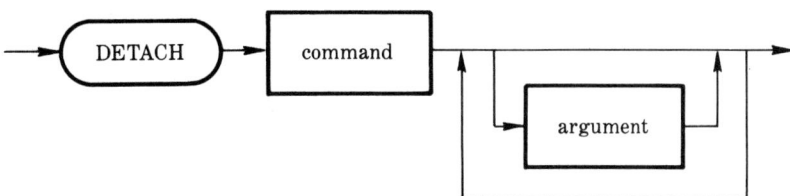

Notes In most cases, you invoke commands to execute in the foreground, which ties up an OS/2 session until the commands complete. The OS/2 DETACH command enables you to start a job in the background and to return the OS/2 system prompt to your protected-mode session. As you continue to enter commands at the OS/2 prompt (foreground), OS/2 executes the background task concurrently.

Most detached commands cannot perform I/O operations to the screen or from the keyboard. As such, if a detached command normally displays output, you must redirect the output by using OS/2 I/O redirection.

For DOS users, visualize OS/2 background tasks in the same fashion as the DOS PRINT command, which allows you to execute commands from the DOS prompt while it prints files in the background.

The OS/2 CONFIG.SYS entry RUN also allows you to create background processes.

OS/2 detached processes must complete on their own. OS/2 does not provide facilities to cancel them.

Examples In the following case, OS/2 performs the CHKDSK command as a background process and redirects the output of the command to the file DISK.STS:

```
[C:\] DETACH CHKDSK > DISK.STS
The Process Identification Number is 7.

[C:\]
```

In a similar manner, OS/2 will write the directory listing of drive B to the file B.LIS as a background process.

```
[C:\] DETACH DIR B: > B.LIS
The Process Identification Number is 9.

[C:\]
```

DIR

Function   Display a directory listing of files.

Mode   Real/Protected

Format

DIR [*file_specification*] [/P] [/W]

where the following is true:

file_specification is the complete OS/2 file specification for the file(s) of which DIR is to display the directory listing. It can contain a disk drive identifier and path name. If you do not place a file specification in the command line, DIR displays a directory listing of all of the files in the current directory. DIR fully supports OS/2 wildcard characters.

/P directs DIR to pause after each screenful of information to display the following prompt:

```
Press any key when ready.
```

/W directs DIR to display the files in short form (filename) only with five file names across the screen.

Syntax Chart

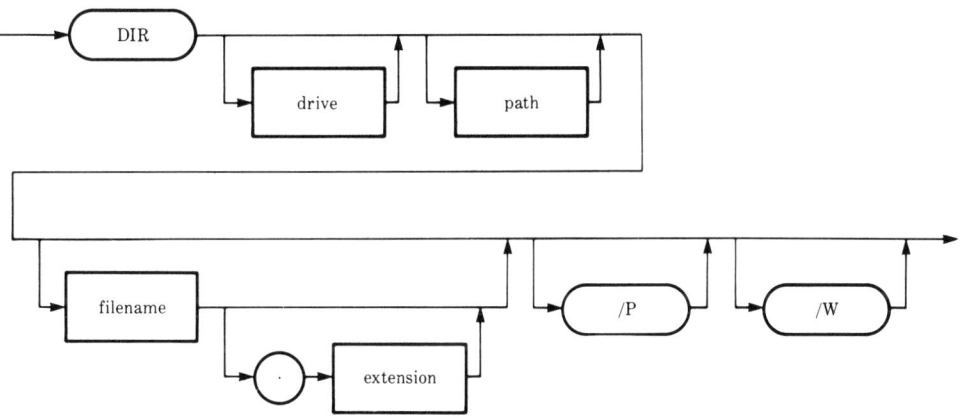

Notes For each file, DIR displays the complete name, size in bytes, and the date and time of creation (or last modification).

The DIR command also displays the amount of free disk space in bytes.

Use the TREE command to list all of the files on disk, including files in OS/2 subdirectories.

The DIR command always displays the drive and directory in which the files are stored, as shown here:

```
Volume in drive A is OS2DISK
Directory of  A:\

SUBDIR        <DIR>      11-01-87  12:53p
         1 File(s)    1213440 bytes free
```

Examples In the following case, OS/2 displays a directory listing of each of the files in drive B:

```
[C:\] DIR B:
```

This command is functionally equivalent to the following:

```
[C:\] DIR B:*.*
```

If several files exist on drive B, many may scroll off of the screen during the directory listing. If this happens, invoke DIR with the /P qualifier, as shown here:

```
[C:\] DIR B:*.* /P
```

Each time DIR completes a screenful of files, it pauses to display the following prompt:

```
Press any key when ready.
```

When this occurs, simply press any key and DIR will continue.

The file specification of the DIR command can be quite specific, as shown here:

```
[C:\] DIR \OS2\CONFIG.OLD
```

In this case, DIR displays the directory listing of the file CONFIG.OLD that resides in the subdirectory \OS2 of the current disk.

If you are not interested in file sizes or date and time stamps, simply invoke DIR with the /W option, as follows:

```
[C:\] DIR /W
```

In this case, DIR displays a directory listing of file names only, five files across the screen, as shown here:

```
Volume in drive C is OS2DISK
Directory of  C:\OS2

.                  ..              ANSI    EXE   APPEND   COM   ASSIGN    COM
ATTRIB   EXE   BACKUP    COM   CHKDSK  COM   COMP     COM   DISKCOMP  COM
DISKCOPY COM   EDLIN     COM   FDISK   EXE   FIND     COM   FORMAT    COM
FORMATS  TBL   GRAFTABL  COM   GWBASIC EXE   HELPMSG  EXE   JOIN      EXE
KEYB     EXE   LABEL     COM   MODE    COM   MORE     COM   PATCH     EXE
PRINT    COM   README          REPLACE EXE   RESTORE  COM   SORT      EXE
SPOOL    EXE   SUBST     EXE   SYS     COM   TREE     COM   XCOPY     EXE
         35 File(s)    7106560 bytes free
```

Many people also use the OS/2 redirection operators with DIR. In this example, OS/2 displays a sorted directory listing:

```
[C:\] DIR | SORT
```

DISKCOMP

Function   Compare two floppy disks.

Mode   Real/Protected

Format

*[drive:][path]*DISKCOMP *[primary_drive: [secondary_drive]]*

where the following is true:

drive: specifies the disk drive that contains the file DISKCOMP.COM. If you omit the drive specifier, OS/2 uses the current default.

path specifies the OS/2 subdirectory name that contains the file DISK-COMP.COM. If you do not specify a path name, OS/2 uses the current default.

primary_drive: specifies one of the floppy-disk drives to be used in the disk comparison. If you do not specify a primary drive, DISKCOMP prompts you for one.

secondary_drive specifies the second drive to be used in the disk comparison. If you do not specify a secondary drive, DISKCOMP prompts you for one.

Syntax Chart

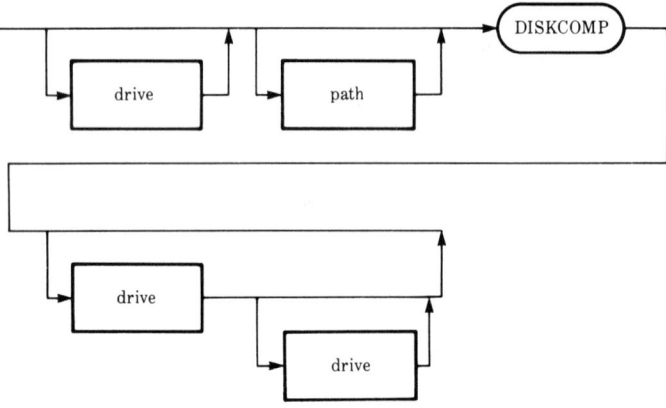

Notes If you have a single-floppy system, DISKCOMP performs a single-drive comparison and prompts you to enter the source and target disk at the correct time.

If the contents of the disk are identical, DISKCOMP displays the following message:

```
Compare OK.
```

Otherwise, DISKCOMP displays the side and track (in hexa-decimal) of the first ten differences.

Example If you do not specify a primary or secondary drive

```
[C:\] DISKCOMP
```

DISKCOMP prompts you for them, as shown here:

```
Enter drive letter for source. A:
Enter drive letter for target. B:
```

If the disks are identical, DISKCOMP displays the following:

```
Compare OK.
```

Otherwise, DISKCOMP displays the locations of the first ten differences, as shown here:

```
Comparison error on side n track n.
```

DISKCOPY

Function   Copy a source floppy disk to a target disk.

Mode   Real/Protected

Format

[*drive:*][*path*]DISKCOPY [*source_drive:* [*target_drive*]]

where the following is true:

drive: specifies the disk drive containing the file DISKCOPY.COM. If you do not specify a disk drive, OS/2 uses the current default.

path specifies the OS/2 subdirectory that contains the file DISKCOPY.COM. If you do not specify a path name, OS/2 uses the current default directory.

source_drive: specifies the disk drive containing the floppy disk to copy. If you do not specify a source drive, DISKCOPY prompts you for one.

target_drive specifies the disk drive containing the disk to be copied to. If you do not specify a target drive, DISKCOPY prompts you for one.

Syntax Chart

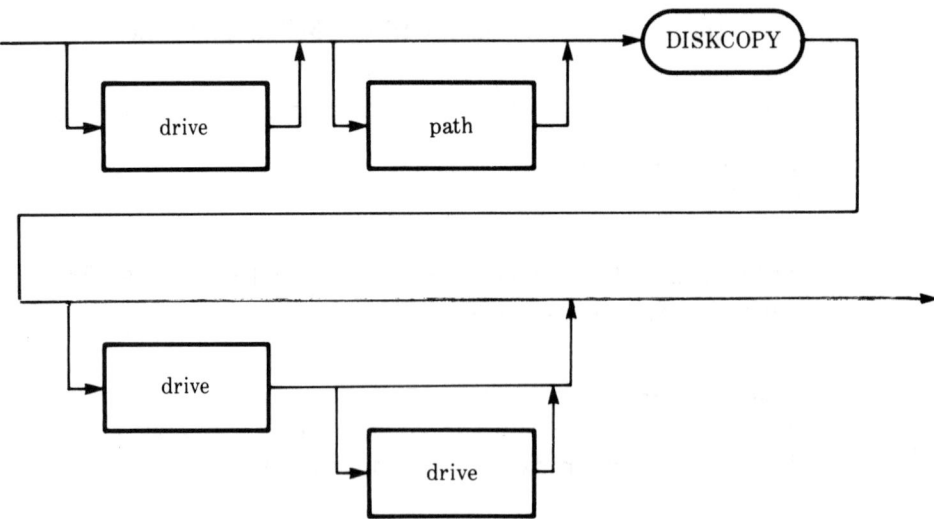

Notes The DISKCOPY command copies the contents of one floppy disk to another. If you have a single-floppy system, DISKCOPY performs a single-drive copy and prompts you to enter the source and target disks at the correct time.

The DISKCOPY command will FORMAT an unformatted disk during the copy. The DISKCOPY command does not correct disk fragmentation. The DISKCOPY command destroys the previous contents of the target disk.

If the source and target disks are not the same type (a 360K and 1.2MB disk, for example), DISKCOPY displays the message:

```
DOS1240: Drive types or diskette types are
incompatible.
Copy process ended.
Copy another diskette (Y/N)?
```

Do not use DISKCOPY with disks that have been used with the JOIN or SUBST command.

Examples The following command assumes that you have two compatible floppy-disk drives on your system:

```
[C:\] DISKCOPY A: B:
```

If you do not specify a source and target disk, DISKCOPY prompts you for one, as shown here:

```
Enter drive letter for source. A:
Enter drive letter for target.
```

Once DISKCOPY begins copying a disk, it reads several tracks of data from the source and then writes them to the target disk. In a single-floppy drive system, DISKCOPY repeats this process and prompts you for the source and target disks, as shown here:

```
Insert source diskette in drive A:

Press Enter to continue.
Copying 40 tracks, 9 sectors per track, 2 side(s).
Insert target diskette in drive A:

Press Enter to continue.
Copy process ended.
Copy another diskette (Y/N)?
```

DPATH

Function   Define the data-file search path that OS/2 uses each time it fails to locate a file in the current directory, or as specified.

Mode   Protected

Format

DPATH [*drive:*][*path*] [;[*drive:*][*path*]...]

where the following is true:

drive: specifies a disk drive that OS/2 is to include in the data search path.
path specifies an OS/2 subdirectory to include in the data search path.
... states that the disk drive and subdirectories may be specified several times.

Syntax Chart

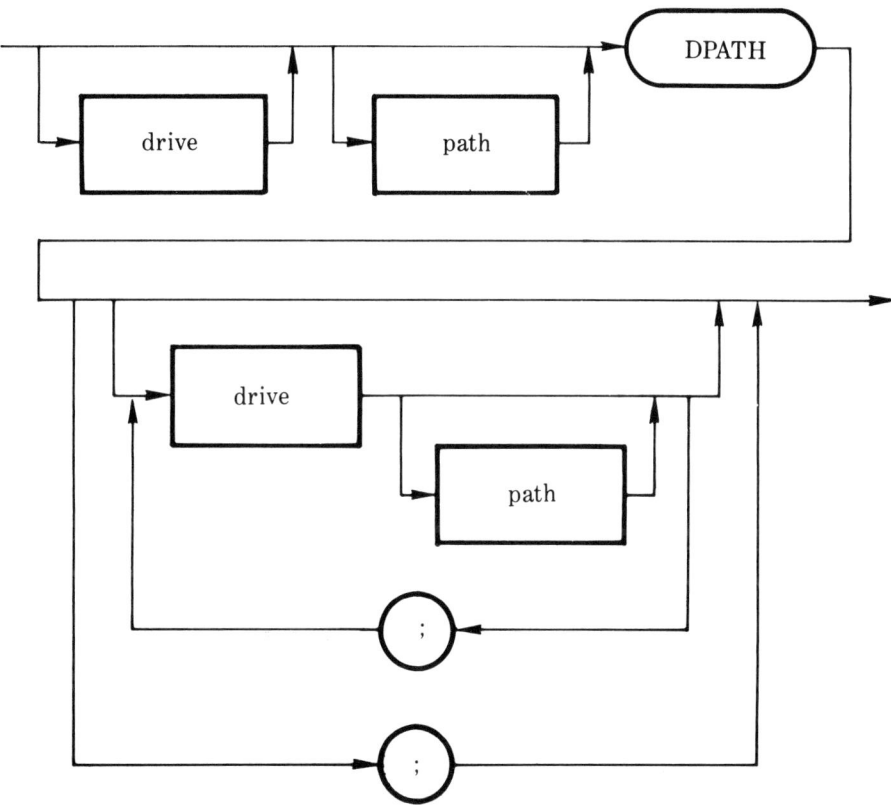

Notes   Each time OS/2 protected mode cannot find a data file as specified or in the current directory, it searches to see if the user has defined a data-file search path (see Figure B-5).

The OS/2 DPATH command enables you to define disk drives and subdirectories to be included in the protected-mode data-file search path. In a similar manner, the OS/2 APPEND command enables you to define a real-mode data-file search path.

Examples   In the following case, if OS/2 cannot find the data file in the current directory, OS/2 searches the root directories on drives C, B, and A (in that order), as shown in Figure B-6.

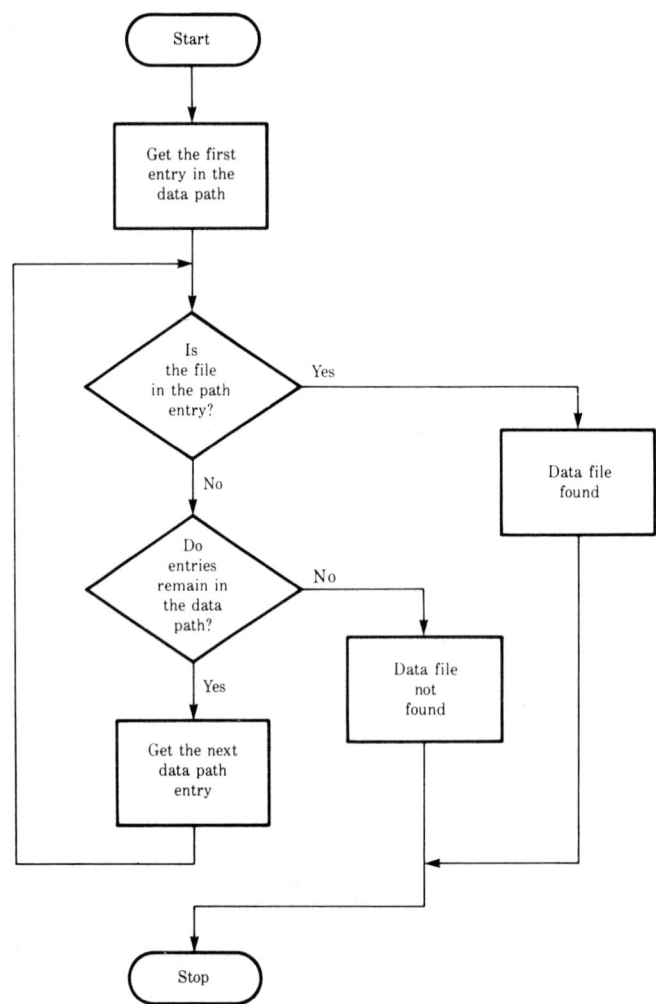

Figure B-5. *Flowchart for determining if file is in data path*

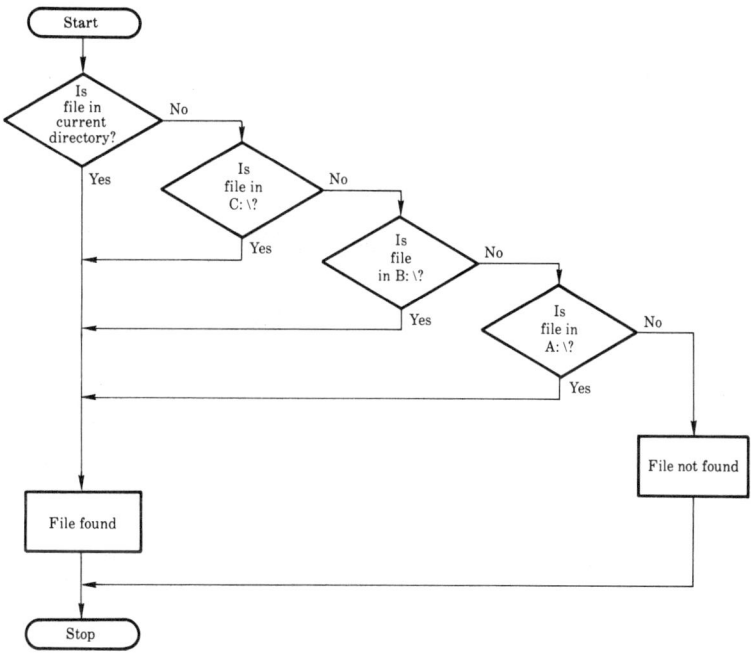

Figure B-6. *OS/2 searching root directories*

```
[C:\] DPATH C:\;B:\;A:\
```

In similar manner, the following DPATH command directs OS/2 to search \OS2, \UTIL, and then \MISC in that order:

```
[C:\] DPATH \OS2;\UTIL;\MISC
```

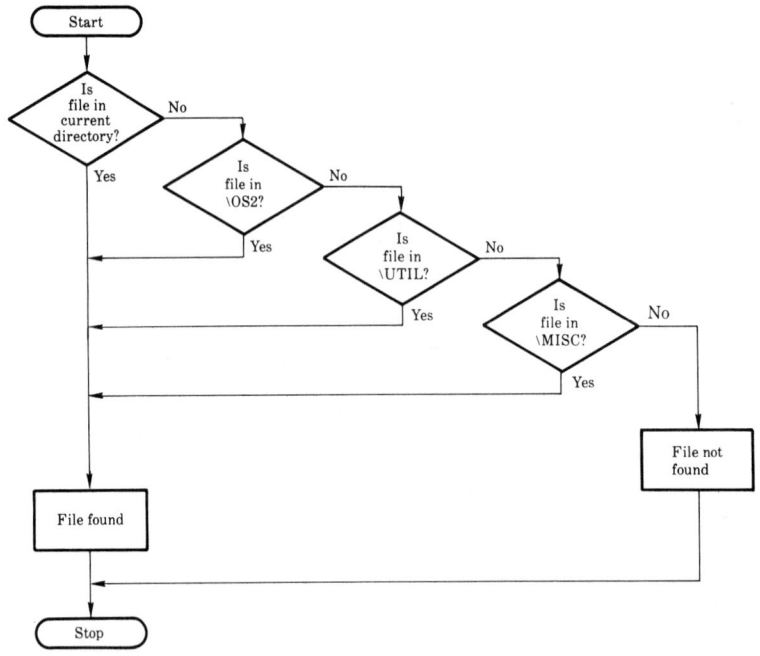

Figure B-7. *DPATH searching \OS2, \UTIL, and \MISC*

Figure B-7 illustrates the processing performed.

ECHO

Function   Display or suppress batch command messages.

Mode   Real/Protected

Format

ECHO [*ON¦ OFF¦ MESSAGE*]

where the following is true:

ON enables the display of batch commands as they execute.
OFF disables the display of batch command names as they execute.
MESSAGE is a text message ECHO is to display to the user.

Syntax Chart

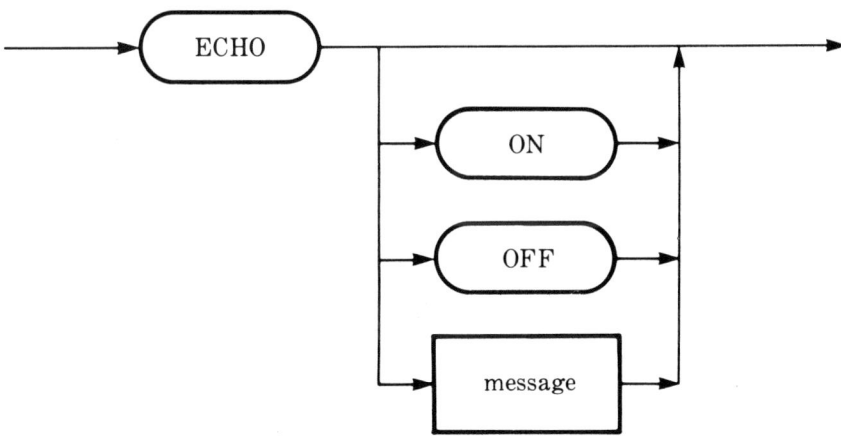

Notes By default, each time you execute OS/2 batch files, OS/2 displays the names of each command as it executes. For example, the file

A
B
C

will display the following:

```
[C:\]A

[C:\]B

[C:\]C
```

The ECHO command enables you to suppress the display of command names within an OS/2 batch file as the command executes. In this case, the file

```
ECHO OFF
A
B
C
```

will display

```
[C:\] ECHO OFF
```

The ECHO command also provides a convenient method of displaying messages to the end user.

If you invoke ECHO without a command-line parameter, ECHO displays its current state (ON or OFF).

Examples In the following case, OS/2 continues to display command names within an OS/2 batch file as it executes:

```
ECHO ON
```

In a similar manner, this batch command disables command-name display:

```
ECHO OFF
```

The ECHO command can be used with batch parameters, as shown here:

```
ECHO %0
```

This batch command displays the name of the batch file that is currently executing.

In a similar manner, this batch procedure displays each of its command-line parameters:

```
ECHO OFF
:LOOP
SHIFT
IF '%0'== '' GOTO DONE
ECHO %0
GOTO LOOP
:DONE
```

This ECHO batch command displays a simple message to the user:

```
ECHO This is a message via ECHO
```

This batch file fully exploits ECHO by displaying copyright information on the screen:

```
ECHO OFF
ECHO ************************************
ECHO * Kevin Schafer Software, Inc. 1988   *
ECHO *                                     *
ECHO * 49rs Football Predictions -- 1988   *
ECHO *                                     *
ECHO ************************************
```

Upon invocation the procedure displays the following:

```
ECHO OFF

****************************************
* Kevin Schafer Software, Inc. 1988   *
*                                     *
* 49rs Football Predictions -- 1988   *
*                                     *
****************************************
```

ENDLOCAL

Function   ENDLOCAL works in conjunction with SETLOCAL to preserve the current drive, directory, and environment settings within a batch file to ensure that the batch file changes are only temporary.

Mode   Real/Protected

Format

ENDLOCAL

Syntax Chart

Notes By default, each time you execute an OS/2 batch procedure, any changes you make to the current drive, directory, or environment entries remain in effect upon completion of the batch file. Consider the following batch procedure:

```
CD \FILES
C:
PROMPT YES$G
PROGRAM
```

Upon completion, the current directory, drive, and system prompt will be changed. Such side effects of batch processing are not always desirable.

The OS/2 ENDLOCAL command works in conjunction with the SETLOCAL command to save and restore the current directory, drive, and environment specifications in a batch file.

The SETLOCAL command saves the current settings that the ENDLOCAL command later restores.

Example In the following case, although the batch file changes the current drive, directory, and prompt, once the batch file completes, SETLOCAL and ENDLOCAL have worked in conjunction to prevent the side effects from remaining:

```
SETLOCAL
CD \FILES
C:
PROMPT YES$G
PROGRAM
ENDLOCAL
```

EXIT

Function   Terminate a secondary command processor.

Mode   Real/Protected

Format

EXIT

Syntax Chart

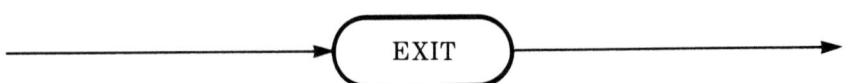

Notes   The EXIT command enables you to terminate either a real- or protected-mode secondary command processor.

If you invoke EXIT from a protected-mode command processor, OS/2 returns control to the OS/2 Session Manager.

Examples   The EXIT command terminates a protected- or real-mode secondary command processor.

```
[C:\] EXIT
```

EXTPROC

Function   Define an external command processor to execute the commands that follow within the batch file.

Mode   Real/Protected

Format

EXTPROC *processor_name* [*argument* [...]]

where the following is true:

processor_name is the name of the file containing the desired command processor. It is a complete OS/2 file specification with an optional disk drive and path name.

argument is a command-line argument to the program acting as the command-line interpreter.

... states that several command-line parameters can be placed on the command line.

Syntax Chart

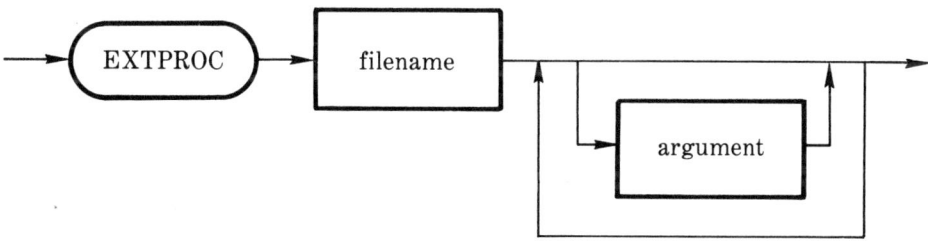

Notes Periodically, you may create a batch procedure that you want executed by a command interpreter other than CMD.EXE. The OS/2 EXTPROC command enables you to define such a processor.

The EXTPROC command must be the first line in your batch file.

Example In the following case, you use the OS/2 executable file SOMEPROG.EXE as the command-line interpreter for this specific batch file. Note that the EXTPROC is the first command in the batch file (as required).

```
EXTPROC SOMEPROG.EXE
CLEARSCR
DATE
```

FDISK

Function   Define disk partitions on an OS/2 fixed disk.

Mode   Real/Protected

Format

FDISK [*drive:*][*path*]

where the following is true:

drive: specifies the disk drive containing the file FDISK.COM. If you do not specify a disk drive identifier, OS/2 uses the current default.

path specifies the name of the OS/2 subdirectory that contains the file FDISK.COM. If you do not specify a subdirectory path, OS/2 uses the current default.

Syntax Chart

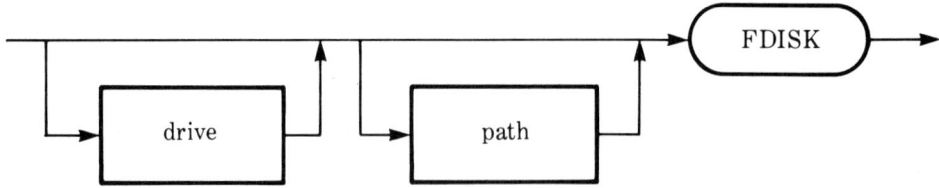

Notes   OS/2 allows you to divide your fixed disk into logical collections of cylinders known as partitions. In so doing, you can actually place several different operating systems on one fixed disk, as shown in Figure B-8.

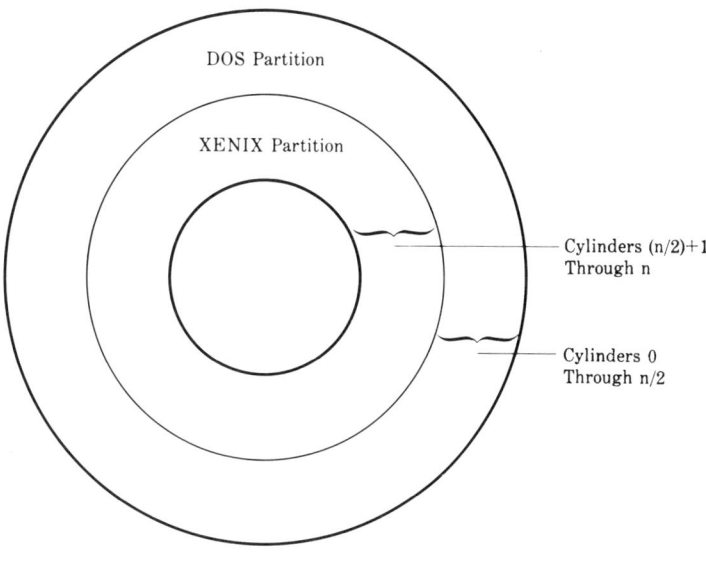

Figure B-8. *Hard disk with partitions for multiple operating systems*

The OS/2 FDISK command allows you to add, change, display, and delete disk partitions.

The first sector on every fixed disk contains a master boot record. This record actually contains partition information. This defines from which partition the computer boots. The FDISK command is your interface to the master boot record.

The FDISK command does not work with the SUBST or JOIN commands.

FIND

Function   Search a file(s) or piped input for a string.

Mode   Real/Protected

Format

[*drive:*][*path*]FIND [/C][/N][/V] "*string*" [*file_spec* ...]

where the following is true:

drive: specifies the disk drive containing the file FIND.COM. If you do not specify a disk drive identifier, OS/2 uses the current default.

path specifies the name of the OS/2 subdirectory that contains the file FIND.COM. If you do not specify a subdirectory path, OS/2 uses the current default.

/C directs FIND to display a count of occurrences of the string.

/N directs FIND to precede each line containing the string with its line number.

/V directs FIND to display each line not containing the string.

string specifies the string for which FIND is to search. It must be in quotation marks.

file_spec is the file name to search for the string. It can be a series of file names separated by spaces. The FIND command does not support OS/2 wildcard characters.

... specifies that several file names can reside in the command line.

Syntax Chart

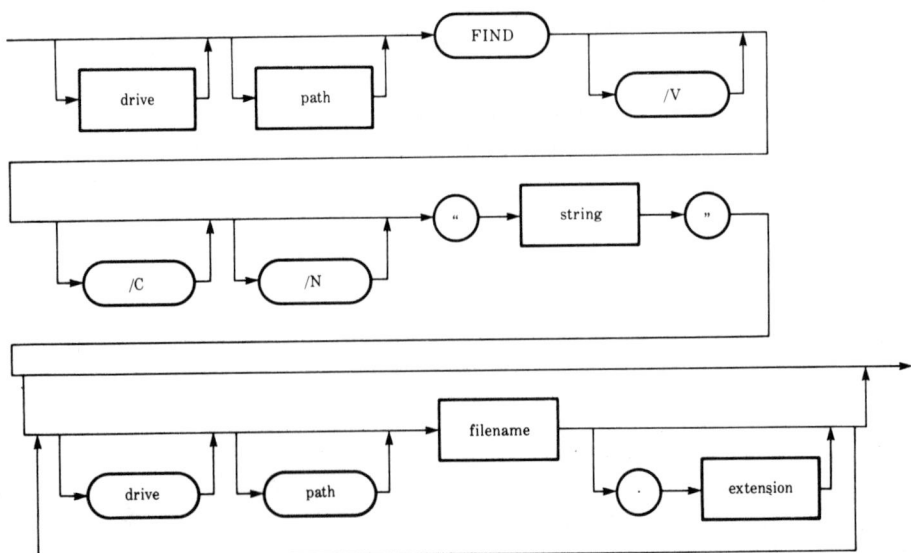

Notes The FIND command enables you to quickly locate a sequence of characters within a file or redirected output. Many people use FIND as a filter of piped input.

If /C and /N are used together, FIND ignores /N.

The string for which FIND is searching must be in quotation marks. If the string has nested quotation marks within it, you must use two quotation marks at each nested quotation mark, as shown here:

```
[C:\] FIND """Look"" he said" FILENAME.EXT
```

Examples In the following case, the user is using FIND as a filter to list each subdirectory in the current directory:

```
[C:\] DIR A: ¦ FIND "<DIR>"
```

If the current directory contains

```
    Volume in drive A is OS2DISK
    Directory of  A:\

SUBDIR         <DIR>        11-01-87    12:53p
A              <DIR>        11-01-87     1:44p
B              <DIR>        11-01-87     1:44p
C              <DIR>        11-01-87     1:44p
WSSTRIP   EXE      2816     10-03-84    10:33p
TAB       EXE     12326      5-05-85     6:25p
SUM       EXE      2834     10-24-87     2:20p
PIPE      EXE      2814     10-26-87     6:47p
PIPE2     EXE      7528     10-23-87    12:37p
          9 File(s)    1182208 bytes free
```

the previous command displays the following:

```
SUBDIR          <DIR>       11-01-87   12:53p
A               <DIR>       11-01-87    1:44p
B               <DIR>       11-01-87    1:44p
C               <DIR>       11-01-87    1:44p
```

To list all of the files that are not directories, use the FIND /V option, as shown here:

```
[C:\] DIR A: ¦ FIND /V "<DIR>"
```

The following command displays each occurrence of the string "begin" in the file TEST.PAS:

```
[C:\] FIND "begin" TEST.PAS
```

In a similar manner, this command displays each occurrence of the string "begin." However, in this case, each line is preceded by its line number.

```
[C:\] FIND /N "begin" TEST.PAS
```

This command simply displays a count of the number of occurrences of "begin" in the file:

```
[C:\] FIND /C "begin" TEST.PAS
```

FOR

Function   Provide repetitive execution (iterative processing) of OS/2 commands.

Mode   Real/Protected

Format

FOR *%%variable* IN (*set*) DO *OS2_command*

where the following is true:

%%variable is the FOR loop-control variable that OS/2 manipulates with each iteration. The variable name is restricted to a character. The numbers 0-9 cannot be used since they are reserved for OS/2 batch parameters.

set is a list of valid OS/2 file names. The *set* variable can be a list of OS/2 file names separated by commas (A, B, C), or it can contain a wildcard character (*,*), or both (A, B, *.DAT).

OS2_command is the command to execute with each iteration.

Syntax Chart

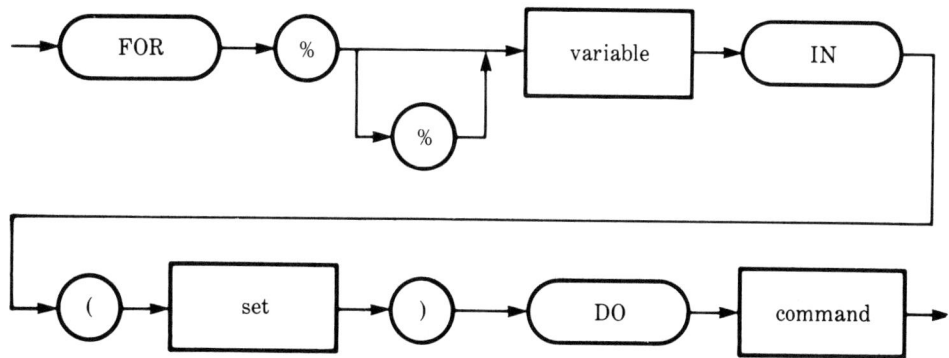

Notes   The FOR command is used most commonly within OS/2 batch files. However, FOR can be used from the OS/2 prompt. The %% before the variable name are used in batch files, while % is used from the OS/2 prompt.

The processing FOR performs is actually quite straightforward. Consider this example:

```
FOR %%V IN (AUTOEXEC.BAT, CONFIG.SYS, STARTUP.CMD) DO TYPE %%V
```

In this case FOR will assign the variable the file name AUTOEXEC.BAT during the first iteration and type its contents, as shown here:

```
TYPE AUTOEXEC.BAT
```

On the second iteration, FOR assigns the variable the file name CONFIG.SYS and displays its contents:

```
TYPE CONFIG.SYS
```

On the third iteration, FOR assigns the variable the file name STARTUP.CMD and again displays the file's contents:

```
TYPE STARTUP.CMD
```

When FOR prepares for the fourth iteration, it fails to find any more file names, so its processing is complete. Figure B-9 illustrates he processing FOR performs.

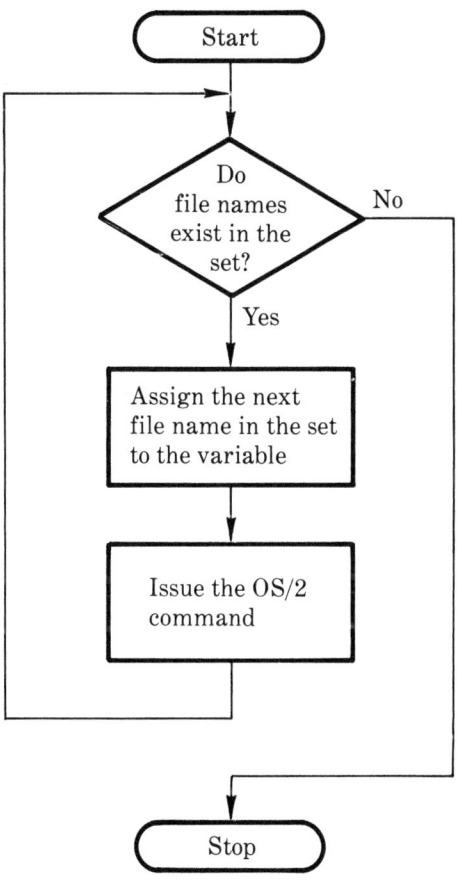

Figure B-9. *Processing performed by FOR command*

Examples In the following case, the user has issued the command from the OS/2 prompt:

```
[C:\] FOR %I IN (*.FOR) DO TYPE %I
```

Note that the variable name is only preceded by one percent sign (%I) when FOR is invoked from the OS/2 command line.

In the following case, an OS/2 batch file is using FOR to compile all of the C files on the current directory:

```
FOR %%F IN (*.C) DO CC %%F
```

FORMAT

Function   Format a disk for use by OS/2.

Mode   Real/Protected

Format

[*drive:*][*path*]FORMAT [*d:*][*/S*][*/V:volume*][*/4*][*/T:tracks*]
   [*/N:sectors*]

where the following is true:

drive: is the disk drive containing the file FORMAT.COM. If you omit the disk drive specifier, OS/2 uses the current default.

path is the OS/2 subdirectory name of the subdirectory containing the file FORMAT.COM. If you omit the subdirectory specifier, OS/2 uses the current default.

d: is the disk drive identifier containing the disk to format.

/S directs FORMAT to place the OS/2 system files on the disk and make the disk bootable.

/V:volume directs FORMAT to include the volume label.

/4 directs FORMAT to format the disk double-sided in a quad-density disk drive.

/T:tracks defines the number of tracks/side.

/N:sectors defines the number of sectors/track.

Syntax Chart

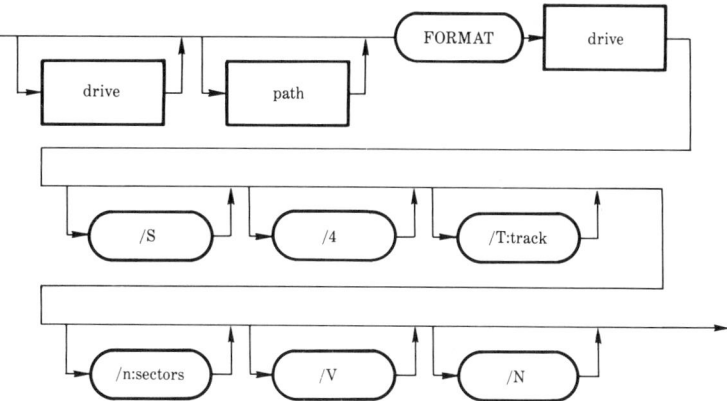

Notes   Each time you purchase floppy disks, the original disk manufacturer has no way of knowing on what computer the disks will be used or with what operating system. As such, before you can use a new disk, you must FORMAT it under OS/2.

Warning: FORMAT destroys any of the information contained on the target disk.

The FORMAT /S command copies to the target disk the OS/2 hidden files that are required to boot OS/2 along with any files specified in FORMAT.TBL.

The final step in the FORMAT processing is to prompt you to enter the desired disk volume identifier. A disk volume is an 11-character name that you can assign to a disk. It is a good habit to utilize disk volume names, as shown here:

```
Type in an 11-character volume label,
or press Enter.
```

Simply type in the name that you desire and press the ENTER key.

Because inadvertently formatting a fixed disk can be disastrous, FORMAT first prompts you with

```
WARNING, ALL DATA ON NON-REMOVEABLE DISK
DRIVE N: WILL BE LOST!
Proceed with Format (Y/N)?
```

before continuing. To proceed with the FORMAT type Y. Otherwise, type N.

Upon completion, FORMAT displays the following information:

- Total disk space

- Corrupted disk space marked as defective

- Total disk space consumed by the operating system

- Total disk space available for file utilization

As you can see, FORMAT reports on defective space that it finds during formatting. In addition, FORMAT places entries for each defective sector into a table called the file-allocation table (FAT), which prevents OS/2 from using the corrupted sectors for data storage.

Do not use FORMAT in conjunction with ASSIGN, JOIN, or SUBST.

Examples   In the following case, the command creates a bootable disk with the disk contained in drive B:

```
[C:\] FORMAT B:/S
```

Many users often must FORMAT double-density disks in their 1.2MB drives. The /4 qualifier in the FORMAT command directs FORMAT to create a 360K disk, as shown here:

```
[C:\] FORMAT A:/4
```

Upon invocation, this command displays the following:

```
Insert a new diskette in drive A:
and press Enter when ready.
```

GOTO

Function Branch to the label specified in a BAT file.

Mode Real/Protected

Format

GOTO *label_name*

where the following is true:

label_name specifies the name of a label within an OS/2 batch procedure.

Syntax Chart

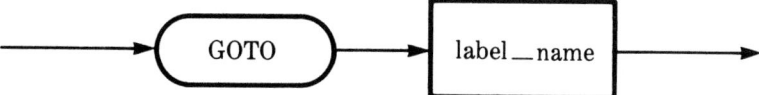

Notes OS/2 label names contain any of the characters valid for OS/2 file names. If the label does not exist, OS/2 terminates execution of the batch file.

OS/2 label names can be virtually any length. However, OS/2 only distinguishes the first eight characters of a label name. As such, OS/2 will consider the label names OS2_LABEL1 and OS2_LABEL2 as equivalent since it only examines the first eight characters of the label name.

Example The following batch procedure displays a continuous directory listing until the user presses CTRL-C or CTRL-BREAK:

```
:LOOP
DIR
GOTO LOOP
```

When OS/2 cannot find a label specified in a GOTO command, it terminates the processing, as shown here:

```
GOTO OS2LABEL
DATE
TIME
:OS2LABL
```

Upon invocation the procedure displays the following:

```
DOS1039: The system cannot find the batch label specified.
```

The following procedure illustrates how OS/2 only examines the first eight characters of a label name. Although the GOTO command branches to the label OS2_LABEL2, OS/2 first finds OS2_LABEL.

```
GOTO OS2_LABEL2
:OS2_LABEL
ECHO LABEL1
GOTO DONE
:OS2_LABEL2
ECHO LABEL2
:DONE
```

GRAFTABL

Function   Enable real mode to display the extended character set when the display is in graphics mode.

Mode   Real

Format

[*drive:*][*path*]GRAFTABL [*codepage*¦ *?*¦ /STA]

where the following is true:

drive: specifies the disk drive containing the file GRAFTABL.COM. If you do not specify a disk drive identifier, OS/2 uses the current default.

path is the OS/2 path name of the subdirectory that contains the file GRAFTABL.COM. If you do not specify an OS/2 path name, OS/2 uses the current default.

codepage specifies the code page to be used for display:

437   United States
850   Multilingual
860   Portugal
863   French-Canadian
865   Nordic

? directs GRAFTABL to display its command-line options.
/STA directs GRAFTABL to display the code page that is currently in use.

Syntax Chart

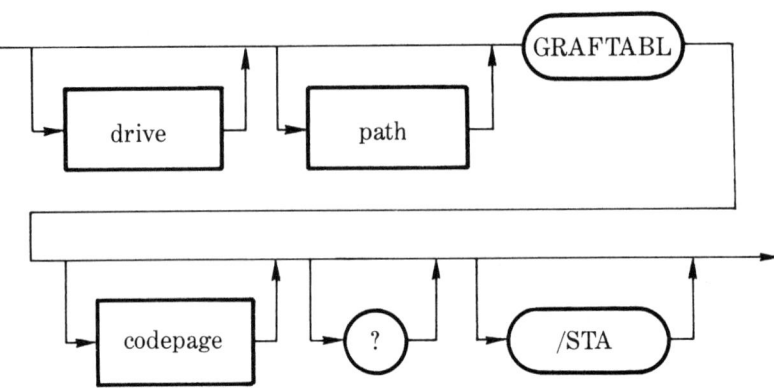

Notes GRAFTABL command loads memory-resident code when it is invoked. As such, GRAFTABL can only be invoked one time. GRAFTABL affects only the real-mode session.

Examples If you specify the ? option in the GRAFTABL command line, GRAFTABL displays its command-line options, as shown here:

```
C> GRAFTABL ?

No version of the graphic character set
table has been loaded.
The acceptable GRAFTABL parameters are:

  /STA - Request status only
  ?      - Display this summary of parameters

  437  - English graphic character set
  860  - Portuguese graphic character set
  863  - Canadian French graphic character set
  865  - Nordic graphic character set

C>
```

In the following case, GRAFTABL uses the code page for the United States when it displays extended characters:

```
C> GRAFTABL 437
```

This command directs GRAFTABL to display the current code page:

```
C> GRAFTABL /STA

The English version of the graphic character
set table is already loaded.

C>
```

HELPMSG

Function   Provide additional help on each OS/2 error message.

Mode   Real/Protected

Format

[*drive:*][*path*]HELPMSG *message_id*

where the following is true:

drive: specifies the disk drive containing the file HELPMSG.EXE. If you do not specify a disk drive identifier, OS/2 uses the current default.

path is the OS/2 path name of the subdirectory that contains the file HELPMSG.EXE. If you do not specify an OS/2 path name, OS/2 uses the current default.

message_id is the OS/2 message on which to display additional help text. Each OS/2 error message comes in the form SYS*nnnn* where *nnnn* is a four-digit number.

Syntax Chart

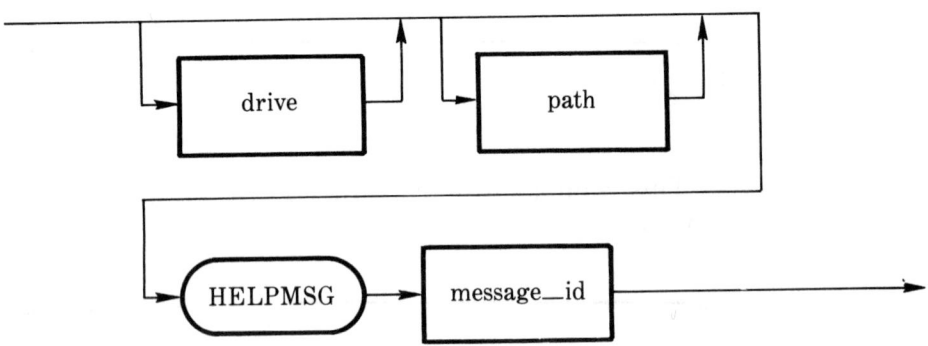

Notes Each time OS/2 displays a protected-mode error message, it uses the format SYS*nnnn* where *nnnn* is a four-digit number that uniquely identifies the error.

Although most OS/2 error messages are self-explanatory, HELPMSG gives you additional help text.

Example In the following case, OS/2 could not find the command specified:

```
[C:\] SOMECMD
DOS1041: The system cannot find the filename specified.

[C:\]
```

If you invoke HELPMSG with the error-message number, it displays the following:

```
[C:\] HELPMSG DOS1041

DOS1041: The system cannot find the filename specified.


EXPLANATION: One of the following errors
occurred:

1. An incorrect filename was entered.
2. A filename was entered that does not
   contain a .BAT, .EXE, or .COM extension.
3. A ? or * character was entered in the filename.
ACTION: Retry the command using a correct filename.

[C:\]
```

Likewise, if OS/2 cannot find a data file,

```
[C:\] TYPE XXX
DOS0002: The system cannot find the file specified.

[C:\]
```

HELPMSG displays the following:

```
[C:\] HELPMSG DOS0002

DOS0002: The system cannot find the file specified.


EXPLANATION: The file named in the command
does not exist in the directory or the drive
specified.  You may have typed the filename
incorrectly, or you may have used an
unacceptable character.  Unacceptable
characters are: . " / \ [ ] : | < > + ; ,
and all control characters.
ACTION: Retry the command using a correct filename.

[C:\]
```

IF

Function   Provide conditional processing within OS/2 batch files.

Mode   Real/Protected

Format

IF [*NOT*] *condition OS2__command*

where the following is true:

NOT performs a Boolean NOT on the result of the condition.
condition must be one of the following:

> ERRORLEVEL value (true if program exit status >= value)
> EXIST file__spec (true if the specified file exists)
> string1==string2 (true if both strings are identical)

OS2__command is the name of the command that OS/2 is to perform if the condition is true.

Syntax Chart

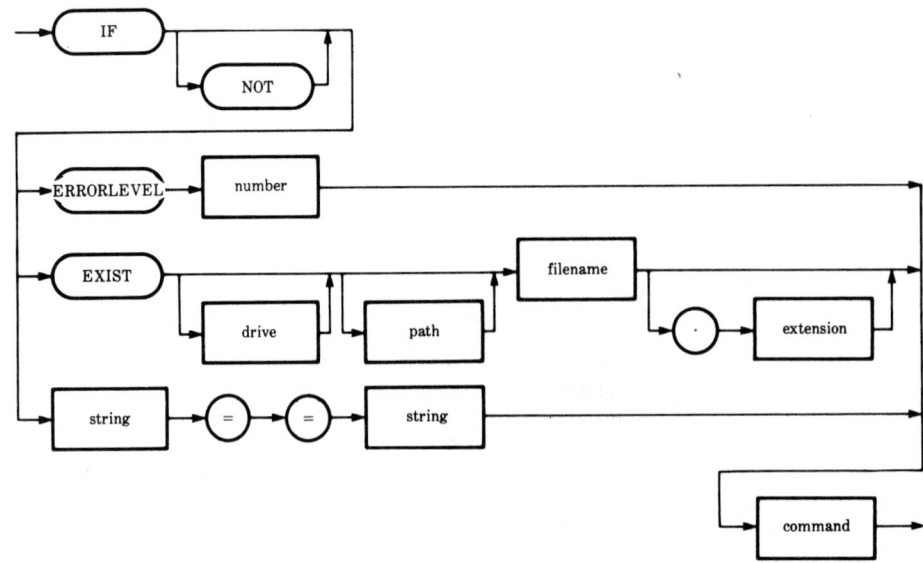

Notes   Although most users only utilize the OS/2 IF statement from within OS/2 batch files, OS/2 fully supports IF from the command line.

Examples   In the following case, if the file CONFIG.SYS exists in the current directory, OS/2 copies the file to drive B:

```
[C:\] IF EXIST CONFIG.SYS TYPE CONFIG.SYS
```

The processing becomes that shown in Figure B-10.

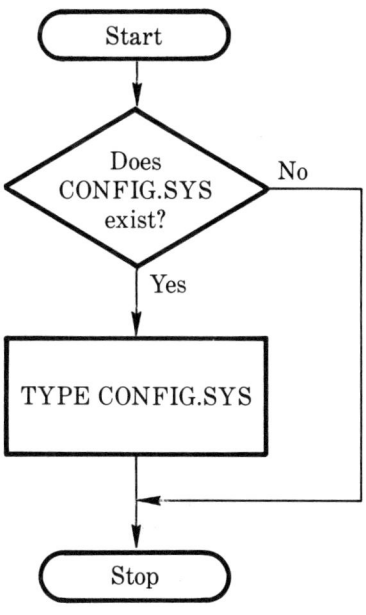

Figure B-10.   *Processing performed by IF command*

In the following case,

```
ECHO OFF
OS2PGM
IF ERRORLEVEL 3 ECHO T H R E E
```

if the program OS2PGM exits with a status greater than or equal to 3, OS/2 displays the following message:

```
T H R E E
```

Note how you can simply add the Boolean NOT to the previous expression to direct the program to terminate if the exit status is less than 3:

```
ECHO OFF
OS2PGM
IF NOT ERRORLEVEL 3 GOTO DONE
ECHO T H R E E
:DONE
```

Again, the processing is that shown in Figure B-11.

Lastly, in the following case, you use the OS/2 IF command to determine whether or not the value of the batch parameter is NULL:

```
IF '%1' == '' GOTO NULL
```

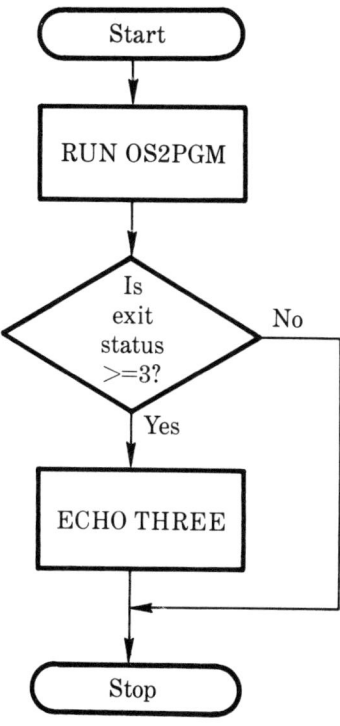

Figure B-11. *Processing performed by IF command with exit status value included in statement*

If you use this expression within the following batch file, you can ECHO each of the batch-file parameters to the screen:

```
ECHO OFF
:LOOP
SHIFT
IF '%0'== '' GOTO DONE
ECHO %0
GOTO LOOP
:DONE
```

If you invoke the procedure with

```
[C:\] ECHOTEST 1 2 3 4 5
```

it will display the following:

```
[C:\] ECHOTEST 1 2 3 4 5
1
2
3
4
5
```

Figure B-12 illustrates the processing performed.

JOIN

Function   Join a disk drive to an OS/2 path.

Mode   Real

Format

[*drive:*][*path*]JOIN [*d1:* [*d2:path*]][/D]

where the following is true:

drive: is the disk drive identifier of the disk that contains the file JOIN.EXE. If you do not specify a disk drive, OS/2 uses the current default.

path is the name of the OS/2 subdirectory that contains the file JOIN.EXE. If you do not specify a disk drive, OS/2 uses the current default.

d1: specifies the disk drive to join to the path provided.

d2:path specifies the join directory.

/D directs JOIN to undo a previous JOIN procedure.

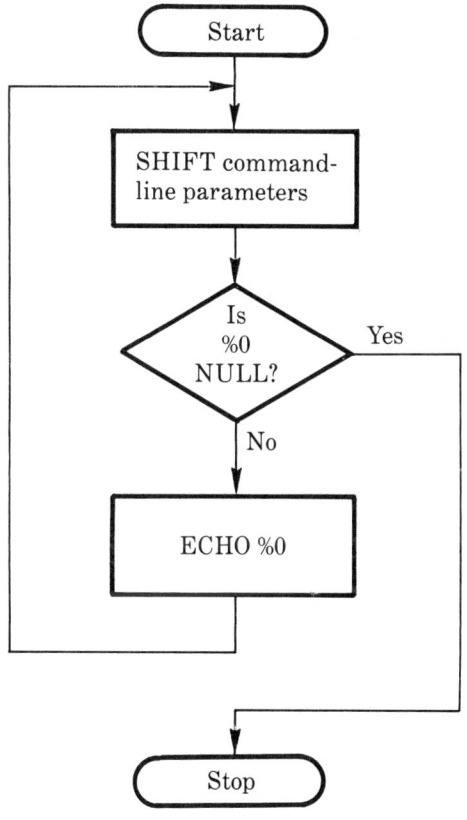

Figure B-12. *Processing of echoing batch procedures to screen*

Syntax Chart

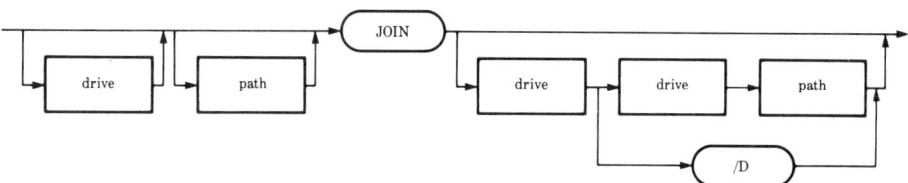

Notes The JOIN command makes two disks appear as one by joining a disk to an OS/2 path.

If you issue a JOIN command without any parameters, JOIN displays the current JOINS.

OS/2 only joins a disk to an empty OS/2 directory.

Do not use JOIN in conjunction with the following commands:

CHKDSK
DISKCOPY
FDISK
FORMAT
LABEL
RECOVER
SYS

Examples Before you can JOIN a disk to a directory, you must create an empty directory by using the MKDIR command:

```
[C:\] MKDIR \JOINDIR
```

Next, use JOIN to connect a disk to the subdirectory, as shown here:

```
[C:\] JOIN B: \JOINDIR
```

In this case, references to C: \JOINDIR are identical to references to drive B. If drive B contains OS/2 subdirectories, simply refer to them as follows:

```
[C:\] DIR \JOINDIR\SUBDIR
```

If you invoke JOIN without any command-line parameters, JOIN displays the current JOINs, as shown here:

```
[C:\] JOIN
```

Lastly, to remove a JOIN, use the /D qualifier, as shown here:

```
[C:\] JOIN A: /D
```

KEYBXX

Function   Load foreign keyboard set.

Mode   Real/Protected

Format

[*drive:*][*path*]KEYB^XX

where the following is true:

drive: is the disk drive identifier of the disk that contains the KEYBCOM file. If you do not specify a disk drive identifier, OS/2 uses the current default.

path is the OS/2 name of the subdirectory that contains the KEYBCOM file. If you do not specify a subdirectory name, OS/2 uses the current default.

Syntax Chart

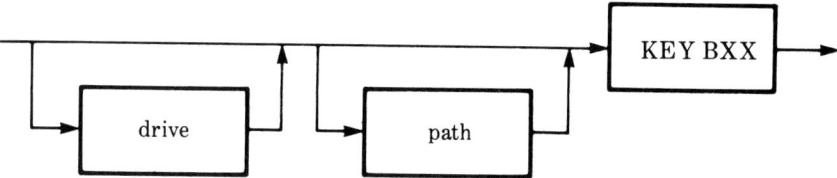

Notes   In order to fully support international configurations, OS/2 provides support for various keyboard templates.

The KEYBXX command loads memory-resident software to replace the standard keyboard layout supported by the ROM-BIOS.

Once a new keyboard is installed, you can toggle between it and the default keyboard by pressing CTRL-ALT-F1 for the default, and CTRL-ALT-F2 for the foreign keyboard.

Common keyboard layouts include

KEYB FR	France
KEYB GR	Germany
KEYB IT	Italy
KEYB SP	Spain
KEYB UK	United Kingdom
KEYB US	United States

Example   In this case, OS/2 uses the United Kingdom keyboard template.

```
C> KEY BUK
```

LABEL

Function   Specify a disk volume label.

Mode   Real/Protected

Format

[*drive:*][*path*]LABEL [*target_drive:*] [*volume_label*]

where the following is true:

drive: is the disk drive identifier of the disk containing the file LABEL.COM. If you do not specify a disk drive, OS/2 uses the current default.

path is the name of the OS/2 subdirectory that contains the file LABEL.COM. If you do not specify a disk drive, OS/2 use the current default.

target_drive: is the disk drive containing the disk to label.

volume_label is the desired 11-character volume label. All of the characters that are valid in OS/2 file names are valid volume-label characters.

Syntax Chart

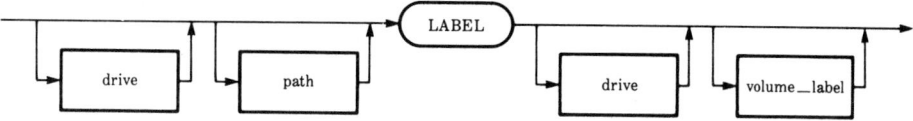

Notes OS/2 allows you to define a name for each of your disks. Each time you issue the OS/2 DIR command, DIR displays the volume label of the disk, as shown here:

```
Volume in drive A is OS2LABEL
Directory of  A:\
```

By using software, you can also obtain the disk volume label from within your OS/2 programs. In so doing, you can ensure that the user has the correct disk in each drive.

The OS/2 VOL command also displays the disk volume label, as shown here:

```
[C:\] VOL A:

Volume in drive A is OS2LABEL

[C:\]
```

If you do not specify a volume label in the command line, LABEL prompts you for one, as follows:

```
Volume in drive C is OS2DISK
Type a volume label of up to 11 characters
or press Enter for no volume label update.
```

If you do not want to change the disk label, simply press ENTER. Otherwise, type in the desired volume name.

Example In the following command, the label name is not specified in the command line:

```
[C:\] LABEL
```

As such, LABEL prompts as follows:

```
Volume in drive C is OS2DISK
Type a volume label of up to 11 characters
or press Enter for no volume label update.
```

Again, either type in the volume label that you desire or press the ENTER key to leave the current label name unchanged.

MKDIR

Function   Create the specified OS/2 subdirectory.

Mode   Real/Protected

Format

MKDIR [*drive:*]*path* [...]

or

MD [*drive:*]*path* [...]

where the following is true:

drive: specifies the drive on which to create the subdirectory. If a drive is not specified, MKDIR uses the current default.
path specifies the name of the OS/2 directory that MKDIR is to create.
... specifies that in OS/2 protected mode you can create several OS/2 subdirectories in one command line.

Syntax Chart

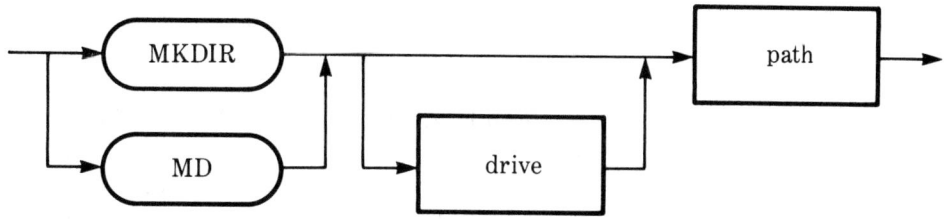

Disk space	Maximum number of subdirectories in the root directory
160K	64
180K	
320K	112
360K	
1.2MB	224
Fixed disk	Based upon partition size

Table B-4. *Subdirectories Supported by Root Directory*

Notes If you do not use OS/2 subdirectories, your disks are restricted to a limited number of files, as shown in Table B-4.

Every OS/2 directory has a root directory (\ ) from which all other subdirectories grow.

The maximum path name that OS/2 can process is 63 characters, as follows:

```
C> MD \COMMANDS\UTILITY\DATAFILE\INPUT\LOWLEVEL\PASCAL\SOURCE\ROUTINES
```

Each time you create an OS/2 subdirectory, MKDIR has two choices. First, if the directory name starts with a backslash (such as \SUBDIR), OS/2 starts with the root directory to create the subdirectory. However, if the name does not start with a backslash (SUBDIR), OS/2 creates the subdirectory within the current directory.

Use the following rules of thumb when you create your OS/2 directories:

■ OS/2 directory names conform to the same format as OS/2 file names with an eight-character file name followed by an optional three-character extension. As such, the following are valid OS/2 directory names: FILENAME.EXT, HARDWARE.SAL, and SOFTWARE.INV.

■ If you do not specify a complete OS/2 path name when you create a subdirectory, OS/2 assumes that you are creating the subdirectory in the current directory.

■ To manipulate directories contained on other disks, simply precede the directory name with a disk drive identifier (such as B:\FINANCE\CAR).

■ Do not create directory names identical to files contained in the same directory.

■ Do not create a directory called \DEV. OS/2 uses a hidden directory called \DEV to communicate with hardware devices. For example, enter the following command:

```
[C:\] COPY \STARTUP.CMD \DEV\PRN
```

■ OS/2 path names cannot exceed 63 characters.

■ Root directories on each disk are restricted to a specific number of files because of the disk layout. However, subdirectories can contain an unlimited number of files.

■ Logically divide your disk into subdirectories.

Examples Assume for the following examples that you have a newly formatted disk that only contains the root directory, as shown here:

```
Root
Directory
```

In each case, the directories will be shown as OS/2 creates them.

For example, the command MKDIR creates a directory called IBM in the root.

```
[C:\] MKDIR \IBM
```

The disk now contains the following:

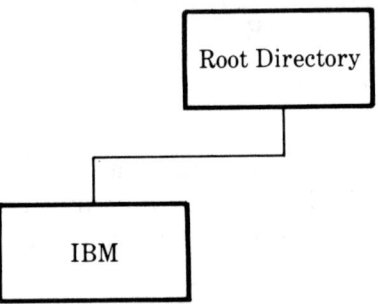

In a similar manner, the following command creates a subdirectory called NOTES in the IBM root directory:

```
[C:\] MKDIR \IBM\NOTES
```

This command is equivalent to the following commands:

```
[C:\] CHDIR \IBM
[C:\] MKDIR NOTES
```

Note that the second command does not have a backslash in front of the directory name NOTES. If it did, MKDIR would create the directory in the root as opposed to the subdirectory \IBM. The disk now contains the following:

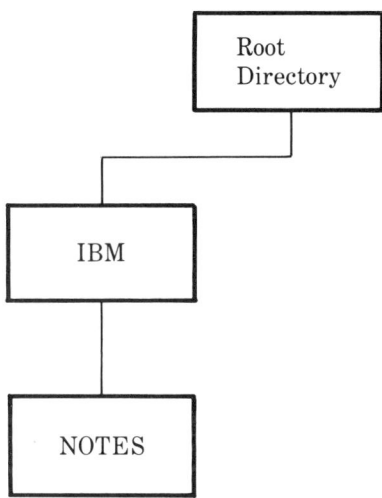

Assuming that the current directory is still the root, the following command also creates a subdirectory off of the root:

```
[C:\] MKDIR MISC
```

In this case, the subdirectory name does not contain a backslash. As such, MKDIR creates the directory in the current directory, which, in this case, is still the root. The disk contains the following:

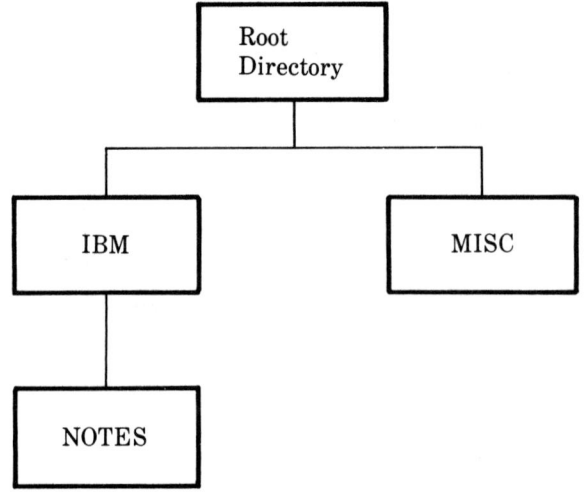

MODE

Function   Specify device characteristics.

Mode   Real/Protected

Format

[*drive:*][*path*]MODE *n*[, C]

or

[*drive:*][*path*]MODE *COM#*[:] *baud*[,*parity*[,*data*[,*stop*[,*P*]]]]

or

[*drive:*][*path*] MODE *LPT*#[:] [*cpl*][,*vli*][,*P*]

where the following is true:

drive: specifies the disk drive identifier of the disk containing the file MODE.COM. If you do not specify a disk drive, OS/2 uses the current default.

path specifies the name of the OS/2 subdirectory that contains the file MODE.COM. If you do not specify a subdirectory name, OS/2 uses the current default.

baud specifies the device baud rate (110, 150, 300, 600, 1200, 2400, 4800, 9600, or 19200). MODE only requires you to specify the first two digits of the baud rate.

n specifies the screen-display attribute. It must be one of the following:

40	Specifies 40-column display
80	Specifies 80-column display
BW40	Specifies a black-and-white 40-column display
BW80	Specifies a black-and-white 80-column display
CO40	Specifies a color 40-column display
CO80	Specifies a color 80-column display
C#	Specifies the number of display lines 25, 43, or 50

parity specifies the device parity: E for even parity, N for no parity, O for odd parity. The default is even parity.

data specifies the number of data bits (7 or 8). The default is 7 data bits.

stop specifies the number of stop bits (1 or 2). For 110 baud, the default is 2. Otherwise, it is 1.

cpl is characters per line (80, 132).

vli is vertical lines per inch (6, 8).

P specifies continuous retries on time-out errors.

LPT# specifies the parallel printer number (such as LPT1).

COM# specifies the serial port number (such as COM1).

Syntax Chart

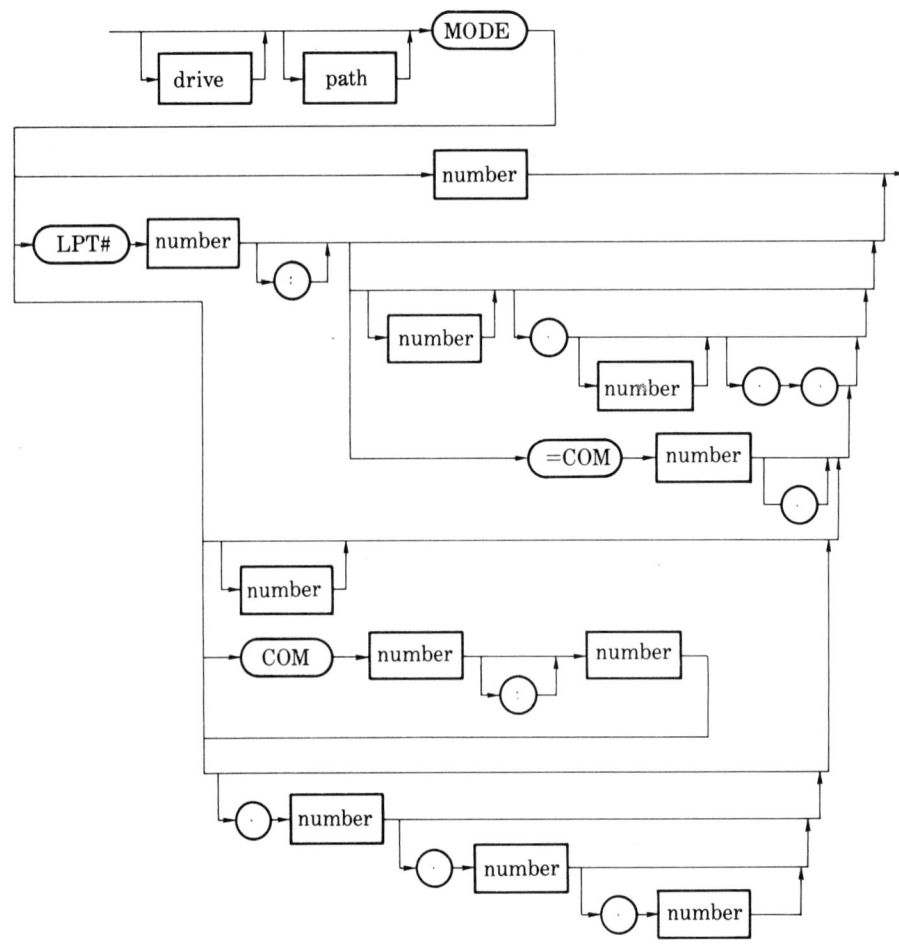

Notes Many hardware devices require unique data communications setups (such as 4800 baud, even parity). The OS/2 MODE command enables you to set the characteristics of a port on the computer.

By default, OS/2 uses the parallel printer port for printed data. If your printer is connected to a serial device, you can redirect the parallel output to the serial device by using the MODE command.

If a device requires modification each time it is used, place the MODE command in either AUTOEXEC.BAT or STARTUP.CMD.

Examples   The following command

```
[C:\] MODE 40
```

sets the screen display to 40-column mode, as shown here:

```
[C:\]
```

To restore the screen to 80-column mode, enter the following:

```
[C:\] MODE 80
```

This command specifies the data-communication parameters for COM1:

```
[C:\] MODE COM1: 48,N,7
```

MORE

Function   Display a command's output, a screenful at a time.

Mode   Real/Protected

Format

OS2_COMMAND ¦ [*drive:*][*path*]MORE

or

[*drive:*][*path*]MORE < OS2_COMMAND

where the following is true:

drive: is the disk drive identifier of the disk containing the file MORE.COM.
If you omit the disk drive, OS/2 uses the current default.

path is the name of the OS/2 subdirectory that contains the file MORE.COM.
If you omit the subdirectory name, OS/2 uses the current default drive.

Syntax Chart

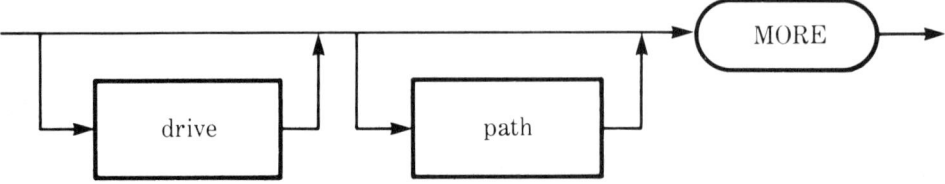

Notes   The OS/2 MORE command reads data from the standard
input device and displays the information to the standard output
device a page at a time until end-of-file is encountered. Each time
a page of data is displayed on the screen, MORE displays the

following message:

— MORE —

Simply press any key to continue the output, or press CTRL-C to terminate the command.

Example By entering the following command,

```
[C:\] SORT < DATA.DAT ¦ MORE
```

the user is using MORE as a filter to obtain input from the standard input device (stdin) as shown in Figure B-13.

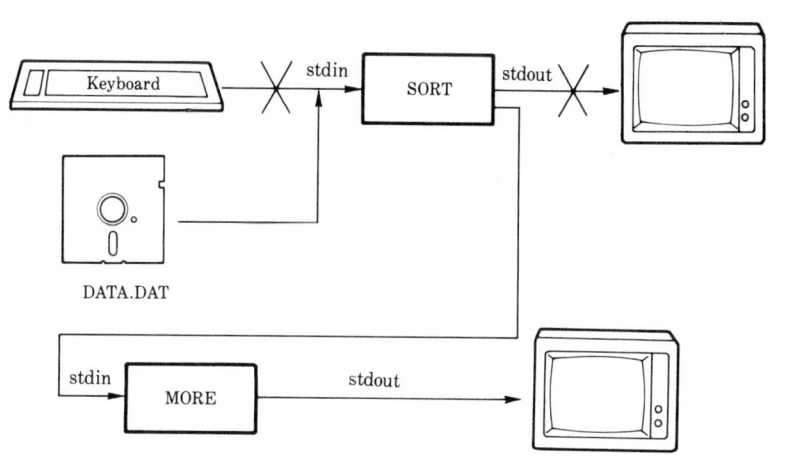

Figure B-13. *Using MORE as a filter to obtain input from the stdin*

To simply display the contents of DATA.DAT one screenful at a time, use MORE as shown here:

```
[C:\] MORE < DATA.DAT
```

This command is processed as shown in Figure B-14.
Simply issue the MORE command from the OS/2 prompt.

```
[C:\] MORE
```

In this case, MORE expects its input from the keyboard. Simply type in a screenful of information and then press CTRL-Z. The MORE command will process as normal.

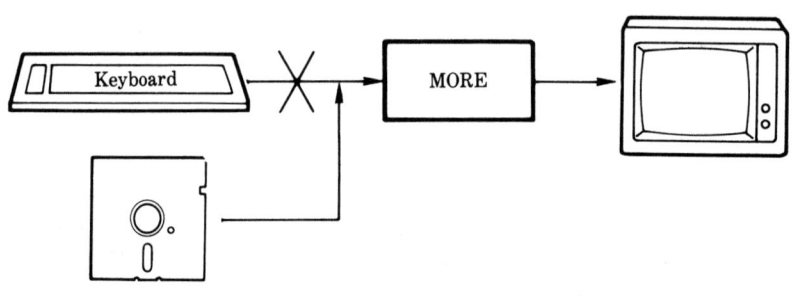

Figure B-14. *Using MORE to display contents of DATA.DAT*

PATCH

Function Make changes to an executable file.

Mode Real/Protected

Format

[*drive:*][*path*]PATCH *file_specification* [*/A*]

where the following is true:

drive: specifies the disk drive containing the file PATCH.EXE. If you do not specify a disk drive identifier, OS/2 uses the current default.

path is the OS/2 path name of the subdirectory that contains the file PATCH.EXE. If you do not specify an OS/2 path name, OS/2 uses the current default.

file_specification is the complete OS/2 file specification of the file to which PATCH is to apply the changes. The *file_specification* variable can contain a disk drive identifier and OS/2 path name.

/A directs PATCH to execute in automatic mode and to obtain its inputs from a file (as opposed to the user).

Syntax Chart

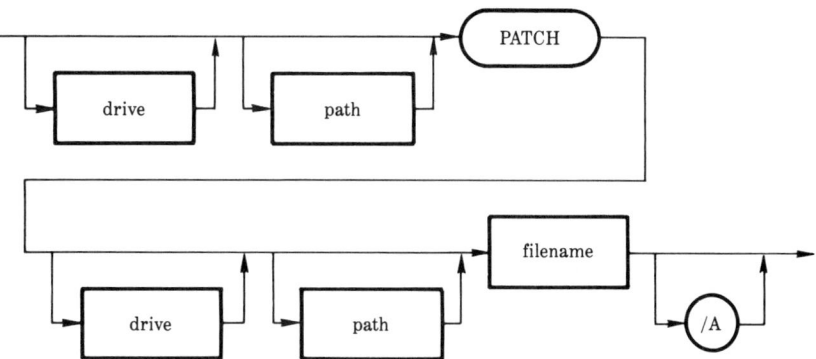

Notes Executable files are difficult to change, should a solution to a known bug be found. In the past, programmers used the DOS DEBUG command to apply fixes (patches) to an executable file.

PATCH provides a standard for changing files.

Most people will never use this command. In many cases, software developers will publish fixes called patches for software programs. The OS/2 PATCH command allows you to apply these fixes.

All values specified to patch are in hexadecimal.

Examples In the following case, you apply a patch to the file FILENAME.EXE.

```
[C:\] PATCH FILENAME.EXE
```

PATCH prompts you for the hexadecimal offset in the file for the first patch, as shown here:

```
Patching FILENAME.EXE
End of file is at AFE
Enter the hexadecimal offset of patch:
```

Enter 0 and press the ENTER key:

```
00000000    4D 5A 40 00 01 00 00 00 04 00 FF FF FF FF 00 00    MZ@...
```

PATCH displays the current byte value at this location. Enter 11 to change the current value. PATCH moves the cursor to the right, allowing you to change the next value.

```
00000000    11 5A 40 00 01 00 00 00 04 00 FF FF FF FF 00 00    MZ@...
```

Simply press ENTER. PATCH will respond with the following:

```
Do you want to continue patching FILENAME.EXE? (Y/N)
```

To continue with the patch type Y. Otherwise, type N. In this case type N.

```
Patching FILENAME.EXE
End of file is at AFE
Enter the hexadecimal offset of patch: 0

00000000    00 5A 40 00 01 00 00 00 04 00 FF FF FF FF 00 00    .Z@...

Do you want to continue patching FILENAME.EXE? (Y/N)

Patches entered for FILENAME.EXE

00000000    11 5A 40 00 01 00 00 00 04 00 FF FF FF FF 00 00    .Z@...

Do you want these patches applied to FILENAME.EXE? (Y/N) Y

Patches applied to FILENAME.EXE
```

PATCH displays the changes that you have made to the file and prompts you as to whether or not you want the patch actually written to disk. To write the patch type Y. Otherwise, type N.

PATH

Function   Define the command-file search path that OS/2 uses each time it fails to locate a command as an internal command, within the current directory, or specified directory.

Mode   Real/Protected

Format

PATH [*drive:*][*path*] [;[*drive:*][*path*]...]

where the following is true:

drive: specifies a disk drive that OS/2 is to include in the command-file search path.
path specifies an OS/2 subdirectory to include in the command-file search path.
... states that the disk drive and subdirectories may be specified several times.

Syntax Chart

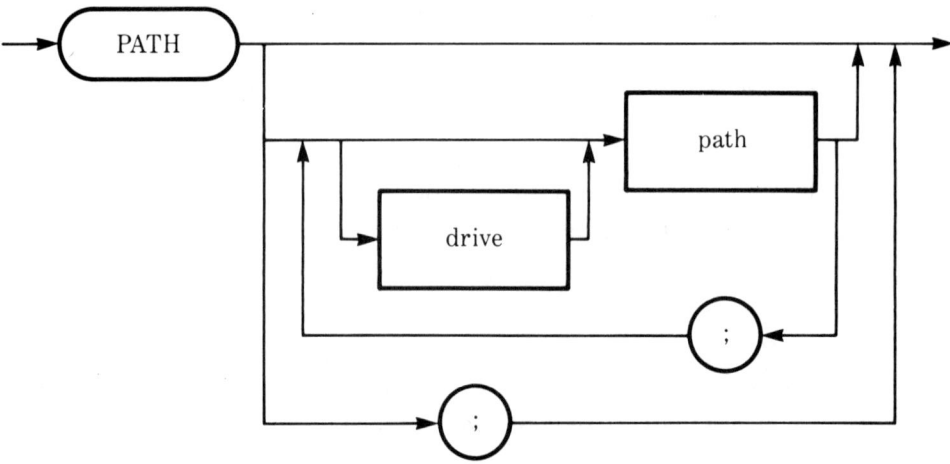

Notes   Each time OS/2 real mode cannot find a command as an internal command, or as an EXE, COM, BAT, or CMD file in the current directory, it searches to see if the user has defined a command-file search path (see Figure B-15).

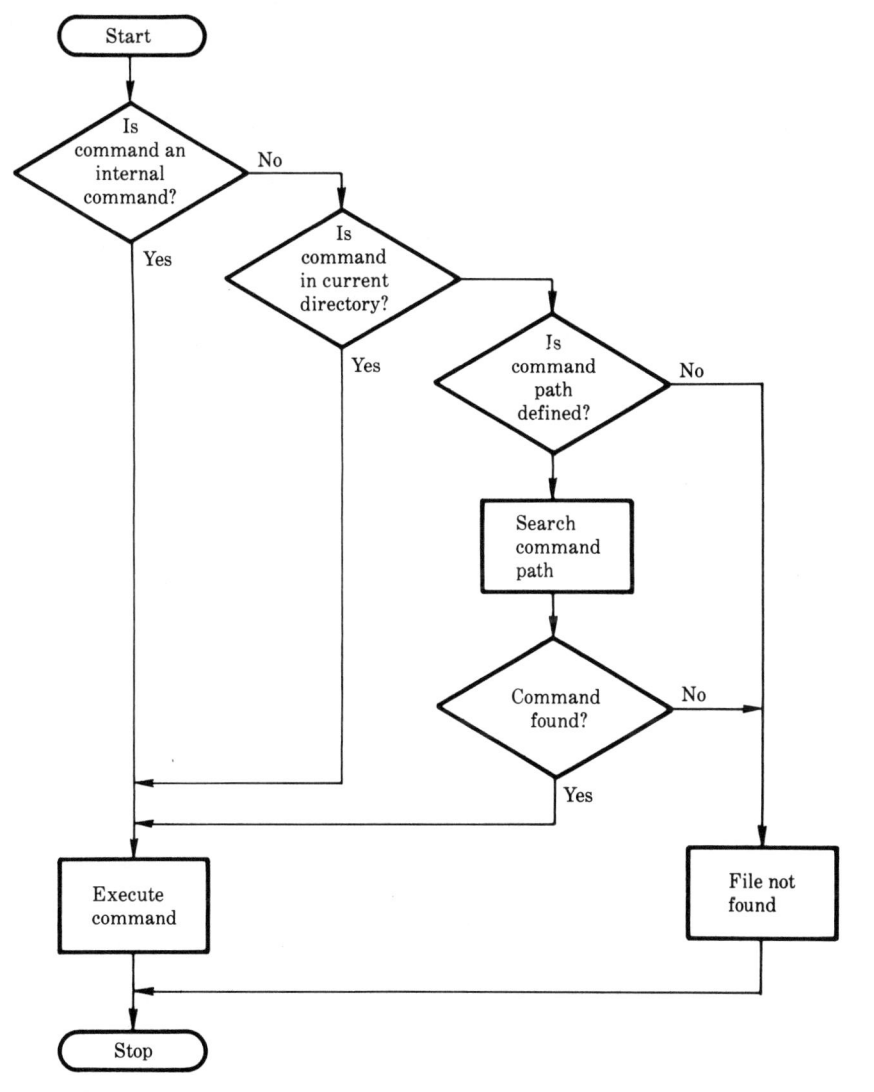

Figure B-15. *OS/2 searching to see if command-file search path has been defined*

The OS/2 PATH command enables you to define disk drives and subdirectories to be included in the command-file search path.

Examples In the following case, if OS/2 cannot find the command, OS/2 searches the root directories in drives C, B, and A (in that order) as shown in Figure B-16:

```
[C:\]  PATH  C:\;B:\;A:\
```

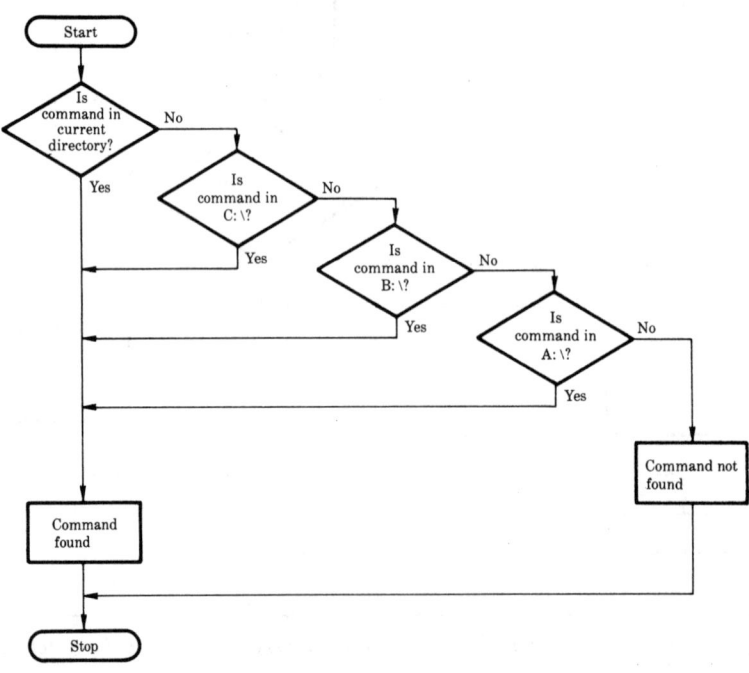

Figure B-16. *OS/2 searching root directories for defined command-file search path*

In similar manner, the following PATH command directs OS/2 to search \OS2, \UTIL, and then \MISC (in that order):

```
[C:\] PATH \OS2;\UTIL;\MISC
```

Figure B-17 illustrates the processing performed.

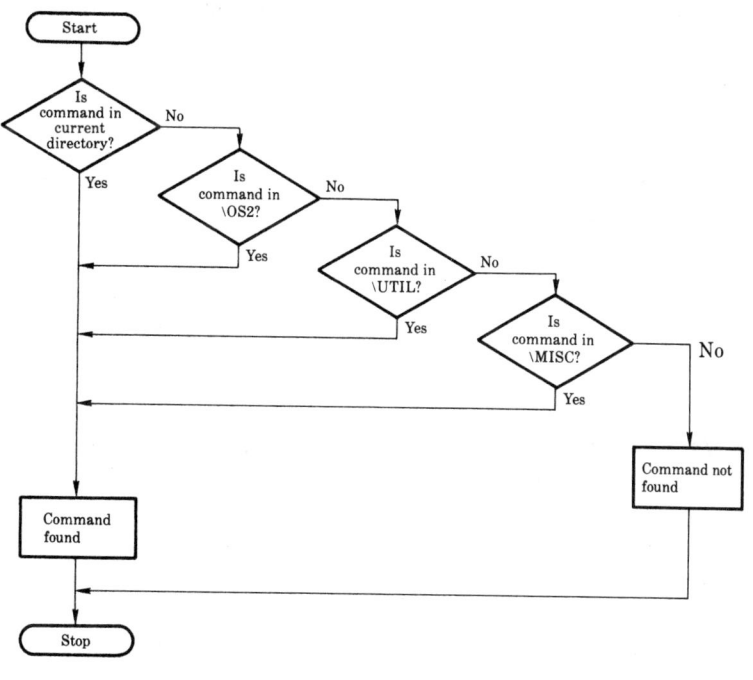

Figure B-17. *PATH searching \OS2, \UTIL, and \MISC*

PAUSE

Function Display an optional message while pausing batch-file execution.

Mode Real/Protected

Format

PAUSE [*message*]

where the following is true:

message is an optional message that PAUSE is to display each time it suspends batch processing. The *message* can contain up to 123 characters.

Syntax Chart

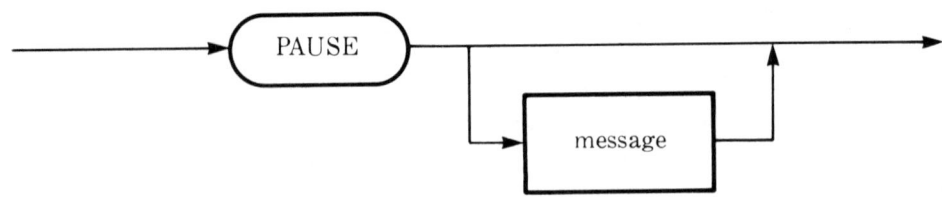

Notes Each time OS/2 encounters PAUSE within a batch file, it displays the following:

[optional message text]
Strike a key when ready . . .

To continue batch processing, press any key. Otherwise, press CTRL-BREAK.

If you press CTRL-BREAK in real mode, OS/2 displays the following:

```
   Terminate batch job (Y/N)?
```

To terminate the batch file, type Y. Otherwise, type N. In protected mode, OS/2 simply terminates the batch file.

The OS/2 ECHO OFF command suppresses the display of messages from PAUSE.

Examples Consider the following:

```
PAUSE Enter a blank disk in drive B
```

In this case, when OS/2 encounters the PAUSE command with the batch procedure, it pauses and displays the following:

```
[C:\] PAUSE Enter a blank disk in drive B
Strike a key when ready . . .
```

In a similar manner, this command

```
PAUSE
```

displays the following:

```
[C:\] PAUSE
Strike a key when ready . . .
```

Predefined Function Keys

Function   OS/2 function keys.

Notes   OS/2 buffers each entered command in a location in memory that you can access to simplify your command entry. The following are the predefined settings for function keys:

F1	Copy one character from the previous command buffer
F2	Copy all characters in the buffer that precede the next character typed
F3	Copy all of the characters in the command buffer
F4	Copy all characters including and following the next character typed
F5	Edit the current command buffer
F6	Place a CTRL-Z (^Z) end-of-file marker at the end of a file
INS	Insert characters in the current command buffer
DEL	Delete the character that precedes the cursor
ESC	Cancel the current command line without executing it

PRINT

Function   Print an OS/2 file by way of the print queue.

Format

[drive:][path] PRINT *[/D:device_name][/C][/T] file_spec* [...]

where the following is true:

drive: is the disk drive identifier of the disk that contains the file PRINT.COM. If you do not specify a disk drive, OS/2 uses the current default.

path is the name of the OS/2 subdirectory that contains the file PRINT.COM. If you do not specify a disk drive, OS/2 uses the current default.

/D:device_name specifies the name of the device OS/2 is to use for the printer (such as LPT1). The default device is LPT1.

/C directs PRINT to cancel the current print job.

/T directs PRINT to cancel all of the print jobs in the printer queue.

file_spec is the complete OS/2 path name of the file to add to or remove from the print queue. PRINT supports OS/2 wildcard chracters.

. . . states that several file names can be placed on the PRINT command line.

Syntax Chart

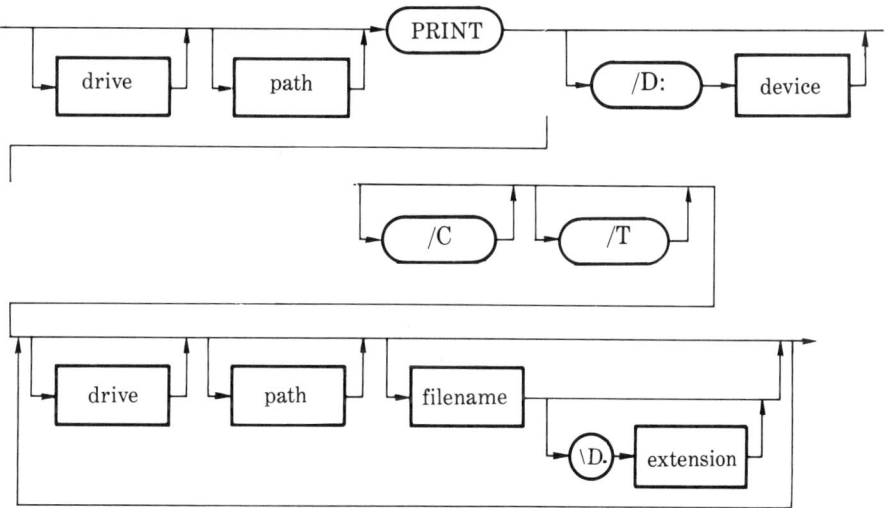

Notes The PRINT command sends files to the spooler in background mode and allows you to continue your processing in the foreground.

If you are using a serial printer, you must first issue the OS/2 SPOOL command before PRINT will work. In addition, you may need to install a device driver in the CONFIG.SYS file for the serial port.

Examples The following command sends to the printer all of the files in the current directory that have the DAT extension:

```
[C:\] PRINT *.DAT
```

In a similar manner, this command simply prints the file CONFIG.SYS:

```
[C:\] PRINT CONFIG.SYS
```

This command terminates all of the current print jobs:

```
[C:\] PRINT /T
```

PROMPT

Function   Define the OS/2 prompt.

Mode   Real/Protected

Format

PROMPT [*prompt_string*]

where the following is true:

prompt_string is the character string that defines the OS/2 prompt. It can contain characters or the following metastrings:

$a	& character
$b	¦ character
$c	(character
$d	Date
$e	ESC
$f	) character

$g	> character
$h	Backspace
$l	< character
$n	Current drive
$p	Current directory
$q	= character
$t	Current time
$v	OS/2 version number
$_	CR LF
$$	$ character

Syntax Chart

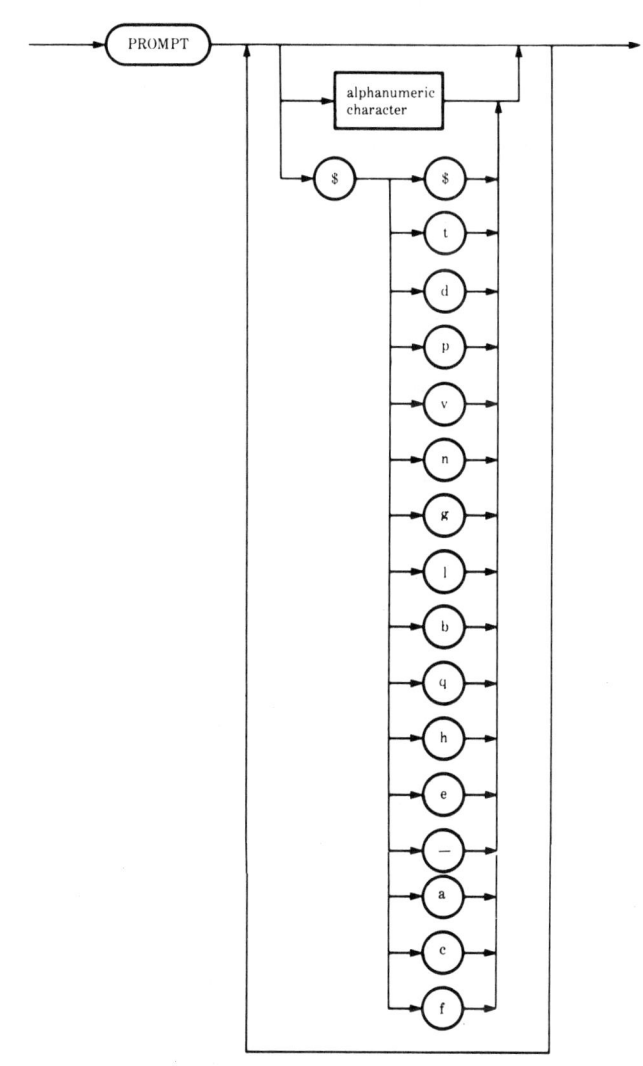

Notes If no string is specified, PROMPT resets the system prompt to the current default drive.

Determine a distinct real- and protected-mode prompt to ensure that you can always easily track where you are.

Examples In the following case, you simply set the real-mode prompt to REAL>. In so doing, you are always aware of the mode in which you are executing.

```
[C:\] PROMPT REAL$g
REAL>
```

The following command

```
[C:\] PROMPT $t
```

sets the system prompt to the current system time, as shown here:

```
15:20:18.81
15:20:43.78
15:20:87.12
```

To only display the hours and minutes, you can change the prompt to the following:

```
[C:\] PROMPT $t$h$h$h$h$h
```

Many people use the OS/2 prompt to help them keep track of their current directories. In the following case, the PROMPT command

```
[C:\] PROMPT [$p]
```

directs OS/2 to display the current directory name as the system prompt, as shown here:

```
[C:\SUBDIR]
```

RECOVER

Function   Recover a damaged disk or file.

Mode   Real/Protected

Format

*[drive:][path]*RECOVER *[d:][p]filename.ext*

where the following is true:

drive: specifies the disk drive containing the file RECOVER.COM. If you do not specify a disk drive identifier, OS/2 uses the current default.

path is the OS/2 path name of the subdirectory that contains the file RECOVER.COM. If you do not specify an OS/2 path name, OS/2 uses the current default.

d: is the disk drive identifier of the file or disk to recover. If you do not specify a disk drive, RECOVER uses the current default.

p is the OS/2 path name of the subdirectory containing the file to recover. If you do not specify an OS/2 path name, OS/2 uses the current default.

filename.ext is the name of the damaged file to recover.

Syntax Chart

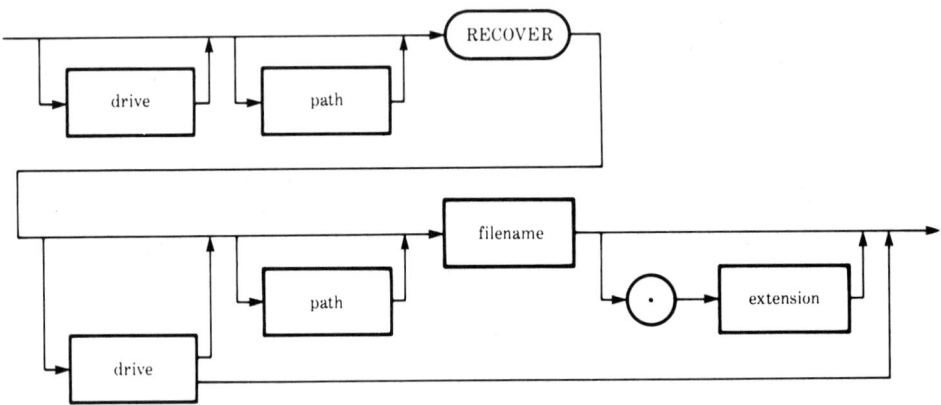

Notes If an OS/2 disk or file becomes damaged and loses sectors, the OS/2 RECOVER command enables you to retrieve portions of the file up to the point of the corruption.

If the file is a text file, you can later edit the file to restore the missing contents. However, if the file is an executable file, you should not execute it. Remember, the file is missing sectors. Instead, maintain a good backup of your files so that you do not have to rely on RECOVER.

If you use RECOVER to recover a complete disk, RECOVER creates files in the root directory with names in the form FILE*nnnn*.REC, where *nnnn* is a four-digit number beginning with 0001 (FILE0001.REC).

Examples The following command attempts to recover the contents of the disk in drive A.

```
[C:\] RECOVER A:
```

The RECOVER command creates several files whose names are in the format FILE*nnnn*.REC.

Likewise, the following command simply recovers the contents of the file FILENAME.EXT up to the point of the damaged sector:

```
[C:\] RECOVER FILENAME.EXT
```

REM

Function   Display comments during batch-file execution.

Mode   Real/Protected

Format

REM [*message*]

Syntax Chart

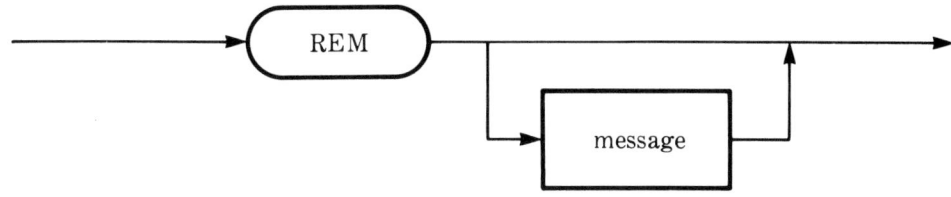

Notes   REM allows you to display messages to the standard output device during the execution of batch (BAT) files. The message is an optional command-line parameter that contains the message. The OS/2 command ECHO OFF inhibits the display of messages by REM.

Example

```
:LOOP
REM About to display the directory listing
DIR
REM Directory listing complete
REM
GOTO LOOP
```

RENAME

Function   Rename the specified file(s).

Mode   Real/Protected

Format

REN *file_specification filename*[.ext]

or

RENAME *file_specification filename*[.ext]

where the following is true:

file_specification is the complete OS/2 path name of the file to rename. It can contain a drive and OS/2 subdirectory path. RENAME supports OS/2 wildcard characters.

filename is the target file name to be renamed. It cannot have a drive or OS/2 subdirectory path. The RENAME command supports OS/2 wildcard characters.

Syntax Chart

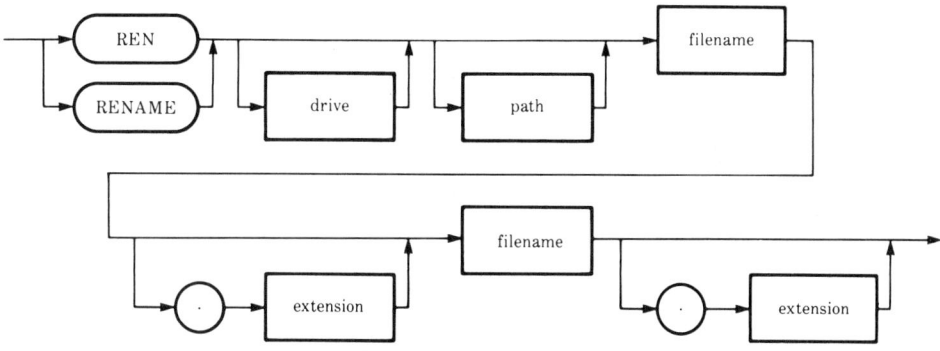

Notes   The target file must reside in the same directory on the same disk drive as the source file. This is because RENAME does not copy file contents. Rather, the command simply renames the file in its directory entry (see Table B-5).

Examples   The following command renames all of the files on drive B that have the BAK extension to the same file name with

Field	Offset
File name	0
Extension	8
Attribute byte	11
Reserved for DOS	12
Time	22
Date	24
Starting cluster number	26
File size	28

Table B-5.   *Entry in Directory Structure*

only the extension changed to SAV:

```
[C:\] REN B:*.BAK *.SAV
```

In a similar manner, this RENAME command changes the extension of all of the files with the SYS extension that are contained in the directory \DOS to the XXX extension:

```
[C:\] RENAME \DOS\*.SYS *.XXX
```

The target file must reside on the same disk and in the same directory as the source. For example, if you specify a disk drive identifier on the target file, REN displays the following:

```
DOS1043: The system cannot accept the parameter
specified.
```

Note how the HELPMSG command provides insight into your error:

```
[C:\] HELPMSG DOS1043

DOS1043: The system cannot accept the parameter
specified.


EXPLANATION: One of the following errors
occurred:

    1. An incorrect parameter was
       specified in the DIR command,
```

> 2. The second parameter used in the
>   RENAME command is incorrect
> 3. An incorrect parameter was used
>   in the COPY command
> 4. A parameter was used with a command
>   that does not require a parameter.
> ACTION: Retry the command using a correct
> parameter.
>
> [C:\]

REPLACE

Function   Allow selective file replacements and updates when new versions of software become available.

Mode   Real/Protected

Format

[*drive:*][*path*]REPLACE *source__filespec* [*target__filespec*]
[*/A*][*/P*][*/R*][*/S*][*/W*]

where the following is true:

drive: specifies the disk drive containing the file REPLACE.EXE. If you do not specify a disk drive identifier, OS/2 uses the current default.

path is the OS/2 path name of the subdirectory that contains the file REPLACE.EXE. If you do not specify an OS/2 path name, OS/2 uses the current default.

source__filespec is the complete OS/2 file specification of the files that REPLACE is to use in the file replacement. The REPLACE command supports OS/2 wildcard characters.

target__filespec is the complete OS/2 file specification of destination of the files being added or released.

/A directs REPLACE to add files to the target directory instead of replacing them. With this qualifier, REPLACE only places those files onto the target that are not currently present.

/P directs REPLACE to prompt you with

> ```
> Do you want to replace drive:filename.ext (Y/N)?
> ```

before replacing files.

/R directs REPLACE to also replace files on the target location that are currently marked as read-only. Without this qualifier, REPLACE stops replacement operations with the first file marked as read-only.

/S directs REPLACE to search the subdirectories on the target location for other occurrences of the file to replace. This qualifier cannot be used with /A.

/W directs REPLACE to prompt

> ```
> Press Enter to begin replacing files.
> ```

before starting the file-replacement operations.

Syntax Chart

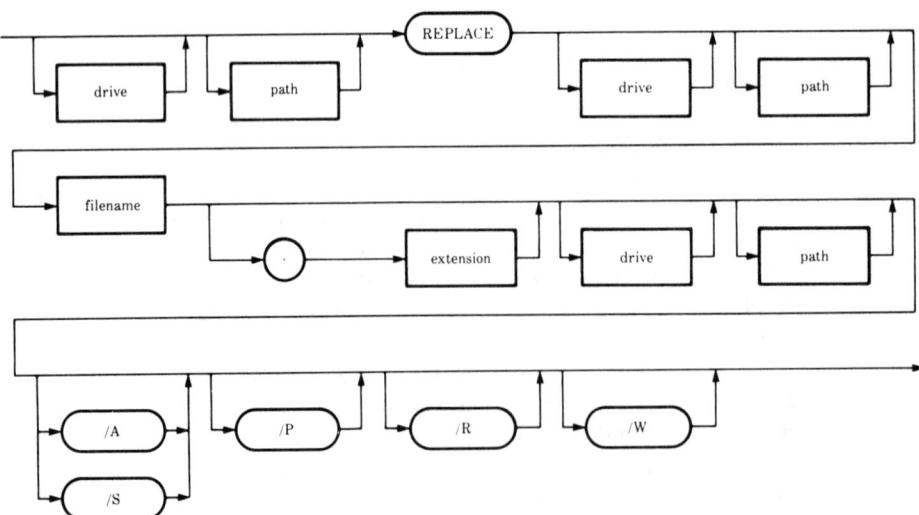

Notes   The REPLACE command is a convenient utility for software developers. It allows them to easily select specific files for replacement.

Examples Assume that your target disk in drive A has the following directory structure:

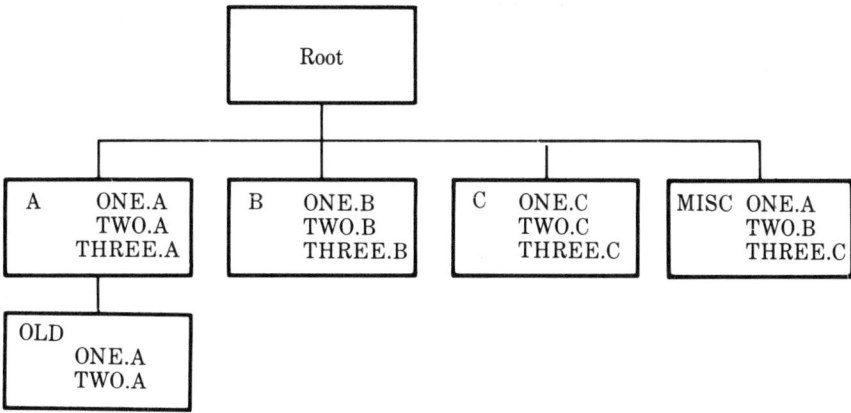

Also assume that the source disk contains the following files:

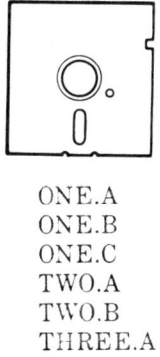

ONE.A
ONE.B
ONE.C
TWO.A
TWO.B
THREE.A

The following REPLACE command does not replace any files since the root directory in drive A does not contain any files:

```
[C:\] REPLACE *.A A:\
```

However, the following command

```
[C:\] REPLACE *.A A:\A
```

replaces the files, as shown here:

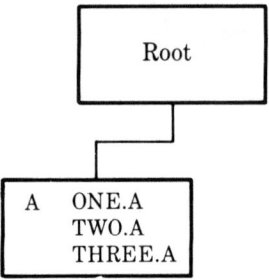

In a similar manner, the command

```
[C:\] REPLACE *.* A:\ /S
```

replaces the following files on the target disk:

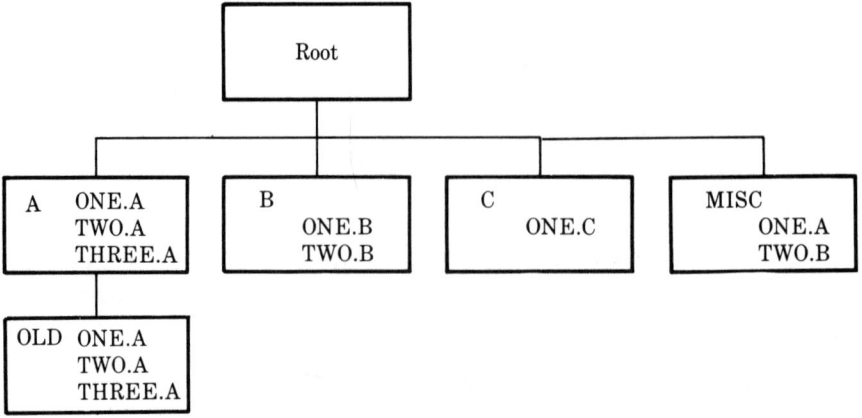

The REPLACE command makes your file updates straightforward.

RESTORE

Function Restore files saved by the BACKUP command.

Mode Real/Protected

Format

[*drive:*][*path*]RESTORE *source_drive:file_spec target_drive:file_spec*
[*/P*][*/S*][*/B:mm-dd-yy*][*/A:mm-dd-yy*][*/E:hh:mm:ss*][*/L:hh:mm:ss*][*/M*][*/N*]

where the following is true:

drive: is the disk drive identifier of the disk that contains the file
RESTORE.COM. If you omit the disk drive specifier, OS/2 uses the current
default.

path is the name of the OS/2 subdirectory that contains the file
RESTORE.COM. If you do not specify a path name, OS/2 uses the current
default.

source_drive:file_spec specifies the files to restore. The file name must
match the name of the file as it was originally backed up. The *source_drive*
qualifier is the drive that contains the back-up files.

target_drive:file_spec is the disk drive identifier to which the files will be
restored.

/P directs RESTORE to prompt to the user before restoring files that have
been modified or set to read-only since the backup.

/S directs RESTORE to restore files contained in subdirectories.

/B:mm-dd-yy directs RESTORE to only restore files modified on or before
the specified date.

/A:mm-dd-yy directs RESTORE to only restore files modified after the
specified date.

/E:hh:mm:ss directs RESTORE to only restore files modified on or before the
specified time.

/L:hh:mm:ss directs RESTORE to only restore files modified on or after the
specified time.

/M directs RESTORE only to restore files modified since the last backup.

/N directs RESTORE only to restore files that no longer exist on the target
disk.

Syntax Chart

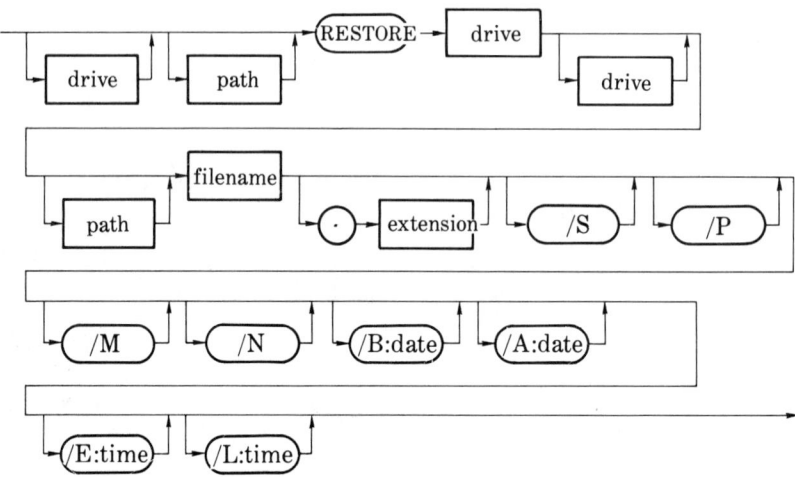

Notes The OS/2 BACKUP command places files onto a disk in a manner only accessible by the RESTORE command. To copy a file from the back-up disk, you must use RESTORE.

The RESTORE command will not restore the hidden system files or the OS/2 command processors CMD.EXE and COMMAND.COM.

To support OS/2 batch processing, RESTORE provides the following exit status values:

0 Successful restoration
1 No files found to restore
2 Shared files not restored
3 User termination by way of CTRL-C
4 Restoration error

Examples The following command restores all of the files from the back-up disk in drive A, including those in subdirectories:

```
[C:\] RESTORE A: C:*.* /S
```

If the backup used several floppy disks, RESTORE prompts you to enter the next disk as required each time it needs a new back-up disk.

This command restores all of the files from the back-up disk that contain the DAT extension:

```
[C:\] RESTORE A: C:*.DAT /P
```

The RESTORE command will prompt the user with

```
Warning! File FILENAME.EXT was changed after backed up.
Replace the file (Y/N)?
```

before it restores files that have been modified since the backup.

RMDIR

Function Remove the specified directory.

Mode Real/Protected

Format

RMDIR [*drive:*] *path* [. . .]

or

RD [*drive:*] *path* [...]

where the following is true:

drive: specifies the drive from which to remove the subdirectory. If a drive is not specified, RMDIR uses the current default.
path specifies the name of the OS/2 subdirectory to remove.
... states that RMDIR can remove several subdirectories with one command line.

Syntax Chart

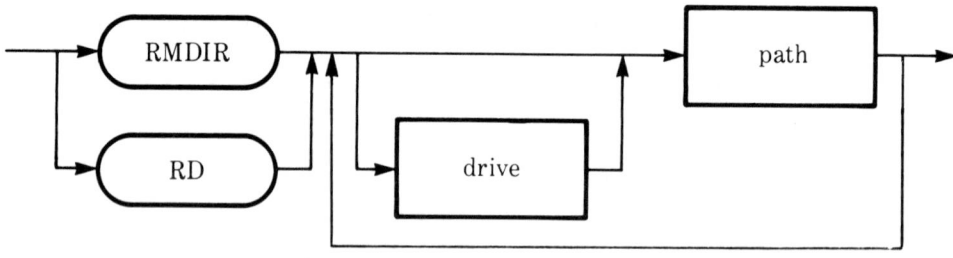

Notes   The RMDIR command only removes empty subdirectories that do not contain files.
The maximum path name that OS/2 can process is 63 characters.

Examples   For the following examples, assume that the current directory structure is as follows:

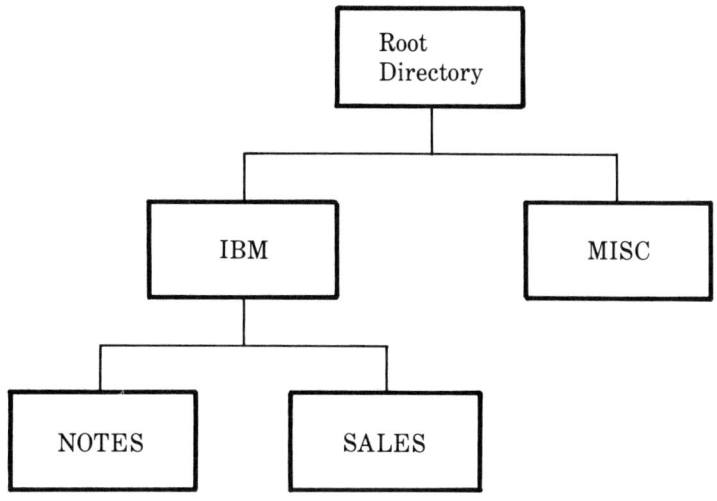

The following command attempts to remove the IBM subdirectory. However, since the directory contains files, RMDIR cannot remove the directory.

```
[C:\] RMDIR \IBM
```

However, the command

```
[C:\] RMDIR \IBM\NOTES
```

succeeds and makes the directory structure as follows:

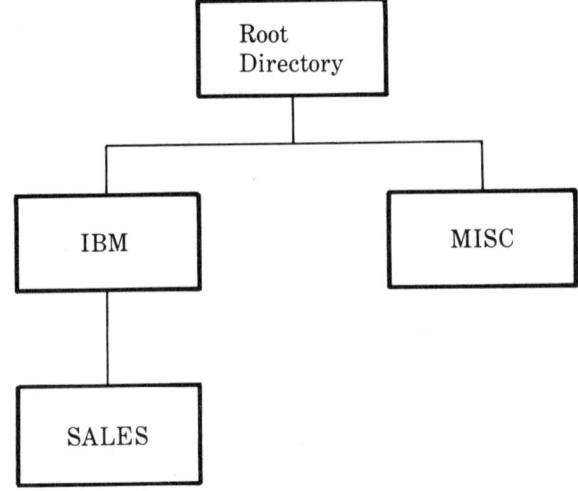

The following command illustrates that OS/2 protected mode can remove several subdirectories in one command line:

```
[C:\] RMDIR MISC \IBM\SALES
```

The directory structure becomes as follows:

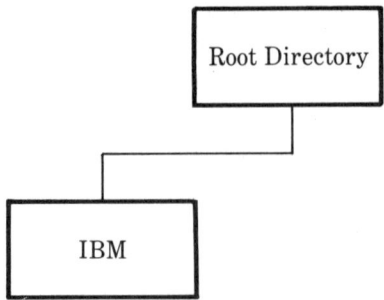

SET

Function Place or display OS/2 environment entries.

Mode Real/Protected

Format

SET [*name*=[*value*]]

where the following is true:

name is the name of an OS/2 environment entry to which you are assigning a value.
value is the character string that defines the assigned value.

Syntax Chart

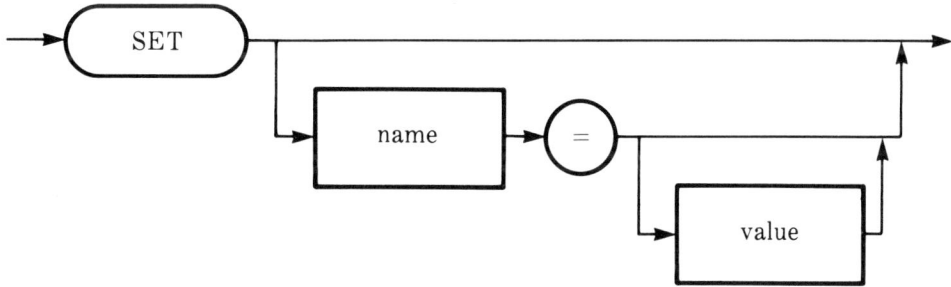

Notes Each OS/2 session has an area of reserved memory called the environment.

The OS/2 SET command sets or displays entries in the OS/2 environment. The OS/2 environment provides a storage location for system specifics. OS/2 commands such as PROMPT and PATH place entries in the environment.

The SET command converts all entry names to uppercase.

The SET command with no parameters displays the current environment.

Examples The SET command with no command-line parameters directs SET to display the current environment entries:

```
[C:\] SET
COMSPEC=c:\command.com
PATH=c:\;c:\os2;c:\tools
INCLUDE=c:\include
LIB=c:\lib
INIT=c:\init
PROMPT=[$p]

[C:\]
```

In the following case, SET creates a new environment entry called FILE and assigns it the value TEST.DAT:

```
[C:\] SET FILE=TEST.DAT
```

You can verify this by issuing the SET command, as shown here:

```
[C:\] SET
COMSPEC=c:\command.com
PATH=c:\;c:\os2;c:\tools
INCLUDE=c:\include
LIB=c:\lib
INIT=c:\init
PROMPT=[$p]
FILE=TEST.DAT

[C:\]
```

To remove the value for an entry, use SET as shown here:

```
[C:\] SET FILE=
```

Invoking SET now displays the following:

```
[C:\] SET
COMSPEC=c:\command.com
PATH=c:\;c:\os2;c:\tools
INCLUDE=c:\include
LIB=c:\lib
INIT=c:\init
PROMPT=[$p]

[C:\]
```

SETLOCAL

Function   SETLOCAL works in conjunction with ENDLOCAL to preserve the current drive, directory, and environment settings within a batch file, to ensure that the batch-file changes are only temporary.

Mode   Real/Protected

Format

SETLOCAL

Syntax Chart

Notes By default, each time you execute an OS/2 batch procedure, any changes you make to the current drive, directory, or environment entries remain in effect upon completion of the batch file. Consider this batch procedure:

```
CD \FILES
C:
PROMPT YES$g
PROGRAM
```

Upon completion, the current directory, drive, and system prompt will be changed. Such side effects of batch processing are not always desirable.

The OS/2 ENDLOCAL command works in conjunction with the SETLOCAL command to save and restore the current directory, drive, and environment specifications in a batch file.

The SETLOCAL command saves the current settings that the ENDLOCAL command later restores.

Example In the following case, although the batch file changes the current drive, directory, and prompt, once the batch file completes, SETLOCAL and ENDLOCAL have worked in conjunction to prevent the side effects from remaining:

```
SETLOCAL
CD \FILES
C:
PROMPT YES$g
PROGRAM
ENDLOCAL
```

SHIFT

Function   Shift each batch parameter left one position.

Format

SHIFT

Syntax Chart

Notes   If more than 10 parameters are passed to an OS/2 batch procedure, you can use the SHIFT command to access each parameter past %9. If no parameter exists to the right of a parameter, SHIFT assigns the parameter a NULL string.

Example   This batch file displays all of the batch parameters specified on the command line:

```
ECHO OFF
:LOOP
SHIFT
IF '%0'== '' GOTO DONE
ECHO %0
GOTO LOOP
:DONE
```

SORT

Function OS/2 sort filter.

Mode Real/Protected

Format

OS2_COMMAND ¦ [*drive:*][*path*]SORT [/*R*][/+n]

or

[*drive:*][*path*]SORT [/*R*][/+n] < file

where the following is true:

drive: is the disk identifier of the disk containing the file SORT.EXE. If you do not specify a disk drive, OS/2 uses the current default.

path is the name of the OS/2 subdirectory that contains the file SORT.EXE. If you do not specify a subdirectory name, OS/2 uses the current default.

/*R* directs SORT to sort the data in reverse order.

/+n allows you to specify the column on which to sort the data.

Syntax Chart

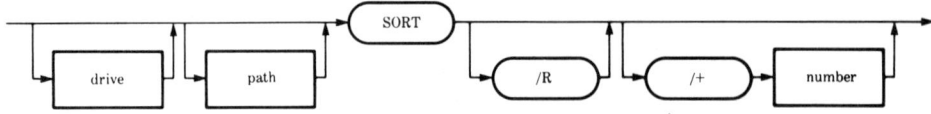

Notes The OS/2 SORT command reads data from the standard input device, and then sorts and displays the information to the standard output device until end-of-file is encountered.

Most people use the SORT command as a filter by way of the OS/2 redirection operators < or ¦.

Examples The following command directs SORT to sort the information contained in the file DATA.DAT:

```
[C:\] SORT < DATA.DAT
```

In a similar manner, this command directs SORT to sort the same file, this time in reverse order:

```
[C:\] SORT /R < DATA.DAT
```

If your data file contains

```
Bill M
Mary F
Kris M
Kal  M
Andy F
Jim  M
Mike M
Ed   M
```

the following command directs SORT to sort the file based on the data starting in column 6:

```
[C:\] SORT /+6 < FILENAME.EXT
```

In this case, SORT displays the following:

```
Andy F
Mary F
Kris M
Kal  M
Bill M
Jim  M
Mike M
Ed   M
```

If you do not redirect input to SORT

```
[C:\] SORT
```

SORT expects its input from the keyboard. As such, type in the following letters and then press CTRL-Z:

```
[C:\] SORT
A
F
D
E
B
C
^Z
```

SORT will sort the data and display the following:

```
[C:\] SORT
A
F
D
E
B
C
^Z

A
B
C
D
E
F

[C:\]
```

SPOOL

Function   Initialize the OS/2 print spooler for operations from multiple applications. The OS/2 print spooler allows programs to perform their print operations in the background.

Mode   Real/Protected

Format

[*drive:*][*path*]SPOOL [*pathname*] [*/D:device*] [*/O:devicename*]

where the following is true:

drive: specifies the disk drive identifier of the disk containing the file SPOOL.EXE. If you do not specify a disk drive identifier, OS/2 uses the current default.

path specifies the name of the OS/2 subdirectory that contains the file SPOOL.EXE. If you do not specify a subdirectory name, OS/2 uses the current default.

pathname is the OS/2 name of the path into which OS/2 will place spooled files. By default, OS/2 uses the path \SPOOL.

/D:device specifies the name (LPT1, COM1) of the device to which OS/2 is to print.

/O:devicename specifies the name of the output print device. By default, OS/2 uses the name given by */D:device*.

Syntax Chart

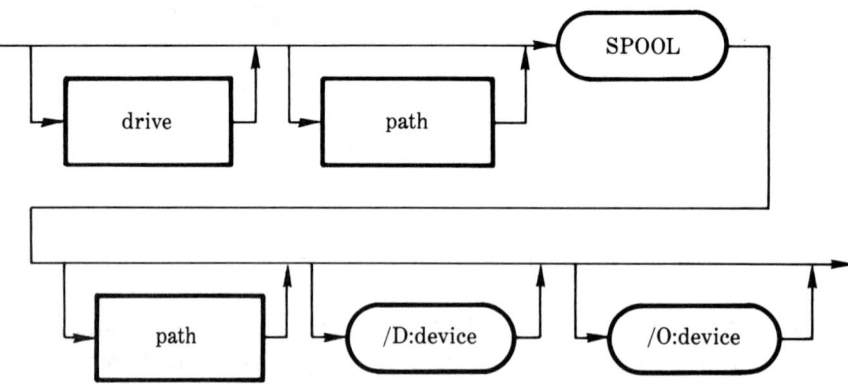

Notes Before you output to a serial printer, you must install the OS/2 spooler.

Once the spooler is installed, OS/2 allows you to use the SHIFT-PRINTSCREEN keyboard combination to print the screen contents, or CTRL-PRINTSCREEN to echo screen data to the printer.

Examples The following command installs the OS/2 spooler with the default device and uses the subdirectory \MYSPOOL:

```
[C:\] SPOOL \MYSPOOL
```

Upon invocation, SPOOL displays the following:

```
SPOOL is running and printing data on device LPT1.
```

Once the spooler is installed, you must create another protected-mode session to issue commands. The following command installs the OS/2 spooler and directs output to the serial port COM1:

```
[C:\] SPOOL \MYSPOOL /O:COM1
```

Users with serial printers should also refer to the OS/2 MODE command.

SUBST

Function   Substitute a drive name for an OS/2 path name.

Mode   Real/Protected

Format

[*drive:*][*path*]SUBST [*d:*] [*pathname*][*/D*]

where the following is true:

drive: is the disk drive identifier of the disk containing the file SUBST.EXE. If you do not specify a disk drive, OS/2 uses the current default.

path is the subdirectory name of the OS/2 subdirectory that contains the file SUBST.EXE. If you do not specify a subdirectory name, OS/2 uses the current default.

d: is the disk drive identifier that will be used to reference the path.

pathname is the OS/2 path name to abbreviate.

/D directs SUBST to remove a previous disk substitution.

Syntax Chart

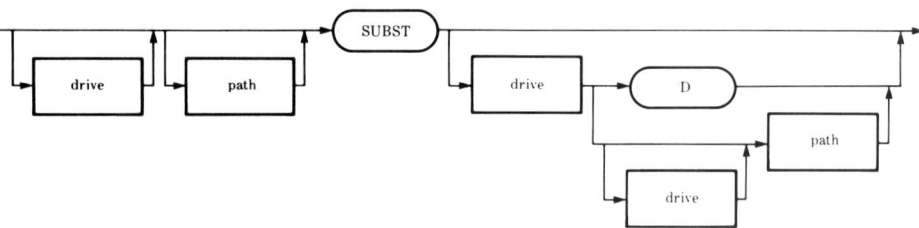

Notes   Because OS/2 path names can become quite large, OS/2 allows you to substitute a drive identifier for a path name.

If you invoke SUBST without any parameters, current substitutions are displayed.

Examples   In the following case, OS/2 will now allow you to abbreviate the subdirectory \OS2 \HELPFILE \COMMANDS with the drive letter E:

```
[C:\] SUBST E: \OS2\HELPFILE\COMMANDS
```

As such, a command like

```
[C:\] DIR E:
```

will display the contents of the directory \OS2\HELPFILE-\COMMANDS. If that subdirectory contains other subdirectories, you can still use the drive letter, as shown here:

```
[C:\] DIR E:SUBDIR
```

If you invoke SUBST without any command-line parameters, SUBST displays the current substitutions, as shown here:

```
[C:\] SUBST
E: is substituted for C:\OS2\HELPFILE\COMMANDS
```

SYS

Function Transfer the hidden operating system files that perform the initial system start-up processing to the target disk.

Mode Real/Protected

Format

*[drive:][path]*SYS *target_drive:* [/S]

where the following is true:

drive: specifies the disk drive containing the file SYS.COM. If you do not specify a disk drive identifier, OS/2 uses the current default.

path is the OS/2 path name of the subdirectory that contains the file SYS.COM. If you do not specify an OS/2 path name, OS/2 uses the current default.

target_drive: specifies the target disk drive for the hidden operating system files.

/S directs SYS to also copy the files specified by the file FORMAT.TBL to the target drive.

Syntax Chart

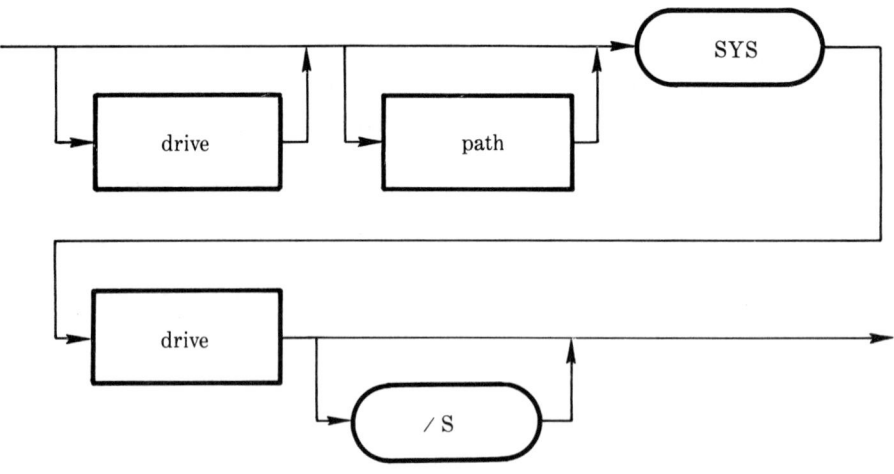

Notes The SYS command does not copy either of the files CMD.EXE or COMMAND.COM to the target disk. You must do so by using the OS/2 COPY command.

The SYS command does not work with the JOIN or SUBST commands.

OS/2 will only transfer files to an empty target disk.

Example   If you enter the following command,

```
[C:\] SYS A:
```

SYS will transfer the hidden operating system files to the disk in drive A. Verify this by issuing the CHKDSK command, as shown here:

```
[C:\] CHKDSK A:
```

TIME

Function   Set the OS/2 system time.

Mode   Real/Protected

Format

TIME [*HH:MM*[*:SS*[*.hh*]]]

where the following is true:

HH is the desired hours (0-23).
MM is the desired minutes (0-59).
SS is the desired seconds (0-59).
hh is the desired hundredths of seconds (0-99).

Syntax Chart

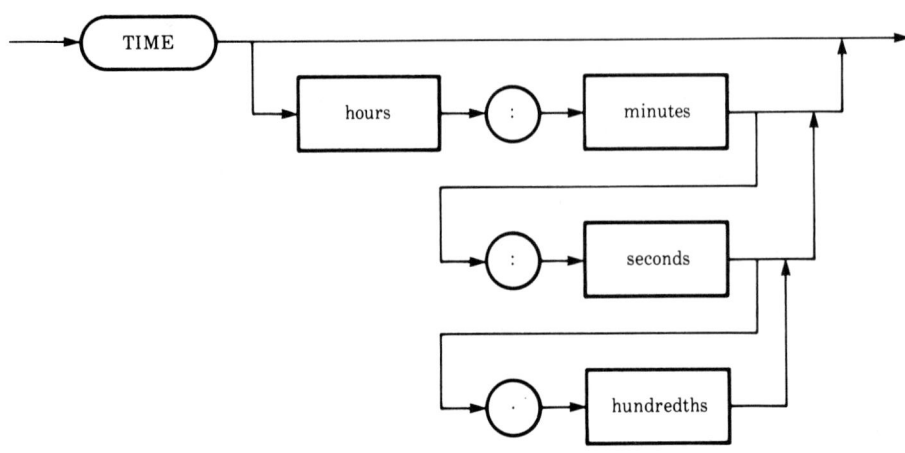

Notes   If you do not specify a time, TIME displays the current time.

In the past, most DOS users had to use the SETUP disk provided in the *Guide to Operations* manual to set their system clocks. The OS/2 TIME command modifies the AT system clock, thus removing this requirement.

Examples   If you do not specify a time on the command line,

```
[C:\] TIME
```

TIME will prompt you for one, as shown here:

```
Current time is 16:08:41.15
Enter new time:
```

To leave the time unchanged, simply press ENTER. Otherwise, type in the desired time.

This command sets the clock to noon:

```
[C:\] TIME 12:00
```

Similarly, this command sets the clock to midnight:

```
[C:\] TIME 00:00:00.000
```

If the time that you specify is invalid

```
[C:\] TIME 15:65:00
```

TIME displays an error message and prompts you for the time, as shown here:

```
Invalid time
Enter new time:
```

TREE

Function   Display directory structure.

Mode   Real/Protected

Format

[*drive:*][*path*]TREE [*d:*][*/F*]

where the following is true:

drive: specifies the disk drive identifier of the disk containing the file TREE.COM. If you do not specify a disk drive, OS/2 uses the current default.

path specifies the name of the OS/2 subdirectory that contains the file TREE.COM. If you do not specify a subdirectory, OS/2 uses the current default.

d: is the disk drive identifier of the disk for which TREE is to display the directory structure.

/F directs TREE to also display the name of each file in a directory.

Syntax Chart

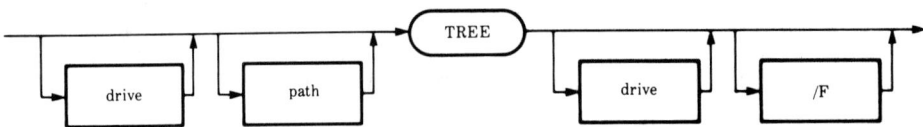

Notes   By default, TREE displays the name of each directory on a disk. To also display each file name, use the /F qualifer.

Examples   For the following examples, assume that you are using a disk with the following structure:

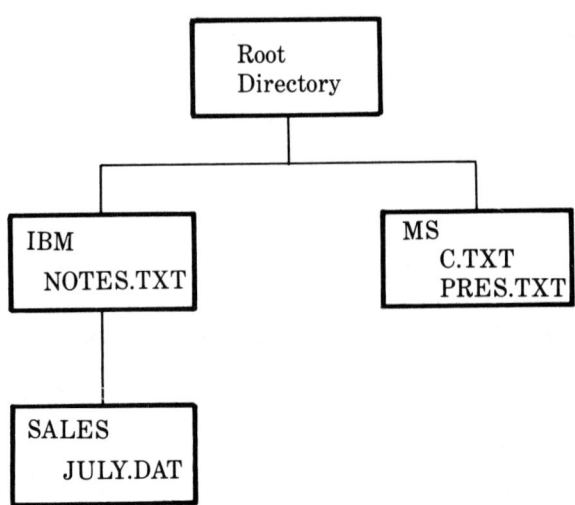

In this case, the command

```
[C:\]  TREE
```

displays the following directory structure of the disk:

```
Directory path listing

Path: \IBM

Subdirectories:   SALES


Path: \IBM\SALES

Subdirectories:   None


Path: \MS

Subdirectories:   None
```

To also display the files in each directory, use /F, as shown here:

```
[C:\]  TREE  /F
```

Upon invocation, the command displays the following:

```
Directory path listing

Files:          None


Path: \IBM

Subdirectories: SALES

Files:          NOTES   .TXT


Path: \IBM\SALES

Subdirectories: None

Files:          JULY    .DAT


Path: \MS

Subdirectories: None

Files:          C       .TXT
                PRES    .TXT
```

TYPE

Function Display the contents of a file.

Mode Real/Protected

Format

TYPE *file_specification* [...]

where the following is true:

file_specification is the complete OS/2 file specification for the file to display. It can contain a disk drive identifier and OS/2 path name.

... states that OS/2 protected mode will display several files in one TYPE command.

Syntax Chart

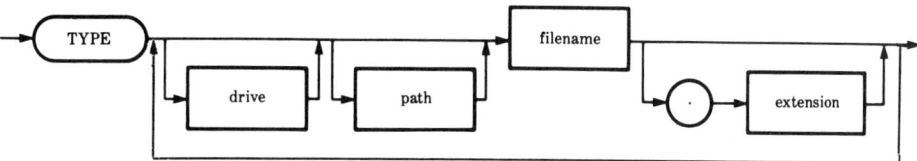

Notes The TYPE command is restricted to ASCII files. Do not TYPE COM or EXE files. These file types contain unprintable characters that cause your computer to beep and screen to display uncommon characters.

Examples The following command directs TYPE to display the contents of the file CONFIG.SYS:

```
[C:\] TYPE CONFIG.SYS
```

In a similar manner, the following command directs TYPE to display the contents of the file AUTOEXEC.SAV in the sub-directory \DOS in drive B:

```
[C:\] TYPE B:\DOS\AUTOEXEC.SAV
```

OS/2 protected mode allows you to display the contents of multiple files with one TYPE command, as shown here:

```
[C:\] TYPE CONFIG.SYS STARTUP.CMD INITENV.CMD
```

VER

Function   Display the OS/2 version number.

Mode   Real/Protected

Format

VER

Syntax Chart

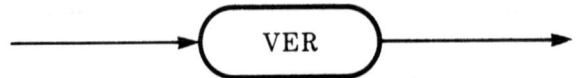

Notes   OS/2 version numbers are comprised of a major and minor number combination. For example, DOS 3.2 has a major version number of 3 and a minor version number of 2.

Example   This command directs VER to display the current version number:

```
[C:\] VER
```

Invoke the command from OS/2 real and protected mode, and OS/2 displays the same version number in each mode.

VERIFY

Function   Enable or disable disk verification.

Mode   Real/Protected

Format

VERIFY [*ON¦ OFF*]

where the following is true:

ON enables OS/2 disk verification.
OFF disables OS/2 disk verification.

Syntax Chart

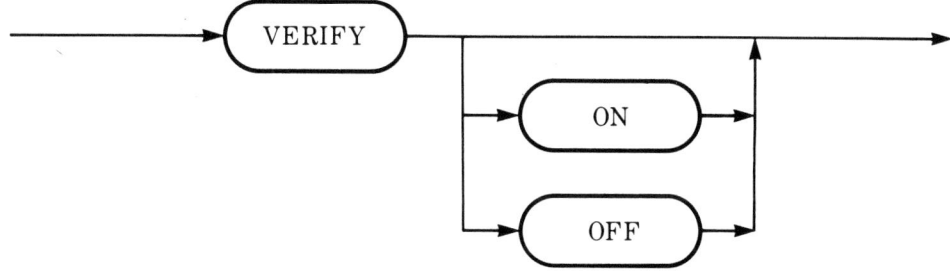

Notes Periodically, a disk drive may not correctly record the information on disk as OS/2 intended. Although rare, such occurrences can leave incorrect data on disk.

If you enable disk I/O verification, OS/2 double-checks the data it writes to disk by rereading each sector and comparing it to the original data, as shown in Figure B-18.

If a discrepancy exists, OS/2 can detect it. Figure B-19 illustrates the processing that OS/2 normally performs for a command such as the following:

```
[C:\] COPY SOURCE.DAT TARGET.DAT
```

However, once you enable disk verification, OS/2 performs processing as shown in Figure B-20.

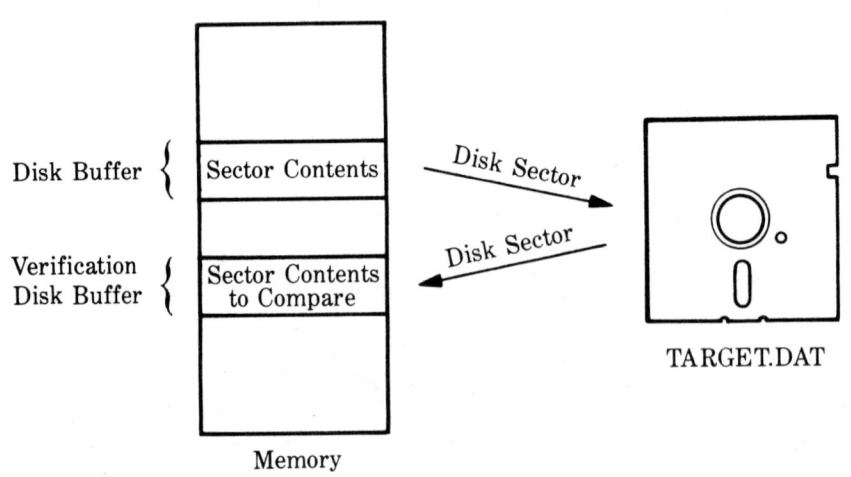

Figure B-18. *OS/2 verifying that target and source sectors are the same*

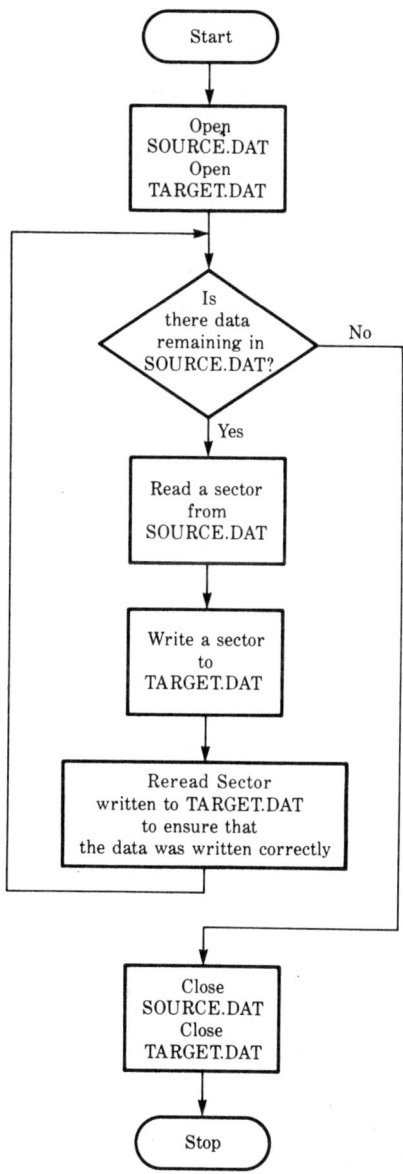

Figure B-19. *Process of OS/2 reading and writing sectors*

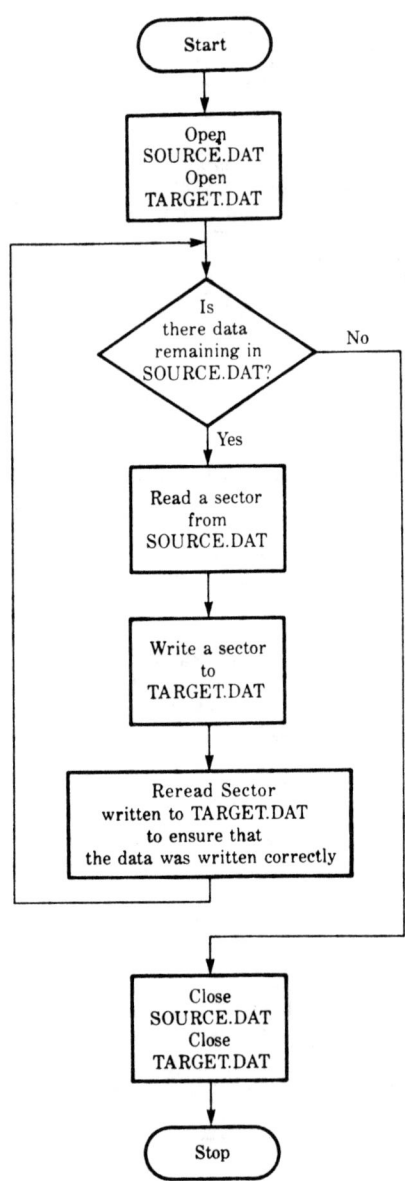

Figure B-20.   *OS/2 recognizes differences between source and target sectors*

If you invoke VERIFY without a command-line parameter, VERIFY displays its current state (ON or OFF).

Because OS/2 must now reread each sector that it writes to disk, disk verification has significant system overhead.

Examples This command enables disk I/O verification:

```
[C:\] ATTRIB +A \*.* /S
```

If you invoke VERIFY without command-line parameters, VERIFY displays its current state (ON or OFF), as shown here:

```
[C:\] VERIFY
VERIFY is on.

[C:\]
```

VOL

Function Display a disk volume label.

Mode Real/Protected

Format

VOL [*drive:*]

where the following is true:

drive: specifies the disk drive identifier of the disk for which VOL is to display the disk volume. If you do not specify a disk identifier, VOL uses the current default.

Syntax Chart

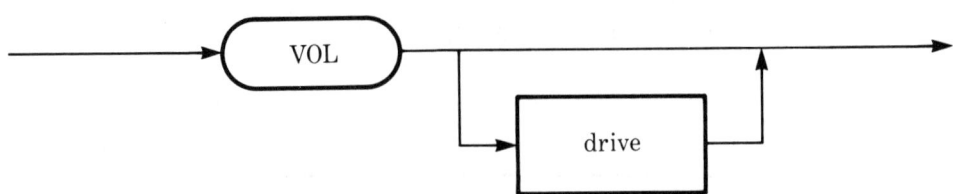

Notes   OS/2 volume labels are 11-character names assigned to a disk.

Volume names use the same characters as OS/2 file names.

If you do not specify a target drive, VOL uses the current default.

To assign a volume label, use the OS/2 LABEL command.

Example   In the following case, VOL displays the disk volume name of the disk contained in the current drive:

```
[C:\] VOL
Volume in drive C is OS2DISK

[C:\]
```

XCOPY

Function   Copy source files and subdirectories to a target destination.

Mode Real/Protected

Format

[*drive:*][*path*]XCOPY *source__filespec* [*target__filespec*]
[*/A*][*/D:mm-dd-yy*][*/E*][*/M*][*/P*][*/V*][*/S*]

where the following is true:

drive: specifies the disk drive containing the file XCOPY.EXE. If you do not specify a disk drive identifier, OS/2 uses the current default.

path is the OS/2 path name of the subdirectory that contains the file XCOPY.EXE. If you do not specify an OS/2 path name, OS/2 uses the current default.

source__filespec is the complete OS/2 file specification for the source files that XCOPY is to copy.

target__filespec is the destination name for the files copied by XCOPY.

/A directs XCOPY to only copy files that have archive bits set.

/D:mm-dd-yy directs XCOPY only to copy files created since the specified date.

/E directs XCOPY to place subdirectories on the target disk if the subdirectory is currently empty.

/M provides the same functionality as the */A* qualifier. However, */M* directs XCOPY to clear each file's archive bit as it copies.

/P directs XCOPY to prompt

```
FILENAME.EXT (Y/N)?
```

before copying each file.

/V directs XCOPY to verify the contents of target file to source file to ensure that the file copy was successful.

/S directs XCOPY to copy files contained in subdirectories below the current directory.

Syntax Chart

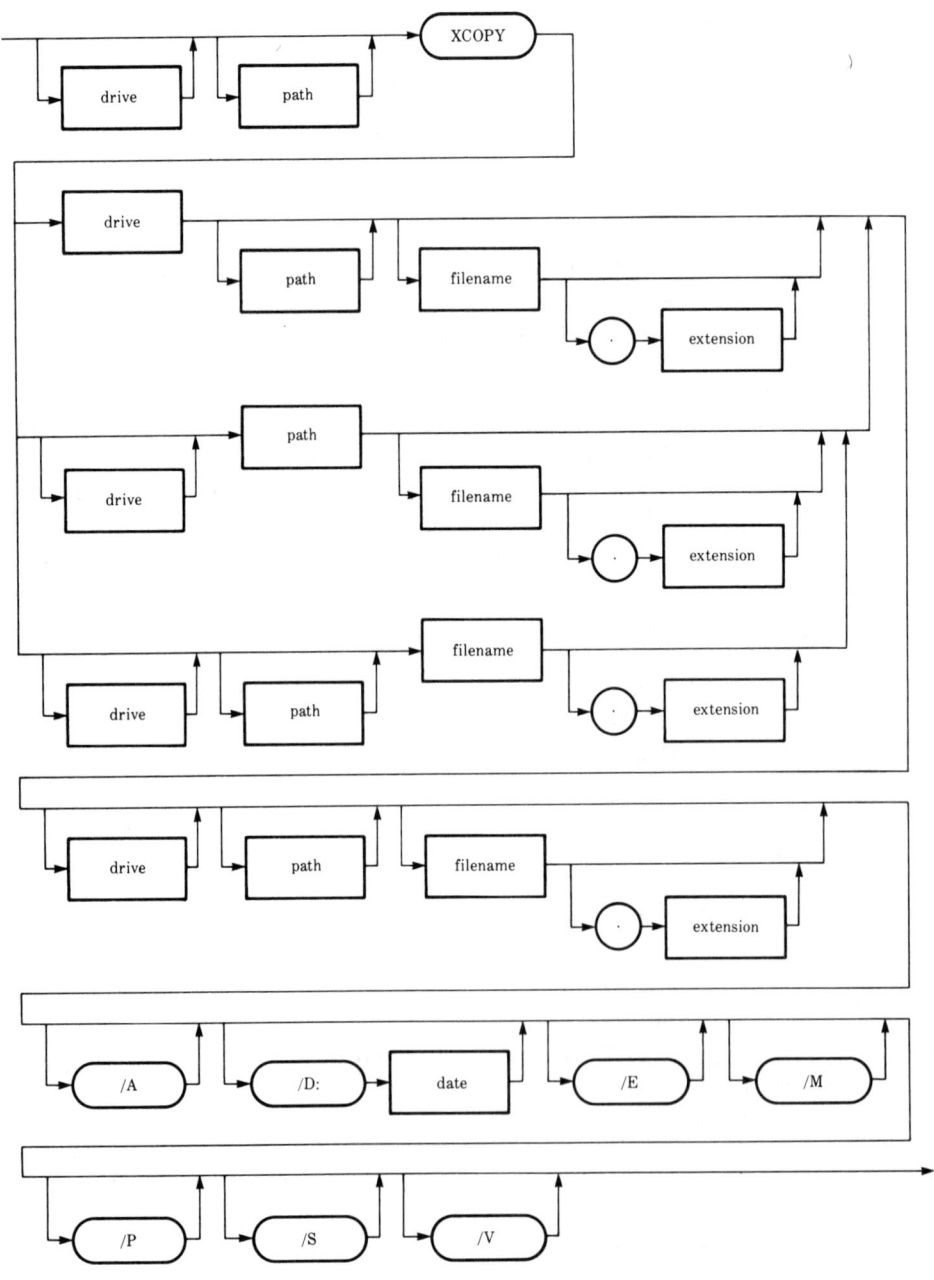

Notes The XCOPY command provides increased functionality over the COPY and DISKCOPY commands in that it will copy files contained in OS/2 subdirectories on a selective basis. In fact, many people use XCOPY to repair disk fragmentation or as a system back-up mechanism.

Examples Assume that your source disk in drive A contains the following file structure:

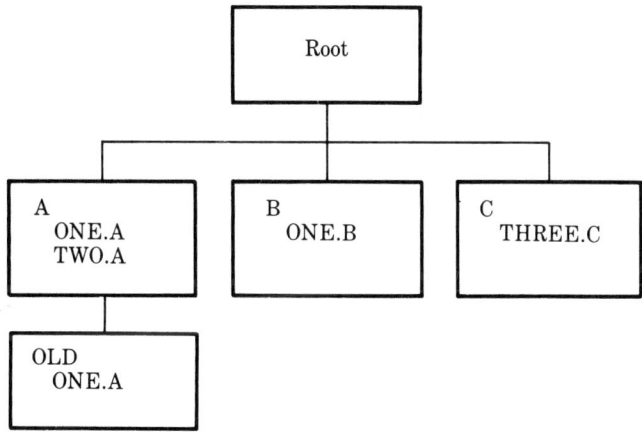

Given a blank disk in drive B, the command

```
[C:\] XCOPY A:\*.* B:\ /S
```

will create an identical disk structure on the disk in drive B. Likewise, the command

```
[C:\] XCOPY A:\A\*.* B:\ /S
```

will create a disk with the following structure:

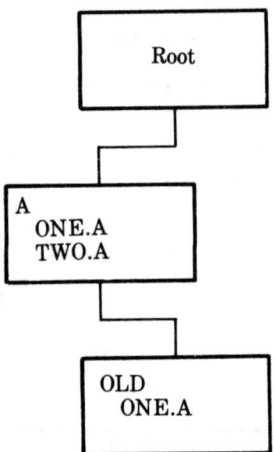

To use XCOPY to copy the entire contents of a fixed disk to floppy disks, first set each file on the fixed disk as requiring a backup, as shown here:

```
[C:\] VERIFY ON
```

Next, issue the following command:

```
[C:\] XCOPY \*.* A:\ /M /E /S
```

XCOPY will begin transferring files to the floppy disk and maintaining the existing disk structure. Once the target disk becomes full, simply insert a new floppy disk in drive A and again invoke the following command:

```
[C:\]  XCOPY A:\*.* B:\ /S
```

XCOPY will continue right where it left off since it has been clearing the archive bit on each file it successfully copies to the target disk.

C OS/2 Fixed Disk Installation

Although it is possible for you to run OS/2 simply by booting it from a floppy disk, to exploit OS/2 fully you must eventually migrate to a fixed disk drive. Other operations can be performed in conjunction with fixed disk installation. If you have been using a fixed disk drive for some time, the migration to OS/2 will provide you with the opportunity to format your fixed disk and to detect any errors that have developed in past usage.

Although your OS/2 documentation provides a complete guide to setting up your fixed disk drive, you should perform the following steps before proceeding. First, be sure that you have sufficient disks to perform two complete system backups. By completing two system backups, you greatly reduce the possibility of a single disk corruption rendering your backup incomplete. Refer to the OS/2 BACKUP command in Chapter 10 to determine the number of floppy disks that you will require.

Next, make sure that your original OS/2 disks are write-protected. This will prevent an error from destroying data during the DISKCOPY process. At this point, boot OS/2 from floppy disk.

Using the OS/2 DISKCOPY command, create a working copy of your OS/2 disks. Once the copy is complete, place your originals in a safe location.

With your OS/2 working disks, back up your fixed disk to floppy disk, as shown in Chapter 10.

Next, using the OS/2 FORMAT /S command, format your fixed disk. This process will detect any media corruptions on the disk as well as build a bootable disk. Perform this step only if your backup completed successfully. The FORMAT command places the boot files on the disk along with all of the files contained in the file FORMATS.TBL. Take time now to examine this file by entering the following:

```
[C:\] TYPE FORMATS.TBL
```

Next, follow the procedures specified in the OS/2 documentation. In most cases this will require you to create a subdirectory called \OS2 and place the OS/2 commands into it. In addition, you will probably need to create the files CONFIG.SYS, AUTOEXEC.BAT, and STARTUP.CMD, which are explained in detail within the text. Each of these files must reside in the root directory.

The OS/2 migration to fixed disk should be fairly straightforward. If you take your time and follow the steps just outlined, you should not encounter any problems.

Trademarks

AT™	International Business Machines Corporation
COMPAQ®	COMPAQ Computer Corporation
dBASE®	Ashton-Tate
DeskPro™	COMPAQ Computer Corporation
IBM®	International Business Machines Corporation
Lotus®	Lotus Development Corporation
Microsoft®	Microsoft Corporation
Mouse Systems Mouse®	Mouse Systems Corporation
1-2-3®	Lotus Development Corporation
OS/2™	International Business Machines Corporation
PS/2™	International Business Machines Corporation
UNIX®	AT&T
VisiOn™	VisiCorp
WordStar®	MicroPro International Corporation
XT™	International Business Machines Corporation

Index

The manuscript for this book was prepared and submitted to Osborne/McGraw-Hill in electronic form. The acquisitions editor for this project was Cynthia Hudson, the technical reviewer was Kevin Shafer, and the project was Fran Haselsteiner.

Text body set in Century Expanded for text body and display in Megaron.

Cover art by Bay Graphics Design Associates. Color separation by Colour Image. Cover supplier, Phoenix Color Corp. Book printed and bound by R.R. Donnelley & Sons Company, Crawfordsville, Indiana.

OS/2 Command Card

ANSI [ON¦OFF]	Controls ANSI support for protected mode
[drive:][path]APPEND [drive:][path][;[drive:][path]...] or APPEND ;	Define or display the data file search path. OS/2 real mode
[drive:][path]ASSIGN [drive1 [=] drive2 [...]]	Route disk I/O request for drive 1 to drive 2 for OS/2 real mode
[drive:][path]ATTRIB [+R¦−R][+A¦−A] [drive:][path]filename[.ext][/S]	Set the file's read-only and archive-attribute bits
[drive:][path]BACKUP [drive:[path][filename[.ext]] d: [/S][/M][/A][/D:mm-dd-yy][/F][/L¦file] [/T:hh:mm:ss]	Back up one or more files to another disk
BREAK [ON¦OFF]	Allow or inhibit CTRL-BREAK checking when OS/2 functions finish
CALL batchfile [parameters]	Invokes a second batch file from within an OS/2 batch file
CHCP [codepage]	Set or display the current code page
CHDIR [drive:][path] or CD [drive:[path]	Change or display the current directory on the specified drive
[drive:][path]CHKDSK [drive:][path][filename[.ext]] [/F][/V]	Analyze and (optionally) repair directories, files, and the FAT
CLS	Clear the screen display
[drive:][path] CMD [drive:][path] [[/C¦/K]string]	Start a secondary protected-mode command processor
[drive:][path]COMMAND [drive:][path][/P][/C string][/E:nnnnn]	Invoke a secondary real-mode command processor
[drive:][path]COMP [drive:][path][filename[.ext]] [drive:][path][filename[.ext]]	Compare the contents of the files specified
COPY [/A][/B] [drive:][path]filename[.ext] [/A][/B] [+[[,,]drive:][path]filename[.ext][/A][/B]...] [drive:][path][filename[.ext]][/A][/B][/V]	Copy the contents of the source file(s) to the target file(s)
DATE [mm-dd-yy] ¦ [dd-mm-yy] ¦ [yy-mm-dd]	Set or display the current system date
DEL [drive:][path]filename[.ext][...]	Delete the specified file names from disk
DETACH OS/2_command [arguments]	Execute an OS/2 command in background mode
DIR [drive:][path][filename[.ext]][...][/P][/W]	List the files as specified
[drive:][path]DISKCOMP [drive1: [drive2:]]	Compare the contents of the disks in drive 1 and in drive 2
[drive:][path]DISKCOPY [drive1: [drive2:]]	Copy the contents of the disk in drive 1 to the disk in drive 2

DPATH [drive:][path][;[drive:][path]...] *or* DPATH;	Define data-file search path for OS/2 protected mode
ECHO [ON¦OFF¦message]	Allow or suppress the screen display of OS/2 command names as the command executes within a batch file
ENDLOCAL	Restore drive, directory, and environment saved by SETLOCAL
ERASE [drive:][path]filename[.ext][...]	Delete the specified file names from disk
EXIT	Exit current command processor
EXTPROC [file__specification][arguments]	Define OS/2 batch-file command processor
[drive:][path]FDISK	Define fixed-disk partitions
[drive:][path]FIND [/V][/C][/N] "string" [[drive:][path][filename[.ext]]	Display all of the lines that contain the specified string
FOR %%variable IN (set) DO command	Allow iterative processing of OS/2 commands
[drive:][path]FORMAT drive:[/S][/4][/ V:label][/T:tracks][/N:sectors]	Format the disk in the specified drive
GOTO label__name	Allow branching within batch files
[drive:][path]GRAFTABL[codepage¦?¦/STA]	Load software to support the display of extended ASCII characters for the color/graphics adapter in real mode
HELPMSG message__id	Provide on-line help for OS/2 error messages

IF [NOT] condition command	Allow conditional batch processing
	    condition is one of the following:
	        ERRORLEVEL number
	        string1==string2
	        EXIST [drive:][path]filename[.ext]

[drive:][path]JOIN [drive: /D]¦ [drive: path]	Connect a disk drive to a directory OS/2 real mode
[drive:][path]KEYBxx	Load software for a foreign keyboard
[drive:][path]LABEL [drive:] [volume__label]	Create or modify an 11-character volume label
MKDIR [drive:][path][...] or MD [drive:][path][...]	Create the specified subdirectory
[drive:][path]MODE LPT#[:][cpl][,[vli][,P]] *or* [drive:][path]MODE n *or* [drive:][path]MODE COM#[:]baud[,[parity][,[databits][,[stopbits][,P]]]]	Set the characteristics of the system printer, monitor, or asynchronous communications adapter

Using OS/2™

or

[drive][path]MODE LPT#[:]=COM#   Display data obtained from standard input
                                                   to standard output a screen at a time

[drive:][path]MORE

[drive:][path] PATCH [drive:][path]   Allow patches to executable code
[filename[/A]

PATH [[drive:]path[;[drive:]path]...]]   Define the optional command search path
or
PATH ;

PAUSE [remark]   Suspend batch processing and display a
                                                   prompt for the user to
                                                   Strike a key when ready...

[drive:][path]PRINT   Install the OS/2 print queue and print the
[/C][/D:device__name]   specified file(s)
[/T]
[[drive:][path]filename[.ext]...]

PROMPT [prompt-string]   Set the system prompt as specified. The
                                                   following metastrings can be used:
                                                   $$ Dollar-sign character
                                                   $_ carriage return linefeed
                                                   $a &
                                                   $B ¦ character
                                                   $C (
                                                   $D System date
                                                   $E ESCape character
                                                   $F)
                                                   $G > character
                                                   $H Delete previous character
                                                   $L < character
                                                   $N Default-drive letter
                                                   $P Current directory
                                                   $Q = character
                                                   $T System time
                                                   $V OS/2 version number

[drive:][path]RECOVER   Recover the specified file(s) or disk drive
[drive:][path]filename[.ext] ¦ [drive:]

REM [remark]   Display remarks from within a batch file

REN[AME] [drive:][path]filename[.ext]   Rename the file provided as specified
filename[.ext]

[drive:][path]REPLACE   Allow selective replacement/addition of
[drive:][path]filename[.ext]   files from the source to the target location
[drive:][path] filename, ext. [/A][/P][/R][/S][/W]

[drive:][path]RESTORE drive: Restore the specified file(s) from the
[drive:][path]filename[.ext][/S][/P]   backup device
[/B:MM:DD:YY][/A:MM:DD:YY][/E:HH:MM:SS]
[/L:HH:MM:SS][/M][/N]

RMDIR [drive:]path[...] ¦ RD [drive:]path[...]   Remove the specified subdirectory

SET [name=[string]]   Define an item in the command environment

SETLOCAL   Stores the current drive, directory, and
                                                   environment in OS/2 batch files

Command	Description
SHIFT	Shift the batch parameters %0-%n left one parameter
[drive:][path]SORT [/R][/+ column]	Sort and display data received from standard input
[drive:][path] SPOOL [d:][spoolpath] [/D:device][/O:device]	Install the OS/2 spooler to control printer operations
[drive:][path]SUBST [drive: drive:path] ¦ [drive: /D]	Substitute an OS/2 path name with a disk-drive specifier
[drive:][path]SYS drive: [/S]	Copy the system files to the specified disk, making it bootable
TIME [hh:mm[:ss[.hh]]]	Set or display the system time
[drive:][path]TREE [drive:][/F]	Display all of the directory paths on a disk and (optionally) the files that they contain
TYPE [drive:][path]filename[.ext][...]	Display the contents of the specified file
VER	Display the OS/2 version number
VERIFY [ON ¦ OFF]	Enable or disable disk-write verification
VOL [drive:]	Display the 11-character volume label of the specified drive
[drive:][path]XCOPY [drive:][path]filename[.ext] [drive:][path][filename[.ext]][/A][/D:mm-dd-yy][/E][/M] [/P][/S][/V] or [drive:][path]XCOPY [drive:]path[filename[.ext]] [drive:][path][filename[.ext]][/A][/D:mm-dd-yy][/E][/M] [/P][/S][/V]	Provide selective copies of the specified file(s) to the target destination

I/O Redirection Operators

Operator	Description
<	Input redirection
>	Output redirection
>>	Append operator
¦	Pipe operator
&	Command separator
&&	AND operator
¦¦	OR operator
^	Escape operator

CONFIG.SYS Entries

BREAK=[ON¦OFF] default OFF
BUFFERS=n default 3
CODEPAGE=nnn,yyy
COUNTRY=nn
DEVICE=[drive:][path]filename[.ext]
DEVINFO=device_type,subtype,[file_specification,[ROM=[( ]aaa[,bbb)]]
FCBS=n,n default 4,0
IOPL=[YES¦NO] default No
LIBPATH=drive:path[;drive:path][...]
MAXWAIT=n default 3
MEMMAN=swap_option,move_option
PRIORITY=[absolute¦dynamic] default dynamic
PROTECTONLY=[YES¦NO] default No
PROTSHELL=file_specification command_interpreter /K CMD_file
RMSIZE=kbytes
RUN=file_specification [command_line_arguments]
SHELL=[drive:][path]filename[.ext][/C string][/P][/E]
SWAPPATH=drive:[path]
THREADS=n default 48
TIMESLICE=n,y